ISLAMIC SPIRITUALITY
Manifestations

World Spirituality

An Encyclopedic History of the Religious Quest

1. Asian Archaic Spirituality
2. European Archaic Spirituality
3. African and Oceanic Spirituality
4. South and Meso-American Native Spirituality
5. North American Indian Spirituality
6. Hindu Spirituality: Vedas through Vedanta
7. Hindu Spirituality: Postclassical and Modern
8. Buddhist Spirituality: Indian, Sri Lankan, Southeast Asian
9. Buddhist Spirituality: Chinese, Tibetan, Japanese, Korean
10. Taoist Spirituality
11. Confucian Spirituality
12. Ancient Near Eastern Spirituality: Zoroastrian, Sumerian, Assyro-Babylonian, Hittite
13. Jewish Spirituality: From the Bible to the Middle Ages
14. Jewish Spirituality: From the Sixteenth-Century Revival to the Present
15. Classical Mediterranean Spirituality: Egyptian, Greek, Roman
16. Christian Spirituality: Origins to the Twelfth Century
17. Christian Spirituality: High Middle Ages and Reformation
18. Christian Spirituality: Post-Reformation and Modern
19. Islamic Spirituality: Foundations
20. Islamic Spirituality: Manifestations
21. Modern Esoteric Movements
22. Spirituality and the Secular Quest
23. Encounter of Spiritualities: Past to Present
24. Encounter of Spiritualities: Present to Future
25. Dictionary of World Spirituality

Board of Editors and Advisors

Volume 20 of
World Spirituality:
An Encyclopedic History
of the Religious Quest

ISLAMIC SPIRITUALITY

MANIFESTATIONS

Edited by
Seyyed Hossein Nasr

CROSSROAD • NEW YORK

1991
The Crossroad Publishing Company
370 Lexington Avenue, New York, NY 10017

World Spirituality, Volume 20
Diane Apostolos-Cappadona, Art Editor

Printed in the United States of America

Library of Congress Cataloging-in-Publication Data

Islamic spirituality : manifestations / edited by Seyyed Hossein Nasr.
p. cm.–(World spirituality ; v. 20)
Includes bibliographical references (p.
ISBN 0-8245-0768-1
1. Sufism. I. Nasr, Seyyed Hossein. II. Series.
BP189.I85 1990
297'.4–dc 20 89-25272
CIP

Contents

In the Name of God, Most Merciful, Most Compassionate

قُلِ الرُّوحُ مِنْ أَمْرِ رَبِّي

Say, the Spirit is from the Command of my Lord

Preface to the Series

THE PRESENT VOLUME is part of a series entitled World Spirituality: An Encyclopedic History of the Religious Quest, which seeks to present the spiritual wisdom of the human race in its historical unfolding. Although each of the volumes can be read on its own terms, taken together they provide a comprehensive picture of the spiritual strivings of the human community as a whole—from prehistoric times, through the great religions, to the meeting of traditions at the present.

Drawing upon the highest level of scholarship around the world, the series gathers together and presents in a single collection the richness of the spiritual heritage of the human race. It is designed to reflect the autonomy of each tradition in its historical development, but at the same time to present the entire story of the human spiritual quest. The first five volumes deal with the spiritualities of archaic peoples in Asia, Europe, Africa, Oceania, and North and South America. Most of these have ceased to exist as living traditions, although some perdure among tribal peoples throughout the world. However, the archaic level of spirituality survives within the later traditions as a foundational stratum, preserved in ritual and myth. Individual volumes or combinations of volumes are devoted to the major traditions: Hindu, Buddhist, Taoist, Confucian, Jewish, Christian, and Islamic. Included within the series are the Jain, Sikh, and Zoroastrian traditions. In order to complete the story, the series includes traditions that have not survived but have exercised important influence on living traditions—such as Egyptian, Sumerian, classical Greek and Roman. A volume is devoted to modern esoteric movements and another to modern secular movements.

Having presented the history of the various traditions, the series devotes two volumes to the meeting of spiritualities. The first surveys the meeting of spiritualities from the past to the present, exploring common themes that

A longer version of this preface may be found in Christian Spirituality: Origins to the Twelfth Century, *the first published volume in the series.*

can provide the basis for a positive encounter, for example, symbols, rituals, techniques. Finally, the series closes with a dictionary of world spirituality.

Each volume is edited by a specialist or a team of specialists who have gathered a number of contributors to write articles in their fields of specialization. As in this volume, the articles are not brief entries but substantial studies of an area of spirituality within a given tradition. An effort has been made to choose editors and contributors who have a cultural and religious grounding within the tradition studied and at the same time possess the scholarly objectivity to present the material to a larger forum of readers. For several years some five hundred scholars around the world have been working on the project.

In the planning of the project, no attempt was made to arrive at a common definition of spirituality that would be accepted by all in precisely the same way. The term "spirituality," or an equivalent, is not found in a number of the traditions. Yet from the outset, there was a consensus among the editors about what was in general intended by the term. It was left to each tradition to clarify its own understanding of this meaning and to the editors to express this in the introduction to their volumes. As a working hypothesis, the following description was used to launch the project:

> The series focuses on that inner dimension of the person called by certain traditions "the spirit." This spiritual core is the deepest center of the person. It is here that the person is open to the transcendent dimension; it is here that the person experiences ultimate reality. The series explores the discovery of this core, the dynamics of its development, and its journey to the ultimate goal. It deals with prayer, spiritual direction, the various maps of the spiritual journey, and the methods of advancement in the spiritual ascent.

By presenting the ancient spiritual wisdom in an academic perspective, the series can fulfill a number of needs. It can provide readers with a spiritual inventory of the richness of their own traditions, informing them at the same time of the richness of other traditions. It can give structure and order, meaning and direction to the vast amount of information with which we are often overwhelmed in the computer age. By drawing the material into the focus of world spirituality, it can provide a perspective for understanding one's place in the larger process. For it may well be that the meeting of spiritual paths—the assimilation not only of one's own spiritual heritage but of that of the human community as a whole—is the distinctive spiritual journey of our time.

EWERT COUSINS

Introduction

See the One, utter the One, know the One,
For this is the seal of the root and branches of faith.

THUS SINGS THE Persian Sufi poet Maḥmūd Shabistarī in his *Gulshan-i rāz* (*The Rose Garden of Divine Mysteries*). Islamic spirituality is precisely this seeing the One, uttering the Name of the One, and knowing the One who is God in His absolute Reality beyond all manifestations and determinations, the One to whom the Quran refers as Allah. All of Islam is in fact based on the central doctrine of Unity (*al-tawḥīd*), but what can specifically be called Islamic spirituality is the experience and knowledge of this Unity and its realization in thoughts, words, acts, and deeds, through the will, the soul, and the intelligence. This spirituality is ultimately to live and act constantly according to God's Will, to love Him with one's whole being, and finally to know Him through that knowledge which integrates and illuminates and whose realization is never divorced from love nor possible without correct action.

God is the One but man[1] in his ordinary condition lives in the world of multiplicity deprived of both knowledge and experience of the One. The attainment of the One is made possible by revelation, which is a message from the One to man, who is immersed in the world of multiplicity. Revelation must of necessity descend into the world of outwardness and multiplicity, where its recipient, man, resides. Although its formal expressions exist in the world of outwardness, its inner dimension remains wed to the world of Unity, and it is to this inner dimension that one must turn in order to see, utter, and know the One. In Islam this dimension of inwardness is the domain *par excellence* of Islamic spirituality, and in fact the Spirit (*al-rūḥ*) is identified with this dimension, which is at once beyond and within the macrocosm and the microcosm.

In Islamic cosmology, the *rūḥ* is mentioned distinctly with the other supreme angels and stands at the pinnacle of cosmic reality, the highest point of creation and the nexus between the cosmos and God. The *rūḥ* is also identified with the very center of man's existence and is the principle of life, for it was by breathing His Spirit into Him (Quran XXXVIII, 72) that God bestowed man with life and consciousness. The *rūḥ* is therefore both beyond the human and the cosmic realities and at the very center of man's being; the *rūḥ* is the gate to Divine Transcendence and Immanence. Islamic spirituality, which in Arabic is called *rūḥāniyyah,* can therefore be defined as that aspect of Islam which leads to the transcendent and immanent Divine Reality. The essential nexus between Islamic spirituality and inwardness is accentuated by another term for spirituality used especially in Persian, namely, *ma'nawiyyat,* which connotes literally "meaning" or the inward, in contrast to *ṣūrat* or outward form.

All of Islam is, of course, concerned with God and His Will as embodied in the *Sharī'ah,* the Divine Law of Islam, obedience to which is sufficient in order to live a life of balance and happiness in this world and to be saved at the moment of death. A study devoted to Islamic spirituality, however, could not be synonymous with one devoted solely to the *Sharī'ah.* While taking into account the great significance of the spiritual dimension of everyday piety and the *Sharī'ah,* such a study must pay special attention to those aspects of the Islamic tradition which in the Islamic context itself would be most concerned with *rūḥāniyyah* and *ma'nawiyyat* as defined above. A study of spirituality, therefore, must turn most of all to the inner dimension of Islam. It is precisely such a path that we have sought to tread in these two volumes on Islamic spirituality. Moreover, we have had to take full consideration of the limits that have been imposed on the subject because of the very nature of this project that is part of a major encyclopedic history. The space devoted to each religion has been predetermined, and the language and content must be tailored to the predominantly Western audience addressed by these volumes.

Plan of the Volumes on Islamic Spirituality

From the beginning, two volumes were allotted for Islamic spirituality despite the vast expanses of the Islamic world and the many ethnic, linguistic, and cultural areas which that world embraces. As a result, we planned these volumes in such a way as to present what is essential to the understanding of Islamic spirituality. We attempted to penetrate the specific areas of the Islamic world sufficiently to present an adequate picture of the whole, even if details of certain areas, schools, or historical periods are incomplete.

In order to deal with Islamic spirituality authentically, we sought to avoid a number of ideas prevalent in the West concerning scholarship in the field of religion—ideas that are alien to the Islamic point of view. These include

(1) historicism, inherited from the nineteenth century, which reduces all religion and even spirituality to merely historical phenomena without a transhistorical reality, and (2) rationalistic and post-rationalistic skepticism and nihilism, which refuse to take seriously the claim of spiritual authorities to have access to an objective knowledge of the cosmic and metacosmic realities.

As mentioned in the introduction to the previous volume, these considerations led us to formulate a plan that would do justice to the Islamic perspective and yet be comprehensible to the Western scholarly public. We devoted the first volume to the foundations of Islamic spirituality. It deals with the Quran, the Prophet[2] and his *Ḥadīth,* the Islamic rites and practices, especially prayer, Sunnism, Shīʿism and female spirituality, the nature, origin, and basic practices of Sufism and the doctrines of Islam concerning God, the angels, the cosmos, man, and eschatology. These doctrines and realities have had an ubiquitous and perennial presence throughout Islamic history. They have been the ever-living spring from which many streams have gushed forth over the centuries. They are therefore foundational, possessing a transhistorical reality, an immutability and a permanence that characterize Islam as a religion.

Islam has also been a community that has had a life of over fourteen centuries, affecting billions of human beings from the Atlantic to the Pacific. It has created a major world civilization and a rich intellectual, cultural, and artistic tradition. In the second volume, we have sought to deal with the manifestations of Islamic spirituality in both time and space. We have dealt with this spirituality as it has developed and manifested itself in various periods of history as well as in various areas of the Islamic world.

The Present Volume

Islamic spirituality, as defined above and more extensively in the introduction to the first volume, has revealed itself in Islamic history most of all in Sufism, which has been the guardian of the path of inwardness (*al-bāṭin*). Most of this volume is therefore devoted to Sufism and the teachings, practices, writings, and impact of the Sufi orders. There are several histories of Sufism and Sufi orders in European languages, but they do not, for the most part, deal with the spiritual reality of Sufism. This volume contains the first global study in English of Sufism that is concerned with the distinct spiritual climate of the Sufi orders and the spiritual significance of their teachings. The study is not complete or exhaustive, but it takes the whole of the Islamic world into account.

Considering the vastness of the Islamic world and the long history of Sufism with its immense impact on art and thought as well as the social, economic, and political life of Muslims from Nigeria to the Philippines and from China to Albania, it became obvious that it would be simply impossible to be all-embracing and exhaustive. Therefore, we decided to devote a number of chapters to some of the most important Sufi orders, such as the Qādiriyyah and the Naqshbandiyyah, in order to bring out their particular color and spiritual essence. The choice of orders was based on the length of their existence, the geographical extent of their influence, and their general cultural and religious impact. We regret that space limitations prevented us from including a number of orders that also have had a wide following, such as the Rifā'iyyah and the Tijāniyyah, but hard choices had to be made. Some of these orders are dealt with in the second section of Part 1, which is concerned with Sufism in the main regions of the Islamic world. This regional study complements the study of individual orders, which reveals the particular traits of each order across ethnic boundaries. The study of regions brings out the local ethnic, social, and cultural factors that have colored the manifestations of Islamic spirituality over the ages. Unfortunately, not all the areas of the Islamic world have been treated with the same thoroughness, largely because of the different approaches of the contributors to this volume, who come from different backgrounds and regions. Islam in China had to be left out, because it was impossible to find a scholar who could deal with this subject from within and who would also have freedom of expression. The present volume, therefore, propagates unwillingly the lack of attention in current scholarship to the spiritual, religious, and cultural life of Muslims in China, who comprise numerically one of the major Islamic communities in the world.

It was necessary to deal with two other subjects in the section on Sufism: Ibn 'Arabī and his school and spiritual chivalry or *futuwwah.* Although a current within Sufism called Akbarian (from Shaykh al-Akbar, the title of Ibn 'Arabī) has manifested itself over the centuries, there is no major Sufi order established by Ibn 'Arabī that compares with the Mawlawiyyah Order founded by Rūmī or the Shādhiliyyah Order founded by Abu'l-Ḥasan al-Shādhilī. The teachings of Ibn 'Arabī, however, have had an immense impact on members of many of the orders, from the Naqshbandiyyah to the Shādhiliyyah. He also exercised great influence on later Islamic philosophy and theology. It was therefore necessary to deal with him and his school separately. As for *futuwwah,* it too cuts across various Sufi orders and has manifested itself over the centuries in many climes and under very different circumstances. Hence, it also had to be treated separately. Without a knowledge of *futuwwah,* one could not gain a clear understanding of many of the major ramifications of Islamic spirituality.

Islamic spirituality is also reflected in the literatures of the Islamic people. Because the Word of God was revealed in the Islamic universe in the form of a book with supreme literary excellence, literature—especially poetry—has always occupied a position of honor in Islamic civilization. The deepest yearnings of the Muslim's soul for God and the spiritual world are reflected in the various literatures that have developed and flourished in the Islamic world over the centuries. Therefore, Part 2 of this volume is devoted to literature as a mirror of Islamic spirituality. The major literary traditions, that is, Arabic, Persian, Turkish, the literatures of the Indian subcontinent, Malay and the literatures of Africa have been treated. For reasons mentioned above, the Chinese world has been left out.

The study of these literatures is brief, and in fact the original contributions had to be greatly shortened. What is presented is neither the history of these literatures nor a detailed account of mystical and spiritual poetry. Rather, our aim has been to present something of the spiritual significance of these literatures with a brief historical account of their development and mention of major figures as a mirror of Islamic spirituality. The literature of the Islamic peoples has never been treated completely in a single study, nor has it been possible to do so here.

The last part of this volume deals with Islamic thought and art. Islamic philosophy and theology are treated again in their relationship with spirituality, as are the so-called hidden sciences—especially the science of letters, whose symbolic significance is closely allied to Islamic esoteric doctrines and therefore to the inwardness that characterizes Islamic spirituality. Finally, there is an extensive treatment of the arts, including music, sacred dance, and the plastic arts. Sacred and traditional art issues from the inner dimension of a religion and reflects the religion's essence and spirit in the world of outward forms, thereby supporting spiritual life. This universal truth certainly holds in the case of Islam, whose art reflects directly both the spirit and form of the Islamic revelation. Islamic art is perhaps the most accessible means of appreciating the spiritual realities and inner beauty of Islam. The call of beauty in the contemplative life is always from the Beautiful and to the Beautiful, who is God, *al-Jamīl.*

It is hoped that through the study of the Sufi orders, Sufism in different regions, Islamic literature, and Islamic thought and art, the manifestations of Islamic spirituality in time and space will become known at least in their grand outline. One cannot expect to deal with all the manifestations of this spirituality among so many diverse ethnic groups, in so many languages and literatures and with such diverse artistic and intellectual expressions. But perhaps by grasping the major manifestations studied here, the reader will also gain at least indirect knowledge of areas, periods, ethnic groups and languages that have been left out either because of lack of knowledge in the present state of scholarship or because of limitations imposed upon the scholarly task at hand by external human and even political factors.

The Authors and the Editing of This Volume

Considering the differences between traditional scholarship in the domain of spirituality and current Western scholarship, which we discussed in the introduction to the previous volume, the selection of scholars for the present opus presented great difficulties. It was essential to choose scholars who were familiar with Islamic spirituality from within, who knew what a Sufi order is, who had felt deeply the message of a poem in this or that Islamic language, and who had participated in a Muslim's appreciation of a particular work of art or idea. Yet these scholars had to be able to transmit their thought in a language that would be comprehensible or could be made comprehensible to the Western public. Therefore, as in the first volume, we sought first the help of Muslim scholars, both the young and the well-established, who were fully conversant with their own tradition, especially in its spiritual dimension, and at the same time able to convey their thought to a Western audience. But we sought also the collaboration of those Western scholars who have lived with the reality of Islamic spirituality and who can speak about it from within.

After an extensive search that was made difficult by long distances, the busy schedule of a number of suitable scholars who could not participate, and even in certain cases local wars, a number of scholars agreed to write the essays presented here. As in the first volume, the authors are from diverse regions of the Islamic world and also from the West. The Western scholars are all authorities in their fields and have had intimate contact with the Islamic tradition. In the section on literature, our aim was to try especially to select scholars whose mother tongue would be that of the literature in question. This goal was achieved for Arabic, Persian, Turkish, and Malay. In the case of the literatures of the Indian subcontinent and Africa, however, many languages were involved and we were fortunate in being able to benefit from the vast knowledge and experience of two of the most eminent Western authorities in these fields. They possess a knowledge of many languages and literatures in the two areas in question and a general perspective that it was not possible for us to discover among available scholars of those regions.

The task of editing this volume has been great, requiring several years of hard labor. To transform an essay by some of the Muslim scholars to one that can be easily studied and readily assimilated by a reader accustomed to the norms of Western scholarship was not always easy. In a few cases, it required almost an alchemical transmutation, despite all the care that had been taken in the selection of the authors. We were forced to carry out heavy editing in several cases and to translate in others. Our goal has not been, however, to create uniformity. The scholars have written in diverse styles and have treated their subjects somewhat differently. These differences, far from being a negative factor, reveal something of the richness and diversity of Islamic spirituality and the perspectives in the light of which it is studied. The only uniformity we have sought to impose concerns the form of presentation of references, punctuation, transliteration,[3] and the like. We also have had to take the liberty to edit the language in several cases and to remove or change certain passages where there was some overlapping between two or more essays. As far as quotations from the Quran are concerned, we have followed the practice of the previous volume. The translations are either by Arberry, Pickthall, or this editor.

The Essays in the Present Volume

Part 1 of this work begins with a short prelude by Seyyed Hossein Nasr on the significance of Sufism as the main repository of Islamic spirituality, the early period of Sufism, the reasons for the rise of the Sufi orders, manifestations of Islamic spirituality outside of the Sufi orders, and the reasons for choosing the particular orders that are discussed in separate chapters.

Khaliq Ahmad Nizami writes in the first chapter about the most universal of Sufi orders, the Qādiriyyah. He deals with the life and the exceptional spiritual power of the founder, ʿAbd al-Qādir al-Jīlānī, and his attempt to regenerate Islamic society through the organization and spread of his order. He treats also ʿAbd al-Qādir's extant writings and analyzes in some detail his metaphysical and mystical teachings and the spiritual discipline of the order.

In the second chapter of Part 1, Victor Danner discusses the Shādhiliyyah Order and North African Sufism. He deals in detail with the life of Shaykh Abu'l-Ḥasan al-Shādhilī and mentions the prayers that have survived from the saint and his spiritual and mystical methods. He then turns to the early successors of al-Shādhilī, the relationship between the Shādhiliyyah Order and both Ashʿarism and Mālikism, and its establishment as a major order in predominantly Mālikī North Africa. Danner continues with the later history of the order and its many branches and discusses Maraboutism. He turns finally to the revivals of Shādhilism in the thirteenth/nineteenth and fourteenth/twentieth centuries in both North Africa and the eastern lands of Islam.

The Shādhiliyyah Order became one of the main transmitters of the teachings of Ibn ʿArabī, to whom William C. Chittick turns in the next chapter. He gives an account of the exceptional life of the sage and his voluminous writings. Chittick discusses the influence of the master throughout the Islamic world and his teachings on the Divine Names, the One and the many, evil, and the perfect man. He concludes with a number of diagrams which in a sense "summarize" Ibn ʿArabī's vast studies of cosmology.

In chapter 4, Muhammad Isa Waley discusses an order that has remained almost completely bound to the eastern lands of Islam, the Kubrawiyyah, associated with the Central Asian School of Sufism. He treats the life of the founder, the spiritual methods of the Kubrawiyyah, their emphasis on the journey through the seven inner states of the microcosm, and their particular attraction to visionary apperception and the spiritual significance of photisms. He then turns to some of the major figures of the order and discusses the significance of this predominantly Persian order in both the Sunni and Shīʿite worlds and its vast impact in the Indian world (especially Kashmir) and in Central Asia.

William C. Chittick turns to another major Persian Sufi figure, Jalāl al-Dīn Rūmī, who founded the Mawlawiyyah Order, an order whose main locus of activity has been Turkey and certain provinces of the Ottoman Empire. Chittick deals briefly with the life of Rūmī and his encounter with Shams-i Tabrīzī and discusses the *Dīwān* of Rūmī named after Shams as well as the *Mathnawī* and other works of the greatest mystical poet of the Persian language. Rūmī's followers, the sources of his poetry and ideas, and his relation with Ibn ʿArabī are treated. Chittick concludes with an analysis of Rūmī's teachings, which are studied under the title "the religion of love."

Another major Sufi order, whose founder was Persian but which spread almost exclusively in the Indian subcontinent, was the Chishtiyyah. Sayyid Athar Abbas Rizvi discusses the life of the founder and some of his early successors, the phenomenal spread of the order in India, and its role in the spread of Islam. He treats Chishtī literature and turns finally to spiritual discipline, social ethics, ritual practices, and the significance and influence of the order in India.

Javad Nurbakhsh, who is himself the supreme master of the Nimatullahi Order today, discusses the life of the founder of the order, quoting many of his poems. Nurbakhsh traces the later history of the order, concentrating on Sayyid Maʿṣūm ʿAlī Shāh, who came from Deccan to revive the order in Persia in the twelfth/eighteenth century. A section by Nurbakhsh's disciples, who have also translated the chapter from Persian, deals with the order under Nurbakhsh himself and its spread to the West. The chapter concludes with a description of contemplative methods and spiritual discipline.

Chapter 8 of Part 1 turns to one of the most widespread and influential of the Sufi orders, the Naqshbandiyyah. K. A. Nizami discusses the general features and initiatic chain (*silsilah*) of the order and gives an account of the life of the founder and the mystical practices established by him. He deals with the major successors of the founder and their role in the spread of the order in Central Asia as well as their immense influence in public life. He discusses ʿAbd al-Raḥmān Jāmī, the celebrated Persian poet, one of the main figures of the order. Nizami treats in detail the order's spread into India and its vast influence in the life of the subcontinent. He treats the importance of the Naqshbandiyyah in the political domain as a pivot of the Muslim resistance against the British and the subsequent activities of the order in other parts of the Islamic world, including Turkey and the Muslim areas in the Soviet Union. Nizami concludes with a reference to the spread of the order in the West in recent years.

The major orders discussed thus far cover vast areas of the Islamic world and embrace much of what is central to Sufism. The authors of the next six chapters turn their attention to other aspects of Sufism in particular areas. S. Abdullah Schleifer discusses Sufism in the Arab East and especially Egypt, where Sufism has been very active over the centuries and remains so to this day. He mentions the Badawiyyah and Rifāʿiyyah orders and their offshoots in Egypt and their immense influence down to the present day. He deals with the relation of al-Azhar University to Sufism and the reason for the harmony that has existed for the most part between the religious scholars (*ʿulamāʾ*) and the Sufis in that land. He treats the revival of Sufism in Egypt and other eastern Arab lands during the past two centuries and important recent Sufi figures. He brings his personal knowledge of Sufism in the Arab East to bear on the description of Sufi practices such as the *mawālīd* (birthdays of the Prophet and the saints) and the account of some of the figures who have kept Sufism alive.

In his essay on Sufism and spirituality in Persia, S. H. Nasr begins by indicating how widespread Sufism was in Persia from the early centuries of Islamic history. Leaving aside the orders covered already, many of which had Persian founders, he traces the later history of Sufism in Persia and the reasons for its eclipse during the Safavid period. He then turns to an important dimension of Sufism associated with the Malāmatiyyah (People of Blame), which began in Khurasan but spread later to other Muslim lands. He discusses the wandering dervishes (*qalandars*), such groups as the

Uwaysīs and Ahl-i Ḥaqq and the revival of Sufism during this century.

In her treatment of Sufism and spiritual life in Turkey, Annemarie Schimmel draws from her profound knowledge based not only on scholarly study but also on long personal experience. She gives an account of her encounter with Sufism in Turkey and its deep impact on Turkish culture and especially literature. She mentions the immense impact of Rūmī on the spiritual life of the Turkish people. She discusses the very different climate of the Baktāshī Order and its literature and points in conclusion to the great love of the Turks for Sufism, as exemplified by their attachment to their Sufi poets and their love for calligraphy, many of whose Turkish masters were Sufis.

In a note on the Khalwatiyyah-Jarrāḥiyyah Order, Shems Friedlander draws from intimate personal experience to describe the teachings and practices of an important Turkish Sufi order that has now spread into America and Europe. His study begins with a brief history of the Khalwatiyyah Order founded by the Persian Sufi ʿUmar Khalwatī, its spread into the Ottoman world, and the appearance of Nūr al-Dīn Jarrāḥī.

Although many aspects of Sufism in the Indian subcontinent had been treated in nearly all the chapters dealing with the Sufi orders (especially the Chishtiyyah), the life of Sufism in that region has been so rich and diverse that it was necessary to devote a separate chapter to Sufism in the Indian world. In his study of Sufism in the Indian subcontinent, S. A. A. Rizvi deals with such orders as the Kāzirūniyyah, the Suhrawardiyyah, the Kubrawiyyah, and the once politically and socially powerful Shaṭṭāriyyah. He discusses the *qalandars* and *majdhūbs* (enraptured Sufis), who have been common in the Indian scene, and he writes of the significance of Sufi poetry in the local languages of India.

In general works dealing with Islam or Sufism, attention is rarely paid to the Malay world; however, this region has had a rich Sufi tradition closely allied to both the Arab and Persian worlds. Osman Bakar deals with this tradition, beginning with a discussion of the significance of Sufism in the Islamization of the Malay-Indonesian archipelago and the role of Sufism in molding Malay as a major Islamic language. Bakar analyzes the practices of the Rifāʿiyyah Order, such as *dabbūs* (the ceremony of inflicting wounds upon the body). The specific forms that these practices have taken are particular to that world. Bakar discusses the general characteristics of Malay Sufism and the litanies and invocations of the orders; he concludes with a study of the impact of Sufism upon the culture of the Malays.

In his study of Sufism in Africa (exclusive of North Africa, which was treated earlier), Abdur-Rahman Ibrahim Doi begins by studying the role of Sufism in the spread of Islam in the African continent and the structure and activities of the Sufi orders in that region. He traces the spread of such major orders as the Qādiriyyah and Rifā'iyyah into both East and West Africa, emphasizing the remarkable expansion of the Tijāniyyah in much of West Africa. He points to the gradual degeneration of some of the orders and the later attempts at their reform. He deals extensively with the establishment of the Sanūsiyyah Order, which spread mostly in Libya but also became powerful in Chad and much of the rest of Central Africa and the Sudan. An appendix contains the names, the dates of the beginning of the impact, and the region of influence of Sufi orders that have been active in Africa over the centuries.

Without a consideration of the dimension of Islamic spirituality called *futuwwah* in Arabic and *jawānmardī* in Persian, Part 1 would have been incomplete. These words can be translated roughly as "spiritual chivalry." Throughout Islamic history *futuwwah* has been connected with Sufism on the one hand and with the knightly orders and craft guilds on the other. S. H. Nasr discusses the origin of *futuwwah,* the virtues of generosity and courage associated with it, and its history from the earliest period to its later development in Persia and then the Arab East and Turkey. He analyzes the content of the *Futuwwat-nāmahs* (*Books of Spiritual Chivalry*), the goal of *futuwwah* and its relation to the various crafts and professions. He concludes with the highest meaning of *futuwwah* discussed in the writings of Rūmī and Ibn 'Arabī.

Part 2 of this volume deals, albeit briefly, with the major literatures of the Islamic world as mirrors of Islamic spirituality, no attempt having been made to provide a detailed history or literary analysis of these literatures. In the essay on Arabic literature, Safa Abdul Aziz Khulusi points out that within the vast literary tradition of the Arabs there are four classes of works that reflect Islamic spirituality most strongly. He discusses each of these genres and its characteristics, pointing especially to the significance of the *adab al-Ṭaff,* or literature associated with the martyrdom of al-Ḥusayn in Karbala', and Sufi poetry.

In discussing Persian literature, S. H. Nasr and Jalal Matini first turn to the genesis of Persian as the language of Persian Muslims who accepted Islam but did not become Arabs. They deal with the rise of religious and mystical literature, concentrating mostly upon the major Sufi poets. Some space is devoted to religious poetry, chiefly by Shī'ites, in the Safavid period, and the later development of Persian Sufi poetry after Jāmī is outlined. The study concludes with a discussion of Persian Sufi literature in India and Sufi literature in other Iranian languages, such as Kurdish and Baluchi.

In her discussion of Turkish literature, Gönül A. Tekin points out that two major forces helped to create Turkish religious and mystical literature: the formal aspect of Islam itself and Sufism. She discusses both *dīwān* and *tekke* literature, concentrating more on the latter as typifying what is most Turkish in form and spirit. She deals with later "orthodox Sufi poetry" as well as Malāmī-Ḥamzāwī and 'Alawī-Baktāshī poetry colored by extremist Shī'ite ideas. Tekin points to the emulation of Persian models by certain Turkish poets and a return to purely Anatolian and Turkish imagery and form by others.

A. Schimmel treats the Islamic literature of the Indian subcontinent in the context of the spiritual life of that region. She turns to the general characteristics of Sufism in the subcontinent, emphasizing the influence of Ḥallāj and Rūmī and the significance of Chishtī literature. She delves into other manifestations of Sufism, complementing the discussions of earlier chapters, deals with exchanges between Sufism and Hinduism, and then discusses the influence of Sufism on the growth of literature in the subcontinent.

Baharudin Ahmad turns farther east to give a synopsis of Malay literature, most of whose early works are in fact connected with Sufism. He discusses the importance of translations of Sufi classical works into Malay from Arabic and Persian, such as the books of Ibn 'Aṭā' Allāh and Jāmī, along with the appearance in Malay of stories dealing with the life of the Prophet, the Muḥammadan Light (*al-nūr al-muḥammadī*), and early episodes of Islamic history including the tragedy of Karbala'. He then turns to the major figures of Malay Sufi literature, mentioning some of the traits of Malay Sufism and the influence of the major figures on Malay intellectual and spiritual life. He concludes with a study of an almost contemporary author, Amir Hamzah of Indonesia.

In the last chapter of Part 2, Jan Knappert deals with the complex and vast subject of the literatures of the Islamic people of Africa, beginning with some of the problems involved in the study of the subject and the question of the alphabet as well as written and oral literatures. He surveys Berber, Harari, Fulani, Swahili, and several other languages. A number of poems are presented in translation, and the close relation in theme between these forms of literature and religious models in Arabic literature is brought out. The author makes clear that these literatures have kept a distinctively African character while being imbued with Islamic piety and reflecting Islamic spirituality as it has penetrated the soul of the African people.

The third and final part of this book discusses Islamic thought and art as reflections and expressions of Islamic spirituality. S. H. Nasr deals with the major schools of theology (*kalām*), especially the Mu'tazilite and Ash'arite, their history and their teachings as they touch on Islamic spirituality. He discusses different schools of philosophy, including the early Peripatetics, the Spanish philosophers, the followers of the school of Illumination, and such later figures as Mullā Ṣadrā and Shāh Walī Allāh of Delhi. Special attention is paid to the profound interactions between Sufism and theology and particularly philosophy in later Islamic history beginning with Suhrawardī. Themes in Islamic philosophy and theology that involve Islamic spirituality directly are accentuated, and the Islamic intellectual tradition is presented as a major dimension of Islamic spirituality.

In Islam a whole series of "hidden" or "occult" sciences (*al-ʿulūm al-khafiyyah* or *gharībah*) reveal through their symbolism certain aspects of inner knowledge and are related in some of their most important branches, such as the science of letters, to the text of the Quran and the symbolism of the Arabic alphabet. They correspond to the Kabbalistic and Hermetic sciences in the West and must be dealt with in any complete treatment of Islamic spirituality. Jean Cantiens turns to some of these sciences to reveal their esoteric meaning, concentrating especially on the sacred science of *al-jafr*, or the science of letters. He studies the Arabic letters as they appear at the beginning of certain chapters of the Quran and their cosmological symbolism and relation to the human hand as understood in Islamic sources. He turns to the view expounded by Ibn ʿArabī and many other Sufis concerning the relation of the generation of the letters and words, which have a cosmogonic and cosmological function, to the "breath of the Compassionate." He brings out something of the symbolism and metaphysical significance of the letters of the Supreme Divine Name *Allāh* and its relation with the *shahādah*, or the Islamic testimony of faith. He concludes with a brief reference to the other "hidden sciences," especially alchemy and its spiritual and cosmological significance.

Jean-Louis Michon deals with the spiritual significance of sacred music and dance in Islam, commencing with the question of the legality of music, which was never settled categorically by the Muslim jurists. He then turns to the philosopher-musicologists of Islam and their views on the effect of music on the soul. He discusses the views of Sufi authorities concerning the *samāʿ*, or spiritual concert, and its elements—instruments, the human voice, melody, and rhythm. He deals with the supreme sonoral art of Islam, the Quranic psalmody, and complements this by mentioning the call to prayer (*adhān*) and its musical significance as well as musical and poetic celebrations of the Prophet and praises upon him. He turns to the ecstatic dance of the Sufis, *qawwālī* in the Indian subcontinent, the music of the Kurds, and the Shīʿite religious music in Persia. This geographical survey is followed by an extensive study of the classical music of the Islamic people including the Arabo-Andalusian, Iranian, Turkish, and Hindustani.

The volume ends with the last essay of Titus Burckhardt, the foremost Western exponent of the spiritual meaning of Islamic art, written shortly before his death. In an illuminating study, Burckhardt summarizes a lifetime of devotion to Islamic art and points to its deepest and most salient features. He begins with certain general comments on art and what distinguishes Islamic art from Western art. He turns to the Kaʿbah as the proto-architecture of Islam and brings out the relation of the Kaʿbah and the rites performed around it to Islamic art in general. He deals with the Arabic element in Islamic art and the impact of the Quran on that art wherever it was cultivated. He discusses the particular characteristics of Persian art and Turkish art, which constitute the other major expressions of Islamic art besides the Arabic. Burckhardt turns to calligraphy, the arabesque, and the use of light in Islamic art and answers the oft-posed question of why Islamic art is aniconic. After a brief discussion of the Persian miniature, Burckhardt writes of the architecture of the mosque and its various components and concludes with the relationship between art and craft in Islamic civilization. The author brings out in a lucid and poetic fashion that the traditional art of Islam is a crystallization of the inner dimension of the Islamic revelation and the direct manifestation of Islamic spirituality.

Islamic Spirituality Today

It is our hope that these two volumes on Islamic spirituality will open a new chapter and inaugurate a new category in Islamic scholarship being carried out in the West today. Too often the spiritual aspects of Islam have been studied in the West only historically and as being irrelevant to the present-day world. They have usually been treated as separate from and somehow "added to" Islam from outside sources. It has been our aim in these volumes to present Islamic spirituality in all its depth, length, and breadth as issuing directly from the sources of the Islamic revelation while adapting itself to very different climes from the Pacific to the Atlantic and through numerous centuries from what the West calls the early Middle Ages to the present.

Islamic civilization today has been eclipsed in many of its aspects by modernism. Much of Islamic art and architecture has been destroyed. Many traditional schools of thought have been either forgotten or mutilated by modernistic interpretations. Even the Sufi orders have suffered in many areas of the Islamic world through both inner decadence and outer opposition and suppression. Yet the inner message of Islam still survives. The spring of Islamic spirituality still gushes forth, and the religious life of Islam today cannot be limited to the political eruptions that are themselves mostly the consequence of the pressure of an alien civilization upon the Islamic world. The most inward teachings of Islam, which make possible the journey from the circumference of existence to the Divine Center, are still available for those who seek and who are qualified to receive them. Even the arts and schools of thought studied in this volume have not disappeared completely but continue to survive in a world dramatically opposed to their very existence. Nor could Islamic spirituality, which lies at the heart of the last plenary revelation of present humanity, die out completely before the end of time, for according to traditional sources God will never leave the earth without His "proof" (*ḥujjah*). The lamp lit by the Divine Light cannot be extinguished by men, although its light can become eclipsed and dimmed temporarily.

A Final Note

In concluding this introduction, we want to draw attention to the illustrations in these volumes. They have been far from perfect and, furthermore, in some cases their selection has been beyond our control. Limitations of budget and available material prevented us from including what we would have considered to be ideal. Nevertheless, we hope that the illustrations will reveal something of the visual dimension of the world of Islamic spirituality.

The task of editing these volumes has been a long and arduous one. We thank God for having made its accomplishment possible and pray that its fruit will be of benefit, whatever its shortcomings. We wish to thank all the authors for their contributions and Katherine O'Brien for translating some of the essays and helping also in the editing of the English of certain others. We are grateful to Dr. William Chittick, who has taken a great deal of time to go over the whole of the manuscript and the proofs. Finally, we thank Dr. Diane Apostolos-Cappadona for the research and preparation of the illustrations and Sarolyn Joshua for typing the manuscript. The collaboration of all concerned has made possible this first work in the English language devoted to Islamic spirituality in both its foundations and manifestations in time and space. May these volumes make more accessible the treasures of Islamic spirituality in a world so much in need of the liberating message of the Spirit.

Wa mā tawfīqī illā bi'Llāh
Our success comes only through God.

Notes

1. As stated in the introduction to the earlier volume of this series, *Islamic Spirituality: Foundations,* throughout this volume the term man is used not in its meaning of male but as the human being corresponding to *homo, vir,* or *Mensch* or as far as Islamic terms are concerned, *al-insān* in Arabic.

2. For reasons mentioned in our introduction to the previous volume (p. xxix n. 2), we have refrained from using the traditional Islamic terms of honor and respect for the Quran, the Prophet of Islam, and other prophets. In Islamic languages, the Quran is usually referred to as the Noble or Glorious Quran (*al-Qur'ān al-karīm* or *al-majīd*). After the name of the Prophet of Islam, who will be referred to throughout this volume with a capital *P,* the formula *salla'Llāh*[u] *'alayh*[i] *wa sallam* (blessings and peace be upon him) or one of its variants is uttered, while the formula *'alayh*[i]*'s-salām* (peace be upon him) is used for other prophets and in Shī'ism also for the Imams.

3. The system of transliteration for Arabic and Persian is given on p. xxx of the first volume. We have left words in other Islamic languages such as Turkish and Malay in the form provided by the authors. The question of transliteration from various Islamic languages is a complex one, and there is no single system covering all the different languages of the Islamic world which would be acceptable to all Western scholars.

Part One

ISLAMIC SPIRITUALITY AS MANIFESTED IN SUFISM IN TIME AND SPACE

Prelude: The Spiritual Significance of the Rise and Growth of the Sufi Orders

Seyyed Hossein Nasr

The truth and reality of the inner teachings of Islam became crystallized mostly in Sufism. Sufism therefore embodies more than any other facet of Islam the various aspects of Islamic spirituality, although this spirituality also manifests itself in the religious life of Shari'ite Sunni Muslims, in Shī'ite piety as well as in the intellectual and artistic life of Islam. Within the world of Sufism itself, the traditional teachings were transmitted from generation to generation going back to the origin of the revelation as seen in the essays in the previous volume of this Encyclopedia devoted to the foundations of Islamic spirituality. It was only later in the history of Sufism that the orders or *ṭuruq* (pl. of *ṭarīqah*) appeared on the scene and became the main depositories and guardians for the teachings of Sufism.

During the first four to five centuries of Islam, Sufi instruction was transmitted by an individual master around whom disciples would gather. Gradually the downward flow of time and further removal of the Muslim community from the source of the revelation necessitated a more tightly knit organization revolving once again around the master (called *shaykh, pīr,* or *murshid*), and usually named after the founder, but based on a definite set of rules of etiquette and behavior, litanies, forms of meditation, etc. Gradually Sufi orders appeared throughout the Islamic world having at the heart of their teachings the truth of Divine Unity (*al-tawḥīd*) and methods of reaching the Truth based on the invocation (*dhikr*) of various Divine Names and the acquiring of virtues (*faḍā'il* or *iḥsān*), which alone allow the *dhikr* to penetrate into the depth of the human soul and which are at the same time the fruit of the *dhikr.*

Each order emphasized some element of the path and adapted itself to various ethnic and psychological climates in a vast world which included such different human types as Arabs and Berbers, Nigerians and Persians, Turks and Malays. While the basic practices of *dhikr* and the Shariʿite foundation remained the same for all orthodox orders, other elements of the path, including the use of artistic forms ranging from music and poetry to the sacred dance, differed from order to order. As a result, an incredibly rich diversity of spiritual possibilities came into being in the Islamic world, which enabled men and women of very differing ethnic, mental, and psychological types to participate in the teachings of Sufism. At the same time the orders guaranteed the perpetuation of the teachings of Sufism, the continuity of initiation and initiatic transmission, and brought into being organizations that could protect the flame of Sufism in the storm of outward human life with all its vicissitudes.

During the nine centuries since the beginning of the organization of the Sufi orders, numerous orders have appeared in various parts of the Islamic world. Some have remained of importance in only one locality, and others have spread over vast areas. Some have lived for a short period only to decay and then die out, and others have survived over the centuries and continue to attract disciples to this day. Among the surviving orders some still make possible traveling upon the path (*sulūk*), whereas others only provide the grace of Sufism (*tabarruk*) without the possibility of a vertical ascent. In the major orders one can observe the occasional decay and death of one branch and the birth of another branch through the appearance of a veritable master. It is also possible for an order to be dormant and in a state of decadence only to be revived at a later time, as long as the chain of initiation and the initiatic transmission have remained intact.

A work such as the present one cannot deal with all the Sufi orders that have existed or continue to exist in the Islamic world.[1] The manifestations of Islamic spirituality in the form of Sufism have been presented by treating separately the major orders and schools and then adding complementary essays for various regions of the Islamic world. In this way it is hoped that most of the central manifestations of Sufism have been covered and that the teachings and history of the major orders have been brought out in an integral manner.

It is important to add, however, that despite the overwhelming importance of the orders as the major depositories of Sufi teachings during the past eight or nine centuries, the teachings of individual masters who cannot be identified with a particular order remain important. This is true not only of the earlier centuries, when Sufism was identified with the teachings of individuals, but also of later times, when the orders had already become established. Such a major figure as Ibn ʿArabī did not establish a specific *ṭarīqah,* although there is a distinct Akbarian current to be found during later centuries and he wielded great influence among members of several orders.[2] There are also a variety of Sufi figures guided by al-Khiḍr, the ever-living "prophet of initiation" or by members of the "invisible hierarchy" who form a part of the Sufi universe.[3]

The choice of the orders that have been treated separately in this section is based on several factors: their long history, geographical spread, impact on Islamic society, and intellectual and artistic significance. Some of the oldest orders such as the Rifāʿiyyah have not been treated separately because of their relatively limited geographical extension, although the order has been mentioned in the discussion of Sufism in the Arab world. Others like the Tijāniyyah have also not been treated separately, since, although such an order has spread over large areas, it is of fairly recent origin. In any case, the limitation of space forced a choice upon us that has resulted in the present treatment of the orders. What is certain is that the orders that have been treated separately are all major orders which have had a profound impact on Islamic history. They have been vibrant centers and guardians of Islamic spirituality and esoteric teachings starting with the Qādiriyyah Order, the most universal of all Sufi orders, whose centers are spread from the Philippines to Morocco.

Notes

1. A number of historical works have surveyed the Sufi orders throughout the Islamic world, the most thorough being J. Spencer Trimingham, *The Sufi Orders in Islam* (London: Oxford University Press, 1971). But even this work is not complete; moreover, there is no single work that covers the history of all the Sufi orders thoroughly. For the organization of the orders, see L. Massignon, "*ṭuruq*" in the old *Encyclopaedia of Islam.*

2. That is why a separate chapter has been devoted to Ibn ʿArabī and his school despite the fact that he did not establish a distinct Sufi order such as the Shādhiliyyah or Qādiriyyah, both of which espoused his teachings during later centuries.

3. This issue has been dealt with in chapter 10, "Sufism and Spirituality in Persia."

1

The Qādiriyyah Order

KHALIQ AHMAD NIZAMI

The Founding of the Order and Its Characteristics

THE QĀDIRIYYAH ORDER, so named after Shaykh ʿAbd al-Qādir Jīlānī (470/1077–561/1166), occupies a preeminent place in the spiritual history of Islam. Although its organizational structure came into prominence several decades after the death of the saint, its teachings had a profound influence on the thought and behavior of many Muslims during the lifetime of the Shaykh, who came to be looked upon as an ideal of spiritual excellence and achievement. Later generations, however, developed all sorts of legends surrounding his personality, and the real nature of his spiritual activity became shrouded in innumerable miracle stories woven around him by his followers and circulated by his biographers, such as ʿAlī ibn Yūsuf al-Shaṭṭanawfī (d. 713/1314).[1]

Shaykh ʿAbd al-Qādir was endowed with a remarkable power of persuasion and eloquence, and he used these gifts to extricate people from excessive engrossment in material pursuits by awakening their spiritual sensibilities. In inculcating a respect for moral and spiritual values, he found the supreme talisman of human happiness, and to it he dedicated his whole life. His intensely religious way of life and sincerity of purpose impressed his contemporaries, who thronged around him. Himself punctilious in obedience to every minute detail of Islamic Law (*Sharīʿah*), he demanded from his followers strict adherence to it. He looked upon the *Sharīʿah* as a *sine qua non* for all spiritual advancement and culture. This approach not only bridged the gulf between the jurists (*faqīhs*) and the mystics (Sufis) but also created a balance between varying degrees of emphasis laid on the spirit and the letter of Islamic Law.

The saint's association with the Ḥanbalī school of Islamic jurisprudence shaped his attitude in many matters of religious significance. He often cites in his works and sermons Imam Aḥmad ibn Ḥanbal (d. 241/855) and draws ideological sustenance from him. His adherence to Ḥanbalī law, to which later reformists like Ibn Taymiyyah (635/1263–728/1328) and Muḥammad ibn ʿAbd al-Wahhab (1115/1703–1201/1787) also adhered, saved him from much of the criticism to which other mystic teachers were subjected by the externalist scholars. In fact he made *fiqh* (jurisprudence) and *taṣawwuf* (mysticism) supplement each other and created an identity of approach among the jurists and the mystics. While propounding his mystical ideas, he never lost sight of their juristic implications, and in explaining juristic principles he underlined their spiritual value.

The Shaykh looked upon "showing people the way to God" not only as the leitmotif of all mystic effort but as a legacy of the Prophetic mission, which it was incumbent upon all Muslims to continue under all circumstances. He tackled the problem of imbuing people with spirituality from the point of view of both knowledge and faith and used the media of *madrasah* (college) and *ribāṭ* (hospice) for this purpose. A careful study of his sermons as contained in *al-Fatḥ al-rabbānī* ("Divine Victory"), some of which were delivered in the *madrasah* and some in the *ribāṭ*, would illustrate the subtle difference of orientation and emphasis. Like most religious figures of medieval Islam who became centers of a revival movement, Shaykh ʿAbd al-Qādir believed that he was divinely inspired and ordained to guide people on the path of spirituality. This consciousness of his mission gave not only a depth but also a sense of divine purposiveness to his efforts. He considered himself an agent of God for the moral and spiritual resuscitation of society.

The Regeneration of Islamic Society and the Expansion of the Order

In the era in which ʿAbd al-Qādir lived, his mystic activity contained a response to the challenges of the time. Adam Mez's *The Renaissance of Islam* portrays the condition of Muslim society in the fourth/tenth century.[2] The disintegration of Muslim political power and the degeneration of Muslim morals weakened the fabric of society while materialistic pursuits froze the heat of spiritual life. The innumerable sects that appeared during this period were expressions of intellectual anarchy and religious confusion rather than indications of spiritual virility and intellectual curiosity. The horrifying activities of the Assassins, the endless internal broils among the Seljuq princes, the disintegration of the Abbasid power, and the holocaust caused by the Crusades had created an atmosphere in which Muslim society needed moral animation and spiritual resurrection.

Shaykh ʿAbd al-Qādir's movement for the spiritual regeneration of society crossed the boundaries of Iraq and reached many countries, initially in the form of a vigorous religious activity by individual mystic teachers, later in the form of the *ṭarīqah* (small body of like-minded people devoted to the spiritual life) propagating the Qādirī mystic ideals, and subsequently as a *silsilah* (chain of a spiritual order) aiming at a mass effort for the spiritual culture of humanity and society. Initially the Qādirī teachings spread in and around Baghdad, but later on Arabia, Morocco, Egypt, Turkestan, and India came under their influence and large numbers of people entered the fold. The social milieu and the religious background of these regions being different, the order was confronted with diverse problems of response and adjustment. In African countries, it had to adjust to the conceptual framework of the tribes, and many customs and ceremonies of the earlier period were continued under new rubrics of Qādirī ideals and practice; in Ghur, Gharjistan, Bamiyan, Khurasan, and Central Asian regions where the Karrāmiyans dominated the religious scene,[3] Qādirī activities paved the way for the rejection of anthropomorphic ideas and attracted people toward the "personal God" without physical features. In many areas the activity and doctrinal orientation of the Qādirī saints were determined by the nature of activities of other mystic orders which had reached these areas earlier.

Because the crystallization of the Qādiriyyah Order did not take place during the lifetime of the saint, many of the spiritual exercises and litanies that were later consolidated into a system were not initiated by the Shaykh himself. Significantly enough, these spiritual exercises absorbed the attention of the people more than the thought of the saint.[4] The Shaykh's books being in Arabic, their direct impact on people of non-Arab regions was limited. Persian commentaries and translations of his works no doubt appeared in India and other countries, but the standard of spiritual life and the doctrines preached by the Shaykh were so elevated that it was beyond the capacity of ordinary individuals to follow them meticulously. Later generations, consequently, relied more on the *litanies* of the Qādiriyyah Order than on the *teachings* of the Shaykh.

The Organization of the Order and Its Spread

As stated earlier, the Shaykh combined in his person the twin roles of a mystic mentor and a college teacher, but after him the two functions became separated. His son ʿAbd al-Wahhāb (552/1151–593/1196) succeeded him in the *madrasah,* and his other son ʿAbd al-Razzāq (528/1134–603/1206-7) turned to spiritual discipline and looked after the *ribāṭ*. It was he who built near the grave of his father a mosque with seven gilt domes. Hulagü's sack of Baghdad (658/1258) brought to an end both the *madrasah* and the *ribāṭ*, and the Shaykh's descendants became scattered and dispersed. Thereafter, those associated with his family turned their attention to organizing the order in different regions. Those of his family members who remained in Baghdad constituted what has been called "the moral center of the order"; others settled in Cairo and Aleppo. ʿAlī ibn Ḥaddād carried his mystic ideas and his discipline to Yemen. In Syria, Muḥammad al-Baṭā'inī of Baalbek popularized his religious ideas. In Egypt, Muḥammad ʿAbd al-Ṣamad worked for the propagation of the order. According to E. Mercier, the order was prevalent in Berbery in the sixth/twelfth century and was in close contact with the Fāṭimids, who ruled there until 566/1171.[5] A. Le Chatelier says that the Shaykh's religious and mystical ideas were taken to Morocco, Egypt, Arabia, Turkestan, and India during his own lifetime by his own sons,[6] but this assertion has not been confirmed by contemporary sources. It took several centuries for the order to reach some of these countries.

In India, for instance, the order did not make any significant impact before the tenth/sixteenth century. North Africa saw the rise of the Jilālah communities, which attributed great spiritual and supernatural powers to the saint. Such developments were criticized by Ibn Taymiyyah and Ibrāhim al-Shāṭibī.[7] The order was introduced in Fez by the descendants of the Shaykh, Ibrāhīm (d. 592/1196) and ʿAbd al-ʿAzīz. Their descendants later migrated to Spain, but before the fall of Granada in 897/1492 all of them returned to Morocco. In Asia Minor and Istanbul, the order was introduced by Ismāʿīl Rūmī (d. 1041/1631). He founded some forty *takiyyahs* (Sufi centers in Turkish) in that region and a *khānqāh* (Sufi center in Persian—also transliterated as *khānaqāh*) known as *Qādirī-khānah*. In Arabia *zāwiyahs* (Sufi center in Arabic) were set up at Jedda, Madina, and Mecca. There was a time when the entire Nile Valley was studded with Qādirī centers, and Cairo was an important center of the Qādiriyyah Order. In Africa, Khartoum, Sokoto, and Tripoli had numerous *zāwiyahs* of the Qādirīs. The Qādirī missionary activity has been particularly noticed among Berbers. In fact, the sack of Baghdad by Hulagü in 658/1258, the fall of Granada in 897/1492, and the rise of the Ottoman Empire in 923/1517 are the three major developments of the Islamic world in the background of which the history of the Qādiriyyah Order may be traced in Africa, Central Asia, and Turkestan.

As the order spread out in different regions, many sub-branches and offshoots also appeared, but these were designated by the name of the local Qādirī saints. For instance, in Yemen, the ʿUrabiyyah after the name of

'Umar ibn Muḥammad al-'Urabī (tenth/sixteenth century), the Yāfi'iyyah after the name of 'Afīf al-Dīn 'Abd Allāh al-Yāfi'ī (718/1318–768/1367), and the Ahdaliyyah after the name of Abu'l-Ḥasan 'Alī ibn 'Umar al-Ahdal; in Syria, the Dā'ūdiyyah after the name of Abu'l-Bakr ibn Dā'ūd (d. 806/1403); in Egypt, the Fāriḍiyyah after the name of 'Umar ibn al-Fāriḍ (d. 632/1235); and in Turkey, the Asadiyyah after the name of 'Afīf al-Dīn 'Abd Allāh ibn 'Alī al-Asadī. These offshoots of the Qādiriyyah Order became known after the names of their immediate founders but retained their affiliation with the central figure of the *silsilah.*

The Life of the Founder

The district of Gilan lies in northern Iran south of the Caspian Sea. Here, in a village called Nif (*Bahjat al-asrār,* 88),[8] Shaykh 'Abd al-Qādir was born in 470/1077-78. His line of descent is traced to Imam Ḥasan (the grandson of the Prophet). His maternal grandfather, Sayyid 'Abd Allāh Sumā'ī was a pious and saintly person. 'Abd al-Qādir's father having died early, Sumā'ī looked after the orphan's upbringing. It was at the age of eighteen (in 488/1095), that 'Abd al-Qādir left Gilan for Baghdad, which was then humming with unprecedented intellectual activity and where the renowned Niẓāmiyyah College, founded in 457/1065, was in its full bloom. He did not, however, like to study at this seminary and completed his education with other teachers of Baghdad. His truthful character and the impact that it was to make on those who happened to come into contact with him were evident from his very early years. It is said that when he left his native place for Baghdad, his mother gave him forty gold coins—his share in the patrimony—and safely stitched them in his cloak. Her parting advice to his son was to be always truthful and honest. 'Abd al-Qādir promised to abide by it.

On the way robbers intercepted the caravan and plundered it. One of the robbers asked 'Abd al-Qādir if he had anything with him. He replied that he had forty gold coins. The robber did not believe it and moved on. One after the other robbers asked him and he gave the same reply. The leader of the gang interrogated him further and asked him to show where the money was. He placed his cloak before him and the robber found the money concealed there. Startled and puzzled at this truthfulness, the robber asked him why he had disclosed it; he could say that he had nothing and thus save this money. 'Abd al-Qādir replied that he had made a promise to his mother to be truthful under all circumstances. The revelation came as a terrible shock to the leader of the gang and he fell at his feet and repented for his conduct saying: "You keep the promise you made to your mother and we forget the promise that we made to our Creator." The gang returned the entire plunder to the owners and repented for their sins.

'Abd al-Qādir spent his early years in Baghdad under extremely straitened circumstances, but starvation and penury could not dampen his zeal for knowledge. He studied with particular care *Ḥadīth* (sayings of the Prophet), *fiqh* (law), and literature. Names of his sixteen teachers of *Ḥadith* and five teachers of *fiqh* have come down to us from Shaṭṭanawfī (*Bahjat al-asrār*, 106). It was in Baghdad that he became attracted to the Ḥanbalite school of Islamic jurisprudence. He received his spiritual training from Shaykh Abu'l-Khayr Ḥammād ibn Muslim al-Dabbās (d. 525/1131),[9] a saint who was illiterate but renowned for his spiritual excellence. His reputation at this time was one of a jurist, and the Sufi circles resented his admission to the mystic fold. But since some of the Ḥanbalite jurists of this period were inclined toward mysticism, this resentment was short-lived. Qāḍī Abū Sa'īd Mubārak al-Mukharrimī, head of a school of Ḥanbalite law in Baghdad, is reported to have initiated Shaykh 'Abd al-Qādir into the mystic discipline and to have conferred upon him his mystic robe.

Having completed his academic and spiritual training in Baghdad, he took to seclusion and spent eleven years in the ruins near Baghdad away from human company. In the words of Henri Bergson this seclusion of a mystic is "like the repose of a locomotive standing in a station under steam pressure." When he came out, he turned with great vigor and enthusiasm to public speeches. Apart from his own spiritual intuition in the matter, he was advised by Khwājah Yūsuf Hamadānī (d. 534/1140)[10] to preach in public. All contemporary and later writers refer to his extremely powerful role as a preacher. Unlike many mystics who impressed people by individual attention and personal care, the Shaykh addressed huge crowds and brought about a change in their lives. In the long and checkered history of Islamic mysticism, hardly any saint can match him so far as mass appeal and stentorian impact are concerned. In fact, with his advent begins a new phase in the history of Islamic mysticism, when mass activity is inaugurated and the mystic teachers of *dā'irahs* (small mystic centers of like-minded persons) and *zāwiyahs* (centers for mystics to live and pray) come out into the open and address huge congregations and convey their message of spiritual and moral enlightenment to the people at large. According to Shaṭṭanawfī, the number of those who attended his sermons reached seventy thousand (*Bahjat al-asrār*, 92). These figures may be exaggerated, but the popular response to his sermons was no doubt tremendous, and people came to him from Mesopotamia, Persia, and Egypt. According to his son, 'Abd al-Wahhāb, he delivered sermons three times a week: on Friday morning and Tuesday evening in his college, and on Sunday morning in his hospice. Four hundred scribes recorded whatever he uttered (*Bahjat al-asrār,* 95).[11] Jews and Christians also came to his meetings and were so moved by his orations that often they embraced Islam then and there. Speaking about his impact as a preacher, Abu'l-Faraj al-Jawzī, a contemporary writer, says that his hearers sometimes died of emotions. People gave up their sinful activities and adopted the path of morality and virtue as a result of his exhortations (*Bahjat al-asrār,* 96).

The Shaykh's teacher Qāḍī Abū Sa'īd Mubārak al-Mukharrimī was in charge of a large *madrasah,* which he entrusted to his pupil. The Shaykh took such interest in its development that the area became almost a *madrasah* town. The Shaykh himself used to instruct in several religious sciences. With the *madrasah* on one side and the *ribāṭ* on the other, the Shaykh had all the necessary instruments for the dissemination and propagation of his ideas. He delivered sermons for forty years (521/1127–561/1165) and gave lessons in religious sciences and pronounced religious opinion as *muftī* for thirty-five years (*Bahjat al-asrār,* 95). Thus, in his person he combined the mystical zeal for spiritual life with the adherence of a *faqīh* (jurist) to Islamic Law. Though his ideological commitment seems to have been with the Ḥanbalite school, he was not exclusive in his approach, and according to a report he acted as the guardian of the tomb of Imam Abū Ḥanīfah.

The doubt cast on his position as a mystic teacher (*Ṣūfī*) during his lifetime is based on misunderstanding. The Shaykh's entire approach was mystical, and he looked after a community center for giving instruction in mystic discipline. But since the regular organization of *silsilahs* was a later phenomenon, his mystic efforts also did not crystallize into a well-knit system. In his *Ghunyat al-ṭālibīn* (*That Which Is Sufficient for Seekers*) there is a very profound and penetrating discussion of the mystical ideal.

The Shaykh's family life began at a very advanced age. He married at the age of fifty-one and according to one report had forty-nine children. He was so meticulous in following the laws of the *Sharī'ah* in every minute detail of his life that even the food prepared for him was strictly according to *Sunnah* (practice of the Prophet). It is said that even grain was particularly cultivated for him (*Bahjat al-asrār,* 104).

'Abd al-Qādir as the Supreme Pole

According to traditional Sufi teachings, there exists a hierarchical system of saints who control the entire world order. Hujwīrī says: "But of those who have power to loose and to bind and are the officers of the Divine Court there are three hundred, called *Akhyār,* and forty called *Abdāl,* and seven, called *Abrār,* and four called *Awtād,* and three called *Nuqabā,* and one called *Quṭb* or *Ghawth.*"[12] Ibn 'Arabī calls Shaykh 'Abd al-Qādir the *quṭb* (or Pole) of the times;[13] generally among the people he is known as *al-Ghawth al-a'ẓam* (the greatest *ghawth*), which places him at the apex of the mystical hierarchy. His contribution to spirituality in Islam cannot be exaggerated. He initiated a powerful movement for the spiritual culture of Muslim society. Some of the founders of mystic orders—like Khwājah Mu'īn al-Dīn Chishtī and Shaykh Najīb al-Dīn 'Abd al-Qāhir Suhrawardī—were influenced by his mystic ideas and had benefited from his company. The Shaykh is reported to have remarked: "My foot is on the head of every saint." While in the case of other mystics such utterances made in a state of spiritual exhilaration have become the subject of criticism, his remark was taken seriously and according to Jāmī some of the eminent saints of the age actually put their heads under his feet.[14]

The Works of 'Abd al-Qādir

Shaykh 'Abd al-Qādir's mystic and religious ideas are contained in the following works: (1) *al-Ghunyah li-ṭālibī ṭarīq al-ḥaqq* (*That Which Is Sufficient to the Seekers of the Path of Truth*)[15] (generally known as *Ghunyat al-ṭālibīn*), a comprehensive work on the duties enjoined by Islam and the Islamic way of life; (2) *al-Fatḥ al-rabbānī*,[16] a record of sixty-two sermons delivered by him during the years 545/1150–546/1152; and (3) *Futūḥ al-ghayb* (*Victories of the Invisible*),[17] a record of seventy-eight sermons compiled by his son 'Abd al-Razzāq. C. Brockelmann has listed twenty-four titles of manuscripts ascribed to Shaykh 'Abd al-Qādir.[18] A critical study of these manuscripts would, however, reveal the apocryphal nature of some of the treatises ascribed to him by later generations.

While the large number of legends and litanies attributed to him reveal the nature of popular and credulous appraisals of his personality, the treatises ascribed to him throw light on the interpretations put on his teachings by the succeeding generations. Both of these may be important in estimating the popular response to his teachings, but a real assessment of his thought and spiritual ideals can be made only in the light of his three main works listed above.

The *Ghunyat al-ṭālibīn* was written in response to the request of his followers and friends for a detailed exposition of his religious views. Unlike the two other works, the *Futūḥ al-ghayb* and *al-Fatḥ al-rabbānī,* this is a complete work on Islamic Law and mystical thought. The compilers of his sermons, however, had to work under certain limitations. They could not take down every word that he uttered. Gaps and lacunas were inevitable and a coherent exposition of ideas remained a pious wish of the recorders. Sometimes the scribes recorded powerful sentences that the Shaykh uttered to emphasize his point of view, leaving aside the argument that preceded those remarks. In the two collections of his sermons, the Shaykh appears as a totally otherworldly person, but in the *Ghunyat* his views have a greater balance between the spiritual and mundane obligations of life. His discussions pertaining to faith, charity (*zakāt*), fasts, and *ḥajj* (pilgrimage) are followed by details of etiquette and decorum to be followed in daily life. The last portion of the book contains an exposition of his mystic ideas. It was within this framework—faith, devotion to God, and dealings with human beings—that the Shaykh interpreted his approach to religion and morality. In a section of this work he deals with sects that he considered to have gone astray.

The sermons contained in *Futūḥ al-ghayb* have a somewhat thematic arrangement but contain no dates. It is possible that discussions on particular themes dispersed in different assemblies were arranged and put together by the compiler under one heading. The *Fatḥ al-rabbānī* contains an account of forty sermons of the Shaykh delivered either in the *khānqāh* or in the *ribāṭ* in 545/1150. It is thus an account of the Shaykh's assemblies held only in one year and that too with long gaps. The scribe has not been able, and in fact could not be expected, to reproduce verbatim the speeches of the Shaykh. Naturally therefore gaps have been filled by the translators and commentators of his works.

The need to popularize his views and the insistence of Shaykh ʿAbd al-Wahhāb Qādirī Shādhilī of Mecca and Shāh Abu'l-Maʿālī of Lahore led Shaykh ʿAbd al-Ḥaqq Muḥaddith of Delhi to translate *Futūḥ al-ghayb* into Persian. The *Ghunyat* was translated into Persian by ʿAbd al-Ḥakīm Sialkotī (d. 1068/1657). Many abridgments, recensions, and commentaries of his works have also appeared.

The biography of the saint was compiled more than a hundred years after his death by ʿAlī ibn Yūsuf al-Shaṭṭanawfī (d. 713/1314) and named *Bahjat al-asrār* (*Splendor of Secrets*). Then followed the accounts prepared by Dhahabī (d. 748/1348), Taqī al-Dīn al-Wāsiṭ (d. 744/1343), al-Yāfiʿī (d. 768/1367) and others. Adulation and credulity have marred the historical value of many of the hagiological works written about the saint.

Mystical and Metaphysical Teachings of the Shaykh

Shaykh ʿAbd al-Qādir's spirituality had its roots in his concept and experience of God. For him God was neither a theological myth nor a logical abstraction of unity but an all-embracing personality present in man's

1. Sufis studying and contemplating in a garden.

ethical, intellectual, and aesthetic experience. He felt as if he were always in His Presence. This consciousness of the Divine Presence around him was the guide and motive of his active waking life and gave it a transcendent value. The Prophet's exhortation to people "to pray as if you see Him; and if you see Him not then He sees you" was the motto of his life and he translated it into practice. His sermons illustrated the extent of his own realization of the Omnipresence of God. He believed that this realization purged and purified the heart of an individual and put it in tune with the world of the Spirit (*al-Fatḥ al-rabbānī,* XXIII 133). He did not, however, allow this consciousness to blur the distinctness of the Creator and the creation. His discussions about *fanā'* (annihilation) and *baqā'* (subsistence) were also careful insofar as they scrupulously avoided any pantheistic implications, although many later Qādirī saints, such as Miyān Mīr (d. 1045/1635) and Mullā Shāh Badakhshānī (d. 1071/1661) of India were not so careful.[19]

One day when Shaykh 'Abd al-Qādir's mind was in a state of ferment, he said to himself:

> I want a death which has no life in it and
> a life which has no death in it.

Then he began to explain:

> So I was asked what kind of death it is that has no life in it and what kind of life it is that has no death in it. I said: "The death that has no life in it is my death from my own species . . . so that I do not live in any of these and am not found in them. And as for the life that has no death in it, it is my life with the act of my Lord in such a manner that I have no existence in it and my death in it is existence with Him." Since I have attained understanding, this has been the most precious of all purposes of mine. (*Futūḥ al-ghayb,* 167)[20]

As a result of the teachings of Muḥammad ibn Karrām, anthropomorphic ideas were current in certain regions of Central Asia and Iran.[21] The Shaykh firmly combatted such ideas. "Our Creator is on the *'arsh* (heavenly throne) but He has no body" (*al-Fatḥ al-rabbānī,* XIX, 124).

The ideal life in the eyes of the Shaykh was one which was absolutely devoted and dedicated to God. For this purpose alone did God create mankind, as the Quran says, "I have not created *jinn* and mankind except to serve Me" (LI, 56). The more a man strives to "live for the Lord," the nearer he comes to realizing the divine purpose of life. One has to surrender his life, his will, and his material means to God if he aims at divine realization. "God-conscious existence" gives man spiritual strength; it lifts him from mundane struggles for petty gains and joys of life to a life of spiritual solace and serenity and sets him in tune with the real source of spiritual power (*al-Fatḥ al-rabbānī,* XXI, 122–25).

An introspective study of one's own self is the first step in the direction of divine realization. "Whoever understands his own self, also understands God," said the Shaykh. This interiorization of spiritual experience paves the way for a deeper study of both noumena and phenomena. Creation points to the existence of its Creator, "because creation indicates the existence of the Creator and strong power is an indication of the wise actor behind it; because all things are in existence through Him. And it is this which is reported from Ibn 'Abbās in his explanation of the word of God: 'God has subjected to you whatever is in the heavens and earth'" (XXXI, 20) (*Futūḥ al-ghayb,* ed. Muḥammad 'Ālam Qayṣarī, 151–54). This power, however, comes to man when he identifies himself with the Divine Purpose of Existence and leads a life in consonance with the Divine Will. The Divine Will is revealed in the *Sunnah* (sayings and doings of the Prophet). So whoever follows it meticulously and in all details of life in effect subordinates himself to the Divine Will.

The Shaykh looked upon this world as a veil (*ḥijāb*) that hides from view the world of the hereafter. The more one involves his heart in this world and all that it has to offer, the greater become the thickness and darkness of the veil between him and the noumenal world (*al-Fatḥ al-rabbānī,* XXI, 122).

Whoever desires spiritual progress must come out of his "self" and develop an attitude of detachment toward all things worldly and material. Engrossment in material pursuits deadens man's spiritual sensibilities and makes his heart irresponsive to divine communications. In developing his ideas about "detachment," the Shaykh went to the extent of saying that unless one cuts oneself off completely, both physically and mentally, from the world around him and stops putting reliance on his own effort, action, and intelligence, his spiritual being remains dormant.

Spiritual life, he used to say, is not possible unless one controls his natural urges and adopts the path of the Law (*Sharī'ah*). In every matter, whether it is related to food and drink, dress and marital relationship, or habits and predilections, one has to subordinate himself to the injunctions of the Law. He recited this Quranic verse in support of his exhortations: "Whatever the Messenger gives you, take; Whatever he forbids you, give over" (LIX, 7) (*Futūḥ al-ghayb,* 159).

The Sources of Man's Thoughts

The Shaykh was of the opinion that transient ideas (*khāṭirāt*) which flash across the mind originate from any one of the following sources: (1) *nafs* (lower soul), (2) *shayṭān* (Devil), (3) *rūḥ* (Spirit), (4) *malak* (angel), (5) *'aql* (intellect-reason), (6) *yaqīn* (certitude). Ideas which owe their origin to the lower soul and the Devil lead man astray; those arising out of the Spirit and generated by angels are the genuine and truthful ideas and lead one to the path of righteousness and piety. Ideas that are created by reason may be either good or bad. A discriminating eye alone can make the distinction. Ideas that emanate from certitude are the source of spiritual solace and come to the saints, martyrs, and truthful people. The development of a man's spiritual personality ultimately depends on the care and meticulousness with which he analyzes the source of such transient ideas (*Ghunyat al-ṭālibīn*, 220–22).[22] The Shaykh laid down ten principles for the guidance of those who wished to lead a life of piety: (1) Abstain from speaking ill of an absent person. (2) Refrain from developing a suspicious attitude against anybody. (3) Abstain from gossip and whispering. (4) Abstain from looking at things prohibited. (5) Always utter the truth. (6) Always be grateful to God. (7) Spend money in helping people who deserve help. (8) Abstain from running after worldly power and status. (9) Offer five time prayers regularly. (10) Follow the *Sunnah* of the Prophet and cooperate with Muslims (*Ghunyat*, 275–76).

While developing his views about the path of spiritual progress, the Shaykh highlights the role of a spiritual mentor. He compares the spiritual teacher to a wet nurse who feeds the baby (*Futūḥ al-ghayb*, trans. Ahmad, 54). The Shaykh is needed only so long as one is infested with low desires and mean purposes. When one overcomes these baser appetites, the need for the Shaykh also disappears (*Futūḥ al-ghayb*, 54). What follows from this discourse is that although the guidance of a spiritual master is absolutely indispensable in the early stages of one's spiritual career, it is not required for all of one's life. Once the Shaykh has weaned a disciple away from earthly attractions, the need of his guidance comes to an end.

Determinism and Free Will

The Shaykh's discussions about determinism and free will were frequent, but while he talked about free will as far as human responsibility for actions is concerned, he basically advocated that destiny has decreed everything and that God's Will predominates in determining one's course of action.

On Dhu'l-Ḥijjah 12, 401/July 7, 1011, he saw a dream which again emphasizes the same attitude toward evil. He says:

> I saw Satan the accursed in a dream as if I were in a big crowd and I intended to kill him. Then he said to me, "Why are you going to kill me and what is my sin? If providence sets the evil in motion I have no power to change it and transform it into good. And if providence sets the good in motion I

> have no power to change and transform it into evil. And what is there in my hand?" I found his appearance resembling that of a eunuch, soft in speech, a line of hairs fringing his chin, miserable looking and ugly faced, as if he were smiling before me, full of shame and fear. (*Futūḥ al-ghayb,* 65)

It seems as if the Shaykh's attitude of extreme otherworldliness emanated from his faith in determinism. At times he was so distressed at the attitude of his contemporaries, whom he found weltering in the mire of sordid materialism, that he preached total renunciation of worldly pursuits and went to the extent of saying that as soon as a child was able to suck the stone of dates, one's responsibility to look after his children came to an end. At another place he says: "Teach some craft to your son and then turn your attention from him to prayers of the Almighty" (*al-Fatḥ al-rabbānī,* XXII, 130). Such expressions of disgust seem to have been prompted by excessive indulgence of the people in material pursuits and worldly struggles. In his *Ghunyat al-ṭālibīn,* however, he takes a more practical view toward family affairs, although spiritual obligations are never ignored.

Trials in Life

Referring to divine purpose in inflicting calamities on pious people, the Shaykh states that God tries and tests believers in proportion to the firmness of their faith. *Rasūls* (prophets), *nabīs* (apostles), *abdāls* (saints entrusted by God with the administration of the world), *walīs* (saints) were and are all put to tests and tribulations (*Futūḥ al-ghayb,* 66). These divine trials and calamities are a source of strength for their hearts and create confidence in them, establish their faith in the Lord, generate patience, and weaken the animal self and its desires (*Futūḥ al-ghayb,* 67).

Sometimes, however, calamities come as punishment for violation of Divine Law or for the commission of sin. Sometimes the divine purpose in sending calamities on man is to refine his nature and reform his ways (*Futūḥ al-ghayb,* 128). If patience in calamities is not linked with deep and unshakable faith in God, it can lead to frustration and pessimism. The Shaykh believed that good and evil were both acts of God and cited the following Quranic verse in support of his view: "God has created you as well as what you do" (LXXXVII, 96). It is therefore incumbent upon every human being to bear all calamities with patience and fortitude. To grudge and grumble is not the prescribed way. "Hold on to patience even if you get exhausted through your cheerful submission to and harmony with God. Hold on to cheerful resignation to and concord with Him" (*Futūḥ al-ghayb,* 66).

The Posthumous States

The Shaykh's account of hell to which the evildoers would be condemned is full of horrible scenes of punishment and torture.

> When the curtain would be lifted from hell, squalls would burst and smoke would spread everywhere and the sinners would painfully smell its offensive fetor. Nineteen angels would be wardens of hell and every angel would be assisted by seventy thousand assistants. . . . Every one would be with a cane in hand. When the angel would order, hell would start breathing like the braying of horses. It would emit fire and its flames would rise and spread as if they would swallow all. . . . The sparks coming out would be as numerous as the stars on the sky. Every spark would be like a cloud rising from the west. . . . There would be seven sectors of hell. . . . The seventh one would have pits, fire, smoke, snakes, scorpions in it. Its trees would have fruits, each having seventy thousand insects in it. . . . Hell has seven gates—every gate has seventy jungles, each jungle is spread over a distance of seventy years; the pits have seventy chasms—each full of snakes, scorpions, dragons, etc. . . . The wardens of hell would be armed with terrible weapons, iron rods, whips and chains. The scenes of torture would make the eyes of people turn stone blind. Their flesh would burn and fall down from their bodies; the brain would melt; puss would gush out of their bodies. (*Ghunyat*, 307–20)[23]

After describing the horrors of hell in several pages, the Shaykh refers to sins that would be punished in hell and particularly refers in this connection to adultery, theft, false evidence, polytheism, and tyrannical behavior toward human beings.

The Shaykh's account of heaven is as luring and enchanting as his account of hell is horrible and awe-inspiring. He says that in heaven there would be beautiful gardens laid out all around with trees laden with fruits. The roots of trees would be of gold and their branches would be silvery. The fruits would be softer than butter, sweeter than honey, and better in smell than *kastūrī* (a fruit). The palaces in heaven would be made of pearls, diamonds, and precious stones. Thousands of servants and a houri would be in attendance in each palace. In the mirror-like skin of houris one would be able to see one's own face. "The greatest pleasure for people in heaven," remarks the Shaykh, "would be the vision of God" (*Ghunyat*, 321–39). The descriptions of hell and heaven given by the Shaykh in his discourses and sermons reveal his tremendous power of exposition and his capacity to move the people.

Social Attitude and Ideals

Sharp awareness of contemporary social problems determined the nature and direction of the spiritual activities of the Shaykh. From the middle of the fifth/eleventh century, to use the terminology of A. Toynbee, Muslim society became a prey to "schism of the soul" and "schism of the body-politic." The Shaykh was deeply disturbed at this degeneration of Muslim morals and the intellectual anarchy that characterized the thought and behavior of the Muslim people. He found in the spiritual resurrection of society the panacea for all its ills and concentrated all his energies in strengthening the spiritual fiber of the community which, in his opinion, ultimately determined the stability and well-being of the social order.

Shaykh 'Abd al-Qādir used to say that time is like a pregnant woman; no one knows what is in its belly (*al-Fatḥ al-rabbānī*, 57).[24] This pithy sentence may be interpreted as an indication of the Shaykh's ideas of determinism, but in the context of his discussions it has far wider implications. He emphasized that human action and behavior ultimately assume a concrete shape and there is no escape from the process of cause and effect. One has to reap the consequences of one's actions. Time gives birth to what a man's own efforts have generated.

To strive for the welfare of society is, in the eyes of Shaykh 'Abd al-Qādir, a religious and spiritual obligation. He widened the horizon of spiritual effort when he identified "service of mankind" with the highest spiritual activity of man. He looked upon all people as "children of God on earth" (*al-Fatḥ al-rabbānī*, 19) and found in helping the poor and the needy the real spirit of religious devotion. "Whoever fills his stomach while his neighbor starves is weak in his faith" (*al-Fatḥ al-rabbānī*, 109). He advised his followers to desire for others what they desired for their own selves and to abstain from wishing for others what they did not wish for themselves (*al-Fatḥ al-rabbānī*, 107). He quoted the Quranic verse "Surely God loves the doers of good to others" (III, 133) and derives from it the principle that service to mankind is an act of spiritual value. His philanthropic spirit reaches its sublimity when he says that "he would like to close the doors of hell and open those of paradise to all mankind."[25] It is incumbent upon whoever desires to tread the path of righteousness and piety first to abstain from doing anything tyrannical against human beings and second to perform his duties toward them with care and consideration (*Ghunyat*, 295–96). Quoting a saying of the Prophet from his wife Haḍrat 'Ā'ishah, he says that human errors and sins are of three categories: (a) sins one commits against oneself—God may pardon such acts; (b) sins committed against God by developing polytheistic concepts—God would not forgive such sins against Him; (c) tyrannical acts perpetrated upon other human beings—God would not forgive even a small item of such tyrannical actions (*Ghunyat*, 262–63).

In his *Ghunyat* he equates hypocrisy with polytheism (*Ghunyat*, 478). People with hypocritical temperaments will incur divine displeasure. Even a scholar (*'ālim*) who does not act upon his knowledge is guilty of hypocrisy. He warned people against the company of those *'ūlamā'* who did not act upon the knowledge they had acquired (*al-Fatḥ al-rabbānī*, 83). He particularly condemns people who are like lambs in appearance but are really wolves in thought and action (*Ghunyat*, 480).

Although at times the Shaykh exhorts people to cease being entangled in the struggle to acquire worldly means—an attitude born of the painful realization that people were becoming too engrossed in mundane affairs—he was opposed to parasitism and advised the people to (a) live on permitted sources of income, (b) earn their bread with their own effort, and (c) share with others whatever they earned. But he advised his followers not to place complete reliance on people through whom they received their sustenance nor on the arts and crafts that helped them in earning their bread (*al-Fatḥ al-rabbānī*, 47, 27, 19, 130, 145, 160ff.).

The Shaykh gave a wide berth to the rulers of the day and held that most of their wealth was acquired through illegal means and exploitation.[26] Any contact with the ruler was, therefore, looked down on by him as a negation of the true spirit of religion. Although the Abbasid caliphs were anxious to seek his blessings, he never encouraged their visits. Sultan Sanjar is reported to have offered the province of Sistan (in southern Persia) for the expenses of his *khānqāh*, but he declined the offer with this verse on his lips: "My face may turn black like the canopy of Sanjar, / If except poverty I desire anything from Sanjar's country."[27]

Notwithstanding his critical attitude toward rulers, he believed that the type of rulers that a people had was what they deserved in accordance with their own life and character. "As you are, so shall be your rulers," he used to say. His constant advice to the people was that if they reformed their own thought and behavior, their rulers would also be good (*al-Fatḥ al-rabbānī*, 51).

Litanies and Rituals of the Qādiriyyah Order

During the course of its expansion, the Qādiriyyah Order developed many litanies and rituals, particularly when it spread in Turkey, Egypt, India, and Africa. The origin of some of the rituals has been ascribed to Shaykh 'Abd al-Qādir,[28] while others are obviously later accretions. Symbols have sometimes been adopted to highlight special features of the order in different areas. The Turkish Qādirīs have adopted a green rose as their symbol. When a candidate is admitted to the order, the Qādirī shaykh attaches to his felt cap a rose of eighteen sections, with Solomon's Seal in the center. This cap is called *tāj* (crown),[29] and is highly coveted in mystic circles.

In Egypt the Qādirīs use white turbans and white banners. Some fishermen who are members of the order carry upon poles nets of various colors when they move in a procession. In Morocco some Qādirīs recite invocations (*dhikr*) to the accompaniment of instruments. In Tangier the Jilālah, when they make vows, deposit white cocks in the *zāwiyah.* These are called *muḥarrar* and are not killed.[30]

Some relics of Shaykh ʿAbd al-Qādir were taken to different regions and a halo of sanctity came to surround these places. In Uchh there is a turban claimed to have belonged to the saint.[31]

Invocation and Contemplation

Of the spiritual practices adopted by the Qādiriyyah Order, *dhikr* (reciting the Name *Allāh*) is the most important.[32] Various degrees of intensity and emphasis are involved in the performance of *dhikr.* There is *dhikr* with one stroke, two strokes, three strokes, and four strokes. *Dhikr* with one stroke means repeating the Name *Allāh* with long drawn breath firmly, as if from high above, with force of heart and throat, and then stopping so that the breath returns to normal. This is to be repeated continuously for a long time. The *dhikr* with two strokes means sitting in the posture of prayer and invoking the Name *Allāh* first on the right side of the breast and then on the heart. This is done repeatedly without interval and with force. It is deemed effective in developing concentration of heart and in dispelling worries and distractions. The *dhikr* with three strokes is performed sitting cross-legged and repeating the Name *Allāh* first at the right side, second at the left, and the third time on the heart. The third stroke is to be with greater intensity and is to be continued longer. The *dhikr* with four strokes is also performed sitting cross-legged and consists of uttering the Name *Allāh* first on the right side, second on the left, the third time toward the heart, and the fourth time in front of the breast. The last stroke is expected to be stronger and longer.

These *dhikr* practices can also be performed by groups, loudly or silently, sitting in circles after morning and afternoon prayers. If a man utters *Allāh* four thousand times a day regularly for two months, he is usually expected to have qualified for some kind of spiritual experience.

After *dhikr* the Qādirīs recommend *pās-i anfās,* which means regulating the breath in such a way that in the process of inhaling and exhaling, the Name *Allāh* circulates automatically in the body. Then comes the *murāqabah* (contemplation). One is advised to concentrate on some Quranic verse or Divine Quality and become completely absorbed in contemplation.

Some of the practices developed by the later followers register local influences and are inexplicable with reference to the saint's own ideas and ideals. For instance the followers of the Qādiriyyah Order in North Africa, who are called *Gīlānīs,* have developed the practice of the *khalwah* (spiritual retreat) in a very special manner. Reeds are planted between heaps of stones, rags are attached to them by women, and benzoin and styrax are burnt. Both men and women visit this type of *khalwah* and pray for the fulfillment of their wishes.

An almost inevitable concomitant of such practices was the deification of the saint by extreme groups. Those who did not go to that length attributed a remark to him: "All the saints are under my feet"[33] –an expression that, if uttered by the Shaykh, could best be interpreted as referring to an extreme condition of spiritual elation without any other implications.[34] But later admirers wrote to defend his position and sought to establish his pre-eminent place in the mystical hierarchy. Even an otherwise very cautious and critical scholar such as Shaykh 'Abd al-Ḥaqq Muḥaddith of Delhi paints the Shaykh in colors borrowed from these exaggerated hagiological tales. The greatness of Shaykh 'Abd al-Qādir lay not in his miracles, but in his "God-conscious" existence and dedication to the supreme ideal of Islamic mysticism: to realize God, to show people the way to God, and to bring happiness to disturbed hearts and distracted souls.

Notes

1. He is the author of *Bahjat al-asrār* (Cairo, 1304).
2. A. Mez, *The Renaissance of Islam,* trans. Salahuddin Khuda Bakhsh and D. S. Margoliouth (London: Luzac, 1937).
3. K. A. Nizami, *Some Aspects of Religion and Politics in India during the 13th Century* (Aligarh: S. Nural Hasan, 1961) 48–49.
4. That is why a number of works on invocations and litanies are attributed to him. *Evradi Sherifeh* (Constantinople, 1869) is one such collection.
5. E. Mercier, *Histoire de l'Afrique septentrionale* (Paris: E. Leroux, 1881–91) 3:14.
6. A. Le Chatelier, *Les confreries musulmanes du Hedjaz* (Paris: E. Leroux, 1887) 35.
7. *I'tiṣām,* I, 348ff. (Reprint of the 1914 Cairo edition by Dār al-Manār).
8. Yāqūt Ḥamawī, however, says that he was born at Bashtir (*Mu'jam al-buldān,* II, 187). 'Abd al-Maḥāsin names a village between Baghdad and Wasit as his birthplace (Abū al-Maḥāsin Yūsuf ibn Taghribirdī, *al-Nujūm al-zāhirah,* ed. Popper, *Annals* [Berkeley: University of California Press, 1909]).
9. For a biographical notice, see Jāmī, *Nafaḥāt al-uns* (Lucknow, 1915) 456–58.
10. A very distinguished saint of the time who influenced many founders of spiritual orders. For a biographical notice, see *Nafaḥāt al-uns,* 337–39.
11. If this figure is correct, the surviving record of his speeches is infinitesimally small. One whose speeches were preserved by so many people must leave a fairly large number of records.
12. Hujwīrī, *Kashf al-maḥjūb,* trans. R. A. Nicholson (London: Luzac, 1911) 214.
13. Ibn 'Arabī, *al-Futūḥāt al-makkiyyah* (Beirut: Dār Ṣādir, n.d.) I, 262.

14. *Nafaḥāt al-uns,* 457–58. See also 'Abd al-Ḥaqq Muḥaddith Dihlawī, *Akhbār al-akhyār* (Delhi: Maṭba' Mujtabā'ī, 1331 A.H.) 10.

15. Cairo, 1322/1905.

16. Cairo, 1302/1884.

17. Text on the margin of *Bahjat al-asrār* (Cairo, 1304/1886), trans. W. Braune (Leipzig: W. de Gruyter, 1933).

18. C. Brockelmann, *Geschichte der arabischen Literatur* (Weimar: E. Felber, 1898) 1:435.

19. For Miyān Mīr, see Dārā Shikoh, *Sakīnat al-awliyā',* ed. S. M. R. Jalālī Nā'īnī and D. Tarachand (Tehran: 'Ilmī Press, 1965).

20. Except where noted, citations of this work are from the English translation by Aftab-ud-Din Ahmad (Lahore: Sh. M. Ashraf, 1958).

21. For Muḥammad ibn Karrām and the Karrāmiyyah doctrines, see Abu'l Fatḥ al-Shahrastānī, *Book of Religions and Philosophical Sects* (*Kitāb al-milal wa'l-niḥal*) (London: Society for the Publication of Oriental Texts, 1846) 85–96.

22. Delhi, 1979.

23. This and the following citations of this work are from the translation by Amanullah Arman.

24. This and the following citations of this work are from the translation by 'Ashiq Ilahi.

25. His *Ghunyat* breathes a spirit of deep humanism and concern for the welfare of society.

26. 'Abd al-Ḥaqq Muḥaddith Dihlawī, *Akhbār al-akhyār,* 17.

27. Ibid., 198.

28. The litanies ascribed to Shaykh 'Abd al-Qādir in *al-Fuyūḍāt al-rabbāniyyah* are cited on the authority of 'Abd Allāh ibn Muḥammad al-'Ajamī, who lived some 185 years after the saint.

29. J. P. Brown, *The Dervishes: Or Oriental Spiritualism* (London: Oxford University Press, 1927) 98.

30. G. Salmon, *Archives marocaine* (1905) 2:108.

31. *Encyclopedia of Religion and Ethics,* 1:69.

32. For details, see Walī Allāh Dihlawī, *Intibāh fī salāsil-i awliyā' Allāh* (Delhi, 1311 A.H.) 21–17; *Qawl al-jamīl* (Kanpur, 1291 A.H.) 34–45.

33. Shaykh 'Abd al-Ḥaqq Muḥaddith Dihlawī, *Tanbīh al-'ārif bi mā waqa' fī'l-'awārif,* MS, Rampur Library; see K. A. Nizami, *Ḥayāt-i Shaykh 'Abd al-Ḥaqq Muḥaddith Dihlawī* (Delhi: 1953) 180–81.

34. Shaykh Shihāb al-Dīn Suhrawardī holds this view.

2

The Shādhiliyyah and North African Sufism

Victor Danner

The Background

Sufism reaffirmed itself in a decisive fashion in the seventh/thirteenth century, which allowed the works of Ibn 'Arabī (d. 638/1240) and the new Sufi orders of the day to come to the fore. The political and dynastic readjustments made in both the East and the West of the Islamic world provided a new social framework or political state of affairs within which Sufism could exert a revitalizing spirit within the community as a whole. In the West the end of the Almohades gave rise to several dynastic regimes. Under one of these, the Ḥafṣids of Tunis, the Shādhilī Order of Sufism began its existence.[1] In the middle of the century, the Ayyūbid power in the East disintegrated and there came upon the scene the great Mamlūk state. The Mamlūks stopped the westward march of the Mongols and transplanted to Cairo the caliphal institutions that had been eradicated by the Mongol conquest of Baghdad in 656/1258, some months before the death of the founder of the Shādhiliyyah, the Imam Abu'l-Ḥasan al-Shādhilī. His order would flower under the Mamlūks in Egypt and elsewhere in the Near East in the latter part of that century. But the origins of the Shādhiliyyah were in the same Maghrib (Spain, Morocco, Algeria, Tunisia, and parts of Libya) that saw so many other great manifestations of the Sufi way of life. More or less contemporaneous with the founder of the Shādhilī Order were such luminaries as Abū Madyan Shu'ayb al-Maghribī (d. 594/1197), Ibn 'Arabī (d. 638/1240), 'Abd al-Salām ibn Mashīsh (d. 625/1228), Ibn Sab'īn (d. 669/1271), and al-Shushtarī (d. 688/1270), just to mention a few.

The role of the Maghrib in the spiritual life of Islam prior to the seventh/thirteenth century remains a largely unstudied question,[2] but its role after that epoch seems clear enough. Practically all of the previously mentioned Sufis wound up in the East. The Shādhilīs themselves, after their initial start in the Maghrib, put out new roots in the East in the very lifetime of the founder. For centuries after, down to the present day, the order would furnish a steady stream of shaykhs moving from the Maghrib to the eastern or other parts of the Islamic world. The brilliance of the personalities and schools of the seventh/thirteenth century makes us aware of the eastward migration of Sufism almost as if it had suddenly begun in that time. The paucity of records for the period from the third/ninth to the sixth/twelfth centuries accounts in part for the lack of historical studies of Maghribī Sufism in the early days. But also the concentration of attention on the eastern types of Sufism has stymied the understanding of what actually took place in Maghribī Sufism prior to the days of Ibn al-ʿArīf (d. 536/1143).[3] The foundations of Sufism in the Maghrib came, of course, from the East, as did Islam. Yet the peculiar genius of Islam in the West, its life-style, its calligraphic art, its mosque architecture, and the lucidly crystalline nature of its urban architecture—to say nothing of its Mālikism—existed from the very early generations of Islam. These general traits were reinforced when, with the rise of the Abbasids in the second/eighth century, the West cut itself off from the East and began to develop organically in its own fashion. It was in such an ambiance that Shādhilism arose in the seventh/thirteenth century.

The Life and Works of Abu'l-Ḥasan al-Shādhilī

In the history of Islam, there are numerous Sufi types. The universality of the Sufi tradition balks at any attempt to reduce it to a single, controllable pattern. Nominalistic and antinomian Sufism have always coexisted. Over the centuries, however, there has emerged a type of Sufi master who embodies in his person what one could call "normative Sufism." This Sufi is characterized by a kind of spiritual sobriety, so to speak, that excludes all flamboyance and singularity. While his mind is fixed on the Real (*al-Ḥaqq*), he affirms nevertheless the relative validity of both the Law and the dogmas of Islam. Such a Sufi tends to be self-effacing and to pass unnoticed by ordinary Muslims. It is he who is the characteristic flower of Sufism and the one who typifies the contemplative path throughout the centuries. Altogether of a different stamp is al-Ḥallāj (d. 309/922), who is well known outside the Islamic world but who can in no way be considered as embodying the normative Sufi typology before or after his time.[4] The agonies, the persecutions, and the eventual martyrdom on the gibbet of this great Sufi saint contrast with the absence of all drama and pathos in the lives of the Sufis who follow the usual way. It is this normative Sufism, nevertheless, that furnishes the real measure of the spiritual path in Islam. That is the kind of Sufism that characterizes the founder of the Shādhiliyyah, who nonetheless exercised a tremendous influence on the world around him and, through his order (or his *ṭarīqah*, "spiritual path," "Sufi order"), on the history of Islam.

He was born in the region of Ghumārah, near present-day Ceuta, in northern Morocco, in the year 593/1197, at a time when the Almohades had reached the end of their vigor.[5] A *sharīf* of Ḥasanid descent, he was a Mālikī who wandered far afield in search of knowledge. Immensely learned, even as a young man, he was famous for his ability to engage in legal argumentation with the religious scholars of his day. It was in a hermitage on top of Jabal al-ʿAlam, near Tetuan, that he met the shaykh who was to have the greatest influence on his life, ʿAbd al-Salām ibn Mashīsh (d. 625/1228), subsequently known as "the Pole of the West," just as ʿAbd al-Qādir al-Jīlānī (d. 561/1166) would be called "the Pole of the East." Remaining with his master for a while, Abu'l-Ḥasan then departed for Shādhilah, in Tunisia, on orders from his teacher; and from there he received the name of al-Shādhilī. After intense spiritual exercises in the Jabal Zaghwan region, he was ordered in a vision to teach Sufism.

Accordingly, he set up his first *zāwiyah* in Tunis in the year 625/1228, just when the new governor and future founder of the Ḥafṣids, Abū Zakariyyā', arrived there too. His new *ṭarīqah* was a stunning success, drawing masses of people from all walks of life, including the sultan's family. On one of his trips to the East, an Ayyūbid sultan conferred on him and his descendants, by way of a religious endowment, one of the enormous towers that arose from the walls formerly encompassing the city of Alexandria in Egypt. In the year 642/1244, the shaykh, once again in obedience to a vision, left the Maghrib for the last time and, accompanied by other Sufi shaykhs and many of his own disciples, moved to Alexandria, where he established both his residence and the *zāwiyah* of his order in the tower the Ayyūbid sultan had given him. On the top floor he lived with his family; another floor was converted into a tremendous mosque where he gave public instruction; and yet another floor was turned into a great *zāwiyah* for his disciples, with cells for meditational retreat. In Egypt, likewise, his order met with great success, drawing into its ranks many court officials, great religious scholars like ʿIzz al-Dīn ibn ʿAbd al-Salām (d. 660/1262) or the Shāfiʿī traditionist al-Mundhirī (d. 656/1258), a host of Sufi figures, and individuals from different levels of society. In the year 646/1248, he became blind, and it was in that state that he participated, in his own way, in the Battle of al-Manṣūrah in Egypt, which stopped the Seventh Crusade headed by Saint Louis of France, one of the few instances in history where saints in opposing armies actually clashed without knowing of one another's presence. Shortly before Shaykh Abu'l-Ḥasan started on his last pilgrimage to Mecca, the city of Baghdad fell to the conquering Mongols, thus ending the long reign of the Abbasids there and ushering in a new epoch in the history of Islam. The shaykh was accompanied by a mass of his disciples; but he fell ill in the eastern desert of Egypt, in a place called Ḥumaythirah, and there he died in the year 656/1258.

The shaykh never composed any books or treatises on Sufism, but he did compose litanies (*aḥzāb*, pl. of *ḥizb*), which are prayers of a mystical origin containing Quranic formulations as well as particular Sufi inspirations.[6] These were immediately diffused throughout the Islamic world. Since then, they have become some of the most widely used litanies in Islam and are considered to possess special graces. They have names that he or others gave to them, such as *Ḥizb al-baḥr* (*Litany of the Ocean*) or *Ḥizb al-anwār* (*Litany of Lights*), and the like. Well over a dozen of them are famous and have been glossed by eminent Sufi teachers of later times. They are said to possess certain theurgical properties, and the shaykh claimed that he received them from the mouth of the Prophet in visions. Their fundamental teaching has to do with the Oneness of Allah (*tawḥīd*) and the spiritual consequences that flow therefrom in the soul of the believer. Both mystical and nonmystical Muslims can find their own levels within the litanies, and that is no doubt why they have been so popular over the centuries. But apart from that pedagogical function, they seem to have been used by the early and later Shādhilīs as themes of meditation on death, the hereafter, purification, vigilance, detachment, patience, and the Attributes of God. We read in one Sufi text that they were used three times a day—in the morning, in the afternoon, and in the evening—which implies that they functioned as part of the Shādhilī methods of concentrating the mind on the Divinity. It was perhaps in relation to these meditations that the other compositions by the shaykh, the *dawā'ir* (pl. of *dā'irah*, "circle"), are to be situated. These were geometric representations, generally of circles within squares or vice versa, containing Quranic verses or Divine Names or the names of the archangels, which seem to have been used as visual supports of meditation. The same *dawā'ir* had theurgical functions too, as protective amulets and talismans, and the shaykh prescribed them for some of his disciples. They were transmitted by later Shādhilīs through a regular chain of authorities going back to the founder of the order. The Shādhilī biographer, Ibn 'Iyāḍ, in his *al-Mafākhir al-'Aliyyah* (*Lofty Glorifications*) gives examples of these *dawā'ir*. A considerable amount of the material found in the cosmological work called *Shams al-āfāq fī 'ilm al-ḥurūf wa 'l-awfāq* (*The Sun of the Horizons concerning the Science of Letters and Harmonies*) by 'Abd al-Raḥmān al-Busṭāmī (d. 858/

1454), goes back to Shaykh Abu'l-Ḥasan through one of his greatest disciples, Shaykh Abu'l-ʿAzā'im, who died in Tunis at the age of 116 (718/1318). The cosmology in question is purely esoteric and related to the Divine Names of Allah and a number of disciplines, such as alchemy and astrology, in their symbolic meanings. This cosmological, talismanic, and theurgical development of the *dawā'ir,* in conjunction with the symbolism of the Arabic letters, must not be confused with either black magic (*al-siḥr al-aswad*), which is sorcery, or with white magic (*al-siḥr al-abyaḍ*), which is more positive in nature, to be sure, but is still not of a purely theurgical characteristic, for this has spiritual graces and blessings as its fruits. Moreover, all of this constitutes a secondary development of the symbolism of the *dawā'ir* anyway, a kind of popular extension of what must have had meditational values or higher meanings for Sufi adherents.

Shādhilī Teachings

The *ṭarīqah* that Shaykh Abu'l-Ḥasan established was based on the metaphysical and spiritual contents of the Islamic doctrine of the absolute Oneness of Allah (*tawḥīd*). The goal of his path was the gnostic realization of Allah, gnosis (*maʿrifah*) implying perfect wisdom and sanctity of soul in the contemplative. The *maʿrifah* he preached reposed on simple faith, on the strictures of the Law (*Sharīʿah*), and on the dogmatic formulations of Ashʿarism as regards creed (*ʿaqīdah*). Although the gnosis in question also had cosmological implications in a spiritual sense, it was in no way enshrouded in the complex philosophical notions of *waḥdat al-wujūd* ("Oneness of Being") propounded by Shaykh Abu'l-Ḥasan's contemporary, Ibn ʿArabī (d. 638/1240),[7] although the Shādhilī masters defended the Shaykh al-Akbar against his detractors, particularly against Ibn Taymiyyah (d. 728/1328), the Ḥanbalī canonist of later times. Moreover, the *tawḥīd* taught by Shaykh Abu'l-Ḥasan carried with it the implication of "remembering God" (*dhikru'Llāh*), or the invocation of the Divine Name *Allāh,* the prime spiritual art of concentration in Sufism. The two, *tawḥīd* and *dhikr,* constituted the essential pillars of his way, the former with respect to doctrine, the latter with respect to spiritual methodology. Yet it was not in these two elements that one can discern a difference between his Sufi order and the others of his day or earlier: they were all more or less based on the same Quran and *Sunnah* of the Prophet, on the same Islamic teachings and practices as seen from an esoteric viewpoint, varying only in emphases or accents and applications. True, the gnostic teachings of the Shādhiliyyah set them apart from the orders that stressed devotionalism and asceticism carried to great lengths; but there were, of course, other orders of the day, such as the

Qādiriyyah, the Suhrawardiyyah, and the like, that were gnostic also and that approached things from an intellectual, not an emotional or sentimental, attitude.[8]

Rather, it was in the external self-effacement of the early Shādhilīs that we must look for differences and contrasts with other Sufi communities of the times. The Shādhilī Order was not discernible from the outside. Although its masters gave public lectures on *taṣawwuf* from time to time, which made their presence in a given locality obvious, the members of the order, the rank and file, were not distinguishable from the generality of Muslims. In the days of Shaykh Abu'l-Ḥasan, a number of his disciples became eminent shaykhs in Tunisia and elsewhere in the Maghrib. All of them had disciples, as one can well imagine; but their tracks in history cannot be pinpointed because they had no visible signs of adherence to the Shādhiliyyah. If we did not know through one of the biographical accounts of the early masters of the order that the Sultan al-Malik Muʿizz al-Dīn (d. 655/1257) had been a disciple of Shaykh Abu'l-Ḥasan, there would have been no way of discovering this either from the practices of the sultan or from his external garb.

Likewise, the *zāwiyahs* of the order were nowhere obvious, the masters very often holding forth in their own homes, as did Shaykh Abu'l-Ḥasan himself when he founded his path in Tunis or when he later moved to one of the towers of the wall surrounding Alexandria. For the *zāwiyahs* of the Shādhilīs had none of the semi-official characteristics of the imposing *khānqāhs* built by the rulers of the day for the other Sufi orders. In a similar effort toward discretion, the *fuqarā'* of the order wore no distinctive garments, such as the *khirqah* or the *muraqqaʿah*, which were the coarse, patched-up woolen garments of the other orders. They had no bowl or staff, nor did they lead wandering, eremitical lives as mendicants. Quite the contrary, they dressed like all other Muslims did; and some of them, like the founder of the order himself, very often wore magnificent clothing, so that more than one ascetic would have reason to wonder if he were in the presence of a genuinely spiritual person or not. Their garments reflected the particular social class to which they belonged, whether it was that of a shoemaker, a doctor of the Law, a minister, a professor, or some other group. There was a reason for that effacement of the *faqīr* in the professional world around him: the rule of the early Shādhilīs was that all members of the order must gain their livelihood through the exercise of a trade or a profession. They were not to flee from the world to lead a contemplative life as recluses; rather, they followed the contemplative life in the very midst of society, in their actual professions or trades. Those disciples who had no means of livelihood were frowned upon. All in all, the Shādhilī way was a kind of remanifestation of the *tawḥīd* or *dhikr* of the early Islamic community in the time of the Prophet, when there were no distinguishing marks among the Muslims that separated the contemplatives from the faithful who followed a life of action: the inner life of the Spirit was accentuated, while externally everyone seemed to follow his own particular calling in the world. It is for this reason that the historical traces of the Shādhilīs in early times are practically impossible to track down in Spain, Morocco, Algeria, and elsewhere, unless one already knows in advance the names of certain masters or of their disciples.

The Early Successors of Shaykh Abu'l-Ḥasan al-Shādhilī

Shortly before he passed away, in 656/1258, Shaykh Abu'l-Ḥasan designated Abu'l-'Abbās al-Mursī as his successor in the order. The latter was born in Murcia, Spain, in the year 616/1220, the same city that witnessed the births of Ibn 'Arabī and Ibn Sab'īn, this last coming into the world only a few years before al-Mursī himself. At the age of around twenty-four, al-Mursī set out for the pilgrimage to Mecca with his family, but his ship foundered off the Algerian coast. He lost his parents in the calamity, and he narrowly escaped death by swimming to shore with his brother. After wandering for a while in North Africa, they finally encountered Shaykh Abu'l-Ḥasan and joined his order. Shortly afterward, in the year 642/1244, the shaykh moved the center of his *ṭarīqah* from Tunis to Alexandria. In Egypt, al-Mursī proved to be what the shaykh had anticipated and became a teacher of the path himself. After Shaykh Abu'l-Ḥasan's death, in 656/1258, al-Mursī moved into the great tower that the founder of the Shādhiliyyah had used as residence, mosque, and *zāwiyah*, and remained there until his death (686/1288) some thirty years later, seldom moving out to travel about in Egypt. Whereas Shaykh Abu'l-Ḥasan al-Shādhilī had no compunction of mind in mingling with the officials of state in his days, if he felt that some just cause could be served thereby, Shaykh Abu'l-'Abbās al-Mursī was made of a different cloth altogether and would have nothing to do with officials of any kind, refusing all provisions or stipends offered him by the Mamlūks. Occasionally, he ventured forth to Cairo, like his teacher, to lecture on *taṣawwuf* before the principal religious scholars of his day, but in general he occupied himself with the affairs of the *ṭarīqah* until his death. Also like his master, he wrote no books or treatises on Sufism and considered all such works to be nothing but foam cast up on the shores of the infinite ocean of spiritual realization; but, like his teacher, he did compose *aḥzāb*, some of which are still in circulation. Perhaps the most widely known of his disciples in the Islamic world at large is the legendary al-Būṣīrī (d. 694/1295), the Egyptian poet of Berber origins who is famous for his two great poems in praise of the Prophet, the "Mantle Poem" (*al-Burdah*) and the *Hamziyyah,* both of which are recited every year on the Prophet's birthday. The other great Sufi disciples of al-Mursī are not well known in the Islamic world, but they play an important role in Near Eastern Sufism. Among them is Shaykh Yāqūt al-'Arshī (d. 732/1332), the Alexandrian teacher of Abyssinian origins whom Ibn Baṭṭūṭah visited in 725/1325 during his travels in the East. Still another was the incomparable Shaykh Najm al-Dīn al-Iṣfahānī (d. 721/1321), the Persian disciple of al-Mursī, whose long residence at Mecca spread the Shādhilī Order among the pilgrims. He was the Shādhilī teacher of the Sufi al-Yāfi'ī (d. 768/1367), and it was through the latter that the Shī'ite Sufi order of the Ni'matu'llāhiyyah is connected with the Shādhiliyyah. Finally, there was Shaykh Ibn 'Aṭā' Allāh (d. 709/1309), who is the third eminent Shādhilī master in most of the chains of transmission for the order, but who is also the first of the early teachers to write down the doctrines of the order in books that have since become indispensable for understanding the perspectives of the Shādhiliyyah in those days.

Shaykh Abu'l-'Abbās al-Mursī's long tenure as guardian over the affairs of the Shādhiliyyah was contemporaneous with the reign of al-Malik al-Ẓāhir Baybars (658/1260–676/1277), who brought the Mamlūks to the pinnacle of power and success in Egypt and Syria. The time for a fresh outpouring of Sunni Islam was at hand. The old caliphal seat at Baghdad was transferred by him to Cairo in 659/1261, converting Egypt into the prestigious center of the Islamic community. Then, turning his attention to Sunnism, he consecrated the four Sunni schools of jurisprudence as having equal voice with the ruler, thus sounding the death knell for other schools, such as the Ẓāhirī and the Shī'ite. He crushed once and for all the power of the so-called Assassins (the Ismā'īlīs) of the Near East; he regained numerous lands from the Christians of the Levant; and, by reuniting Egypt and Syria, he laid the foundations for the brilliant Mamlūk cultural manifestations in the arts and architecture that were to have such lasting influences in the region. But the Mamlūks were also the patrons of Sufism, and it was in that regenerated sociopolitical atmosphere that the influence of the early Shādhilī masters made itself felt on the world around them.

The early Shādhilīs were concerned not only with the teachings and practices of Sufism but also with the Law of Islam and the creedal forms of belief, or with what is usually called exoteric Islam. They were Sunni Muslims, and, although Sufism as such has nothing to do with theological dogmatism, they nevertheless tended to favor the Ash'arite school of theology, one of the important currents of creedal formulations in Islam. But the Ash'arism they adhered to was perhaps not quite the same as that preached by Abu'l-Ḥasan al-Ash'arī (d. 324/935), since by the seventh/thirteenth century other great figures, such as al-Ghazzālī (d. 505/1111), had added their own contributions to the school, changing its nature somewhat. When all is said and done, Ash'arism was not too far removed from the rather strict system of beliefs embodied in Ḥanbalism. Ash'arism allowed for a limited use of reasoning, whereas the Ḥanbalī school of thought rejected all speculative theology and defended its particular interpretations of the Quran through a powerful display of dogmatic voluntarism. Although the Shādhilīs of those days were Ash'arites, this does not mean that their Sufism was Ash'arite dogmatism, nor does it mean that they themselves were dogmatists. In the eyes of the early teachers, Ash'arism was perhaps a better approach to the articles of belief than Ḥanbalism. But they did not require their disciples to be Ash'arites, nor can their Sufism be reduced to a merely theological program of studies. Thus, the fact that Abu'l-'Abbās al-Mursī studied the *Irshād* of Imam al-Ḥaramayn al-Juwaynī (d. 478/1085), the Shāfi'ī theologian of Ash'arite inspiration, because it contained theology (*uṣūl al-dīn*), must not mislead us into thinking that Ash'arism was an indispensable element of his *ṭarīqah.*

In many ways, the Shādhilī path was a reform in the spiritual and religious sense of that word. It was not an iconoclastic or puritanical reform that brutally sought to destroy the external institutions of Islam in the name of a return to the ways of the pious ancestors (*salaf*). But in its own way it did point an accusatory finger at the exaggerated formalism and literalism of the exoteric Islam of those days, just as it also had something to say against the armies of ascetics and wandering *fuqarā'*, who moved under the banners of Sufism and who could not all be sincere treaders of the path, to say the least. Perhaps out of all the great Sufi orders that saw the light of day in the seventh/thirteenth century, the Shādhiliyyah most conformed not simply to normative Sufism, in the sense previously defined, but also to normative Islam, if only because the Shādhilī initiates, unlike those of other orders, never stood out in the midst of the faithful and could thus easily pass unperceived more or less like the early Muslim contemplatives of Umayyad times, when Islam was still pristine and fresh.

Mālikism among the Shādhilīs

Although Sufism in its Shādhilī guise represents the spiritual path (*ṭarīqah*), it is worth recalling that early Shādhilism was based on the Mālikī school of jurisprudence, and this association between the two would continue largely undisturbed down to the present day. Not only was the founder of the order a Mālikī, but the Maghrib, in which Shādhilism first saw the light of day, was a vast region stretching from Spain to the Libyan desert near Egypt that was uniformly Mālikī in coloration. Although it is not surprising that the origins of Shādhilism, in Tunis, were under the governance of Mālikism, it may come as a surprise to learn that the second center of the order, Alexandria, was likewise a stronghold of Mālikī jurisprudence in Egypt. The city of Alexandria was then second in importance only to Cairo. It was a port city on the Mediterranean, a point of entrance to and exit from Egypt. It was also a great fortress, with immense walls—a double series of them, to be exact—surrounding it, giant towers arising from them at regular intervals. We have already seen that, in one of those towers, Shaykh Abu'l-Ḥasan al-Shādhilī established his home and *zāwiyah*. In the Mamlūk period, those towers would often serve as places of confinement for persons deemed to be troublemakers; thus, Ibn Taymiyyah spent some time in one of them, although under comfortable conditions of exile. Alexandria was also a trading mart; Christian merchants and consuls from distant lands had their quarters there; and, indeed, within the symmetrically laid out streets (a plan that was peculiar to the city), a tremendous amount of commercial activity was always going on.

Mālikism was firmly implanted in the city precisely because it was the meeting-place between the West of the Islamic community and the East, and had been for centuries. In the course of time, many Maghribīs had settled in the city and brought with them their Mālikism. A flourishing colony of Muslims from the Maghrib was to be found there, and inevitably influences from both the East and the West joined forces within its walls. The Ayyūbids built *madrasahs* in the city for the teaching of Mālikism, and great authorities in the *madhhab* were to be found in the city, some of whom, like Ibn al-Ḥājib (d. 646/1248) or Ibn al-Munayyir (d. 683/1285), were actually disciples of Shaykh Abu'l-Ḥasan al-Shādhilī. A young Mālikī would begin as a boy with the Quranic school (the *maktab*), and then go on afterward to a local religious college (*madrasah*) or to the private home of an Alexandrian religious scholar for further instruction. Like the other schools of jurisprudence, Mālikism had developed its own manuals and textbooks over the centuries, and these formed the fundamental core of instruction. All of the early Shādhilī masters—and this holds true even for the later ones—had studied their Mālikī jurisprudence from such works, and a number of them, including Shaykh Abu'l-Ḥasan himself, were past masters of Islamic Law. Moreover, as was previously mentioned, some of the eminent authorities of Mālikism were influenced by the early Shādhilī teachers; thus, the famous Mālikī *faqīh*, Ibn al-Ḥājj (d. 737/1337), the author of the *Madkhal*, knew Shaykh Ibn 'Aṭā'Allāh quite well, and he often cites the words of Shaykh Abu'l-Ḥasan al-Shādhilī. In fact, Shaykh Ibn 'Aṭā' Allāh was himself considered to be one of the foremost figures in Mālikī jurisprudence in his day, thus perpetuating the dynasty of religious scholars founded by his grandfather in Alexandria.

The Sufi Heritage of Shādhilism

While Mālikism was the dominant *madhhab* of the early Shādhilīs, their Sufism, as we can see in the works of Shaykh Ibn 'Aṭā' Allāh, was not limited to any one particular school of thought. Shādhilī intellectuality fastened on the gnostic works of earlier teachers, such as the *Khatm al-walāyah* (*Seal of Sanctity*) of al-Ḥakīm al-Tirmidhī (d. ca. 285/898), or the *Mawāqif* (*Spiritual Stoppings*) of the fourth/tenth century Sufi al-Niffarī. Nor did it recoil at the words and deeds of the martyred Sufi al-Ḥallāj (d. 309/922), who was viewed as a saintly sage and not as some eccentric in the path. Great respect was held for the *Qūt al-qulūb* (*The Nourishment of Hearts*) of Abū Ṭālib al-Makkī (d. 386/996), a work that was said to confer spiritual light on its readers. Similarly, the *Iḥyā' 'ulūm al-dīn* (*The Revival of the Religious Sciences*) by al-Ghazzālī (d. 505/1111) was much appreciated; its author was ranked among the eminent saints of Islam.

It is possible that Shaykh Abu'l-Ḥasan al-Shādhilī actually had contacts with Ibn 'Arabī, given the former's numerous travels in the Near East. We are on surer ground when it comes to the Shaykh al-Akbar's disciple, Ṣadr al-Dīn al-Qūnawī (d. 673/1275), author of numerous works in the same spirit of *waḥdat al-wujūd* as characterized by his master. He came to Cairo to meet the Shādhilī sage, so that we do know that the two Sufi schools of thought—analogous versions of metaphysical *tawḥīd*, to be sure—met briefly in their early period. Moreover, the Shādhilīs were vigorous defenders of Ibn 'Arabī's teachings, as we see in the tumultuous confrontation between Shaykh Ibn 'Aṭā' Allāh and the Ḥanbalī fundamentalist critic of the Shaykh al-Akbar, Ibn Taymiyyah, in the Citadel of Cairo early in the eighth/fourteenth century. In this connection, it is well worth remembering that the acerbic remarks made by Shaykh Ibn 'Aṭā' Allāh against the doctors of the Law who restrict the meaning of the Islamic message to the level of their own comprehension really apply, first and foremost, to the Ḥanbalī canonist.

In the days of Ibn Taymiyyah, it was not unusual for many of the religious scholars to have Sufi masters; we have already seen this in the case of some of the well-known doctors of the Law attached to the early Shādhilī masters. Ibn Taymiyyah was no exception to the general rule; he too had his Sufi teacher. But this must not lead us to believe that the Ḥanbalī *faqīh* was something of an esoterist in his own right, for it is clear from his very

2. The tomb of Moulay Idrīs, the Patriarch of North African Sufism, in Fez in Morocco.

writings that the contemplative esoterism of Islam was not altogether to his liking. Even those Sufis of whom he approved, such as the founder of the Qādiriyyah, ʻAbd al-Qādir al-Jīlānī (d. 561/1166), were acceptable only to the degree that they embraced Ḥanbalī creedal positions, which was the case for Shaykh ʻAbd al-Qādir, and not to the extent that they embodied in their teachings or persons the contemplative nature of the Sufi path. For the Shādhilī teachers to defend the Shaykh al-Akbar against the attacks of Ḥanbalīs or religious scholars belonging to other schools of jurisprudence is not in the least surprising: his *waḥdat al-wujūd*, in the final analysis, was the same as their own teachings on *tawḥīd*. They were themselves intellectuals and highly speculative in their doctrinal elaborations. Shaykh Ibn ʻAṭā' Allāh has left us a kind of catalogue of the only subjects that his master, Shaykh Abu'l-ʻAbbās al-Mursī, used to speak about: the Great Intellect (*al-ʻaql al-akbar*), the Supreme Name, the Names of God, the letters of the alphabet, the circles of the saints, the stations of those who have certitude, the angels near the Throne, the sciences dealing with the inner mysteries, the graces in invocations, the "day" of those in the graves, the question of self-direction, the science of cosmology, the science of God's Will, the question of God's "Grasp" (*qabḍah*) and of the men belonging to it, the sciences of the "solitary saints" (*afrād*), the Day of Resurrection and God's dealing with His servants with gentleness and gracefulness, and the existence of God's revenge. In other words, while the first two Shādhilī teachers did not leave behind books, they nevertheless discussed more or less the same subjects we find treated in the works of the Shaykh al-Akbar, who put down in writings inspirations similar to those that the other shaykhs uttered in assemblies surrounded by their intimate disciples. The gnostic positions of Ibn ʻArabī found a ready echo in the teachings of the Shādhilīs, whose intellective way is best summarized in Shaykh Abu'l-ʻAbbās al-Mursī's rejection of the cult of charismatic phenomena: the greatest miracle, he claimed, was in the purification of the intellect in the heart.

To that body of Sufi literature antedating or contemporaneous with the first two teachers of the Shādhiliyyah, there soon came to be added the works of Shaykh Ibn ʻAṭā' Allāh himself: *Kitāb al-ḥikam* (*The Book of Aphorisms*), a summary of the Sufi way in its perennial elements;[9] *al-Tanwīr fī isqāṭ al-tadbīr* (*Illumination on Rejecting Self-Direction*), an exposition of the errors to be found in all egocentric self-direction; *Laṭā'if al-minan* (*The Subtleties of Grace*), a biographical sketch of the first two Shādhilī masters; *al-Qaṣd al-mujarrad fī maʻrifat al-ism al-mufrad* (*The Sole Aim Concerning Knowledge of the Unique Name*), an excellent spiritual and metaphysical discussion of the Divine Name *Allāh* and the other Names; *Miftāḥ al-falāḥ wa miṣbāḥ al-arwāḥ* (*The Key of Success and the Lamp of Spirits*), a compendium on the remembrance of God in the widest sense of the word *dhikr;* and a number of other, minor works. The whole corpus of his writings came to be the dominant Shādhilī writings precisely because he was the first of the early teachers to put pen to paper and expound the doctrines of the order. Others later on would also compose works of different sorts; these were added to the ensemble of writings within the Shādhilī tradition that would be referred to and cited by later generations as authoritative expositions of the order's teachings.

The Spiritual Movement Eastward

The already mentioned trait of Maghribī Sufism to move from West to East in the Islamic world can be seen not only in the life and travels of the Shaykh al-Akbar, who wound up in Damascus, but also in the teaching career of Shaykh Abu'l-Ḥasan al-Shādhilī himself, who moved from Tunis to Alexandria. Other Shādhilī teachers in subsequent centuries would follow in his footsteps, or else their disciples would settle here and there in the East. How to account for this phenomenon? Of course, one can point to Mecca as the pilgrimage center of the Islamic world, so that it is only natural that Sufis, like other Muslims, should go eastward; but it is one thing to go on the pilgrimage and return, and another thing to go to the East and stay there. Initially, the movement of Sufism was the reverse: it came from different parts of the eastern world of Islam and settled in the lands of the Maghrib with the same waves that brought Islam to the region. We know very little about that earlier period of Sufism, because historians, both Muslim and non-Muslim, tend to concentrate on events and sects or movements that broke out in the Near East, the homeland of the faith. The Maghrib became, in due time, an independent cultural entity, with its own style of life, its own artistic forms, and its own sociopolitical system, which set it off altogether from the eastern regions of Islam, so much so that Ibn 'Arabī, when he arrived in Egypt from the Maghrib, found that the Sufis there were unaware of Sufism in the Maghrib. Perhaps it would be closer to the mark to say that the archaic nature of Islam, its primordial character, had been preserved within the Maghribī bastion and leavened with infusions of Sufism coming from the East until finally the West, by virtue of having maintained a reservoir of spirituality within its ancient forms of Islam, was in a position to reverse the movement and to influence the East, to say nothing of the African South.

We should bear in mind that the Maghrib, more than any other part of the Islamic world, developed an extraordinary Islamic civilization that preserved the earlier Umayyad culture that was purely Arab and gave to it a startlingly original imprint in the course of time. Even after the Christian Reconquest of Spain had come to an end in the ninth/fifteenth century, North Africa remained a real bastion of Sufi spirituality,[10] especially when one realizes that, after that epoch, the Near East began a long, slow decline. The gradual weakening of the Ottoman and Safavid empires heralds that coming spiritual decadence. It is within this context that we can understand the movement of Shādhilism, in later times, from the Maghrib to the East, reawakening in the eastern lands the spirit of gnostic *taṣawwuf*, particularly in the Arab region. The Maghrib, as was said, had changed roles with the East, a process that began with the founder of the Shādhiliyyah, one of the greatest Sufis of Islam, whose *ṭarīqah* would become a powerful force for the regeneration of Islam in century after century down to the present day, testifying in that manner to the central part that Shādhilism would play in the midst of vast areas of the Islamic community.

The Shādhilī Branches of Later Times

A great *ṭarīqah* like the Shādhiliyyah can be compared to a tree: as it grows from a sapling to a fully matured tree, it throws out branches, and these in turn sometimes develop still other, lesser branches. The same holds true for the Sufi orders: originally, they are named after their founders, such as ʿAbd al-Qādir al-Jīlānī, as mentioned in the last chapter, but as time goes by the main trunk gives rise to branches, likewise named after their founders. It is not a question here of a schismatic movement or of some sort of sectarianism; rather, it is that the new branch, by virtue of some outstanding quality in its founder—or perhaps even a fresh reorientation within the framework of the order—receives a new name. We see this in the eighth/fourteenth century, in Egypt, with the Shādhiliyyah: a branch emerged called the Wafā'iyyah, founded by Shams al-Dīn Muḥammad ibn Aḥmad Wafā' (d. 760/1359), who was known as Baḥr al-ṣafā' ("The Ocean of Purity") and was the father of the illustrious ʿAlī ibn Wafā' (d. 807/1404). The Wafā'iyyah developed in their own way as the generations passed, spreading into parts of the Near East outside of Egypt. After the ninth/fifteenth century, they wore their own type of Sufi garments, as if the original unobtrusive style of the Shādhiliyyah no longer was observed or was applicable, for a number of reasons. Likewise, they gradually took on an institutional life that was certainly much more complex and rigid than was the case for the earlier Shādhiliyyah.

Much the same can be said of the numerous other branches that emerged from the parent trunk of the order: the Ḥanafiyyah, the Jazūliyyah, the Nāṣiriyyah, the ʿĪsawiyyah, the Tihāmiyyah, the Darqāwiyyah, and the like, correspond to readaptations and readjustments of the original Shādhilī message. Very often they arose because historical and social circumstances called for a Sufi response of a special type. It is not easy to determine in every single case what might have been the causal relationship between the historical milieu and the rise of one of these branches. The Jazūliyyah, for example, which goes back to the famous Imam al-Jazūlī (d. ca. 875/1470), one of the patron saints of Marrakesh, seems to have arisen largely as a powerful devotional manifestation of love for the Prophet, as we can see in his well-known litany on the Prophet, *Dalā'il al-khayrāt* (*The Signs of Benedictions*), which has been recited since his day in great parts of the Islamic world. By then, the spiritual substance of Morocco was in need of a powerful symbol to allow it to dedicate itself once again to the roots of its collective well-being. And what more regenerative a source could be found than the love of the Prophet? Especially was this the case in view of the *jihād* that was then going on against the Portuguese colonies on the coast that threatened the security of *dār al-islām*. But also—and this needs to be stressed—the devotional fervor generated by the *Dalā'il al-khayrāt* was a testimony to its otherworldly origins; and thus it was a kind of celestial message that the Jazūliyyah were destined to spread over other Islamic lands.

If we look at the causes that might have given rise to the Zarrūqiyyah, named after its founder Shaykh Aḥmad Zarrūq (d. 899/1493), they probably have to do with the restoration of piety and conformity to the Law. Not only was the shaykh an indefatigable commentator on the *Ḥikam* of Ibn 'Aṭā' Allāh, writing something like thirty glosses, but he was also a great traveler. Wherever he went, he inculcated the strict observance of the Law as a necessary accompaniment to the contemplative path. His works on Sufism, like the *Qawā'id al-taṣawwuf* (*The Principles of Sufism*), demonstrate a meticulous regard for legal rules that strikes one at first glance as inappropriate in a contemplative esoterist; but, after reflection, one discerns here and there in his book that he is seeking to reestablish some kind of balance between the Law and the Path, so that neither of the two will impinge on the other's domain. The Zarrūqiyyah, no doubt, considered the balancing of Sufism and the Law as an indispensable quality in the would-be *faqīr*, something that he had to be aware of, or something that he had to assimilate.

The branching out of different orders from the original Shādhilī trunk also implied adaptations to a variety of spiritual vocations. Although the Shādhiliyyah retained throughout the centuries a characteristic intellectual orientation, with time, some of the orders, like the 'Īsawiyyah, established by the tenth/sixteenth-century shaykh Muḥammad ibn 'Īsā, were hardly intellectual in nature. Like the Rifā'iyyah of the Near East, the 'Īsawiyyah engaged in practices designed to demonstrate the immunity of their adherents to fire, swords, scorpions, and so on. No doubt all of this had a certain disciplinary function with some of the shaykhs of the order; but sooner or later the pursuit of such immunities became an end in itself, so that the order was reduced simply to a kind of exhibitionism in the minds of many Muslims. It drew into its ranks a particular mentality, not only in Morocco, of course, where it originated, but also in Egypt and elsewhere. It is generally the likes of the Rifāʿiyyah and the ʿĪsawiyyah that, on a popular plane, give to Sufism a circuslike ambiance that was certainly not intended by their founders. But it was easy for the critics of Sufism, particularly the religious scholars of puritanical bent, to point to such orders as examples of the deviations and subversions of Islam which Sufism produces. Nevertheless, and whatever might be the opinions of the strait-laced believers and scholars concerning such orders, they served the purpose of integrating into Sufism various classes of society that might otherwise have been left out of its precincts altogether. In any case, not all such deeds as characterize the ʿĪsawiyyah, for example, can be attributed to motivations that are incompatible with the spiritual life: everything depends on the teacher and how such unconventional practices are seen by him within the deeper perspective of the order. Without him, of course, the practices succumb easily to the charge of charlatanism or fraud and lose their real value.

The Question of Maraboutism

A peculiarity of Moroccan Sufism is something called Maraboutism.[11] In parts of the Moroccan regions, pious hermits or missionaries would establish their hermitages in order to raise the religious standards of the local population. The religious edifice they used was called a *ribāṭ*, and the ascetic teacher was a *murābiṭ*, from which the French derived the word Marabout. The pious missionary would leave behind a legacy of saintliness and grace (*barakah*) attaching not only to the place but also to his descendants. Fusion with Sufism turned some of these places into *zāwiyahs*, presided over by the descendants of the original hermit. When the families were also descendants of the Prophet, or the *sharīfs* of Morocco, who were mostly of Idrīsid lineage, there was an amalgamation of Sufism, Maraboutism, and Sharīfism revolving around the key term of *barakah*, the grace that emanates from a person, who can be a holy man or a descendant of the Prophet, or both together at one and the same time. It is at times an inextricable association of Sufism properly speaking, the cult of saints, and the honor due the *sharīfs* as descendants of the Prophet, for all three categories have something to do with spiritual grace (*barakah*) in one way or another, not only in

Morocco, but elsewhere in the Islamic world. But what makes for Maraboutism, especially as it manifested itself in late medieval Morocco, was the combination of all these elements. Not that Sufism in Morocco was uniquely in alliance with Sharīfism; on the contrary, as in other parts of the Muslim world, it had its own independent existence as a contemplative path and was in no need of Maraboutism. Nevertheless, side by side with that contemplative version of Sufism is the socioreligious phenomenon of Maraboutism that has left its imprint on the Moroccan scene. Even dynasties of a political nature, like the Sa'dians of the tenth/sixteenth century, came to power with the help of the religious leaders of Sharīfian status. Sooner or later, the entire religiopolitical structure of the country was tinged with Sharīfism. Only the descendants of the Prophet could be entrusted with ruling powers, and this carried over into other domains, affecting even Sufism. While all of this particular blending of Sufism and Maraboutism is a characteristic of Morocco, the fact of the matter is that in other Islamic lands one finds elements that are similar: the cult of Sufi saints' tombs exists all over the Islamic world, as does the notion that the descendants of the Prophet are possessed of a certain grace.

The constants of the Sufi path—its doctrines on *tawḥīd*, its methods of concentration having to do with the *dhikru'Llāh*, its initiatic transmission, and the like—can be detected in all ages within the rich variety of its historical forms. The Sufi contemplative way has nevertheless certain essential characteristics without which it ceases to be Sufism. At what point Maraboutism was no longer Sufism, in the strict sense of that word, is something that is not easy to determine. What is evident throughout the centuries of the Sufi tradition is that all kinds of customs and practices grafted themselves onto the core of Sufi teachings and methods and became identified with Sufism as such, whereas in reality they are merely peripheral or tangential aspects of the path and in any case are not central. One can imagine a religiomilitary society, like the medieval *futuwwah,* being integrated into the Sufi path, just as one can imagine artisanal guilds that function as expressions of Sufism in the arts. Such activities in no way constitute an essential aspect of Sufism, for we know quite well that Sufism can very easily exist without them. Thus, the societal manifestations of Sufism—including the sacred forms of Maraboutism—cannot really be included in a definition of the essential nature of the path. There is Sufi poetry, Sufi architecture, Sufi music, Sufi dance, and so on, but these are outpourings of a contemplative path that is centered on a spiritual realization of Allah through direct knowledge or love. They are the fruits of the path, but not the path itself. Similarly, the numerous practices of a negative characteristic, such as the use of drugs, that crept into some of the decadent orders cannot be ascribed to Sufism as such. These are abuses and corruptions that the eminent shaykhs of the path have always inveighed against because they detract from the reputation of the authentic spiritual way of Islam and tend to confuse the outsider in his estimation of the contemplative life. That the religious scholars of the community have seized upon such corruptions by way of criticizing all Sufism is understandable, for many of the *'ulamā'* have never had more than a very limited grasp of the nature of the Islamic message to begin with. In their eyes, the multiple manifestations of Sufism are simply heretical forms of the Islam that they recognize as legitimate. But one must be careful not to include all of the *'ulamā'* in this assessment: many of them—including the most illustrious—not only understood that Sufism was the spiritual content of Islam but also were themselves members of Sufi orders. In sum, it is of great importance not to confuse the essential in Sufism with the accidental, not to give the societal elements of the path more than their proper due. There is a historical side to the path, to be sure, but the path as such is intrinsically transhistorical by nature, for the simple reason that its teachings and practices are all centered on the absolutely Real (*al-Ḥaqq*), which transcends the entire creation.

The Thirteenth/Nineteenth-Century Revival in the Maghrib

After the gradual collapse of the Ottoman, Safavid, and Mughal empires in Turkey, Persia, and India, respectively, a period of decadence set in over great regions of the Islamic world. The brilliant cultural achievements of those dynasties in the arts, the sciences, the architectural forms, and in intellectual life in general now came to an end. The inner spiritual resources of the Islamic East had been largely consumed in the intellectual and artistic manifestations of the tenth/sixteenth and eleventh/seventeenth centuries. It is simply not possible for great dynasties to go on indefinitely producing cultural flowerings one after another with no finality to the process. It is true that the fruits of civilization—the arts and architecture, the sciences, literature, great political, military, or economic systems—are not always the result of spiritual vitality: they can also stem from reservoirs of purely psychical powers that lie dormant in people until leaders appear who know how to tap those sources of strength. Such was not the case for the previously mentioned dynasties: their achievements were largely the consequences of strong spiritual currents, as we can see so clearly in their arts, for the arts mirror the collective soul. The same arts also mirror the decline, and this involves the attenuation of the spiritual vitality of a people in different ways.

What made the decadence that came over the Islamic community all the more dangerous was that the process of decline coincided with the coming of the modern Western secular civilization produced by the French Revolution and the Industrial Revolution of Europe. Western civilization, which had already begun the task of stripping Europe of its Christian culture, now pounced on the Islamic world in the form of colonialist systems that brought secularism and materialism in all their guises to that community. This accelerated the interior decadence of Islamic culture and added a new corrosive and destructive power that could not be stopped altogether but could only be slowed down temporarily or even neutralized partially. Yet the establishment by the West of colonies all over the Islamic world ensured that the traditional civilization there would have to contend unequally with the powerful industrial and materialistic culture coming from the West.

One part of the Islamic world that retained a spiritual vibrancy was the Maghrib, even though in the latter half of the thirteenth/nineteenth century France would establish its colonial regime in Algeria and Tunisia.[12] At the very moment that France was beginning to colonialize parts of North Africa, a veritable spiritual rebirth was taking place in the Maghrib, which proved that the decadence existing elsewhere in *dār al-islām* was not uniform throughout the community. When Western Europe, through the French Revolution, was destroying its own Christian world, the Maghrib was undergoing a spiritual efflorescence under the direction of the Shādhilī masters of the day. Previous Shādhilī regenerations had occurred in the eleventh/seventeenth century with the Nāṣiriyyah of Shaykh Muḥammad ibn Nāṣir and one or two other branches. But at the end of the twelfth/eighteenth century, a powerful spiritual rebirth took place under yet another branch of the Shādhilīs, the Darqāwā, founded by the Sharīf Mawlay al-ʿArabī al-Darqāwī (d. 1239/1823).[13] This new branch sought to restore the purity of early Shādhilism through a return to an equilibrated view of the Law (*Sharīʿah*) and the Path (*ṭarīqah*), which was what characterized the first teachers.[14] Numerous branches would in turn emerge out of the Darqāwā and have a profound influence not only in North Africa but also in the Hijaz, Turkey, and in the Levant.[15] These were the Būzīdiyyah, the Kattāniyyah, the Ḥarrāqiyyah, and the Madaniyyah, and some of these would in turn give rise to still other branches. Thus, the Madaniyyah, founded by Muḥammad Ḥasan ibn Ḥamzah al-Madanī (d. 1363/1846) of Medina, spread out from Libya, but it created the Raḥmāniyyah in the Hijaz and the Yashruṭiyyah in the Levant. In addition, other Shādhilīs would move southward into Africa.[16] From all of this proliferation of Sufi orders in different directions, revivals of the inner life of Islam took place. Of course, no revival is permanent, and for that reason history records numerous ups and downs within the annals of the Islamic faith. Nevertheless, the thirteenth/nineteenth-century revivals here and there in the community were carried out very often under the pressures of European colonialism, which was then beginning to make itself felt in a number of Islamic lands. It is this which confers upon the Maghribī spiritual reformation of the time a good deal of its cyclical importance, for it was being carried out very often under the colonialist systems that the imperialist powers of Europe brought to the Islamic countries.

The Fourteenth/Twentieth Century

Among the many branches of the Shādhiliyyah that arose in the past century or so, the one that would have a very impressive flowering is the 'Alawiyyah. This was founded by the Algerian shaykh Aḥmad al-'Alawī, who died in 1934, and whose Shādhilī lineage takes him back to Abu'l-Ḥasan al-Shādhilī through Mawlay al-'Arabī al-Darqāwī.[17] Shaykh Aḥmad al-'Alawī was thought to embody in his person the renovator (*mujaddid*) of Islam for this epoch, in accordance with the words of the Prophet to the effect that a reviver of his community would appear at the beginning of each century.

The Algerian master was at once a great saint, metaphysician, scholar, and poet. He pointed in his teachings to the "transcendent unity" which underlies the formal diversity of religions and respected the truly pious Christians who came to see him. Yet he was fully aware of the false suppositions upon which modernism is founded and spoke against any compromise with the secularist and humanistic tendencies prevalent in the modern world. He combined in himself the manifestation of quintessential Sufism seen in his several works on Sufi metaphysics with the deepening of Islamic ethical norms through an aura of sanctity which attracted a large number of disciples from near and far.

Indeed, the 'Alawiyyah had a direct hand in the regeneration of Islam, not only in the Maghrib but elsewhere in the community, or wherever Shādhilism spread. The shaykhs who emerged from the 'Alawiyyah, most of whom were direct disciples of Shaykh al-'Alawī, wound up in different parts of the Islamic world. Likewise, the order has played an extremely important role in the intellectual revival of Islam along traditional lines. The hundreds of thousands of disciples who were members of the order themselves came from different parts of the Maghrib as well as from other parts of the Islamic world. We do not need much imagination to see how these individuals, once returned to their own lands, were indirectly involved in the reformative work of the founder himself.

It was always in that fashion, as a general rule, that the Sufi masters affected the populations of their day: their disciples, their books, and their own spiritual influence would generate a kind of transformation of the milieu around them, so that a collective psychical substance would result that was receptive to the influences of the Spirit—or at least was much more porous to its presence than had been previously the case. This would result in widespread consequences, not only in the moral attitudes of the population but also in the fruits of their hands, in the arts and architecture, and even in the intellectual lucubrations of the principal thinkers of their time. It was in that way that spiritual rebirths took place in the long history of Islam, and it was in the absence of such influences that we find numerous periods of decline and stultification.

Shādhilism in general has also played a most remarkable role in the revival of Western traditional intellectuality in the twentieth century. We see a clear-cut example of this in the famous French thinker, René Guénon, himself a Shādhilī known in the Muslim world as Shaykh ʿAbd al-Wāḥid Yaḥyā. His numerous works on the metaphysical underpinnings, the cosmological aspects, and the spiritual foundations of the great religions of the world have had an incalculable influence on a large number of Westerners, especially those in search of the spiritual path, since the end of the First World War. Shaykh Aḥmad al-ʿAlawī, for his part, directly influenced yet another Western authority on the traditional spiritual life, Frithjof Schuon, who knew the Algerian master personally. Schuon's own numerous works on Islam and the other great religions of the world have perpetuated into our times the theses of the great medieval Sufis on the universality of revelation and have shed further light on the principal arguments found in the brilliant school of metaphysicians left behind by René Guénon. This entire current of Western intellectual and spiritual life, which continues to vibrate at the present day and to produce many important formulations of doctrine, could not have existed without an initial Shādhilī impetus and guidance.[18]

Given that the Shādhiliyyah have always considered their *ṭarīqah* to possess a central role in the unfolding of the spiritual life of the community—they have actually affirmed that the axial sage of the epoch (*quṭb al-zamān*) would always be found in their midst—it is clear that the last word on the order cannot yet be said. This is all the more so in that the order has now taken root in Europe and North America and has begun yet another revival of the traditional intellectual spirit, this time based on the Quranic teaching, long dormant, of the universality of revelation, with all that this implies in a metaphysical and spiritual sense.

Notes

1. On the rise of Shādhilism, see R. Brunschvig, *La Berbérie orientale sous les Hafṣides des origines à la fin du XV siècle* (Paris: A. Maisonneuve, 1947) 2:322–30.

2. See A. M. M. Mackeen, "The Early History of Sufism in the Maghrib Prior to Al-Shādhilī (d. 656/1258)," *Journal of the American Oriental Society* 91 (1971) 398–408.

3. His *Maḥāsin al-majālis* (*The Beauties of Spiritual Gatherings*), on the inner life and the contemplative virtues, has been translated by W. Elliott and A. K. Abdulla into English (Amersham, England: Avebury, 1980).

4. See L. Massignon, *The Passion of al-Hallāj, Mystic and Martyr of Islam,* trans. H. Mason (4 vols.; Princeton, NJ: Princeton University Press, 1982).

5. See E. H. Douglas, "Al-Shādhilī, a North African Sufi, According to Ibn Ṣabbāgh," *Muslim World* 38 (1948) 257–79; and A. M. M. Mackeen, "The Rise of al-Shādhilī (656/1258)," *Journal of the American Oriental Society* 91 (1971) 477–86.

6. Examples of these litanies can be found here and there in C. Padwick's *Muslim Devotions* (London: S.P.C.K., 1961).

7. For Ibn 'Arabī's ideas, see T. Burckhardt, *An Introduction to Sufi Doctrine* (Wellingborough, England: Thorsons, 1976), Part Two, 57–97; and M. Asín Palacios, *El Islam cristianizado* (Madrid: Editorial Plutarcho, 1931), a long account of Ibn 'Arabī's life and teachings.

8. O. Depont and X. Coppolani's *Les Confréries religieuses musulmanes* (Algiers: A. Jourdan, 1897) has a wealth of material on the orders, as does J. Spencer Trimingham's *The Sufi Orders in Islam* (London: Oxford University Press, 1971).

9. See P. Nwyia, *Ibn 'Aṭā' Allāh (m. 709/1309) et la naissance de la confrérie šaḏilite* (Beirut: Dār al-Mashreq, 1972), a translation and study of the *Ḥikam;* and V. Danner, *Sufi Aphorisms* (New York: Paulist Press, 1978), for an English version of these famous spiritual maxims.

10. North African Sufi spirituality influenced also Spanish Christian mysticism indirectly, as we see in Asín Palacios, "Šadhilies y alumbrados," vols. 9 (1944) to 16 (1951) of *Al-Andalus,* and his *Saint John of the Cross and Islam,* trans. H. W. Yoder and E. H. Douglas (New York: Vantage, 1981).

11. See E. Lévi-Provençal, s.v. "Shorfā'," *Encyclopedia of Islam,* 1st ed.

12. T. Burckhardt gives numerous translations from Sufi and other works that depict the spiritual vitality of Morocco in its traditional setting (*Fes, Stadt des Islam* [Olten: Urs Graf Verlag, 1960]).

13. In *Letters of a Sufi Master* (Bedfont, Middlesex: Perennial Books, 1969), T. Burckhardt has translated some of al-Darqāwī's treatises on the spiritual path.

14. See J. L. Michon, *Le Soufi marocain Aḥmad ibn 'Ajîba et son mi'rāj* (Paris: J. Vrin, 1973), for a study of one of the Darqāwī teachers who sought to restore primitive Shādhilism to the order.

15. F. de Jong's *Ṭuruq and Ṭuruq-Linked Institutions in Nineteenth-Century Egypt* (Leiden: Brill, 1978) has numerous references to the Shādhilīs in that country and their social and religious structures.

16. See B. Martin, *Muslim Brotherhoods in Nineteenth-Century Africa* (Cambridge: University Press, 1976).

17. A biographical and doctrinal treatment of the great Sufi shaykh is to be found in M. Lings, *A Sufi Saint of the Twentieth Century* (Berkeley: University of California Press, 1975). See also his article on the Algerian sage in *The Encyclopedia of Islam,* 2nd ed., s.v. "Aḥmad b. 'Alīwa."

18. 'Abd al-Ḥalīm Maḥmūd, former rector of the Azhar in Cairo, who knew Guénon personally, has written an important Arabic work on contemporary Shādhilism, wherein he mentions the work of Guénon as a Western offshoot of Shādhilī intellectuality: *al-Madrasah al-shādhiliyyah al-ḥadīthah wa imāmuhā Abu'l-Ḥasan al-Shādhilī* (Cairo: Dār al-kutub al-ḥadīthah, 1968).

3

Ibn ʿArabī and His School

William C. Chittick

Life, Works, and Influence

IBN ʿARABĪ (560/1165–638/1240) is probably the most influential author of works on Sufism in Islamic history. Known in the Arabic world as Ibn al-ʿArabī with the definite article *al-*, he indicates in his autographs that his full name was Abū ʿAbd Allāh Muḥammad ibn al-ʿArabī al-Ṭāʾī al-Ḥātimī. He was called Muḥyī al-Dīn, "The Revivifier of the Religion," and al-Shaykh al-Akbar, "The Greatest Master." Though he is not considered the founder of a Sufi order, his influence quickly passed beyond his immediate disciples to all Sufis who expressed their teachings in intellectual or philosophical terms. He was able to combine the various esoteric currents existing within the Islamic world—such as Pythagoreanism, alchemy, astrology, and different viewpoints within Sufism—into a vast synthesis shaped by the Quran and the *Sunnah* of the Prophet.

Ibn ʿArabī's father ʿAlī was apparently employed by Muḥammad ibn Saʿīd ibn Mardanīsh, the ruler of Murcia in Spain. In 567/1172 Murcia was conquered by the Almohad dynasty and ʿAlī took his family to Seville, where again he seems to have been taken into government service. His high social standing is indicated, among other things, by the fact that one of his wife's brothers, Yaḥyā ibn Yughān, was the ruler of the city of Tlemcen in Algeria. More interesting is the fact that this uncle renounced all worldly power in the midst of his reign and became a Sufi and an ascetic. Ibn ʿArabī mentions two other uncles who were also Sufis.

In his youth Ibn ʿArabī was employed as a secretary by the governor of Seville and married a girl named Maryam from an influential family. When he was thirty he left Spain for the first time, traveling to Tunis. Seven years later, in 597/1200, a vision told him to go to the East. In 599/1202 he performed the pilgrimage at Mecca and became acquainted with a shaykh from Isfahan, whose beautiful and spiritually accomplished daughter became, like Dante's Beatrice, his inspiration in the composition of the *Tarjumān al-ashwāq* (*Interpreter of Desires*). Also in Mecca he met Majd al-Dīn Isḥāq, a shaykh from Malatya whose yet unborn son was to be Ṣadr al-Dīn al-Qūnawī (606/1210–673/1274), Ibn 'Arabī's greatest disciple.

Accompanying Majd al-Dīn back to Malatya, Ibn 'Arabī stayed for a time in Mosul, where he was invested with the power of spiritual initiation by Ibn al-Jāmi', who himself had received it from the hands of al-Khiḍr. For some years Ibn 'Arabī traveled from city to city in the regions of Turkey, Syria, and Egypt, and the holy cities of Mecca and Medina. In 608/1211–12 he was in Baghdad, perhaps accompanied by Majd al-Dīn, who had been sent there by Sultan Kay Kā'ūs I (607/1210–616/1219) of Konya on a mission to the caliphal court. Ibn 'Arabī himself was on good terms with this sultan and wrote him a letter of practical advice. He was also a companion of the ruler of Aleppo, al-Malik al-Ẓāhir (582/1186–615/1218), a son of Saladin (Salāḥ al-Dīn al-Ayyūbī).

In 620/1223 Ibn 'Arabī settled down permanently in Damascus, where a circle of disciples, including al-Qūnawī, served him until his death. According to a number of early sources, he had married Majd al-Dīn's widow, al-Qūnawī's mother. Among those who studied with him during this time was the Ayyūbid Muẓaffar al-Dīn (d. 635/1238), the ruler of Damascus. In a precious document dated 632/1234, Ibn 'Arabī grants him permission (*ijāzah*) to teach his works, of which he lists 290; he also mentions seventy of his own masters in the sciences, noting that the list is incomplete. It is clear from this source that, as a complement to his Sufi studies, Ibn 'Arabī had spent long years learning the exoteric sciences such as the seven recitations of the Quran, Quranic commentary, jurisprudence, and especially *Ḥadīth*.

Ibn 'Arabī's outward life demonstrates nothing very exceptional for a Muslim man of learning. His special place in Islamic history is determined more by his life's inward events, his writings, and his encounters with spiritual men. In this respect, his youthful meeting with the great philosopher Ibn Rushd (Averroes) is of great symbolic importance, since it demonstrates the wide gulf Ibn 'Arabī perceived between the formal knowledge of the "men of reason" and the mystical "unveiling" (*kashf*), or vision of spiritual realities with the eye of the heart, that characterizes his own doctrines and teachings. It is significant that Ibn 'Arabī says he was a "beardless youth" when the meeting took place. Though certain authorities have inferred from an ambiguous passage in his *Futūḥāt* that he did not enter Sufism until he was twenty, the meeting with Ibn Rushd certainly took place before he had reached this age, and in recounting it he alludes to specifically Sufi practices that he had undertaken. Ibn Rushd "had wanted to meet me because . . . of what had reached him concerning the 'opening' (*fatḥ*) God had given me in the spiritual retreat (*khalwah*)." The spiritual retreat, performed exclusively by the Sufis, is never undertaken without initiation and the guidance of a shaykh; "opening," defined for example as "the unveiling of the uncreated Lights," is constantly mentioned in the works of Ibn ʿArabī and his followers as a primary goal of the Sufi. One of Ibn ʿArabī's closest disciples, Ismāʿīl ibn Sawdakīn, relates that when his master first entered the Path, he went into the spiritual retreat in the early morning and attained to opening before dawn. He remained in the retreat for fourteen months and received, through an overpowering attraction to God (*jadhbah*), everything that he was later to write down in his works. Al-Qūnawī's disciple al-Jandī (d. ca. 700/1300) provides a similar account on the authority of his master.[2] These points help to explain the significance of the exchange that took place during Ibn ʿArabī's meeting with Ibn Rushd:

> He said to me, "Yes." I replied, "Yes," and his joy in me increased. When I perceived why he had become happy, I said, "No." He became constricted, his color changed, and he began to doubt himself. He asked, "How have you found the situation in unveiling and the Divine Effusion? Is it the same as is given to us by rational consideration (*al-nazar*)?" I replied, "Yes and no. Between the yes and the no spirits fly from their matter and heads from their bodies." . . . He used to thank God that in his own time he had seen someone who had entered the spiritual retreat ignorant and had come out as I had come out, without study, discussion, investigation, or reading.[3]

The idea put forth by certain authorities that Ibn ʿArabī's initial spiritual growth took place at the hands of al-Khiḍr is unfounded. In fact, his earliest encounter with the "Men of the Unseen World" was with Jesus, as he states repeatedly, and his first spiritual master, Abu'l-ʿAbbās al-ʿUryabī, was dominated by Christ's spiritual influence.[4] Jesus is considered the "Seal of Universal Sanctity," while Ibn ʿArabī, at least in certain passages of his works, claimed to be the "Seal of the particular, Muḥammadan Sanctity" (see below), so the connection between the two is not fortuitous.

Ibn ʿArabī relates innumerable inward experiences and visions that helped determine the course of his life and the nature of his teachings; a number of these have been translated into English in *Sufis of Andalusia.* Here allusion can be made to a few similar accounts provided by al-Qūnawī. Ibn ʿArabī tells us that his decision to go to the East resulted from a command he received during a vision of the Divine Throne. Al-Qūnawī's account makes clear that he had known about this journey when he first decided to leave Spain permanently. Arriving at the Mediterranean, he decided not to sail without knowing the details of what was to come. He turned his attentiveness toward God with total presence and was shown everything that would happen to him inwardly and outwardly until the end of his life. "Then I set sail on the sea, with vision and certainty. What has happened has happened and what will come to be will come to be, without defect or deficiency." In a similar vein al-Qūnawī writes that the great saints have knowledge of what is destined to come about. Hence, they never pray for something whose existence is not predestined. "I witnessed that in our shaykh for many years in innumerable things. He told me he once had a vision of the Prophet, who said, 'God answers your prayers more quickly than you can utter them!'" Again, al-Qūnawī writes that Ibn ʿArabī used to contemplate the objects of God's knowledge at the ontological level of that knowledge itself. He would gaze at anyone whose innermost reality he desired to perceive and then "give news about his future becoming until his final resting place. . . . He was never wrong."[5]

Ibn ʿArabī's Works

In his comprehensive study of the 850 different works attributed to Ibn ʿArabī, Osman Yahya estimates that 700 are authentic and that of these, over 400 are extant. Though many of these are only a few pages long, many more are full-sized books, and the *Futūḥāt* alone contains more words than most authors write in a lifetime. Ibn ʿArabī provides the reason for his almost miraculous output. He never set out to write a single book. "On the contrary, influxes from God have entered upon me and nearly burned me alive. In order to find relief . . . I have composed works, without any intention on my own part. Many other books I have composed because of a divine command given during a dream or unveiling."[6]

Among Ibn ʿArabī's well-known works are the following:

(1) *al-Futūḥāt al-makkiyyah* (*The Meccan Openings*). This compendium of all the religious and gnostic sciences in Islam is a vast and bewildering ocean of inspirations. Among the subjects treated are the meanings of all the Islamic ritual observances, the stations and states the travelers undergo on their journey to God and in God, the significance and nature of each ontological level in the cosmos, the spiritual and ontological meaning of the letters of the Arabic alphabet, the meaning of different Quranic verses and *ḥadīths* from the points of view of various stations of mystical knowledge, the sciences embraced by each of the ninety-nine Names of God, and the "psychological" states of those travelers who are dominated by the spiritual influences of various prophets.

(2) *Fuṣūṣ al-ḥikam* (*The Ringstones of Wisdom*). Judging from the more than one hundred commentaries written on this work and the great esteem

in which it has always been held by Ibn ʿArabī's followers, one can accept H. Corbin's view that it is "no doubt the best compendium of Ibn ʿArabī's esoteric doctrine."[7] In al-Qūnawī's view, it is "one of the most precious shorter writings of our shaykh."[8] Basing himself on the Quran and the *Ḥadith*, Ibn ʿArabī discusses the divine wisdom revealed to twenty-seven different prophets or Words of God from Adam to Muḥammad; he shows how each prophet is the theophany of the wisdom implied by one of the Divine Names. The first to comment on the *Fuṣūṣ* was al-Qūnawī, although he discusses only the general themes of each chapter.

A second early commentator was ʿAfīf al-Dīn al-Tilimsānī (d. 690/1291), a direct disciple of Ibn ʿArabī and then a constant companion of al-Qūnawī; so close were they that al-Qūnawī willed all of his own works to ʿAfīf al-Dīn. In his commentary he deals with a few salient points which appear unclear or with which he is in disagreement (such as the question of the immutability [*thubūt*] of the entities). Undoubtedly, the most influential of the commentators was al-Jandī, who tells us that when al-Qūnawī was explaining to him the preface of the work, he was overcome by his spiritual influence and was given an opening through which the purport of the whole work was revealed to him. When apprised of this experience, al-Qūnawī told him that the same thing had happened to him when Ibn ʿArabī had begun to explain the work to him.

A famous commentator is al-Jandī's student al-Kāshānī (d. 730/1330); T. Izutsu's outstanding exposition of Ibn ʿArabī's ontology is based largely on al-Kāshānī's work. More influential in Iran and the eastern lands of Islam has been the commentary of al-Kāshānī's student al-Qayṣarī (d. 751/1350), who directed a *madrasah* in Anatolia. Bābā Rukn al-Dīn Shīrāzī (d. 744/1344) studied with both al-Kāshānī and al-Qayṣarī and wrote the first Persian commentary. Sayyid Ḥaydar Āmulī (d. ca. 786/1384) in *Naṣṣ al-nuṣūṣ* (*The Text of Texts*) integrated the *Fuṣūṣ* into the context of Shīʿite gnosis. ʿAbd al-Raḥmān Jāmī (d. 898/1492) wrote both an Arabic commentary on the *Fuṣūṣ* and a mixed Persian and Arabic commentary on Ibn ʿArabī's own summary of the *Fuṣūṣ*. In India Muḥibb Ilāh Ilāhābādī (d. 1058/1648) wrote commentaries on the *Fuṣūṣ* in both Arabic and Persian; his many works on Ibn ʿArabī's teachings earned him the title of "the Second Ibn ʿArabī." In the Turkish-speaking part of the Islamic world ʿAbd Allāh of Bosnia (d. 1054/1644), known as ʿAbdi Efendi, wrote several Arabic treatises showing a remarkable spiritual and intellectual affinity with al-Qūnawī and is the author of commentaries on the *Fuṣūṣ* in Arabic and Turkish, both of which have been published. Perhaps the most widely read commentary on the *Fuṣūṣ* in the Arab world was written by the prolific Sufi author ʿAbd al-Ghanī al-Nābulusī (d. 1143/1730); his care to define and explain practically every single word and his often questionable interpretations suggest that already by his time the general ability to read and understand the *Fuṣūṣ* in the Arab world had severely declined.

(3) *Tarjumān al-ashwāq*. This short divan of love poetry referred to above was the first of Ibn 'Arabī's works to be translated into English. It is particularly famous because he himself wrote a commentary on it to prove to certain exoteric *'ulamā'* that it dealt with spiritual truths and not profane love. Ibn 'Arabī is also the author of at least two other divans and many thousands of verses scattered throughout his prose works; he is one of the best and most productive of all Arab poets.

(4) *Shajarat al-kawn* (*The Tree of Engendered Existence*). Developing the symbolism of the Quranic verse, "a good word is like a good tree . . ." (XIV, 24), this relatively short treatise on cosmology, extant in English translation, describes the Prophet Muḥammad as the embodiment of the Perfect Man.

Among the many works wrongly attributed to Ibn 'Arabī, *Risālat al-aḥadiyyah* (*The Treatise on Unity*) has been translated into English. It has recently been shown to be the work of Awḥad al-Dīn Balyānī; though influenced by Ibn 'Arabī, Balyānī interprets a number of his teachings in a manner unacceptable to the mainstream of his school.

Ibn 'Arabī's Influence

Ibn 'Arabī's doctrines have been taught either in conjunction with a practical spiritual method, or independently as "mystical philosophy." It is highly likely that Ibn 'Arabī himself taught his own works both to initiated Sufis and to those who were intellectually attracted to Sufism but had not taken the practical step of swearing allegiance to a shaykh. The chief disciple to whom he transmitted both his spiritual and intellectual authority was al-Qūnawī; all sources agree that he was the major spokesman for Ibn 'Arabī's teachings. Al-Qūnawī himself refers to his special role in recounting a vision of Ibn 'Arabī fifteen years after his death. He asked from him the "attainment of the direct vision of that theophany after which there is no veil and which does not endure for any other Perfect Man," that is, apart from Ibn 'Arabī. After granting this request, Ibn 'Arabī tells him that he has had many sons and disciples, especially the son of his own loins, Sa'd al-Dīn (d. 656/1258, the author of a divan), "but what you have asked was not made possible for any of them. How many sons and disciples have I killed and then revived! But he who died, died, and he who was slain, was slain, and none of them attained to this!"[9]

Al-Qūnawī is the author of about thirty works, of which five or six are of central importance for the spread of Ibn ʿArabī's teachings, since they determined how he was to be interpreted by most of his followers. In style of expression, he stands at the antipodes of his master. While Ibn ʿArabī's works are torrents of inspiration, continual flashes of light often with no apparent interconnection, al-Qūnawī provides a model for the systematic and rational formulation of ideas, though he constantly deals with the world of unveiling. In the words of the great Sufi poet Jāmī, "It is impossible to understand Ibn ʿArabī's teachings concerning the Oneness of Being in a manner consistent both with intelligence and with the religious law without studying al-Qūnawī's works."[10] Among the most important of these are *Miftāḥ al-ghayb* (*The Key to the Unseen*), a systematic account of Ibn ʿArabī's metaphysics and cosmology; *Tafsīr al-fātiḥah* (*Commentary on the Opening Chapter of the Quran*), an exposition of the nature of the "three books" (the Quran, the cosmos, and man); and a correspondence with Naṣīr al-Dīn al-Ṭūsī (d. 672/1274), the foremost representative of Ibn Sīnā's Peripatetic philosophy. In this last work, al-Qūnawī demonstrates concurrences between Ibn ʿArabī's teachings and those of the Peripatetics, while clearly showing where they diverge.

Al-Qūnawī directed a flourishing center in Konya, where he was a close friend of Rūmī, though he represents a very different mode of formulating Sufi teachings. Scholars came from much of the Islamic world to study *Ḥadīth* with him. Often, after delivering a formal lecture on this subject in Arabic, he would change to Persian and comment on Sufi poetry. This was his method in teaching the great *Poem of the Way* of Ibn al-Fāriḍ (d. 632/1235). Al-Qūnawī's disciple al-Farghānī (d. 695/1296) took careful notes during these lectures and then rewrote them in the form of the Persian work *Mashāriq al-darārī al-zuhar* (*Orients of Radiant Stars*), to which al-Qūnawī added a short introduction. Later al-Farghānī revised his own work in Arabic with the title *Muntaha'l-madārik* (*The Utmost Limit of Perception*); concerning the latter work Jāmī writes, "No one else has ever been able to explain the intricacies of the Science of Reality with such interconnectedness and order."[11]

Another important disciple of al-Qūnawī was al-Jandī, referred to above; his Persian *Nafḥat al-rūḥ* (*The Breath of the Spirit*) provides valuable information concerning the practices connected with Ibn ʿArabī's teachings. A third student, Fakhr al-Dīn ʿIrāqī (d. 688/1289) was inspired by al-Qūnawī's lectures on the *Fuṣūṣ* to write *Lamaʿāt* (*Divine Flashes*), a digest in exquisite Persian prose of Ibn ʿArabī's teachings on metaphysics and divine love. A fourth, Abū Bakr ʿAlī al-Malaṭī or al-Sīwāsī is known only because he transmitted al-Qūnawī's power of initiation to later Sufis.[12] Among later members of the same *silsilah* is Muḥammad ibn Muḥammad Shīrīn

Maghribi (d. 809/1406-7), whose Persian divan has long been highly esteemed for its exposition of Ibn 'Arabī's teachings. Famous later masters descended from Ibn 'Arabī's line include the prolific Moroccan author Abu'l-'Abbās Aḥmad known as al-Zarrūq (d. 899/1493), and the *amīr* 'Abd al-Qādir al-Jazā'irī (d. 1300/1883), exiled from Algeria to Damascus by the French for his role in leading the resistance to their rule and author of a number of important works.

Outside of the small number of *silsilahs* that trace a line of descent to Ibn 'Arabī, practically all Sufis who have expressed themselves in intellectual terms have followed the lead of his school. Even those Sufis who opposed certain of his teachings, such as 'Alā' al-Dawlah Simnānī (d. 736/1336), employed his terminology and concepts. In the same way, Rūmī's commentators lived in Ibn 'Arabī's intellectual universe and employed his teachings to explain those of their own master. Besides the commentators on the *Fuṣūṣ* mentioned above, the majority of whom are also authors of independent works, Ibn 'Arabī's most important followers include 'Abd al-Karīm al-Jīlī (d. ca. 832/1428); in contrast to most authors of this school, he shows relatively little influence from al-Qūnawī and represents an independent reinterpretation and revivification of Ibn 'Arabī's teachings. The most famous of his thirty or so works is *al-Insān al-kāmil* (*The Perfect Man*). In contrast, the writings of Shah Ni'mat Allāh Walī (d. ca. 832/1429; see chapter 7) are dominated by the influence of al-Qūnawī's followers, especially al-Kāshānī and al-Qayṣarī. Shaykh Maḥmūd Shabistarī (d. 720/1320) is famous for his one-thousand-verse Persian poem *Gulshan-i rāz* (*The Rose-garden of Mystery*); its lengthy commentary by Shams al-Dīn Muḥammad Lāhījī (d. 912/1506-7) is one of the most masterly presentations of Ibn 'Arabī's teachings in Persian.

In the Arab world 'Abd al-Wahhāb al-Sha'rānī, who died in Cairo in 973/1565, did much to popularize Ibn 'Arabī's teachings through more than fifty works written in an easily intelligible style. Two figures in Turkey well known to historians for their political role but not yet widely recognized as members of Ibn 'Arabī's school are Qāḍī Burhān al-Dīn (d. ca. 800/1398), the sultan of Sivas and author of an important summary of al-Qūnawī's teachings, and Sultan Mehmet, the conqueror of Istanbul (855/1451–886/1481). At the latter's command, several important commentaries were written on al-Qūnawī's works and his *Miftāḥ al-ghayb* was translated into Persian.[13] Among the numerous followers of Ibn 'Arabī who lived in the subcontinent, one should mention Muḥammad ibn Faḍl Allāh Burhānpūrī (d. 1029/1620), who wrote a ten-page "Gift addressed to the Prophet's Spirit," which is a summary of Ibn 'Arabī's teachings seen largely through the eyes of Jāmī. It was the object of several commentaries both in the Arab countries and farther east, was translated into Javanese, and according to its English translator, is one of the most important texts for the history of the development of Sufi thought in Indonesia. Although Burhānpūrī's famous contemporary Aḥmad Sirhindī (d. 1034/1624) criticized Ibn ʿArabī on certain points, he supported him on many others and must be considered an adherent of his school. In Indonesia, Ḥamzah Fansūrī (fl. tenth/sixteenth century) wrote extensively on Ibn ʿArabī's doctrines. In Iran and farther east, numerous figures who are known primarily as philosophers, such as Ṣā'in al-Dīn Turkah Iṣfahānī (d. ca. 836/1432) and Mullā Ṣadrā (d. 1051/1641), were deeply influenced by Ibn ʿArabī's teachings. Finally, let it be mentioned in passing that Asín Palacios and others have suggested that Ibn ʿArabī exercised considerable influence in the medieval West, especially on Raymund Lull and Dante.

Ibn ʿArabī's Teachings

In formulating his teachings, Ibn ʿArabī made use of every available source, beginning with the Quran and the *Ḥadīth.* He borrowed extensively from the written and oral tradition of Sufism that had been developing for several hundred years; his works are a vast repository of references to the words of earlier shaykhs, including such lesser-known but important Andalusian masters as Ibn Masarrah (d. 319/931) and Ibn Qasī (d. 546/1151). He made free use of the terminology of the philosophers, especially those belonging to the more esoteric schools, such as the Ikhwān al-Ṣafā' and various pre-Islamic schools such as Hermeticism and Neoplatonism. He was thoroughly versed in *Kalām,* especially Ashʿarism. But all these schools of thought were so many building blocks that became part of Ibn ʿArabī's own intellectual edifice; his repeated testimony and the very nature of his writings and influence show that his unveiling and mystical perception gave a new form to the raw material with which he worked.

Most of Ibn ʿArabī's works remain unedited, unpublished, and/or unstudied. Though the *Futūḥāt* was first printed in the nineteenth century, a critical edition has begun to appear only recently. Even if this were finished, years of effort on the part of a large number of scholars would be needed before a thorough analysis of its contents could be carried out, and there would still remain his other works. Thus, all scholars who have attempted to explain Ibn ʿArabī's thought have pointed out the tentative nature of their endeavors. Nevertheless, certain central themes, highlighted for example in the *Fuṣūṣ,* can be discerned throughout his works. We can be sure of their primary importance because they were emphasized by his immediate disciples and followers. These same themes have been taken up and elaborated upon by generations of Sufis and philosophers. It is to some of these that we will limit our attention here.

The Divine Names

As early as 1914, Asín Palacios saw that "the whole of the *Futūḥāt* is based on "belief in the esoteric virtue of the divine names."[14] Other authorities, such as T. Burckhardt, H. Corbin, and S. H. Nasr, have in their turn called attention to the primary importance of the Names in Ibn ʿArabī's doctrines. According to the Quran and the *Ḥadīth,* God is the Merciful, the Wise, the Generous, the Forgiving, the Living, the Hearing, the Avenger, and so on. His Names epitomize the knowledge of Him that has been revealed to mankind; through them we can grasp something of the Divine Nature, though we must remember the Prophet's saying: "Meditate upon God's blessings [e.g., upon the effects of His Bounty and Generosity], but not upon His Essence (*dhāt*)," since God as He is in Himself is unknowable to us, at least in terms of discursive thought. Here we should recall Ibn ʿArabī's well-known teaching concerning transcendence and immanence—or, more precisely, "incomparability" (*tanzīh*) and "similarity" (*tashbīh*): On the one hand, God is unknowable; on the other, we can understand Him through the Names. True knowledge of Him must combine the two points of view. Ultimately, this coincidence of opposites can be grasped only at the stage of unveiling. The apparent incompatibility of the two standpoints is one reason that the highest stage of mystic knowledge is often referred to as "bewilderment" (*ḥayrah*).

Everything we can know about God, and ultimately everything we can know about "other than God" (*mā siwa'Llāh*)—that is, "the world" or "the cosmos" (*al-ʿālam*)—is prefigured by the Names. They delineate God's perfections inasmuch as He is Being (*al-wujūd*) and the source of all that exists. Ranked in a hierarchy, some are broader in scope than others; the "Universal Names" are said to number 99, 300, or 1001, whereas the "particular Names" in the last analysis correspond to all things. Hence Ibn ʿArabī can say that the Divine Names are infinite in keeping with the infinity of the creatures (*Fuṣūṣ*, chap. 2).

The formula "In the Name of God, the All-Merciful, the All-Compassionate," which begins practically every chapter of the Quran, mentions three Names: *Allāh, al-Raḥmān,* and *al-Raḥīm.* The latter two both derive from the word *raḥmah,* "mercy" (which in turn derives from the same root as *raḥim,* "womb"). For Ibn ʿArabī, mercy is Being. When God says, "My Mercy embraces all things" (Quran VII, 156), this means, "I bestow existence on all things," since existence is the only quality in which all things share.

In a *ḥadīth* the Prophet refers to the "Breath of the All-Merciful" (*nafas al-Raḥmān*). According to Ibn ʿArabī, the All-Merciful's exhalation of His Breath is equivalent to the bestowal of existence (*ījād*). In the same context he and his followers constantly quote the *ḥadīth* in which God says, "I was a Hidden Treasure and I wanted to be known, so I created the creatures that I might be known." The Hidden Treasure refers to the possibilities of outward manifestation prefigured by the Names. Since "God encompasses all things in knowledge" (Quran LXV, 12), the Hidden Treasure corresponds to all things as known by Him before their creation.

The All-Merciful, whose very nature is to have mercy on all things (*al-ashyāʾ*) and thus bring them into existence, feels distress (*kurbah*) within Himself; by the "possibility" (*imkān*) the things possess to display their own special qualities, they beg Him to bestow existence upon them. So God "exhales" and relieves His distress; He deploys His Breath and the cosmos is born. But this is not a simple exhalation. It is articulated speech: "Our only word to a thing, when We desire it, is to say to it 'Be!,' and it is" (Quran XVI, 40). The myriad types and grades of existents can be divided into letters, words, phrases, sentences, and books. Ibn ʿArabī and others have developed a complicated cosmology based on the symbolism of letters and words understood in this ontological sense.

The "things embraced by God's Knowledge" (*al-maʿlūmāt*) are also referred to as the "nonexistents" (*al-maʿdūmāt*), the "immutable entities" (*al-aʿyān al-thābitah*), and the "possible things" (*al-mumkināt*). They are "nonexistent" as long as they remain only in God's Knowledge and do not appear in the world, "immutable" since He knows them for all eternity, and "possible" because He may or may not bestow existence upon them in any given circumstances. They are also called "concomitants" (*lawāzim*) of the Names. All of these "realities" (*ḥaqāʾiq*) can be divided into the "divine" (*ilāhī*), which are the Names and the immutable entities, and the "engendered" (*kawnī*), which are the entities when given existence by the Breath.

The Universal Divine Names or Attributes can be classified from a number of points of view. According to one such classification, four of them are the most fundamental, the "pillars" (*arkān*) of Divinity: Will, Knowledge, Power, and Speech. Other formulations add three more Attributes—Life, Generosity, and Equity—to give the "seven Leaders" (*al-aʾimmat al-sabʿah*). The remaining Names derive from these four or seven. The Leaders or Pillars are then embraced by the Name Allah, the All-Comprehensive Name (*al-ism al-jāmiʿ*) that points to the Divine Essence.[15]

The hierarchical relationship among the Names is reflected in the structure of the cosmos, which is composed of descending levels of existence (*marātib*), though from creation's viewpoint they are ascending. Thus, we have the "arc of descent" (*qaws al-nuzūl*) and the "arc of ascent" (*qaws al-ṣuʿūd*), which together make up the "Circle of Existence" (*dāʾirat al-wujūd*). At each descending level, different realities interrelate or "marry" (*nikāḥ*) to bring about the production of succeeding levels. Ibn ʿArabī envisages this hierarchical structure from several different standpoints. In the scheme illustrated by the diagrams accompanying the creation myth (I–V), he describes each higher reality as active and masculine in relation to the next lower reality, which is passive and feminine. The higher is in a state of undifferentiation (*ijmāl*), while the lower is in a state of differentiation (*tafṣīl*). Thus, for example, the Supreme Pen contains all spiritual realities in undifferentiated form; then it deploys them in their differentiated details by writing them out in the Guarded Tablet. But Ibn ʿArabī indicates that every reality in the scheme is a pen from one point of view and a tablet from another.

The One and the Many

The Names, and so also the immutable entities, are no different in their existence from God Himself; there is only one Being, God, who is called by many Names, each of which denotes one of His ontological modes. But God in His very Essence, which is beyond the limitation implied by any of the Names, is One in a different sense than God considered as the Possessor of Names (*dhāt al-asmāʾ*). Here lies a distinction fundamental to Ibn ʿArabī's teachings. At the beginning of chapter 7 of the *Fuṣūṣ,* he writes, "Know that He who is called Allah is one in His Essence and all through His Names." He often refers to the Oneness of the Essence as *al-aḥadiyyah* ("Exclusive" or "Absolute Unity") and the Oneness of the Names, through which God is all, as *al-waḥdāniyyah* ("Inclusive" or "Infinite Unity"), although for the second kind his followers usually prefer the term *al-wāḥidiyyah.*

Ibn ʿArabī is well known as the founder of the school of the "Oneness of Being" (*waḥdat al-wujūd*). Though this teaching permeates his works, he does not himself employ the term. One of the first members of his school to use it in a technical sense is al-Farghānī, who normally contrasts it with the "Manyness of Knowledge" (*kathrat al-ʿilm*): One in His Reality, God possesses the principle of manyness in His knowledge. He is One and All.

In God's knowledge, the nonexistent things are known in all their differentiated details. This is the level of the "Most Holy Effusion" (*al-fayḍ al-aqdas*) or the "Unseen Theophany" (*al-tajallī al-ghaybī*). It is also the level of the Hidden Treasure and the "distress" of the All-Merciful. The manifestation of the Hidden Treasure, or the exhalation of the Breath, is called the

"Holy Effusion" (*al-fayḍ al-muqaddas*) or the "Visible Theophany" (*al-tajallī al-shahādī*). The entities, still nonexistent and immutable within God's Knowledge, are manifested outwardly within the various levels of existence.

The One Being does not, through the manifestation of the entities, become many beings, since Being is a single reality. True, the entities are now provisionally called "existents" (*mawjūdāt*) or "engendered things" (*kā'ināt*), but Being/Existence retains Its original property of nondelimitation (*iṭlāq*) and transcendence. Light remains eternally unaffected by Its outward effusion, just as the sun is unaffected by its rays. As Ibn ʿArabī and his followers explain through many images, "the entities have never smelt—and will never smell—the fragrance of existence." "The possible existents remain nonexistent in their original state; existence is nothing but the Being of God" (*Fuṣūṣ*, chap. 8). The entities we perceive are only the different modalities of the One Being. In the words of al-Qūnawī,

> The greatest obscurity and veil is the plurality that arises in the One Being because of the effects of the immutable entities within It. People imagine that the entities become outwardly manifest in existence and through existence. But only their effects (*athar*) become manifest in existence. Manifestation and outwardness belong only to Being, but on condition of having become plural through the effect of the entities.[16]

Each entity displays a perfection of Being, thus veiling and revealing It at one and the same time: "God made the creatures like veils (*ḥijāb*). He who knows them as such is led back to Him, but he who takes them as real is barred from His Presence" (*Futūḥāt*, II, p. 460). As long as we do not perceive the things for the veils that they are, the whole world is naught but fantasy.

> Everything engendered in existence is imagination (*khayāl*)
> —but in fact it is Reality.
> Whoever understands this truth has grasped the mysteries
> of the Way. (*Fuṣūṣ*, chap. 16)

One mark of the essential nonexistence of all "existent" things is that they must be recreated at each instant. According to Ibn ʿArabī, God places dreams in the animal world so that people may witness the ontological level of Imagination and come to know that there is another world, similar to the sensory world. Through the rapid transformations of imaginal forms in dreams, God wants to show us that the sensory world is changing at every instant. "If the world were to remain in a single state for two units of time, it would possess the attribute of independence from God. 'But men are in doubt as to the renewed creation' (Quran L, 15)" (*Futūḥāt*, III, p. 199).

Here two basic meanings of the term "imagination" can be discerned. In the first sense, everything that is "other than God" is "imaginary" and in the ultimate sense unreal. This is the level of "nondelimited imagination" (*al-khayāl al-muṭlaq*), which Ibn ʿArabī identifies with the Breath of the All-Merciful. Through it "That which can not possibly exist [since it is not Allah, the only Being there is] comes to exist" (*Futūḥāt,* II, p. 312). "The reality of imagination is change in every state, and manifestation within every form. There is no true being that does not accept change except Allah. So there is nothing in realized existence (*al-wujūd al-muḥaqqaq*) except Allah. As for everything else, that is in imaginal existence. . . . So everything other than the Essence of God is imagination in the process of change" (*Futūḥāt,* II, p. 313). It is from this point of view that all things in the world must be "interpreted" (*taʿbīr*) as if they were dreams (*Fuṣūṣ*, chap. 9).

Second, "imagination" refers to an ontological realm between the spiritual world and the corporeal world, also called the "isthmus" (*barzakh*) and the world of "image-exemplars" (*mithāl*). Here spiritual realities become manifest as sensory forms, and, after death, the attributes and moral qualities of men become personified. Just as the animal soul acts as the means whereby the disengaged (*mujarrad*) spirit can maintain a connection with the corporeal body, so the world of imagination acts as an intermediary between the disembodied spirits and the corporeal world. This intermediate world is in turn divided into two kinds of imagination, one of which is "contiguous" (*muttaṣil*) to our psyches, and the other of which is "discontiguous" (*munfaṣil*).

> The difference between contiguous and discontiguous imagination is that the former disappears with the disappearance of the imaginer, while the latter is a self-subsistent ontological level which continuously acts as a receptacle for disengaged meanings and spirits, to which it gives corporeal forms, though only in accordance with their specific characteristics. Then contiguous imagination derives from discontiguous imagination. (*Futūḥāt, II,* p. 311)

The nature of the realities that become manifest within nondelimited imagination or the cosmos is determined by their preparedness (*istiʿdād*), that is, the extent to which they are able to act as receptacles (*qābil*) that display the perfections of Nondelimited Being. Preparedness in turn is determined by the "Lord" (*rabb*) of each existent, the particular Name that governs it, its immutable entity. "The All becomes entified in keeping with each existent; then that entification (*taʿayyun*) is that thing's Lord. But no one takes from Him in respect of His Absolute Unity" (*Fuṣūṣ*, chap. 7). The difference between the prophets and saints on the one hand and ordinary people on the other is that the former are loci of manifestation (*maẓhar, majlā*) for Universal Names, while the latter manifest particular Names.

The former display the myriad perfections of Being, while the latter only display a few, and these imperfectly.[17]

Closely connected to the entity's preparedness is the question of "destiny" (*qadar*). Since each existent thing is determined by its Lord, its destiny is foreordained. But the "mystery of destiny" (*sirr al-qadar*) is that God does not do the foreordaining; on the contrary, the entity foreordains itself. The entity, after all, is in essence a nonexistent object of God's Knowledge. God did not make (*jaʿl*) it the way it is, since it is uncreated—He has known it for all eternity. "So no one possesses in himself anything from God, nor does he have anything from any other than himself" (*Fuṣūṣ*, chap. 2). God's only role is to bring the entity from nonexistence in knowledge to existence in the world, that is, to show mercy upon it through His Breath. Once in existence, the entities themselves determine how they will act and what their ultimate destiny will be. "So let them blame none but themselves, and let them praise none but themselves: 'God's is the conclusive argument' (Quran VI, 149) through His Knowledge of them" (*Fuṣūṣ*, chap. 8).

Here Ibn ʿArabī distinguishes between God's engendering command (*al-amr al-takwīnī*), through which He gives existence to the entity, and His prescriptive command (*al-amr al-taklīfī*), through which He requires men to follow the religious law. In the practical terms of human experience, men freely choose whether or not to follow the latter. Since they cannot know their destiny until it overcomes them, they must follow the command of God and trust in Him; but in the final analysis, their ends are determined by their beginnings. This is one significance of such Quranic verses as "To your Lord you shall return" (VI, 164).

In the same context, Ibn ʿArabī states that men worship "the God created by their beliefs." Men can only conceive of Nondelimited Being—God—to the extent allowed by their own preparedness, which is determined by their immutable entity, their Lord. The prophets and saints are theophanies of God's Universal Names, through which they know and realize Him. In the same way the sciences and laws which they bring for mankind are manifestations of these Names—this is the whole theme of the *Fuṣūṣ*. Other men are theophanies of particular Names, which do not manifest the same ontological perfections. Thus, their "beliefs" concerning God will be determined by their own preparedness for knowledge and existence. In effect, the God they worship—their own Lord—will be "created" by their limited preparedness. Only the greatest prophets and saints—the Perfect Men—worship God as such, since they are loci of manifestation for the All-Comprehensive Name *Allāh*.

Each "existent" in the world is a mixture of existence and nonexistence, or of light and darkness. To the extent that it exists, it is a theophany of

Being; to the extent that it is nonexistent, it is a veil over Reality. "So you are situated between existence and nonexistence, or good (*khayr*) and evil (*sharr*)" (*Futūḥāt*, II, p. 304). "Existence is light, while nonexistence is darkness. We are in existence, so we are encompassed by good" (*Futūḥāt*, III, p. 486). God or Nondelimited Being is Sheer Good (*al-khayr al-maḥḍ*); hence the Prophet said, "All good is in Thy hands, while no evil is ascribed to Thee." Ibn 'Arabī concludes that evil has no fundamental reality, even though it is totally relevant to our everyday lives; otherwise, religion would have no role to play and God's prescriptive command would be meaningless.

> To whom can evils be ascribed? For the cosmos is in the hand of Sheer Good, which is Total Being. However, the possible existent can be envisaged as nonexistent; to the extent this is so, evil is ascribed to it. For it does not possess in its very essence the property of Necessary Being; hence evil befalls it. (*Futūḥāt*, III, p. 315)

The creatures are given existence through the Breath of the All-Merciful, and in the end they return to Mercy. "God showed us favor through the Name All-Merciful, thus bringing us out of evil, which is nonexistence, to good, which is existence. . . . So from the beginning, He entrusted us to Mercy" (*Futūḥāt*, II, p. 157). From this point of view Ibn 'Arabī maintains that hell itself is a mercy and that the chastisement (*'adhāb*) of the unbelievers will eventually be changed to "sweetness" (in accordance with the root meaning of the word *'adhāb*; cf. *Fuṣūṣ*, chap. 10).

Instead of attributing evil to nonexistence, al-Qūnawī follows the lead of many passages in the *Futūḥāt* by calling attention to the ontological qualities evil does in fact reflect and the manner in which religion protects mankind from evil's consequences. The various phenomena connected with religion and salvation—such as the prophets, the Scriptures, religious teachers, mosques, faith, the remembrance of God, and piety—are loci of manifestation for the Divine Name the Guide (*al-Hādī*), while phenomena that manifest evil—such as satanic men and *jinn*, unbelievers, immorality, and thoughts that turn the mind away from God—display the properties of the Name the Misleader (*al-Muḍill*). Al-Qūnawī is thus able to discuss suffering and damnation without minimizing their practical significance. In this context, he recalls Ibn 'Arabī's definition of evil as "that which is incompatible with man's goal and disagreeable to his nature and constitution" (*Fuṣūṣ*, chap. 11). Al-Qūnawī remarks that when the soul leaves the state of equilibrium established by the *Sharī'ah* and the *ṭarīqah*, it falls under the sway of the Names of Severity, such as the Misleader, the Wrathful, He-who-harms (*al-Ḍārr*), and the Avenger. "As a result, the effects of these Names become manifest in this world, or in the next world, in forms disagreeable to the soul, such as suffering, chastisement, illness, punishment, distance from God, and veils."[18]

As the theophany of Sheer Good, the cosmos is the locus of beauty and the object of love (*maḥabbah*). The root of all love, whether for God or for "others," is God's Love, through which the world was created. In the *ḥadīth* of the Hidden Treasure, God does not in fact say that He "wanted" to be known, but that He "loved" (*aḥbabtu*) to be known. "Through this Love God turned His Will toward the things in the state of their nonexistence . . . and said to them 'Be!'" (*Futūḥāt,* II, p. 167). In God Himself, Love, Lover, and Beloved are one, since the nonexistent objects of Love are none but the perfections of His own Self. So also in creation, Love manifests Itself in all things, each and every one of which is both lover and beloved.

> Nothing is loved in the existents except God, since He is manifest within every beloved to the eye of every lover. And nothing exists but lovers. So all the cosmos is lover and beloved, and all is reducible to Him. . . . No one loves any but his own Creator, but he is veiled from Him by the love of Zaynab, Suʿād, Hind, Laylā, the world, dirhams, position, and all other objects of love. (*Futūḥāt,* II, p. 326)

Ibn ʿArabī's teachings on love, expressed poetically by such figures as ʿIrāqī, extend explicitly to the domain of sexuality. He views man's contemplation of God in himself and in woman during the sexual act as one of the highest forms of spiritual vision (*Fuṣūṣ*, chap. 27).

The Perfect Man

The Perfect Man, a key term in Ibn ʿArabī's vocabulary, is the all-comprehensive engendered existent (*al-kawn al-jāmiʿ*) discussed at the beginning of the *Fuṣūṣ*. Ontologically the origin and goal of the cosmos, he is also the model of spiritual perfection and the guide of men. In his inmost reality, he is known as the Cloud (*al-ʿamāʾ*). The Prophet was asked, "Where was God before He created the creatures?" He replied, "In a cloud, neither above which nor below which was any space." The Cloud in fact is the All-Merciful Breath, the theophany of Sheer Being, within which letters and words become articulated. The Cloud surrounds God "before" He creates the creatures and is thus the intermediary between Him and them; it is the Reality of Realities (*ḥaqīqat al-ḥaqāʾiq*), within which all immutable entities are englobed.

But the Perfect Man is both "all-comprehensive," in the sense that he embraces all realities, and "engendered," that is, he belongs to the world of created things, at least in his outward dimension. He is an isthmus (*barzakh*) between God and the cosmos, since he comprehends both the divine and the engendered realities. In God, the One and the Many are united; in the cosmos the Many are dispersed, but in the Perfect Man the One and the Many are reunited in the midst of their very separation and dispersion.

As al-Qūnawī makes explicit, the Perfect Man contains within himself the "Five Divine Presences," the five universal levels where God makes Himself known. Al-Qūnawī enumerates these as (1) the Reality of Realities, or the Presence of Knowledge; (2) the World of the Spirits; (3) the World of Imagination; (4) the World of Corporeal Bodies; (5) the All-Comprehensive Presence, that is, the Perfect Man in his total deployment. The Perfect Man is the macrocosm, while individual man is the microcosm. "God only created the cosmos outside of man to strike an example for him and so that he might know that everything manifest in the world is inside himself, while he is the goal. . . . In him all the Divine Names and their effects are displayed" (*Futūḥāt,* III, p. 417).

If the Perfect Man is the ontological prototype of both the cosmos and the individual man, he is also man perfected, the human state realized in its full breadth and depth. According to the Prophet, "Allah created Adam upon His own Form"; in the Quran God says, "He taught Adam the Names, all of them" (II, 31). As the Name that embraces all other Names, *Allāh* is the Reality of Realities. To say that man is created upon Allah's form means that God is the "meaning" (*maʿnā*) or immutable entity of mankind, while man is God's outward form or existent entity; though other things also reflect Him, they do so incompletely, since they manifest lesser Names. But it is only the Perfect Man who is able to live up to this human potential and truly actualize this station. He alone is the "vicegerent of Allah" (*khalīfat Allāh;* cf. Quran II, 30). A human being who does not attain perfection in this world is only a "rational animal," not a "man." He is related to humanity as a corpse is related to a living person. "He is a man in shape, not in reality, for a corpse lacks all faculties. Thus is he who does not attain perfection. . . . Only the Vicegerent is worthy to act as a receptacle for (all) the Divine Names" (*Futūḥāt,* II, p. 441).

According to the Quran, God "governs the Command (*al-amr*) from heaven to earth; then it ascends to Him in a day whose measure is a thousand years of your counting" (XXXII, 5). This descent of the Command is the exhalation of the All-Merciful's Breath. When it reaches its lowest point, at the level of mankind, it reverses. If a man is destined to become a Perfect Man, he will enter the spiritual path, through which he can return to his Source and complete the Circle. Then he becomes established at the "Point at the Center of the Circle" (*nuqṭah wasaṭ al-dāʾirah*), also known as the station of Equilibrium (*al-iʿtidāl*), since the Perfect Man is equidistant from each and every reality, whether created or uncreated. Having realized the full human potential, he manifests the All-Comprehensive Name *Allāh* and escapes the domination of every limited Name and entity. Al-Qūnawī writes that Equilibrium is the center from which no one deviates except him who is attracted to what is less than himself. "If a man veers away from the Center to one side because of an attracting and overpowering affinity, and if the property of certain Names and levels predominates so that he leaves Equilibrium, . . . then he will worship God from the standpoint of that [limited] Name's level. . . . It will become the utmost limit of his hopes . . . unless he passes beyond it."[19]

The spiritual stature of the Perfect Men, those who truly act as God's vicegerents, explains the meaning of such Quranic verses as "He has subjected to you what is in the heavens and what is in the earth, all together, from Him" (XLV, 13; cf. *Fuṣūṣ*, chap. 16).

> Through the activity of his mind every human being is able to create in his imagination that which has no existence in the outside world; this is the situation with all of us. But through his concentration (*himmah*) the gnostic creates that which possesses existence outside of the locus of his concentration so long as his concentration continues to preserve it. (*Fuṣūṣ*, chap. 6)

If the saints normally refrain from employing this power, it is because of their knowledge that everything occurs according to God's Will. "Whenever the gnostic does exercise his concentration in the world, it is because of a divine command; he does so because he is compelled to do so, not out of free choice" (*Fuṣūṣ*, chap. 13).

In order to turn his concentration toward its ultimate object and actualize its creative power, man must follow the path of purification and perfection. For Ibn ʿArabī, as for all Sufis, the basis of this path is the practice of Islam. He takes the daily prayers, the fast during Ramadan, etc.—in short, the "pillars" of Islam—for granted. In words of advice to disciples, we even find him telling them, "Do not play with your beard or any part of your clothing during the ritual prayer . . . , and make sure that your back is straight when you bow down" (*Futūḥāt*, IV, p. 497). A work like *Kunh mā lā budd minhu'l-murīd*, translated into English as *Instructions to a Postulant*, shows that he considered the sincere and scrupulous practice of both the mandatory commands of the *Sharīʿah* and the supererogatory acts recommended by the *Sunnah* as the *sine qua non* of all Sufism.

Ibn ʿArabī also explains in great detail the practices specific to Sufism, which amount to extensions and intensifications of the required practices of Islam. Al-Jandī summarizes Ibn ʿArabī's teachings in ten principles: (1) constant ritual and moral purity, (2) unceasing remembrance/invocation (*dhikr*) of God, (3) the elimination of all distracting thoughts, (4) constant examination of conscience (*murāqabah*), (5) daily review of one's actions (*muḥāsabah*), (6) attentiveness to the inward consciousness of one's shaykh, (7) hunger, (8) vigil, (9) silence, and (10) inward humility and tears. If there is anything remarkable about these instructions, it is that they are basically the same as those found in most other Sufi orders.

The Seal of the Muḥammadan Saints

Islam calls the Prophet of Islam the "Seal of Prophecy," meaning among other things that no prophet will come after him until the end of time. In a number of passages, Ibn 'Arabī speaks of two "Seals of Sanctity": the Seal of General Sanctity, or Jesus when he returns at the end of time, and the Seal of Muḥammadan Sanctity. Sometimes Ibn 'Arabī declares that he himself is the latter, and most of his followers held this to be the case; elsewhere he implies that someone else is this seal, as in a passage where he says that the Seal of Muḥammadan Sanctity is an Arab whom he met in the year 595/1198-99. He goes on to explain the function of this person:

> Just as, through Muḥammad, God has sealed the prophecy of Law-giving, so, through the Muḥammadan Seal, He has sealed the sanctity which derives from the Muḥammadan inheritance, not that which derives from other prophets—for among the saints there are those who inherit from Abraham, Moses, and Jesus. Such will continue to be found after the Muḥammadan Seal; but after him, there will no longer be found any saint "upon the heart of Muḥammad (*'alā qalb Muḥammad*)." (*Futūḥāt*, II, p. 49)

One of the clearest explanations of how Ibn 'Arabī's title as the Seal of Muhammadan Sanctity was understood by those of his followers who ascribed it to him is provided by al-Jandī. He writes that true knowledge of God's Essence, Attributes, and Acts and of the realities of things as they are in God's Knowledge cannot be acquired in the most perfect and complete manner from secondary stations, sources, and doctrines, but only from the doctrines of, first, the Seal of the Prophets, and second, the Seal of the Saints, who is the perfect inheritor of Muhammad. The spiritual vision of the seals comprehends all spiritual perceptions, contains all doctrines, and encompasses all stations and levels. Just as there must be a Name more perfect and comprehensive than all others—that is, the Name *Allāh*—so also there must be a prophet and a saint more perfect than all other prophets and saints, and these are the seals.[20]

The claim that Ibn 'Arabī was the Seal of the Muḥammadan Saints thus implies that his teachings embrace all Islamic teachings. And, in fact, practically every intellectual formulation of Sufism after him derives directly or indirectly from his own works or those of his followers. In this respect, at least, it is difficult to dispute this claim. In the words of Seyyed Hossein Nasr, Ibn 'Arabī "has provided over the centuries the precious doctrinal language in terms of which Sufi masters have sought to expound the mysteries of gnosis,"[21] and to explain their vision of the Truth as gained through mystical perception and the unveiling of the Uncreated Lights.

Notes

1. Although the name of this sage in Arabic is Ibn al-ʿArabī, he is often referred to as Ibn ʿArabī among his Muslim disciples and also in European languages. We have therefore kept the Ibn ʿArabī version throughout the Islamic volumes of this series.—ED.

2. M. Profitlich, *Die Terminologie Ibn ʿArabīs im "Kitāb wasāʾil as-sāʾil" des Ibn Saudakīn* (Freiburg im Breisgau: Klaus Schwarz Verlag, 1973), Arabic text, p. 21. Al-Jandī, *Sharḥ fuṣūṣ al-ḥikam* (MS), commentary on the word *mubashshirah* in the *khuṭbah;* also *Nafḥat al-rūḥ* (MS Istanbul, Haci Mahmud 2447) f. 23b.

3. *Al-Futūḥāt al-makkiyyah* (Beirut: Dār Ṣādir, n.d.) I, 153–54.

4. Ibn ʿArabī's encounter with Jesus in the spiritual world and his repentance (*tawbah*) at his hands are mentioned by Ibn ʿArabī in *al-Futūḥāt al-makkiyyah,* I, 155.26; III, 43.20, 341.22; IV, 77.30. On al-ʿUryabī's connection to Jesus, see I, 223.21 (cf. II, 365.19); he is the same as the Abū Jaʿfar " ʿUryanī" discussed as no. 1 in R. W. J. Austin, *Sufis of Andalusia* (London: Allen & Unwin, 1971). See Michel Chodkiewicz, *Le Sceau des saints* (Paris: Gallimard, 1986) 98–99.

5. Al-Qūnawī's three accounts are found respectively in al-Jandī, *Sharḥ fuṣūṣ al-ḥikam,* commentary on the second chapter; al-Qūnawī, *al-Nuṣūṣ,* appended to al-Kāshānī, *Sharḥ manāzil al-sāʾirīn* (Tehran: Ibrāhīm Lārījānī, 1315/1897-98) 284; al-Qūnawī, *al-Fukūk,* on the margin of the previous work, 233.

6. Ibn ʿArabī, *Fihrist al-muʾallafāt,* ed. A. E. Affifi, "The Works of Ibn ʿArabī," *Revue de la Faculté de Lettres de l'Université d'Alexandrie,* 8 (1954) 194.

7. H. Corbin, *Creative Imagination in the Ṣūfism of Ibn ʿArabī* (Princeton, NJ: Princeton University Press, 1969) 73.

8. Al-Qūnawī, *al-Fukūk,* 184.

9. Al-Qūnawī, *al-Nafaḥāt* (Tehran: Shaykh Aḥmad Shīrāzī, 1316/1898–99) 152–53.

10. Jāmī, *Nafaḥāt al-uns,* ed. M. Tawḥīdīpūr (Tehran: Saʿdī, 1336/1957) 556.

11. Ibid., 559. For an excerpt, see p. 71 below.

12. This name is to be found in different forms in a number of *silsilahs;* see Claude Addas, *Ibn ʿArabī* (Paris: Gallimard, 1989) 374–77. See also M. Chodkiewicz (trans.), Emir Abd al-Kader, *Ecrits spirituels* (Paris: Seuil, 1982) 183. A *silsilah* apparently drawn up by ʿAlī himself or by one of his disciples is found appended to three manuscripts of al-Qūnawī's works in Istanbul: Şehid Ali Paşa 1441/1, Yeni Cami 1196/1, Laleli 1499/1.

13. On these two figures, see W. Chittick, "Sulṭān Burhān al-Dīn's Sufi Correspondence," *Wiener Zeitschrift für die Kunde des Morgenlandes* 73 (1981) 33–45.

14. M. Asín Palacios, *The Mystical Philosophy of Ibn Masarra and His Followers,* trans. E. H. Douglas and H. W. Yoden (Leiden: Brill, 1978) 174–75.

15. See "An Islamic Creation Myth," p. 70 below.

16. Al-Qūnawī, *al-Nuṣūṣ,* 299.

17. See "The Lord of Men and the Lords of Men," p. 71 below.

18. Al-Qūnawī, *Marātib al-taqwā,* Istanbul MSS Şehid Ali Paşa 1340/3, Carullah 1001/3, Feyzullah 2163.

19. *Iʿjaz al-bayān fī tafsīr umm al-Qurʾān* (Hyderabad-Deccan: Osmania Oriental Publications Bureau, 1949) 271.

20. Al-Jandī, *Nafḥat al-rūḥ*, f. 4b.
21. S. H. Nasr, *Three Muslim Sages* (Cambridge, MA: Harvard University Press, 1964) 121.

Excursuses

An Islamic Creation Myth

The Names gathered together in the Presence of the Named and, gazing upon their own realities and meanings, sought the outward manifestation of their properties. They desired that their own entities might become mutually distinct through the effects that they make manifest. The Creator, who makes ordainments, the Knower, the Governor, the Deployer, the Producer, the Form-giver, the Nourisher, the Life-giver, the Slayer, the Inheritor, the Grateful, and all the rest of the Divine Names gazed upon their own essences but found none created, none governed, none deployed, none nourished. So they said, "What can be done so that these entities might become outwardly manifest? For through them our properties and authority are deployed."

So the Names, having seen their own entities, . . . had recourse to the Name the Producer. They said, "Perhaps you can give existence to our entities so that our properties may appear and our authority be established. For at the moment we reside in an ontological degree that allows us no effectivity." The Producer replied, "That depends upon the Powerful, for I am under His sway. . . ."

Then the Names had recourse to the Powerful, who said, "I am under the sway of the Willing. I can not bring into existence a single one of your entities without His designation. The possible existent in itself is not sufficient for me. First the command of the Commander must come from its Lord. Once He commands that a possible existent enter into engendered existence—once He says to it 'Be!'—then I will be able to act upon it. . . . So have recourse to the Name the Willing. Perhaps He will choose the side of existence over the side of nonexistence. Then I will join with the Commander and the Speaker and give you existence."

[After hearing similar words from the Willing, the Names proceed to the Name the Knowing, who tells them that the entities under their sway are indeed destined for outward manifestation. But first courtesy (*adab*) must be observed.]

So all the Names came together in the Presence of the Name *Allāh* . . . and told Him about their state. He said, "I am the Name that comprehends all your realities and I denote to the Named (*al-musammā*), who is an All-Holy Essence, possessing qualities of perfection and transcendence. Stay here while I enter upon the object of my denotation. So the Name *Allāh* entered that Presence and repeated the words of the possible existents and the Names. He was told, "Go out, and tell all the Names to undertake among the possible existents what their realities require. . . ."

So the Name *Allāh* went out, next to Him the Name the Speaking, acting as His spokesman to the possible existents and the Names. He related to them what the Named had said. So the Knowing, the Willing, the Speaking, and the Powerful undertook their tasks and the first possible existent became outwardly manifest. (Ibn al-ʿArabī, *al-Futūḥāt al-makkiyyah* [Beirut: Dār Ṣādir], n.d., I, 323)

The Lord of Men and the Lords of Men

The Universal Name "Lord" courses through all other Names, whether universal or particular, principal or derivative, down to the least of the derivatives. It manifests itself in every Name in keeping with the properties of that Name.... The Name from which any human being derives his existence . . . is in reality his "Lord". . . . It will also be his place of return and his ultimate end. The theophanies he receives in keeping with his states within this world's plane, and his vision of God in the next world, are tied specifically to this Name and take place through it.

But . . . "Lordship" has two properties, one general and one specific. The general property derives from the fact that, for example, the Name *Allāh* is related to all worlds and ontological levels and to all their inhabitants, in respect both to the receptive reality, i.e., the entity, and to the existence that it receives. Hence the Lordship attributed to the Name *Allāh* is all-comprehensive. This is indicated, for example, by God's words, "Praise belongs to *Allāh,* the Lord of the worlds" (Quran I, 1). . . . As for the specific property pertaining to Lordship, that is what we said above: Whenever a thing's existence becomes entified from the Presence of a Name, that Name is its specific Lord. This is why we find that in the Quran and the *Ḥadīth,* vision of God is attributed only to Lords ascribed to various levels. For example, "Upon that day faces will be radiant, gazing upon *their* Lord" (LXXV, 23). . . .

The source of the outward existence of the Perfect Men among the prophets and saints is the Ocean of the Second Entification, i.e., the level of the Name *Allāh* in respect of the Second Isthmus, which englobes the seven principle Names, which in turn embrace the realities of each Perfect Man. However, a faint trace of that Perfect Man's distinguishing characteristics remains, so his Lord is the Second Entification in respect of the faint trace peculiar to him. Then the source of the existence of those prophets, messengers, and saints who are near to the Perfect Men in receptivity, preparedness, scope, universality, spiritual perception, and contemplation is those Seven Principles themselves, but in respect of their manyness and their special relationship with particular effects and properties. . . . Finally the existence of other human beings below the prophets and saints in rank derives from the tributaries of these Oceans, i.e., these Seven Principles, or the rivers of the tributaries, or the streams of the rivers, or the brooks, or the pools, or the tankards, or the jugs, or the infinite drops. So their original entification and their ultimate return follow their preparedness as determined by their Lords.

As for our Prophet Muḥammad—God bless him and give him peace—he possesses the Supreme Watering Place, which is the First Theophany. That is his Light and his Lord. It is the source, origin, return, and end of all Names and all entifications within knowledge and existence. That is why God says, addressing the Prophet specifically, "Surely unto thy Lord is the ultimate end" (Quran LIII, 43), and, "Surely unto thy Lord is the return" (Quran XCVI, 8). (al-Farghānī, *Muntaha'l-madārik,* Cairo: ʿAbd al-Raḥīm al-Bukhārī, 1293/1876, I, 43-44).

I. The Divine Names and the Cosmos

(*See diagram I, p. 75.*)

The outward existence of the entities presupposes these nine Names. The Living is the "Lord of the Lords," while the next four are often called the Four Pillars, though sometimes the Four Pillars are said to include the Living. They are the principle of all "quaternity" in creation. Among the correspondences Ibn ʿArabī points out are the following:

Attribute	*Existent*	*Element*	*Humor*	*Power of the Soul*
Knowledge	First Intellect	Earth	Melancholy	Sustaining
Will	Universal Soul	Air	Blood	Attracting
Power	Universal Nature	Water	Phlegm	Repulsing
Speech	Materia Prima	Fire	Choler	Digesting

He-who-governs and He-who-deploys are the "primary Names related to the cosmos"; the other Names are called the Seven Leaders or the Seven Mothers and are their daughters. Just as the spirit "governs" the body, while the body "deploys" the properties of the spirit, so the Unseen World becomes manifest from He-who-governs, while the visible world becomes manifest from He-who-deploys. By means of these two Names God creates male and female, activity and passivity, generation and corruption. The Generous and the Just bring about the existence of well-being and misfortune, the Garden and the Fire, profit and loss. (*al-Futūḥāt al-makkiyyah,* I, 100, 120, 260; II, 232, 430, 685; III, 198, 427, 441)

II. From the Cloud to the Dust

(*See diagram II, p. 76.*)

The first creatures to become manifest within the Cloud are the Enraptured Angels; their attention is turned totally toward God such that they have no knowledge of any "others." Through a special theophany, one of them, called the First Intellect or the Supreme Pen, is given knowledge of everything that will come into engendered existence until the Day of Resurrection. Perceiving the Perfect Man in the Cloud, it turns its attention toward creation to bring his potentiality into actuality. There it sees its own shadow, the Universal Soul, whom it "marries," just as Adam married Eve. According to another image, it looks for something upon which to write and the Guarded Tablet is born from its search. The union of the Pen and the Tablet gives rise to the Throne, where the All-Merciful Breath, having created all things, comes to rest: "The All-Merciful sat Himself upon the Throne" (Quran XX, 5). The Tablet possesses two basic attributes, which manifest He-who-governs and He-who-deploys: knowledge of itself and action; the latter is attributed to it just as light is attributed to the sun. Knowledge is connected to destiny; action to the bestowal of existence upon the known entities; the first is the father, the second the mother. Universal Nature has no existence as such, only through the ontological modalities prefigured in the Soul: heat (which is a manifestation of Life), dryness (Will), cold (Knowledge), and wetness (Speech). In a similar way, the Dust exists not in itself but through the forms that appear within it as a result of Nature's activity. (*Futūḥāt,* I, 139–40; II, 427–31; III, 90, 390, 399, 420–21, 429–30)

III. From the Dust to the Footstool

(*See diagram III, p. 77.*)

The marriage of Nature and Materia Prima results in the birth of the Universal Body; its length reflects the Intellect, its breadth the Soul, and its depth the Void, which it fills. Within the Body's compass God brings all the world's forms into existence in an order that comes to be known as "time." The first sensory form to appear is the Throne; supported by four columns, it encompasses all sensory existents. Its parents, the Intellect and the Soul, look upon it with the eye of mercy, the attribute that defines its nature. Within the Throne stands the Footstool, upon which God places the Foot of Surety (Quran X, 2) and the Foot of the All-Compeller (*ḥadīth*), the first of which is in the Garden, and the second in the Fire. The Two Feet mark the division of pure mercy into mercy on the one hand and mercy mixed with wrath on the other. God mixes these two because He wants to manifest all the opposites embraced by His Names, such as He-who-exalts and He-who-debases, the Contractor and the Expander, and the Bestower and the Taker. (*Futūḥāt,* II, 433–37; III, 431–32)

IV. From the Footstool to the Sphere of the Fixed Stars

(*See diagram IV, p. 78.*)

On the underside of the Footstool, God creates a transparent, spherical body divided into twelve parts. It is referred to by the verse "By the heaven of the constellations!" (Quran LXXXV, 1). In each constellation dwells an angel; the twelve of them play the same role toward the inhabitants of the Gardens as the elements play for the inhabitants of the earth. Hence each angel is related to one of the four elements: earth, air, water, and fire. When the Shīʿites refer to the infallibility of the Twelve Imams, says Ibn ʿArabī, in fact they are referring to these angels. The angels construct six of the Gardens, while, according to the *ḥadīth,* God constructs Eden with His own hand. Each of the Gardens has 100 degrees, reflecting the Divine Names (the ninety-nine "Most Beautiful Names" plus the Greatest Name); the number of stations in each Garden is equivalent to the number of verses in the Quran. The floor of the Gardens is the surface of the sphere of the fixed stars, which in turn is the roof of hell. Hell, however, does not become manifest until the Day of Resurrection, "The Day the earth shall be changed into other than the earth, and [in the same way] the [seven] heavens [shall be changed]" (Quran XIV, 48), since they become the locus of hell. (*Futūḥāt,* II, 440; III, 433–35)

V. From the Sphere of the Fixed Stars to the Darkness

(*See diagram V, p. 79.*)

The twenty-eight mansions of the moon correspond to the twenty-eight letters that become articulated in the Breath of the All-Merciful. To each of them pertains a Divine Name, a letter of the Arabic alphabet, and an ontological level (see the diagram in Burckhardt, *Mystical Astrology According to Ibn ʿArabi* [Gloucestershire: Beshara, 1977] pp. 32–33). Each constellation possesses thirty treasuries of generosity (cf. Quran XV, 21), from which it sends down effusions upon the four elements, which combine in varying proportions to yield the three kingdoms. The last existent is animal man, who comprehends all created realities, just as the Perfect Man comprehends all uncreated realities. The latter is the Pillar extending from earth to heaven upon which the world's preservation depends (cf. Quran XIII, 2). The seven spheres reflect the Seven Leaders and have affinities with various other realities:

Sphere	*Planet*	*Attribute*	*Prophet*	*Day of the Week*	*Clime*
1	The Moon	Life	Adam	Monday	7
2	Mercury	Will	Jesus	Wednesday	6
3	Venus	Knowledge	Joseph	Friday	5
4	The Sun	Hearing	Enoch	Sunday	4
5	Mars	Sight	Aaron	Tuesday	3
6	Jupiter	Power	Moses	Thursday	2
7	Saturn	Speech	Abraham	Saturday	1

The seven earths are referred to in the Quran (LXV, 12), while the Water, Air, and Darkness upon which they rest are mentioned in a *ḥadīth*. Below the earths, which mark the lowest limits of the world embraced by the Throne, is the Water about which God says, "His Throne is upon the Water" (Quran XI, 7). The Water is in fact ice; it rests upon frigid Air that is exhaled by the Darkness. This last is the Unseen, which none knows but God. (*Futūḥāt,* I, 155; II, 438-40; III, 432, 437)

I. The Divine Names and the Cosmos

(*Diagram I*)

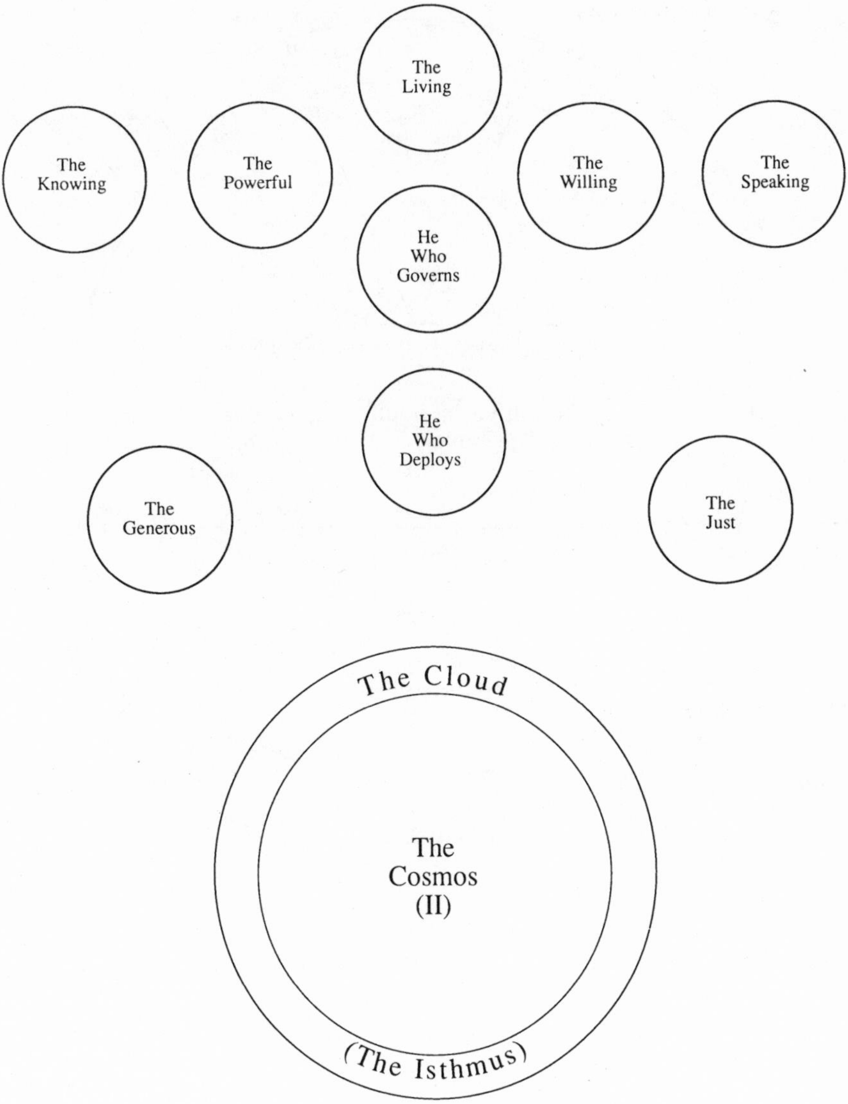

II. From the Cloud to the Dust
(*Diagram II*)

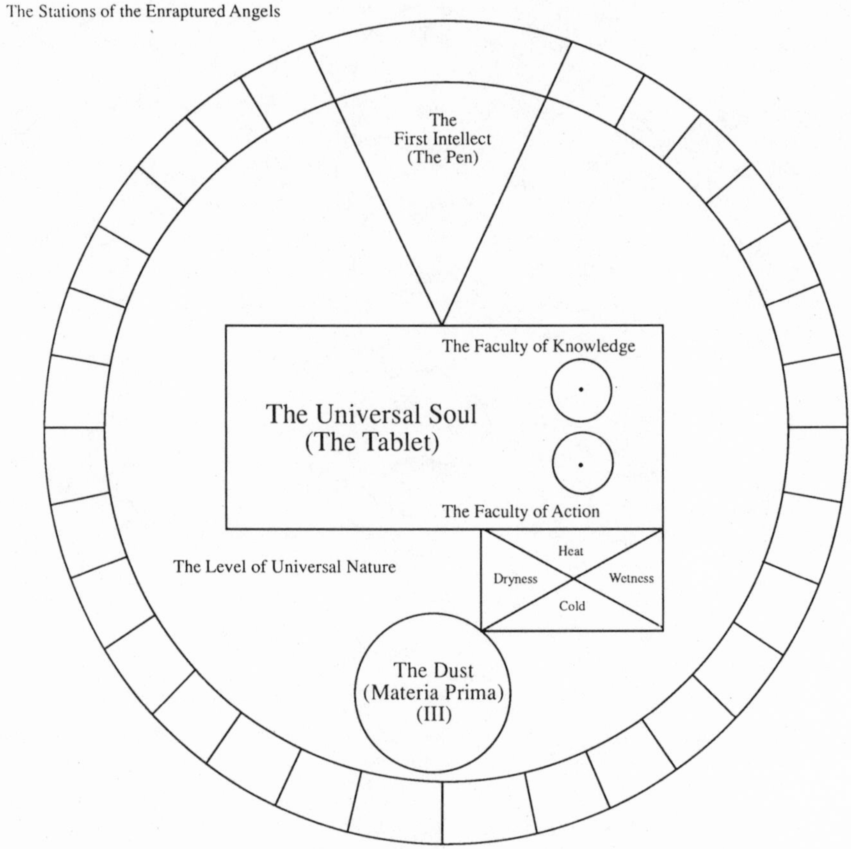

III. From the Dust to the Footstool

(*Diagram III*)

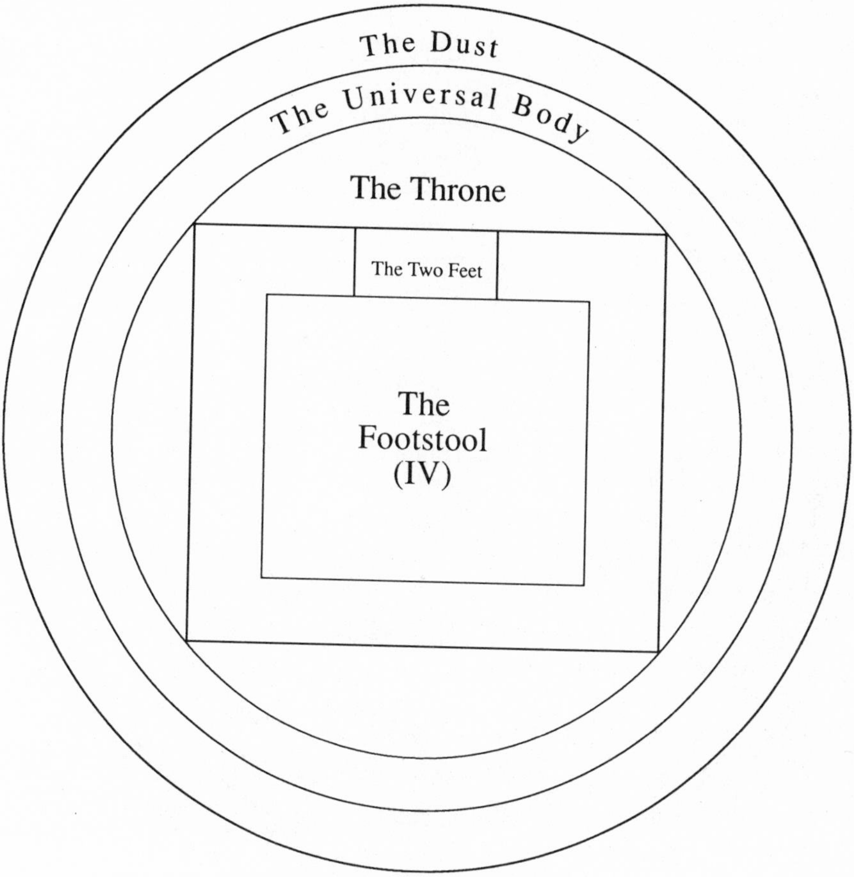

IV. From the Footstool to the Sphere of the Fixed Stars

(*Diagram IV*)

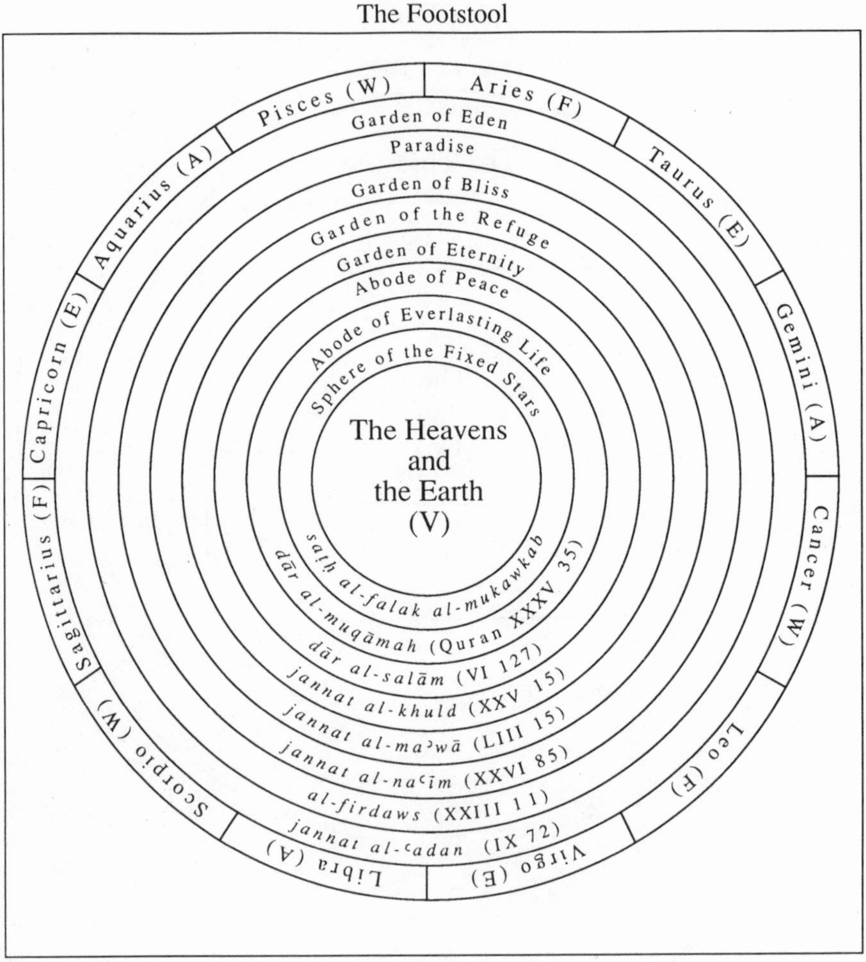

V. From the Sphere of the Fixed Stars to the Darkness
(*Diagram V*)

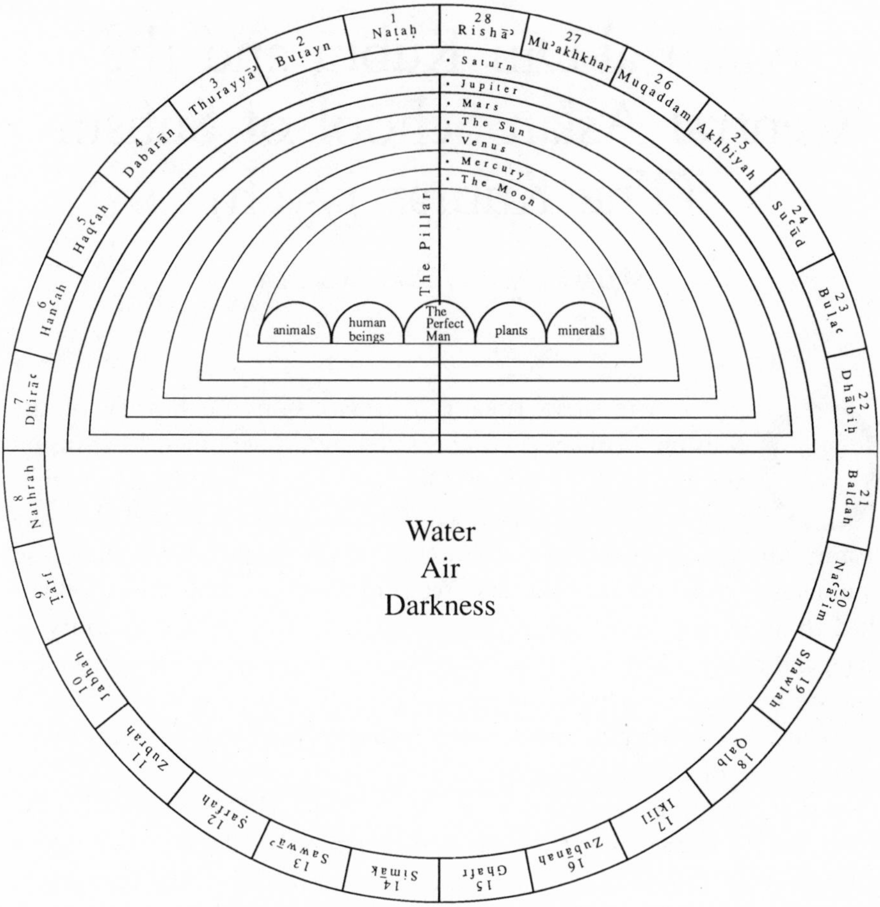

4

Najm al-Dīn Kubrā and the Central Asian School of Sufism (The Kubrawiyyah)

Muhammad Isa Waley

One of the most turbulent periods in the history of the Muslim world was compensated by a phenomenal expansion and flowering of Sufism. During the later twelfth and the thirteenth centuries A.D. (550–700 A.H.) there occurred the cataclysmic Mongol invasion, the destruction of the Baghdad caliphate, and innumerable concomitant disasters. Yet Muslim saints and scholars flourished to an extent rarely seen since the early days of the Community of Islam, and many major Sufi orders were founded or revived: these include—to name but a few—the Qādiriyyah, Rifāʿiyyah, Suhrawardiyyah, Shādhiliyyah, and Mawlawiyyah, as well as the Kubrawiyyah *ṭarīqah* (order) which is the subject of the present essay.

The Kubrawiyyah derives its name from Najm al-Dīn Kubrā (d. 618/1221), founder of the order. From its beginnings in the Central Asian region of Khiva (then known as Khwarazm) to the south of the Aral Sea—where it survives to this day—it spread, with its offshoots, to Persia, Afghanistan, India, and even to China. During its long history the Kubrawiyyah produced several masters of great eminence who in addition to training disciples left for posterity a body of writings many of which are as yet unpublished. These works contain some highly interesting and innovative elaborations of Sufi methodology and doctrine. The contribution of Kubrā and certain of his successors in what has come to be known as the Central Asian school of Sufism to the phenomenology and analysis of spiritual vision and gnosis merits the attention of all who are interested in visionary experience and its place in spirituality.

Najm al-Dīn Kubrā: His Life and Spiritual Masters

Abu'l-Jannāb Najm al-Dīn ibn 'Umar al-Kubrā, founder of the Kubrawiyyah, was born at Khwarazm in about 540/1145. Najm al-Dīn's intellectual powers became evident at an early age. While still a student, he acquired the nickname *Kubrā* (literally, "the greatest"), an abbreviated form of the Quranic phrase *al-tāmmat al-kubrā*, "the Greatest Calamity" (LXXIX, 34). This appellation apparently alluded to the formidable talents which made Najm al-Dīn the downfall of those who contended with him in disputation. Having received the normal formation in the Islamic religious sciences, Kubrā left Khwarazm to pursue his studies in other lands, as was the wont of many medieval scholars. His chief interest at that time was in the science of *Ḥadīth*, which he studied for several years in Persia and Egypt.

At some time between 573/1177 and 576/1180, however, an interest in esoteric matters was kindled in Najm al-Dīn. He was initiated into the Suhrawardiyyah Order in Egypt by a shaykh named Rūzbihān al-Wazzān al-Miṣrī. According to one account, this followed—or else coincided with—a vision of the Prophet. At all events, we know from Najm al-Dīn's own writings that he had undergone at least one striking spiritual experience in his childhood.[1] Nonetheless, he continued for some time to pursue the study of Prophetic Tradition. The turning point in Kubrā's life may have been his encounter at Tabriz with a certain Bābā Faraj Tabrīzī, whose bearing greatly impressed him and who urged him to forsake the pursuit of exoteric knowledge in favor of the Sufi path.

Najm al-Dīn's first Sufi master was Ismā'īl al-Qaṣrī (d. 589/1193), at Dizful in western Persia. But after he had spent only a short while there, Ismā'īl advised him to go to 'Ammār ibn Yāsir al-Bidlīsī. This shaykh, who died in 582/1186, was the disciple of Abu'l-Najīb al-Suhrawardī; his treatise entitled *Bahjat al-ṭā'ifah* (*Splendour of the Tribe*) is extant in manuscript. Kubrā underwent spiritual retreats (*khalwah*) with both Qaṣrī and Bidlīsī, and his writings include accounts of some experiences with them. Next, Kubrā returned to Egypt on the orders of 'Ammār; here Rūzbihān al-Miṣrī continued Najm al-Dīn's training until he pronounced him qualified to initiate and instruct disciples of his own. During this period Najm al-Dīn married Rūzbihān's daughter.

Probably between 581/1185 and 586/1190, Rūzbihān sent Najm al-Dīn back to Khwarazm. The remainder of Kubrā's life was devoted to the spiritual path and the training of disciples. These were relatively few in number, but such was their stature that Najm al-Dīn was to earn a second epithet: *Walī-tarāsh*, "Fashioner of Saints." He also wrote a number of treatises, the most important of which is the *Fawā'iḥ al-jamāl wa fawātiḥ al-jalāl* (*Aromas of Beauty and Preambles of Majesty*). We shall have occasion to refer several times to this key Arabic text, which constitutes a personal record of Najm al-Dīn's visionary experiences combined with a guide to the theory and practice of the Sufi path for initiates. Najm al-Dīn Kubrā died at Urgench, near Khwarazm, in 618/1221, when the city was overrun by the Mongol army. It is related that Najm al-Dīn was offered protection if he took refuge with the Mongols, but he refused and fought to defend the city, earning the further glory of a martyr's death in battle. The founder of the Kubrawiyyah became, as it were, a patron saint in Central Asia; his memory continues to be venerated in and around Khiva.

The Affiliation of the Kubrawiyyah

Like all the authentic orders of Sufism, the Kubrawiyyah possesses an *isnād* or spiritual pedigree tracing the succession of shaykhs back to the Prophet himself, this being an indispensable condition for the transmission of the initiatic *barakah* or blessing. According to the Kubrawīs' spiritual genealogy, the principal line of descent runs through ʿAmmār al-Bidlīsī and Rūzbihān al-Miṣrī to Abu'l-Najīb al-Suhrawardī. He in turn was a disciple of Aḥmad Ghazzālī, whose initiatic line descends through such figures as Abū Bakr al-Nassāj and Abū ʿAlī Rūdbārī to Abu'l-Qāsim al-Junayd of Baghdad (d. 297/902), one of the most renowned Sufis, whose name appears in the lines of the Shādhilī, Qādirī, and other orders. An alternative genealogy, current among the Shiʿite offshoots of the Kubrawiyyah, includes the names of the first eight Imams of the Shīʿah. The various branches of the Kubrawiyyah will be discussed briefly later in this essay.[2]

Kubrā's Methodology: The Discipline of the Order

Like all masters of authentic Sufism, Najm al-Dīn Kubrā insisted on certain prerequisites in those whom he accepted as disciples. A sound knowledge of the essentials of Islamic theological doctrine and law was required. The disciplinary rules of the Kubrawiyyah were founded on the Eight Principles laid down in the third/ninth century by Junayd of Baghdad, to whom Najm al-Dīn frequently refers (six times in the *Fawā'iḥ* alone).

The Eight Principles are similarly cited and expounded in treatises by several later Kubrawī masters, including Baghdādī, Rāzī, Simnānī, and Badakhshī.[3] As transmitted by Kubrā himself, the first five rules of Junayd prescribe constant observance of the following: ritual purity (*wuḍū'*), fasting (*ṣawm*), silence (*ṣamt*), seclusion (*khalwah*), and invocation or recollection (*dhikr*) of God using the formula *lā ilāha illa'Llāh.* Sixth: the disciple must keep his heart forever fixed upon the shaykh, abandoning his own will entirely, and refer to him for interpretation and guidance concerning any spiritual experiences he may have. Seventh: all thoughts and mental impulses (*khawāṭir*) are to be put aside the moment they occur. Finally, the disciple must surrender entirely to the Will of God and never refuse what He imposes upon him; and he must neither pray to be granted paradise nor spared from hell.

These rules are added to and commented on by Kubrā in a work on Sufi methodology which bears the title *Risālah ila'l-hā'im al-khā'if min lawmat al-lā'im* (*Epistle to the Dozing* [*Seeker*] *Fearful of the Blamer's Blame*).[4] The two additional rules are to take the bare minimum of sleep and to observe moderation in eating and drinking when breaking the (daytime) fast. In the same treatise Kubrā touches on several other important aspects of Sufi doctrine and method. Another treatise, *al-Uṣūl al-'asharah* (*The Ten Principles*), circulated widely both among Kubrawīs and in other orders. Among the more significant commentaries on the text are those composed in Ottoman Turkish by Ismā'īl Ḥaqqī Burūsawī, who belonged to the Khalwatiyyah *ṭarīqah* and in Persian by 'Abd al-Ghafūr Lārī.

Although most of the principles of discipline outlined above are more or less self-explanatory, others call for some comment. We shall take up those points further on in this essay. One reason for enumerating the Principles of Junayd here is to emphasize their importance to the methodology of an order that stresses solitary retreat and gnosis. The impulsion to court visionary experience, which arises from the lower soul's desire for self-aggrandizement, is one of the greatest dangers that can beset the initiate—let alone the seeker who attempts the esoteric path without the guidance of a qualified spiritual master.

Kubrā on the Microcosm and Its Faculties

In this and the following sections we shall explore the main distinctive elements of Najm al-Dīn Kubrā's theory, description, and empirical analysis of the initiatic Sufi path: the journey to God being in reality an inward one. Inevitably, our exposition owes much to the work on this subject by Henry Corbin.[5] In a brilliant and wide-ranging study, Corbin examines the leitmotif of gnostic vision as reflected in the works of Najm al-Dīn Kubrā and his successors of the Central Asian school of Sufism, at the same time relating these both to the "visionary recitals" of the *ishrāqī* shaykh Shihāb al-Dīn Suhrawardī and Rūzbihān Baqlī and to a number of cognate elements of Zoroastrian, Manichaean, and other gnostic doctrines.

One of the cornerstones of Kubrā's understanding of the initiatic path is the doctrine that everything that exists in the macrocosm (in Islamic terminology the terms used are, according to the context, *al-insān al-kabīr,* "the great man," or *al-insān al-kāmil,* "perfect man") exists also within every individual human being; each man is none other than the microcosm (*al-insān al-ṣaghīr,* "small man"). Thus, the seeker's journey to God is an *inward* journey which, like the Divine Being Itself, has no limit.

> Know that the lower soul, the Devil, and the Angel are realities that are not external to you. You *are* they. So, too, Heaven, Earth and the Divine Throne are not located outside you; nor are Paradise, Hell, Life or Death. All of these exist within you, as you will realize once you have accomplished the initiatic journey and become pure. (*Fawā'iḥ,* par. 67:32)

> You can only see or witness an object by means of some part of that same object. As we said, it is only the mine whence it came which a precious stone sees, desires, and yearns for. So when you have a vision of a sky, an earth, a sun, stars, or a moon, you should know that the particle in you which has its origin in that same mine has become pure. The more pure you become, the purer and more radiant will be the sky that appears to you, until in the last stages of the journey you travel within the Divine Purity. But Divine Purity is limitless, so never think that there is not something more exalted still ahead. (*Fawā'iḥ,* par. 60:28–29)

All the realms of principal and manifested existence, then, are to be found within the human soul. Were that not the case, the possibility of gnosis would not exist. This is evident in the light of one of the cardinal metaphysical doctrines relating to epistemology. An object can be known only by a cognate subject: like is known only by like. Furthermore, it is by virtue of the innate and spontaneous attraction of like to like that man, as theomorphic creature containing the Spirit of the Divine, is moved and enabled to seek God or the Transcendent Selfhood.

According to a *ḥadīth qudsī* (a Sacred Tradition, related from the Prophet but comprising the very words of God), "Neither My heaven nor My earth has space to contain Me; yet the heart of My truly-believing servant containeth me." This *ḥadīth,* not surprisingly, is widely quoted by Sufis; it is a statement of the vastness and elevation of the human state and the responsibility (*amānah*) that it entails. In respect of his primordial creation, every man is potentially a "truly believing servant." This dictum further adumbrates, without explicitly stating it, an aspect of the supreme mystery: ultimately, the seeker has no identity apart from that of the Sought. Najm al-Dīn broaches this subject at the very beginning of the *Fawā'iḥ al-jamāl:*

> Know this, my dear friend—may God grant you success in achieving that which He loves and is pleasing to Him: the Goal (*murād*) is God, and the seeker (*murīd*) a light proceeding from Him. God never acts unjustly towards anybody. Every individual contains a Spirit, which comes from God, and possesses intelligence; and [God] "has made" for him "hearing, sight and hearts" (Quran XLVI, 26).[6] All men are in a state of [spiritual] blindness save those from whom God has removed the veil. That veil is not something external to them, but is indeed part of them; for it consists of the darkness of their [individual] existences. (*Fawā'iḥ,* par. 1:1)

With this last sentence Najm al-Dīn introduces the question of the imperfections of the soul, and in the paragraphs immediately following he describes the means by which the initiate is to undertake the necessary task of self-purification. In Islamic spirituality, this process is often called "spiritual combat." The foundations of Kubrā's method are theoretical knowledge, initiation, the ascetic disciplines of Junayd and *dhikr.* The latter term here denotes the systematic invocation of God by means of the *shahādah,* or testimony of faith, or the Divine Name. It is essential that the initiate be fully aware of what this practice entails and be prepared accordingly. Like the spiritual masters of certain other traditions, the Sufi shaykhs teach that in the *dhikr* God renders Himself mysteriously present in the Divine Name. Therein lies the secret of the grace and power of the "Way of Invocation" to bestow salvation, purity, and gnosis.

Visionary Apperception: Photisms and Their Analysis

By means of the practices outlined above, the Kubrawī initiate begins to progress along the path. In his *Fawā'iḥ,* Najm al-Dīn Kubrā describes some of the visionary phenomena that he himself witnessed and analyzes their significance. Such manifestations of light are not to be courted. Rather, they are signs of grace, as our author demonstrates, and they provide clear indications as to the stage which the witnessing initiate has reached on his inward journey. Following the terminology employed by Corbin, we shall henceforth refer to these apparitions of light as "photisms." The teachings of Kubrā and his successors concerning photisms form perhaps the most distinctive feature of the Central Asian school of Sufism.

In order to avoid any misunderstanding, it must be stressed that photisms are objective realities of a subtle type and not hallucinations. They are related to the phenomena known as auras, which are perceived not by the physical eyes but by those faculties of the Spirit which one might term "the suprasensory senses." Photisms may even be said to be more "real" than the objects of visual sense perception, for they pertain to a higher order of existence. The faculty that perceives and interprets them is the Spiritual Imagination, whose field of activity is not the realm of corporeal existence but the world of "imaginal forms," also known as *mundus imaginalis,* or the world of image-ideas (*'ālam al-mithāl*). In the hierarchy of being, the imaginal world is situated between the archetypal and the sensory.

At first dark and turbid, the visions of light perceived by the seeker gain in lucidity and beauty as he progresses. The faculties of spiritual vision likewise gain in strength in accordance with the purity of the initiate. They have their center in the various points (*laṭīfah*), comparable to the *chakras* of yogic doctrine, figuratively located in various areas of the body. The aim of the shaykh is to transmute the human substance of the disciple. In Kubrā's words: "Our method (*or* path, *ṭarīq*) is the method of alchemy. It is essential that the subtle center (*laṭīfah*) of light be released from beneath those mountains (i.e., the four elements of corporeal existence)" (*Fawā'iḥ,* par. 12:5). Although the use of the word "alchemy" in connection with the spiritual path is not uncommon, Kubrā here seems particularly to have in mind the fact that, as he puts it elsewhere, "mystical experience (*dhawq*) is caused by a transformation of the being, and of the Spirit . . . this involves a transmutation of the faculties of sense-perception. The five senses are changed into senses of another kind" (*Fawā'iḥ,* par. 42:19).

Here one can quote only one or two of the many passages of the *Fawā'iḥ* in which our author describes the forms and colors of photisms corresponding to the various spiritual states (*aḥwāl*) and stations (*maqāmāt*) of the path. In the following passage, Kubrā is concerned with the circles of light pertaining to each of the three states of the soul:

> Know that "the soul that incites" [to evil-doing] (*al-nafs al-ammārah*) has a sign which renders it perceptible to spiritual vision. It is a large, pitch-black circle which first rises in front of you, then fades away, then rises before you again like a cloud. As it reappears, something is revealed at its edges which is like the crescent moon when one of its horns becomes visible through the clouds. Next, it turns into a complete crescent. When it [the commanding soul] has begun to accuse itself [i.e., has been transformed into the "accusing soul" (*al-nafs al-lawwāmah*)] it rises alongside the right cheek as if it were a red sun whose heat is felt on the cheek; sometimes, though, it is perceived next to the ear, sometimes next to the forehead, and sometimes above the head. This "accusing soul" is the intelligence (*'aql*).
>
> As for the "pacified soul" (*al-nafs al-mutma'innah*), it too possesses a sign perceptible to spiritual vision. It sometimes rises before you like the circle of a great fountain from which light pours forth. Alternatively, you may visualize it, in the realm of the suprasensory, as a circle representing your face, composed of pure light, like a polished mirror. When the circle of light rises

> towards your face and your face disappears in it, then your face is the "pacified soul." On the other hand, you sometimes perceive the circle far away in the suprasensory, and there are a thousand stages of journey between you and the circle of the "pacified soul." Were you to approach any one of those intermediary stages, you would catch fire. (*Fawā'iḥ*, parr. 55–56:26)

Elsewhere, Kubrā speaks of awesome visions in which the mystic beholds with his own eyes (of subtle vision) what he has hitherto known only in theory, by means of reason:

> When you see before you a vast expanse opening out toward the distance, there is clear air above you and you see on the far horizon colors such as green, red, yellow, and blue, know that you are going to pass through that air to where those colors are. The colors appertain to spiritual states. Green is the sign of the life of the heart [this being the highest state]. The color of pure fire indicates the life of "spiritual concentration" (*himmah*), which denotes power [of actualization]. If this fire be dark, that betokens the fire of exertion and shows the seeker to be weary and afflicted after the battle with the lower ego and the Devil. Blue is the color of the life of the ego. Yellow is the color of lassitude. All these are suprasensory realities that speak with him who experiences them in the two languages of inner tasting (*dhawq*) and visionary apperception. These are two realiable, mutually corroboratory witnesses: what you behold with inner vision you also experience within yourself, and what you experience inwardly you also behold with inner vision. (*Fawā'iḥ,* par. 13:6)

Najm al-Dīn Kubrā's interpretation of the colors of light apparitions was elaborated upon by some later Kubrawī masters. Foremost in this respect were Najm al-Dīn Dāyah Rāzī and 'Alā' al-Dawlah Simnānī, whose work will be discussed below.

Love and Union: "The Heavenly Witness"

Reference has already been made to the reciprocal nature of the mystic's quest of the Supreme Reality. Najm al-Dīn Kubrā teaches that the mutual relationship of love between the seeker and the Sought calls into existence, in the *mundus imaginalis,* a being to which Kubrā variously refers by the names "Person of light," "Suprasensory Guide," and "Heavenly Witness" (*Fawā'iḥ,* par. 66:32). As with the other manifestations of light, the form in which this being appears to the disciple indicates the latter's spiritual state. At the outset, it is not the "Person of Light" who will be seen but a black form that will be manifested—this being a projection of the darkness of one's individuated existence, of the "soul inciting to evil." When, however, the initiate attains the state of complete purity in which he is vouchsafed the vision of the green light, the circle of the face reflected before him in visionary apperception becomes pure and extraordinarily luminous, and is accompanied by a sunlike form.

> This Face is in reality your own face and this sun is the Sun of the Spirit which oscillates within your body. Then your entire body is immersed in purity, and at that moment you see before you a person made of light, who generates lights. The spiritual traveller, too, then experiences his entire body as generating lights. It may be that the veil will fall from all individuality, so that you see totality through the totality of your body. The faculty of inner vision is opened first in the eyes, then the face, then the breast, then the whole body. This person of light in front of you is called by the People [Sufis] "the Suprasensory Guide," and is also known as "the Suprasensory [Personal] Master" or "the Suprasensory Scales [of Judgment]" (*Fawā'iḥ,* par. 66:31–32)

The last-mentioned expression leads us to an element in the gnosis of Najm al-Dīn Kubrā which has a further, eschatological significance. As we have seen, the "Person of Light" who guides the initiate is his own beloved, his guide to Heaven—and is none other than himself. Linking this doctrine to Zoroastrian metaphysics and eschatology, Corbin has demonstrated the principle common to both systems.[7] The vocation of all humans (not of initiates alone) being the quest for the True Self, such an *alter ego* in the form of a luminous personification potentially exists for every human being. Whether or not the encounter with the Truth takes place during one's earthly life, it must needs come to pass in the hereafter. If man has betrayed the trust which the human state entails, he will be met in the *barzakh,* the isthmus between this world and the next, by the dark shadow of his own spiritual emptiness. The perfected initiate, however, has already found his heavenly guide and partner in the lower world.

Majd al-Dīn Baghdādī and His Followers

We may now pass on from Najm al-Dīn Kubrā to consider some of his outstanding successors. Majd al-Dīn Baghdādī hailed from a village in Khurasan called Baghdadak. Little is known of his life, which in the account by Jāmī is overshadowed by the circumstances of his death in 616/1219.[8] According to Jāmī, Majd al-Dīn was drowned in the River Oxus by the Mongols as foretold by Kubrā, whom Majd al-Dīn had disobeyed. Whether or not that is correct, Majd al-Dīn was one of Kubrā's authorized representatives, responsible for the formation of many disciples. From his treatise *Tuḥfat al-barārah* (*Gift for the Godly*) we know that Majd al-Dīn, like his teacher, was engaged in the interpretation of the colors and images occurring in gnostic visions and dreams.

One of Majd al-Dīn Baghdādī's disciples was Najm al-Dīn Dāyah, to be discussed below; it is noteworthy that although Baghdādī died before Kubrā, Dāyah never mentions the latter in his writings, apparently regarding Baghdādī as his only shaykh. Also probably a follower of Majd al-Dīn was Farīd al-Dīn 'Aṭṭār of Nayshapur (d. ca. 617/1220), one of the greatest Persian Sufi writers. In his *Manṭiq al-ṭayr* (*Logic of the Birds*, known also as *Conference of the Birds*) and other major poems, 'Aṭṭār explores with profound perceptiveness and feeling the awesome perils and the majestic epiphanies of Divine Beauty entailed in the initiate's quest for the Transcendent Self. In one part or another of his didactic poem *Asrār-nāmah* (*The Book of Secrets*), 'Aṭṭār sets out some principles for the spiritual life. Not only do these visibly parallel the Kubrawiyyah Order's "rules of Junayd" already discussed; four of them are identical.[9]

"Sultan of the Scholars": Bahā' al-Dīn Walad

It is probable, though not certain, that Bahā' al-Dīn Walad of Balkh was another of Najm al-Dīn Kubrā's immediate disciples. Best known as being the father of the great Mawlānā Jalāl al-Dīn Rūmī (see the next chapter in this volume), he is a significant figure in his own right whose work would repay further study. Bahā' al-Dīn was born ca. 540/1145 at the ancient city of Balkh, now in northern Afghanistan. His learning in the exoteric sciences of religion earned him the title *sulṭān al-'ulamā'*, "Sultan of the Scholars," and some prestige at the court of the Khwārazmshāh, ruler of the region. Either court intrigues or the threat of the Mongols, or both, impelled Bahā' al-Dīn to migrate westward with his family. After traveling through the central Islamic lands, he taught at *madrasahs* in various parts of Asia Minor. He finally settled at Konya, where he died in 628/1231, to be succeeded—first as professor, later as Sufi master—by his son Jalāl al-Dīn.

Renowned as a preacher, Bahā' al-Dīn Walad was a strong personality who possessed eloquence and also a vivid spiritual imagination. Fortunately, a large compilation of his discourses, *Ma'ārif* (*Divine Knowledge*), has survived.[10] The discourses reveal a great deal concerning the author's personality, his teachings, his interpretation of the Quran and *Ḥadīth*, and his deep influence on the thought and style of Jalāl al-Dīn Rūmī. They show Bahā' al-Dīn to have possessed some of that ecstatic tendency which is often said (although this is a broad generalization) to characterize the Sufism of Khurasan in contrast to the more "sober" Sufism of Iraq. The language is plain and direct, the message for the most part straightforward, although sometimes opaque. Many chapters of the *Ma'ārif* open with the text of a

Quranic verse or phrase, or a tradition, which provides the theme for exposition. Bahā' al-Dīn Walad often alludes to his own meditations, inspirations, and visions; the following passages may be cited by way of illustration:

> I was saying, "Glory to my Lord, the Immense" [when] He said, "I have at My court lords such as the stars, the moon, the sun, and those who are masters on the face of the earth. But that lordship [alluded to in the glorification] is not for them. Every few days I dismiss them from their lordly position. For they are minor lords, whereas I am the Immense Lord." (*Ma'ārif,* sec. 160; ed. Furūzānfar, 1:252–53)

The striking imagery of the next passage illustrates the affinity between Bahā' al-Dīn Walad and his son Jalāl al-Dīn Rūmī:

> Now whenever I look at something, and my eye alights upon the Earth, the formal universe, the various parts of my body, or the inanimate constituents of the world, I look on each one of these objects as a peachstone containing Divine Gardens. These Gardens provide sustenance for the nurturing of those who possess a spirit and intellect; besides nourishing their understanding, love, taste, true companionship, and hearing, the Gardens provide a myriad refreshing delights. (*Ma'ārif,* sec. 113; ed. Furūzānfar, 2:159)

Najm al-Dīn Dāyah Rāzī: Life and Work

Yet another disciple of Kubrā to emerge as an influential figure himself was Najm al-Dīn Abū Bakr Rāzī (573/1177–654/1256), often known as Najm al-Dīn Dāyah. Leaving his native city of Rayy (south of present-day Tehran) in 599/1202–3, he traveled widely before reaching Khwarazm. There he became the disciple of Kubrā, who put him under the guidance of Majd al-Dīn Baghdādī. In 618/1221 the impending menace of the Mongol invasion impelled Dāyah to take refuge in Asia Minor. He spent most of the remainder of his life either there or at Baghdad. In addition to his other work, Najm al-Dīn Dāyah undertook a diplomatic mission for the Abbasid caliph with the aim of concerting various Muslim rulers' resistance to the Mongols.

Najm al-Dīn Rāzī is one of the outstanding Sufi authors of the seventh/thirteenth century; his influence was widespread and lasting beyond the Kubrawiyyah Order. The first work to mention is his *Baḥr al-ḥaqā'iq* (*The Ocean of Divine Realities*), an esoteric commentary on the Quran, which although extant in manuscript still remains unpublished. This represents the continuation of a commentary which Najm al-Dīn Kubrā planned, but which (in written form, at least) only reached the early

3. The Kubrawī Sufi master Majd al-Dīn al-Baghdādī.

verses of sura II. Dāyah's *tafsīr* covers the Quran from there down to sura LII. It fell to another Kubrawī master, 'Alā' al-Dawlah Simnānī, to complete what is one of the greatest monuments of Quranic *ta'wīl,* or hermeneutics. The most celebrated of Najm al-Dīn Dāyah's works, however, is entitled *Mirṣād al-'ibād min al-mabda' ila'l-ma'ād* (*The Path of God's Servants from the Beginning until the Return to Him*).[11] It exists in two recensions and a shorter adaptation.[12]

The Path of God's Servants: Exposition and Symbolism

Like many of the prose classics of Persian Sufi literature, the *Mirṣād* was almost unknown in the West until recently. In a sense it may be said to parallel the work of Abū Ḥāmid al-Ghazzālī inasmuch as the author affirms the centrality of the perspectives of Sufism in the context of a lucid and systematic exposition of Muslim doctrine. At the same time, its profundity and expository style at times recall the *Mathnawī-yi ma'nawī* (*The Spiritual Mathnawī*) of Najm al-Dīn Dāyah's renowned contemporary Jalāl al-Dīn Rūmī. The main themes treated in *Mirṣād al-'ibād* are these: the hierarchical degrees of existence; the nature and purpose of religion, prophethood, and revelation; laws and rituals and their significance; doctrines, methods, stages, and states of the Sufi path; the nature of the soul; the spiritual tendencies and needs of different types of men; and ethics and its link with eschatology.[13]

Also deserving of attention is the brilliance of Najm al-Dīn Dāyah's style of exposition. Were Dāyah's Quranic commentary alone insufficient proof of his spiritual eminence, it is evident from his lucid metaphysical, cosmological, and psychological exposition of the nature and purpose of existence. Dāyah employs symbolism and imagery drawn largely from natural phenomena and everyday life. Such figurative and symbolic language provides keys to unlock something of the hidden meaning between principles and phenomena, and the correspondences and links between the lower and the higher levels of being. Such is the nature and meaning of symbolism. Far from being luxuries, symbolic language and corresponding spiritual insights provide the heart and soul with vital nourishment. For Islamic spirituality, the prototype of such symbolism and imagery is the figurative and allusive language of the noble Quran itself.[14]

As an example of Najm al-Dīn Dāyah Rāzī's parabolic exposition, let us take the chapter of the *Mirṣād* devoted to a difficult and subtle question: "concerning the original creation of the various spirits, and the degrees of knowledge thereof." Dāyah begins by recapitulating the Islamic doctrine that

God's first creation was *al-Rūḥ al-muḥammadī*, the Muḥammadan Spirit (this term in Islamic cosmology corresponds to the Universal Intellect). From it, God successively created the spirits of the prophets, saints, believers, unbelievers, the angels, *jinn* (subtle beings possessing souls), demonic beings and animals. Dāyah continues:

> These degrees and stages (of manifestation of spirits) are comparable to the processes whereby a sugar merchant extracts raw white sugar from cane: he boils it a first time, and extracts white sugar candy; a second, and extracts white sugar; a third, and extracts brown sugar; a fourth, and extracts caramel; a fifth, and extracts black loaf sugar; and after the sixth boiling there remains only a very dark black residue known as treacle. (*Mirṣād*, ed. Riyaḥī, 38)

After pointing out that each of these refined products of sugarcane has its own peculiar qualities and uses, Najm al-Dīn Dāyah explains that the simile in question casts light not only on the hierarchical order of spirits and created beings but also on the problem of the essential nature of the Spirit.

> Now, with regard to the question of the essential nature of the Spirit, our predecessors have said a great deal without going far towards broaching even its elementary aspects. Here once again the analogy with sugar can be applied. The seven types of sugar product possess seven attributes: whiteness, blackness, lightness, darkness, subtlety, density, and sweetness. The Spirit is a subtle essence appertaining to God Himself and is honored in an exclusive manner by the possessive suffix "My" in the words "of My Spirit."[15] The Spirit likewise has seven attributes: these are luminosity, love, knowledge, forbearance, intimacy (with God), permanence and life. From each one of these, further attributes proceed. . . . (*Mirṣād*, 42)

Najm al-Dīn Dāyah develops this analysis at considerable length. However, we must now turn our attention to his teachings on two subjects already touched upon in relation to Najm al-Dīn Kubrā: "photisms"—luminous phenomena appearing to the "Eye of the Spirit"—and the "Man of Light."

The Phenomena of Light

The section of Dāyah's *Mirṣād al-ʿibād* devoted to the methodology of Sufism contains three chapters (17–19) on the nature and analysis of visionary apperception.[16] In the first, Dāyah discusses the differences between dreams and waking visions. In relation to the former, it is necessary to distinguish in the first place between dreams inspired by Satanic influences and dreams that are "sound," and, second, between those whose meaning is literal and those of which part or all needs interpretation. Where waking visions are concerned, Najm al-Dīn Dāyah shares the viewpoint of exoteric Islam: these can only benefit the visionary if he be a monotheist in the strictest sense. "Monks, philosophers and Brahmins," as he terms them, may enjoy visions as a result of asceticism; but being veiled from the lights of the attributes of Divine Unity, they are unable to transcend the human state and are ultimately led to perdition.

For the true believer, visions possess three potential benefits. First, they show him his present spiritual state or degree, for whatever attribute prevails in his heart is invested by the faculty of spiritual imagination with a form which the vision manifests to him. Thus, for example, a leopard represents arrogance, a donkey lust, and a fox deceit, while visions of walking on air or witnessing angels or celestial lights betoken corresponding spiritual stations. The second benefit of such visions is that they engender in the initiate a "taste" for the pure, subtle realm of the Spirit and the angels by virtue of which he is increasingly induced to love and yearn for the inner rather than the outer, gross world. Third, such visions from the unseen are essential if the initiate is to attain to the total self-effacement (*fanā'*) which is the gateway to "perpetual abiding" (*baqā'*), the end and purpose of the path. It is conceivable that some could traverse certain earlier stages of the Way without direct guidance. By its very nature, however, the state of "non-being" (*fanā'*) cannot be gained by the seeker's own efforts: any striving on his part depends on, and hence affirms, his own existence. Therefore, the realization of *fanā'*—and hence of *baqā'* too—necessitates the seeing of luminous visions deriving from the sanctity of the shaykh, the Prophetic Presence, or the Divine Attributes pertaining to the Dominical Presence.

Nūr al-Dīn Isfarā'inī: Modes of Spiritual Communication

In all forms of esotericism, the maintenance of a close relationship and communication between teacher and disciple is a matter of vital importance. As far as the Kubrawīs of Central Asia are concerned, this is spelled out repeatedly in their writings. An interesting case is that of the exchange of letters, over a period of some thirty-five years, between two shaykhs of the Kubrawiyyah: Nūr al-Dīn 'Abd al-Raḥmān Isfarā'inī Kasirqī (639/1242–717/1317) and his pupil and successor 'Alā' al-Dawlah Simnānī (d. 736/1336).[17] Although Simnānī is the more renowned of the two men, the titles of 150 works by Isfarā'inī are known, and his stature is evident from his surviving letters, which often address complex questions of doctrine and hermeneutics, and from his *Kāshif al-asrār (Unveiler of Mysteries)*, which contains an interpretation of many aspects of the path as well as reflections on his own spiritual life that are both eloquent and instructive.[18]

In addition to written and spoken communication, there is the possibility of suprasensory communication between master and disciple. Sufi literature abounds in examples of this, and Najm al-Dīn Kubrā in *Fawā'iḥ al-jalāl* (sec. 36) describes how he asked his shaykh 'Ammār al-Bidlīsī a question and received the latter's reply by this means. According to Majd al-Dīn Baghdādī, one of the categories of inspiration (*khāṭir*), between which one must learn to distinguish, is "the inspiration from the shaykh" (*Fawā'iḥ*, ed. Meier, *Anhang*, 288). Nūr al-Dīn Isfarā'inī, in reply to a question concerning three types of "indication" or "suggestion" (*ishārāt*) transmitted by the shaykh, states that the disciple can distinguish between the three (although they are fundamentally one and the same) once he can recognize those inspirations which derive from the lower soul or the Devil. When this point has been reached, the physical presence of the shaykh is no longer essential to the *murīd*, who thenceforth may continue to benefit from his guidance even if the shaykh be no longer materially alive, provided that he loves the shaykh and observes the conditions of discipleship.[19] Guidance and inspiration may then come inwardly, from the *alter ego* or *shaykh al-ghayb*, as Najm al-Dīn Kubrā also taught.[20]

The Bākharzīs and the Spiritual Retreat

Two Kubrawīs who each had a significant role in the development of Sufi teachings were Sayf al-Dīn Bākharzī and his grandson Abu'l-Mafākhir Yaḥyā. Sayf al-Dīn established a Kubrawī *khānqāh* at Bukhara, in which he witnessed the embracing of Islam by Berke, the Mongol Khan of the Golden Horde, one of the most powerful rulers of the time.[21] In this way the Kubrawiyyah played its part in safeguarding the future position of Islam in that region. The eighth/fourteenth century Arab traveler Ibn Baṭṭūṭah visited the Kubrawī *khānqāh* at Urgench and also that of Bākharzī, where he attended a *samā'* at which Persian and Turkish Sufi poems were sung.[22]

Sayf al-Dīn is quoted extensively in Yaḥyā Bākharzī's treatise on Sufi doctrine and methodology, of which only the second part, *Fuṣūṣ al-ādāb* (*Bezels of Refinement*), has been published.[23] This is a work of great interest, covering in detail many aspects of the path. Here we shall examine a single aspect of the *Fuṣūṣ al-ādāb:* the chapters on the practice of *khalwah* (Persian *khalwat*), or retreat. As already noted, *khalwah* occupies an important place in the methodology of the Kubrawiyyah and more than one member of the order devoted short treatises to the subject. Yaḥyā Bākharzī's exposition, being full and fairly typical, serves as a convenient example to consider.

The section of *Fuṣūṣ al-ādāb* on *khalwah* is divided into three chapters (*faṣṣ*). In the first, Bākharzī is chiefly concerned with citing justifications and precedents for the practice of retreat with reference to the Quran and the Prophetic Sunnah, as is normal in Sufi treatises. He also quotes from Sayf al-Dīn and other Sufi masters; and he explains why the traditional duration of the *khalwah* is forty days. We may single out for interest the exposition given of this claimed *ḥadīth* (the source is not given): "He [God] kneaded the clay of Adam with His Hands for forty mornings." Bākharzī explains that since the human spirit, or reality (*ḥaqīqat*), has been thoroughly mixed (the number forty is, of course, symbolic) with the four elements of corporeal existence, a like period is required to disengage the spirit from these veils. Until this has been accomplished, the seeker cannot undertake the spiritual journey to the Unseen.

Sayf al-Dīn's second chapter on *khalwah* discusses the spiritual benefits and revelations which the Sufi may experience. Attention is drawn to the dangers that may attend the *khalwah* if performed by one who is insufficiently prepared or instructed by his preceptor. Also emphasized is the importance of observing scrupulously the prescriptions of worship and other acts prescribed by the *Sharī'ah*.

The third and final chapter is entitled "On entry upon forty-day retreat, its nature, and the method of ascetic rigor and spiritual striving." Bākharzī enumerates and expounds the ten principles taught by Najm al-Dīn Kubrā. He also discusses in detail such questions as the following: the importance of offering the ritual prayer regularly and in congregation even during the retreat; the five categories of thought or inspiration (*khāṭir*); and the extent and method of reducing the consumption of food. Unusually, Bākharzī deems it permissible for less-experienced disciples to interrupt from time to time their invocation, normally constant, of the formula *Lā ilāha illa'Llāh* ("No god but God"). At intervals they may perform other acts of worship such as reciting the Quran; they may also remain bowing or in prostration for an hour or two at a time while performing supererogatory prayers in the retreat. The *khalwah* is but one of many facets of Sufi methodology treated in Bākharzī's manual.

'Alā' al-Dawlah Simnānī: Life, Work, Doctrine

Reference has already been made to 'Alā' al-Dawlah Simnānī as the disciple of Nūr al-Dīn Isfarā'inī. But Simnānī is himself one of the foremost figures in the history of the Kubrawiyyah and indeed in Persian Sufism. Born in 659/1261 at Simnan, some distance to the east of Tehran, he served Arghūn, the Mongol Īl-khān of Iran, for twelve years. Discussions with Buddhist priests of the court of Arghūn led Simnānī to an interest in mysticism. According to his own account, he learned through spiritual visions that the Buddhists were unable to attain the ultimate goal because they lacked the essential doctrinal framework of unity, that is, the religion of Islam.[24] Having finally extricated himself from the court, Simnānī went to seek guidance from the Sufis and thereafter devoted himself to the Way. As we have seen, he found a master who was expert in the interpretation of visions. After receiving investiture as shaykh from Nūr al-Dīn Isfarā'inī in 689/1290, he established near Simnan a *khānqāh* named Ṣūfī-ābād-i Khudādād ("God-given Sufi center"); here many followers gathered about him until his death in 736/1336.

'Alā' al-Dawlah left behind a sizable corpus of writings, of which only three can be mentioned here, as well as a very beautiful *Dīwān* or collection of lyric poems. *Chihil majlis* (*Forty Gatherings*) contains an eyewitness account of forty discourses of Simnānī on aspects of Sufism; the teachings are leavened and illustrated with many anecdotes of the spiritual life of 'Alā' al-Dawlah and some of his predecessors. The same applies also to *al-'Urwah li-ahl al-khalwah wa'l-jalwah* (*The Bond concerning the People of Spiritual Retreat and Spiritual Manifestation*), a lengthy treatise of which two versions exist, in Persian and in Arabic.

The most original feature of 'Alā' al-Dawlah's work is his commentary on the Quran, which is highly esoteric. Nevertheless, his strictly orthodox attitude on matters relating to the transcendence of God calls for mention. While on a journey, he took exception to some doctrines asserted by Ḥājjī Ḥasan Āmulī, decided him to be a *kāfir* and almost succeeded in having the man killed. Simnānī also criticized some facets of Ibn 'Arabī's "unitarian" doctrine of *waḥdat al-wujūd*.[25] The critique of the *Shaykh al-Akbar* by Aḥmad Sirhindī of the Naqshbandī Order, who some three hundred years after Simnānī posited the alternative doctrine of *waḥdat al-shuhūd* ("unity of consciousness"), seems to have been based partly on Simnānī's views.[26] Yet the extent and significance of Simnānī's strictures should not be exaggerated; in his *Chihil majlis* he quotes the dictum of Sa'd al-Dīn Ḥamūyah, a fellow Kubrawī shaykh, that Ibn 'Arabī was "a boundless ocean."

Simnānī, *Tafsīr*, and "The Prophets of Your Being"

The most important part of Simnānī's literary and doctrinal legacy is contained in his esoteric commentary on the Quran. Simnānī not only completed the commentary begun as *'Ayn al-ḥayāh* (*Fountain of Life*) by Najm al-Dīn Kubrā and later continued down to sura LI under the title *Baḥr al-ḥaqā'iq* (*The Ocean of Divine Realities*) by Najm al-Dīn Dāyah Rāzī (see above); he also further elaborated certain of the doctrines formulated by those masters. Once again, it was H. Corbin who analyzed the characteristics of 'Alā' al-Dawlah's Quranic *ta'wīl* and their relation to earlier Kubrawī teachings about photisms, their link with the stations of the path to God, and the "Man of Light." The starting point of Simnānī's approach to *tafsīr* is that all events and objects of perception in the outer world have their correspondences in the inner. Time unfolds in two modes: time without (*zamān āfāqī*) and time within the soul (*zamān anfusī*). Every individual's knowledge and understanding of Reality depend, axiomatically, on his or her state of inward being, and vice versa. The noble Quran, the Divine Word, possesses seven esoteric meanings. Those who deny the outward meanings, relating to the domain of human events, are characterized by Simnānī as *bāṭinīs* (heretical esoterists); those who deny the inner meanings, relating to the celestial inner world, are negators of truth and are obscurantist fools; only those who embrace both the inner and outer are Muslims in the true sense.

According to Simnānī, the Quranic Text possesses seven levels of esoteric meaning, each corresponding to one of the subtle centers of light (*laṭīfah*). The reader will recall that these are organs of suprasensory perception which are dormant until activity is engendered by the practices of the Sufi path. Each represents a stage in the seeker's progress toward realization and may be accompanied (as we have seen in the work of Najm al-Dīn Kubrā) by visions of colored lights. Furthermore, Simnānī teaches that each of these suprasensory faculties also corresponds to the mysterious reality (*ḥaqīqah*) of one of the prophets. 'Alā' al-Dawlah's prophetology in some respects recalls that of Ibn 'Arabī, whose *Fuṣūṣ al-ḥikam* (*Bezels of Wisdom*) interprets many Quranic verses in such wise as to relate some twenty-seven prophets to specific aspects of the Divine Word or Wisdom. For Simnānī, the Quranic accounts of the prophets are to be interpreted both literally and also, especially, on the level of "inward time." Macrocosmically, the seven subtle organs and their associated prophets correspond to the seven hierarchical domains of being as classically schematized by Islamic cosmology. These are, in ascending order, the World of Nature (*ṭabī'ah*), Forms (*ṣuwar*), Inner Meaning or Perception (*ma'nā*), the Angels and Imagination (*malakūt*), the Dominion or Supraformal (*jabarūt*), the Divine Being (*lāhūt*), and the Divine Essence (*hāhūt*). This theory is elaborated in great detail; what follows is no more than a short synopsis.

The first and lowest of the organs of suprasensory perception is termed the *laṭīfah qālibiyyah* (subtle center of the mold). It represents the genesis within the spiritual wayfarer of a new body or mold (*qālib*), this being the "resurrection body" of Muslim eschatology whose nature is subtle. Because of its link with the creative process, this first subtle center is named "the Adam of your being" (*Ādam wujūdik*). The color of the corresponding photism, or light apparition, is black shading into smoke-gray.

Next in ascending order comes the organ of the soul in its animative aspect (*laṭīfah nafsāniyyah*). In terms of the path, it represents the conflict between the spiritual and the passional elements of the individual like that of Noah and his defiantly disbelieving people. Hence this *laṭīfah* is "the Noah of your existence." It is heralded by a blue light-apparition.

Progress on the spiritual way potentiates the existence of a new self, a new and true identity. In the third stage, this identity is engendered in embryonic form, like a pearl within its shell, in the subtle organ of the heart (*laṭīfah qalbiyyah*). Because of the spiritual begetting which this *laṭīfah* betokens, it is termed "the Abraham of your existence." The photism is red in color.

In Sufi terminology the *sirr*, or secret, is a subtle faculty of supraconscious perception. It is the *sirr*, Simnānī teaches, that is the locus of intimate discourse with God (*munājāt*). As Moses is known to Muslims as *Kalīm Allāh* ("he who spoke with God"), this fourth *laṭīfah* represents "the Moses of your being." Its photism is white, which recalls the miraculous White Hand of Moses mentioned in the Quran.

The fifth subtle organ of perception relates to the Spirit (*rūḥ*). On account of its high rank, it is endowed with the kingly office of vicegerent (*khalīfah*) of God. The *laṭīfah rūḥiyyah* is "the David of your existence," and the associated photisms are yellow.

Higher still is the *laṭīfah khafiyyah:* the subtle body of the *khafiy*, or arcane mystery, by which Simnānī understands the faculty whereby the aid of the Holy Spirit (*rūḥ al-quds*) is rendered to those approaching the degree of *nabī*, or divinely inspired prophet. This represents "the Jesus of your existence." Simnānī points to a peril that attends this stage of the path. He warns that the Muslim seeker may misunderstand his *fanā'* (effacement of individuality) as complete identity with the Godhead, while Christians, conversely, take God Himself as having fallen into the human condition. The perceptions of celestial light associated with the *khafiy* are a luminous black, entirely distinct from the ordinary black which is the absence of light. The nature of this luminous blackness is also described by Najm al-Dīn Dāyah Rāzī, in *Mirṣād al-'ibād*, and by Maḥmūd Shabistarī, author of the famous Persian metaphysical poem *Gulshan-i rāz* (*The Garden of Divine Mysteries*); these two, however, ascribe it to the final rather than the penultimate stage of the Sufi path.[27]

The seventh and highest suprasensory organ is the *laṭīfah ḥaqqiyyah* (the subtle body of the truth). This is the seeker's True Self (*anā'iyyah*), mysteriously not other than the Divine Self, which began to form within the matrix of the Abrahamic third *laṭīfah*, that of the heart. The Blessed Prophet Muḥammad, descendant of Abraham both physically and spiritually (as *ḥanīf* and *muslim*, according to the Quran) represents pure, primeval religion. The *laṭīfah ḥaqqiyah*, then, is "the Muḥammad of your existence"; its photism, says Simnānī, is an effulgent emerald green in color.

Regarding the hermeneutics (*ta'wīl*) of the Sacred Book, Simnānī exhorts the Kubrawī Sufi to interpret and meditate on each Quranic allusion to one of the seven prophets in question by having recourse to the corresponding *laṭīfah*. For example, he links the relation between the third and seventh subtle centers, those of Abraham and Muḥammad, to two verses: III, 61 and IV, 124.

The foregoing represents no more than a bare outline of the highly complex and articulated theories of 'Alā' al-Dawlah Simnānī. It may, nonetheless, serve to indicate the importance of this Kubrawī shaykh's contribution to Sufi metaphysical thought and methodology.[28]

Sa'd al-Dīn Ḥamūyah

At this point we must move backward in time in order to discuss one more Kubrawī shaykh who was the direct disciple of Najm al-Dīn Kubrā. Sa'd al-Dīn Ḥamūyah, or Hammū'ī, is cited quite frequently in Sufi literature but has received less attention from scholars than his stature seems to warrant, and his work remains largely unpublished. Ḥamūyah and his rather better-known disciple 'Azīz al-Dīn Nasafī are two of the most illustrious Kubrawī shaykhs. Not the least interesting aspect is that both were Imami Shī'ites.

Sa'd al-Dīn was born in 587/1191. During his youth, he lived for a time near Damascus, where he enjoyed discussions with Ṣadr al-Dīn Qūnawī, who was to become the most outstanding pupil and interpreter of Muḥyī al-Dīn ibn 'Arabī. It is not clear if Sa'd al-Dīn actually met Ibn 'Arabī, his high opinion of whom was noted above. At the age of thirty, Ḥamūyah received authorization from Kubrā to take disciples of his own. His *khānqāh* at Bahrabad, in northeastern Iran, became the center of one of the most influential branches of the Kubrawiyyah, remaining so for some time after his death in 650/1252–53. When the Īl-khān Ghāzān Khān, son of Arghūn, announced his conversion to Islam in 694/1295, Ḥamūyah's son Ṣadr al-Dīn Ibrāhīm was summoned to the Alburz mountains in order to act as witness.[29]

Ḥamūyah composed numerous works, chiefly in Arabic, including verse (some quatrains and ghazals are extant); they are particularly difficult to understand fully because of the variety of allusions and subtleties they contain.[30] His surviving writings, as well as the evidence of Nasafī and others, show Sa'd al-Dīn to have specialized in expounding the theoretical principles of the Way and of Imami Shī'ah philosophical cosmology including the doctrines regarding *walāyah*, the Imams' function of extending the cycle of the prophethood of Muḥammad. Some elements of Ḥamūyah's thought are known to us from citations in the works of Nasafī. An important element in Sa'd al-Dīn Ḥamūyah's viewpoint is his close devotion to the Hidden Imam. We may also mention his interest in the mysterious science of the letters of the alphabet and in symbolic diagrams.

'Azīz al-Dīn Nasafī: Shī'ism and "The Perfect Man"

All the Kubrawī masters devoted attention to the actual technique of *dhikr* in addition to its doctrines. An example of the technical instructions is the following, from the sixth treatise in 'Azīz al-Dīn Nasafī's *Insān-i kāmil,* on *dhikr* in retreat:

> Know that invocation (*dhikr*) represents for the traveler on the Path what milk does for any infant. The wayfarer must have received his invocation by direct instruction (*talqīn*) from the shaykh . . . he must commence by purifying himself and performing the prayer of thanks after the minor ablution. He should then sit down facing the *qiblah.* Some say that one should sit down cross-legged, since that is more comfortable; others, that one should kneel as in the ritual prayer, this being closer to respectful comportment [before God]. Our Shaykh used to sit cross-legged, as did his companions. Whilst invoking, the disciple must close his eyes tightly. During the early years [of discipleship] he should recite the *dhikr* aloud, but once the *dhikr* has passed beyond his tongue and established itself inwardly, so that the heart itself begins to invoke, it is fitting for him to recite it softly. It takes a long time for the *dhikr* to establish itself inwardly and for the heart to start invoking. As already stated, he must strive to be aware whilst invoking, and practise the negation and affirmation according to the degree of his knowledge. For his invocation he must prefer the formula *lā ilāha illa'Llāh* ("No god but God"), and each time that he says "*illa'Llāh*" he must strike with the [initial] *alif* of *illā* the flesh on his left side with sufficient force to cause pain.[31]

Nasafī then explains that during prolonged *dhikr* in *khalwah* the disciple will lose his voice and suffer pain. After some days, though, his voice will return and the pain subside. This indicates that the *dhikr* is becoming interiorized as desired. The real expert can tell immediately on hearing a man's invocation whether the heart itself has begun to invoke.

The Kubrawīs in India: Sayyid 'Alī Hamadānī, His Successors, and the Firdawsiyyah

The first offshoot of the Kubrawiyyah Order to reach India was known as the Firdawsiyyah. One of the successors of Sayf al-Dīn Bākharzī (see above) was Badr al-Dīn Samarqandī. It was his successor, Najīb al-Dīn Muḥammad, who migrated to Delhi, where he died ca. 699/1300. The best-known figure to emerge from the Firdawsiyyah was Aḥmad Yaḥyā Manērī (d. 772/1371), whose Sufi letters circulated widely.[32]

More significant for the destiny of Sufism—indeed of Islam—in northern India was the advent of Sayyid 'Alī Hamadānī. Born at Hamadan, western Persia, in 714/1314, 'Alī Hamadānī was descended from Zayn al-'Ābidīn, the Fourth Imam of the Shī'ah, and was the disciple of two *khalīfah*s of 'Alā' al-Dawlah Simnānī. At the age of twelve he became a Sufi and thenceforth spent much of his life traveling, until at length in about 782/1380 he arrived in Kashmir. For some six years he propagated Islam and the Kubrawī Way to great effect in Kashmir and in neighboring Badakhshan, accumulating a large following.

Sayyid 'Alī Hamadānī called himself "a second 'Alī" and has been described as a Shī'ite. In fact, however, the Hamadāniyyah Order, as the Kashmīrī Kubrawīs came to be known, remains Sunni to this day. Sayyid 'Alī Hamadānī died in 786/1385 while on his way back to Persia via Afghanistan. An account of his life was written by one of his disciples, Nūr al-Dīn Badakhshī.[33]

Later History of the Kubrawiyyah

The Hamadāniyyah line founded by Sayyid 'Alī also had lasting offshoots of Shī'ite persuasion. Following the murder of Hamadānī's successor Isḥāq Khuttalānī (ca. 826/1423), the succession was disputed between Isḥāq's nominee, Muḥammad Nūrbakhsh and 'Abd Allāh Barzishābādī. Both branches flourished in Persia: the Nūrbakhshiyyah lasted into the Safavid period, while the Barzishābādī faction, also known at one time as the Ightishāshiyyah, or "rebels," developed into the Dhahabiyyah Order. The reason for this nomenclature is unknown. Although the Dhahabiyyah was described by an early thirteenth/nineteenth-century traveler as being in decline, it is still in existence; its center is Shiraz, and other *khānqāh*s are located at Tehran and Tabriz. There are two branches, associated respectively with two twentieth-century shaykhs: Sayyid Muḥammad Riḍā Āqā

Sharīfī Majd al-Ashrāf, and Waḥīd al-Awliyā'[34], and there are still many active members of the order, especially in Shiraz, where they have produced a large number of works during the past few decades.

Of the later history of the Kubrawiyyah in Central Asia we know rather little.[35] The order remained active at Saktari, not far from Bukhara, at least until the early eleventh/seventeenth century. Remarkably, an offshoot is known to have established itself for a time in eastern or Chinese Turkistan.[36] It is probable that the Kubrawiyyah was largely supplanted, in the course of the ninth/fifteenth century, by the Naqshbandiyyah, which at that time became enormously influential in the western regions of Central Asia and remains a force to be reckoned with even in the Soviet period.

Despite the vicissitudes of history, recent studies by Soviet scholars, to whose sponsors the continuing vigor of Sufism in Central Asia is a matter of some concern and perplexity, show that the Kubrawī Order is far from dead.[37] The spiritual and intellectual heritage of Najm al-Dīn Kubrā and the Central Asian school lives on elsewhere, in treatises and in the perpetual life of the Sufis.

Notes

1. *Fawā'iḥ al-jamāl wa fawātiḥ al-jalāl*, ed. F. Meier (Wiesbaden: Franz Steiner, 1957) par. 107.
2. For full details of the Kubrawiyyah genealogy, see R. Gramlich, *Die schiitischen Derwischorden Persiens: Erster Teil: Die Affiliationen* (Wiesbaden: Abhandlungen für die Kunde des Morgenlandes, 1965).
3. Listed by F. Meier in his introduction to *Fawā'iḥ*, 248.
4. Text published with several others in a critical edition by M. Molé under the title: "Traités mineurs de Nağm al-Dīn Kubrā," *Annales islamologiques*, 4 (Cairo: Institut Français d'Archéologie Orientale, 1963) 1–78.
5. H. Corbin, *L'Homme de lumière dans le soufisme iranien* (Paris: Présence, 1984; Eng. trans. by N. Pearson: *The Man of Light in Iranian Sufism* [Boulder: Shambhala, 1978]).
6. The wording of several other Quranic verses is almost identical.
7. See Corbin, *Man of Light*, 89–92.
8. *Nafaḥāt al-uns*, ed. M. Tawḥīdī-pūr (Tehran: Kitābfurūshī-yi Sa'dī, 1336/1957) 424–28.
9. See C. Tortel's introduction to her French translation of *Asrār-nāmah: Le Livre des secrets* (Paris: Deux Oceans, 1985) 15–21.
10. *Ma'ārif: majmū'a-yi mawā'iẓ wa sukhanān-i-... Bahā' al-Dīn Walad*, ed. B. Furūzānfar (2 vols.; 2nd ed.; Tehran: Ṭahūrī Bookshop, 1352/1973).
11. Edited with a study by Muḥammad Amīn Riyāḥī (Tehran: Bungāh-i Tarjamah wa Nashr-i Kitāb, 1352/1973).
12. *Marmūzāt-i asadī dar mazmūrāt-i dā'ūdı*, ed. M. R. Shafī'ī (Tehran: McGill University Institute of Islamic Studies, Tehran Branch, 1352/1973),
13. For a fuller description and analysis, see the introduction and translation by H. Algar of this work entitled, *The Path of God's Bondsmen from Origin to Return* (Delmar, NY: Caravan Books, 1983).

14. See, e.g., Quran LXIX, 21.
15. Referring to the infusion into Adam of the Divine Spirit (Quran XV, 29).
16. *Mirṣād*, ed. Riyāḥī, 299–329.
17. *Mukātabāt-i ʻAbd al-Raḥmān Isfarāyinī bā ʻAlā' al-Dawla-yi Simnānī* (*Correspondence spirituelle échangée entre Nuroddîn Esfarâyenî et son disciple ʻAlâoddawleh Semnânî*), ed. H. Landolt (Tehran and Paris: A. Maisonneuve, 1972).
18. *Kāshif al-asrār*, ed. and French translation by H. Landolt: *Nuruddin Isfarayini: Le Révélateur des mystères* (Paris: Verdier, 1986).
19. *Rasā'il al-nūr*, in manuscript. See H. Landolt, introduction to *Mukātabāt*, 20–21.
20. See Landolt, introduction to *Mukātabāt*, 21.
21. Ibn Khaldūn, *ʻIbar* (Bulaq: Bulāq Press, 1837) 534; J. Richard, "La conversion de Berke et les débuts de l'Islamisation de la Horde d'Or," *Revue des études islamiques* 35 (1967) 173–79.
22. Ibn Baṭṭūṭah, *al-Riḥlah* (Cairo: Maṭbaʻah Wādī al-Nīl, 1287/1870) 3:5–6.
23. *Awrād al-aḥbāb wa fuṣūṣ al-ādāb, jild-i duwwum: Fuṣūṣ al-ādāb*, ed. Īraj Afshār (Tehran, 1345/1967).
24. H. Landolt, "Simnânî on Waḥdat al-wujûd," introduction to *Mukātabāt*, 94.
25. Ibid.
26. J. S. Trimingham, *The Sufi Orders in Islam* (London: Oxford University Press, 1971) 95; see also K. Nizami, "The Naqshbandiyyah," chapter 8 in this volume.
27. H. Corbin, *Man of Light*, 126–28.
28. For a fuller account, see H. Corbin, *En Islam iranien* (Paris: Gallimard, 1972) 3:275–355.
29. Dawlatshāh Samarqandī, *Tadhkirat al-shuʻarā'*, ed. E. G. Browne (London: Luzac, 1901) 213; Rashīd al-Dīn Faḍl Allāh, *Tārīkh-i ghāzānī*, ed. K. Jahn (Leiden: Brill, 1940) 79.
30. See Najīb Māyil Harawī's introduction to his edition of Ḥamūyah's *Miṣbāḥ al-taṣawwuf* (Tehran: Intishārāt-i Mawlā, 1362/1983) 36–37.
31. Nasafī, *Insān-i kāmil*, ed. M. Molé (Tehran and Paris: A. Maisonneuve, 1341/1962) 106–10; see also Nasafī, *Le Livre de l'homme parfait*, trans. I. de Gastines (Paris: Fayard, 1984).
32. See Sharafuddin Maneri, *The Hundred Letters*, trans. P. Jackson (New York: Paulist Press, 1980).
33. Nūr al-Dīn Badakhshī, *Khulāṣat al-manāqib*, trans. J. K. Teufel as *Eine Lebenschreibung des Scheichs ʻAlī-i Hamadānī* (Leiden: Brill, 1962).
34. Gramlich, *Schiitische Derwischorden*, 18–26.
35. For a summary of the available evidence on the later history of the Kubrawiyyah, see H. Algar's article on Kubrā in *Encyclopaedia of Islam*, 2nd ed.
36. Muḥammad Tawāḍuʻ, *al-Ṣīn wa'l-islām* (Cairo, 1364/1945) 112.
37. E.g., G. P. Snesarev, *Relikty domusul'manskikh verovanii i obriadov u Uzbekov Khorezma* (Moscow: U.S.S.R. Academy, 1969) 269, 433; S. M. Demidov, *Sufizm v Turkmenii: evolutsiia i perezhitki* (Ashkhabad, 1978) 32–38. See also A. Bennigsen and M. Broxup, *The Islamic Threat to the Soviet State* (London: Croom Helm, 1983) 76.

5

Rūmī and the Mawlawiyyah

William C. Chittick

Jalāl al-Dīn Rūmī, known in the East as Mawlānā ("our lord," from which is derived the word Mawlawī), was born on 6 Rabī' I 604/30 November 1207 and died on 5 Jumādā II 672/17 December 1273. No doubt the best known of the Sufi poets, he has inspired constant interest among Western scholars and seekers for over a hundred years. In the East his poetry has been popular at all levels of society wherever the Persian language has been known, from Turkey to India; his works have provided practical instruction for generations of Muslims at every level of spiritual aptitude; and the Mawlawī Sufi Order that he founded has played a major role in the religious and cultural life of Turkey from Ottoman times to the present. From his own lifetime on, superlatives have been heaped upon his person and poetry; here we can refrain from repeating these while attempting to summarize his historical setting and spiritual message.

The History of the Mawlawiyyah

Rūmī's life story has often been told and need not be discussed here in any detail. His father, Bahā' al-Dīn Walad (d. 628/1231), a well-known and learned divine residing in Balkh in present-day Afghanistan, preached to the faithful about the necessity of spiritual rejuvenation as the context for all moral action; at the same time he was a Sufi master, so he also trained a group of followers in the discipline of the spiritual path. His *Ma'ārif* (*Gnostic Sciences*), a collection of sermons and meditations on Quranic verses, combines the ethical tone of the preacher with the visionary imagery of the contemplative. In ca. 615/1218, with the Mongols gradually approaching Balkh, Bahā' Walad left for the pilgrimage to Mecca with his family and many followers; Balkh was destroyed in 617/1220. Bahā' Walad stayed for some time in Syria and then moved to Karaman in present-day Turkey, where Jalāl al-Dīn was married, his wife giving birth to a son, Sulṭān Walad, in 623/1226. Bahā' Walad was soon invited by the Saljuq ruler, 'Alā' al-Dīn Kayqubād, to come to his capital at Konya, some sixty miles northwest of Karaman, and there he settled in about 627/1228. When Bahā' Walad died on 18 Rabī' II 628/23 February 1231, Jalāl al-Dīn was appointed to take over his official duties. At this point Rūmī was already learned in the sciences of his day, especially jurisprudence, theology, and Arabic and Persian literature, and he was thoroughly familiar with the Sufi ethical teachings constantly stressed in his father's writings. He also must have been well advanced on the path of realizing the inward significance of the outward forms of ritual and practice; but the sources suggest that he only began to dedicate himself to methodical Sufi training around the year 629/1232, when Burhān al-Dīn Muḥaqqiq Tirmidhī (d. 638/1240–41), a disciple of his father, came to Konya and undertook his spiritual instruction. Rūmī continued to fulfill the functions of a respected man of knowledge, wearing the clerical dress and ministering to the religious and spiritual needs of the populace for several years; but on 26 Jumādā II 642/29 November 1244—note that the exact date has been preserved—an event took place that was to transform him outwardly and inwardly: Shams al-Dīn of Tabriz came to Konya.

Shams-i Tabrīzī

Shams is certainly one of the most mysterious and enigmatic figures in Sufism; it is not without reason that Sulṭān Walad likens him to Khiḍr and Rūmī to Moses (*Walad-nāmah,* 41).[1] The recent publication of Shams's *Maqālāt* (*Discourses*), which were apparently noted down by someone close to both him and Rūmī, should put to rest speculation that Shams was some sort of supernatural apparition rather than a human being. Shams speaks of having seen and recognized Rūmī fifteen or sixteen years earlier in Syria when Rūmī had gone there to study (ca. 630–34/1233–37). He mentions a spiritual awakening he had experienced as a child that set him apart from others; when his father questioned him about his strange behavior, he compared himself to a duckling hatched among chickens. "So, father, I see the ocean: It has become my mount; it is my homeland and spiritual state. If you belong to me or I to you, then come into the ocean; otherwise, stay with the chickens" (*Maqālāt,* 78).[2] Of his father he could say, "He was a good man and had a certain nobility . . . , but he was not a lover of God. A good man is one thing, a lover something else" (*Maqālāt,* 124).

According to the traditional accounts, and as Shams himself indicates, he was directed to Rūmī through a dream. It is said that Rūmī was aware of his coming and went out to meet him; they sat opposite each other in front of a shop for some time without speaking. Finally Shams asked Rūmī a question about the comparative stations of the Prophet and Bāyazīd Basṭāmī, and Rūmī answered by explaining the incomparable superiority of the former. Then they embraced and "mixed like milk and sugar." For six months they were inseparable, and Rūmī's way of life changed completely; the transformation of the great divine was noted by the whole city, especially when he abandoned his clerical garb, ceased teaching and delivering sermons, and began to attend regular sessions of *samāʿ*. Sulṭān Walad says that when Shams invited Mawlānā Jalāl al-Dīn to participate in a special form of *samāʿ*, "Mawlānā took it as his rite (*madhhab*) and orthodoxy (*raʾy-i durust*)—his heart blossomed into a hundred gardens" (*Walad-nāmah,* 17).

Rūmī himself alludes to the change that he underwent in such verses as the following:

> My hand always used to hold a Quran, but now it holds Love's flagon.
> My mouth was filled with glorification, but now it recites only poetry and songs. (D 24875–76)

Rūmī's total devotion to Shams incited the jealousy of some of his followers; the unfriendly atmosphere they created made Shams leave Konya after a stay of about sixteen months. In his sorrow, Rūmī cut himself off from practically everyone; soon his disciples realized that they were even more deprived of his presence than before. When a letter came from Shams in Syria, Rūmī sent him a number of ghazals, describing his state in Shams's absence:

> Without your presence, *samāʿ* is forbidden; like Satan, revelry is accursed.
> I wrote not a single ghazal without you; when your message arrived,
> The pleasure of hearing (*samāʿ*) it brought five or six into verse. (D 18457–59)

Rūmī sent Sulṭān Walad after Shams, who this time remained in Konya until 645/1247–48, when he disappeared. According to one of the earliest accounts, now accepted by many scholars, he was murdered by jealous disciples. The involvement of Rūmī's son, ʿAlāʾ al-Dīn, in the plot would explain the coldness of his father's relationship with him and the fact that Rūmī refused to attend his funeral when he died in 658/1260. But Rūmī exhibited no signs that he thought Shams was dead, nor did he withdraw into himself as he had at Shams's first disappearance. Instead he devoted himself to *samāʿ* and to singing songs of heartache and separation. Still hoping to find Shams, on two occasions he went to Damascus looking for him. During his second trip, at least two years after Shams's disappearance, he came to the conclusion that Shams would only be found within himself. In the words of Sulṭān Walad,

> He said, "Though in body I am far from him, without body and spirit we two are one light. . . .
> Since I am he and he is I, why do I seek? We are one—now I will sing of myself." (*Walad-nāmah,* 60–61)

Many of Rūmī's own verses make the same identification; his constant praise of Shams must be viewed as praise of his own Self.

> Shams of Tabrīz is in fact a pretext—it is I who display the beauty of God's Gentleness, I.
> To cover up, I say to the people, "He is a noble king, I am but a beggar. . . ."
> I am obliterated in Shams's beauty—in this obliteration, there is neither he nor I. (D 16532–35)

What manner of person was Shams? This question was already being asked by his contemporaries, and in a sense one could say that Rūmī devotes thousands of verses to answering it, though he usually keeps in view the otherworldly side of Shams's nature. Shams himself was well aware that most people considered his appearance and manner strange or even outrageous.

> These people are justified in being unfamiliar with my way of talking. All my words come in the mode of Grandeur (*kibriyā*)—they all appear as baseless claims. The Quran and Muhammad's words come in the mode of need (*niyāz*), so they all appear as meaning (*ma'nā*). Hence people hear words from me that are not in the mode of seeking or need—my words are so high that when you look up, your hat falls off. (*Maqālāt,* 147).

Remarks like the following must have scandalized the more sober members of Rūmī's entourage:

> I speak two kinds of words: dissimulation (*nifāq*) and truth (*rāstī*). In the case of my dissimulation, the souls and spirits of all the saints hope to meet and sit with me; but as for that which is true and without dissimulation—the spirits of the prophets wish that they might have lived during my time to share my companionship (*ṣuḥbat*) and listen to my words. (*Maqālāt,* 108)

Shams shows no surprise at the effect his presence had on Rūmī: "The sign that a person has attained to companionship with me is that companionship with others becomes cold and bitter for him—not such that he continues their companionship in spite of its having become cold, but such that he is no longer able to bear it" (*Maqālāt,* 75). Shams was fully aware of Rūmī's spiritual stature and found it natural that Rūmī alone should realize his true worth: "In this world I have nothing to do with the common people

(*ʿawāmm*)—I have not come for their sake. I take the pulse of those who guide the world to God" (*Maqālāt,* 84).

He explains his relationship with Rūmī in a parable:

> A merchant had fifty agents who traveled in every direction on land and sea and traded with his property. But he set out in search of a pearl, knowing that there was a certain pearl diver. He passed by the diver, and then the diver came after him. The nature of that pearl was hidden between the merchant and the diver. The merchant had earlier seen a dream concerning the pearl, and he trusted his dream, like Joseph. . . . Today that diver is Mawlānā, the merchant is myself, and the pearl is between us. (*Maqālāt,* 119)

Prefiguring many verses of the *Dīwān* named after him, Shams compares himself and Rūmī to the sun and the moon:

> Mawlānā is the moonlight; eyes cannot reach the sun of my existence, except by means of the moon. The sun is so bright and radiant that eyes cannot bear to look at its light, nor can the moon reach the sun, unless the sun reaches the moon. "Eyes cannot embrace Him, but He embraces the eyes" (Quran VI, 153). (*Maqālāt,* 120)

It is clear from certain of Shams's remarks quoted above and from other passages in his *Maqālāt* that he made no claim to be Rūmī's spiritual guide in the usual sense of the word—Rūmī was already a great pearl diver when Shams set out to meet him. In fact, Shams states explicitly that there was no master-disciple relationship in either direction: "When I came to Mawlānā, the first condition was that I should not come as a shaykh. God has not yet brought to earth the man that can act as Mawlānā's shaykh. Nor am I someone who can be a disciple—I have passed beyond that stage" (*Maqālāt,* 33). It is also true that Rūmī influenced Shams in ways similar to Shams's influence on him: "I speak well and talk sweetly, inwardly I am bright and radiant. I was water, seething and turning in upon myself and beginning to stink, until Mawlānā's existence struck upon me—then that water began to flow and it keeps on flowing, sweet, fresh, and pleasant" (*Maqālāt,* 245–46).

Whatever the secret of Shams's existence, there can be no doubt that one of the happy consequences of his meeting with Rūmī was the latter's incredible outpouring of poetry. Rūmī's *Dīwān-i Shams-i Tabrīzī,* containing his collected ghazals and other miscellaneous verses, comprises some forty thousand lines, and his *Mathnawī*—called by Jāmī the Quran in the Persian language—includes about twenty-five thousand verses more. The *Dīwān* consists mainly of love poetry, celebrating the joys of union with the Beloved and the agonies of separation from Him. In general, the ghazals average eight to ten lines and represent the spontaneous expression of particular spiritual states; they were often composed while Rūmī was participating in the *samā'* and are usually appropriate for musical accompaniment. In contrast, the *Mathnawī* consists of a single poem in six books written over a period of some sixteen years; it contains over three hundred long and short anecdotes and stories drawn from a wide variety of sources and retold to illustrate various dimensions of the spiritual life. As in the *Dīwān,* love remains the central theme, but the *Mathnawī* was written with the conscious intention of elucidating "the roots of the roots of the roots of religion"–the spiritual essence of Islam–in relatively didactic language. Since it is designed to guide disciples and lovers of God on the spiritual path, it differs in style from the ghazals of the *Dīwān,* which are largely extemporaneous expressions of spiritual perceptions. The poems in the *Dīwān* pertain to all periods of Rūmī's spiritual unfolding after the coming of Shams, whereas the *Mathnawī* appears as the intentional testament of the saint who has reached the highest stages of human perfection and has returned to this world to guide others to God.

Rūmī has also left three relatively short prose works. *Fīhi mā fīhi* (translated into English as *Discourses*) covers many of the same themes as the *Mathnawī*. *Majālis-i sab'ah* (*Seven Sermons*) was apparently written down long before the coming of Shams; the sermons are mystical in tone, but have a strong moralistic and ethical emphasis, like Bahā' Walad's *Ma'ārif.* Finally, about 150 of Rūmī's letters have been preserved; many of these were written to high officials on behalf of disciples or friends looking for jobs, redress of some grievance, or various other favors. In general the letters are interesting for the light they throw on the social role that the head of a great Sufi order had to play.

Rūmī's Followers

Two of Rūmī's companions deserve special mention. Shaykh Ṣalāḥ al-Dīn Zarkūb (d. 657/1258) was a goldsmith without formal education who had been Muḥaqqiq Tirmidhī's disciple and whose daughter became the wife of Sulṭān Walad. Two or three years after Shams's disappearance, Shaykh Ṣalāḥ al-Dīn became Rūmī's closest companion and remained so until his death. He is the object of praise of over fifty of Rūmī's ghazals. Ḥusām al-Dīn Chalabī (d. 683/1284–85) became Rūmī's closest companion after Ṣalāḥ al-Dīn's death. He had been a favorite disciple for many years, and when Shams was living in Konya he had been given the important duty of looking after his affairs and acting as an intermediary between him and various people who wanted to meet him. A dated ghazal (D 1839) is dedicated to him already in Dhu'l-qa'dah 654/November 1256, and modern scholars have marshaled strong evidence to show that the *Mathnawī*, which Rūmī dedicated and dictated to Ḥusām al-Dīn, was begun some eighteen months before Ṣalāḥ al-Dīn's death.

In 672/1273, when Rūmī was nearing the completion of the *Mathnawī*'s sixth book, which he had already announced would end the work, his health began to decline seriously, though his physicians were unable to diagnose any specific illness. He left the *Mathnawī* unfinished; one of his last ghazals, composed on his deathbed, begins with this line:

> How should you know what kind of King is my inward companion? Look not at my yellow face, for I have legs of iron! (D 1426)

At Rūmī's death, Ḥusām al-Dīn was his caliph, that is, his highest ranking disciple, in charge of directing most of the affairs of the order. Nevertheless, Ḥusām al-Dīn came to Sulṭān Walad and asked him to take his father's place as the supreme spiritual guide. According to his own account, Sulṭān Walad replied as follows:

> During my father's time, you were his caliph—no change can now be allowed.
> You were the leader and I the follower; the king himself made this known to us.
> You are our caliph from first to last, our leader and shaykh in the two worlds. (*Walad-nāmah*, 123)

Ḥusām al-Dīn remained supreme master of the order until his death ten years later. The disciples then gathered around Sulṭān Walad and installed him in Ḥusām al-Dīn's place. He undertook a vigorous expansion of the order, sending caliphs throughout Anatolia. He also codified the characteristic Mawlawī rites and rules of dress and behavior. His *Dīwān*, three *mathnawīs*, and collected "Discourses" cannot compare to the works of his father on any level, yet they provide important and straightforward clarifications of many of Rūmī's central teachings. Sulṭān Walad states that one of his purposes in beginning his first *mathnawī* (in 690/1291) was to tell of the spiritual stations and miraculous deeds of those who have lived "in our own times," just as his father's *Mathnawī* was concerned with the deeds of earlier generations. He also points out that Shams al-Dīn, Ṣalāḥ al-Dīn, and Ḥusām al-Dīn were not well known, but would become famous through his accounts. It is certainly true that Sulṭān Walad's works are one of the most important sources for the early history of the order, rivaled only by Sipahsālār's *Risālah* and Aflākī's *Manāqib al-ʿārifīn* (both written in the years 718–19/1318–19).

Concerning Sulṭān Walad, Rūmī said, "You are the closest of mankind to me in physical constitution and character (*khalqan wa khulqan*)" (*Walad-*

nāmah, 3), and people often mistook them for brothers. Indeed, perhaps Sulṭān Walad's most important contribution to the Mawlawiyyah was his transmission of the human qualities of his father: after Sulṭān Walad's death in 712/1312 three of his four sons ('Ārif Chalabī, d. 719/1319; 'Ābid Chalabī, d. 729/1329; and Wājid Chalabī, d. 733/1333) followed him successively as masters of the order, and his daughter, Muṭahharah Khātūn, was the mother of another master. Except for two sons of 'Ābid Chalabi and Muṭahharah's son, all other masters of the order down to recent times have been descendants of 'Ārif Chalabī (whose mother, in contrast to his siblings, was the daughter of Ṣalāḥ al-Dīn Zarkūb).

It would be impossible to provide even a brief outline of the subsequent expansion and influence of the Mawlawī Order here. Suffice it to say that the Mawlawīs played a major role in the history of the Ottoman Empire, spiritually, culturally, and also politically. The development of Turkish music is intimately connected with the Mawlawī "rites" (*ā'īn*), and many of the greatest Turkish calligraphers have been members of the order. Turkish poetry owes a great deal, both stylistically and thematically, to Rūmī's Persian verse; a master like Mehmed Esad Ghālib (d. 1218/1799) can only be understood in the context of the *Mathnawī.* The political role of the order becomes especially apparent during the reign of Sultan Selim III (1789–1808), who was himself a Mawlawī dervish whose musical talents allowed him to compose an *ā'īn.*

Rūmī's radiance was not held back by the boundaries of the Ottoman Empire. As A. Schimmel has amply demonstrated, to speak of his influence is to speak of the development of poetry in all major Islamic languages except Arabic and of the popular expansion of the Sufi orders.[3] The vast majority of Muslims at all social and educational levels have always appreciated the beauty of poetry and its subsidiary arts, such as music and calligraphy. Wherever these have been valued from Turkey to India, Rūmī has been a central figure.

Rūmī's Sources

Schimmel has shown that a vast range of works are reflected in Rūmī's poetry and ideas, beginning with the Quran and the *Ḥadīth;*[4] here it will be sufficient to allude to the influence of various earlier Sufis. Besides those figures who were so important in shaping all later formulations of Sufi teachings, such as al-Ghazzālī, it seems that two major strands of influence can be discerned: First, there are the great Sufi poets who preceded Rūmī, in particular Sanā'ī (d. 525/1130–31) and, to a lesser degree, 'Aṭṭār (d. ca. 618/1221). The former is often praised by Rūmī; Shams held that he was "marvellously detached from self: his words are the words of God" (*Maqālāt,* 156).

The other major strand of influence is that of Rūmī's own immediate masters and companions, in particular his father, Bahā' Walad, and Shams-i Tabrīzī, both of whose works influenced him in numerous specific instances, as the editors of the *Ma'ārif* and *Maqālāt* have shown. More importantly, these two masters prefigure in their own personalities two complementary dimensions of Rūmī's spirituality. Bahā' Walad's *Ma'ārif* is infused with the emphasis on love and beauty that characterizes Rūmī and the Mawlawiyyah in general; God's Attributes of Gentleness (*luṭf*) and Beauty (*jamāl*) set the tone throughout. In contrast, Shams's *Maqālāt* are often marked by displays of Severity (*qahr*) and Majesty (*jalāl*). In one passage, Shams alludes to the fact that Mawlānā reveals God's Gentleness, while he himself displays both Gentleness and Severity (*Maqālāt,* 74). If it is true that Rūmī used to carry his father's *Ma'ārif* with him and study it constantly until Shams forbade him to read it, Shams's act may have symbolized his intention to strengthen within Rūmī the capacity to display the Attributes of Majesty and Severity. Here one should recall the close connection, obvious in Rūmī's teachings, between Severity and the pain and heartache of separation. Indeed, separation from Shams may have been necessary before Rūmī could realize this Attribute fully. Moreover, the many ghazals in which Rūmī displays the divine Majesty and Grandeur while speaking in the first person seem to pertain to the latest period in his life, when he had fully realized Shams al-Dīn–"religion's Sun"–within himself; it can rightly be said that in these ghazals Rūmī speaks from such a high vantage point that, looking up at him, "one's hat falls off." In brief, one might say that Bahā' Walad's influence on Rūmī was "feminine," whereas Shams's was "masculine"; Bahā' Walad was Rūmī's father "in form" (*dar ṣūrat*) but his mother "in meaning" (*dar ma'nā*), whereas Shams was his spiritual father.

Rūmī and Ibn 'Arabī

It has often been suggested or stated explicitly that Rūmī was influenced by Ibn 'Arabī and/or his followers, but this judgment has been based largely on speculation and can safely be rejected. It is true that Ṣadr al-Dīn al-Qūnawī (d. 673/1274), Ibn 'Arabī's son-in-law and foremost disciple, was one of Rūmī's close friends, but Rūmī was far too advanced spiritually to come under the influence of "friendship," even that of a great master. (Nor is there any sign that al-Qūnawī was influenced by Rūmī.) Sipahsālār reports that Rūmī became a "companion" of Ibn 'Arabī during the years Rūmī stayed in Damascus (ca. 630–34/1233–37), and it would indeed be strange if there had been no contact whatsoever. But again, the question of influence must be discussed separately from that of contact or companionship. It is not without significance that certain passages in Rūmī's biographies and Shams's *Maqālāt* suggest that the Mawlawī shaykhs looked upon the systematized theosophy characteristic of Ibn ʿArabī and his followers with disdain; the differences in style are so consistent and deep that it would be inconceivable for these not to reflect a fundamental difference in perspective. The spiritual resources of Islam are certainly broad enough to embrace both of these oceans of spirituality, without excluding other possibilities as well.

Henry Corbin overstates his case when he says that "it would be quite superficial to dwell on the contrast between the two forms of spirituality cultivated by Mawlānā and Ibn ʿArabī."[5] For those who look at Sufism from the perspective of the spiritual needs of the twentieth century, this judgment may be true, but profound differences remain in the texts; nor should one forget that the two forms of spirituality are, generally speaking, aimed providentially at two different types of mentality. Ibn ʿArabī's complicated theosophy, no doubt grounded in practice to the same extent as Rūmī's "religion of love," appealed primarily to those who had undergone the technical training of the Islamic sciences, especially theology and philosophy. It provided sophisticated answers to sophisticated questions. In contrast, Rūmī's spirituality attracted everyone who could appreciate beauty and music, whatever one's educational level. Rūmī employed the most ordinary phenomena and experiences of everyday life as imagery to explain the profoundest levels of metaphysics and spiritual psychology. He also employed a wide variety of technical terms, but these were drawn primarily from the language spoken by the people, not that of the philosophers and theologians. Hence the Mawlawī dervishes came from every level of society; they ranged from the most educated to the illiterate, the richest to the poorest, the governing elite to the street sweepers. Any Muslim with "taste" (*dhawq*) could follow Rūmī's way (although not necessarily understand the *Mathnawī*), but only a small minority would have the necessary specialized training to understand the doctrines of Islam as expounded by Ibn ʿArabī. An anecdote related to this author by the contemporary Iranian *ḥakīm* Sayyid Jalāl al-Dīn Āshtiyānī conveys the contrast between the two modes of expression succinctly: After listening to Rūmī explain a point of doctrine to his disciples, al-Qūnawī asked him, "How are you able to express such difficult and abstruse metaphysics in such simple language?" Rūmī replied, "How are you able to make such simple ideas sound so complicated?"

It must also be kept in mind that there could be no question of spiritual links between Rūmī and Ibn ʿArabī of the master–disciple kind, since two clear and distinct lines of transmission (*silsilah*) can be discerned. Hence, the

4. The Sufi master and poet Jalāl al-Dīn Rūmī.

5. The meeting of Rūmī and Shams-i Tabrīzī.

problem comes down to one of doctrinal links, in the sense that Rūmī might have borrowed certain formulations from Ibn ʿArabī. Anyone who reads works by the two masters will see similarities, but these can be traced to sources earlier than Ibn ʿArabī. Nor is it true that because "references to the works of Ibn ʿArabī are frequent in the abundant commentaries on the *Mathnawī* produced in India and in Iran," it is therefore "necessary to study these commentaries if we wish to learn what Mawlānā's spirituality meant to his mystic following."[6] During Rūmī's own lifetime and through the time of Sulṭān Walad, no reference was made to Ibn ʿArabī's teachings in order to clarify Rūmī's. Thus, for example, Aḥmad Rūmī's *Daqāʾiq al-ḥaqāʾiq* (written in 720/1320) explains in a relatively systematic manner many of Rūmī's important teachings; each of its eighty chapters is preceded by a quotation from the Quran or the *Ḥadīth,* illustrated by verses from Rūmī's *Mathnawī* or *Dīwān* and amplified by the author's own poetry. Works such as this demonstrate that Rūmī's verses do not need to be explained through Ibn ʿArabī's terminology and ideas; Rūmī's works are in fact self-sufficient, especially when accompanied by the practices that went along with them. Moreover, if Rūmī were indeed a follower of Ibn ʿArabī, one would expect other followers of Ibn ʿArabī to quote his poetry in their works, since it is exquisitely suited to express many of their teachings. But, in fact, none of Ibn ʿArabī's immediate followers who wrote in Persian and quoted Persian verse (i.e., al-Qūnawī, ʿĪrāqī, Farghānī, and Jandī) ever quotes from Rūmī. At the very least this suggests that in their view Rūmī did not share their perspective.

Why, then, do Rūmī's commentators insist on interpreting his ideas in terms of Ibn ʿArabī's teachings? The major reason is that intellectual discourse had come to be dominated by Ibn ʿArabī's modes of expression. Thus, to "explain" Rūmī's views meant to translate a poetical idiom with its own characteristic imagery and technical terminology into a more intellectual mode of expression largely determined by the concepts and terms of Ibn ʿArabī's school. There is no fundamental incompatibility between the two modes of spirituality, but to translate one form of expression into another meant a dilution of the specific virtues and, in particular, the spontaneity of the former.

The mere fact that Rūmī's commentators refer to Ibn ʿArabī's teachings does not mean that all Rūmī's followers understood him in such terms. Most commentaries were written precisely by and for scholars trained in the Islamic sciences, that is, "intellectuals." But the vast majority of disciples in most orders, drawn as they were from every level of Islamic society, would have been satisfied with the poetry itself without feeling any need for "explanation." The beauty of the poetry when recited or sung was sufficient "commentary" on its intellectual content. Even today when Sufi orders meet in places like Iran and listen to the recitation of the *Mathnawī,* every dervish appreciates the beauty of the poetry, which makes available the intellectual content in a direct manner, but few are interested in technical explanations of the intellectual bases of Rūmī's thought.

Finally, perhaps it still needs to be stressed that there is no evidence in Rūmī's works of influence by Ibn 'Arabī or al-Qūnawī. Even Henry Corbin, the outstanding proponent of harmony between the two modes of spirituality among those who have studied the texts, never claims any direct influence, since none of Ibn 'Arabī's original terminology or discussions is found in Rūmī's works.

The Religion of Love

When Ibn 'Arabī speaks of the "religion of love" in the famous poem from his *Tarjumān al-ashwāq,* he is alluding to the nonspecificity or "nonentification" of the heart of the Perfect Man, who experiences continuous theophanies of the Divine Essence, theophanies that "never repeat themselves." Hence, his heart becomes "a receptacle for every form, a pasture for gazelles, a cloister for Christian monks." Once one has understood what this means in the context of Ibn 'Arabī's teachings, it would not be totally inaccurate to say that Rūmī is alluding to the same thing when he says, for example, that "the intellect is bewildered by the Religion of Love" (D 2610). But to consider the meaning of the term "religion of love" as identical in the two instances would be to ignore certain fundamental differences in perspective between the two schools. Thus, for Rūmī love, along with the beauty and joy that it implies, is the heart and marrow of religion, the central theme of all spirituality, whereas for Ibn 'Arabī, love is a possible mode of realizing the Nondelimited Truth. When reading Rūmī, one is constantly pulled toward the experience of love as the central reality beyond any possible conceptualization; when reading Ibn 'Arabī, one does not feel that Love is all-important. The emphasis is on the experience and comprehension of Ultimate Reality, but love is not necessarily the primary means to achieving this, while the theoretical description of that Reality and of the means to reaching It remains a central concern.

In no sense did Rūmī attempt to set down, in the manner of his friend al-Qūnawī, a metaphysical or theological system, or a comprehensive philosophy of the nature of existence. His aim is to tell of the wonders of love and to "open a door to the Unseen world for the creatures" (D 14324). Above all, he wants to ignite the fire of love in the heart of man: "The worst of all deaths is to live without love" (D 13297).

> How long this talk, these figures of speech, these metaphors? I want burning, burning—accustom yourself to that burning.
>
> Ignite the fire of love in your spirit and burn away all thoughts and concepts! (M II 1762–63)

The overwhelming impression that the reader receives from studying Rūmī's works is the necessity and urgency of following the spiritual life and abandoning oneself to the Divine Mercy. But this does not mean that no coherent "philosophy of existence" underlies his works. Quite the contrary: His clear perception of man's place in the universe helps make his message so persuasive.

Rūmī does not set out to discuss metaphysics, theology, cosmology, anthropology, or psychology, but his views on all these become clear while he sings the praises of Love; in retrospect numerous commentators have recognized a coherent world view underlying his poetry and have attempted to clarify it from their own perspectives. But in doing to they invariably throw water on the burning fire of his poetry.

The Quranic doctrine of *tawḥīd* shapes everything that Rūmī says. As Schimmel remarks, "one may say without exaggeration that Rūmī's poetry is nothing but an attempt to speak of God's grandeur as it reveals itself in the different aspects of life."[7] This, precisely, is the essence of *tawḥīd:* to show that everything sings the praises of the One, since all multiplicity is ultimately reducible to Unity.

Rūmī's world view has been outlined in detail elsewhere;[8] here one can only allude to a few of its distinguishing characteristics. Like other Sufis, Rūmī sees the universe as the theophany of God's Names and Attributes, while man or Adam, "the lord of 'He taught the Names'" (M I 1234), carries God's Trust because he is made in His image. The Divine Attributes can be divided into two categories, those of Mercy (*raḥmat*) or Gentleness, and those of Wrath (*ghaḍab*) or Severity, though only the former is intrinsic to God's very Essence, since "My Mercy precedes My Wrath."

As theophanies of all the Names and Attributes, human beings embrace both Gentleness and Severity. In general, the prophets and saints maintain a perfect balance between the two Attributes, but since Gentleness or Mercy is in fact prior, it dominates over them. In contrast, God's Wrath dominates over the unbelievers. In the same way the angels are theophanies of Gentleness and Mercy, whereas the satans are theophanies of Severity and Wrath; microcosmically, the intellect (*'aql*) pertains to Gentleness, whereas the ego (*nafs*) manifests Severity. The ordinary human situation, as perceived by Rūmī, is for man to have faith in God and practice his religion, yet to be caught in the struggle between angel and devil, intellect and ego, since it is not yet clear whether Mercy or Wrath will determine any particular individual's resting place in the next world, that is, whether he will enter paradise or hell. "The saints are waiting to bring the believers into their own houses and make them like themselves, while the satans are also waiting to drag them down toward themselves to 'the lowest of the low' (Quran XCV, 5)."[9]

The cosmic drama, at the center of which stands man, results from the manifestation of the Hidden Treasure: "I loved to be known, so I created the creatures." The Love and Mercy that lie at the base of the creative urge bring the universe into existence and determine its final end; Wrath comes into play only in subordination to Mercy and with Mercy in view. Thus Rūmī defends the function of Iblīs in the cosmic harmony and shows that evil is a necessary concomitant of the world's creation; but never does he claim that Iblīs is equal to Adam, hell to paradise, or the ego to the intellect, since Mercy and Gentleness remain forever the precedent Attributes.

Unique among the creatures, man is able to choose the path he is to follow in the unfolding of the primordial possibilities embraced by the Hidden Treasure. Rūmī's appeals to everyday experience provide some of the most convincing arguments in Islamic literature for man's free will and responsibility. Moreover, the overall thrust of his works—to encourage his fellow humans to enter the spiritual path—would be meaningless without human freedom. "Man is mounted upon the steed of 'We have honored Adam's children' (Quran XVII, 70): the reins of free will are in the hands of his discernment" (M III 3300).

Rūmī's view of man's relationship to God, discussed or alluded to in innumerable passages in his works, provides a comprehensive doctrine of the nature of existence. A second dimension of his teachings has to do with the path man must follow to attain spiritual perfection and actualize the form upon which he was originally created; here Rūmī describes the attributes and the practices—such as prayer, fasting, and the remembrance of God—of the spiritual warrior, who "cuts the throat of sensuality" (D 36120) and "rides his stallion joyfully into a sea of blood" (D 18700). Then a third major dimension of Rūmī's works describes in a vast range of imagery and symbolism the various degrees of spiritual development leading to the station where man may rightfully say with al-Ḥallāj, "I am the Real."

The One Beloved

While affirming that Love cannot be defined, Rūmī describes its qualities and attributes in a thousand images and anecdotes. In summarizing his words, one might say that Love is a divine power that brings the universe into existence, motivates the activity of every creature, and wells up in the human heart to establish unity in the midst of multiplicity. Ultimately, Love is God as Creator, Sustainer, and Goal of the universe; it is the One Reality that reveals itself in infinite forms.

Intimately connected with Love is beauty or loveliness, that which is lovable. Probably no Sufi order emphasizes beauty in theory and in practice as much as the Mawlawiyyah. Certainly Sufis in general are the first to recall the Prophet's saying, "God is beautiful, and He loves beauty," but the Mawlawīs have been especially thorough in drawing all the consequences of this teaching for the spiritual life. In the context of Rūmī's teachings, "God is beautiful" means that "There is none beautiful but God"; true (*ḥaqīqī*) beauty belongs to Him alone, while the beauty of all other things is "derivative" or "metaphorical" (*majāzī*).

> Love for God has struck fire in the spirit's bush, burning away all derivative realities. (D 36080)

Everything lovable derives its reality from the divine Beloved, the only reality that truly is; this is perhaps the central theme of Bahā' Walad's *Ma'ārif.* A typical passage speaks of God's Beauty as follows:

> "Glory be to God!" means this: O God, how pure and holy Thou art! For every contour of the houris and the black-eyed beauties, the loveliness of all kinds of animals, the freshness and sparkle of all flowers, herbs, sweet waters, and blowing winds, all joys, all hopes, are spots on the face of Thy unique Beauty, dust and debris in Thy lane.[10]

Rūmī repeats his father's message in numerous verses, though his insistence that we derive the consequences for our spiritual lives is clearer and more compelling. The Way of Love is to discern the True Beloved from the false, to cut away everything illusory and evanescent with the sword of the *shahādah*—"no god but God"—and to turn totally toward the One Beloved.

> Listen! Open a window toward Joseph, then behold a delightful spectacle!
> "To love God" is to open that window, for the Friend's Beauty brightens the breast.
> Always look toward the face of the Beloved! This is in your own hands—listen to me, my friend!
> Open the way into the depths of your own self! Banish any perception that thinks of "others"! (M VI 3095–98)

The lover discerns that there is only a single Beloved; "others" are veils over the Real.

> Love is that flame which, when it blazes up, burns away everything except the Beloved.

> It drives home the sword of "no god" to slay "other than God". . . . (M V 588–589).

The mistake of worldly people is not their love for things of this world but their inability to perceive that all things of this world are but shadows of the true Beloved.

> The bird is flying on high, while its shadow runs across the ground, flying like a bird.
> The fool hunts that shadow, running until he becomes exhausted,
> Not knowing that it is the reflection of the bird in the sky, unaware of the shadow's source. (M I 417–19)

Imperfect loves, loves for "other than God," will eventually disappoint the lover, since only God is real. Felicity lies in discerning this truth in the present life and attaching ourselves to the One Beloved here and now. But we will not find the Beloved in the world around us. This is the message of many anecdotes in the *Mathnawī,* such as the famous story of the Sufi who sat in a beautiful garden meditating, only to have a busybody interrupt and tell him to gaze upon the marks of God's Mercy in the garden.

> The Sufi answered, "Mercy's marks are in the heart, O self-seeker! On the outside are only the marks of the marks." (M IV 1362)

Similarly, Rūmī begins a ghazal as follows:

> Without thinking I mentioned the name of roses and gardens—that Rose-Faced Beauty came and slapped me on the mouth!
> "I am the Sultan, I am the Spirit of all rosegardens. In the face of a Presence like Me, do you think of so-and-so?
> You are My tambourine—do not let yourself be beaten by just anyone! You are My flute—beware, do not play just anyone's tune!" (D 21748-50)

Heartache and Joy

For the spiritual traveler, the goal is to reestablish the human connection with the Gentleness, Love, and Mercy that brought man into existence. Since "this world is the house of God's Severity" (M VI 1890), he must cling to the Gentleness that pertains to the other world. In cosmological terms, the contrast between the lower and the upper worlds, or material and spiritual existence, is expressed in such pairings as body and spirit, form and meaning, outward and inward, dust and air, foam and ocean; in general, all these pairs correspond to Severity and Gentleness ("in general," since Rūmī sometimes takes other relationships into account).

The cosmological relationship between Gentleness and Severity manifests itself spiritually and psychologically in the contrast between "union" (*wiṣāl*) and "separation" (*firāq*). Nearness to God and union with Him result from Mercy and Gentleness, whereas distance and separation from Him are the consequence of Wrath. Spiritual perfection involves a harmony between these two Attributes, always with Mercy taking precedence. Initially man is caught in the "House of Severity" and seeks Gentleness:

> His Mercy is prior to His Wrath. If you want spiritual priority, go, seek the prior Attribute. (M IV 3205)

But finally, when the traveler reaches the station of sanctity, he combines the two Attributes in a harmonious balance, since he has actualized the theomorphic form upon which he was created. Thus Rūmī speaks of the perfect guide on the path, the shaykh:

> At one moment the wave of his Gentleness becomes your wing, at the next his Severity's fire carries you forward. (M IV 545)

In the process of attaining to spiritual perfection, the lover will traverse a path that carries him through alternating experiences of separation and union, or "contraction" (*qabḍ*) and "expansion" (*basṭ*). Rūmī's ghazals speak of various degrees of these experiences in a great variety of images, the most common being those of "derivative love" (the beautiful face, the tresses, the kiss), wine drinking (the cup, intoxication, sobriety), and the garden (flowers, spring, autumn).[11] The imagery is not chosen arbitrarily; rather, it grows up as it were "naturally" because of the possibilities and limitations of human language within the context of Islamic civilization and, more specifically, because the experiences themselves assume a particular imaginal form within the given context. Rūmī discusses the nature of "imagination" (*khayāl*) in great detail; here a single quotation must suffice:

> First there were intoxication, loverhood, youth, and the like; then came luxuriant spring, and they all sat together.
> They had no forms and then became manifested beautifully within forms—behold things of the imagination assuming form!
> The heart is the antechamber of the eye: For certain everything that reaches the heart will enter into the eye and become a form. (D 21574–76)

Much of Rūmī's poetry must be understood as an attempt to render spiritual and "imaginal" perceptions intelligible to those who have not perceived them. His father before him had devoted a good portion of the *Ma'ārif* to the same task. For example, we read there as follows:

> In my every part streams of light flow like molten gold. . . . All my thoughts and tastes come into existence from God and all have turned their faces toward Him. He is like a handsome king sitting in the midst of young brides: one nibbles on his back, another bites his shoulder, and still another presses

herself against him. Or [my thoughts are] like children who surround their young father like pearls and play with him; or they are like pigeons and sparrows circling the person who feeds them and landing upon him wherever they can. Just as all existents, like motes, turn round about God's Beauty, so my ideas and thoughts turn round about God.[12]

Rūmī's message is that all joy and all delight are found in God, and that God is to be found at this moment in the heart. The following ghazal, employing typical imagery, is perhaps more explicit than most:

Have you heard about the Emperor's edict? All the beauties are to come out from their veils.
His words were these: "This year I want sugar *very* cheap."
Wonderful year! Splendid, blessed day! Wonderful Emperor! Splendid, laughing fortune!
It is now forbidden to sit in the house, for the Emperor is strolling toward the square.
Come with us to the square and see a joyful banquet, manifest and hidden.
Tables have been set, abundant blessings spread out: halva and roasted fowl.
Serving boys stand like moons before the saki; minstrels play tunes sweeter than life.
But love for the King has delivered the spirits of the drunkards from saki and table.
You say, "Where could this be?" I answer: "Right there, at the very point where the thought of 'Where' arose." (D 1903)

But it is not easy to turn in upon oneself and establish contact with the innermost core of one's being. To do so, one must follow the discipline laid down by the prophets and saints. The Mawlawī path is grounded firmly in the *Sharī'ah* and the *sunnah,* centering upon the remembrance (*dhikr*) of the Beloved through various outward and inward supports, ranging from prayer and fasting to music and dance. Discipline is central, for without the practice of religion one will never be able to leave the confines and limitations of one's own individuality and enter into the Divine Presence: "Since you are not a prophet, enter the Way!" (M II 3453).

Our distance from God stems from our own self-existence, our mistaken impression that we are somehow independent of our Source. The ego veils us from perceiving the spirit and what lies beyond; like Iblīs, we see only the outward side of things. We must actualize the inward angelic light known as the Intellect, which by its very nature is a "finder of God" (M III 3195). Then the ego, which is one in origin with Satan (M III 3197, 4053), can be overcome. At the same time, we need to avoid the calculating attitude of the "partial intellect" (*'aql-i juz'ī*), which is still veiled by the ego's clouds, and abandon ourselves to infinite Love. At the final stages of the Path, "everything other than God"—even the Universal Intellect itself, since it too is a created reality—must be left behind.

Escape from the Ego

In the context of Rūmī's spiritual psychology, the life of the ego is the death of the spirit; union with the lower world is separation from God. Pain and heartache derive from our illusory selfhood and our distance from Self. To pass beyond Wrath and reach the Mercy which is the source of all, we must escape from the ego and dwell in the heart. Pain and suffering, then, are the necessary concomitants of the life of the ego. They cannot be overcome on this level of existence, but must be transformed inwardly into the joy that lies at the center of the heart. In fact, true pain can be known only by the prophets and saints, since they alone are given a vision of things as they are in themselves. As Rūmī often remarks, until a bird has drunk fresh water, it will never realize that it lives on brine; until the traveler tastes union, he will never understand that he dwells in the infinite heartache of separation. "Whoever is more awake has greater pain" (M I 629). Hence also, the greatest misfortune a human being can suffer occurs when he does not feel the pain of separation:

> He that is without pain is a brigand, for to be without pain is to say "I am God." (M II 2521)

As long as we have no pain, we will not strive for ease; as long as we have no love, we will not seek the Beloved.

> Where there is pain, cures will come; where there is poverty, wealth will follow. . . .
> Spend less time seeking water and acquire thirst! Then water will gush forth from above and below. (M III 3210, 12)

To acquire thirst and pain, we must realize our own imperfection and inadequacy—or, rather, our utter nothingness before the One Reality. Rūmī's central teaching, like that of other Sufis, comes down to this: "Remove self from the midst, so that you may grasp Self in your embrace!" (D 12280). Our selfhood is empty and illusory, yet we remain bound to it. Once it has been nullified and annihilated through the discipline of the Path and the fire of love and desire, nothing remains but God. As Rūmī expresses it, employing the words of the *shahādah:*

> After "no god," what else remains?
> There remains "but God," the rest has gone. Bravo, great, idol-burning Love!
> (M V 589–90)

Selfhood, then, is separation; selflessness is union and human perfection. A typical ghazal calls the seeker to this realization:

Revelers, beg the minstrel for wine! Come to pleasure, ask for the song of the reed!
Become royal riders on the steed of delights, fortunate men! Pass beyond heartache's horse with galloping revelry!
O you who sit with self, annihilate intellect, awareness, and foresight with pure wine from the Vat of Oneness!
Behold a new spring with gardens and meadows of a hundred colors—abandon the cold, dryness, and adversity of December!
When you see decapitated corpses row upon row, you will be apostates, O lovers, if you weep and wail!
You must seek the Chinese Idol in China—what kind of intellect tells you to go to Rayy?
At the Ruins of Subsistence in the *samā'* of the spirit's ear, abandon this childlike repetition of the alphabet!
Fill your skull's cup with the unmixed eternal wine—for God's sake, roll up the carpet of intellect and circumspection!
O lovers, come out of the attributes of selfhood—obliterate yourselves in the vision of the Living God's Beauty!
Along with Shams al-Dīn, the lord of kings, king of Tabrīz, sacrifice your spirit! For his sake, dedicate yourself to God! (D 747)

God's Mercy

Rūmī and those of his followers who have been faithful to his teachings tell us that God's Love, Mercy, and Gentleness pervade the cosmos and determine our destinies. The universe is fundamentally good and beautiful, though our own self-centeredness may prevent us from seeing this. God's Mercy hides behind the veil of every manifestation of Wrath, pulling us toward our ultimate felicity. But it remains for us to open ourselves to the "precedent Attribute," lest we remain forever veiled. Our task as humans is to return to the Mercy from which we arose and thus to integrate all multiplicity into Oneness and to see all phenomena as veils upon the Beloved's Face. Speaking for the saints who are mankind's guides on this path, Rūmī sings:

Accustom yourself to us, not to the unaware! Don't be a donkey—why do you sniff at the tail of every she-ass?
Your beginning and end are eternal Love—don't be a whore, taking a different husband every night.
Set your heart upon that Desire from which it can never be detached. Lion-man, don't make your heart the dog of every lane!
When in pain, you seek a remedy—turn your eyes and heart toward the Remedy, not to this and that.

Run not like a camel toward every thornbush—abandon not the garden, spring, meadow, and stream.

Pay attention! The Emperor has set out a kingly banquet. For God's sake, don't continue to starve in this dustbin!

Our polo-playing Prince has come onto the field—make your heart and spirit a ball before His horses!

Wash your face clean—don't blame the mirror! Refine your gold—don't blame the scales!

Part your lips only toward Him who gave you lips, run only toward Him who gave you feet! Know that the faces and hair of these beauties are false—don't call them "moon-faced, silken locked"!

Cheeks, eyes, and lips were loaned to a clod of earth—don't be so eager to look lovingly on the eyeless.

Love's beauty called out, "The *samā'* will last forever"—shout and dance only in pursuit of that beauty!

Breathe no more words, poet, or breathe them silently beneath your lips. Speech is a veil—make it a single veil, not a hundred! (D 1992)

Notes

1. Citations are from *Walad-nāmah,* ed. J. Humā'ī (Tehran: Iqbāl, 1316/1937).
2. Citations are from *Maqālāt-i Shams-i Tabrīzī,* ed. M. 'A. Muwaḥḥid (Tehran: Dānishgāh-i Ṣan'atī-yi Āryāmihr, 2036/1977).
3. A. Schimmel, *The Triumphal Sun* (London: Fine Books, 1978) 367ff.
4. Ibid., 37ff.
5. H. Corbin, *Creative Imagination in the Ṣūfism of Ibn 'Arabī* (Princeton: Princeton University Press, 1969) 70.
6. Ibid., 71.
7. Schimmel, *Triumphal Sun,* 225.
8. See W. Chittick, *The Sufi Path of Love: The Spiritual Teachings of Rumi* (Albany, NY: State University of New York Press, 1983).
9. Rūmī, *Fīhi mā fīhi,* ed. B. Furūzānfar (Tehran: Amīr Kabīr, 1348/1969) 78; see also Chittick, *Sufi Path,* 86.
10. *Ma'ārif,* ed. B. Furūzānfar (Tehran: Chāpkhāna-yi Majlis, 1333/1954) I, 111–12.
11. See Chittick, *Sufi Path,* Part III; cf. Schimmel, *Triumphal Sun,* Part II; and "Sun Triumphal—Love Triumphant: Maulana Rumi and the Metaphors of Love," in her *As Through a Veil: Mystical Poetry in Islam* (New York: Columbia University Press, 1982) 83–133.
12. *Ma'ārif,* 134–35.

6

The Chishtiyyah

SAYYID ATHAR ABBAS RIZVI

History

THE ORIGIN OF THE CHISHTIYYAH ORDER goes back to the third/ninth century. It originated in the town of Chisht, from which it received its name, some one hundred kilometers east of Harat in modern Afghanistan. The order, however, achieved fame only in India. Other branches, which spread to Transoxiana and Khurasan did not survive long. The Chishtiyyah trace their lineage back to Ḥasan al-Baṣrī (21/642–110/728). They believe that Ḥasan was ʿAlī ibn Abī Ṭālib's disciple, a doctrine which they defend spiritedly. Of the later Sufis, the Chishtiyyah give a prominent place to Abū Saʿīd ibn Abiʾl-Khayr (357/967–440/1049). He was born and died at Mayhana (the present Meʾana near Sarakhs) but lived for a long time in Nayshapur. The hard ascetic exercises practiced by some Chishtīs, such as hanging head downward into a well continuously for forty nights, are a legacy from this shaykh. His teachings also inspired the Chishtīs to devote themselves unquestioningly to their *pīrs* (spiritual guides), to prostrate themselves before their *pīrs* and to practice self-abasement and service to mankind.

The founder of the Chishtiyyah Order in India was Khwājah Muʿīn al-Dīn Ḥasan. No information is available regarding his early life. On the basis of his death, which occurred on 6 Rajab 633/16 March 1236, when he was reputed to be ninety-seven years old, it is presumed that he was born in 536/1141–42 in Sijistan (Sistan). He was fifteen years old when his father died. The Khwājah inherited a garden and a water mill, but he left his property to adopt a life of study and travel. At Harwan, a suburb of Nayshapur, he became the disciple of the greatest contemporary Chishtiyyah *pīr*, Khwājah ʿUthmān Harwanī. For about twenty years, he accompanied his *pīr* to various places and later traveled independently. In Baghdad he visited the Qādiriyyah Sufi, Shaykh ʿAbd al-Qādir Jīlānī and other eminent Sufis. Leaving there, he traveled through Iraq and Iran and arrived in the Ghazni region at the age of fifty-two. There his Chishtiyyah *pīr,* Khwājah ʻUthmān, met Khwājah Muʻīn al-Dīn again and encouraged him to leave for India. Sufism was already firmly established there in the Punjab and Sind.

Leaving Ghazni for India, Khwājah Muʻīn al-Dīn went to Lahore and then to Delhi. Later he moved to Ajmer, which was annexed to the Delhi sultanate in 592/1195–96 and had a Muslim governor. The Khwājah settled in Ajmer fort. His simple and ascetic life was an inspiration to both the Turkic warriors and the Hindu converts to Islam. In ca. 606/1209–10 the Khwājah married the daughter of a brother of the local governor. He also took a second wife, the daughter of a local Hindu chieftain who had been taken as a prisoner of war.

Medieval and modern scholars recount fantastic miracles supposedly performed by the Khwājah at Ajmer. Modern scholars also assert that he eradicated the Hindu practice of untouchability and converted a large number of Hindus to Islam. The Khwājah's known character and sayings however, do not corroborate any of the legends about him. The rules of spiritual life he carved out are as follows: (1) One should not earn money. (2) One should not borrow money from anyone. (3) One should not reveal to anyone nor seek help from anyone if one has eaten nothing, even for seven days. (4) If one gains plenty of food, money, grain, or clothing, one should not keep anything until the following day. (5) One should not curse anyone; if anyone is very hurt, one should pray to God to guide one's enemy toward the right path. (6) If one performs a virtuous deed, one should consider that the source of the virtue is either the kindness of one's *pīr,* the intercession of the Prophet Muḥammad on one's behalf, or the Divine Mercy. (7) If one performs an evil deed, one should consider one's evil self responsible for the action and try to protect oneself from such deeds. Fearing God, one should be careful to avoid actions which may involve oneself in evil. (8) Having fulfilled all the above conditions, one should regularly fast during the day and spend the night in prayer. (9) One should remain quiet and speak only when it is imperative to do so. The *Sharīʻah* makes it unlawful both to talk incessantly and keep totally silent. One should utter only such words as those which please God.[1] The Khwājah's teachings became the cornerstone of the superstructure of Chishtiyyah life, although adjustments and modifications were made from time to time.

In close contact with Khwājah Muʻīn al-Dīn during his lifetime was his young disciple, Shaykh Ḥamīd al-Dīn Ṣūfī (d. 673/1274), who made the rural surroundings of Nagawr in Rajasthan the center of his activity. Another of Khwājah Muʻīn al-Dīn's disciples, Khwājah Quṭb al-Dīn Bakhtiyār Kākī, settled in Delhi, which Sultan Shams al-Dīn Iltutmish

(607/1211–633/1236) had made his capital. Quṭb al-Dīn had chosen in Baghdad to become Khwājah Mu'īn al-Dīn Chishtī's disciple, although Shaykh 'Abd al-Qādir Jīlānī as well as the eminent founders of the Suhrawardiyyah and Kubrawiyyah orders also lived there. After leaving Baghdad, Quṭb al-Dīn spent a long time traveling and arrived in Delhi only ca. 618/1221. There he became immensely popular. The *'ulamā'* failed to make Sultan Iltutmish stop Khwājah Quṭb al-Dīn's assemblies of *samā'* (Sufi music and dance, literally, audition).

On 14 Rabī' I 633/27 November 1235, he died in a state of ecstasy aroused by the following verse in the *samā'*:

> The martyrs of the dagger of *taslīm* ("surrender")
> Each moment get a new life from the Unseen World.

Khwājah Quṭb al-Dīn's successor, Shaykh Farīd al-Dīn Mas'ūd "Ganj-i Shakar" (popularly known as Bābā Farīd) was born at Kahtwal, near Multan in 571/1175–76. He received his education at a local seminary, but it was his mother's pious life that influenced his future the most. After obtaining initiation from Khwājah Quṭb al-Dīn, he practiced hard ascetic exercises. He spent forty nights in prayer while he hung, head downward in a well, with his legs tied to logs at the top. This exercise, said to have been invented by Shaykh Abū Sa'īd ibn Abi'l Khayr, was known as *chilla-yi ma'kūs* ("inverted forty-day retreat"). For a long time he lived in Hansi in the Hisar district west of Delhi but finally he settled down in Ajodhan (Pak Pattan), where he died on 5 Muḥarram 664/17 October 1265. Bābā Farīd was in touch with a wide cross-section of society; even the Nath Yogis called on him and uninhibited discussion on Ultimate Reality took place. He wrote poetry in Arabic, Persian, and the local Punjabi dialect. His spiritual sensitivity is reflected in the following verses which he frequently repeated:

> I pray to live only for the sake of loving Thee,
> I wish to become dust and dwell eternally under Thy feet.
> My principal expectation from both worlds is that
> I should die and live for Thee.[2]

Bābā Farīd's successor, Shaykh Niẓām al-Dīn Awliyā', who lived in Delhi until his death on 18 Rabī' II 725/3 April 1325, crystallized the Chishtī traditions in northern India. The order was also introduced into the Deccan during his lifetime. The shaykh possessed a deep understanding of human nature from his experience in dealing with all types of people. His visitors were generally more than satisfied with his advice. His inspired knowledge, known in mystic language as *'ilm-i ladunnī*, greatly helped those who sought his help. Even the *'ulamā'*, many of whom were notorious for their enmity toward Sufis, were overwhelmed by his conversation. The shaykh was a master of the Sufi method of teaching by anecdotes.

Shaykh Niẓām al-Dīn's favorite disciple was Amīr Khusraw. He was born in 651/1253 at Patyali, about 250 kilometers east of Delhi. He belonged to a distinguished family of administrators and warriors but was passionately fond of writing poetry. He had commenced composing verses at the age of eight. Amīr Khusraw wrote historical *mathnawīs* and produced an enormous corpus of *ghazals.* He was also the composer of a number of musical modes and melodies and a master musician. Moreover, he wrote verses combining Hindi dialects with Persian. The death of his *pīr* shocked him so deeply that he only survived him by six months.

Shaykh Niẓām al-Dīn Awliyā's spiritual successor was Shaykh Naṣīr al-Dīn of Awadh, who became known as the Chirāgh or "Lamp" of Delhi. Sultan Muḥammad ibn Tughluq (725/1325–752/1351) tried to compel him and other distinguished disciples of Shaykh Niẓām al-Dīn to help streamline the administration and arouse popular interest in his grandiose schemes. They refused to obey him and suffered great hardship. Most of them were forced to move from Delhi to Devagiri (Dawlatabad), which the Sultan had made his second capital. The shaykh died on 18 Ramaḍān 757/14 September 1356.

At the time of Shaykh Naṣīr al-Dīn's death, the disciples of Bābā Farīd and Shaykh Niẓām al-Dīn Awliyā' had established many new Chishtiyyah centers. Of these, the most important was the Ṣābiriyyah branch, founded by Bābā Farīd's disciple, 'Alā' al-Dīn 'Alī ibn Aḥmad Ṣābir (d. 691/1291), at Kaliyar in Saharanpur east of Delhi. His successors established branches in Lanipat, Rudawli (east of Lucknow) and Gangoh (Saharanpur). Aḥmad 'Abd al-Ḥaqq (d. 839/1434), who lived at Rudawli, was well known. He promoted Bābā Farīd's custom of writing poetry in the local dialect. This was perfected by Shaykh 'Abd al-Quddūs Gangōhī (d. 944/1537), a distinguished Sufi of this order. Shaykh 'Abd al-Quddūs's *Rushd-nāmah* (*The Treatise on Right Conduct*) contains some Hindi verses written by his predecessors as well as a large number of his own compositions. They highlight the similarities between the Chishtiyyah Sufi and Nath Yogi teachings. The most notable among the successors to Shaykh 'Abd al-Quddūs Gangōhī's order was Shaykh Muḥibb Allāh Ṣadrpūrī of Allahabad (d. 1058/1648). Shaykh Muḥibb Allāh was decidedly the most learned Chishtī interpreter of Ibn 'Arabī's *waḥdat al-wujūd.*

Shaykh Niẓām al-Dīn's disciples founded Chishtiyyah centers in Jawnpur, Malwa, Gujarat, and the Deccan. Shaykh Sirāj al-Dīn (d. 759/1357) made

Gawr in Bengal the center of his activity. Nūr Quṭb-i ʻĀlam (d. 813/1410) of Pandwa was the most distinguished Sufi of this branch. In Dawlatabad, the Chishtiyyah center was established by Shaykh Niẓām al-Dīn's disciple, Shaykh Burhān al-Dīn Gharīb (d. 741/1340). The local ruler of the Khandesh dynasty was so impressed by the shaykh that he named Burhanpur after him.

The most famous Sufi in the Deccan, however, was Shaykh Naṣīr al-Dīn Chirāgh Dihlawī's *khalīfah* ("successor"), Sayyid Muḥammad ibn Yūsuf al-Ḥusaynī, popularly known as Khwājah Bandah Nawāz or Gīsū Darāz (d. 825/1422). After Tamerlane's massacre in Delhi in 801/1398, Gīsū Darāz left the area and moved to Gujarat; from there he went to the Deccan. Around 815/1412–13, he arrived in Gulbarga at the advanced age of ninety. He survived for only ten years more but firmly established the Chishtiyyah center there. He was a prolific author and a poet. Toward the end of his life, he abandoned the ideas of Ibn ʻArabī and became an exponent of the beliefs of Shaykh ʻAlāʼ al-Dawlah Simnānī.

Among Shaykh Niẓām al-Dīn Awliyā's disciples, Mawlānā Shihāb al-Dīn acted as his *imam* (prayer-leader). Shaykh Shihāb al-Dīn's first disciple, Shaykh Rukn al-Dīn, was not well known, but his disciple, Maʻsūd Bakk (d. 836/1432) was a profound scholar. He had no inhibitions in expressing ideas based on *waḥdat al-wujūd* in his works. His *Dīwān*, called *Nūr al-yaqīn* (*Light of Certainty*), and the prose work entitled *Mirʼāt al-ʻārifin* (*Mirror of Gnostics*) are very important contributions to Sufi literature.

Masʻūd Bakk's contemporary, Sayyid Muḥammad Ḥusaynī ibn Jaʻfar al-Makkī, renounced his position in state service to become a Sufi and traveled throughout Arabia, Persia, and Iraq. A collection of his letters, some dated 824/1421 and 825/1422, embody his keen observations on both spiritual and worldly life. He believed that gaining mastery of *fiqh* had kept him as far away from the true faith as a dog from a mosque.[3]

Toward the beginning of twelfth/eighteenth century, the Niẓāmiyyah branch of the Chishtiyyah in Delhi was reinvigorated by the leadership of Shāh Kalīm Allāh Jahānābādī (d. 1142/1729). Mawlānā Fakhr al-Dīn, the son of Shāh Kalīm Allāh's disciple Shāh Niẓām al-Dīn, directed the Niẓāmiyyah-Chishtiyyah center in Delhi from 1165/1751–52 till his death in 1199/1785. He tried to infuse a balanced spiritual life into Delhi, which was now torn by Sunni–Shīʻite controversies. His disciples established new centers in the Punjab, Bareilly, and Rajasthan.

At present all the Chishtiyyah centers in the Indian subcontinent are actively engaged in disseminating the Chishtiyyah way of life and spiritual discipline.

Chishtī Literature

There is a mass of Chishtī literature, most of which is in Persian. Chishtī Sufis also wrote in local dialects, particularly in their poetry, but some treatises were composed in Arabic. Below we mention some important works in different categories of Chishtī literature.

Malfūẓāt (Conversations)

The early Chishtiyyah before Shaykh Naṣīr al-Dīn Chirāgh-i Dihlī did not write any books, or so the shaykh asserts.[4] Nevertheless, apocryphal Sufi *malfūẓāt* began to appear from Shaykh Niẓām al-Dīn Awliyā's time on. These were designed to serve the popular demand for Chishtiyyah anecdotes. The anonymous authors of these apocryphal books were neither conversant with historical facts nor with the spiritual environment of the great Sufis whose conversations they ventured to fabricate. Their works tend to give the impression that the Chishtiyyah were endowed with incredible miraculous powers, that they had crushed Hindu spiritual power and had made Islam triumphant throughout India.

In Shawwāl 708/March 1309, Shaykh Niẓām al-Dīn Awliyā' admitted to his disciple, Amīr Ḥasan Sijzī, that he had tried to write down Bābā Farīd's discourses but had been unable to record a single word. Amīr Ḥasan then produced a draft he had prepared of the shaykh's lectures over thirteen months. After reading the draft, the shaykh approved it and filled in a few gaps. The first authentic account of Shaykh Niẓām al-Dīn Awliyā''s discourses, from 3 Sha'bān 707/28 January 1308 to 19 Sha'bān 722/2 September 1322, was thus written by Amīr Ḥasan Sijzī. It was given the title *Fawā'id al-fu'ād* (*Benefits of the Heart*). These are not daily or even weekly accounts. Amīr Ḥasan's official duties kept him outside Delhi, but, during his stay in the capital, he attended the shaykh's assembly at least once a week. The most closely covered period is the year 708–9/1308–9.

Usually the lectures answered questions put by those gathered around the shaykh. They dealt with a variety of subjects, religious, social, political, and economic. The shaykh's answers, which took the form of a sermon, included references to the Quran, *Ḥadīth,* anecdotes, and the sayings of earlier Sufis, and they were intended to satisfy the spiritual and ethical needs and emotions of the audience. They were not necessarily derived from authentic sources. These discourses never included an analysis of opposing views and were believed to be infallible.

Like the *Fawā'id al-fu'ād,* the discourses of Shaykh Naṣīr al-Dīn Chirāgh-i

Dihlī, as recorded by his disciple Ḥamīd Qalandar in the *Khayr al-majālis* (*The Best of Gatherings*), are not dated. Nevertheless, they are more voluminous. Earlier, a section of *malfūẓāt* written by the shaykh's nephew had so disappointed the shaykh that he had rejected the draft. Although he had sufficient confidence in Ḥamīd, the shaykh regularly supervised the work himself. The *Khayr al-majālis* gives a lively account of Shaykh Naṣīr al-Dīn's spiritual life against a background of political, social, and economic change. These two *malfūẓāt* works set the mold for other scholars who recorded the conversations of their *pīrs*.

Biographical Literature

The earliest known biography of an Indian Chishtī is the *Siyar al-awliyā'* (*Biographies of the Saints*) by Sayyid Muḥammad ibn Mubārak 'Alawī Kirmānī (d. 770/1368–69), known as Mīr Khwurd. The Kirmānī family was deeply devoted to Bābā Farīd and Shaykh Niẓām al-Dīn Awliyā'. They served the shaykh from his youth till his death. Mīr Khwurd himself flourished during the shaykh's last days and after his death lived in the company of the shaykh's disciples. Around 727/1327, he was forced to move from Delhi to Dawlatabad with the other *'ulamā'* and Sufis of Delhi. A few years later, when he returned to Delhi, he was filled with nostalgic memories of the spiritual environment of Shaykh Niẓām al-Dīn Awliyā''s days. He therefore wrote the *Siyar al-awliyā'* as a monograph on Shaykh Niẓām al-Dīn Awliyā', his teachings, and his disciples. The biographical notes on the Sufi *pīrs* preceding the shaykh, are given only as an introduction. The work draws heavily on the *Fawā'id al-fu'ād*, the *Khayr al-majālis*, and other sources no longer available. It is loaded with a large number of verses, some of which are hardly essential, and the style is verbose.

Ḥamīd ibn Faḍl Allāh, known as Jamālī (d. 942/1536), was a Suhrawardī Sufi and poet. He had traveled the Islamic world widely and collected the traditions of the Indian Sufis prevalent in various regions. His *Siyar al-'ārifīn* (*Biographies of Gnostics*) includes anecdotes of the Chishtī Sufis in Persia and Iraq, which, although common knowledge in his days, are not necessarily correct.

From the tenth/sixteenth century on, the apocryphal Sufi *malfūẓāt* of earlier Sufis were frequently used by authors who were interested mainly in the stories of miracles and freely gave vent to their own imagination in elaborating them. The *Jawāhir-i farīdī* (*The Jewels of Farīd*) by 'Alī Aṣghar ibn Shaykh Mawdūd completed in 1033/1623, and the *Siyar al-aqṭāb* (*Biographies of Poles*) by Ilāhdiyah, begun in 1036/1626–27 and completed in 1056/1646–47, describe incredible Chishtiyyah miracles.

Some of the eleventh/seventeenth and twelfth/eighteenth century biographical works deal with contemporary saints such as the *Chishtiyya-yi bihishtiyyah* (*Heavenly Chishtīs*) of 'Alā' al-Dīn Muḥammad Chishtī Barnāwī (eleventh/seventeenth century). This contains an account of Barnawa Sufis, while *Manāqib-i fakhriyyah* (*Virtues of Fakhr al-Dīn*) by 'Imād al-Mulk Ghāzī al-Dīn Khān Fīrūz Jang (d. 1215/1800) comprises a biography of Mawlānā Fakhr al-Dīn. Another biography, the *Manāqib-i sulaymānī* (*The Virtues of Sulayman*) by Ghulām Muḥammad Khān Jhajjarī, written in 1255/1839–40, gives an account of Khwājah Muḥammad Sulaymān Chishtī of Tawnsa (d. 1267/1850). Equally interesting is the *Manāqib al-maḥbūbayn* (*Virtues of the Two Beloveds*) by Najm al-Dīn Nāgawrī, which contains the history of some twelfth/eighteenth-century Chishtīs.

Some general biographical works such as the *Akhbār al-akhyār* (*Annals of Pious Men*) by Shaykh 'Abd al-Ḥaqq Muḥaddith Dihlawī (d. 1052/1642–43), the *Gulzār-i abrār* (*The Garden of the Godly*) by Muḥammad Ghawthī Shaṭṭārī and the *Mir'āt al-asrār* (*Mirror of Secrets*) by 'Abd al-Raḥmān Chishtī (d. 1094/1683), provide reliable records. The *Ma'ārij al-wālāyah* (*Ascensions of Sanctity*) by 'Abd Allāh Khweshgī Qaṣūrī is an early twelfth/eighteenth-century work, but it deserves special mention because it contains reproductions of a number of important treatises which no longer survive.

Maktūbāt (Letters)

Letters from Chishtīs, particularly those of Sayyid Nūr Quṭb-i 'Ālam, Shaykh 'Abd al-Quddūs Gangōhī, and Shāh Kalīm Allāh Jahānābādī, give interesting glimpses of their spiritual beliefs and environment.

Hindi Poetry

Chishtī poems in Persian also reveal the spiritual life of the order. More important, however, are the Chishtī poetical works in Hindi. The Hindi verses of Shaykh Ḥamīd al-Dīn are quoted in his *malfūẓāt*, entitled *Surūr al-ṣudūr*, (*Joy of Breasts*), which was compiled by his grandson. In 772/1370–71, Mullā Dāwūd, who came from Dalmau in Rae Bareli district near Lucknow, commenced his famous *mathnawī*, *Chandā'in*, in Hindi and completed it in 781/1379–80. He was a successor to Shaykh Zayn al-Dīn, who, in turn, was the son of the sister of Shaykh Naṣīr al-Dīn Chirāgh-i Dihlī. His story is based on a local folktale, but the spiritual significance of the romance in the *Chandā'in* is very deep. It highlights the constant Sufi effort to be united with the Divine in a symbolic form. In 990/1583 Quṭbān, a Sufi who lived in Jawnpur, wrote a Hindi *mathnawī*, *Mrigāwatī*. The story revolves around an Elysian beauty called Mrigāwatī. In this *mathnawī,* Quṭbān describes the Essence as Light and calls it Niranjan "Eternal Soul." Defining Muḥammad as the cause of creation, the poet compares Islamic cosmological concepts with those of the Hindus.

A high standard of perfection in Hindi *mathnawī* was attained by Malik Muḥammad Jā'isī (of Ja'is in Rae Bareli near Lucknow), who in 947/ 1540–41, wrote the *Padmāvatī*. Reconciling Yogic concepts with Sufi ideas, the *Padmāvatī* set a model for the Hindi *mathnawīs* written by later Sufis. Jā'isī himself wrote more than a half dozen Hindi *mathnawīs* of deep symbolic significance. Non-Chishtīs also frequently drew on the verses of Jā'isī, and other Sufi poets who wrote in Hindi, to defend their spiritual concepts and doctrines.

Chishtiyyah Spiritual Life

The Chishtīs mingled freely with the common people and did not build *khānqāhs* with four walls and gateways. Instead they constructed simple halls with mud walls covered by thatched roofs for their disciples. These were called *jamā'at-khānah* and were the principal center of their spiritual and social life. The halls had no furniture except torn mats and blankets. A string bed was supplied only to distinguished mystics and *'ulamā'*. A separate cell for the Sufi leader's or shaykh's meditation was attached. The shaykh's family lived in a simple house containing one or two rooms near the *jamā'at-khānah.* The shaykh and the members of the *jamā'at-khānah* lived on *futūḥ,* or unsolicited gifts. In the early years of Bābā Farīd's stay at Ajodhan, a *zanbīl* (a basket made of palm leaves hung round the neck), was carried by some members of the *jamā'at-khānah* twice a day to the town and the offerings placed in it were shared by all. The Bābā preferred to eat the bread from the *zanbīl* in order to be more fully integrated into the life of his *jamā'at-khānah.* He also refused to allow small amounts of money for household needs to be borrowed, although this was permitted by other Chishtī shaykhs, including his own teachers. Nothing received as *futūḥ* was kept by the Chishtīs for longer than a day. Any surplus was distributed to the poor. The Sufi emphasis is on trust in God. Each new day brought a new hope in God and concern for future needs was seen as opposed to this trust.[5]

Visits by Nath Yogis to the Bābā's *jamā'at-khānah* on three different dates are recorded in Shaykh Niẓām al-Dīn Awliyā''s conversations. Other anecdotes indicate that the Chishtī *jamā'at-khānah* was open to all kinds of visitors, and ideas on a very wide range of topics were exchanged.

Social Ethics

According to the Chishtīs, the first lesson of Sufism was not related to prayers or organized rituals, but began with the mastery of the maxim "Do as you would be done by." The Chishtī *pīrs* accepted that family responsibilities entailed involvement in worldly affairs and that few men were capable of becoming totally dedicated ascetics. But they opposed those who acquired more money than they needed. Although it might appear that supporting a family was a worldly occupation, certain material goods were essential. For instance, clothes were necessary to cover the body, but spare garments could not be kept. The indiscriminate distribution of goods, however, was also extravagant. Only charity to please God had spiritual merit.[6]

Khwājah Mu'īn al-Dīn took two wives at an advanced age in order to follow the Prophet Muḥammad's traditions of leading a family life, but Shaykh Niẓām al-Dīn favored celibacy. He believed that marriage was permissible for a Sufi, but that celibacy was preferable as it called for a degree of determination. Those totally involved in divine contemplation had no need to marry, since contemplation left no room for sexual desire, and the eyes, tongue, and limbs would be completely protected from sin. If a Sufi was unable to attain this absorption and obliterate the sex drive, then he should marry. The essence of mystic contemplation was found in the heart. Those who were completely absorbed in God were totally affected. If their heart was disturbed by other matters, a reaction would be felt throughout their whole being.[7]

The Chishtīs encouraged people to work in trade and commerce as a means of earning their living. They also approved of farming and practicing crafts. They insisted that these occupations be followed honestly although they should not interfere with spiritual exercises. The Chishtīs believed that working for the government provided an opportunity to serve mankind.[8] Bābā Farīd's favorite son was in the army and various distinguished disciples of Niẓām al-Dīn Awliyā', such as Amīr Khusraw and Amīr Ḥasan, held important positions under the contemporary ruler. The Chishtīs opposed government service, however, insofar as it made people authoritarian, reckless, greedy, and cruel. They also contended that government servants were dependent on worldly authorities, which was contrary to the Sufi practice of trust in God.

Chishtī Rituals

Disciples were generally initiated after they had attained a fair knowledge of the *Sharī'ah*. The *ṭarīqah*, or the Sufi path, required an advanced spiritual discipline. Like other Sufi orders, the Chishtīs also administered *tawbah* (repentance) before initiation, *dhikr-i khafiy* (mental recollection), *fikr* (reflection or meditation), *murāqabah* (mystical contemplation), and *chillah* (forty days of retreat). These, however, had a unique significance for the Chishtīs. For example, to them, *tawbah* meant a complete revolution in life. It combined the past, present, and future. The repentance of past sins did not mean simply feeling guilty but involved offering compensation to all who had been wronged. For example, if someone had taken ten *dirhams* (a coin) from another, the simple repetition of *tawbah* was not sufficient. It was essential to repay the amount and take steps to please the person who had been robbed. If someone abused another, it was necessary to go to the person concerned, apologize, and try to please him. A drunkard was required to distribute sherbet and water to complete his *tawbah*.[9] *Tawbah* for the present meant regret for past sins and *tawbah* for the future involved the determination to refrain from further wrongdoing.

Dhikr is the rhythmical repetition of God's Name in order to feel the Divine Presence throughout one's being. Generally one of the ninety-nine Names of God is invoked. Bābā Farīd had translated *Huwa* "He" into Hindi and invented a Hindi formula of *dhikr* in order to make his local disciples penetrate deeply into its significance.

The Chishtī *dhikr* was incomplete without recollection in the heart in the presence of one's *pīr* or spiritual guide. The practice amounted to a belief that the shaykh's spirit was divinely inspired both in its emanation and in its power.

According to the twelfth/eighteenth-century Chishtī Sufi Shāh Kalīm Allāh Jahānābādī, *dhikr* was an Attribute of God. When Sufis performed *dhikr*, they turned to the Divine Essence, for *dhikr* was the product of *ma'rifah*, or gnosis, and love. When they practiced *fikr*, they were involved in an examination of the self, time, and ecstasy. In short, according to Shāh Kalīm Allāh, *dhikr* was the most perfect, lofty, and pure of the two states and led to union with God.[10]

The Chishtiyyah developed carefully the technique of *pās-i anfās* (controlled breathing) on the pattern of the sitting postures of the Hindu Yogis and Siddhas (perfect sages). To Shaykh Naṣīr al-Dīn Chirāgh-i Dihlī, the essence of Sufi discipline was controlled breathing. This should be practiced during meditation. Each breath was related to the mystic state. When breathing was controlled, thoughts were not diffused nor was time ill-used. Initially, breath control was deliberate, but later it became automatic. A Sufi could count his breaths and the perfect Sufi was a *ṣāḥib-i anfās*, "the master of articulated breath." The Siddhas, who were faultless Yogis, also measured their breaths. One dervish claimed that he had learned concentration from watching a cat waiting in front of a mouse hole. The cat had such full control over its breathing that not a single whisker moved.[11]

The Chishtiyyah practiced *samāʿ* (see chapter 25 of this volume) to arouse spiritual ecstasy. This was a most controversial issue. The Chishtiyyah were, however, inspired by the following justification by Hujwīrī:

> In short, all foot-play (*pāy-bāzī*) is bad in law and reason, by whomsoever it is practised, and the best of mankind cannot possibly practise it; but when the heart throbs with exhilaration and rapture becomes intense and the agitation of ecstasy is manifested and conventional forms are gone, that agitation (*idṭirāb*) is neither dancing nor foot-play nor bodily indulgence, but a dissolution of the soul. Those who call it "dancing" are utterly wrong. It is a state that cannot be explained in words: "without experience no knowledge."[12]

The Spiritual Significance of the Chishtiyyah Order

The Chishtiyyah belong to the Sunni branch of Islam. To them the first four successors to the Prophet Muḥammad are paragons of spiritual eminence, righteousness, and self-sacrifice. They strictly follow the *fiqh* of Abū Ḥanīfah but, like all Sufis, the world view of the early Chishtiyyah was not restricted to the letter of the law; it was concerned mainly with its spirit. They believed that out of the first four caliphs, it was ʿAlī on whom the Prophet Muḥammad chose to bestow the *khirqah* (patched cloak) which he had received on the night of *miʿrāj* (ascent to Divine Proximity).[13] The early Chishtiyyah drew heavily on the teachings of ʿAlī and his eleven successors (the twelve Shīʿīte Imams) for their spiritual regeneration. Following ʿAlī, they believed that God manifests "His Essence by His Essence." Khwājah Muʿīn al-Dīn Ḥasan Sijzī asserts:

> When like a snake I shed my slough and perceived attentively, I found that lover, beloved and love were identical. In the realm of Divine Unity there is no distinction between them. The pilgrims circumambulate the Kaʿbah but the hearts of the *ʿārifs* (gnostics) circumambulate the heavens and the Hijaz of Divine Majesty. They yearn for beatific vision.[14]

It was only after the death of Khwājah Muʿīn al-Dīn Ḥasan that the impact of the doctrine of *waḥdat al-wujūd* (unity of being) of the great Ibn ʿArabī began to be felt by the Indian Sufis. This doctrine deeply impressed the Chishtīs from the end of the eighth/fourteenth century on. The doctrine of *waḥdat al-wujūd* was most exuberantly expressed in the work of Masʿūd Bakk. Its framework enabled the Chishtī Sufis to enter into a meaningful dialogue with the Hindu ascetics. This had commenced in the eighth/fourteenth century and was widely prevalent from the ninth/fifteenth to the thirteenth/nineteenth centuries.

The Sufi literature in Hindawi, or the local dialects of the subcontinent, made a distinctive contribution in this field and tried to bridge the gulf between Islamic and Hindu mysticism. The Chishtī shaykh, Ḥamīd al-Dīn Ṣūfī Nāgawrī, blamed linguistic problems and difficulties in communication for the failure to realize that "Reality is One." An object can assume hundreds of different forms and be known by the same number of names, but this does not alter the fact that they all emanate from the One.[15] The *Rushd-nāmah* by Shaykh ʿAbd al-Quddūs Gangōhī seems to have overcome the problems of terminologies and hurdles of dialects. The *sine qua non* of spiritual life to Shaykh ʿAbd al-Quddūs, his contemporary Hindu sages, and the Nath Yogis is to discipline the body, the senses, and the mind. Their mutual objective is to transmute the physical body into a rarified state enabling it to obtain tranquillity. The Nath Yogis describe the Supreme Creator as *Alakh-Nāth* (the Inconceivable or Unseeable Lord) or as *Niranjana* (the Eternal). Shaykh ʿAbd al-Quddūs also uses the name *Alakh Niranjana* (the Unseeable and the Eternal) in the same sense. He says that his Lord is *Alakh Niranjana* and those who are able to comprehend Him are lost to themselves. In another verse, the shaykh identifies *Niranjana* with *Khudā* ("God" in Persian) and calls Him the Creator of different worlds.

The Nath Yogic *sahaja* (the state of bliss) is of great significance to Shaykh ʿAbd al-Quddūs. It leads to the achievement of ontological immortality or the Sufi *baqāʾ*. In a state of perfect equilibrium, it transcends perceptual knowledge with positive and negative experience. The Nath in such a state is simultaneously both meditator and meditation with Divinity as object. This idea was predominant in the Sufism of Khwājah Muʿīn al-Dīn Chishtī but, from the eighth/fourteenth century on, it was represented in the *Hama ūst* ("All is He") framework of *waḥdat al-wujūd.*

The Prophet Muḥammad is the last of the prophets in the Islamic system, but in the framework of the doctrine of *waḥdat al-wujūd*, as explained by Shabistarī in the *Gulshan-i rāz* (*The Garden of Divine Mysteries*), the *mīm* (M) of Muḥammad is a great mystery. Shaykh ʿAbd al-Quddūs also could not comprehend Muḥammad by the mere crying of his name. To him Muḥammad and *Aḥad*, which means "the One" or "God," are the same, and everyone in the world is misled because of a failure to understand the true significance of the intervening *mīm* (M) in the words Aḥmad (a name of the prophet Muḥammad) and *Aḥad.* The Chishtiyyah discourage the mechanical invoking of the name of Muḥammad or Allah. They urge the development of spirituality after Muḥammad and the death of the self before the death of the earthly body.[16]

Like other followers of *waḥdat al-wujūd*, the Chishtiyyah identify Reality with Being and assert that, in the stage of nondetermination (*lā ta'ayyun*), Being is the Absolute per se. They deny, however, that Divine Self-manifestation and determination imply a belief in the unification of the world with God (*ittiḥād*), or His descent or incarnation (*ḥulūl*) into existence. Therefore, Sufis seeking God should first obey the Prophet Muḥammad (in both word and deed, inwardly and outwardly) and then move on to contemplation of the Unity of Being. Shāh Kalīm Allāh Jahānābādī, says that mystical union (*waṣl*) means denial of everything except God, indifference to all phenomenal existence, and absorption and extinction in the *Bērangī*, or the Absolute. Initially this state appears as "unconsciousness" and a trancelike state resembling death, except that in death one does not enjoy the Divine Mystery, whereas in mystic "unconsciousness" one's whole being partakes of it.

When the seeker emerges from this stage of partaking of the Divine Mystery, even though it may last for no longer than an hour, he is known as *walī* (protege or friend of God), one who has attained knowledge of the Divine. The mystic completes his course of mystical ascension if he tends to destroy his self when contemplating the Essence. He strays from the correct path by ignoring this goal and casting his eyes to the right and left and involving himself with other determinations.[17]

The earlier Chishtīs believed that Sufism demanded humility, modesty, patience, fortitude, and the cleansing of the heart from all conceit. Self-abnegation involved careful concern not to offend others, and, in the event of this happening, sincere and plentiful apologies were essential. According to Shaykh Niẓām al-Dīn Awliyā', there would be no end to hatred and strife if animal soul (*nafs*) met animal soul; animal soul should, however, be met with the heart (*qalb*). It was customary, the shaykh said, to meet evil with evil and good with good. The dervishes, however, offered good will on all occasions, whether meeting with evil or good.[18]

To Shaykh Niẓām al-Dīn Awliyā', Islam was not an empty round of prayers and rituals but a highly ethical code. To illustrate this he told a story concerning Shaykh Bāyazīd Basṭāmī and his Jewish neighbor. The Jew was questioned after Basṭāmī's death as to why he had not converted to Islam. The Jew answered that if by Islam was meant the path of Basṭāmī, it was because he could not follow such a difficult course; if, on the other hand, his inquisitors implied following their way, he would be ashamed to pursue it.[19]

Shaykh Niẓām al-Dīn Awliyā' was deeply impressed with the devotion of the Brahmins to their faith and urged his disciples to follow their example. He watched the crowds of Hindus bathing in the Jamuna with interest and passed no adverse comments. Although his main concern was to improve the conditions of the Muslims, he also tried to help the Hindus. Amīr Ḥasan tells a story that illustrates this. Ḥasan's servant bought a slave girl for five *tankās* in Devagiri. The time came for them to leave for Delhi with the army. The distraught parents begged to be allowed to buy their daughter back even if it cost twice as much as the servant had originally paid for her. The sum was paid by Amīr Ḥasan himself and the girl returned to her family. Shaykh Niẓām al-Dīn approved of the Amīr's action because his teacher, Mawlānā ʻAlāʼ al-Dīn Uṣūlī, had set a precedent. At one time the Mawlānā had owned a female slave who had been parted from her son in Katihar. When the Mawlānā learned of her sorrow at the separation, he gave her some food and told her to return home. Shaykh Niẓām al-Dīn was greatly impressed by this policy, although he knew the *ʻulamāʼ* disapproved of it.[20]

Masʻūd Bakk wrote that a true devotee did not concern himself with the difference between the seventy-two sects of Islam; instead he was concerned with the illumination concealed at the door of the Divine, not the veil hiding it. It was the objective, not faith or sectarianism, which was all-important to the seeker. To Masʻūd Bakk faith was the vehicle for the attainment of the objective, and *kufr* (infidelity) made the objective unobtainable because it meant involving oneself with other objects. Those who worshiped themselves naturally neglected to adore God; those who ignored themselves worshiped the Truth (*Ḥaqq*). On the assumption that all names referred to the One Name, Masʻūd Bakk contended that in all forms only the One Face was concealed and that in all religions only One Road was hidden. All religions would appear identical if only the subtle truth of this path, gleaned from these different forms, were understood.[21]

Another distinguished Sufi, dwelling on the idea that the paths to God were as numerous as human souls, Ḥusaynī ibn Jaʻfar, a contemporary of Masʻūd Bakk, classified human souls into three groups. The first category comprised the common Muslims whose right path was a scrupulous observance of the *Sharīʻah,* although he believed that the true goal did not lie at the end of this path. In the second group, he placed people who performed hard ascetic exercises with a view to purifying the self and the heart and to changing their natural disposition. This was an inward-looking path and was suitable only for the pious and holy. The third category included the spiritual elite who had reached the stage of understanding *lāhūt* (Divinity).[22]

Defining *kufr* (infidelity), Jaʻfar claimed that in its common form it contradicted the *Sharīʻah,* but its most significant aspect involved worship by the carnal soul. All externalists, he asserted, were guilty of this type of infidelity. A true perception of *kufr* was required for a realistic understanding of Satan. *Kufr* and *īmān* (faith) were merely two veils, and a seeker who remained involved in arguments about them would be unable to understand God. The true seeker should be neither a *kāfir* (infidel) nor a "Muslim," but a lover and an axis around which both *kufr* and *īmān* revolved.[23]

An interpretation of paradise was given by Khwājah Bandah Nawāz Gīsū Darāz. He claimed that paradise was an awareness of the "Divine Form" hidden in human beings. He interpreted the Sufi *ḥadīth* "He who knows himself knows his Lord" as referring to the consciousness of the secret archetype by which God manifests Himself in and through human beings. The awareness of this reality amounted to achieving the pleasure of paradise. For Gīsū Darāz the Day of Resurrection would reveal no secrets.[24]

Influence

The spiritual influence of the Chishtiyyah on society was far-reaching. Political developments in the eighth/fourteenth century, however, resulted in some of them becoming missionaries. Khwājah Bandah Nawāz Gīsū Darāz, for example, learned Sanskrit in order to enter into polemical discussions with the Brahmins, whom he claims to have defeated. Shaykh ʿAbd al-Quddūs Gangōhī wrote to Sultan Sikandar Lōdī (894/1489–923/1517), Bābur (932/1526–937/1530), and Humāyūn (937/1530–947/1540 and 962/1555–963/1556) demanding they inject Sunni orthodoxy into their administration. These actions were, however, a minor aspect of Chishtī life; the Chishtī majority strictly adhered to the tradition of peaceful coexistence.

The Mughal emperors from Akbar (963/1556–1014/1605) to the end of the dynasty in 1274/1857 were deeply attached to the Chishtiyyah. Some Chishtīs entered the imperial service, but the leading *pīrs* maintained their independence and treasured the spiritual traditions of their ancestors. Khwājah Muʿīn al-Dīn's tomb at Ajmer became an important center for pilgrims after his death. The tomb of the great founder and those of his spiritual descendants all over the subcontinent attract to this day hundreds of thousands of devotees throughout the year. The death anniversary (*ʿurs*) of the Chishtī *pīrs* is observed at their tombs with great ceremony. The *samāʿ* gatherings held there transport those of spiritual bent into ecstasy, and there is no dearth of people who gain spiritual satisfaction from these ceremonies.

The impact of modern scientific thought and twentieth-century political developments in the subcontinent has not been able to kill Sufism. The richness and the range of the Sufi message both in prose and in poetry continue to arouse interest in knowledge, action, and humanity. That message reveals those universal aspects of Reality as all sages and saints of different religions, including Muslims, perceived them and directs torn personalities and split minds to a more fruitful way of life.

Notes

1. Farīd al-Dīn Muḥammad, *Surūr al-ṣudūr* (Habibganj Collections, Mawlānā Āzād Library, Aligarh University Manuscript) 51–52.
2. Ḥamīd Qalandar, *Khayr al-majālis* (Aligarh, 1959) 224.
3. Ḥusaynī ibn Ja'far, *Baḥr al-ma'ānī* (India Office Library; London: Ethé, 1867) f. 37a.
4. Ḥamīd Qalandar, *Khayr al-majālis,* 150.
5. Mīr Khwurd, *Siyar al-awliyā'* (reprint; Lahore, 1978) 76.
6. Ḥasan Sijzī, *Fawā'id al-fu'ād* (Bulandshahr).
7. Ibid., 171.
8. Ḥamīd Qalandar, *Khayr al-majālis,* 156–57.
9. Ḥasan Sijzī, *Fawā'id al-fu'ād,* 154–55.
10. Shāh Kalīm Allāh Jahānābādī, *Kashkūl-i kalīmī* (Delhi, 1315/1897–98) 8–12.
11. Ḥamīd Qalandar, *Khayr al-majālis,* 59–60.
12. Hujwīrī, *Kashf-al-maḥjūb,* trans. R. A. Nicholson (London: Luzac, 1911) 416.
13. Mīr Khwurd, *Siyar al-awliyā',* 18–19.
14. Ibid., 55–56.
15. Farīd al-Dīn Muḥammad, *Surūr al-ṣudūr,* 69.
16. S. A. A. Rizvi, *A History of Sufism in India* (New Delhi: Munshiram Mansharlal, 1978) 1:335–41.
17. Shāh Kalīm Allāh Jahānābādī, *Kashkūl-i kalīmī,* 3–4.
18. Ḥasan Sijzī, *Fawā'id al-fu'ād,* 139.
19. Ibid., 197.
20. Ibid., 215–16, 179–80.
21. Mas'ūd Bakk, *Mir'āt al-'ārifīn* (India Office Library; London: Ethé, 1854) f. 160a.
22. Ḥusaynī ibn Ja'far, *Baḥr al-ma'ānī,* ff. 154b–155b.
23. Ibid., f. 37a.
24. Gīsū Darāz, *Istiqām al-sharī'ah* (India Office Library; London: Ethé, 1861) f. 20b.

7

The Nimatullāhī

JAVAD NURBAKHSH

THE NIMATULLĀHĪ ORDER,[1] one of the most well-known Sufi orders, has many followers in the United States, Europe, and especially Persia at the present time. As the name suggests, the order was founded by Shāh Ni'mat Allāh Walī, a renowned master of the Ma'rūfiyyah Order, which is known as the mother of the orders (*umm al-salāsil*). This is due to the fact that almost all the orders of Sufism were started by Ma'ruf Karkhī, after whom the Ma'rūfiyyah Order is named. It must, however, be remembered that nearly all the orders consider 'Alī ibn Abī Ṭālib, the son-in-law of the Prophet, as the first master of the spiritual path.

Masters of the Nimatullāhī Order

The spiritual chain of the Nimatullāhī Order from 'Alī up to Shāh Ni'mat Allāh is as follows:

1. 'Alī ibn 'Abī Ṭālib (d. 41/661)
2. Ḥasan al-Baṣrī (21/642–110/728)
3. Ḥabīb al-'Ajamī (d. 119/737)
4. Dā'ūd al-Ṭā'ī (d. 165/781)
5. Ma'rūf al-Karkhī (d. 200/815-16)
6. Sarī al-Saqaṭī (d. 253/867)
7. Abu'l-Qāsim al-Junayd (d. 298/910)
8. Abū 'Alī Rūdbārī (d. 322/934)
9. Abū 'Alī al-Kātib (d. after 340/951)
10. Abū 'Uthmān al-Maghribī (d. 373/984)
11. Abu'l-Qāsim al-Gurgānī (d. 469/1076)
12. Abū Bakr al-Nassāj al-Ṭūsī (d. 487/1094)
13. Aḥmad Ghazzālī (d. 520/1126)
14. Abu'l-Faḍl al-Baghdādī (d. 550/1155)
15. Abu'l-Barakāt (d. 570/1174)

16. Abu'l-Su'ūd al-Andalusī (d. 579/1183)
17. Abū Madyan (d. 590/1194)
18. Abu'l-Futūḥ al-Sa'īdī
19. Najm al-Dīn Kamāl al-Kūfī
20. Abū Bakr Ṣāliḥ al-Barbarī
21. 'Abd Allāh al-Yāfi'ī (d. 768/1367)
22. Shāh Ni'mat Allāh Walī (731/1331–834/1431)

The Life and Works of Shāh Ni'mat Allāh

Nūr al-Dīn Shāh Ni'mat Allāh Walī, the *quṭb* (pole) of those who realize Oneness, the best of those perfected, was one of the greatest Sufi masters and most renowned mystics of the eighth/fourteenth and ninth/fifteenth centuries.[2] His teachings spread to all the followers of the Spiritual Path (*ṭarīqat*) of Islam. In truth, it can be stated that he was the reviver of the Spiritual Path of Muḥammadan Poverty (*faqr-i Muḥammadī*) throughout all the Muslim lands, especially Persia and the subcontinent. Moreover, it was the order bearing his name that was able, in the twelfth/eighteenth century, to revive the *ṭarīqat* in Iran and to quench the thirst of those who were searching for mystical truth.

Shāh Ni'mat Allāh was born on 14 Rabī' al-awwal 731/1331, in Aleppo in present-day Syria. His father, Mīr 'Abd Allāh, was one of the great Sufi masters of his time. His mother was of the royal lineage of Fars, in southern Persia. It is said that during his childhood Shāh Ni'mat Allāh memorized the whole of the Quran and had a great capacity for comprehending spiritual truths and expressing mystical meanings. He writes:

> Know for certain that the knowledge
> in which they instructed my heart
> Wasn't taught anywhere.
>
> What the shaykh of the forty-day retreat
> never realized at the age of thirty
> Was revealed to me at the age of three.

Although in his youth he studied both theosophy (*ḥikmat-i ilāhī*) and scholastic theology (*kalām*), he was discontent with the lack of application that he discovered in those who pursue these disciplines, and so he set out in search of a perfect master and an enlightened guide. He encountered many of the great spiritual teachers of his day, until at last he found his own master in Shaykh 'Abd Allāh al-Yāfi'ī. Shaykh Yāfi'ī, whom Shāh Ni'mat Allāh considered to be the chief among the saints of the world, was endowed not only with esoteric perfection but also with such a great mastery of exoteric knowledge that he was considered one of the greatest jurisprudents and historians of his time.

Shāh Ni'mat Allāh served Shaykh al-Yāfi'ī for seven years. Blessed by the grace of Shaykh al-Yāfi'ī's presence and the *barakah* (grace) of his breath, Shāh Ni'mat Allāh attained the rank of a master after having been a disciple. After taking leave of Shaykh al-Yāfi'ī, Shāh Ni'mat Allāh began his second period of travels through different countries. This time, however, he went as a spiritual pole of his age, quenching the spiritually thirsty by the grace of his breath, directing the hands of the seekers and soothing the pain of the lovers of God. In this second period of travels, Shāh Ni'mat Allāh first set out toward Egypt and then went to Transoxania, where he settled in Shahrisabz near Samarqand. It was on this journey that an encounter took place between Shāh Ni'mat Allāh and Tamerlane. Tamerlane, like Genghis Khan, was a savage conqueror who tyrannized Persia during his reign from 771/1335 to 807/1405. Tamerlane did not appreciate the worth of Shāh Ni'mat Allāh. Therefore, to avoid trouble, Shāh Ni'mat Allāh decided to leave Shahrisabz and set out for Harat.

In Harat, Shāh Ni'mat Allāh married the granddaughter of Mīr Ḥusayn Harawī (d. 720/1329), whose questions had prompted Maḥmūd Shabistarī to compose *Gulshan-i rāz* (*The Garden of Divine Mystery*). The issue of this marriage was both a physical and a spiritual son, Burhān al-Dīn Khalīl Allāh (born 885/1373), who succeeded Shāh Ni'mat Allāh as the *quṭb* of the order.

From Harat, Shāh Ni'mat Allāh traveled to Mashhad, residing for a while in Yazd and Baft, and then settling in Kubana. From there he went to Kirman, then to the nearby town of Mahan, where he remained for almost all of the last twenty-five years of his life, sometimes living in Kirman and sometimes in Mahan. During Shāh Ni'mat Allāh's stay in Mahan, his fame spread to most areas of Persia and India, and those longing to meet him would make the pilgrimage there. However, Aḥmad Shāh Bahmanī, the king of the Deccan, had requested Shāh Ni'mat Allāh to come to India. In response, Shāh Ni'mat Allāh sent his grandson, Shāh Nūr Allāh, thus providing the basis for the subsequent transfer of the Nimatullāhī Order to the Deccan in India and Shāh Khalīl Allāh's later exodus there.

Shāh Ni'mat Allāh lived nearly a hundred years. On 23 Rajab 732 A.H. (21 April A.D. 1332), he "vacated his *khirqah*" in Kirman. His body was carried by government officials, servants, dervishes, and nobles, shoulder to shoulder, to Mahan, and was there entombed.[3]

Say then, here was a "Shah," free from this world,
who went,
Who when he heard the call "Return"
from the Truth,

Surrendered his soul, with a heart alive
in Love, and went.[4]

ʿAbd al-Razzāq Kirmānī had written:

His lordship [Shāh Niʿmat Allāh] was outstanding among the great people of his time in the field of discourse and exceptional among the masters of spiritual struggle (*mujāhadah*) of his day. There was neither pride nor laxity in his nature; he was totally devoid of all greed and blameworthy qualities. He was always courteous and civil, and he never neglected, either inwardly or outwardly, the observation of the proper manners and behavior necessary for the performance of the exact requirements of the Muḥammadan Spiritual Path. He chose his words with hesitation, speaking with gravity yet constancy, never raising his voice or using unbecoming words. His perfect morality inclined him to regard all human beings as worthy of being treated with good-will.[5]

Shāh Niʿmat Allāh, in addition to directing large numbers of disciples, spent his free time in farming, making his occupation a model for his disciples to emulate and visibly demonstrating to his followers that the best form of austerity and the most excellent way to purify the heart and purge the self was by service to society and kindness to other human beings.

My friend! Remember God and invoke
his Name constantly;
If you are able, work within your "work."[6]

By Divine Grace, this tradition of kindness to people and service to society has caused the state of "expansion" (*basṭ*) to prevail over that of "contraction" (*qabḍ*)[7] in the hearts of the Nimatullāhī Sufis. By his own actions, Shāh Niʿmat Allāh demonstrated that retirement from the world and laziness resulted solely in apathy, lethargy, and depression, and that social activity and association with people, combined with service to them in the Name of God, resulted in contentment and expansion of the soul and mind. Following his example, the Nimatullāhī Sufis abandoned seclusion and retreat as a mode of life; the vulture of apathy, lethargy, and depression flew off, while in its place the falcon of joy spread its wings in the sky of the heart.

Another of Shāh Niʿmat Allāh's "innovations" was his prohibition against the wearing of any particular costume or publicly appearing in any special Sufi attire. It was his opinion that inner and spiritual affairs had to be free from any kind of show and pretense, colorlessness being far closer to God than black or white. In the words of a Sufi poet:

The king's associates are liberated
from black and white.

Adorned with the vestment of the
Divine Attributes,
They're beyond cloak and cap.[8]

Shāh Ni'mat Allāh insisted on following his predecessors in not separating the *ṭarīqat* from the Divine Law (*Sharī'at*) because of his belief that the Truth (*ḥaqīqat*) could only be attained through the integration of both. To quote his own words:

The *Sharī'at* is knowledge of the theory of religion,
the *ṭarīqat* its application.
And if you combine theory and practice sincerely,
Solely for the sake of God, that is the *ḥaqīqat*.[9]

One of the most important steps taken by Shāh Ni'mat Allāh, however, was that he did not consider Sufism limited to a certain group of people. In contrast with other Sufi masters of his time, who accepted only some seekers of God and rejected others as unworthy, he left his door open to all seekers, instructing in the way of Love (*maḥabbat*) all those in whom he perceived a longing for the school of Unity. Shāh Ni'mat Allāh regarded all people as being equally deserving and in need of the school of Sufism. He said, "All those whom the saints have rejected, I will accept, and, according to their capacity, I will perfect them." Celebrating these ideas in verse, Riḍā Qulī Khān Hidāyat wrote:

Trusting in the knowledge of God, that pivot
of all saints, Shāh Ni'mat Allāh, declared:
"Any disciple on the path of Ultimate Attainment
who all the other masters have cast away,
Liberate him from the bait and snare of the world
and send him to me. Though by others he was rejected
and turned away, I'll accept him into the holy poverty of God
and make him drunk as befits him."[10]

After he was sixty years old, Shāh Ni'mat Allāh began to compose poetry.[11] It is said that the poetry of Shāh Ni'mat Allāh reveals the same fluency of expression and directness of meaning that have been reported about his discourses:

If the unity of the essence of God
manifests itself,
Like a knower, I'll declare it openly.
And if the images of multiplicity appear in imagination,
I'll deny them and refuse to say two.[12]

Yet the greatness and fame of Shāh Ni'mat Allāh do not by any means rest upon his poetry. This "Shāh" in reality was not a poet; rather he was a gnostic (*'ārif*) and a mystic who clothed Reality (*ḥaqīqat*) in the garment of verse. The poems of Shāh Ni'mat Allāh have a purely gnostic content and are the expressions of the state of a person who has spent a lifetime engaged in the sorrow of Divine Love. Like an infatuated and distraught lover, he stands before his Beloved enraptured in praise:

> Ah! We're prisoners
>   in the shackles of an immense passion,
> Afflicted, tormented,
>   manacles on our ankles!
>
> We are *les miserables*
>   in the desert of love,
> Skilled in the field
>   of riot and revolution.
>
> Sometimes we're thunder,
>   sometimes bolts of lightning.
> Sometimes we're clouds,
>   sometimes the sea.
>
> Sometimes earth-like,
>   abased and debased,
> Sometimes sky-like,
>   exalted and transcendent.[13]

The main form on which Shāh Ni'mat Allāh expended most of his inspiration was the lyric or *ghazal*. The poems that he wrote in other verse forms such as the *qaṣīdah* (ode), *tarjī'-band* (strophe poem), *mathnawī* (rhyming couplet), and the *rubā'ī* (quatrain) are insignificant in comparison with his lyric poetry or *ghazals*. Though it may seem that the poems of Shāh Ni'mat Allāh are repetitious, upon reflection it becomes apparent that he was in fact expressing but a single Reality while experiencing different spiritual states. It is one Truth (*ḥaqīqat*) expressed in different forms, ornamented and communicated by intuitive vision to lovers according to their respective capacities. His poetry is the chant of the ode of life; it is a tune of the flute of being, a melody of the music of God:

> The wave, the sea and the bubble
>   are all one.
> All is one, nothing else,
>   whether less or more.

In most of his poems, Shāh Ni'mat Allāh speaks in some manner of the unity or identity of the "seer" (*nāẓir*) with the "Seen" (*manẓūr*), or the "witness (*shāhid*) with the "Witnessed" (*mashhūd*), or the "seeker" (*ṭālib*) with the Sought (*maṭlūb*). Often he dwells on the lover, the Beloved, and Love. The meaning of these metaphors, however, revolves around one single idea: the transcendent unity of being (*waḥdat al-wujūd*):[14]

According to our faith, lover and Beloved are one;
To us, what is desire?
The desirer and the Desired are one.

They tell me, "Seek Him in His essence."
But how should I seek?
Seeker and Sought are one.[15]

These ideas on the transcendent unity of being, which Shāh Ni'mat Allāh set to verse in his *Dīwān* of poetry, were also expressed by him in his prose treatises. Other subjects dealt with in these treatises related to the more practical aspects of the spiritual path and to other esoteric doctrines of Sufism. Of the many treatises of Shāh Ni'mat Allāh, 130 have thus far been located, edited, and published in four volumes by Khaniqahi-Nimatullahi Publications in Tehran.[16]

The Continuation of the Nimatullāhī Order from the Ma'rūfiyyah Order

Although the Nimatullāhī Order is essentially a continuation of the Ma'rūfiyyah Order, after the death of Shāh Ni'mat Allāh, the name of the order was altered for some of the following reasons: (1) Shāh Ni'mat Allāh attracted a vast number of disciples from every walk and class of society. He was a powerful and great propagator of the principles and ideas of Sufism both as a master in the sphere of popular culture and as a poet and an author in the field of its most advanced philosophical and literary expressions. (2) He encouraged Sufis to work and involve themselves with social activities, and he discouraged them from hiding away in seclusion and retreat. (3) He insisted that his disciples should wear clothes according to the times and the place in which they lived. He prevented his disciples from wearing a particular type of clothing. (4) He encouraged the Sufis to observe faithfully the exoteric practices of the *Sharī'ah.* (5) Unlike other masters, he did not turn anyone away who came to him for the love of God, but instructed them according to their capacity in the path of self-purification. (6) He prohibited his disciples from the use of opium and hashish at a time when these were used by some ordinary people and certain Sufis as well.

After the death of Shāh Ni'mat Allāh, his son and successor, Shāh Khalīl Allāh I, the twenty-third master in the initiatic chain of the order, chose to live in the Deccan, India. This resulted in the settlement of the Nimatullāhī masters in the Deccan up to the time of Sayyid Ma'ṣūm 'Alī Shāh Deccani, who moved back to Persia.

Nimatullāhī Masters Who Lived in India from Shāh Khalīl Allāh to Sayyid Ma'ṣūm 'Alī Shāh

23. Shāh Khalīl Allāh I (775/1373–860/1455)
24. Shāh Ḥabīb al-Dīn Muḥibb Allāh I (d. 914/1508)
25. Shāh Kamāl al-Dīn I
26. Shāh Khalīl Allāh II (d. 925/1508)
27. Shāh Shams al-Dīn Muḥammad I
28. Shāh Ḥabīb al-Dīn Muḥibb Allāh II
29. Mīr Shāh Shams al-Dīn Muḥammad II
30. Mīr Kamāl al-Dīn 'Aṭiyyat Allāh II
31. Mīr Shāh Shams al-Dīn Muḥammad III
32. Mīr Maḥmūd Deccani
33. Shams al-Dīn Deccani
34. Sayyid Riḍā 'Alī Shāh Deccani
35. Sayyid Ma'ṣūm 'Alī Shāh Deccani (martyred 1211/1796)

The Life and Works of Sayyid Ma'ṣūm 'Alī Shāh

Ma'ṣūm 'Alī Shāh is particularly important in the revival of the Nimatullāhī Order in Persia. Mīr 'Abd al-Ḥamīd, or Ma'ṣūm[17] 'Alī Shāh, as he was known in the *ṭarīqat,* was born in Hyderabad, India. His ancestors were wealthy members of the aristocracy. After having undergone the conventional education in exoteric learning, he hastened to devote himself to the masters of rapture and mystical states (*arbāb-i wajd wa ḥāl*), sincerely submitting himself to the service of Riḍā 'Alī Shāh Deccani. He served his master for many years until he reached the rank of mastership and received permission to guide others.

In India, before becoming a Sufi, Sayyid Ma'ṣūm 'Alī Shāh was said to have possessed great wealth, power, and prestige. It is reported that whenever he ventured forth, eight men would follow in procession behind him carrying gold and silver staves. When he first came to see Riḍā 'Alī Shāh together with this impressive retinue, Riḍā 'Alī told him to return the next day alone. In response, Sayyid Ma'ṣūm immediately gave away everything he had, only then setting out for the *khānqāh* of Riḍā 'Alī. Having given away all his belongings, he was so poor that all he could find to take as an offering to Riḍā ʿAlī was some camel dung (for fuel), which he picked up along the way. As Niẓām ʿAlī Shāh[18] has written in the *Jannat al-wiṣāl* (*The Paradise of Union*):

So he set out, this unique man,
  hastening for the King's court,
Alone and unequalled, seeking
  the Divine Grace,
And bringing only camel-droppings
  as an offering.

By the order of Riḍā ʿAlī Shāh, in 1190/1775 Sayyid Maʿṣūm traveled to Persia by way of the Sea of Oman. Upon reaching Shiraz, a number of people submitted to him, among whom were Fayḍ ʿAlī Shāh and Nūr ʿAlī Shāh.[19] After disciplining and perfecting these two disciples, Maʿṣūm ʿAlī Shāh gave them each the authority (*ijāzah*) of guidance and delivered over to Nūr ʿAlī Shāh the affairs of the Nimatullāhī Order.

Maʿṣūm resided peacefully in Shiraz with his disciples for two or three years until Karīm Khān Zand, the ruler of Fars who had made Shiraz his capital, began to turn against him. Karīm Khān had fallen under the influence of a man named Jānī, an Indian who coveted a higher place in the court and who sought to have Maʿṣūm expelled from Shiraz. Jānī had bribed some of the attendants at the Khān's court to support him in this venture. One day when Karīm Khān left the city for a tour of the countryside, Jānī, together with some of the attendants of the court whom he had bribed, approached Karīm Khān and, after paying homage to the ruler, declared in the guise of being a devoted friend and servant:

There is in your city
  A fire-worshipping dervish.
Sometimes he claims Divinity,
    Sometimes says he's a Shāh,
Sometimes a beggar.
A sorcerer – he steals hearts.
    He's a descendant of the "King of
      Najaf."[20]
Like moths about candles,
    Men gather about him.

O fortunate monarch, if in the city
    This man remains, it's certain
      he'll rob you
Of crown and throne.[21]

Upon saying this, Jānī had the group that he had brought with him give testimony as to the truth of what he had said. The king believed these allegations and ordered that Ma'ṣūm 'Alī Shāh and his disciples be banished from Shiraz. Accompanying Ma'ṣūm in leaving the city were Fayḍ 'Alī Shāh, Nūr 'Alī Shāh, Mushtāq 'Alī Shāh, Naẓar 'Alī Shāh, and Darvīsh Ḥusayn 'Alī.

Ma'ṣūm and his disciples then made their way from Shiraz to Isfahan. At this time, there was anarchy in every section of the country, 'Alī Murād Khān (a relative of Karīm Khān Zand) making claims for his own kingship in Isfahan. The Qājār tribe, with the assistance of their leader, Āqā Muḥammad Khān Qājār, had risen to defend 'Alī Murād Khān, hoping to conquer and rule Arak and Fars. For a short time, 'Alī Murād Khān had been forced to flee from Isfahan, and groups of Sufis of the Jalālī Order had at his departure celebrated and reveled in the marketplace and on the streetcorners of that city. Thus 'Alī Murād Khān held a general grudge against all dervishes, so that when he regained power in Isfahan and slanderers reminded him that Ma'ṣūm 'Alī Shāh and his followers, like the Safavids,[22] might also have aspirations toward political power, he turned against them.

The superintendent of police in Isfahan along with Rustam Khān and Aṣlān Khān, two brothers who were close confidants of 'Alī Murād Khān, were authorized to expel Ma'ṣūm and his disciples with the utmost humiliation from the *khānqāh* of Fayḍ 'Alī Shāh, where they were staying. Government agents assaulted the Sufi house and pillaged everything they had. Ma'ṣūm 'Alī Shāh and Nūr 'Alī Shāh were then taken in chains to the house of the police captain.

Finally, Sayyid Ma'ṣūm, accompanied by Nūr 'Alī Shāh and a few devoted disciples, was expelled from Isfahan. They took the road to Kashan, intending to reach Khurasan. It is related that when they stopped to rest under a tree in Murchih-khurt, a village between Isfahan and Kashan, Ma'ṣūm bowed his head in contemplation for an hour and when he raised it declared, "the police captain has not yet finished bothering us. A few of our limbs still have to be cut off. Anybody who wants to save himself can leave." Upon hearing this, two horsemen sent by the governor of Isfahan galloped up. One cut off the ears of Nūr 'Alī Shāh and Ma'ṣūm 'Alī Shāh, taking back the cropped ears to Rustam and Aṣlān Khān; the other took the two Sufis in custody through Kashan to Tehran.

Āqā Muḥammad Khān Qājār, however, who had been under the surveillance of Karīm Khān Zand earlier while staying in Shiraz, had become an intimate confidant of Ma'ṣūm 'Alī Shāh through contact with a famous mullah and thought well of the Sufis. Upon learning of Ma'ṣūm's circumstances, he arranged for the dervish to be treated with respect and generosity and to journey to the holy city of Mashhad at his expense. Thus, Ma'ṣūm 'Alī Shāh traveled to Mashhad along with some of his closest disciples, including Nūr 'Alī, Ḥusayn 'Alī, Mushtāq 'Alī, Naẓar 'Alī, Ṣafā 'Alī, and Shawq 'Alī.

After making the pilgrimage to the tomb of Imam Riḍā in Mashhad, Ma'ṣūm and his disciples set out for Harat where many of the nobles of that area became his disciples, including Prince Fīrūz al-Dīn Afghān, Muḥammad Kāẓim Khān Shāmlū, and Aḥmad Khān Taymūrī. After a short stay there, the best of Ma'ṣūm's disciples who accompanied him, including Nūr 'Alī, Ḥusayn 'Alī, Mushtāq 'Alī, Rawnaq 'Alī, and Sayyid Maẓhar 'Alī, were dismissed from his presence. Ma'ṣūm 'Alī Shāh then set out for Kabul, Zabul, and India.

After traveling through these lands, Sayyid Ma'ṣūm traveled by sea to Iraq, taking up residence in Najaf. Shortly thereafter he moved to Karbala', where he resided once again in the company of Nūr 'Alī, Rawnaq 'Alī, Majdhūb 'Alī, and Riḍā 'Alī.

After a while, Sayyid Ma'ṣūm resumed his travels and set out to make the pilgrimage to the tomb of Imam Riḍā in Mashhad. When he reached Kirmanshah, however, Āqā Muḥammad 'Alī Bihbahānī—an Iraqi theologian and scholar fanatically opposed to the Sufis and the son of Muḥammad Bāqir Bihbahānī—had Ma'ṣūm 'Alī arrested and imprisoned. The author of the *Ṭarā'iq al-ḥaqa'iq* (*Paths of Truths*) writes:

> It has been related from the most reliable persons in Kirmanshah as well as from other sources that Sayyid Ma'ṣūm was martyred and then buried in the garden of the 'Arsh-i Barīn, where there now exists a building, and that this deed was done at his [Bihbahānī's] insistence.[23]

As is obvious from all of the foregoing, Sayyid Ma'ṣūm 'Alī Shāh must be considered one of the renewers of the Nimatullāhī Order in Persia. It should be noted that Sufism had been on a steady decline in Persia ever since the end of the Safavid era. The Afghan invasion, the frequent military expeditions of Nādir Khan, and the rule of the Zand dynasty had all caused the people to pay less and less attention to spirituality. At the time of the arrival of Ma'ṣūm 'Alī Shāh, nothing but the mere name remained of the Safavid Sufi orders. A small number of people in Mashhad from the Nūrbakhshī Order and a small group of Dhahabī dervishes in Shiraz were all that remained. The coming of Ma'ṣūm 'Alī Shāh, his spiritual charisma, and the readiness of the Persian people after all the years of murder, bloodshed, and misbehavior on the part of a small number of the exoteric *'ulamā'*, all caused the progress and reviviscence of the school of Sufism and gnosis. It seemed that everywhere that Sayyid Ma'ṣūm and his companions placed their feet, people unconsciously inclined toward Sufism. From then on, the masters of the Nimatullāhī Order settled in Persia, after many centuries in India.

Ma'ṣūm 'Alī Shāh's age at the time of his martyrdom (1211/1796) was said to have been a little over sixty. Concerning his outward appearance, the author of the *Ṭarā'iq* has written:

> He was a man of pleasing countenance and graceful appearance. He always wore the costume of the Sufis and left his hair disheveled and uncombed. He was weak physically and of a short stature. He was long in thinking and deliberating, and short in words. He never inclined towards anything of the world or any of its vanities, nor ever attempted to amass wealth. Whatever was given in charity to him, he immediately distributed among the dervishes, never accepting more than a single portion for himself, considering himself one of the dervishes.[24]

Masters of the Nimatullāhī Order after Ma'ṣūm 'Alī Shāh

The spiritual chain of the Nimatullāhī Order from Ma'ṣūm 'Alī Shāh until the present day is as follows:

1. Nūr 'Alī Shāh (d. 1212/1797)
2. Ḥusayn 'Alī Shāh Iṣfahānī (d. 1234/1818)
3. Majdhūb 'Alī Shāh (d. 1239/1823)
4. Mast 'Alī Shāh (d. 1253/1837)
5. Raḥmat 'Alī Shāh (d. 1278/1861)
6. Munawwar 'Alī Shāh (d. 1301/1883)
7. Wafā 'Alī Shāh (d. 1336/1918)
8. Ṣādiq 'Alī Shāh (d. 1340/1922)
9. Mūnis 'Alī Shāh (d. 1373/1953)
10. Nūr 'Alī Shāh II (Javad Nurbakhsh)

Divisions of the Nimatullāhī Order in Persia

After the death of Raḥmat 'Alī Shāh, two of his representatives (shaykhs),[25] Ṣafī 'Alī Shāh and Muḥammad Kāẓim, known as Sa'ādat 'Alī, rejected the mastership of Munawwar 'Alī Shāh, the legal successor of Raḥmat 'Alī Shāh, and provided the basis for the Gunābādī lineage and the Ṣafī 'Alī Shāhī brotherhood.

The Ṣafī ʻAlī Shāhī Brotherhood

After the death of Raḥmat ʻAlī Shāh, Ṣafī surrendered himself to Munawwar ʻAlī Shāh but after some time for various reasons their paths became separated. After this separation, Ṣafī ʻAlī Shāh's disciples, including Ẓahīr al-Dawlah, founded the Society of Brotherhood (*anjuman-i ukhuwwat*), which became an influential organization within Persian society as a whole. The first members of the Society of Brotherhood were:

1. Ẓahīr al-Dawlah (President)
2. Sayyid Muḥammad Khān Intiẓām al-Dawlah
3. Sālār Amjad
4. Niẓām al-Dawlah
5. Yamīn al-Mamālik
6. Niẓām al-Lashkar
7. Mīrẓā Muḥammad ʻAlī Khān Nuṣrat al-Sulṭān
8. Mīrẓā ʻAlī Akbar Khān Surūsh
9. Mīr Bāqir Khān Ṣafāmanish
10. Mīrzā ʻAbd al-Wahhāb Jawāhirī
11. ʻAlī Riḍā Ṣabā

Many of these men were eminent figures of their day and their presence in the Society of Brotherhood did much to extend the influence of Sufism in the Persian upper classes. An important point to note here is that Ṣafī ʻAlī never appointed a successor for himself.

The Gunābādī Lineage

Ḥājjī Muḥammad Kāẓim, known as Saʻādat ʻAlī, was a shaykh in the order of Raḥmat ʻAlī Shāh but, as mentioned, did not surrender himself to Munawwar ʻAlī Shāh, the legal successor to Raḥmat ʻAlī. While in Mashhad, Ḥajjī Mullā Sulṭān Gunābādī met Saʻādat ʻAlī and became his disciple and founded the Gunābādī lineage. After the death of Ḥājjī Muḥammad Kāẓim, his son Ḥājjī Mullā ʻAlī, and after him, his son Muḥammad Ḥasan, known as Ṣāliḥ ʻAlī, and after him, his son Tābandih, successively claimed the leadership of the Gunābādī lineage. The latter is the present head of that lineage in Persia.

The Nimatullāhī Order Today under Javad Nurbakhsh

Javad Nurbakhsh was born in Kirman, Iran. He completed his early schooling in that city, often skipping grades and always the top student in his class. At the age of sixteen he was initiated into the Nimatullāhī *ṭarīqah* by Āqā Murshidī, one of the shaykhs of Mūnis 'Alī Shāh. Finishing secondary school, he moved to Tehran to complete his studies in the University of Tehran, attending to his master, Mūnis 'Alī Shāh, during his free time. At age twenty he was appointed by Mūnis to the position of shaykh and over the next two years composed three slim volumes in honor of his master, called the *Gulzār-i Mūnis* (*The Garden of Mūnis*), concerning various aspects of theoretical and practical Sufism. The final volume of this work appeared in 1949.

In 1952 he received his M.D. and moved to Bam, west of Kirman, where he was appointed head of the town clinic. There, on June 15, 1953, when Mūnis 'Alī Shāh passed away in Tehran, J. Nurbakhsh received news of Mūnis 'Alī Shāh's posthumous investiture of him as *quṭb* of the Nimatullāhī Order. For the last thirty-four years, Javad Nurbakhsh (Nūr 'Alī Shāh II) has directed the affairs of the Nimatullāhī Order, during which time he has supervised the construction of more than one hundred Sufi houses or *khānqāhs* in the major cities and towns throughout Persia.

Javad Nurbakhsh has been the author or editor of over ninety publications in Persian, printed in Tehran by Khaniqahi Nimatullahi Publications (Intishārāt-i Khānqāh-i Ne'matu'llāhī). These publications fall basically into two categories: (1) compositions by J. Nurbakhsh and (2) critical editions of the prose and poetical works of classical Sufi writers.[26] J. Nurbakhsh has also published many articles on psychology, consideration of which is, however, beyond the scope of this article.[27] It should also be mentioned that the Nurbakhsh Library in Tehran houses one of the largest collections of ancient manuscripts and books on Islamic mysticism in Iran, the complete index of which was published in 1973 by Ibrāhīm Dībājī.[28] From 1962 until 1977, Javad Nurbakhsh practiced psychiatry as professor at Tehran University and the head of one of the country's leading psychiatric hospitals. He also spent some time studying and doing research in this field at the Sorbonne. He is one of the first Sufi authorities to be well versed at once in the traditional science of the soul and modern psychiatry.[29]

The Nimatullāhī Order in the West

Javad Nurbakhsh made his first visit to the United States in 1974, and, in response to the requests of an increasing number of America disciples, in 1975 he established the first Nimatullāhī Sufi house (*khānqāh*) in the United States in New York City. This was followed by a number of other centers in several other American cities. During the past decade, the number of *khānqāhs* has continued to increase in America, and an important *khānqāh* in London has become the center for the order in the West.

Javad Nurbakhsh has resided in London since 1983, at which time he initiated a series of publications in Persian.[30] Two series of these works deserve particular mention, since they comprise an important contemporary chapter in this ancient tradition of Sufi literature: (1) *Ma'ārif-i ṣūfiyyah* (*The Gnosis of the Sufis*), a concise description of the basic theosophical concepts of classical Sufi authors in seven volumes (four of which have been translated into English); and (2) *Farhang-e Nūrbakhsh,* a fifteen-volume encyclopedia of Sufi terminology that discusses in detail the esoteric meaning of the poetic symbolism in the Sufi lexicon (three volumes have been translated into English under the title *Sufi Symbolism*). Furthermore, a learned journal, *Sufi,* dedicated to the study of the literature, philosophy, and practice of Sufism, has recently begun publication in London in Persian and English, reaffirming the basic and perennial tenets, metaphysical grounds, and poetic truths of Islamic spirituality.

Nimatullāhī Spirituality and Contemplative Disciplines

The Nimatullāhī Order stresses the fraternity and equality of all human beings, unbiased respect for all the religions of the world, as well as service and love of all humanity regardless of differences in creed, culture, and nationality. In this order the practice of Sufism aims to create in the outer personality (*ẓāhir*) a highly ethical character, and in the interior soul (*bāṭin*) it aims to guide hearts to concentrate on human qualities and virtues and to achieve a unitarian insight and vision. Any propagation of Sufism should aim at the reality of Islam so that an attitude of love may be generated capable of unifying followers of divergent faiths. By the energy of Sufism, sectarian differences and disagreements are eliminated, since the Sufi directs his or her attention toward the sphere of Divine Unity (*tawḥīd*), regarding everyone from this standpoint in fraternity and equality.

Nimatullāhī contemplative disciplines consist of five basic practices: (1) *dhikr-i khafiy* (interior invocation or prayer of the heart), (2) *fikr* (contemplation, reflection), (3) *murāqabah* (meditation), (4) *wird* (litany, supplication), and (5) *muḥāsabah* (self-examination).[31] The Nimatullāhī Sufis congregate twice a week in the Sufi house wherein ritual prayers (*ṣalāt, namāz*) are conducted. This is followed by the Sufi assembly (*majlis*). A period of silent meditation is first observed and then the mystical poetry of the great masters in the Persian Sufi tradition, such as Rūmī, 'Irāqī, Maghribī, or Shāh Ni'mat Allāh is sung, sometimes with musical accompaniment. In the

Nimatullāhī *ṭarīqat* the practice of musical audition (*samā'*) is quite a living tradition.[32] Although the silent or nonvocative remembrance of God (*dhikr-i khafiy*) is the major emphasis of this order, several times a year special gatherings of the Nimatullāhī *fuqarā'* are held, known as *dīk jūsh*, wherein the vocative remembrance (*dhikr-i jaliy*) is practiced.

Obedience to and faith in the master, as well as fidelity (*wafā*) to the order are also fundamental principles. In the relationship of the disciple to the master, the master is conceived of as a mirror reflecting the disciple's attention and devotion back toward God, rather than directing it at himself, so as to foster an idolatrous "cult of personality."

The Nimatullāhī Order particularly emphasizes service (*khidmat*) within the Sufi house itself. This service is performed according to an ancient and well-defined code of etiquette (*adab*), for as it is sometimes said, "the whole of Sufism is *adab*" (*al-taṣawwuf kulluhu ādāb*).[33] The attitude of the Sufi in this service is one of altruistic "purity" (*ṣafā*) so that in interactions with others each Sufi considers himself below the other. Furthermore, the Sufis are generally encouraged to seek proximity to God, the Creator (*al-Khāliq*) through service to His creatures (*khalq*) in society. According to the dictum "Selfhood is blasphemy even if it be holy" (*khudī kufr ast agar khud pārsā'īst*), the Sufis' service has worth only to the degree that it is selfless and altruistic. Insofar as selfishness and egocentricity are the natural enemies of all spirituality, from the unitarian standpoint of the Nimatullāhī Sufis, giving offense to a person is an offense to the Creator, whereas feeling offended by a creature is tantamount to maintaining an attitude of polytheism before the One Creator.

The teachings of the Nimatullāhī Order remain alive today. Within Persia this order is by far the most widespread of the Sufi orders, and it continues to attract a large number of people in Europe and America and even in certain regions of the Islamic world such as black Africa, where this strongly Persian Sufi order had not penetrated until today.

Notes

1. Since the name of this order has become known in the West as the Nimatullāhī, this form will be used throughout this essay rather than Ni'mat Allāhī or Ni'mat Allāhiyyah, which would be the correct transliteration according to the system adopted in this book.
2. The historical sections of this article have been adapted from the author's *Masters of the Path: A History of the Masters of the Nimatullahi Sufi Order* (New York: Khaniqahi Nimatullahi Publications, 1980) 39–81.
3. His beautiful mausoleum in Mahan remains a great center of pilgrimage to this day.

4. See *Kulliyyāt-i ash'ār-i Shāh Ni'mat Allāh Walī Kirmānī* (*The Complete Poetical Works of Shāh Ni'mat Allāh Walī Kirmānī*), ed. J. Nurbakhsh (Tehran: Intishārāt-i Khāniqāh-i Ni'mat Allāhī, 1968; 6th reprint, 1982) *ghazal* 424.

5. 'Abd al-Razzāq Kirmānī, *Tadhkirah dar manāqib-i ḥadrat-i Shāh Ne'mat Allāh Walī*, in *Matériaux pour la biographie de Shāh Ni'matullāh Walī Kirmānī*, ed. J. Aubin (reprint; Tehran: Ṭahūrī Bookshop, 1983) 26.

6. See the editor's introduction, *Kulliyyāt-i ash'ār-i Shāh Ni'mat Allāh Walī Kirmānī*, 12.

7. Classical Sufi texts speak of these two contrasting states of soul, which are technical terms in the Sufi lexicon treated by the author in his *Sufism: Fear and Hope, Contraction and Expansion, Gathering and Dispersion, Intoxication and Sobriety, Annihilation and Subsistence* (New York: Khaniqahi Nimatullahi Publications, 1982).

8. See editor's introduction, *Kulliyyāt-i ash'ār-i Shāh Ni'mat Allāh Walī Kirmānī*, 14.

9. *Kulliyyāt-i ash'ār-i Shāh Ni'mat Allāh Walī Kirmānī*, 880, *rubā'ī* 79.

10. See the editor's introduction, *Kulliyyāt-i ash'ār-i Shāh Ni'mat Allāh Walī Kirmānī*, 15.

11. Although the *Dīwān* of Shāh Ni'mat Allāh has been published often in Iran, the most complete edition is that by J. Nurbakhsh, cited above.

12. See the editor's introduction, *Kulliyyāt-i ash'ār-i Shāh Ni'mat Allāh Walī Kirmānī*, 19.

13. *Kulliyyāt-i ash'ār-i Shāh Ni'mat Allāh Walī Kirmānī*, *tarjī'-band* I, 715.

14. See chapter three in this volume on Ibn 'Arabī and the school in which this basic metaphysical doctrine was first explicitly elaborated.

15. *Kulliyyāt-i ash'ār-i Shāh Ni'mat Allāh Walī Kirmānī*, *rubā'ī* 52, 876.

16. *Risālahā-yi Shāh Ni'mat Allāh Walī Kirmānī* (*The Complete Treatises of Shāh Ni'mat Allāh Walī Kirmānī*) (4 vols.; Tehran: Intishārāt-i Khāniqāh-i Ni'mat Allāhī, 1976–78).

17. *Ma'ṣūm* means inerrant and sinless.

18. Niẓām 'Alī Shāh was one of the shaykhs of Majdhūb 'Alī Shāh (a later *quṭb* of the Nimatullahi Order) and the author together with Nūr 'Alī Shāh and Rawnaq 'Alī Shāh of the *Jannat al-wiṣāl*, ed. J. Nurbakhsh (Tehran: Intishārāt-i Khāniqāh-i Ni'mat Allāhī, 1969) 862.

19. Before Fayḍ 'Alī Shāh's encounter with Ma'ṣūm, he had been a shaykh of the Nūrbakhshiyyah, another Sufi order, and had directed a *khānqāh* in Isfahan. Nūr 'Alī Shāh was the next *quṭb* of the order.

20. I.e., a descendant of 'Alī ibn Abī Ṭālib.

21. *Jannat al-wiṣāl*, ed. Nurbakhsh, 109.

22. The Safavids were originally a Sufi order which became a dynasty of Shī'ite kings who ruled Persia from 905/1500 to 1135/1722.

23. Muḥammad Ma'ṣūm Shīrāzī, *Ṭarā'iq al-ḥaqā'iq*, ed. Muḥammad Ja'far Maḥjūb (3 vols.; Tehran: Kitābkhāna-yi Sanā'ī, 1940) 3:175.

24. Ibid.

25. The term "shaykh" is used in the Nimatullahi Order to refer to the main representative of the supreme master or *quṭb* of the order. In other Sufi orders the master is usually called "shaykh" while the representative is called *muqaddam* or *khalīfah*.—ED.

26. Complete lists of these publications are provided in the bibliography to this volume.

27. See Ibrāhīm Hāshimī, *A Bibliography of Persian Books in Psychology and Education* (Tehran, 1350/1971) s.v. "Nurbakhsh."

28. *Fihrist-i nuskhahā-yi khaṭṭī-yi kitābkhāna-yi Nūrbakhsh (Khāniqāh-i Ni'mat Allāhī)* (Tehran: Intishārāt-i Khāniqāh-i Ni'mat Allāhī, 1971 [vol. 2], 1973 [vol. 1])

29. This section is adapted from extracts of a biography of J. Nurbakhsh composed by some of his disciples.

30. See the bibliography.

31. See J. Nurbakhsh, *In the Paradise of the Sufis* (New York: Khaniqahi Nimatullahi Publications, 1979).

32. See J. Nurbakhsh, *In the Tavern of Ruin: Seven Essays on Sufism* (New York: Khaniqahi Nimatullahi Publications, 1978) chapter 4.

33. Ibid., 67.

8

The Naqshbandiyyah Order

K. A. Nizami

The Silsilah and Its Features

Perhaps no mystic order in the long and checkered history of Islamic mysticism has had such far-reaching impact on the attitude of Muslim peoples in different regions as the Naqshbandiyyah. Named after Khwājah Bahā' al-Dīn Muḥammad Naqshband (717/1317–791/1389), a native of Bukhara, the order first established itself in Central Asia and then spread out to Turkestan, Syria, Afghanistan, and India. In Central Asia not only important towns but even small villages came to have Naqshbandī *takiyyahs* (mystic corners) and hospices which carried on brisk religious activity. In the tenth/sixteenth century the Naqshbandī Order reached India, and a new phase of its spiritual activity began under the leadership of Shaykh Aḥmad of Sirhind (972/1564–1033/1624), known as Mujaddid-i Alf-i Thānī (Reformer of the second millennium).[1] According to Emperor Jahāngīr (1014/1605–1037/1628) his disciples reached every town and city of the Mughal Empire.[2] Under him the influence of the Naqshbandī Order traveled back to Turkish lands with renewed vigor. The Naqshbandī center of Sirhind (in the Punjab) eclipsed in importance many Naqshbandī centers of Central Asia. Early during the thirteenth/nineteenth century, a Naqshbandī saint of Delhi—Shāh Ghulām 'Alī[3] (1156/1743–1240/1824)—had his disciples spread over "Rum, Syria, Baghdad, Egypt, China and Abyssinia."[4] One of his disciples, Mawlānā Khālid Kurdī, revitalized the Naqshbandiyyah in Syria and sent his followers far and wide.[5] The network of Naqshbandī *khānqāhs* covered several continents, and its saints worked both in national and international perimeters.

Muslim reaction to Western presence in many countries during the thirteenth/nineteenth century found its expression in the activities of the Naqshbandī saints. The revivalist movements in Turkey and West Asia owed their intellectual support and sustenance to the Naqshbandiyyah. Sayyid

Aḥmad Shahīd (d. 1247/1831), leader of the Mujāhidīn movement in India, was a Naqshbandī.[6] The renowned Arab reformer Muḥammad Rashīd Riḍā (1282/1865–1354/1935) followed the Naqshbandī teachings in his early years.[7] Snouck Hurgronje has noted the influence of the Naqshbandiyyah even in Sumatra, Java, and Borneo.[8] To this day, in fact, the order is a factor of importance in the life of the Muslim people of several countries. The publication of a Naqshbandī journal, *Sohbet Dergisi,* from Istanbul, though shortlived (1952–53), was an expression of continuing Turkish interest in the ideas of the order.

Throughout its history the Naqshbandī Order had two prominent characteristics determining its role and impact: (1) strict adherence to Islamic Law (*Sharī'ah*) and the traditions of the Prophet (*Sunnah*); (2) determined effort to influence the life and thought of the ruling classes and to bring the state closer to religion. Unlike other Sufi orders, it did not adopt an isolationist policy toward the government of the day. On the contrary, it encouraged confrontation with political powers in order to change their outlook. "The King is the soul and the people the body. If the King goes astray, the people will follow suit," Shaykh Aḥmad Sirhindī used to say.[9] The approach of the other orders, which gave greater importance to society than the government in their reformist efforts, was "As you are, so shall be your rulers." The Naqshbandīs, however, laid the responsibility squarely on the rulers and considered their reform a prerequisite to the reform of society.

Organizationally, an important aspect of the Naqshbandiyyah is its spiritual affiliation with Haḍrat Abū Bakr, the first caliph. Though a few of its sub-branches have traced their origin to Haḍrat 'Alī also,[10] the main affiliation of the order has remained with Abū Bakr. Many other Sufi orders trace their origin to 'Alī alone and consider him to be the main fountain of spiritual life in Islam.

Spiritually, the Naqshbandiyyah stand out in visualizing a whole universe of spiritual experience and adventure. They have laid out with great conceptual clarity a world of spiritual development indicating the stages and stations (*aḥwāl wa maqāmāt*) through which a mystic adventurer has to pass. Perhaps no other Sufi order has ever attempted this task so meticulously.

One other distinctive feature of the Naqshbandī saints was their "consciousness of mission." Most of them believed that they were divinely ordained to play their role in history. From Khwājah Bahā' al-Dīn Naqshband to Shāh Ghulām 'Alī of Delhi, different concepts of *mujaddid* (renewer), *qayyūm* (lasting), *qā'im* (steadfast), and *mahdī* (the guided one) determined the nature and scope of their activities.

Notwithstanding the great reverence that Naqshbandīs generally had for their spiritual mentors, they displayed unusual freedom of thought in giving up any idea or practice of their shaykh if they found it at variance with their own understanding of the *Sharī'ah* or the *Sunnah.* Shaykh Aḥmad Sirhindī disagreed with his mentor Khwājah Bāqī Bi'Llāh as well as all elders of the order on the question of the "oneness of being" (*waḥdat al-wujūd*), while Shāh Walī Allāh's father emphasized his faith in the "oneness of being," ignoring Shaykh Aḥmad's views. Mīrzā Maẓhar declared the Vedas to be a revealed book and explained away the polytheistic character of many Hindu practices, while Shāh Ghulām 'Alī, his disciple, disagreed with these ideas. The concept of *taṣawwur-i shaykh* (visualizing the image of the shaykh in meditation) was popular among the Naqshbandiyyah, but Sayyid Aḥmad Shahīd rejected it. Thus, a certain independence of thought always characterized the Naqshbandiyyah. Taken as a whole, these distinctive features provided the Naqshbandī saints with direction and a motive power for their activities.

Khwājah Bahā' al-Dīn Naqshband: The Founder

Khwājah Bahā' al-Dīn Naqshband, the founder of the order, was born at Kushk-i Hinduwan, a village near Bukhara.[11] He received instruction in Sufism from Muḥammad Bābā of Sammās (a village three miles from Bukhara). Later he visited Bukhara, Samarqand, and other adjoining towns. At Nasaf he studied under Amīr Kulāl and, after his death, lived for several years with 'Ārif al-Dikkirānī, a successor of Amīr Kulāl. For about twelve years he lived in Samarqand in the service of Sultan Khalīl and, when in 748/1347 the ruler was overthrown, he went to Ziwartun. There, as a part of his mystic training, he looked after herds of animals for seven years and spent another period of seven years in road mending. The purpose of such exercises was to deepen the sources of compassion and philanthropy and to awaken a sense of service in the entrant to the mystic fold. He died in his native village in 791/1389.

The Khwājah popularized his order in Central Asia and attracted people belonging to different walks of life. Though some incidents of his contact with the rulers and the nobles are recorded, he generally avoided mixing with them.[12] He did not like to partake of food with them, as he considered the sources of their income illegal.[13] Despite all this, he was held in high esteem by the rulers. It is said that once when Tīmūr's procession was passing through the streets of Bukhara, the carpets of the saint's *khānqāh* were being dusted; Tīmūr stood there till the cleaners had finished their work.[14]

The saint had some land in his native village which he caused to be cultivated through some person,[15] but never involved himself in cultivation. He lived a simple life and when asked why he did not have a slave or slave-girl, he replied: "Ownership does not go with sainthood." According to Jāmī, the Khwājah used to say that his mystic path was *al-'Urwat al-wuthqā* (the firmest bond), which meant holding fast to the ways of the Prophet and his Companions.[16] The saint's remark that it is easy to reach the highest pinnacle of the knowledge of monotheism (*tawḥīd*), but it is difficult to attain gnosis (*ma'rifah*) shows the subtle distinction that he made between spiritual knowledge and spiritual experience.[17] From what Ṣāliḥ has recorded about his life and activities, it appears that he was deeply concerned with the moral and spiritual training of his disciples and did not like them to have ill will or strained relations with anyone. Once he sought forgiveness from a person on behalf of a disciple by rubbing his face at his door.[18]

According to Shāh Walī Allāh, the details of spiritual discipline as laid down by Khwājah Bahā' al-Dīn Naqshband for his disciples were based on a thorough appreciation of the Turkish character and were therefore rigorous and exacting.[19]

Antecedents of the *Silsilah:* The Khwājagān

Khwājah Yūsuf Hamadānī (440/1048–534/1140), a seminal personality in the early history of the *silsila-yi Khwājagān* (the initiatic chain of the order), influenced a number of eminent saints who later became founders of independent orders.[20] Well versed in Islamic Law and a follower of the school of Imam Abū Ḥanīfah, Khwājah Yūsuf taught at Baghdad, Isfahan, Khurasan, Samarqand, and Bukhara. Subsequently he turned to spiritual culture and started delivering sermons. Four of his successors, Khwājah 'Abd Allāh Barqī, Khwājah Ḥasan Andaqī, Khwājah Aḥmad Yisiwī, and Khwājah 'Abd al-Khāliq Ghujdawānī played important roles in the history of the order.[21] The organization of the *silsilah* was the result of the efforts of Khwājah Aḥmad; its doctrines emanated from Khwājah 'Abd al-Khāliq Ghujdawānī.

Khwājah Aḥmad Yisiwī (d. 561/1166) is called *ātā* (father) by the Turks out of respect for his role in their spiritual history.[22] Farīd al-Dīn 'Aṭṭār reverentially refers to him as "the spiritual mentor of Turkistan (*pīr-i Turkistān*)."[23] He was born at Yisi and received his early education there. Later he moved to Bukhara and joined the spiritual discipline of Shaykh Yūsuf Hamadānī. In 555/1160 he succeeded him as the chief saint of the hospice. He is reported to have converted large numbers of Turks to Islam.[24] Tīmūr built his tomb, which has remained through the ages a place of pilgrimage for Turks and Mongols and has recently been renovated by the Kazakhistan government.[25] It was through the successors of Khwājah Aḥmad, Manṣūr Ātā (d. 593/1197), Sa'īd Ātā (d. 615/1218), and others that the order spread in Transoxiana, Khwarazm, Khurasan and the rest of

Persia, Anatolia and other places.[26] Ḥājjī Biktāsh and Sari Saltuq also joined it.[27]

Apart from his place in the history of Islamic mysticism in Turkey, Khwājah Aḥmad occupies a position of eminence in the history of Turkish literature. He is called Father of Turkish poetry, as it was he who first started composing verses in that language. His collection of poems, called *Dīwān-i Ḥikmet*, is very popular among the Turks.[28]

Khwājah ʿAbd al-Khāliq (d. 575/1179) was born at Ghujdwan, modern Gighduvan in Uzbekistan, which was a brisk center of trade, its weekly markets attracting people from neighboring villages.[29] As a consequence, the people were generally materialistic in their outlook. The Khwājah used to criticize their ways vehemently. "You have *zunnārs* [the sacred threads of idol worshipers] hidden inside your bodies," he told them. His mystical thought finds expression in his treatises (1) *Risāla-yi ṭarīqat* (*Treatise on the Spiritual Path*), (2) *Naṣīḥat-nāmah* (*Treatise of Advice*), and (3) *Risāla-yi ṣāḥibiyyah* (*The Ṣāḥibiyyah Treatise*).[30]

His spiritual will and testament (*Naṣīḥat-nāmah*) contains the following instructions to his descendants:

> Learn Islamic jurisprudence (*fiqh*) and the traditions of the Prophet (*aḥādīth*). Do not mix with illiterate mystics. . . . Offer prayers in congregation. . . . Do not seek after fame. . . . Do not accept any office. . . . Do not be a surety for anybody. . . . Do not go to the court. Do not mix with rulers or princes. . . . Do not construct a *khānqāh*. . . . Do not hear too much mystic music. . . . Do not condemn mystic music. . . . Eat only what is permitted. . . . So far as you can, do not marry a woman who wants material comforts. . . . Laughter kills one's heart. Your heart should be full of grief, your body as if of an ailing person, your eyes wet, your actions sincere, your prayers earnest, your dress tattered, your company dervishes, your wealth poverty, your house the mosque and your friend God.[31]

Khwājah Ghujdawānī provided the Naqshbandiyyah with its mystic practices by consolidating the thought of the preceding saints of the order in the form of aphorisms which later became the cornerstone of the mystical thought of the order. These principles were the following:

1. *hūsh dar dam:* conscious remembrance of God as one inhales and exhales one's breath.

2. *naẓar bar qadam:* keeping an eye on every step that one takes. It meant that every movement was regulated and directed toward achievement of some divine purpose.

3. *safar dar waṭan:* introspective study of oneself, that is, an effort to investigate and explore, analyze and understand one's own universe of internal experience.

4. *khalwat dar anjuman:* solitude when in company, that is, carrying on spiritual practices internally and being alone with God while outwardly busy with people.
5. *yād kard:* recollection.
6. *bāz gard:* restraining one's thought.
7. *nigāh dāsht:* keeping a watch on the drift and direction of thought.
8. *yād dāsht:* treasuring God in memory through concentration.

Saints who followed 'Abd al-Khāliq Ghujdawānī wove around these aphorisms a whole philosophy of mystic discipline and added the following three concepts to it:

9. *wuqūf-i 'adadī:* keeping an eye on the heart's remembrance of God so that concentration is not disturbed.
10. *wuqūf-i zamānī:* keeping an account of how one spends one's time; thanking Him for the time spent in good works and repenting for wrongs done.
11. *wuqūf-i qalbī:* keeping the heart in a state of alertness, responsive to divine communication.

These practices, which are aimed at regulating the entire inner life of man, may not have been new in spirit or content, but they gave clear and categorical expression to fleeting moments of spiritual experience and identified every spiritual state, permanent or transitory.

Among the disciples of 'Abd al-Khāliq Ghujdawānī, Khwājah Aḥmad Ṣiddīq, Khwājah Awliyā' Kabīr, and Khwājah Sulaymān Karmaynī were active and dynamic figures.[32] They extended the influence of the order in Bukhara and its neighboring areas. Khwājah Muḥammad Bukhārī, a disciple of Khwājah Sulaymān's disciple Shaykh Abū Sa'īd Bukhārī, wrote *Maslak al-'ārifīn* (*The Regulations of the Gnostics*), a book of great value on the doctrines of the order.[33] Another important figure of the *silsilah* was Khwājah 'Alī Rāmitīnī, whose spiritual eminence has been praised by no less a person than Jalāl al-Dīn Rūmī.[34] The Naqshbandīs generally refer to him as *Ḥaḍrat-i 'azīzān.*[35] He had correspondence with Shaykh 'Alā' al-Dawlah Simnānī. His following remark is quoted in Naqshbandī sources: "Had there been at that time a single descendant of Khwājah 'Abd al-Khāliq Ghujdawānī living on this earth, Manṣūr could never have been hanged." Once Khwājah 'Alī was asked why he practiced the repetition of the Name *Allāh* loudly (*dhikr-i jaliy).* He replied: "For a novice loud repetition of the Name *Allāh* is needed; advanced mystics could do it through (silent repetition in) the heart."

The way he entered Khwarazm and settled there throws light on his method of spiritual training and work. When at the gate of Khwarazm, he sent some of his disciples to the Shah with a message: "A weaver dervish stands at the gate of your city. If you permit him, he would come; otherwise he would go elsewhere." The king and his courtiers laughed at this request and the king, in a light mood, acceded to it by putting his signature to an edict. The saint entered the city and settled in a lonely corner. Every morning he went out to the labor market and engaged some laborers. Throughout the day he instructed them in the principles of Islamic hygiene and taught them the way to offer prayers and repeat continuously the Name *Allāh.* At the end of the day he gave them their wages and let them go home. In this way he continued to impart religious and spiritual education to laborers. In the course of time the circle of his admirers increased. Some courtiers created suspicion in Khwārazm Shah's mind about his increasing popularity. The Shah would have expelled him, but the saint showed the *farmān* or royal edict to the Shah and was allowed to live there. He died in Khwarazm working ceaselessly for the spiritual culture of the people of the region.

The teachings of all these saints and their religious and spiritual ideals were consolidated and channeled into a movement by Khwājah Baha' al-Dīn Naqshband.

Successors of Khwājah Naqshband

Muḥammad Pārsā and 'Ubayd Allāh Aḥrār

Among the disciples of Khwājah Bahā' al-Dīn Naqshband, Khwājah 'Alā' al-Dīn 'Aṭṭār and Khwājah Muḥammad Pārsā were the most outstanding. Khwājah 'Aṭṭār (d. 803/1400) had shared the burden of his master in looking after the spiritual training of the new entrants to the mystic fold.[36] He developed a persuasive and inspiring method of spiritual instruction. Khwājah Muḥammad Pārsā recorded the master's table talks, as they contained the essence of Naqshbandī doctrine presented in practical terms. According to him, of the ten stages of spiritual progress, nine could be covered by earning a livelihood through personal effort and from permitted sources. He preferred cultivation to trade.[37]

Khwājah Muḥammad Pārsā (d. 822/1419) accompanied his master on *ḥajj* and received his spiritual training during the journey.[38] He was very fond of the *Mathnawī* of Rūmī and used to consult it even for omen and augury. Citing elder saints as his authority, he used to say that one should always pray to God with the same fear and faith with which a dying person turns to Him in supplication.

Khwājah Muḥammad Pārsā displayed both ingenuity and psychological insight in describing his experiences of the enjoyment of the Infinite. Iqbāl remarked in one of his lectures: "But it is really religious Psychology, as in 'Irāqī and Khwājah Muḥammad Pārsā, which brings us much nearer to our modern way of looking at the problem of space and time."[39] A careful study of Khwājah Pārsā's thought, which takes his exegetical work also into consideration, would reveal the depth and originality of his ideas. Ulugh Beg, Shāh Rukh, and other Central Asian princes treated him with respect on account of his scholarship and piety.

An important aspect of the literary and religious activity of the followers of Khwājah Bahā' al-Dīn was their interest in Quranic studies. Some of them, like Khwājah Muḥammad Pārsā and Ya'qūb Charkhī, wrote commentaries on the Quran in order to attract people to a study of the basic source of the Faith.[40]

In influence and material means Khwājah 'Ubayd Allāh Aḥrār (806/1403–896/1490) was perhaps the most powerful saint of the order. He was born at Shash (Tashkand) in 806/1403 during the month of Ramaḍān. Kāshifī says that he did not suck milk from his mother's breast during the first forty days, as she did not have proper ablutions at that time. If anybody planned anything for him which was a deviation from the traditions of the prophet, it never materialized. He was one year old when the ceremony of shaving his head (*'aqīqah*) was arranged in a way that was not consistent with the tradition of the Prophet. Exactly on the day of celebration, the death of Tīmūr occurred and the whole function was disturbed.[41]

In his boyhood he saw Jesus Christ in a dream and fell at his feet. Jesus pulled him up and said: "Do not be worried, we will train you." Khwājah Aḥrār interpreted this dream to mean that he would be blessed with the power to revive dead hearts as Christ used to revive dead bodies.[42]

Khwājah Aḥrār had little interest in formal education during his youth and frustrated all efforts of his maternal uncle, Khwājah Ibrāhīm, to arrange regular and methodical instruction for him. He was taken to Samarqand for this purpose, but to no avail. His father, Khwājah Maḥmūd Shāshī, was a man of very small means. He cultivated some land at Gulshan. Khwājah Aḥrār spent his early years under extremely straitened circumstances. With an old and tattered garment (*qabā*) on his body, he lived in Shahrukhiyyah in a house that was below the road level so that rain water would run into it and it would become uninhabitable. During winter days half of his body remained cold for want of clothing. This early period of destitution and penury, which was in sharp contrast to his later affluence and plenty, remained ever present in his mind, and he developed a keen concern for the poor and the destitute. Throughout his life, he never accepted *futūḥ* (unasked-for gifts), which were permitted for mystics.

After visiting many important saints in Transoxiana and Herat, Khwājah

Aḥrār returned to his homeland and took to cultivation. With a pair of bulls which he shared with a partner, he started ploughing the fields. Very soon his economic position began to improve. Eventually he came to own thirty-three hundred villages (*mazra'ah*) and many extensive farms. Even the famous village of Pashaghar once belonged to him.[43] Jāmī refers to his villages in his *Yūsuf wa Zulaykhā* (*Joseph and Potiphar's Wife*). Kāshifī once stayed with one of his clerks at Qurshi and was informed by him that in a single village of that area three thousand laborers and double that number of bulls were engaged every year for irrigating the land. From the villages in Samarqand alone eighty thousand *maunds* of corn went to Sultan Aḥmad Mīrzā as land tax (*'ushr*, i.e., one-tenth of the produce).[44] Jāmī says in a verse that when poverty desired to appear in the garb of royalty, it came in the form of 'Ubayd Allāh Aḥrār.

In the history of the Naqshbandī Order no other saint has ever possessed so much land, property, or wealth as Khwājah 'Ubayd Allāh Aḥrār. He was respected by high and low alike. Respectful references to him are found in contemporary histories and records. Bābur looked to him as the source of his spiritual guidance and solace.

Khwājah Aḥrār, who possessed an extremely humble and humane temperament, received his visitors with great humility. His urbanity, culture, and courtesy were almost proverbial. He disdained haughtiness and pride and cited a saying of the Prophet to this effect: "Behaving with pride toward the proud is like spending money in charity." He considered pride an obnoxious habit and cited an incident from the life of Abū Yazīd to highlight its evil effect on a mystic. While walking in a street, he came across a dog with a wet body and tried to save his skirt from getting polluted. The dog said, "If your skirt had touched my body, a little water would have cleaned it, but what about the filth that you have put on your skirt by considering yourself purer than myself. Which water would clean this?"[45] Khwājah Aḥrār believed that pride and arrogance lowered a man's moral stature and weakened his spiritual fiber. Service of mankind was of supreme spiritual value in his opinion, and his concern for the poor and the downtrodden won for him the love and affection of the people.

Once an epidemic broke out in Samarqand. The Khwājah, who was staying at the *madrasah* of Mawlānā Quṭb al-Dīn Ṣadr, looked very devotedly after the patients and did not hesitate to wash their soiled beds. This continued to such a degree that he himself fell victim to the disease. But he did not stop looking after those who needed more care. "Different have been the gates," he used to say, "through which people have reached their spiritual goals; in my case it has been the door of service [to mankind]." A person was cruel and pitiless, in his eyes, if his heart did not throb in sympathy with those in distress and pain. Even cruelty to animals should touch the chords of sympathy in the human heart. He mentioned the story of a saint whose body started bleeding at the sight of a horse which was being whipped.

Though possessing considerable material means, Khwājah Aḥrār did not attach his heart to worldly things and believed that the secret of human happiness lay in contentment, which he explained as the attitude of that person who lived in a jungle where there was no water, no companion, and no hope of getting food from any source, and yet he maintained his peace of mind.

Khwājah Aḥrār's source of spiritual inspiration was Ibn 'Arabī, whose views he often cited in his assemblies. He was also an admirer of Rūmī, and in elucidation of his own mystical concepts, he relied on the *Mathnawī*. The Naqshbandī saints of this period, particularly Khwājah Aḥrār, played a very important role in popularizing the *Mathnawī* in Central Asia.

Two aspects of Khwājah Aḥrār's thought deserve particular mention. First, he believed in the development of man after death (*taraqqī ba'd al-mawt*).[46] For him death was merely a stage in the process of man's growth; he continued to grow even after his death. This idea, which was taken up by his followers also, had an impact on human character and perspective. Second, the Khwājah believed that even fossils and rocks have life and respond to human action. He referred to Ibn 'Arabī's researches in this regard and expressed the view that stones and rocks accept the influence of man.[47]

The Khwājah's spiritual discipline was based on his conviction that the purpose of human life was to be busy with the remembrance of God at all times. This did not mean that a person could cut himself off from all contact with society and sit in a corner meditating and praying. It meant an attitude of mind which, while attending to all routine works of life, remained really engaged with God. In fact, *dhikr* (remembrance of God) should permeate one's whole being. He quoted Khwājah Muḥammad 'Alī Ḥakīm Tirmidhī, who said that the life of the heart depends on remembering God day and night. He once punished his servants who were talking while putting wood in the stove to heat water for ablutions. He expected them to be busy with God even while doing odd jobs. When he permitted visitors to go back to their homes, he advised them to keep busy in contemplation all the way and take stock of their involvement with God at every stage of their journey. While he laid great emphasis on the remembrance of God, he did not permit penitences or fasts beyond a point. Excessive indulgence in them, he used to say, created mental imbalance.

Despite all the consideration that he had for his visitors, he did not like to associate with people who were opposed to mystic ways (*bīgānah*). He believed and quoted Khwājah Aḥmad Yisiwī in support of his views that even if an article belonging to one hostile to the mystic way of life remained in the *khānqāh,* it disturbed concentration in prayers.

Khwājah Aḥrār did not like to see the mystics dressed shabbily or neglecting the cleanliness of their bodies. "Unless a spiritual teacher possesses outward comeliness, he can neither infuse love in the hearts of his followers nor inspire them," he used to say. In support of his views he cited the practice of the Prophet, who combed his beard and put on an attractive headdress before he came out.

The Khwājah advised his visitors that once they selected a spiritual mentor they were obliged to put full faith and reliance in him. Lack of faith in the spiritual guide obstructed the growth of one's spiritual personality. But he rejected the view that nothing could be achieved without a spiritual mentor. He cited from the Quran: "This day have I perfected for you your religion and completed My favor on you and chosen for you Islam as a religion" (III,5). He said that the Quran and the traditions of the Prophet were enough for guidance and the idea of the indispensability of a shaykh was not valid. On the question of celibacy, his attempt was to reconcile two palpably contradictory positions. Although he expressed full faith in the sayings of the Prophet and the Quranic verses which enjoined married life, he put forward arguments in favor of celibacy. He said that prophets could marry because they had full control over their time and their thoughts and there was no risk of their becoming distracted. Marriage was necessary for the common man also, because he needed the satisfaction of his animal soul. For the middle category, in which he included the mystics, celibacy was preferable. "A single breath," he used to say, "that one draws from inside with God is better than seventy-two thousand sons." He said that in recommending celibate life to his followers, he was guided by the exigencies of the time.

According to the Khwājah, the real work of a mystic was not merely concentration and meditation but a continuing effort to subordinate all his actions to a supreme ideal and to infuse that spirit into all his actions. Being in the Divine Presence and the mental concentration that came to an individual as a result of his own struggle upon the mystic path were more abiding than spiritual states that appeared spontaneously. Communication through the tongue was more important than influencing the hearts of people through spiritual communication. Had it been otherwise, prophets would not have used their tongues to attract people but would have relied on their spiritual powers to bring about change in people's lives.

A bold and activist strain appeared in the thought of Khwājah Aḥrār when he talked about resistance to injustice and tyranny. When a man with a just cause is confronted with any difficult situation, two courses are open to him: either to adopt a low-lying posture and save himself or to fight the evil with full determination, regardless of the consequences. Technically the first course is called that of *rukhṣat,* and the second *'azīmat.* The Khwājah told his followers that those who acted on *'azīmat* were superior to those who acted on *rukhṣat.* It was a spiritually impoverished personality which adopted the course of least resistance; *'azīmat* was the path of the spiritually powerful.

Spiritual exercises should be indulged in only to the extent that one retained joy in them and did not become stale. He told his disciples to dispel from their hearts both attraction of heaven and fear of hell. Love of God alone, he used to emphasize, should be the leitmotif of all spiritual activity.

Khwājah Aḥrār considered it necessary to keep contact with the rulers and influence them for the good. Once he was told in a dream that the law of the Prophet (*Sharī'at*) would be strengthened through the rulers. This determined the direction of his thought and activity. He used to say: "If we had concentrated on admitting people to spiritual discipline, no spiritual leader of these days would have found a single disciple for himself. But we have been entrusted with another responsibility. We have to protect the Muslims from the [highhandedness of the] tyrants. For this reason we have to keep contact with the rulers and captivate them."[48] With this approach his contact with the ruling classes increased continuously. The Tīmūrid princes treated him with deep respect. They used to receive him "standing at a distance with their eyes fixed on the ground."[49] Yūnus Khān, Sulṭān Aḥmad Mīrzā, 'Umar Shaykh Mīrzā and others referred their internecine conflicts to him for arbitration. Bābur's father, 'Umar Shaykh Mīrzā, was his disciple.[50] Referring to his father's devotion to the saint, Bābur remarks: "As his Highness the Khwājah was there, accompanying him step by step, most of his affairs found lawful settlement."[51] Before his conquest of Samarqand, Bābur saw him in a dream, lifting him above the ground and predicting his occupation of Samarqand.[52] Khwājah Aḥrār's sons Khwājakā Khwājat and Khwājah Yaḥyā also had close relations with Bābur.[53]

Khwājah Aḥrār did not leave any literary work except a booklet which he wrote at the insistence of his father, Khwājah Maḥmūd Shāshī, entitled *Risāla-yi wālidiyyah* (*Treatise Presented to the Father*). Bābur translated this Persian treatise into Turkish verse during a period of his illness. He believed that as Būṣīrī, the author of the poem *Qaṣīda-yi burdah,* was rid of his paralytic disease upon composition of that poem, so would he recover from illness on versifying Khwājah 'Ubayd Allāh Aḥrār's work.[54]

'Abd al-Raḥmān Jāmī

In the literary and spiritual history of the Naqshbandiyyah, Mawlānā 'Abd al-Raḥmān Jāmī (827/1414–898/1492) stands out as one of its outstanding figures. In 832/1419 when Khwājah Muḥammad Pārsā visited Herat, Jāmī's father, Niẓām al-Dīn, took him to the saint. He was only five years of age at that time, but he was so deeply impressed by the aroma of spiritual serenity and grandeur that hallowed Khwājah Pārsā that throughout his life he remembered his features.

After completing his education in traditional subjects, Jāmī joined the discipline of Khwājah Sa'īd al-Dīn Kāshgharī (d. 864/1459), a *khalīfah* of Khwājah Bahā' al-Dīn Naqshband. For years he subjected himself to penances under his supervision. When Kāshgharī died, Jāmī joined the discipline of Khwājah 'Ubayd Allāh Aḥrār and gave to one of his *mathnawīs* the title *Tuḥfat al-Aḥrār* (*Present to Aḥrār*). It was with him that he learned difficult portions of Ibn 'Arabī's *al-Futūḥāt al-makkiyah* (*Meccan Revelations*). Strangely enough, one of the greatest exponents of Ibn 'Arabī's thought had learned the great mystic's works from one whose formal education did not go beyond a few elementary books.[55] Jāmī, however, used to send his disciples from Khurasan to Khwājah Aḥrār for guidance and inspiration. The Khwājah told them: "When Mawlānā Jāmī is there, why do you take the trouble of coming over to me? How strange it is that a river of light flows in Khurasan and people come rushing here to receive light from a candle!"

Jāmī's chief contribution to Sufism lies in presenting the thought of Ibn 'Arabī in more intelligible terms and in writing commentaries on the works of Ibn 'Arabī, Rūmī, Pārsā, etc. which elucidated many abstruse concepts of the oneness of being (*waḥdat al-wujūd*). Jāmī's own poetic compositions also helped in propagating such concepts and ideas. During his lifetime, he was looked upon as an authority on Ibn 'Arabī and people from regions as distant as the Deccan wrote to him for elucidation of the mystical concepts of Ibn 'Arabī.[56]

Jāmī's *Nafaḥāt al-uns* (*Breath of Familiarity*) has not only preserved the account of many saints of Central Asia and Persia but has also inspired many others to attempt similar compilations. Encouraged by him, Kāshifī wrote his *Rashaḥāt* (*Sprinklings*), which is invaluable for reconstructing the history of the Naqshbandī Order.

Jāmī's mystical attitude was determined by his deeply aesthetic temperament. He believed in divine and cosmic love (*'ishq*) as a necessary condition for all spiritual advancement. Though this emotion was basically mystical and cosmic, at times it appears that it became erotic, and appreciation of things beautiful made his love appear sensual and mundane. But in his day an impression had developed that the love of some human being (*'ishq-i majāzī*) was necessary for developing the love of God (*'ishq-i ḥaqīqī*). Love centralized and integrated a personality by giving it an emotional peg. A mystic mentor's task was made easy when a man was in the grip of *'ishq-i majāzī*, because he could cut his connection at one point and divert his emotions toward *'ishq-i ḥaqīqī*. As for one who did not experience *'ishq-i majāzī* but was desirous of traversing the mystic journey, his mentor would have to sever his connection with the world at too many points. But this whole approach, whatever its psychological basis, involved grave risks, and Khwājah Bāqī Bi'Llāh told his disciples that even Jāmī had dispensed with it in his later life.

The Naqshbandī *Silsilah* in India and the Role of Khwājah Bāqī Bi'Llāh

In the closing years of the tenth/sixteenth century, the center of Naqshbandī activity, as well as its intellectual gravity, shifted to India. Khwājah Bāqī Bi'Llāh (971/1563–1012/1603) was born in Kabul.[57] He traveled in Transoxiana, Samarqand, Bukhara, Kashmir, etc., and then came to India. In his own words, he "brought the sacred seed (of the order) from Samarqand and Bukhara and sowed it in the fertile soil of India." Fully conversant with the Naqshbandī principles of organization and its methods of training, he bestowed equal attention on the common man and Mughal nobles. During the short span of five years that he was destined to work in India, he conveyed the message of the *silsilah* to the *'ulamā'*, the Sufis, the *māliks* (landowners), and the *manṣabdārs* (officials) with equal effectiveness. His discerning eye selected the best talent in different spheres—Nawāb Murtaḍā Khān among the political figures,[58] Shaykh Aḥmad Sirhindī among the Sufis, and Shaykh 'Abd al-Ḥaqq among the *'ulamā'*.

What endeared Khwājah Bāqī Bi'Llāh to the people was his extremely amiable personality. People came to him not merely for mystic training but also for that spiritual bliss and solace which are the deepest longing of the human heart. Like the Naqshbandī saints of Central Asia, he was addressed as Ḥaḍrat-i Īshān. His *khānqāh* was a big establishment where food and stipend were given to the inmates. But he extended his hospitality to others for three days only. In his view permitted sources of livelihood and faith in one's spiritual guide were necessary prerequisites for spiritual training. The following proceedings of his meeting held on 23 Dhi'l-qa'dah 1009/17 May 1601 throw light on the principles of his discipline:

> I [the compiler] was privileged to kiss the ground [received access to meeting with the saint]. Conversation turned to the circumspection that should be

exercised in the matter of food. [The Khwājah said: "One should not merely satisfy himself that the food before him is permitted. One should see to it that the wood, the water, and the cooking utensils used are all from permitted sources of income. The cook also should be a God-conscious person. Cooking should be done at the proper time with a heart conscious of God and His Presence. Food prepared without due care generates a smoke inside which closes the sources through which divine benediction descends [upon the human heart]. Pious souls which are the reflection of divine grace do not come near such a heart. . . . People with weak minds should take food which is soft [easily digestible] and invigorates the mind. For instance, if a man with a feeble mind makes bread of barley his diet, aridity will affect his mind and stop the passage of [divine] benediction. . . . There is a bounty [of God] which specifically pertains to the mind. When dryness gets into the brain [as a result of uncongenial food], this bounty cannot reach there. So be very cautious in the matter of your food. Do not eat food which does not suit your temperament. Do not observe many [supererogatory] fasts which cause the weakness of mind. People endowed with spiritual unveiling (*kashf*) should be extra cautious about it and should take care to make their mind vigorous. Often the dryness of mind leads to deceptive [spiritual] revelations.

At this stage a man submitted that such and such a person—he named a notable contemporary saint—has said that your good self keeps away his followers from faith in earlier saints and thinks that their spiritual well-being depends on this [segregation]. [The Khwājah] replied: "It is not so. When I find that some aspirants for spiritual training are fickle in their faith, I advise them to concentrate on one [saint and one order]. There is a lot of discussion on this subject in mystic treatises. One [author] says: 'One who remains at one place, is [virtually] everywhere; and one who is everywhere is [really] nowhere.' Another writer says: 'Hold to one door and hold it fast.' Others have said: 'Oneness of objective is a prerequisite of the mystic path' and so on.

"This being the truth of the matter, why should not I tell them and save them from distraction? Those who come to me, come for their [spiritual] benefit and not for any other purpose. . . . No one else has the faith which we have in the Chishtiyyah, the Qādiriyyah and the Suhrawardiyyah [saints]. But the people of India in general have a faith in [these saints of different orders] which borders on *shirk* (polytheism). In our view the saints of these orders have [so] lost themselves in God (*fanā' fi'Llāh*) [that their separate existence has ceased], but these people consider them as independently existent and effective."[59]

A staunch believer in the doctrine of the oneness of being of Ibn 'Arabī, Bāqī Bi'Llāh explained away the criticism of 'Alā' al-Dawlah Simnānī as a result of a misunderstanding. The claim of the followers of Shaykh Aḥmad Sirhindī that he had accepted the other theory propound by Shaykh Aḥmad lacks confirmation.

Khwājah Bāqī Bi'Llāh breathed his last when he was hardly forty. Some time before his death he showed his palm to his wife and said: "See, my life line has come to an end." What the Khwājah had achieved at that age was really remarkable. He had effectively delivered the message of the Naqshbandiyyah in India and had prepared the ground for its further expansion. Though he ran a large *khānqāh,* when he breathed his last his property comprised one rupee in cash, a few books, a horse, and an ordinary carpet.[60]

Khwājah Bāqī Bi'Llāh used the medium of poetry also to communicate his ideas, mostly of the school of the oneness of being, but elucidating other mystical concepts also.[61] In his table talks the spirit of his discipline is made clear in a single sentence: "Not mystic emotions but adherence to *Sharī'at* Law should be the ideal." His eldest son, known as Khwājah Kalān, wrote *Mablagh al-rijāl* (*Perfection of Men*) in which he discussed some contemporary trends of thought and religious sects in India and Persia. His younger son, Khwājah Khurd, wrote a treatise, *Ta'līm-i sālik* (*Instruction of the Traveler upon the Path*) providing basic instruction to the entrants of the mystic fold.[62]

Shaykh Aḥmad of Sirhind and Shaykh 'Abd al-Ḥaqq Muḥaddith of Delhi were eminent disciples of Khwājah Muḥammad Bāqī. Shaykh 'Abd al-Ḥaqq concentrated on academic work and looked after the seminary where the traditions of the Prophet (*aḥādith*) were the main subject of instruction.[63] He wrote about sixty books on different religious themes and prepared also the first reliable biographical dictionary of the Indian mystics, the *Akhbār al-akhyār* (*Annals of Pious Men*).

Mujaddid-i Alf-i Thānī and the Reorganization of the Naqshbandiyyah

Shaykh Aḥmad was born in 971/1563 in Sirhind, a town in the Punjab.[64] After completing his education there, he came to Agra for further studies and came into contact with Abu'l-Faḍl and Fayḍī, who were to enjoy great prestige at the court of Akbar. He is reported to have helped Fayḍī in writing his Arabic commentary on the Quran, known as *Sawāṭi' al-ilhām* (*Radiance of Inspiration*). This work has the amazing peculiarity of containing no letter with a dot—and the Arabic alphabet has fifteen dotted letters! At the age of twenty-eight he went to Delhi and joined the circle of Khwājah Bāqī Bi'Llāh's disciples.

Shaykh Aḥmad's position is unique in the intellectual history of the Naqshbandī Order. While adhering to the basic and fundamental principles of the order, he gave its doctrines a new orientation by discarding the doctrine of the oneness of being (*waḥdat al-wujūd*) as propounded by Ibn 'Arabī and accepted by almost every important saint of the Naqshbandiyyah, like Khwājah Bahā' al-Dīn Naqshband, Khwājah 'Ubayd Allāh Aḥrār, and Mawlānā Jāmī. His predecessors had not merely accepted the ideas of

Ibn 'Arabī, but in fact the key and kernel of their higher thought was derived from his *al-Futūḥāt al-makkiyah* (*Meccan Revelations*) and *Fuṣūṣ al-ḥikam* (*Bezels of Wisdom*). Shaykh Aḥmad declared: "We do not need the *Futūḥāt al-makkiyah;* we need the *Futūḥāt al-madaniyyah* (Medinan Revelations)" and rebutted Ibn 'Arabī's doctrines of the oneness of being, propounding the other concept of *tawḥīd* generally termed *waḥdat al-shuhūd* (unity of consciousness). Burhān Aḥmad Fārūqī explains the implications of his thought as follows:

> The Mujaddid insists that there is absolutely no relation between the world and its unique Creator except that the world has been created by Him and is a sign that indicates His hidden attributes. All other assertions, viz., *ittiḥād* or union or identity, *iḥāṭa* or comprehension or *ma'iyyat* or co-existence are due to *sukr* or the ecstatic condition of mystics. Those who have reached the higher state of *ṣaḥw* or sobriety are free from such so-called *ma'ārif* or cognitions. True, they too came across such cognitions in the course of their mystic journey; but they have left them behind and they criticise them in the light of Revelation. Indeed, to speak of the relations of *ittiḥād* or union, *'ainiyyat* or identity, etc. between God and the World is an awful misconception. It is a misconception of this sort: Suppose a highly accomplished man invents an alphabet and certain sounds to display his ingenuity and capacity. Someone comes forward and maintains that the alphabet and the sounds are identical with the inventor.[65]

Shaykh Aḥmad propounded his ideas so cogently and based them on his personal spiritual experience that after him the doctrine of *waḥdat al-shuhūd* became the doctrine of the Naqshbandī saints. In India the mystic doctrine till then was based mainly on the doctrine of *waḥdat al-wujūd,* and a number of commentaries had been written on the works of Ibn 'Arabī. It was but inevitable that a conflict of mystical concepts took place as a result of Shaykh Aḥmad's exposition of his doctrine. Even the French visitor François Bernier noticed the controversy that was raging in Indo-Muslim religious thought in those days.[66]

Shaykh Aḥmad, like preceding Naqshbandī saints of Central Asia, demanded from his disciples meticulous adherence to the Quran and the traditions (*Sunnah*) of the Prophet. He was opposed to all innovations that were not confirmed by the practice of the Prophet and dubbed them *bid'at.* He trenchantly criticized the attitude of mind which looked to any source of inspiration except the Prophet.[67] This approach led him to criticize Akbar's religious experiments.

Akbar had had long discussions with different religious thinkers in his Hall of Religious Discussions. He had inquired into the religious principles and practices of Hinduism, Buddhism, Jainism, Zoroastrianism, and Christianity. In his *Dīn-i ilāhī* (Divine Religion) he made an attempt to mix elements of different religions and to evolve a new eclectic system of thought with himself as its head. Shaykh Aḥmad considered these experiments a serious blow to the monotheistic principles of Islam and made up his mind to oppose them. His three volumes of letters (containing 534 letters) show that he had approached eminent Mughal nobles of the period and had established intellectual understanding with them. When Jahāngīr ascended the throne, one of the closest supporters of Shaykh Aḥmad's point of view, Nawāb Murtaḍā Khān Shaykh Farīd, elicited a promise from the Emperor that he would "defend the law of Islam."[68] The impact that Shaykh Aḥmad had on the Mughal emperors and their religious attitude may be gauged from the fact that Aurangzeb received his spiritual instruction from the sons and grandsons of Shaykh Aḥmad. Shaykh Aḥmad's spiritual eminence as well as the Tīmūrid tradition of looking to the Naqshbandī Order as their spiritual umbrella determined the attitude of Aurangzeb.[69] Even the Chishtī saints realized the Naqshbandī hold on Aurangzeb's mind, and Shāh Kalīm Allāh of Delhi told his disciples in the Deccan that they were trying in vain to influence the religious outlook of Aurangzeb.[70]

Apart from his concept of *waḥdat al-shuhūd*, which gave a new direction to Muslim mystical thought in India and elsewhere, Shaykh Aḥmad's contribution in the broader framework of mystical thought was in two directions: (a) he gave greater exactness to mystical terms already current in mystical circles and added some new terms to the mystical vocabulary with very clear connotations; (b) he described his personal spiritual experience with such clarity and guided his followers on the mystic path with such confidence that he made the world of spirit look like a world of tangible reality. Iqbal was constrained to observe that some of his letters give us an idea of "a whole universe of inner experience."[71] No earlier saint had penetrated the world of spirit in this manner. In fact, his predecessors became either mythical or abstruse while describing their spiritual experiences. Shaykh Aḥmad's clarity of thought invested the world of spiritual experience with a touch of realism which is unique. We may quote the same letter through which Iqbal illustrated his point of view. The experience of one 'Abd al-Mu'min was thus described to the shaykh:

> Heaven and Earth and God's Throne and Hell and Paradise all have ceased to exist for me. When I look around I find them nowhere. When I stand in the presence of somebody I see nobody before me: God is infinite. Nobody can encompass Him, and this is the extreme limit of spiritual experience. No saint has been able to go beyond this.

The shaykh said in reply:

> The experience which is described has its origin in the ever-varying life of the *qalb* (heart); and it appears to me that the recipient of it has not yet passed even one-fourth of the innumerable "stations" of the *qalb*. The remaining three-fourths must be passed through in order to finish the experiences of this first "station" of the spiritual life. Beyond this "station" there are other "stations" known as *rūḥ* (Spirit), *sirr-i khafiy* (hidden secret) and *sirr-i akhfā* (the most hidden secret). Each of these "stations," which together constitute what is technically called *'ālam-i amr* ("the world of Divine Command"), has its own characteristic states and experiences. After having passed through these "stations," the seeker of truth gradually receives the illuminations of the "Divine Names" and "Divine Attributes" and finally the illuminations of the Divine Essence.[72]

No reader of Shaykh Aḥmad Sirhindī's letters, however, can fail to notice that in describing some of his spiritual experiences, particularly those which relate to his own self, he has become controversial. His views about two individuations—the bodily-human and the spiritual-angelic—for the Prophet[73] and the process of "Muḥammad" becoming "Aḥmad" belong to this category and have evoked considerable criticism.

The Descendants of Shaykh Aḥmad Sirhindī

In the history of Islamic mysticism, there has hardly been any saint whose sons and grandsons have involved themselves in mystical work as keenly as the descendants of Shaykh Aḥmad Sirhindī: his four sons, Muḥammad Ṣādiq, Muḥammad Sa'īd, Muḥammad Ma'ṣūm, and Muḥammad Yaḥyā, and their descendants. A consciousness of mission and an urge to reform and regenerate society in the light of Islamic Law motivated their activities.

Khwājah Muḥammad Ma'ṣūm (1008/1599–1069/1668) pursued his father's mission with such enthusiasm that the Naqshbandī sources credit him with having enrolled nine hundred thousand disciples.[74] The figure may be exaggerated, but it indicates the extent of his influence. When he went on the *ḥajj* in 1068/1657, a large number of disciples accompanied him.[75] His spiritual experiences during his stay in the Hijaz were recorded by his son, Muḥammad 'Ubayd Allāh, in *Ḥasanāt al-ḥaramayn* (*Virtues of the Two Ḥarams*).[76] While in Mecca he sought divine guidance in resolving the contradictions in the statements of Shaykh Aḥmad Sirhindī regarding the position of the *Ka'bah:*

> As the writings of Mujaddid-i Alf-i Thānī contain diverse opinions about the position of the *Ka'bah,* the saint [Khwājah Ma'ṣūm] was always anxious to resolve them. . . . He sought divine help in this matter. One day he told his sons in Mecca in a complacent mood: I have been able to understand the reality [of the *Ka'bah* in my spiritual experience]. I felt that the *Ka'bah* was

> superior to all realities and that the "realities" of all things prostrated before it and that all ranks and levels of creation, even prophethood and apostleship, alighted from the *Ka'bah*. . . . When I went deeper into my experience, I came to realize the secret that despite all its high position, ascension and progress are not inherent in it; these are the characteristic of man. No one shares this [power of ascension] with man. . . . Thus, though the sacred *Ka'bah* is superior to the realities of all the individuals of the creation, spiritual progress and ascension are the [exclusive] privilege of man, and [from this point of view] some spiritually perfect individuals have precedence over it. On this account the *Ka'bah* keeps an eye on their spiritual illuminations.
>
> One other difference between perfect persons and the *Ka'bah* was made clear to me, and that difference is based on station and status. Though angels etc. are superior to man, what constitutes real superiority is known to man [alone]. As in the world of *majāz* [allegory] the status of *ḥaqīqat* [the truth] becomes obvious, the slaves and the servants are closer to the kings, but the status enjoyed by the *wazīrs* is not the fortune of the slaves.[77]

One of his spiritual experiences at Medina was as follows:

> It was felt that the person of the Prophet is the Center of all the creations (*'ālam*) and from the high Heavens (*'arsh*) to the earthly center all the creatures—angels, houris, men, *jinn* and all the various *ṭabaqāt* [orders] of the creation of God—are dependent on the Prophet and receive spiritual benedictions from him. No doubt the real giver of spiritual blessings is God, but all the blessings are conferred through the Prophet. All matters of grave importance pertaining to this and the other world are executed through him. I witnessed that from the mausoleum of the Prophet blessings and rewards are being bestowed day and night as if the mouths of the *mashkīzah* [water bag] have been opened. God says: "We have sent you [the Prophet] as blessings for all the world." This blessing includes universal mercy and benediction. Submitting problems to the Prophet and praying for their redress and solution are really in the nature of seeking his intercession. To seek redress of problems without the intercession of the Prophet amounts to disobedience and is troublesome.[78]

Khwājah Muḥammad Ma'ṣūm worked within the perimeters laid down by his father, Shaykh Aḥmad Sirhindī, and mostly explained or applied his views to new situations. In a letter to one of his disciples he refers to the controversies of the day and defends his role as a reformer determined to extricate people from sin and immorality:

> The general view that the principle of the Sufis is to avoid meddling in the ways of the people so that nobody's displeasure or ill-will is incurred is wrong and mischievous. Such a view is fraught with many evils. . . . To tell the people to follow the right path and to warn them against sinful acts is an obligation which should be discharged. If a person loves or hates people for the sake of God, his stature is raised to that of the martyrs. Some so-called

> Sufis are really outside the circle of the *Sharī'at*. . . . The Naqshbandī saints believe in strict adherence to the ways of the Prophet (*Sunnah*). They disdain innovations. Abandoning (the duty of) dissuading people from sin and attracting them towards piety amounts to giving up the ways of the order. . . . Khwājah Mu'īn al-Dīn Chishtī exhorted his disciples to advise and admonish people and create in them fear of divine punishment on the Day of Judgment. Shaykh Muḥyī al-Dīn ibn 'Arabī, who is the leader of the mystics of the *waḥdat al-wujūd* school, criticised his contemporary Sufis who indulged in music. . . . Shaykh 'Abd al-Qādir Gīlānī has a chapter in his book dealing with "commands to do what is right and lawful" and "prohibition of what is wrong and unlawful."
>
> If God had approved of non-interference with the ways of the people, He would not have sent prophets. . . . My grandfather, Shaykh 'Abd al-Aḥad, was an advocate of *waḥdat al-wujūd* and an exponent of the *Fuṣūṣ al-ḥikam* [of Ibn 'Arabī] but he was firm in his adherence to the *Sharī'at*. . . . Khwājah Aḥrār believed in *waḥdat al-wujūd* yet he was firm in following the *Sharī'at*. . . . Shaykh Muḥyī al-Dīn ibn 'Arabī who had the position of *ṣāḥib-i asnād* [possessor of chains of transmission] in *Ḥadīth* and held the status of a *mujtahid* in juristic matters, used to say: "Some saints expect people to scrutinize their actions day and night; I say they should scrutinize even the ideas that flash across their mind (*khāṭirāt*). . . ."
>
> If non-interference in the life of the people had been the practice and view of the followers of *waḥdat al-wujūd*, Mawlānā 'Abd al-Raḥman Jāmī would not have exhorted people to advise and admonish, as he has done in his *Silsilat al-dhahab* (*The Golden Chain*). . . . People who believe in "non-interference" and in a policy of peace with all, are good towards Jews, yogis, Brahmans, heretics, etc. and have contact and company with them, but they cause trouble to and torture people who believe in the faith. Their peace with all is strange: they have ill-will towards the followers of Muḥammad and love and good will for non-Muslims.[79]

Khwājah Muḥammad Ma'ṣūm claimed himself to be the *qayyūm* (lasting or permanent figure) of the age.[80] As such he had a special responsibility toward the reform of contemporary society. The concept of *qayyūmiyyat* (permanence), which was later developed by the Naqshbandīs to assign an exaggerated role to the saint, created some doctrinal confusion in Naqshbandī circles.[81] The *Rawḍat al-qayyūmiyyah* (*The Garden of Permanence*) reveals the effect of this concept both on the organization of the order and the individual approach of the Naqshbandī saints.

The way in which Shaykh Aḥmad Sirhindī and his followers narrated their spiritual experiences publicly in letters and treatises and tried to fathom the depth of the ocean of mystic experience was fraught with serious implications and could lead to intellectual anarchy and emotional confusion. What saved the Naqshbandīs from this eventuality was (a) their repeated and persistent emphasis on adherence to the *Sunnah* of the Prophet, and (b) their open declaration that spiritual experience of a mystic had no social implication and that *ilhām* (inspiration of a mystic) was not binding on other people. This led them to make a clear distinction between the "prophetic consciousness" and the "mystic consciousness." While the consciousness of a prophet had social and religious significance for all people, the mystic consciousness was relevant for that mystic alone and that too within the framework of the *Sharī'ah* and with awareness of the danger of deceptions and imperfect sensibilities lurking throughout his experience.

Among the followers of Shaykh Aḥmad Sirhindī and Khwājah Ma'ṣūm, there were many persons who belonged to countries outside India. For instance, Mawlānā Murād (d. 1132/1720), a native of Bukhara, joined the discipline of Khwājah Muḥammad Ma'ṣūm.[82] After receiving spiritual training, Mawlānā Murād went to Damascus, where Sultan Muṣṭafā II treated his family with deep respect. A number of colleges, like the Madrasat al-murādiyyah and the Madrasat al-naqshbandiyyat al-barrāniyyah, were established by the descendants of Mawlānā Murād. It was entirely due to Shaykh Aḥmad Sirhindī and his sons and followers that for the first time India found itself in a position to pay back the debt that it owed to outside countries in the realm of mystical thought. The letters of Shaykh Aḥmad Sirhindī were translated into the Arabic and the Turkish languages. It appears from *Tārīkh-i manāzil-i Bukhārā* (*History of the Houses of Bukhara*) that a channel in Afghanistan was named after a descendant of the Mujaddid and its income was sent to the shrine of the Mujaddid at Sirhind.[83]

The Naqshbandī Order in Persia

In Persia the Naqshbandī Order is said to have received a setback in influence as a result of the rise of the Safavid dynasty (906/1501–1151/1738).[84] Seyyed Hossein Nasr has, however, brought to light other aspects of the matter when he informs us about Wā'iẓ Kāshifī. "Although a Sunni, [he] was a Naqshbandī Sufi and the author of Shi'ite devotional works which became extremely popular, especially the *Rawḍat al-shuhadā'*, which has given its name to the typically Shi'ite practice of *rawḍah* in which the martyrdom of Ḥusayn and other members of the household of the Prophet (*ahl al-bayt*) is celebrated." He then observes: "All these figures were instrumental in preparing the intellectual background for the Safavid renaissance which was based on both Shi'ism and Sufism."[85] The Safavid attitude toward Sufism, however, needs a comprehensive and critical study. The circumstances in which some Sufis of the Mughal period, particularly the Naqshbandīs, produced polemical literature against Shi'ism were created by both the Indian and the Persian situation.[86] But this phenomenon pertains to the 11th/17th–12th/18th centuries and cannot be pushed back in space or time.

The Later Influence of Sirhindī

Among those spiritual descendants of Shaykh Aḥmad who made a contribution to the teaching and organization of the order, the names of Shāh Walī Allāh (1114/1703–1176/1762), Mīrzā Maẓhar Jān-i Jānān (1112/1700–1195/1781), Shāh ʿAbd al-ʿAzīz (1159/1746–1239/1824), Sayyid Aḥmad Shahīd of Rae Bareli (1200/1786–1247/1831), Shāh Ghulām ʿAlī (1156/1743–1239/1824), and Mawlānā Khalid Kurdi (b. 1190/1776) deserve special mention.

Shāh Walī Allāh headed a seminary, Madrasa-yi Raḥīmiyyah, named after his father Shāh ʿAbd al-Raḥīm.[87] For more than a half century he worked there for the moral and spiritual regeneration of Muslim society and ushered in an intellectual renaissance of the Muslims. Muḥammad Iqbāl thinks that he was perhaps the first Muslim who felt the urge of a new spirit in him.[88] Rising above the traditional exposition of the theological categories of thought, he adopted a comprehensive and integralistic approach which looked at man and his environment from all possible angles--spiritual, biological, psychological, moral, and economic. He evaluated carefully the role of religion in building up the morally autonomous personality of an individual and in establishing a healthy moral order of society. He believed that Islam provided the best opportunity for the self-realization of man. He considered himself *qā'im al-zamān* (the steadfast pole of the times)—in essence a claim to the *qayyūmiyyat* of the Naqshbandīs—and said that he was directed by the Prophet in a dream on 5 May 1731 in Mecca to overthrow all systems (based as they were on exploitation).[89]

Shāh Walī Allāh believed that a man cannot realize the best in him unless he develops faith in God. He thought that old and traditional defenses of religion were fast crumbling and a new scholastic approach (*ʿilm-i kalām*) was the crying need of the hour. Religion had to be explained both as a code of personal morality and as a social ideal.

If Shaykh Aḥmad Sirhindī laid great emphasis on *ʿālams* as stages and station of the spiritual development of an individual, Shāh Walī Allāh developed his theory of *al-mala' al-aʿlā* (an assembly of angels where human activities in the world below find prior reflection), and, going a step further than Shaykh Aḥmad, he tried to show that there was close spiritual connection between what happened in *al-mala' al-aʿlā* and in this world. He wove the higher mystic experience with the destiny of man on this planet and propounded his theory of the spiritual evolution of man based on the continuity of human life hereafter. He presents the operation of Allah's emanations (*tajalliyyāt*) in the physical world in such a manner that our life in this world and in the world hereafter appears as a continuous process, carrying with it the result of our actions on this planet. Like Browning's Grammarian he believed that "Man is forever." Man's biological development might have come to a halt, but his spiritual evolution goes on, and death is only a turning point, not an end of the journey. What appears as a brief hint in the mystical thought of Khwājah 'Ubayd Allāh Aḥrār becomes a whole philosophy of the growth of human soul in the works of Shāh Walī Allāh.

Though a follower of Shaykh Aḥmad Sirhindī's order, Shāh Walī Allāh took a momentous step by attempting a reconciliation between the thought of Ibn 'Arabī and Shaykh Aḥmad Sirhindī.[90] This he did in the same spirit in which Khwājah Bāqī Bi'Llāh had reconciled the thoughts of 'Alā' al-Dawlah Simnānī and Ibn 'Arabī. Shāh Walī Allāh considered the difference between their attitudes as one of simile and metaphor. In fact, his mystic philosophy could hardly be adjusted within the framework of any other theory except the *waḥdat al-wujūd* in the validity of which he, like his ancestors, had firm faith.

Shāh Walī Allāh dealt with the efforts of man in the social sphere under the following headings: organization of livelihood, organization of professions, organization of home, organization of trade, and cooperation. According to him, the ultimate aim of all human efforts should be the creation of an international community, free from all types of tensions and exploitation. He calls the human individual "small man" and humanity as a whole "big man" and works out on this basis the idea of the unity and oneness of mankind, which again derives its strength from the philosophy based on the oneness of being. In the history of the Naqshbandiyyah, the contribution of Shāh Walī Allāh was remarkable for its spiritual depth and social impact.[91]

Shāh Walī Allāh's son, Shāh 'Abd al-'Azīz, elucidated and explained the thought of his father, as Khwājah Muḥammad Ma'ṣūm had elucidated the thought of Shaykh Aḥmad Sirhindī. Under Shāh 'Abd al-'Azīz, the Naqshbandī *silsilah* became more and more involved in the political struggles of the day. He gave a religious verdict declaring all land occupied by the British to be a war zone (*dār al-ḥarb*),[92] toward the retriving of which all effort should be directed. This was a call for action against foreign domination, and his wishes materialized when Sayyid Aḥmad of Rae Bareli joined the circle of his disciples and launched a movement from the frontier town of Balakot to Calcutta for the liberation of the country from British occupation. The Indian branch of the Naqshbandī Order fell in line with the anticolonial activities of the Naqshbandīs in other lands.

Sayyid Aḥmad used the Naqshbandī doctrines and mystic discipline to organize his movement—which incidentally had to deal with Sikh authority in the Punjab and the Frontier regions—but the main thrust of which was against the British domination of the country.[93] For the first time in the history of Indian Islam, he took an oath of allegiance (*bay'at*) from people for waging a religious war (*jihād*). He used the mystic relationship of disciple (*murīd*) and spiritual master (*murshid*) to build an army of warriors inspired by religious zeal and prepared to lay down their lives for the cause. His movement came to be known as the Mujāhidīn Movement.[94] Sayyid Aḥmad fell fighting at Balakot (1247/1831), but his followers looked upon him as Mahdī-yi ākhir al-zamān (The Mahdi Coming at the End of Time) and believed that he had not been killed but would reappear to lead the forces of Islam to victory.[95]

The resistance movement in India in 1273/1857 was organized by many *mujāhids*, generally called Wahhābīs by the British writers. They were, in fact, the followers of Sayyid Aḥmad Shahīd. Though some Chishtī-Ṣābirī saints also played a part in the struggle, the real dash and drive of the movement came from the Naqshbandīs inspired by the ideals of Sayyid Aḥmad of Rae Bareli.

A famous Naqshbandī saint contemporary with Shāh Walī Allāh in Delhi was Mīrzā Maẓhar Jān-ī Jānān.[96] He confined his work to the spiritual sphere alone, whereas Shāh Walī Allāh and his son Shāh 'Abd al-'Azīz had a wider range of activities, covering the academic, spiritual, and political fields. Mīrzā Maẓhar attracted the Afghan tribes, particularly the Rohillas, to the mystic fold. He took a bold step toward the reorientation of the Naqshbandī attitude to the Hindus. He declared the Vedas to be a revealed book and provided a rationale for some of the Hindu practices and institutions that were earlier considered to be polytheistic.[97]

Mīrzā Maẓhar's chief disciple and follower in Delhi was Shāh 'Abd Allāh, popularly known as Shāh Ghulām 'Alī, whose impact on the Naqshbandiyyah was far more important than any of his contemporaries.[98] According to Sir Syed, who had personally seen him and whose family owed spiritual allegiance to him, people from Abyssinia, Syria, Asia Minor, Afghanistan, and other places came to receive spiritual instruction from him.[99] Five hundred inhabitants of the *khānqāh* were daily supplied meals from his kitchen. Hundreds of people joined his *ḥalqahs*—circular arrangement for disciples to sit and invoke loudly the Name of Allah. These *ḥalqahs* filled the entire surroundings with spirituality, and people who joined these people who joined these assemblies carried Naqshbandī ideas and practices to their homes to propagate them further.[100]

Later Naqshbandī Influence outside of India

One of the most outstanding among the foreign disciples of Shāh Ghūlam 'Alī was Khālid Kurdī, whose grave in Damascus is a place of pilgrimage.[101] The present Qāḍī of Damascus, Mufti Kaftaro, is a spiritual descendant of the saint. The descendants of 'Abd al-Ghaniy al-Nābulusī (1050/1640–1142/1730) and Khālid Kurdī played an important role in the spiritual life of the people in Damascus. Yūsuf Genč Pāshā, a Kurdish governor of Damascus, came under Naqshbandī influence and issued decrees aimed at rigid enforcement of religious law.

In Turkey the popularity of the Naqshbandiyyah during the twelfth/eighteenth century is testified to by Mouradja d'Ohsson. According to J. P. Brown, there were fifty-two *takiyyahs* of the Naqshbandiyyah in Istanbul alone.[102] The thirteenth/nineteenth century saw the order active almost from Calcutta to Istanbul. The revolt against Ottoman rule in 1297/1880 was organized by 'Ubayd Allāh Naqshbandī.

The Naqshbandīs organized their movements from the *madrasahs* and the *masjids.* The *takiyyahs* and *khānqāhs* were there to help but were not in the forefront of struggle. In Baghdad Madrasat al-'Abbāsiyyah was an active center of Naqshbandī activity; in Delhi, Naqshbandī political struggle was organized from the Madrasah-yi Raḥīmiyyah, the Masjid-i Akbarābādī, and the Masjid-i Shāhjahānī.

In Central Asia the Naqshbandīs organized resistance to foreign rule on a large scale. At Andijan, Aush, Namangan, and Marghilan, Naqshbandī saints like Ismā'īl Khān Tore and Muḥammad 'Alī led the rebellious movements in 1313/1895–1316/1898. The following account given by Hélène Carrère d'Encausse is revealing:

> An ishan of the Sufi brotherhood of the Naqshbandi, Muhammad Ali . . . had a reputation for wisdom, holiness, and charity. . . . With the help of disciples attracted to him, he had erected a madrasah, two mosques and a library and his power was substantial. Around him gradually gathered Muslims who, for the most part, had been prominent figures before the conquest, and who had been deprived of their functions and often ruined by the Russians. Most important, the movement which the ishan would take over was very amply organized and financed by the Naqshbandi brotherhood. For the first time since 1865, it was no longer a matter of a spontaneous uprising, nor an uprising still looking for an ideology, but of a prepared holy war, beginning according to a plan and not haphazardly on some pretext.[103]

The Russians liquidated them completely.

In the Caucasus the Naqshbandīs resisted the Russian conquest and its leader Shamil sought to establish an imamate so that the Muslims could live according to Islamic Law (*Sharīʿah*). Sayyid Aḥmad Shahīd of Rae Bareli also aimed at the establishment of the imamate at Balakot. In the struggle of 1273/1857 the Naqshbandīs were in the forefront. The revival of the Naqshbandiyyah in Turkey, Afghanistan, Central Asia, and other places in recent times is a phenomenon of great significance and reveals the extent to which the order has and is expected to fulfill the spiritual needs of the people.

Today the Naqshbandī Order is active not only in Afghanistan, where some of the *mujāhidīn* groups are associated with it, and in Turkey, where it is at the forefront of Islamic intellectual activities. It has also spread to Europe and America, where several Naqshbandī masters such as the Cypriot Shaykh Nāẓim have established Sufi centers which have drawn many disciples to themselves. It also continues to be active among the Muslims of the Soviet Union, where it has played a vital role in the preservation of Islam under exceptionally difficult conditions. Altogether, it can be said with certainty that the Naqshbandī Order continues to be one of the most vibrant and spiritually significant of Sufi orders today, as it has been since its founding by Khwājah Bahāʾ al-Dīn Naqshband seven centuries ago.

Notes

1. According to a tradition of the Prophet recorded by Abū Dāʾūd: "On the eve of every century God will raise a person in the *ummah* (Muslim community) who will renew the religion." Shaykh Aḥmad, who was born in 972/1564, was considered as Mujaddid-i Alf-i Thānī. This was considered his special role, and it determined also his position in the mystic calendar. ʿAbd al-Ḥakīm Siālkutī (d. 1066/1656), who popularized the works of Mullā Ṣadrā Shīrāzī in India, was the first to use this title for him. See B. A. Faruqi, *The Mujaddid's Conception of Tawḥid* (Lahore: M. Ashraf, 1940) 103.

2. *Tuzuk-i Jahāngīrī* (Sir Syed edition) 272–73.

3. For an account of his life, see Sir Syed, *Āthār al-sanādīd* (Karachi, 1966) 207–12; Raʾūf Aḥmad, *Jawāhir-i ʿalawiyyah* (Urdu translation; Lahore) 241.

4. *Āthār al-sanādīd*, 209.

5. A. Hourani, *The Emergence of the Modern Middle East* (London: Macmillan, 1980) 73ff.

6. For accounts of his life, see Abu'l-Ḥasan ʿAlī Nadvi, *Sīrat-i Syed Aḥmad Shahīd* (Lahore, 1958); Ghulām Rasūl Mehr, *Syed Aḥmad Shahīd* (Lahore, 1952).

7. A. Hourani, *Arabic Thought in the Liberal Age* (London: Oxford University Press, 1962) 225.

8. C. Snouck Hurgronje, *Mekka in the Latter Part of the Nineteenth Century* (London: Luzac, 1931).

9. Shaykh Aḥmad Sirhindī, *Maktūbāt-i Imām Rabbānī* (Nawal Kishore, 1877) 2:135.

10. Kāshifī, *Rashaḥāt* (Kanpur, 1912) 4–6; J. S. Trimingham, *The Sufi Orders in Islam* (London: Oxford University Press, 1971).

11. For his life, see Jāmī, *Nafaḥāt al-uns* (Lucknow, 1915) 345–49; *Rashaḥāt*, 53–57. Kushk-i Hinduwān later came to be known as Kushk-i ʿĀrifān. Naqshband literally means, "a painter, embroiderer, one who adorns." If his ancestors were embroiderers, the name may be a reference to the family profession; otherwise it is an indication of his spiritual quality to print the Name of God upon a disciple's heart. The expression *naqshband-i ḥawādith* is an epithet of God.

12. Ṣāliḥ ibn Mubārak Bakhārī (ed.), *Anīs al-ṭālibīn* (Lahore, 1323 A.H.) 35.

13. Ibid.

14. Shaykh Aḥmad Sirhindī, *Maktūbāt-i Imām Rabbānī*, 2:162.

15. *Anīs al-ṭālibīn*, 127.

16. Jāmī, *Nafaḥāt al-uns*, 347. E. Motet's remark in *Encyclopedia of Religion and Ethics* (New York: Scribner, 1919) 10:726, that the Khwājah was "an eclectic reformer (combining Sunnite orthodoxy, Shīʿism and Ismāʿīlī teachings)" is incorrect.

17. Jāmī, *Nafaḥāt al-uns*, 348.

18. *Anīs al-ṭālibīn*, 108–9.

19. Shāh Walī Allāh, *Tafhīmāt-i ilāhiyyah*, 1:86.

20. Jāmī, *Nafaḥāt al-uns*, 337–39.

21. Ibid., 339.

22. Besides *Rashaḥāt* (8), see M. Fuad Koprülü's article in *Islam Ansiklopedisi* (Istanbul: Millî Eğitim Basimevi, 1987) 1:210–15; and F. Iz's article in the *Encyclopedia of Islam* (new edition) 1:298–99. In 1898 a detailed article, mainly based on *Rashaḥāt*, *Khazīnat al-aṣfiyā*, and *Mirʾāt al-asrār*, appeared in *Bulletin de l'Academie Impériale des Sciences de St. Petersbourg*, September T–IX, No. 2.

After Khwājah Aḥmad, the title *ātā* came to be used as a mark of respect added to the name of all his important spiritual descendants, e.g., Manṣūr Ātā, Saʿīd Ātā, Ḥakīm Ātā, Zangī Ātā, etc. See *Rashaḥāt*.

23. Farīd al-Dīn ʿAṭṭār, *Manṭiq al-ṭayr* (Tehran, 1287 A.H.) 158. The Turks themselves refer to him as *Ḥaḍrat-i Turkistān*.

24. See V. V. Barthold's article "Turkistan," in *Encyclopedia of Islam*, 4:896.

25. Yazdī, *Ẓafar-nāmah* (Calcutta) 9–10. For the present-day condition, see G. A. Pougatchen Kova, *Chefs-d'oeuvre d'architecture de l'Asie centrale* (Paris: UNESCO, 1981) 102.

26. For accounts, see *Rashaḥāt*, 9ff.

27. For details about the order, see J. K. Birge, *The Betakshi Order of Dervishes* (London: Luzac, 1937). For their political role, see E. E. Ramsaur, "The Bektashi Dervishes and the Young Turks," *Moslem World* (1942) 7–14.

28. *Ḥikmet* means religious poems. The *Dīwān* was published from Kazan. Some scholars have doubted its authenticity; see E. J. W. Gibb, *A History of Ottoman Poetry* (London: Luzac, 1958) 1:71ff.

29. *Rashaḥāt*, 18–27.

30. Published with commentary by S. Nafīsī in *Farhang-i Īrān zamīn* 1/1 (1332/1953) 70–100.

31. *Rashaḥāt*, 20; *Tārīkh-i gharībah* (ms.), ff. 19b, 20a.

32. See *Rashaḥāt*, 27–32.

33. *Rashaḥāt*, 32. A unique manuscript of this work is in the possession of the writer of these lines.

34. Jāmī, *Nafaḥāt al-uns*, 341. Ramitin was a small town near Bukhara.

35. The Naqshbandīs generally gave some title to their saints—*ātā, ḥaḍrat, 'azīzān,* etc. At one stage the epithet *ḥaḍrat-i īshān* (or simply *īshān*) came to be used for every saint of the order. The title *ḥaḍrat-i īshān* was perhaps inspired by the practice of referring to the Prophet as *ān ḥaḍrat.*

36. Jāmī, *Nafaḥāt al-uns,* 349–52; see also *Sayings and Miracles of 'Alā' al-Dīn 'Aṭṭār,* ms. in British museum, Rieu ii, 862b.

37. *Rashaḥāt,* 86.

38. Jāmī, *Nafaḥāt al-uns,* 352–56; *Rashaḥāt,* 57–63.

39. *Reconstruction of Religious Thought in Islam* (Lahore: M. Ashraf, 1944) 135.

40. For the manuscript, see C. A. Storey, *Persian Literature: A Bio-Bibliographical Survey* (London: Royal Asiatic Society, 1971) 8–9.

41. Tīmūr died on 17 Sha'bān 807/18 February 1405.

42. *Rashaḥāt,* 221–22.

43. *The Bābur-Nāma,* trans. A. S. Beveridge (London: Luzac, 1921) 97.

44. It appears that some tax exemption was also given to the Khwājah. Referring to Aḥmad Mīrzā of Samarqand, Bābur says: "Moreover the dependents of his (late) Highness Khwāja Ubaid'llāh, under whose protection formerly many poor and destitute persons had lived free from the burden of dues and imposts, were now themselves treated with harshness and oppression. . . . Oppressive exactions were made from them, indeed from the Khwāja's very children" (*Bābur-Nāma,* 41).

45. *Rashaḥāt,* 230.

46. Ibid., 262.

47. Ibid., 252.

48. Ibid., 295.

49. *The Tārīkh-i Rashīdī,* trans. E. D. Ross (London: Sampson Low & Co., 1895) 97.

50. *Bābur-Nāma,* 33.

51. *Bābur-Nāma,* 34. See also K. A. Nizami, "Naqshbandī Influence on Mughal Rulers and Politics," *Islamic Culture* 39 (1965) 42–43.

52. *Bābur-Nāma,* 132.

53. Ibid., 149, 98.

54. Ibid., 620.

55. Khwājah Aḥrār himself used to say that his regular education did not go beyond a page or two of *Miṣbāḥ naḥw* (*Rashaḥāt,* 232).

56. Maḥmūd Gawān, *Riyāḍ al-inshā',* Shaykh Chand (Hyderabad, Daccan, 1948) 19–23, 152–57; 167–72; 207–11, 227–32; 300–304; 365–66.

57. For his life, see Hāshim Badakhshānī, *Zubdat al-maqāmāt* (Kanpur: Nawal Kishore, 1307 A.H.).

58. Nawāb Murtaḍā Khān was an eminent Mughal noble. For an account, see S. M. Ikram, *Rūd-i kawthar* (Karachi: Firoz Sons, 1968) 178–89.

59. Anonymous, *Kalimāt-i ṭayyibāt,* being a collection of the conversations of Khwājah Bāqī (Delhi, 1332 A.H.).

60. Ibid., 61, 63.

61. *Mathnawī-yi Ḥaḍrat Khwājah Bāqī Bi'Llāh,* ed. Aḥmad Ḥasan Naqshbandī Amrohvī (Hyderabad-Deccan, 1328 A.H.).

62. Urdu translation (Lahore, 1341 A.H.).

63. See K. A. Nizami, *Ḥayāt-i Shaikh 'Abdul-Ḥaqq Muḥaddith Dihlawī* (Delhi, 1953).

64. For biographical accounts, see Hāshim Badakhshānī, *Zubdat al-maqāmāt;* Badr al-Dīn Sirhindī, *Ḥaḍrat al-quds* (Lahore, 1971). For his thought, see Faruqi, *The*

Mujaddid's Conception of Tawḥīd; for assessment, see Abul-Ḥasan 'Alī Nadvī, *Tārīkh-i da'wat-o-'azimat,* vol. 4 (Lucknow: Nadwat al-'Ulamā', 1980); Y. Friedmann, *Shaykh Aḥmad Sirhindī: An Outline of his Thought and a Study of his Image in the Eyes of Posterity* (Montreal: McGill-Queen's University Press, 1971).

65. B. A. Faruqi, *The Mujaddid's Conception of Tawḥīd,* 134–35. This analysis is based on Shaykh Aḥmad's letters, vol. 1, Epistle Nos. 31, 287.

66. François Bernier, *Travels in the Mogul Empire (1656–1668),* ed. A. Constable (London: Constable's Oriental Miscellany, 1891).

67. The Mujaddid wrote a number of books, but his basic ideas are best revealed in his letters, *Maktūbāt.* His book *Ithbāt al-nubuwwah* is also very significant, as it attacks Akbar's attempt at assuming a prophetic role from a very fundamental angle—the relative position of kings and prophets. It may be pointed out that many Muslim scholars of that period expressed their views on that theme. Shaykh 'Abd al-Ḥaqq Muḥaddith discussed it in his life of the Prophet, *Madārij al-nubuwwah* (Delhi, 1269 A.H.).

68. Nawāb Murtaḍā Khān, *Akbar and the Jesuits,* I, 204.

69. Khwājah Muḥammad Ma'ṣūm, Shaykh Muḥammad Sa'īd, Khwājah Sayf al-Dīn, and Ḥujjat Allāh Muḥammad Naqshband II had not only contact but regular correspondence with Aurangzeb. See *Maktūbāt-i Khwājah Muḥammad Ma'ṣūm* (Kanpur: Niẓāmī Press, 1304 A.H.); *Maktūbāt-i sa'īdiyyah* (Lahore, 1385 A.H.); *Wasīlat al-qabūl ila'Llāh wa'l-rasūl* (Hyderabad-Sind, 1963); *Maktūbāt-i sayfiyyah* (Hyderabad Sind, n.d.). See also Nizami, "Naqshbandi Influence on Mughal Rulers and Politics," 49–50.

70. *Maktūbāt-i kalīmī,* Letters of Shāh Kalīm Allāh of Delhi (Delhi: Matba'-i Yūsufī, 1301 A.H.) 75.

71. *Reconstruction of Religious Thought in Islam,* 193.

72. Ibid., 192–93.

73. Neatly described by A. Schimmel in her *Islam in the Indian Sub-Continent* (Leiden: Brill, 1980) 92.

74. For biographical details, see S. Zawwār Ḥusayn Shāh, *Anwār-i ma'ṣūmiyyah* (Karachi, 1980); for Khwājah Muḥammad Ma'ṣūm's thought, see three volumes of his letters: *Wasīlat al-sa'ādah, Durrat al-tāj,* and *Maktūbāt-i Khwājah Muḥammad Ma'ṣūm* (Lucknow, 1960).

On the number of disciples, see Muḥammad Iqbāl Mujaddidī in his introduction to *Ḥasanat al-ḥaramayn,* by Muḥammad 'Ubayd Allāh, 18, on the authority of *Manāqib-i aḥmadiyyah.*

75. The figure given is highly exaggerated as it is said that seven thousand disciples proceeded on the *ḥajj* pilgrimage with him. *Rawḍat al-qayyūmiyyah,* which is the source for this information, is not very dependable about figures and dates.

76. The Naqshbandīs took keen interest in recording such spiritual experiences. Shāh Walī Allāh also wrote his famous *Fuyūḍ al-ḥaramayn* to describe his spiritual experiences in Hijaz. The tenor of such treatises apart, the fact is significant that in times of crisis of any type, the Naqshbandīs turned to Medinah for inspiration and spiritual guidance. Shaykh 'Abd al-Ḥaqq Muḥaddith went to Hijaz disgusted with the atmosphere created by Akbar's religious experiments; many Naqshbandī saints went to Hijaz before and after 1273/1857. Some of them came back after refurbishing themselves spiritually. Their role after their return was determined, consistent, and objective-oriented.

77. *Ḥasanat al-ḥaramayn,* 177–78.

78. Ibid., 192.

79. *Durrat al-tāj,* as translated by Maulvi Nasīm Aḥmad Farīdī, *Maktūbāt-i Khwājah Muḥammad Ma'ṣūm Sirhindī,* 87–100.

80. *Qayyūm* in Naqshbandī parlance would mean one on whom the stability, reform, and resurgence of that age depend. The Mujaddid had himself indicated that his role of *qayyūm* would devolve on his son Muḥammad Ma'ṣūm (*Maktūbāt-i Imām Rabbānī,* vol. 3, Letter 104). See also Syed Zawwār Ḥusayn, *Anwār-i ma'ṣūmiyyah* (Karachi, 1980) 33ff.

81. For a critical evaluation of the concept of *qayyūmiyyat,* see S. M. Ikram, *Rūd-i Kawthar,* 292–304. *Mujaddid, mahdī, qayyūm, qā'im al-zamān* are all expressions of the same consciousness of mission.

82. On Mawlānā Murād, see H. A. R. Gibb in *The Encyclopedia of Islam* (old edition), Supp. 155; A. Hourani, *The Emergence of the Modern Middle East,* 80–81.

83. Ḥāfiẓ Muḥammad Fāḍil Khān, *Tārīkh-i manāzil-i Bukhārā,* trans. and ed. I. H. Siddiqi (Srinagar, 1981) 4, 27.

84. See A. Hourani, *The Emergence of the Modern Middle East,* 75–89.

85. S. H. Nasr, *Sufi Essays* (Albany: State University of New York Press, 1985) 115–16.

86. Shaykh Aḥmad Sirhindī wrote a short treatise entitled *Risālah dar radd-i rawāfiḍ.* Shāh Walī Allāh did not enter the controversy in that manner. As usual, he exercised a moderating influence between two extreme views and produced his historical evaluation of the role of *khilāfat* in his *Izālat al-khifā' 'an al-khulafā'.*

87. Several works on Shāh Walī Allāh have appeared in English and Urdu. The most perceptive and thought-provoking study, however, remains that of Mawlānā 'Ubayd Allāh Sindhī.

For the account of Shāh 'Abd al-Raḥīm, see Walī Allāh, *Anfās al-'ārifīn* (Delhi).

88. *Reconstruction of Religious Thought in Islam,* 97.

89. See K. A. Nizami, "Shah Waliullah of Delhi: His Thought and Contribution," *Islamic Culture* 54 (1980) 141–52.

90. He wrote a small treatise *Fayṣalah waḥdat al-wujūd wa'l-shuhūd* (*Decision concerning the Unity of Being and Consciousness*).

91. See *Ḥujjat Allāh al-bālighah* for a thought-provoking discussion of *irtifāqāt-i ma'āshiyyah* and *irtifāqāt-i ilāhiyyah.*

92. *Fatāwā-yi 'azīzī* (Delhi: Mujtabai Press, 1904) 1:17, 185; also *Malfūẓāt-i Shāh 'Abd al-'Azīz,* 58.

93. In a letter addressed to the Raja of Gwaliyar, Syed Aḥmad clearly states this supreme objective of his struggle. See Abul-Ḥasan 'Alī Nadvī, *Musalmanon kay tanazzul say dunya ko kiya nuqsan poncha,* 273–74.

94. Ghulām Rasūl Mehr has given details about the persons involved in the struggle in the supplementary volumes to his study of the life of Syed Aḥmad, entitled *Sargu-zasht-i mujāhidīn* (Lahore, 1956). In the words of W. C. Smith, this work "seems to mark a new stage in Urdu historiography" (*Islam in Modern History* [Princeton: Princeton University Press, 1957] 52n).

95. Ghulām Rasūl Mehr, *Syed Aḥmad Shahīd,* 2:443–55.

96. For his life, see Nā'im Allāh Bahra'ichī, *Bishārat-i maẓhariyyah,* ms. British Museum, Rieu Vol. 1, 363a; Nā'im Allāh Bahra'ichī, *Ma'mūlāt-i maẓhariyyah* (Kanpur, 1275 A.H.); also Nabahānī, *Jam' karāmāt al-awliyā'* (Beirut, 1329 A.H.) 1:388–89.

97. *Kalimāt-i ṭayyibāt* (being a collection of the letters of Mīrzā Maẓhar, Shāh Walī Allāh, etc.) (Moradabad, 1303 A.H.) 37–40.

98. For his life, see Ra'ūf Aḥmad, *Jawāhir-i 'alawiyyah;* also Sir Syed, *Āthār al-sanādīd,* 209–12.

99. *Āthār al-sanādīd,* 209.

100. *Durr al-ma'ārif,* being conversations of Ghulām 'Alī compiled by Ra'ūf Aḥmad (Bareilly, 1304 A.H.).

101. A. Hourani, *The Emergence of the Modern Middle East,* 75–89; see also K. A. Nizami, *Tārīkh-i maqālāt* (Delhi, 1965) 215–20.

102. J. P. Brown, *The Dervishes: Or Oriental Spiritualism* (London: Oxford University Press, 1927).

103. H. Carrère d'Encausse in *Central Asia: A Century of Russian Rule,* ed. E. Allworth (London: Columbia University Press, 1967) 168.

9

Sufism in Egypt and the Arab East

Abdullah Schleifer

For more than a millennium Egypt has served as a fertile culture for the flourishing of Sufi doctrine and institutions first formulated elsewhere in the Muslim world. The most dramatic example is provided by the Shādhiliyyah, whose founder, Shaykh Abu'l-Ḥasan al-Shādhilī, and his immediate successor, Abu'l-'Abbās al-Mursī, were from North Africa and Muslim Spain respectively. Yet it was in Egypt that the doctrine and method of the Shādhilī Order were elaborated and widely disseminated, and the order has flourished ever since as a spiritual brotherhood.[1]

Egypt has played a similar nourishing role for individual Sufis drawn from the Arab East. Thus, the most popular luminary in Egyptian spiritual life is Sayyid Aḥmad al-Badawī (d. 675/1276). His disciples in Egypt—where the Aḥmadī or Badawī Order is considered the second largest line among the *ṭuruq*[2]—number in the hundreds of thousands, and the main religious festival (*mawlid*) held in his honor each year in the Nile Delta city of Tanta, where he lived and died, attracts more than two million Egyptians.

Sayyid Aḥmad, whose family had emigrated from Arabia to North Africa and then returned within a few short years, spent his youth in Mecca among the bedouin and won a reputation as a daring horseman and courageous knight. While still a young man, he experienced a spiritual transformation, devoting himself to the recitation of the Quran and to meditation. Sayyid Aḥmad traveled to southern Iraq, where he received training in the way of the Rifā'ī, followers of the great Arab Sufi Aḥmad ibn 'Alī al-Rifā'ī.[3]

The Rifā'iyyah

The Rifā'ī Order, which is one of the oldest in Islam and is widely spread in Egypt, is of Iraqi origin. Its founder, Abu'l-'Abbās Aḥmad ibn 'Alī, known as Ibn al-Rifāʿī, who was born in 499/1106 and died in 578/1182, hailed from the marshlands of southern Iraq, where he lived nearly the whole of his life. He was at once a scholar of Islamic Law (*faqīh*) and a Sufi. His center at Bata'ih in Iraq (hence the occasional use the name Baṭā'iḥiyyah for Rifāʿiyyah) became a major center for those drawn to Sufism and was visited by many outstanding Sufis of other orders including Sayyid Aḥmad al-Badawī. The Rifāʿiyyah came to be known for their extraordinary psychic powers and such acts as walking on fire and eating snakes to prove the mastery of the spirit over the body. Even to this day they continue to be known for their strange feats, especially walking in a fire or eating fire. Such practices are traced back to the founder himself, who is considered to have performed them while in a state of ecstasy, although some later Sufi authorities consider accounts of these practices to be later accretions.

The Rifāʿī Order spread rapidly into many areas of the Islamic world, including Egypt, Syria, Palestine, Anatolia, Persia, India, and as far east as Malaya. In fact, up to the eighth/fourteenth and ninth/fifteenth centuries, it was probably the most widespread Sufi order before it became partially eclipsed by the Qādiriyyah. The Rifāʿiyyah became very popular in Egypt as a result of the activities of Abu'l-Fatḥ al-Wāsiṭī (d. 632/1234) and has remained a major Sufi order in Egypt to this day. Today the Rifāʿiyyah mosque in Cairo is the center of the order in that city, where most of the adherents continue to be drawn from the masses. Throughout the Islamic world, wherever the Rifāʿiyyah survives, whether it be in Turkey, Syria, or South Africa, its members continue to be known for their extraordinary physical feats, although the teachings of this important Sufi order must not be equated with such practices. At the heart of the order there exists the doctrine of *tawḥīd* and means of its attainment through *dhikr*, much as one finds in other Sufi paths.

Sayyid Aḥmad al-Badawī

Sent to Egypt by the Rifāʿiyyah upon the death of the Rifāʿī representative in Egypt, Sayyid Aḥmad al-Badawī settled in Tanta and quickly acquired a large following that ranged from vast numbers of ordinary Egyptians to Mamlūk amirs. The Mamlūks were the newly empowered slave rulers of Egypt, who were to reign in Cairo and serve as patrons and protectors of one of the most glorious phases of Islamic civilization for more than four hundred years. The Mamlūks almost invariably allied themselves as a ruling establishment to the *ṭuruq* as institutions out of personal conviction and/or a quest for legitimacy; Sufism (*taṣawwuf*) was not simply a popular religious attitude to be supported, but in many cases a spiritual discipline to be pursued personally.[4]

Sayyid Aḥmad lived in Tanta for forty-one years, during which time he received divine permission to establish his own order independent of the Rifāʿī. Many miracles have been attributed to him, before and after his death, as a vehicle for God's grace, and he is viewed as one who, by that grace as a "friend" or "favorite" of God (*walī*), may intercede in heaven for the ordinary believer.

Al-Wāsiṭī and al-Dasūqī

Sayyid Aḥmad's immediate predecessor in Egypt, Shaykh Abu'l-Fatḥ al-Wāsiṭī, also traveled to Iraq to become a representative (*khalīfah*) of Aḥmad al-Rifāʿī and later came to Egypt to provide spiritual guidance to Abu'l-Ḥasan al-Shādhilī, who also had traveled in his youth to Iraq on a spiritual quest. Al-Wāsiṭī is responsible more than any other figure for the introduction of the Rifāʿī Order into Egypt, an order that was to become one of the most popular of all *ṭuruq*, particularly in the countryside. It is the point of origin for still another popular and enduring order in Egypt, the Dasūqiyyah, whose Egyptian-born founder, Shaykh Ibrāhīm al-Dasūqī (d. 687/1285), derived his training and spiritual understanding from those emigrant spiritual guides Abu'l-Ḥasan al-Shādhilī and Sayyid Aḥmad al-Badawī—both students or disciples of al-Wāsiṭī and the Iraqi Rifāʿī line. It was from Egypt that all of these orders and their subsequent subdivisions spread to the entire Arab world and beyond, to Africa and southeast Asia.[5]

Al-Azhar University and Sufism

One of the factors that facilitated this transmission was the gradual emergence of al-Azhar University in Cairo as the great center of Sunni orthodoxy. The religious scholars (*ʿulamāʾ*) of this institution dominated all aspects of professional life in Egypt over and above the more narrowly defined religious offices, and they functioned as intermediaries between the popular classes and the Mamlūk and later Mamlūk-Ottoman ruling elites. In addition, they developed far-reaching student–teacher networks with students of the Islamic disciplines who increasingly made their way to al-Azhar from all parts of the Muslim world.[6]

Although much is made of the inescapable tensions between the Sufi or esoteric dimension of Islam and the exoteric or *Sharīʿite* dimension, up until the modern colonial and post-colonial periods, these dimensions overlapped to a great degree at al-Azhar. The *ʿulamāʾ* of the Islamic sciences typically served as *shaykh* or as *murīd* (disciple) of a Sufi *ṭarīqah*. Azharī scholars also served as administrators of Sufi-related institutions such as the shrines of Sufi *awliyā'* and the extensive properties endowed (*awqāf*) by Mamlūks and merchants alike to support the *ṭuruq*.[7]

The student–teacher networks of al-Azhar that reached into every corner of the Egyptian countryside and well beyond to other Arab centers of scholarship and religious activity in Africa and Asia often developed into parallel networks for the diffusion of the Egyptian-based *ṭuruq*. At the same time, the popularity of Sufism in Egypt with its large population and the positive attitude toward *taṣawwuf* taken by both the ruling circle and the orthodox religious establishment would all continue to draw founders or representatives of the occasional new order, or more likely, new suborders reviving one of the older lines in some distant part of the Arab world.

Thus, it was inevitable that the thirteenth/nineteenth-century Sufi revivalist movements, be they reformist as in the case of the Tijāniyyah and the Idrīsiyyah, or traditionalist as in the case of the Darqāwiyyah, also found followings in Egypt. But the impact of these revivalist orders was greater in other areas of the Arab world, in which the interpenetration of *ṭuruq*, orthodox religious establishment, and ruling circle was not as complete as in Egypt and in which the reformist motivations of many of the new lines were more likely to be challenged by the firmly entrenched traditionalist orders. It was to sub-Saharan Africa rather than to Egypt that the Tijāniyyah of Morocco and Algeria flowed more effectively. So too, the Idrīsī subgroups proved far more successful in Libya (in the case of the Sanūsiyyah) or in Sudan (in the case of the Mirghāniyyah/Khatmiyyah) than in Egypt.

Traditionalist Revivalist Sufi Orders

More likely of success in Egypt and the Arab East heartland were the more traditionalist revivalist groups, such as the Darqāwiyyah, which reached Egypt from Morocco via Medina as a branch of the Madaniyyah, whose *shuyūkh* were closely associated with al-Azhar. The present shaykh of this now relatively negligible *ṭarīqah*, known as *al-ṭarīqat al-shādhiliyyat al-qādiriyyah*) is Sayyid 'Alī Ḥasan Zayn al-'Ābidin 'Abd al-Qādir (often written as Abdul-Kader), who is the former Dean of the Faculty of *Uṣūl al-dīn* (theology) at al-Azhar, former director of the Islamic Centers of Washington D.C. and London, and the translator into English of Junayd, the great third/ninth century Sufi of Baghdad.[8]

The Darqāwiyyah also spread to Palestine and Lebanon in its Madaniyyah form as the Yashruṭiyyah, taking its name from Shaykh 'Alī Nūr al-

Dīn al-Yashruṭī (d. 1308/1891), who established the central *zāwiyah* in Acre. While the leadership of the *ṭarīqah* passed on to his male lineage, it was his extraordinary daughter, Sayyidah Fāṭimah Yashruṭī, raised, educated, and spiritually trained in the *zāwiyah* by her father, who was to be a major contemporary instrument of spiritual guidance for several generations of Muslims in this century. The author of three books on *taṣawwuf*, including *al-Riḥlah ila'l-Ḥaqq* (*Journey to the Truth*), she died in Beirut at a very advanced age in 1978.[9]

Sufism in Thirteenth/Nineteenth- and Early Fourteenth/Twentieth-Century Egypt

In the early thirteenth/nineteenth century the Sufi *ṭuruq* in Egypt were popular to the degree that to be a Muslim—especially in the urban areas—was all but synonymous with being affiliated in one manner or another with the *ṭuruq*. It has been suggested that the formal following of the *ṭuruq* actually reached an all-time high at this point in time rather than in earlier centuries. The changing social-economic conditions (the European capitulations, penetration of cheap European manufactured goods, etc.) radically weakened or destroyed the *ṭuruq*-allied system of guilds, which had provided a sufficient social integration into a spiritual perspective for many Muslims, so that they felt little need to pursue the more intense spiritual discipline of the *ṭarīqah*.

Several forces, often otherwise opposed on geopolitical or ideological planes, combined at this point to undermine the position of the *ṭuruq*. The first was the emergence (in the wake of the brief but startling French occupation at the beginning of the thirteenth/nineteenth century) of an energetic effort by the new, modernizing dynasty established by Muḥammad 'Alī to strengthen central authority in Egypt, in other words to build in Egypt the equivalent of a modern European state.

It is in the nature of *étatism* to undermine cohesive voluntary institutions which possess a legitimacy (and frequently extensive financial assets) that appears as great or greater than the emerging centralizing state. This process can take abrupt and obvious forms of repression, as in the case of Ataturk's Turkey, where the *ṭuruq* were simply outlawed in the early 1920s, or it can assume the form of a more delicate operation that gradually weakens and isolates once relatively autonomous voluntary institutional life by employing the political technique of divide and rule.

Such was the case in Egypt from 1227/1812, when Muḥammad 'Alī singled out the leadership of one particularly prestigious *ṭarīqah*, the *shaykh al-sajjādat al-bakriyyah,* and gave to that *shaykh* authority over all the *ṭuruq* and *ṭuruq*-linked institutions, as a government-imposed *shaykh al-mashāyikh al-ṭuruq al-ṣūfiyyah* or grand shaykh of the Sufi *ṭuruq.*[10] Regardless of the popularity and legitimate qualifications of the *shaykh al-sajjādat al-bakriyyah* for this position, the nature of its evolution meant that effectively the emerging modern Egyptian state had created a formal office that counterbalanced that of Shaykh al-Azhar and undermined the role of Azharī *'ulamā'* within the *ṭuruq.* Inevitably, this was to reopen a competitive relationship between the scholars of the exoteric religious sciences and the Sufi *shaykhs.* Indeed, over the next hundred years the decline of the role of the *'ulamā'* within the *ṭuruq* (as in all other branches of Egyptian life) was to be matched by the decline of *taṣawwuf* as a discipline to be formally studied at al-Azhar.

By the late thirteenth/nineteenth century the authority of the *shaykh al-sajjādat al-bakriyyah* in his capacity as *shaykh al-mashāyikh al-ṣūfiyyah* was to be enrolled in a new cause that inevitably accompanies the rise of the modern state in an Islamic society—the "reform" of *ṭarīqah* practices.[11]

With its stress on inner (and thus not necessarily apparent) intention rather than upon legalism, and upon intuitive knowledge and poetic expression rather than discursive reason, and with its priorities fixed firmly within the domain of the invisible world, the domain of angels and of dreams, as a mode for the transmission of spiritual illumination by both living and dead Sufi guides—of whom the foremost is the Prophet—Sufism by its very nature has always been vulnerable to exploitation by charlatans, exhibitionists, and madmen. To the degree that Sufism secured a profound hold on the masses and the institutional life of the community, this danger became particularly acute, given the charitable wealth that was so often showered upon Sufis.

In part the traditionalist revivalism, such as that of the Darqāwiyyah, had always been the solely significant response to this danger; it functioned by deepening the spiritual depth of *ṭarīqah* life through sincere practice. Now other responses, classified as "reformism" and inspired in part by the secularizing example of the European colonial elites that now dominated Egypt and in part by certain puritanical currents in Islam which until this time had always been insignificant, combined with legitimate concern by traditionalist Sufi revivalists and modernists alike in the attempt to eliminate charlatanism and exhibitionism. Periodically measures were imposed—some successfully, others less so—to eliminate the more ecstatic rites of the *ṭuruq* and to curtail the use of musical instruments in street processionals and in the practice of *ḥaḍrah* (the collective *dhikr* or invocation of God's Names).

The *Mawlid*

Through the late thirteenth/nineteenth century and through most of the fourteenth/twentieth, the thrust of these measures was directed in particular at the *mawlid*—popular festivals organized on the often-symbolic birth date of *awliyā'* and the *ahl al-bayt* (the direct descendants of the Prophet). Wherever Sufism is strong, some form of *mawlid* is practiced, but *mawlid* is a particularly significant phenomenon in Egypt.[12] With the collapse of other Sufi-related institutions (nearly all the vast private properties that were specifically endowed in perpetuity for the benefit of Sufi meeting halls, hospices, schools, hospitals, and free kitchens have been periodically confiscated by the modern state), it is the tenacity of the *mawlid* as a popular festival that has to a large measure enabled Sufism to maintain its ties to the popular classes in Egypt.

Aside from the *mawlid al-nabī* (the Prophet's birthday) most *mawlids* are centered at a specific local site—invariably the tomb of a great *walī* or one of the *ahl al-bayt* buried in Egypt. Cairo contains a number of such sites: the mosque tombs of Sayyidnā Ḥusayn (the Prophet's beloved grandson and exemplary *walī*) and other members of the Prophet's family such as Sayyidah Zaynab (who all but rivals Sayyidnā Ḥusayn as "patron saint" of Cairo), as well as such women saints as Sayyidah Fāṭimah al-Nabawiyah, Sayyidah Ruqayyah, and the great scholar and Sufi Sayyidah Nafīsah, whose mosque, tomb, and *mawlid* remain to this date the most wondrous of all.

The *mawlid*, according to one very acute observer, is "to glorify God by venerating one of His favorites" as well as to acquire blessings by praying *for* the *walī* (not *to* him or her) and to acquire the intercession in heaven of these holy men and women. Because the *mawlid* is a joyous occasion to be shared by women and children as well as men, its ambience is a blend of the sacred and the humanly festive. Children play on swings and slides, and carnival games and sweet shops are nearly as visible as the tents of the Sufi orders. Within those tents the Sufis practice *khidmah*—service to God's creatures—in the form of hospitality that ranges from the minimal offer of tea to full meals for every visitor for the glory of God and the honor of the *ṭarīqah*.

Despite the somewhat embattled survival of the *mawlid*, Sufism as both a legitimate institution and as a personal practice declined drastically among the educated middle classes in the first half of the fourteenth/twentieth century. This decline was accentuated by secularism—which always seeks out for first attack the more spiritual dimension of any given religious tradition—Westernization of education, and an increasingly influential "fundamentalist" response to the previous forces. By virtue of its puritanical nature, this latter factor is as opposed to many traditional expressions of Islamic spirituality as the very modernism that "fundamentalism" theoretically opposes.

To these currents must be added the impact of socialism as the ideology of fashion among the middle classes from the 1940s on and the official ideology in Egypt and other Arab states from the late 1950s on. Socialism has always been hostile to any politically quietist "otherworldly" understanding of religion.

The Revival of Sufism in This Century

It is within the context of this early fourteenth/twentieth-century crisis of the *ṭuruq* that an Egyptian echo of the traditionalist and profoundly spiritualizing revival of Sufism in North Africa effected by Shaykh Aḥmad al-ʿAlawī (see chap. 2 of this volume) is to be found in the life and work of Sayyid (Sidi) Salāmah al-Raḍī (d. 1358/1939). His Ḥāmidī Shādhilī Order has strenuously and successfully struggled against those conditions and attitudes which have come to isolate the *ṭuruq* and *taṣawwuf* from the concern of all but the poorest strata of Egyptian Muslim society.[13] The disciplined, highly liturgical yet spiritually intense public *ḥaḍrah* held each Sunday evening in the mosque of Sayyidah Zaynab is one of the most moving testimonies to the enduring nature of spiritual life in Egypt. As many as five hundred followers of the Ḥāmidiyyah rhythmically invoke the Names of God in counterpoint to the singing of the shaykh's *Dīwān* (poetry) in praise of God, His Prophet, and His *awliyā*'.

Although the Ḥāmidiyyah (now led by Shaykh Ḥāmid, the younger son of the late *walī* Sayyid Salāmah) have not directly had the extraordinary impact outside of the Arab world that has been the case of the Algerian Shaykh Aḥmad al-ʿAlawī, it is noteworthy that the late French Muslim scholar and metaphysician René Guénon (d. 1370/1951), who founded the Traditionalist School, frequently attended the *ḥaḍrah* of the Ḥāmidiyyah Shādhiliyyah in the company of Sayyid Salāmah. Sayyid Salāmah also had a formative spiritual impact upon Shaykh Ibrāhīm al-Baṭṭāwī, whose *ṭarīqah* Baṭṭāwiyyah-Shādhiliyyah has functioned for more than three decades in small, relatively informal, and institutionally almost invisible circles of educated Muslims in Alexandria, Cairo, and the Nile Delta in the tradition of the Ḥanafiyyah line of the Shādhiliyyah but with increasing numbers of disciples in Turkey, Holland, the United States, and Indonesia.

Contemporary Sufi Figures of Egypt

An equivalent figure of great spiritual influence on the educated—and, in particular, the educated youth in Alexandria—is Dr. Muḥsin al-Labbān. Although he received a typically modern Egyptian secular education in economics, he stands in the direct line of al-Azhar scholars and is the beneficiary of a private classic Islamic education. Now a faculty member at Alexandria University after a number of years of professional life spent in the West, Muḥsin Labbān has become, in but a relatively short number of years, a spiritual magnet for students and young professionals drawn to a deeper practice and understanding of Islam while disaffected by the politicization and agitation that characterize the "Islamic-oriented protest groups" which have become so politically significant on most Egyptian university campuses.[14] Muḥsin Labbān's circle is considered a branch of the Muḥammadiyyah Shādhiliyyah *ṭarīqah* and, as would be fitting given the Azharī links of this *ṭarīqah,* his guidance stresses the necessity of acquiring *'ilm* (knowledge of the outward religious disciplines) as well as *ma'rifah* (the intuitive knowledge of God).[15]

More parallel in time to Shaykh Ibrāhīm al-Baṭṭāwī's activities[16] has been the impact on the educated middle classes of the work of Dr. Abu'l Wafā' al-Taftāzānī, who serves today as *shaykh al-mashāyikh al-ṣūfiyyah* of the Supreme Sufi Council of Egypt as well as Vice President for Graduate Studies at Cairo University. As a young scholar, al-Taftāzānī published in 1377/1958 his study and commentary on the great expositor of Shādhilī doctrine, Ibn 'Aṭā' Allāh al-Iskandarī (whose mosque and tomb in Besiteen have quietly become a meeting place for those Egyptians involved in the revival of *taṣawwuf* among the educated classes).[17] The publication of this work was particularly noteworthy coming as it did at a time when hostility and ridicule toward *taṣawwuf* were rampant in Egypt, particularly in the mass media.

With the change in ambience over the past twenty years (for reasons many of which are beyond the scope of this study but in no small part due to the efforts of individuals such as al-Taftāzānī) it is now possible for the *shaykh al-mashāyikh al-ṣūfiyyah* to contribute regularly to popular publications articles that touch on Sufi themes—themes he also expounds in his frequent interviews and talks on Egyptian television. Al-Taftāzānī's obvious professional standing in the secular academic world does much to reassure the educated middle classes, who have been culturally conditioned for a number of decades to dismiss Sufism as some sort of shabby, "old-fashioned," low-life cult.

But the single most important figure in the revival of *taṣawwuf* among the educated classes in Egypt is the late Shaykh al-Azhar, Dr. ʿAbd al-Ḥalīm Maḥmūd (d. 1399/1979), who had an extraordinary impact on a generation of influential and educated Muslims. Shaykh ʿAbd al-Ḥalīm published dozens of books and pamphlets which reintroduced the modern educated Egyptian to the great spiritual luminaries of Sufism, such as Dhu'l-Nūn al-Miṣrī (who is considered the *walī* who first introduced Sufism as a "science of spiritual states and stations" to Egypt; d. 245/859),[18] Abu'l-Ḥasan al-Shādhilī, ʿAbd Allāh ibn Mubārak, Shaykh Aḥmad al-Dardīrī, al-Muḥāsibī, Sayyid Aḥmad al-Badawī, Shaykh ʿAbd Allāh ibn Mashīsh, and many others.[19]

These works were more than restatements of Sufi doctrine in a contemporary and popularizing language. Above all they restored to the modern educated Egyptian the lost understanding or insight into the profound spiritual messages expressed by these men and contained within Sufi teachings—messages that have become veiled to most Egyptians by the popular view of the *awliyā'* having solely intercessionary roles.

ʿAbd al-Ḥalīm Maḥmūd's writing and his public lectures influenced hundreds of thousands of Egyptians. On one occasion after giving a lecture on *taṣawwuf* at Cairo University shortly before his death, nearly the entire audience of three thousand stood up and requested *ʿahd* by his hand (initiation administered by a Sufi *shaykh* in which the *shaykh* usually takes the hand of the disciple, in imitation of the Prophet, as a symbol of the spiritual pact the disciple makes with the master and ultimately with God). The *shaykh* apologized to the group and politely said he did not take disciples, but in fact he did quietly initiate a very small number of his most devoted students—a group that included high-ranking military officers, businessmen, merchants, and Azharī *ʿulamā'*. The intensity and station of the spiritual relationship were such that ʿAbd al-Ḥalīm communicated directives to these disciples almost entirely in *ru'yā* (dreams).

ʿAbd al-Ḥalīm Maḥmūd encouraged his disciples to revive the Sufi practice of *khidmah*—service. Calling themselves "The lovers of Sayyidnā Ḥusayn and the students of Shaykh Aḥmad Karāmah and Dr. ʿAbd al-Ḥalīm Maḥmūd,"[20] they have been providing full meals to thousands at all of the major *mawālīd* (pl. of *mawlid*) in Cairo as well as during *ifṭār* and the *saḥūr* meals in the al-Ḥusayn Mosque area during Ramaḍān for more than ten years.[21]

To appreciate the perfume of *barakah* that permeates the activity of the *khidmah* is to first understand that *khidmah* is not an act of "social justice" or "social welfare"; much less is it socialism. It is a religious rite and a spiritual act to serve for the love of God whoever offers himself or herself for the quest—from prince to pauper. But *khidmah* does in fact provide food for thousands of the poor and speaks to the advantages in this world which are inevitably generated by the highest intentions set upon the next world.[22]

Shaykh ʿAbd al-Ḥalīm Maḥmūd's efforts bridged the artificial gap that had been developing since the thirteenth/nineteenth century, separating *ʿilm* from *maʿrifah*, sobriety from ecstasy, *Sharīʿah* from *Ḥaqīqah* (Truth), and al-Azhar from Sufi life and thought, to the detriment of all.

Egypt continues to this day to be a major center of Sufism. It is sufficient to visit the Ra'ʾs al-Ḥusayn mosque in Cairo on any Thursday evening to become aware of the degree to which Sufism is still alive in the land which has been witness to some of the greatest Sufis over the centuries. Nor is Sufism confined to the masses, as can be seen by witnessing the gathering of several of the orders which draw many adherents from highly educated classes. Moreover, Sufism in Egypt remains closely tied to the Arab East, to such countries as Syria and Jordan, as well as to the Sudan, many of whose orders are directly linked with those of Egypt. The *barakah* emanating from the presence of the tombs of such eminent Sufis as Ibn ʿAṭāʾ Allāh al-Iskandarī and Ibn al-Fāriḍ in Cairo or Sayyid Aḥmad al-Badawī in Tanta complement and support the living *barakah* which issues from the sincere practice of Sufism throughout Egypt. The Sufi tradition continues to live in Egypt and the Arab East despite all the obstacles that have been placed in its path, and Sufism remains at the center of the spiritual life of numerous Muslims in these lands who respond to the call of the world of the Spirit as their forefathers have done before them.

Notes

1. See chapter 2 of this volume, "The Shādhiliyyah and North African Sufism," by V. Danner.
2. The estimate was made by Dr. Abu'l-Wafāʾ al-Taftāzānī, the present *shaykh al-mashāyikh* of Egypt.
3. J. Spencer Trimingham, *The Sufi Orders in Islam* (London: Oxford University Press, 1971) 45. On the Rifāʿī Order itself, see pp. 37–40.
4. M. Chodkiewicz, "Introduction," to al-Sulamī, *The Book of Sufi Chivalry* (New York: Inner Traditions International, 1983) 18-20; also A. Schleifer, "*Jihād* and Traditional Consciousness," *Islamic Quarterly* 27 (1983) 195–97.
5. For the general history of Sufism in Egypt, see Trimingham, *Sufi Orders,* 37–51; and Abu'l-Wafāʾ al-Ghunaymī al-Taftāzānī, "Al-ṭuruq al-ṣūfiyyah fī Miṣr," *Ḥawliyyāt Kulliyyat al-Ādāb-Jāmiʿat al-Qāhirah,* vol. 25/2 (Dec. 1963) 55–84.
6. Afaf Lutfi al-Sayyed Marsot, "The *ʿUlamāʾ* of Cairo in the Eighteenth and Nineteenth Centuries," in *Scholars, Saints and Sufis,* ed. N. R. Keddie (Berkeley: University of California Press, 1972) 149–65. Marsot quotes extensively from the early thirteenth/

nineteenth-century chronicle of the Azharī ʿAbd al-Raḥmān al-Jabartī. See also F. de Jong, *Ṭuruq and Ṭuruq-Linked Institutions in Nineteenth-Century Egypt* (Leiden: Brill, 1978).

7. De Jong, *Ṭuruq*.

8. Ali Hassan Abdel Kader, *The Life, Personality and Writings of Al-Junayd* (London: Luzac, 1976).

9. Sayyidah Fāṭimah was a woman of exceptional spiritual attainment whose presence was felt not only in Lebanon and Syria but even in other lands. Many Westerners associated with the Sufi tradition, such as T. Burckhardt and M. Lings, visited her in Beirut, as did such Arab authorities in Sufism as ʿAbd al-Ḥalīm Maḥmūd. She remained the spiritual center of the Yashruṭiyyah until her death and is without doubt one of the outstanding female Sufi figures of this century. Toward the end of her life she wrote her autobiography, *Masīratī ila'l-Ḥaqq* (*My Sojourn to the Truth*) (Beirut, 1981).

10. De Jong, *Ṭuruq*, 3–5.

11. Ibid., 8–39; al-Taftāzānī, "Al-ṭuruq al-ṣūfiyyah fī Miṣr," 66.

12. De Jong, *Ṭuruq*, 155–73; see also J. W. McPherson, *The Moulids of Egypt* (Cairo: Debbane, 1941).

13. See M. Gilsenan, *Saint and Sufi in Modern Egypt* (Oxford: Clarendon Press, 1973).

14. Broader and thus more appropriate than the overworked concept of "Islamic fundamentalists," the term "Islamic oriented protest groups" was coined by Oxford University scholar Māhā ʿAzzām and quoted in J. Johanson's unpublished thesis progress report "The Sheikh, the World and the Problem of Guidance: Some Observations from Sufi Life and Literature" (Oxford, 1989).

15. As a representative work of Muḥsin al-Labbān one may mention *Wa la-dhikr Allāh akbar: dirāsah fī baʿḍ abʿād al-dhikr wa'l-fikr fi'l-kitāb wa'l sunnah* (Alexandria: Liwā al-Ḥamd, 1988). A representative writing by the shaykh of the *ṭarīqah* Muḥammadiyyah Shādhiliyyah, Muḥammed Zakī Ibrāhīm, is *Uṣūl al-wuṣūl: adillah ahamm maʿālim al-ṣūfiyyat al-ḥaqqah min ṣarīḥ al-kitāb wa ṣaḥīḥ al-sunnah* (Cairo: Manshūrāt wa Rasā'il al-ʿAshīrat al-Muḥammadiyyah, 1984).

16. Ibrāhīm Muḥammad al-Baṭṭāwī's representative work is *Miftāḥ al-ism al-aʿẓam wa ṭarīq al-wuṣūl ila'Llāh* (Cairo: Dār al-Insān, 1978).

17. Al-Taftāzānī, *Ibn ʿAṭā' Allāh al-Iskandarī wa taṣawwufuh*^{u} (Cairo: Anglo-Egyptian Publishing House, 1958).

18. Al-Taftāzānī, "Al-ṭuruq al-ṣūfiyyah fī Miṣr."

19. One can enumerate among the works of ʿAbd al-Ḥalīm Maḥmūd, *Dhu'l-Nūn al-Miṣrī* (Alexandria: Jamʿiyyat al-Imām al-Akbar ʿAbd al-Ḥalīm Maḥmūd, 1981); *Bishr ibn al-Ḥārith al-Ḥāfī* (Cairo: Dār al-Miṣriyyah, 1980); *Al-Madrasat al-shādhiliyyah* (Cairo: Dār al-Maʿārif, 1975); *Abu'l-Ḥasan al-Shādhilī* (Cairo: Dār al-Shaʿb, 1969); *Al-Imām al-Rabbānī: ʿAbd Allāh ibn Mubārak* (Cairo: Dār al-Shaʿb, 1979); *Al-Ḥamd*^{u} *li'Llāh: hādhā ḥayātī* (Cairo: Dār al-Maʿārif, 1978); and *Al-Sayyid Aḥmad al-Badawī* (Cairo: Dār al-Shaʿb, 1969). See also Abdel Haleem Mahmud, *The Creed of Islam*, trans. Mahmud Abdel Haleem (London: World of Islam Festival, 1978); this is the only work of the author to have been translated into English so far.

20. Shaykh Aḥmad Karāmah was a pious Muslim who revived the practice of *khidmah* in the al-Ḥusayn area in the 1950s. ʿAbd al-Ḥalīm Maḥmūd encouraged his disciples to work with Karāmah.

21. These terms refer to the meal that breaks the fast at sunset and the last meal prior to the prayer just before sunrise and the resumption of the fast.

22. Schleifer, "*Jihād* and Traditional Consciousness," p. 129 on "the politics of anti-politics."

10

Sufism and Spirituality in Persia

Seyyed Hossein Nasr

Many of the Sufi orders discussed in this volume either arose first in Persia or had a profound influence in that land. 'Abd al-Qādir Jīlānī hailed originally from Gilan and the order has remained alive in certain areas of Persia to this day. The Naqshbandī Order grew within a Persian cultural matrix, as did the Kubrawiyyah. As for the Nimatullahi Order, as was already mentioned, it has been the most influential Sufi order in Persia during the past few centuries, despite its eclipse in the Safavid period. What we wish to do in this chapter is neither to repeat that which has been treated amply in other sections of this work nor to turn to Persian Sufi literature, which will be treated extensively later, but to mention certain manifestations of Sufism in Persia not treated elsewhere in this study and to depict something of the aroma of Sufism and Islamic spirituality in general as they have manifested themselves in Persia since practically the beginning of Islamic history.

Persia has always been one of the main arenas for the flowering of Sufism, and some of the greatest Sufi saints and sages have hailed from this land—not to speak of the poetic creations of Persian Sufis, which transformed the religious and spiritual life of much of Asia. The perfume of Sufism can be sensed in almost every manifestation of Persian culture, whether it be poetry or music, calligraphy or landscape design, philosophy or science—not to speak of social institutions and practices such as *futuwwah* or *jawānmardī* (spiritual chivalry) and the "house of strength" (*zūr-khānah*).[1] The very reverence for 'Alī among Persians in general, whether they be Sunni or Shī'ite, has brought something of the flavor of Sufism, of which he was the first patriarch after the Prophet, even into popular piety, while the most metaphysically rigorous and quintessential type of Sufism has found some of its foremost representatives among Persians.

Persia and Early Sufism: The School of Khurasan

Already in the first century, the first Persian to embrace Islam, Salmān-ī Fārsī, was one of the earliest representatives of Islamic esoterism and is considered by later Sufis as one of their poles. Many of the earliest ascetics (*zuhhād*) of the first/seventh and second/eighth centuries came from Khurasan, such as Ibrāhīm Adham (d. in the later part of the second/eighth century), and some of those who lived in Mesopotamia were also of Persian origin.

In the third/ninth century, the school of Khurasan flowered with the appearance of such masters as Shaqīq Balkhī, Abū Yazīd Basṭāmī, so well known for his ecstatic utterances (*shaṭḥiyyāt*), and Ḥakīm Tirmidhī, whose influence is to be seen as far away as Andalusia and in the writings of Ibn ʿArabī. The school of Khurasan, known for its path of "drunkenness" (*sukr*) rather than sobriety (*ṣaḥw*), produced Sufis of the purely gnostic type such as Abu'l-Ḥasan Kharrāqanī as well as such classical authorities in Sufi doctrine and practice as Abū Naṣr Sarrāj, Abū Bakr Kalābādhī, Abū ʿAbd al-Raḥmān Sulamī, and Imam Abu'l-Qāsim al-Qushayrī. Khurasan was also the home of the first great Persian Sufi writers and poets, such as Khwājah ʿAbd Allāh Anṣarī and Abū Saʿīd Abi'l-Khayr. Later, in the fifth/eleventh and sixth/twelfth centuries, the Khurasani school took unto itself some of the traits of the school of Baghdad associated with Junayd and produced one of the most subtle and metaphysically profound expressions of Sufism in Aḥmad Ghazzālī, whose influence is to be seen not only in his follower ʿAyn al-Quḍāt Hamadānī but also throughout the later history of the Kubrawī Order. It was also in Khurasan that there arose that most celebrated of Muslim scholars, Abū Ḥāmid Muḥammad Ghazzālī, who created a lasting harmony between Sufism and Sunni orthodoxy.[2]

The School of Baghdad and Sufism in Other Regions of Persia

Meanwhile Persians were also numerous in Baghdad and in the circle of Junayd, who himself, although raised in Baghdad, belonged to a family from the Persian city of Nahawand. These included the famous friend of Junayd, Abu'l-Ḥusayn al-Nūrī, who came from Khurasan, and the last outstanding member of the circle of Baghdad, Abū Bakr al-Shiblī, whose family also came from Khurasan. Even the most famous figure of this school, Manṣūr al-Ḥallāj, who was put to death in Baghdad because of his public exposition of esoteric knowledge, hailed originally from the Persian province of Fars.[3] Although Ḥallāj was the greatest of the early Sufi poets of the Arabic language, Persian was his mother tongue. It is a strange fact that during the early history of Sufism most of those who wrote extensively on Sufi doctrine or practice in Arabic were Persian, and the great Arab writers of Sufism belong to the later centuries. The outstanding Arab masters of early Sufism, such as Dhu'l-Nūn al-Miṣrī, seemed to have remained satisfied with short statements and indications (*ishārāt*) which express the deepest truths of Sufism in laconic expressions of great power.

Meanwhile notable Persian Sufis also appeared in other parts of Persia, figures such as Abū Sahl Tustarī from Khuzistan, known for his pioneering esoteric exegesis upon the Quran, which served as model for later Sufi commentaries. Perhaps the most important locus of Sufi activity in Persia outside Khurasan was Shiraz, which has remained over the centuries and to this day a major center of Sufism. Ibn Khafīf, the patron saint of the city, was the spiritual master of Abū Naṣr Sarrāj and many other Sufis from different regions of Persia. Rūzbihān Baqlī Shīrāzī was among the foremost of the Persian *fedeli d'amore* and wrote one of the most important mystical commentaries on the Quran. The two great Persian poets, Sa'dī and Ḥāfiẓ, both of whom were Sufis, hailed from that city and are buried in the northern hills of Shiraz. Even during the present century one of the foremost Sufis, Waḥīd al-awliyā', hailed from the city of Sa'dī and Ḥāfiẓ.

Nor have other parts of Persia remained devoid of the presence of Sufism over the centuries. Azerbaijan has produced a galaxy of important figures of Sufism from Shaykh Maḥmūd Shabistarī to Shaykh Ṣafī al-Dīn Ardibīlī and from the Suhrawardī family, which migrated to Baghdad to found the Suhrawardī Order, to Shams al-Dīn Tabrīzī. Hamadan also had its own great saints, such as Bābā Ṭāhir and Sayyid 'Alī Hamadānī, who exercised such a vast influence in Kashmir. Kerman was the original abode of Awḥad al-Dīn Kirmānī and the place where many later Sufis such as Sayyid Muḥammad Nūrbakhsh and Shāh Ni'mat Allāh Walī flourished. The central cities of Persia, such as Kashan, Na'in, Isfahan, and Yazd, also produced great Sufis.

As one journeys through Persia and Afghanistan today one sees tombs of Sufi saints everywhere in the countryside as well as in the towns. Many a city such as Herat, where Khwājah 'Abd Allāh Anṣārī's mausoleum is to be found, is dominated by the tomb of its patron saint. Such Sufi sites as the tomb of Bābā Rukn al-Dīn in Isfahan, Afḍal al-Dīn Kāshānī near Kashan, Bāyazīd in Bastam, Shāh Ni'mat Allāh Walī in Mahan, and Shabistarī in Shabistar near Tabriz continue to be centers of pilgrimage and focuses of popular piety as well as loci of the Divine Presence and *barakah* which attract travelers upon the Sufi path.

6. The tomb of Salmān-i Fārsī on the Mount of Olives in Jerusalem.

Sufism in the Later History of Persia

The advent of the Mongol invasion was followed by a period of great flowering of Sufism in Persia, as witnessed by the rise of the Kubrawiyyah, Nūrbakhshiyyah, Naqshbandiyyah, and Nimatullahi orders. This was also the period that witnessed the rise of the Ṣafawī Order, leading finally to the establishment of the Safavid dynasty and, paradoxically enough, the beginning of the eclipse of Sufism in much of Persia. The famous battle between Ḥaydarīs and Niʻmatīs in Tabriz and elsewhere bore witness to the eclipse of Sufism during the early Safavid period, which resulted in the migration of many Persian Sufis to India.

Toward the end of the Safavid period, the Shīʻite establishment itself turned against Sufism and Mullā Muḥammad Bāqir Majlisī, the powerful Shīʻite *ʻālim,* attacked the Sufis severely and even denied the Sufi inclinations of his father, Mullā Muḥammad Taqī Majlisī. For a century Sufism remained in eclipse in the central regions of Persia but continued to flourish in the land which was to become Afghanistan as well as in Kurdistan and Baluchistan. It was not until the early Qajar period that Sufism began to flourish once again in the heartland of Persia with the return of the Nimatullahi masters from India, as already mentioned in a previous chapter. Henceforth, often with the support of the Qajars, various branches of the Nimatullahi Order, as well as other orders such as the Dhahabiyyah and the Khāksār, began to flourish. Besides the main branch of the Nimatullahi Order already treated, the most important offshoot of the order was the Gunābādī with its center in Gunabad in Khurasan. This branch has always had a strong Sharīʻite color and has drawn to itself many people who possess strong Shīʻite piety.

The Malāmatiyyah (People of Blame)

A special movement within Sufism which began in Khurasan and spread later to many parts of the Islamic world is the Malāmatiyyah. Called the Malāmatiyyah as well as Malāmiyyah and in certain cases *Ahl al-malāmah,* the followers of this strand of spirituality exercised great influence on many aspects of Sufism and were for some periods of Islamic history associated closely with *futuwwah* or spiritual chivalry.[4] The name of this important group is derived from the word *malāmah,* which means literally "blame." The Malāmatiyyah were people who blamed their lower soul (*nafs*) and sought to control and discipline it while also bringing the blame of people upon themselves by avoiding all pretention and ostentation in matters pertaining to religion and even religious rites. They were often perceived as not being devout Muslims. In reality, however, before the movement decayed in the sixth/twelfth and seventh/thirteenth centuries, the Malāmatiyyah represented a high degree of spiritual realization achieved through sincerity in action (*ikhlāṣ*), which was emphasized above all else. Such later Sufis as Anṣārī practically identified *malāmah* with sincerity.[5]

The founder of the Malāmatiyyah was a third/ninth-century Sufi named Ḥamdūn Qaṣṣār from Nayshapur in Khurasan, and this city remained for some time the center of the movement. The famous saying *al-malāmah tark al-salāmah* ("blame is to give up one's well-being") is attributed to him. The Malāmatiyyah, following him, lived inwardly in union with God, while outwardly they behaved as if they were separated from Him. This trait was recognized by Sulamī, who was one of the first Sufi writers to discuss the Malāmatiyyah.[6] This tendency to perform outwardly unseemly acts—which brought down the criticism of the community—while living inwardly in the Divine Presence seemed to become, once the Malāmatiyyah movement began to decay, a dangerous disregard for the *Sharī'ah*. As a result, a number of people pretended to be members of the group and avoided all outward ostentation as far as religious practices were concerned without following inwardly any Malāmatī practices. As early as the fifth/eleventh century, Anṣārī had alluded to these people when he said, "Now a group has brought forth licentiousness and treating lightly of the Divine law and heresy and lack of etiquette and respectfulness—but *malāmat* was not that somebody would act by showing no respect to the law; it was that they did not care for the people in their service of God."[7]

The veritable Malāmatiyyah, in contrast to pretenders who used the name to disregard the *Sharī'ah* and traditional *adab* or etiquette, rose in Khurasan in opposition to both the school of drunkenness (*sukr*) and sobriety (*ṣaḥw*) and also to the Karrāmiyyah, who emphasized the miracles of saints. The masters of the movement such as Ḥamdūn and, following him, Abū Ḥafs al-Ḥaddād continued to emphasize the importance of sincerity in action and opposed all ostentatiousness and religious hypocrisy. They also lived simply and near to the people, as a result of which they became ever more closely associated with the guilds of craftsmen and artisans.

By the fifth/eleventh and sixth/twelfth centuries, the original Malāmatiyyah movement had decayed, while a Sufi order called the Malāmatiyyah rose in the Ottoman world, but this group had very little connection with the old Khurasani movement. It was only in the Naqshbandī Order that the devotion and sincerity of the early Malāmatiyyah associated with Ḥamdūn and the circle of Nayshapur continued.

The Malāmatī attitude remained, however, within Sufism as a permanent strand of Islamic spirituality despite the many abuses committed in its name. On the highest level, this type of spirituality signifies a perfect surrender to God combined with becoming the theater for the reflection of all of His Names and Qualities.

> By manifesting all the divine names without a trace of Lordship and thereby displaying perfect servanthood, perfect man becomes, one might say, totally ordinary. In him, nothing stands out, since he flows with all created things in perfect harmony and equilibrium. He is like a tree or a bird in his ordinariness, following the divine will wherever it takes him, with no friction, no protest, complete serenity, no waves. He is so much at ease with the continual flux of secondary causes that he remains unnoticed by his contemporaries.[8]

No wonder that Ibn ʿArabī considers the Malāmiyyah to be the most perfect gnostics and to occupy the highest rank among the Sufis. He writes:

> The People of Blame are those who know and are not known. . . .
>
> The People of Blame are the unknown, those whose stations are unknown. No divine affair dominates over them such that it might be known that God has a special solicitude towards them. Their states conceal their stations because of the wisdom of the abode: They never become manifest in the locus of contention, since sometimes people contend with their Master—who is God—in this house in respect of His Divinity. But this tribe have realized their Master, so this realization has prevented them from becoming manifest within the abode within which their Master is concealed. Hence they flow with the common people (*al-ʿāmma*) in respect of the outward acts of obedience which the common people perform. . . . No act becomes manifest from them which would distinguish them from the common people. This contrasts with the miraculous breaking of habits through states displayed by some of the friends.
>
> The People of Blame are the masters and leaders of the folk of God's path. Among them is the master of the cosmos, that is, Muhammad, the Messenger of God—God bless him and give him peace! They are the sages, those who put things in their proper places. They do things well and put the secondary causes in their correct locations, while negating them in the places from which they should be negated. They violate nothing of what God has arranged in His creation, leaving it just as He has arranged it. Whatever is required for this world, they leave for this world and whatever is required for the next world, they leave for the next world. They look at things with the same eye with which God looks at things. They never confuse realities.[9]

The Qalandars and Khāksārs

Another important manifestation of Sufism in Persia which had a particular color of its own and spread later to other lands such as India and Anatolia

7. The *miḥrāb* of the mausoleum of Bāyazīd Basṭāmī in Khurasan, Persia.

is the Qalandariyyah Order with its distant offshoot, the Khāksār.[10] The group of *qalandars,* the origin of whose name is not known with certainty, appeared in the early centuries of Islamic history as being associated with those who were in a state of Divine Attraction (*jadhbah*). Such men, precisely because they were in such a state, that is, beside themselves and in an altered state of consciousness, are like "the fools of God." They have always been a channel of grace and revered by those around them, although while in such a state they cannot even perform their daily prayers. To this day in climates of intense piety where Sufism is still alive, such as Pakistan and India, *majdhūbs,* that is, those in the state of *jadhbah,* are seen attached to various Sufi centers and in the vicinity of the tombs of Sufi saints.

The *qalandars* rose from such a background to become a defined group and even constitute an order called the Qalandariyyah. But they also became associated with carelessness in the observation of religious rites and normal social etiquette. Urban society saw in them the manifestation of a wild, unruly, and rebellious nature depicted in their outward comportment, which was usually rough and aggressive. Sometimes the *qalandars* had long hair and unruly beards. They were always in the state of wandering from place to place and carried a begging bowl (*kashkūl*) and axe (*tabarzīn*) in order to receive food and protect themselves in the wilderness. These two paraphernalia became so much identified with later Sufism that a number of *khānqāhs* in Persia use them to this day as their insignia, while one of the most important works on Sufism during the Safavid period is called *al-Kashkūl* (*The Begging Bowl*).[11]

This aspect of undisciplined behavior and unruliness of the *qalandars* became proverbial in Persian Sufi literature, where the term *rind* also became common as its synonym. This term, which signified a person who is free of all constraints and rules and has a sense of craftiness and shrewdness, gained a positive connotation in later Sufi poetry, especially in the *Dīwān* of Ḥāfiẓ, who uses the term to refer to the person who has gained absolute inner freedom through utter devotion to the love of the One. As Ḥāfiẓ says in this famous verse:

> Do not criticize the *rinds,* O pure natured ascetic,
> For the sins of others will not be recorded
> in thy account.

As Suhrawardī mentions in his classical treatise the *'Awārif al-ma'ārif* (*Confessions of Divine Knowledge*), the *qalandars* were originally followers of the Malāmatiyyah but gradually distanced themselves from them and in contrast to them participated in the spiritual concerts (*samā'*) of the Sufis. The *qalandars* had their own center called *langar,* to which Rūmī has referred in his works,[12] and by the seventh/thirteenth century had organized themselves into a distinct Sufi order. Its founder is usually identified as Shaykh Jamāl al-Dīn Sāwajī, who organized the order in 620/1223 in Damascus. He instituted the practice of shaving the head and even the eyebrows, by which the *qalandars* came to be known at that time, although during recent centuries *qalandars* have often been identified by their very long hair. His student Muḥammad Balkhī added the practice of wearing a *jawāl* or sack, so that the order also came to be known as the Jawāliqī. The order sought to pass beyond and transcend everything in this world and referred to this leaving behind of things as *takbīr.* Henceforth Sufi poetry refers to the distancing of oneself from the world as the act of *takbīr* of the *qalandars* as in the verse,

> Come let us wash our hands of this world,
> And recite a *takbīr* like the *qalandars.*

The *qalandars* often acted in strange and shocking ways. Sometimes they walked naked or dressed like clowns. Sometimes they wore the skin of tigers and leopards and begged in bazaars of lands ranging from India to Turkey but always using the Persian langauge.

After the Mongol invasion, the Ḥaydarī Order was established on a similar foundation as the Qalandariyyah by Quṭb al-Dīn Ḥaydar, after whom also the city Turbat-i Ḥaydariyyah in Khurasan is named. The order spread from Khurasan to India and Anatolia, and its members, like the *qalandars,* always wandered from town to town. One of them, Ḥājj Mubārak Ḥaydarī, was dear to Rūmī. The Ḥaydariyyah carried out ascetic practices to the extreme and avoided all sexual activity.

As far as India is concerned, these types of wandering dervishes or *qalandars* were common and in fact exist to this day, but they were not looked upon with favor by such earlier masters of Sufism as Niẓām al-Dīn Awliyā'. The situation changed, however, when the great Persian Sufi poet Fakhr al-Dīn 'Irāqī joined their group. The *qalandars* became especially respected in India when a Persian Sufi from Azerbaijan, La'l Shahbāz Qalandar (d. 673/1274) went to Multan in India and became one of the most respected spiritual figures of that land.

In the eighth/fourteenth century Sayyid Jalāl Thānī, who was a descendant of Sayyid Jalāl al-Dīn Bukhārī, himself a *khalīfah* or representative of Bahā' al-Dīn Zakariyyā', began to propagate the Jalālī Order, which was an offshoot of the Qalandariyyah and followed its teachings. Like the Qalandariyyah, the Jalāliyyah shaved their head and face and journeyed constantly from one place to another. They also became known, like the *qalandars*, for charming snakes and scorpions and having various kinds of psychic powers.

The Khāksār Order, which spread extensively in Persia during the Qajar period and flourishes to this day, is a branch of the Jalāliyyah and therefore goes back to the whole Qalandariyyah-Malāmatiyyah movement of the earlier centuries. The Khāksār Order is said to have been founded by Ghulām ʿAlī Shāh Hindī, who moved the Jalāliyyah of India in the direction of Shīʿism leading to the establishment of the Khāksār, who are definitely a Shīʿite Sufi order. The history of this order is unclear and is based on late sources such as the *Kursī-nāma-yi lā fatā* (*The Throne Treatise of "There is no Chivalry"*) of Shaydā, which is quite eclectic, citing such figures as Bū ʿAlī Qalandar, Shahbāz Baktāsh, and Shāh Niʿmat Allāh Walī as the masters of the order. What is certain is that the Khāksār place special emphasis upon Salmān-ī Fārsī and display affinities with the Ahl-i Ḥaqq and the Ḥurūfiyyah.[13] Their initiation involves drinking the cup of poverty (*piyāla-yi faqr*) and wearing a cloth (*lung*) made of forty patches. This fact reveals their rapport with the *futuwwāt* or guilds. As a matter of fact, it is mostly among members of the guilds that the Khāksār Order has been popular in Persia, although some of the outstanding masters of this order, such as the contemporary figure Mullā Ḥubb-i Ḥaydar, have also had disciples among highly educated circles of Persian society.

Sufism and Islamic Spirituality in Contemporary Persia

The revival of Sufism in the Qajar period continued into the Pahlavi period, and despite the advent of modernism, the Sufi orders prospered and continued to grow during the last few decades. After the Islamic Revolution in Iran, for a while open hostility was shown toward the Sufi orders, but this attitude gradually subsided. The Sufi orders and Sufism in general continue their life in Persia, although several major masters of these orders now reside outside the country.

During the contemporary period, three important Sufi orders with a Shīʿite color have prospered in Persia: the Nimatullahi, the Dhahabī, and the Khāksār. The Nimatullahi Order has been the most influential with several branches including not only the main branch, headed by Javad Nurbakhsh, but also such other branches as the Gunābādī in Khurasan and Tehran, the followers of Niʿmat ʿAlī Shāh in Isfahan, and the remnants of the branch associated with Ṣafī ʿAlī Shāh, mostly in Tehran.[14] The Dhahabī Order with its centers in Shiraz and Tabriz traces its origin to the Kubrawiyyah Order and Maʿruf Karkhī, purported to be the disciple of the

8. The façade of an 8th/14th century *khānqāh* in Natanz in central Persia.

eighth Shīʿite Imam, ʿAlī al-Riḍā. This order has continued to have many disciples and has been very active in the propagation of Sufi learning and literature. Likewise, as already mentioned, the Khāksār have continued to draw disciples especially from the classes of craftsmen, artisans, and laborers.

In the Sunni parts of Iran such as Baluchistan and Kurdistan as well as in Afghanistan, which was part of the Persian world before the thirteenth/nineteenth century, the predominantly Sunni orders such as the Qādiriyyah and Naqshbandiyyah have continued to be strong and act as the main loci for the spiritual activities and aspirations of the people. Interestingly enough, a number of Qādirīs have later joined the Nimatullahi Order, and the distinction between Sufi orders of Shīʿite and Sunni inclination has not been as sharp during the past few decades as it was during the Qajar and Safavid periods.

One cannot discuss Sufism in contemporary Persia without mentioning a number of other groups that are of significance in either specific areas or among distinct circles of Persians. Among these groups the Uwaysīs are worthy of being especially mentioned. The origin of this form of Sufism goes back to the Yemeni saint, Uways al-Qaranī, who embraced Islam without having ever seen the Prophet. He later joined ʿAlī in Iraq and is said to have died at the battle of Siffin. The Uwaysīs do not usually have a human spiritual master but receive their initiation and guidance from the "invisible world" (*ʿālam al-ghayb*) and more specifically from al-Khaḍir, the mysterious prophet of esoterism mentioned in the Quran.[15] Throughout the history of Islam, there have been Sufis of the Uwaysī branch, some great saints and sages, but they have not established a regular Sufi order because of the very nature of their initiatic affiliation, which is not based on regular transmission through an initiatic chain (*silsilah*).

In Persia, however, there appeared in the early part of this century a famous Uwaysī named Mīr Quṭb al-Dīn Muḥammad ʿAnqāʾ, who is the author of several well-known works and around whom an important circle of Sufi adepts gathered.[16] Gradually the group transformed itself into a regular *ṭarīqah* and has spread to Europe and America under the direction of the son of the late Mīr Quṭb al-Dīn, Shah Maghsoud Sadegh Angha.[17] This phenomenon is itself of some interest in that it represents the transformation of the traditional Uwaysī spirituality based on guidance from on high by the "men of the invisible world" (*rijāl al-ghayb*) into a regular Sufi order organized around a human master. Be that as it may, the traditional Uwaysī spirituality continues and remains an important manifestation of Sufism in Persia as it was in the days of old.

In discussing Sufism in Persia, a word must also be said about the Ahl-i Ḥaqq, to which we have already referred. The Ahl-i Ḥaqq represent not one group but a "family" of closely linked religious organizations which flourish to this day in Luristan, Azerbaijan, and among the Turkumans within Persia as well as in Transcaucasia. They combine certain Sufi teachings with extreme forms of Shīʿism in an eclecticism that includes Manichaean elements and is unorthodox from both the Ithnā ʿAsharī Shīʿite and Sunni points of view. The Ahl-i Ḥaqq believe in the "divinization of ʿAlī," similar to what one finds among the Nuṣayrīs and Druzes. Sometimes they are in fact referred to as ʿAlī Ilāhī ("divinizers of ʿAlī"), although this appellation is not justified.[18] The doctrines of the Ahl-i Ḥaqq, literally, "The People of Truth," have remained for the most part secret and rarely have they been divulged. But there are exceptions, as for example the *Kashf al-ḥaqāʾiq* (*Unveiling of the Truth*) by an important fourteenth/twentieth-century master of the order, Nūr ʿAlī Shāh.[19] Although not at all in the mainstream of Sufism, the Ahl-i Ḥaqq nevertheless represent a certain kind of esoteric knowledge which has been preserved in secret and for the most part on a popular level in certain regions of Persia to this day in the context of an unorthodox religious framework.

Altogether one can detect in contemporary Persia three distinct spiritual types with many possibilities within each type. These types include first of all the regular and orthodox Sufi orders, some of which are of Shīʿite inclinations and others Sunni. There is much contact between the two kinds of orders, and they are far from being mutually exclusive. Second, there is spiritual initiation and instruction given by masters of Sufism who do not belong to a distinct Sufi order and who are either independent masters, as in the early centuries of Islam, or are of the Uwaysī type. Many of the great gnostics of contemporary Persia like ʿAllāmah Ṭabāṭabāʾī have received their spiritual instruction through such a channel. Third, there is Shīʿite spirituality and initiatic guidance independent of the Sufi orders but issuing from the same esoteric dimension of Islam which has given birth to both Sufism and Shīʿism.[20] Such masters of gnosis (*ʿirfān*) during this century as Mīrzā Aḥmad Āshtiyānī, Sayyid Muḥammad Kāẓim ʿAṣṣār, and Mahdī Ilāhī Qumshaʾī, all of whom possessed vast metaphysical knowledge and a high station of spiritual realization, did not belong to Sufi orders but received their spiritual guidance from the authorities of Shīʿite gnosis and individual masters.

There is, in fact, a strong spiritual element present in the mystical climate of Shīʿite spirituality, with its emphasis on the inner message of the Quran and the teachings of the Imams. Many of the prayers recited by the faithful such as the *Du'ā-yi Kumayl* and *al-Ṣaḥīfat al-sajjādiyyah* are of a highly spiritual and esoteric nature.[21] Certain Shī'ite schools such as the Shaykhīs, whose center is in Kerman, also possess esoteric knowledge derived directly from the teachings of the Imams. These teachings include an elaborate cosmology and a spiritual alchemy.[22] It is enough to meditate at night at the luminous mausoleum of 'Alī al-Riḍā in Mashhad, the figure who is at once the eighth Shī'ite Imam and a pole in many Sufi chains, to realize the profound rapport between Sufism and Shī'ite spirituality, both of which emanate from the same source but possess their own perfume and distinct characteristics.

It is strange that at the end of the Safavid period because of the decadence of many of the Sufi orders and the opposition of the Shī'ite *'ulamā'* to Sufism, the term *ṣūfī* became anathema in religious circles. The reality, however, did not disappear, and the term *'irfān,* which denotes the intellectual and metaphysical dimension of Sufism, took its place in such circles. Henceforth, *'irfān* became a most respectable term, and its truth was sought by many of the *'ulamā'*, philosophers, and the learned in general and even by certain simple people. From then on Shī'ite gnosis (*'irfān-i shī'ī*) became a major element in the spiritual and intellectual life of Persia along with Sufism as usually understood.

This type of gnosis and Sufism have continued to flourish during this century in Persia. This period has witnessed several great Sufi saints and sages such as Ṣafī 'Alī Shāh, Shams al-'urafā', and Waḥīd al-awliyā' as well as the Shī'ite gnostics mentioned above. The *khānqāhs* flourished over the whole country during the Pahlavi period and continue to draw people to themselves today. Also during the contemporary era numerous great scholars such as Badī' al-Zamān Furuzānfar and Jalāl Humā'ī resuscitated the literary heritage of Sufism, while men like Ḥādī Ḥā'irī kept alive the classical Sufi tradition of interpreting the *Mathnawī*.

Sufism has in fact penetrated so deeply into all aspects of Persian culture that one can hardly hear classical Persian music or recite classical poetry without being reminded of the love of Majnūn for that Laylī who symbolizes the dark beauty of the Divine Essence. The very light of the early morning sun shining upon the exalted mountain peaks of the Persian plateau reminds man of that light which Suhrawardī considered to be nothing other than the descent of the Light issuing from the Divine Empyrean. The countryside and the cities continue to be adorned by the tombs of men and women of God, some Sufis, some descendants of the Imams, and yet others both spiritual and physical descendants of the bearers of the Muḥammadan Light (*al-nūr al-muḥammadī*). When spring comes and the nightingale begins to chant its celestial song, one is reminded that in this land of poetry and the rose and nightingale, the nostalgia for the Divine and means of reaching that Eternal Garden about which the nightingale sings will always be present. Despite all the upheavals of history and events of unprecedented tragedy in this land, Sufism and Islamic spirituality in general live on and the nightingale continues to sing of its love for that rose garden which never perishes nor withers away.

Notes

1. We have dealt with this issue separately in chapter 15 of this volume.

2. The significance of the school of Khurasan has been treated by A. Schimmel in *Mystical Dimensions of Islam* (Chapel Hill: University of North Carolina Press, 1975). See also A. Zarrīnkūb, *Justiju dar taṣawwuf-i Īrān* (Tehran: Amīr Kabīr, 1357 A.H.S.) chap. 3. On early Sufism in Persia, see also S. H. Nasr, "Sufism," in *The Cambridge History of Iran,* vol. 4, ed. R. N. Frye (Cambridge: University Press, 1975) 442–63.

3. Ḥallāj, who represents a Christic form of spirituality within the cosmos of Muḥammadan poverty, is of great significance for the history of Sufism, and his ecstatic utterance (*shaṭḥ*) *ana'l-Ḥaqq* (I am the Truth) has echoed like a refrain throughout the centuries in the annals of Sufism. Although he was put to death on the pretext that he had claimed divinity for himself, what Ḥallāj asserted was that only the supreme I who is the Self at the heart of every self can utter "I" and this "I" *is al-Ḥaqq.* It was not the ego of Ḥallāj which exclaimed "I am the Truth," but the Divine I at the center of his heart. That is why we still hear his exclamation a millennium later. Ḥallāj was also destined to have a major role in the serious introduction of Sufism to the West through the figure of Louis Massignon, who devoted a lifetime to the study of this great saint and through him made many aspects of Sufism available to the Western public for the first time. See especially his *The Passion of al-Ḥallāj,* trans. H. Mason (4 vols.; Princeton, NJ: Princeton University Press, 1982).

4. See chapter 15 of this volume.

5. As the Malāmatiyyah movement decayed, certain Sufis during later centuries became more critical of it, as one can see in the *Kashf al-maḥjūb* of Hujwīrī.

6. He wrote about them in his *Ṭabaqāt al-ṣūfiyyah* and also dedicated an important independent treatise to them entitled *Risālat al-malāmatiyyah* (*The Treatise of the People of Blame*).

7. Quoted by A. Schimmel in *Mystical Dimensions of Islam,* 87.

8. W. Chittick, *The Sufi Path of Knowledge* (Albany: State University of New York Press, 1989) 372. It is remarkable how similar Ibn 'Arabī's description of the Malāmiyyah, to which this quotation refers, is to the description of the perfect Taoist sage.

9. Chittick, *Sufi Path of Knowledge,* 372–73.

10. Much remains to be done to make better known the history and teachings of this particular manifestation of Sufism; see Zarrīnkūb, *Justiju dar taṣawwuf-i Īrān,* chap. 14.

11. This work is by the eleventh/seventeenth-century Sufi master, poet, theologian, jurist, and mathematician of Isfahan Shaykh Bahā' al-Dīn 'Āmilī, who was of Arab origin but was raised in Isfahan. It is a voluminous compendium of diverse sayings like the begging bowl of the dervishes into which various parcels of food are placed.

12. See Zarrīnkūb, *Justiju dar taṣawwuf-i Īrān,* chap. 15.

13. On the Ahl-i Ḥaqq, see the article of V. Minorsky in the new *Encyclopedia of Islam.* The Ḥurūfīs were a heterodox sect founded by Faḍl Allāh Astrābādī in the eighth/fourteenth century. The founder was at first an orthodox Sufi but around

788/1386 while in Isfahan, he had a vision after which he considered himself to have become the locus for the manifestation of the Divinity. He claimed a new religion and tried to convert Tamerlane but without success. He was finally put to death in 796/1394 in Shirwan. His *Jāwīdān-nāma-yi kabīr* (*The Grand Treatise of Eternity*) as well as the works of his chief disciple ʿAlī al-Aʿlā such as the *mathnawī* poem *Tawḥīd-nāmah* (*The Treatise of Unity*) spread the teachings of the movement, which were based on the kabbalistic study of the letters of the alphabet. Although the movement came to an end in the early decades of the ninth/fifteenth century, it left its mark on the Biktāshīs of Anatolia and also on certain later Persian Sufis who emphasized the significance of the letters (*ḥurūf*) of the alphabet as direct manifestations of Divine Qualities. On the Ḥurūfiyyah, see H. Ritter, "Die Anfange der Hurufisekte," *Oriens* 7 (1954) 1–54; and A. Bausani, "Ḥurūfiyyah" in the new *Encyclopedia of Islam*.

14. See chapter 7 in this volume on the Nimatullahiyyah.

15. According to traditional sources, al-Khaḍir or Khiḍr has been bestowed with an ever-continuing life and does not die. He is constantly present to guide those who are qualified upon the spiritual path.

16. Mīr Quṭb al-Dīn was also a fine poet and master of the "hidden sciences" (*al-ʿulūm al-gharībah*). One of his most popular books in Persian dealing with the journey of the soul from the stage of the fetus to paradise, *Az janīn tā janān*, has been translated into English as *Destination: Eternity*, trans. N. Angha (San Raphael: Multidisciplinary Publications, 1975).

17. See his *Hidden Angles of Life* (Pomona: Multidisciplinary Publications, 1975). The order in America has brought out several books and a journal devoted to Sufism.

18. See Minorsky, "Ahl-i Ḥaqq."

19. See Nūr ʿAlī Shāh Ilāhī, *L'Esotérisme kurde: Aperçus sur le secret gnostique des fidèles de vérité*, trans. M. Mokri (Paris: Albin Michel, 1965).

20. The relation between Sufism and Shīʿism is a very complex issue treated in different ways by various authorities over the ages. The works of Sayyid Ḥaydar Āmulī, at once Sufi disciple of Ibn ʿArabī and great Shīʿite theologian, is particularly significant for an understanding of this relationship, especially his *Jāmiʿ al-asrār*. See H. Corbin, *En Islam iranien* (Paris: Gallimard, 1972) 3:149ff. ("Ḥaydar Āmolī, théologien shīʿite du soufisme"); see also S. H. Nasr, *Sufi Essays*, chap. 8.

21. See W. C. Chittick (trans.), *Supplications (Dūʿā) Amīr al-muʾminīn* (London: Muhammadi Trust, n.d.) 19ff.; and Imam Zayn al-ʿĀbidīn ʿAlī ibn al-Ḥusayn, *The Psalms of Islam*, trans. W. C. Chittick (London: Muhammadi Trust, 1988).

22. On the Shaykhīs, see H. Corbin, *En Islam iranien*, 4:205ff. (Livre VI "L'École shaykhie").

11

Sufism and Spiritual Life in Turkey

Annemarie Schimmel

One day in late 1982 I was addressing a letter to a Turkish friend whom I had known as a mystic of deep spiritual experiences despite his seemingly worldly official occupation. The address was known to me, but suddenly I remembered that another friend interested in Sufism had been living in that very area and I wondered whether she, whom I had not remembered for years might still be alive. The next day, the telephone rang, and a Turkish woman's voice said that the very lady I had been remembering the previous day had asked her to see me. She came, an elegant woman in her forties, and in the course of our conversation I discovered that she had been blessed with extraordinary visions and dreams. We became good friends, and whenever her way led her to Germany she used to come and discuss problems of Sufism and Islamic doctrine with me, and I could not but marvel at the way she described what had illuminated her mind. Although she had never studied any of the great handbooks of mysticism or any of the major Sufi works in Turkish, her dreams and visions were completely in tune with those seen by the masters of the path in olden times, and her descriptions of visions of Mawlānā Rūmī or Shams-i Tabrīzī were marvelous and scaring at the same time. And what about the appearance of the Prophet to her mother when she was reluctant to let her daughter marry a non-Muslim? The vision urged her to give the girl freedom. (That the husband embraced Islam later on owing to an inner urge is another story.) In short, to meet this Turkish friend and her family made me feel once more that the Turkish experience of Islam, and of mystical Islam in particular, is something very special, and our discussions led me back to the 1950s when the religious life in the country was again becoming more visible and the observer could see how right Muhammad Iqbal was when he wrote, in the late 1930s: "It is claimed that the Turks have repudiated Islam. A greater lie was never told."

Everyone was, and is, of course aware of the radical changes introduced by Ataturk's reforms—from the abolition of the caliphate in 1924 to the introduction of Western law codes, the dissolving of the dervish orders, and last but not least the introduction of the Roman alphabet instead of the Arabic one. However, even some leading figures in the mystical orders in Turkey expressed the opinion that the abolition of the orders might have a healthy effect in the spiritual life of those affiliated with them. Much mismanagement and many non-Islamic practices had tinged the external life of the fraternities, and the dervish *tekkes*, once source for spiritual education and purification, had often lost this lofty meaning. The Turkish author Samiha Ayverdi, who has expressed this view in her beautiful book *Istanbul Geceleri* (*Nights of Istanbul*) and is herself one of the leading mystics in our time, is here in full agreement with a German orientalist, Richard Hartmann, who was the first scholar of Arabic and Ottoman culture to visit Turkey after the introduction of the republic. He made similar observations after his visit to the shrine of Mawlānā (Mevlana) Rūmī in Konya.

The Turkish relationship with Islam is very old. The Turks were slowly led into Islam and embraced it wholeheartedly to become its ardent defenders during the centuries following their initial encounters with the new, dynamic religion. Suffice it to mention the role of Turkish dynasties, from the Ṭūlūnids to the Great Mughals, from the Seljūqs to the Ottomans, not to mention a number of others who, like the Quṭbshāhīs of Golconda in southern India, were of Turkish origin. One easily forgets the important role Turkish nobles played at the Mughal court not only as soldiers but also as patrons of art and literature, and the outsider rarely realizes the importance of the Turkish element in the structure of the Safavid empire in Iran. Is it not ironical that Shāh Ismāʿīl, the Safavid empire builder, wrote his mystical poetry in Turkish, while his grimmest enemy, Sultan Selīm Yavūz of Turkey, composed elegant Persian verse? (Not to mention the Turkish *Memoirs* of Bābur, the founder of the Mughal empire, and the touching Turkish *Dīwān* of Sulṭān Qanṣawh al-Ghūrī, the last Mamlūk ruler of Egypt before the Ottoman conquest!)

With the advent of the Seljūqs in eastern Anatolia after the decisive battle of Mantzikert in Dhu'l-ḥijjah 463/August 1071, eastern and central Anatolia became a new cultural center whose importance was enhanced when the art-loving Sulṭān ʿAlā' al-Dīn (Alaettin) Kayqubād ruled the area. When he built the Alaettin mosque in Konya in 618/1221, the eastern part of the Muslim world was already under the sway of the Mongol hordes, who had begun to pour forth from Inner Asia under Chingiz Khān and forced thousands of scholars and Sufis to seek shelter in the comparatively safe kingdom of the Seljūqs. Wise and learned men like Najm al-Dīn Dāyah

Rāzī, the author of the *Mirṣād al-ʿibād* (*The Path of God's Servants*), Burhān al-Dīn Muḥaqqiq of Tirmidh, and last but not least Bahā' al-Dīn Walad and his illustrious son Jalāl al-Dīn—later known as Rūmī—settled in and around Konya, where numerous *madrasahs* were found and where also a fruitful interaction between the Muslim rulers and the considerable number of their Christian subjects had taken place. The Turks are well aware of the fact that most of their great religious leaders came from Khurasan, and not only Mawlānā Rūmī but also Ḥājjī Biktāsh, who reached the country somewhat later, are counted among the "Khurāsānian" masters.

To be sure, the Turks had known the Sufi way already earlier in history. Aḥmad Yisiwī (d. 560/1165) in Central Asia is the first to be credited with a collection of *ḥikam* (wise words). He became the pivotal figure in the development of some of the Sufi orders, in particular the Naqshbandiyyah, which grew in the Central Asian areas until it became a strong political force in Afghanistan, India, and later also in the central Islamic lands. While the well-organized Sufi orders like the Qādiriyyah and Suhrawardiyyah had begun to attract followers as far away as India, they apparently did not enter Anatolia at this early stage, that is, in the seventh/thirteenth century. On the contrary, we read of bands of strange dervishes, such as the Ḥaydarīs and Jawālīqīs, who went around in appalling costumes and certainly belonged to the *bī-sharʿ* Sufis (those who consider themselves not at all bound by the religious law). Mawlānā Rūmī makes some scathing remarks about these people who misbehave and do not follow the *adab*, the etiquette, of the Sufis. Their influence was rather obnoxious at a time when even Anatolia was attacked by the Mongol forces and the Seljūq kingdom broke to pieces.

The inhabitants of Konya considered the presence of Mawlānā Rūmī a blessing, however, and attributed to his strong *barakah* the fact that Konya was spared major destructions in 654/1256. Mawlānā Rūmī, in fact, was not the only strong spiritual leader. Ṣadr al-Dīn Qūnawī, the stepson of Ibn ʿArabī, resided also in the capital, and although Mawlānā sometimes teased the learned theologian, they seem to have been good friends—even though Mawlānā's free-soaring spirit could not be captivated in the fine and intricate system of Ibn ʿArabī's thought as it was elaborated by Ṣadr al-Dīn Qūnawī. Ṣadr al-Dīn's influence, however, worked under the surface, and Ibn ʿArabī's theories constitute an important aspect in later Turkish mystical thought and poetry. Mawlānā Rūmī had sometimes reverted to Turkish works and phrases in his lyrical poetry, and he certainly had a good working knowledge of the language of the people (as he also was acquainted to a certain extent with the Greek of the other part of the population). His son, Sulṭān Walad, composed a whole *Dīwān* in Turkish, in which he translated his father's lofty thoughts into words that people could understand more easily. However, it is more or less a cerebral kind of poetry, and the true inspiration for Turkish Sufi poetry was still to come.

That was accomplished by Yūnus Emre, a wandering dervish who—to judge from his verse—served for a long time (he says "forty years," the traditional number for patience and purification) a mystic called Tapduk Emre, about whom nothing is known. Yūnus may have met Mawlānā in Yūnus's youth; Yūnus died in 721/1321, nine years after Sulṭān Walad, and several places in Anatolia claim to house his tomb.[1] Yūnus Emre uses the simple Turkish language of the people. Although some of his poems are written in *'arūḍ*, the quantitative Arabo-Persian meters, his best verses are those in which he uses syllable counting, as was customary among the Turks, and produces touching folksongs in four-lined stanzas. J. Walsh of Edinburgh has shown that many of Yūnus's verses were intended to be sung in dervish *tekkes*;[2] they repeat formulas like *al-ḥamdu li'Llāh* or the blessing upon the Prophet. They reflect all stages of the mystical path, always highlighting the importance of *dhikr*. As one of his finest poems says:

> The rivers all in Paradise
> They flow and say Allah Allah . . .

Everything in Paradise—breathing, growing, fragrant—is nothing but the constant *dhikr* of the Name of God, whose presence permeates everything. The mystery of the *dhikr* has rarely been expressed more beautifully than in these simple lines, which even today school children can enjoy.

Yūnus takes his imagery from nature, and although the complaining nightingale of high Persian poetry occurs frequently, his strongest poems are those in which he sings of the Anatolian landscape. The mountain becomes the enemy that separates him from his Beloved, and the cloud, hanging in clusters over the hills, weeps for his sake. In the hand of Love, he turns into dust on the road, into a torrent, into wind. Listening to the bees he hears them utter the blessing upon the Prophet. Yūnus is a master of concise imagery, and his verse expresses in simple words the main tenets of mystical Islam and dwells upon the secret of love. Not in vain did Adnan Saygun, whose *Yunus Oratoryusu* is based on texts from the *Dīwān,* use one line as the *basso ostinato* for his musical work: it is the line *askīn ver şevkīn ver,* "Give your love, give longing for you!" which beautifully sums up Yūnus's teachings. Some have tried, in more recent times, to see in Yūnus the true representative of a "Turkish" kind of piety, not bound by the words of the Quran and the tradition, or to depict him as a model of Turkish "humanism." Such attempts leave out the whole Islamic vocabulary

9. The mausoleum of Jalāl al-Dīn Rūmī in Konya, Turkey.

in his verse and cut him off from his spiritual moorings. He is, however, as much theocentric as any other mystic, and his love of humanity grows out of his love of and trust in God.

At the time Yūnus was singing his superbly beautiful hymns, the Mevlevi Order was being organized by Rūmī's son Sulṭān Walad. He formalized the mystical whirling by which the Mevlevi dervishes have been known ever since; the whirling was performed on Fridays after the common prayer.[3] However, it was not only the whirling that the aspiring dervish had to learn: in the 1,001 days of his apprenticeship he became acquainted with household services and had to study the *Mathnawī* carefully. Only then would he be able to perform the mystical dance in the true spirit, understanding it as the dance of the atoms around the central sun, as the dance of the stars, and as the symbol of man's death and resurrection in love. (This is symbolized by the casting off of the black coat and the reappearance of the dervishes in their white gown; the earthly body is cast off, and the "second body," the spiritual body of resurrection, appears when the dance takes place.)[4] Turkish culture owes much to the Mevlevis: they were the order that cultivated calligraphy and especially music, as well as poetry in the classical Persian Ottoman style.

Completely different was the contribution of the Biktāshī Order to Turkish life, an order that also developed during the time Yūnus Emre sang his love-intoxicated hymns. This order even took Yūnus's poetry as its central source of inspiration, and it was this kind of verse that was imitated for centuries among the official and nonofficial members of the Biktāshī Order. Ḥājjī Biktāsh, after whom the order is named, had come, as was mentioned above, from eastern Iran. He settled in central Anatolia, and the order that evolved around him is in many respects the opposite of the refined, urbane Mevlevi Order.[5] The Biktāshīs have, in the first place, a strong Shīʿite tendency; they even speak of a kind of trinity Allah–Muḥammad–ʿAlī. Numerous Shīʿite customs have been taken over by them, but there seems to exist also a certain not quite identifiable Christian substratum which scholars have detected (perhaps wrongly) in the communal meal with bread and wine. The most unusual aspect of the Biktāshīs is that women are allowed full access to all practices and participate in the meal and the sessions. The Biktāshīs were deeply influenced by the Ḥurūfī movement, and one finds many representations of human beings and animals, made up of meaningful letters, such as invocations of ʿAlī, in their *tekkes.* Their mystical theories, as expressed in certain poems, are mainly based on Ibn ʿArabī's ideas and speak of the descent and subsequent ascent of the human soul.

It is an amazing fact that the mystical leaders of this order (called *bābā*) attached themselves to the Janissaries, the elite troops of the Ottoman empire, so that every garrison had to have at least one Biktāshī *bābā* attached to it. This apparently worked well, although the Ottoman soldiers more often than not had to fight the Safavids, with whom they were closely united in their Shī'ite outlook. Furthermore, Shāh Ismā'īl the Safavid became one of the most revered poets among the Biktāshīs, and his glowing hymns, which he wrote under the pen-name Khaṭā'ī, are part and parcel of the ritual.

Besides this quite disturbing combination of different trends in the Biktāshī Order, one has to mention here too their contribution to Turkish literature. Their songs, beginning from Yūnus Emre, constitute a valuable part of Turkish literature, even though they have not been taken seriously by the masters of classical Ottoman *divan edebiyatī*, the highflown poetry that grew under Persian, and even Indo-Persian, influence during the high period of the Ottoman Empire. But for a modern reader some of the poems of early Biktāshīs are highly interesting, not only because they contain so many popular images and ideas but even more because they sometimes are permeated by a weird humor.

The best example of this style is Kayğusuz Abdal, a Biktāshī of the ninth/fifteenth century, who is credited with having founded the first *tekke* in Cairo on the Muqaṭṭam Hills. His verse is sometimes nothing but a parody of mystical love songs in which he describes his adventures with a honey-lipped elegant young man who tells him in not uncertain terms to be gone, or he sings of his insatiable hunger and enumerates the hundreds of plates with rice, meat, fowl, and fruit which he wants to eat. He also takes up a topic which Yūnus Emre had dealt with for the first time in the Turkish tradition—the outcry against God who has made such an apparently nonsensical arrangement for Doomsday. Why does He not build a decent bridge over which mankind can walk without falling into the fire, and why does He weigh the dirty sins of man? These ideas were later taken up by another Biktāshī poet, who goes so far as to ask the Lord why he needs hellfire. Is He perhaps a *külhanbeyi*, a destitute wretch who sleeps in the ashes of the bathhouse? Kayğusuz also depicts the struggle with the *nafs*, the disobedient lower soul, as a failing attempt to cook an old tough goose. In such poems, an aspect of Biktāshī life comes to light which is known even today: these are the Biktāshī jokes, of which almost everyone knows some specimens. The jokes often center on the Biktāshī's fondness for wine or *rakī*, the strong anisette brandy which is used during their ceremonies and is lovingly considered to be *āb-i ḥayāt*, the Water of Life.

Kayğusuz Abdal came from the Balkans, and this area has remained a stronghold of the Biktāshīs ever since the early Ottoman conquest. Even in our day Biktāshī convents are found in Bulgaria and Macedonia, and Albania was almost completely under Biktāshī influence. The order continued to flourish until the corps of the Janissaries was dissolved because of their increasing rebellions and misconduct in 1241/1826. After this time the order too fell in disgrace, but continued to function with a low profile. There were more than a dozen *tekkes* in Istanbul at the turn of the century, and one of them is the stage for the Turkish novel *Nūr Bābā*, written in 1922 by Yakup Kadri (Karaosmanoglu). This book can be considered one of the truly great works of modern Turkish literature. Although its topic—the seduction of a young, beautiful society woman by a sensual Biktāshī shaykh—could lead to unpleasant details, the transformation of the heroine into a great lover in the true tradition of Islamic mystical poetry is perfectly well described, and the novel gives also some interesting insights into Biktāshī ritual. It may be, however, that this novel was one of the numerous factors that contributed to Ataturk's decision to close down the dervish *tekkes.*

The Biktāshīs were an important ingredient in Ottoman life, despite their secrecy and their "immoral" practices, which were often criticized, especially the presence of women in their assemblies. But there were also many other mystical movements and orders that developed in Turkey during the Ottoman period and played an important role in the spiritual life of the people. The major fraternities, such as the Qādiriyyah, the Shādhiliyyah, the Khalwatiyyah, the Naqshbandiyyah, and so on had centers both in Istanbul and throughout the country, and their literary activity was remarkable. Their members sang of the love of God and of the love of the Prophet: one of the most beloved poems in the Turkish literature was written around 802/1400 in the then Ottoman capital of Bursa. It is Suleymān Chelebī's *Mevlūd-i sherīf* (*Birth of the Prophet*). There are many imitations of this poem, but none has reached the popularity of the original version, which retells in simple words the birth of the Prophet, describing the miracles his mother Āminah saw, and translates the great *Marḥabā*! "Welcome!" of all created things into unforgettable verses. This *mevlūd* is recited not only at the actual birthday of the Prophet but also at other festive occasions. One can celebrate it at the fortieth day or the anniversary of a bereavement either at home or in a mosque, and one can make vows to have a *mevlūd* recited in case this or that wish is fulfilled.

Sufi poetry in Turkish comprises all genres known in Persian and extends from the simple songs of many of the Biktāshī poets to highly technical poetry like that of Nasīmī, a Ḥurūfī poet, who had to pay with his life for his doctrines, which he claimed to be equal to those of Manṣūr al-Ḥallāj. He was cruelly killed in 808/1405 in Aleppo.[6] The loneliness of the austere

Anatolian highlands is reflected most beautifully in the melancholy songs of Pīr Sulṭān Abdāl in the tenth/sixteenth century. He too was executed, not for exuberant mystical claims but for conspiracy with the Safavids.

Turkish Sufism takes up the great tradition of epical poetry, retelling the story of Yūsuf and Zulaykhā or of Majnūn and Laylā and filling them with the mystical spirit which was given to them by Mawlānā Jāmī (d. 898/1492 in Herat), a model for many of the later Turkish poets. The mystical romance reached its apogee in a comparatively short *mathnawī* by a Mevlevi poet, Shaykh Ghālib, who died in 1214/1799 at the age of thirty-five. His *Ḥusn*ᵘ *'ishq* (*Beauty and Love*) is an intriguing piece of poetry that combines many different strands and shows a deep psychological insight into the mysteries of love and longing, of forgetfulness and enchantment. But mystical poetry was by no means restricted to the members of the Sufi orders. It permeated much of the lyrics written in Turkey, and even the rulers did not hesitate to compose once in a while a poem in which they—like Sultan Murād III—admonished themselves to awaken from the slumber of heedlessness.

The sultans participated also in another activity that was largely supervised by Sufis, that is, calligraphy. The first master of the typically Turkish style of *naskh* calligraphy, Shaykh Ḥamd Allāh of Amasia, was a member of a Sufi order, as were many of his relatives and followers. It is told that he was inspired to his reform of the *naskh* script by a dream of Khiḍr,[7] who initiated him to his inimitable style. It would be easy to give a long list of calligraphers who belonged to Sufi orders, as has been done by the twelfth/eighteenth-century writer Mustaqīmzāde, himself a staunch adherent of the Naqshbandiyyah. Such a list would show not only the social background of the calligraphers but also their predilections in writing certain texts. The Turks are proud enough to claim that "the Quran was revealed in Mecca, recited beautifully in Cairo, and written most beautifully in Istanbul." Indeed, some of the Ottoman Qurans and album pages with Prophetic traditions are so exquisite that one well understands this saying. But besides copying the Quran and the traditions as well as religious books, the Turks were also most imaginative in inventing artistic variations of the Arabic script, forms like the *ṭughrā,* the highly decorated heading of the imperial documents. Often the very word *ṭughrā* was also used for all kinds of script in round or mirrored form, in clever repetitions and in wonderful and unusual shapes. The human and animal forms of the *basmalah*[8] and similar calligrams belong to this category.

There was still another side to Sufism. Now and then we see Turkish Sufis rebel against what seemed to them an unjust government, and the case of

Qāḍī Badr al-Dīn of Simawna in the early ninth/fifteenth century has become a model for this attempt of Sufis to introduce—even by open rebellion—social justice. It was not always easy for the Ottoman sultans to find the right way to deal with such conflicts, as they themselves were after all the official guardians of orthodox Sunni Islam.

The love of the Turks for "their" Mevlana Rūmī and "their" Yūnus Emre has survived the centuries and many political changes. Rūmī's work has been translated and interpreted by many major writers and has been a source of consolation for thousands of people. The first celebration of the anniversary of his death on 17 December took place in 1954 and attracted thousands of pious Muslims. So it remained during the following years until it sometimes came too close to a tourist attraction. Those who perform the whirling on the stage are no longer trained in the old style and see only the outside, unaware of the numerous layers of meaning that can be discovered in every reading of Mawlānā's poetry. The reappearance of certain Sufi leaders on the political scene after 1951 has certainly not endeared this aspect of Sufism—hunger for power—to many observers who saw the traditional spiritual values of Turkish piety in danger. For the spirit of the great Sufis has no doubt been a very strong formative element in Turkish life, and when talking to the people in the villages and small towns I often felt that their unquestioning trust in God, which gave them the strength to survive ever so many trials and tribulations, had been shaped by the Sufis who taught them, like Ibrāhīm Hakkĭ Erzerumlu:

> *Görelim Hakk ne eyler—n'eylerse güzel eyler:*
> Let us see what God does—whatever He
>   does, He does beautifully!

Notes

1. When I lived in Ankara, the location was revealed to a pious Turkish friend in a dream, and subsequently, a celebration was held there.
2. See J. Walsh, "Yūnus Emre: A Medieval Hymnodist," *Numen* 2–3 (1960) 172–88.
3. See chapter 5 in this volume, by W. Chittick on Rūmī and the Mawlawiyyah Order.
4. On the dance of the Mevlevis, see I. Friedlander, *The Whirling Dervishes* (New York: Macmillan, 1975).
5. Concerning the Biktāshī Order, see the classical work of J. K. Birge, *The Bektashi Order of Dervishes* (London: Luzac, 1937).
6. On Turkish literature as related to Sufism, see chapter seventeen of this volume by G. Tekin.
7. As has already been mentioned, Khiḍr or al-Khaḍir is the ever-present prophet who, like Elijah, did not die and who appears to certain persons to guide them upon the spiritual path.
8. *Basmalah* refers to the fundamental Islamic formula *Bismi'Llāh al-Raḥmān al-Raḥīm*, "In the Name of God, Most Merciful and Compassionate."

A Note on the Khalwatiyyah-Jarrāḥiyyah Order

SHEMS FRIEDLANDER

ONE OF THE MOST IMPORTANT Sufi orders in Turkey today is the Khalwatiyyah-Jarrāḥiyyah, which has also spread to the West during the past few years. This order branched off from the Khalwatiyyah Order (Helvetiyye in Turkish), established by the Persian Sufi 'Umar Khalwatī, who died in Tabriz in 800/1397.[1] The second master of the order, Yaḥyā Shīrwānī, continued the work of spreading the order in Anatolia, where it became closely associated with the *Akhī* movement. After Shīrwānī's death in Baku in 869/1464, branches of the order such as the Gulshaniyyah and Damīrdāshiyyah spread in Egypt, where the order has been strong ever since. It experienced a remarkable growth in the thirteenth/nineteenth century, mostly as a result of the teachings of Kamāl al-Dīn al-Bakrī, the founder of the Bakriyyah branch of the Khalwatiyyah. Also in the twelfth/eighteenth century other branches of the Khalwatiyyah Order, such as the Kamāliyyah, spread in other regions of the Arab East, such as Palestine. The Sammāniyyah-Khalwatiyyah Order spread on the one hand into black Africa and on the other hand through Mecca into Southeast Asia. Syria was also one of the important arenas for the activity of the Khalwatiyyah, and such branches of the Order as the Jamāliyyah and Bakhshiyyah have been active in that land up to modern times.

The main arena of activity of the Khalwatiyyah Order remained Turkey, where in the eleventh/seventeenth century it became an important element even in the political life of the Ottoman world. The peak of its spiritual flowering in the Ottoman world was during the rule of Suleymān the Magnificent and Sultan Selīm I. Moreover, the order continued to flourish in Turkey and the provinces of the Ottoman Empire right up to this century. It was strong in Albania until the 1967 cultural revolution and is active in Yugoslavia to this day. It has also continued to survive in Egypt, Syria, Lebanon, and Palestine. In Turkey itself the Khalwatiyyah Order was abolished along with other Sufi orders in 1925 but has nevertheless continued its existence, especially the Khalwatiyyah-Jarrāḥiyyah branch, which is very active and continues to have its center in Istanbul.[2]

The Khalwatiyyah consider themselves heirs to the teachings of Junayd and usually have supported and followed the perspective of Ibn ʿArabī, especially as concerns the doctrine of *waḥdat al-wujūd*. Historically, they have also had a pro-Shīʿite tendency. The order has always emphasized fasting, vigil, ritual cleanliness, silence, and invocation (*dhikr*). It also insists on the spiritual retreat (*khalwah*) from three to forty days. There is an elaborate teaching in the order concerning the stages of *dhikr* of the "Seven Divine Names" (*al-asmāʾ al-sabʿah*), which correspond to the seven stages in the spiritual development of the human soul. The members of the order also participate regularly in the communal invocation and sacred dance (*al-ḥaḍrah*) and are instructed in reading and chanting Shīrwānī's *Wird al-sattār* (*The Covering Litany*) on specific occasions and times established by the masters of the order. Each branch, however, also has its own particular litanies, as can be seen in the case of the Khalwatiyyah-Jarrāḥiyyah.

The members of the Khalwatiyyah-Jarrāḥiyyah Order point to the fact that Imam Aḥmad ibn ʿUthmān Sharnūbī, the *khalīfah* and son-in-law of the *quṭb* Ibrāhīm Dasūqī, wrote in the *Ṭabaqāt al-awliyāʾ* (*Ranks of the Saints*) some three hundred years before the birth of Nūr al-Dīn Jarrāḥī:

> Sayyid Nūr al-Dīn Jarrāḥī will be from Istanbul and will appear in the year 1115 A.H. He will live forty-four years. One of his miracles will be that he will see his station in heaven while in this world, and will enter paradise directly upon his demise. The prayers of those who visit him and of those who pray in his presence will be accepted by God.

Pīr Nūr al-Dīn signed the book, which is currently in the Fātiḥ Library in Istanbul (#3286), near this passage.

The founder of the Khalwatiyyah–Jarrāḥiyyah Order, Pīr Nūr al-Dīn al-Jarrāḥī was born in 1089/1678. Through his father Sayyid ʿAbd Allāh ibn Muḥammad Ḥusām al-Dīn, he was a descendant of Imam al-Ḥusayn and through the line of his mother a descendant of ʿUbayd ibn Jarrāḥ, one of the ten companions whose inclusion in paradise, according to tradition, was announced in this world by the Prophet.

At the age of nineteen he finished his study of law with honors, and the sultan appointed him chief justice (*qāḍī*) of Egypt, which was then an Ottoman province. As he traveled through Istanbul on horseback, trailed by an entourage, in order to bid farewell to his family, he visited Ḥājjī Ḥusayn Efendī, his maternal uncle, across from whose house was the *dergāh* of the Jalwatiyyah branch of the Khalwatī Order of dervishes. It was on the Toygar hill in Uskudar, and the shaykh was al-Ḥājj ʿAlī ʿAlāʾ al-Dīn al-Khalwatī Kostendīlī. His uncle took him to meet the shaykh, who knew his name before the introduction. During the *dhikr* ceremony after prayers,

10. The spiritual concert (*samāʿ*) of the Khalwatiyyah-Jarrāḥiyyah in their center in Istanbul, Turkey.

Nūr al-Dīn experienced a state of ecstasy and was filled with a fervent desire to become a dervish of this shaykh. Shaykh ʻAlī ʻAlāʼ al-Dīn ordered him to put the world behind him. Nūr al-Dīn, therefore, resigned from his honored post, dispersed his followers, and gave all his possessions to members of his family. He then entered the spiritual retreat (*khalwah*), spending a period of forty days in seclusion and fasting. For seven years he studied with his shaykh, until at the age of twenty-six he himself was declared a shaykh.

During his lifetime Pīr Nūr al-Dīn Jarrāḥī had seven *khalīfahs* among his many dervishes. His *dergāh* was an Ottoman structure built for him by the sultan, and it still stands in the Karagumruk area of Istanbul. In the year 1115/1704, when he became shaykh and inaugurated the *dergāh,* he received the Divine Names, recitations, and prayers particular to his order, the *wird-i kabīr-i ṣabāḥiyyah* ("the great morning litany") and the *wird-i ṣaghīr-i masāʼiyyah* ("the great evening litany"), the *ādāb* (rules of behavior), and the rules of his particular branch of the Khalwatī Order, all through divine inspiration.

At one time Pīr Nūr al-Dīn Jarrāḥī had some forty thousand dervishes in many *dergāhs* throughout Turkey. Some of his *khalīfahs* remained in Istanbul, and others went to Bursa, Edirne, and even as far away as Morea (Peloponnesus) in Greece, which at that time was part of the Ottoman Empire. Some of these *khalīfahs* established branches that flourish to this day, while other branches have been established since then elsewhere. Ḥaḍrat Morāvī Shaykh Yaḥyā Efendī, Pīr Nūr al-Dīn Jarrāḥī's fourth *khalīfah,* was one hundred years old when he returned to Istanbul to sit on the post at Karagumruk, after having built forty *dergāhs* in the Morea peninsula. He was *murshid* there for twenty-four years and died during a *khalwah,* that time of spiritual seclusion which is characteristic of the order. The seclusion is not from the world but from the attraction of the world. Pīr Nūr al-Dīn encouraged his dervishes to be in the world, but not of the world.

Initially the *dergāh* at Karagumruk attracted the court of the sultan and administrators, just as the Mevlevi at that time attracted intellectuals and artists, the Biktashī drew the military, and the Naqshbandī the clergy. Today people from all walks of life gather there for *dhikr.* On any given night the minister of protocol or a university professor might be seated next to a shoemaker or a carpenter.

Unique to the Jarrāḥīs is their many-faceted *dhikr,* which originated as particular gifts given in recognition of Pīr Nūr al-Dīn's station. It is said traditionally that the blue post upon which the shaykh of the principal *dergāh* sits was a gift of Ḥaḍrat Hudā'ī of the Jalwatī branch of the Khalwatiyyah. The part of the shaykh's turban that hangs on the left side of the *tāj* was a gift from 'Abd al-Qādir Jīlānī. Aḥmad Rifā'ī sent the metal top of the flag and the *qiyām dhikr. Jalāl* (Power) came from Ibrāhīm Dasūqī and *Jamāl* (Beauty) came from Aḥmad Badawī, who also sent a particular *dhikr* movement known as the *bedevi topu.* From the Naqshbandīs came the recitation of the Quran during the *dhikr.* Shams al-Dīn Sīwāsī sent the first chant sung in the *dhikr* and Shaykh Wafā, the repetitions done during the final circumambulations. From Mawlānā Jalāl al-Dīn Rūmī came the Sulṭān Walad Walk and from Ḥaḍrat Sunbul Sinān the *ism,* or Name, *Yā Ḥayy,* which is repeated as part of the *dawrān* or circular movement in the *dhikr.* Within the Jarrāḥī *ṭarīqah* can be found essential elements of many different Sufi orders.

The Jarrāḥī *dhikr* is *jahrī* (said aloud) and rhythmic, using musical compositions derived from various *ṭarīqahs.* The *Jarrāḥīs* are known as "Howling Dervishes," for the *ism, Hū,* is stretched, coupled with a breathing exercise which creates a controlled sound of the *ism.* This sound is often likened to the heavy rhythm of a saw as the shaykh indicates that the *dhikr* should become *qalbī,* issuing from the heart. Group singers called *dhākirs* stand outside the circle of dervishes along with musicians playing *bendir* and *kudum* (kinds of drums) and cymbals used for rhythm. In the *dhikr* ceremony the dervishes sit in a circle reciting the formula of *tawḥīd* (*lā ilāha illa'Llāh*), which is followed by the Supreme Name, *Allāh,* and then the *ism Hū.* Between each cycle there is a Quranic recitation and a *du'ā.* The dervishes then stand and chant the *uṣūl,* the initial *ilāhī* given by Shams al-Dīn Sīwāsī. They continue with the repetition of *Hū,* which develops into the Divine Name *Ḥayy.* They conclude by repeating *Ḥayy ul-Qayyūm Allāh,* brought to them initially by Shaykh Wafā, and finally *Ḥayy, Ḥayy, Ḥayy, Hū.*

Each dervish is given certain Names or *asmā'*, according to his station. The number increases to twenty-eight *asmā'*, which is a secret of the *ṭarīqah.*

Since Pīr Nūr al-Dīn Jarrāḥī, twenty shaykhs have sat on the blue post (dyed sheepskin) at the principal *dergāh* in Karagumruk and followed Islamic principles in order to bind themselves to Allah. Nineteen of these shaykhs, along with Pīr Nūr al-Dīn and his family are buried in the *dergāh.* The nineteenth, al-Ḥajj Shaykh Muzaffereddin al-Jerrahi al-Khalwati, came to America and initiated a branch of the order in the West. Shaykh Muzaffer's principal goal was to have as many people as possible repeat the phrase of Unity: "There is no god but God, and Muḥammad is His messenger." He died in Istanbul on 12 February 1985, with his head bowed in prayer and his lips and heart repeating the phrase of Unity. Today, Shaykh Sefer Efendi, the twentieth shaykh of the Jarrāḥī Order's principal *dergāh,* leads Muslims in prayer at the original Jarrāḥī *dergāh* in Istanbul, and the order continues to be active in America.

Notes

1. On the Khalwatiyyah, see E. Bannerth, "La Khalwatiyya en Egypte," *Mélanges Institut Dominicain d'Etudes Orientales du Caire,* vol. 8, 1964-66, 11ff. Also F. de Jong, "Khalwatiyya" in the new *Encyclopedia of Islam,* 4:991–93.

2. There is an extensive literature of this order now available in English, thanks to Shaykh Muzaffer Efendi, who brought its teachings to America in the 1970s. See Shaykh Muzaffer, *Irshād* (Warwick, NY: Amity House, 1988); see also Shems Friedlander, *"When You Hear Hoofbeats Think of a Zebra"* (New York: Harper & Row, 1987); and Shaykh Muzaffer, *The Unveiling of Love* (New York: Inner Traditions International, 1981).

12

Sufism in the Indian Subcontinent

Orders and Spiritual Poetry in Regional Languages

SAYYID ATHAR ABBAS RIZVI

ISLAMIC SPIRITUAL TRADITIONS in the Indian subcontinent developed features uniquely their own, but as was the case in other parts of the Islamic world, they remained deeply rooted in the Quran, *Ḥadīth,* and the teachings of the righteous caliphs and those of ʿAlī ibn Abī Ṭālib's descendants. The spiritual guide of the great Persian Sufi Bāyazīd Basṭāmī was Abū ʿAlī Sindī.[1] In ca. 292/904, on his second pilgrimage to Mecca, Manṣūr al-Ḥallāj with his four hundred disciples traveled through Gujarat, the Lower Indus Valley and the northern Indian borders to Khurasan and Turkestan.[2] From time to time other Sufis also moved to different parts of Sind and the Punjab, but the contributions of only those Sufis who settled in India after the conquest of the Punjab and Sind by Sultan Maḥmūd of Ghaznah (388/998–421/1030) are documented.

The Kāzirūniyyah Ṭarīqah

By the fourth/tenth century, the Sufis had formed several orders and fraternities. One of them was founded by Shaykh Abū Isḥāq Ibrāhīm ibn Shahriyār (d. 426/1035), who died at Kazirun, situated between Shiraz and the Persian Gulf coast. He ordered his nephew Shaykh Ṣafī al-Dīn to mount a camel and travel in whatever direction the animal took him; he was then to remain where finally the camel halted. The camel stopped at Uchh (Upper Sind in Pakistan), where Ṣafī al-Dīn founded his *khānqāh.* The shaykh died in Uchh, but the influence of his uncle penetrated very deeply into the life of seamen and mariners who undertook hazardous voyages from the Persian Gulf to China through the Indian Ocean and the Indonesian archipelago. Ibn Baṭṭūṭah, who traveled along the Indian coasts on his way to China between 743/1342 and 747/1346, stayed in the Kāzirūnī *khānqāhs* in Calicut and Quilon on the Malabar coast and at Zaitun in China.[3] A modern scholar compares the chain of Kāzirūnī *khānqāhs* with an insurance corporation,[4] but none can doubt the devotion of seamen who returned to their homes safely because of what they believed to be the efficacy of Shaykh Abū Isḥāq's prayers.

The Junaydiyyah Fraternity

Before long, Lahore also became an important Sufi center. Abu'l-Faḍl Muḥammad ibn al Ḥasan Khuttalī, a disciple of Ḥuṣrī (d. 371/981–82) of the school of Junayd of Baghdad, is the first known Sufi to have ordered a disciple, Shaykh Zanjānī, to move to Lahore. Later Khuttalī asked his young disciple, Abu'l-Ḥasan 'Alī Hujwīrī to follow Ḥusayn Zanjānī. It would seem that he arrived at Lahore in 426/1035, the same day Zanjānī died.

Born at Ghaznah in about 399/1009, Hujwīrī had studied under many teachers, but Khuttalī of Syria was his main spiritual guide. From Lahore, he made long tours of the Islamic world at least twice during his lifetime. According to A. Nicholson, he died sometime between 465/1072–73 and 469/1076–77 at Lahore.[5] Later Muslims posthumously conferred on him the title, Dātā Ganj Bakhsh (distributor of unlimited treasures). Among the early mystics who undertook hard ascetic exercises at his tomb was Khwājah Mu'īn al-Dīn Chishtī, the founder of the Chishtī Order in the Indian subcontinent.

Hujwīrī wrote books on Sufism in both prose and poetry. His *Kashf al-maḥjūb* (*Rending of the Veiled*) is the first known manual of Sufism written in Persian. Composed toward the end of his life, the work draws on the vast source material available in Arabic and is a most authoritative exposition of the sober Sufism of Junayd's school. It indicates that Lahore had become an important center of Sufism, some Sufis being profoundly aware of Hindu spiritual traditions. One of them who was an expert in Quranic exegesis held that *baqā'* (abiding in Allah) meant God's subsistence in man. Some Lahore Sufis identified gnosis with divine revelation. Some Sufis believed in the superiority of saints over prophets. It was an uphill task for Hujwīrī to convince them of the true meanings of Sufism. He considered himself a "captive among uncongenial folk"[6] in Lahore.

It would appear that from its very inception, Sufism in India developed conflicting trends, mainly because of the challenges from movements among local mystics. The analysis of Sufism, its history, and its principles discussed perceptively in the *Kashf al-maḥjūb* went a long way toward stabilizing Sufi thoughts, not only in India but even in Persia and Central Asia.

The Suhrawardiyyah

The only other work able to match the *Kashf al-maḥjūb* in popularity and utility in India was the *'Awārif al-ma'ārif* by Shaykh Shihāb al-Dīn Abū Ḥafs 'Umar (539/1145–632/1234), the founder of the Suhrawardī Order. He obtained training under his uncle Shaykh Ḍiyā' al-Dīn Abu'l-Najīb Suhrawardī (490/1097–563/1168), who built a hospice on a ruined site on the Tigris in Baghdad. The caliph al-Nāṣir li-Dīni'Llāh (575/1180–622/1225) appointed Shaykh Shihāb al-Dīn as his ambassador to different courts of important rulers and built an extensive *khānqāh* for him in Baghdad, which included luxurious bathhouses and gardens. He traveled extensively and made several pilgrimages to Mecca, accompanied by his eminent disciples. Sufis from all over the world flocked to his *khānqāh* to obtain initiation from him. One of them was Shaykh Bahā' al-Dīn Zakariyyā', who was born at Kot Karor near Multan (now in Pakistan) in about 578/1182–83. After studying at different centers of Islamic learning, he arrived in Baghdad. His training period under Shaykh Shihāb al-Dīn lasted for only seventeen days, to the utter disgust of the senior disciples, but the Shaykh silenced them by saying that when they had first come to him they had been like green wood which would not catch fire, whereas Bahā' al-Dīn had been like dry wood, which had begun to burn with a single breath.

In Multan, the eminent Sufis and *'ulamā'* stubbornly opposed Shaykh Bahā' al-Dīn, but his scholarly attainments and a distinctive position among the disciples of Shaykh Shihāb al-Dīn Suhrawardī soon made him a principal figure in Multan. It appears that merchants from Iraq and Khurasan were attracted to him in large numbers. The Shaykh built an extensive *khānqāh* on the pattern of his spiritual guide's *khānqāh* in Baghdad. He fearlessly opposed Qubāchah, the ruler of Multan, and espoused the cause of Sultan Shams al-Dīn Iltutmish (607/1211–633/1236) of Delhi, who seized Multan in 625/1228. The repeated Mongol invasions of Multan made the life of the townsfolk miserable, but the fame of Shaykh Bahā' al-Dīn's piety in Khurasan and Transoxiana facilitated successful negotiations with the Mongol invaders.[7]

Shaykh Bahā' al-Dīn strongly discouraged Sufis from seeking guidance from a number of different *pīrs* (spiritual guides), urging them to lay their heads on one rather than a number of thresholds. He placed great stress on performing obligatory prayers and assigned a secondary place to supererogatory prayers and *dhikr*. He ate normally and did not indulge in incessant fasting. In Ṣafar 661/December 1262 he died at Multan, and his tomb became a center of pilgrimage in the region. He was succeeded by his own son, Shaykh Ṣadr al-Dīn ʿĀrif (d. 684/1286). Shaykh Bahāʾ al-Dīn Zakariyyā's disciple and son-in-law, the poet and mystic Shaykh Fakhr al-Dīn Ibrāhīm, popularly known as ʿIrāqī (d. 688/1289), spread his fame from Syria to Turkey. Irāqī's *Lamaʿāt* (*Divine Flashes*), based on lectures by Shaykh Ṣadr al-Dīn Qūnawī (d. 673/1274) on his master Ibn ʿArābī's *Fuṣūṣ al-ḥikam* (*Bezels of Wisdom*), made a deep impact on the spiritual discipline of the Indian Suhrawardiyyah.

Shaykh Ṣadr al-Dīn ʿĀrif was fortunate to have the poet Amīr Ḥusayn Ḥusaynī (b. 671/1272–73) as his disciple. Ḥusaynī's works, such as *Zād al-musāfirīn* (*Provision of Travelers*), *Nuzhat al-arwāḥ* (*Pleasure of Spirits*), and *Kanz al-rumūz* (*Treasury of Mysteries*) are devoid of ʿIrāqī's spiritual sensitivity, but their deep ethical teachings are of far-reaching importance.[8]

Shaykh Ṣadr al-Dīn's son and successor, Shaykh Rukn al-Dīn Abu'l-Fatḥ, revived the political and spiritual glory of his grandfather. From the reign of Sultan Alāʾ al-Dīn Khaljī (695/1296–715/1316) to his own death in 735/1334–35 in the reign of Sultan Muḥammad ibn Tughluq (725/1325–752/1351), Shaykh Rukn al-Dīn was deeply revered by all the reigning monarchs of the Delhi sultanate. Whenever he visited Delhi, he never forgot to call on the great Chishtī Shaykh Niẓām al-Dīn Awliyāʾ, but he did not care for the latter's strained relations with the sultans. Petitioners filled Shaykh Rukn al-Dīn's palanquin with petitions on his way to the sultan's court. The latter read them carefully and granted the petitioners' requests, thanks to Shaykh Rukn al-Dīn's influence. The shaykh's fame reached as far as Alexandria and Ibn Baṭṭūṭah was recommended to see him. The works of the shaykh do not survive, but some of his authentic conversations with Sufis tend to indicate that he regarded possession of wealth, scholarship, and mystical enlightenment as indispensable for the Sufis. The Chishtīs, however, never agreed with the Suhrawardīs on the question of the accumulation of wealth.[9] Some of the Suhrawardī saints were, however, great ascetics. One of them was Shaykh ʿUthmān Sayyāḥ (d. 738/1337–38) (the traveler) of Sunnam in eastern Punjab. He was a disciple of Shaykh Rukn al-Dīn. With his *pīr*'s permission, he departed on a pilgrimage to Mecca without carrying even so much as a waterpot. After his return from Mecca, his *pīr* allowed him to live in Delhi, where he spiritedly defended the Chishtī practice of *samāʿ* (spiritual music).

Reverting back to Shaykh Shihāb al-Dīn's disciples, who strengthened the

Suhrawardī spiritual movement in India, we may mention Qāḍī Ḥamīd al-Dīn of Nagawr in Rajasthan, not to be confused with the Chishtiyyah Shaykh Ḥamīd al-Dīn Ṣūfī (see chapter 6 in this volume). His family had migrated from Bukhara to Delhi before its conquest by the Turks. He completed his education in Delhi and was appointed the *qāḍī* of Nagawr. After three years of service, he was disgusted with it and left for Baghdad, where he became Shaykh Shihāb al-Dīn's disciple. He visited Mecca and Medina, traveled to many parts of western Asia and then arrived in Delhi around 618/1221. He was a firm friend of the Chishtī Khwājah Quṭb al-Dīn Bakhtiyār Kākī and enthusiastically participated in *samā*ʿ sessions in Delhi. His wit, in conjunction with his deep knowledge of Islamic Law, frustrated the *ʿulamā*'s efforts to defeat him on legal issues. His thirst for unqualified and nondelimited love in his three surviving works, the *ʿIshqiyyah* (*Pertaining to Love*), the *Ṭawāliʿ al-shumūs* (*Risings of the Suns*) and the *Risālah min kalām* (*Treatise of Kalām*), is very profound. In the *ʿIshqiyyah* he says that although Lover and Beloved appear to be different, they are in fact identical. Whoever sees them as two is confused and whoever does not see them at all is insane. One who is lost in Being is a part of God's Attributes. This stage makes Sufis present everywhere. The extinction of "I" leads to the predominance of "He." Both Lover and Beloved mirror each other. Love is the source of everything that exists. Fire is the burning quality of love, air is its aspect of restlessness, water is its movement, and earth is its immutable aspect.[10] In the *Tawāliʿ al-shumūs,* the Qāḍī spells out the mystery of the Names of Allah. He says that the greatest Name of God is *Huwa* (He) and it indicates His eternal nature, hallowed and free from decline and fall. The Qāḍī died in 643/1245–46.

The disciple of Shaykh Shihāb al-Dīn Suhrawardī who made Islam popular in Bengal was Shaykh Jalāl al-Dīn Tabrīzī. He excelled all the shaykh's disciples in serving his *pīr.* Migrating to Bengal, he built a *khānqāh* at Deva Maḥal near Pandua in northern Bengal and converted a large number of Hindus and Buddhists to Islam. In the *Riḥlah* (*Travels*) of Ibn Baṭṭūṭah, Shaykh Jalāl of Sylhet whom he visited has been confused with Shaykh Jalāl Tabrīzī and the mistake has been repeated by several scholars.

The early Suhrawardīs and the Chishtīs had divided different regions of the Indian subcontinent into spheres of their respective spiritual influence and refrained from interfering with those of others. Despite their humility and self-abasement, the Chishtīs encouraged their disciples to exhibit the utmost veneration to their *pīrs* and even permitted the performance of *sajdah* (prostration) before them, but Shaykh Bahā' al-Dīn Zakariyyā' expected his disciples to greet him with the customary *al-salām*^{u} *ʿalaykum* (peace be upon you). He also urged his disciples to finish their obligatory religious duties first and to greet him afterward. The Suhrawardī view of the function of the state, envisaged by Shaykh Shihāb al-Dīn's disciple, Shaykh Nūr al-Dīn Mubārak Ghaznawī, who settled in Delhi and died there in 632/1234–35, encompassed the prosperity of the Sunni upper classes alone; Shī'īs and Hindus were permitted to survive, provided they did so in a deprived economic state. The Suhrawardīs, as depicted in the legends surrounding Shaykh Jalāl al-Dīn Tabrīzī's activities in Bengal, and those of Makhdūm Jahāniyān, as we shall see, were unhesitating in their proselytizing zeal. By contrast, the Chishtīs believed that only the company of pious and ascetic Muslims prompted others to accept Islam. To them, their main mission was to work for the integration of those Hindus who embraced Islam in an attempt to make them genuinely pious Muslims and save them from emulating the example of the haughty governing classes.

Makhdūm Jahāniyān Sayyid Jalāl al-Dīn Bukhārī was a grandson of Shaykh Bahā' al-Dīn Zakariyyā's disciple, Sayyid Jalāl al-Dīn Surkh. Sultan Muḥammad ibn Tughluq, who initiated the policy of controlling the appointment of the heads of Sufi *khānqāhs,* had made him the head of the *khānqāh* of Sehwan. Before long, however, Makhdūm Jahāniyān embarked on a pilgrimage and later traveled to many parts of the Islamic world, earning the title *Jahāngasht* (world traveler) for himself. During the reign of Sultan Fīrūz Tughluq (752/1351–790/1388), he settled down in Uchh and occasionally visited Delhi. A notorious puritan, Makhdūm Jahāniyān strongly deplored the Indian Muslim religious customs and ceremonies which had been borrowed from Hindus and were an Indian accretion.[11] He urged that dervishes, Sufis, and *'ulamā'* visit rulers and government officials in order to elicit assistance for the downtrodden sections of Muslims. He introduced among his disciples the spirit of the *akhī* and *futuwwah* (spiritual chivalry) organizations of Anatolia, Khurasan, and Transoxiana. After his death in 785/1384, he was succeeded by his brother, Ṣadr al-Dīn, who achieved fame under his nicknames Rājū and Qattāl (slayer) for his militant evangelism. A grandson of Makhdūm Jahāniyān moved to Gujarat and before long came to be known as Quṭb-i 'Ālam (The Pole of the Universe). He settled in Ahmadabad, the newly founded capital of an independent provincial ruling dynasty of Gujarat. He died in 857/1453 and was succeeded by his son, who came to be known by the illustrious title Shāh-i 'Ālam (The Emperor of the World), and was also called Shah Manjhan. Quṭb-i 'Ālam, Shāh-i 'Ālam (d. 880/1475) and their disciples made Gujarat a leading Suhrawardī Sufi center of India. The influence of Shaykh Samā' al-Dīn and the fame of his disciple Shaykh Jamālī transformed Delhi into an important Suhrawardī center. Jamālī (d. 942/1536) was passionately fond of traveling and, starting with a pilgrimage to Mecca, he traveled through western Asia and the Maghreb. At Herat he called on the great Persian poet Jāmī and held lively discussions, particularly on 'Irāqī's *Lama'āt.*[12] Jamālī was the author of several Persian *mathnawīs* in which he lyrically delineated the theme of spiritual transmutation through love. The biographical notes on the Chishtīs and Suhrawardīs which he wrote in his *Siyar al-'ārifīn* (*Biography of the Gnostics*) comprise a wealth of information which he collected during his travels to Persia and Iraq. In the eighth/fourteenth century a Suhrawardī center was established in Kashmir, strengthening orthodox Sunnism there.

The Firdawsī Branch of the Kubrawiyyah

Shaykh Najm al-Dīn Kubrā (540/1145–618/1221), the founder of the Kubrawī Order, was the disciple of Shaykh Ismā'īl Qaṣrī (d. 589/1193) of Khuzistan and Shaykh 'Ammār ibn Yāsir al-Bidlīsī (d. 597/1200), who in their turn were disciples of Shaykh Abu'l-Najīb Suhrawardī (see chapter 5 of this volume). A galaxy of eminent Sufis flocked to Kubrā as disciples and a number of branches of his order spread to Baghdad, Khurasan, and India. One of Kubrā's eminent disciples, Shaykh Sayf al-Dīn Bākharzī (d. 658/1260) ordered his disciple, Khwājah Badr al-Dīn Samarqandī Firdawsī to settle in Delhi. After his death in Delhi, he was succeeded by Khwājah Najīb al-Dīn Firdawsī and Khwājah Rukn al-Dīn. The Firdawsīs would have remained unknown, had Khwājah Najīb al-Dīn not been so fortunate as to find a disciple of the fame of Shaykh Sharaf al-Dīn Aḥmad ibn Yaḥyā Munyarī (also known as Maneri)[13] Aḥmad was born in Munyar, near Patna in Bihar, where he obtained his early education. He then moved to Sunargaon, near modern Dacca in Bengal, with Shaykh Abū Tawwāmah of Bukhara, and studied under the latter until his own father's death in 690/1291. From there he visited Delhi and Panipat and finally became Khwājah Najīb al-Dīn's *khalīfah* and returned to Bihar. Instead of going to his village, the shaykh chose to do ascetic exercises in the lonely Rajgir hills of Bihar, where Buddhist monks and Hindu sages loved to establish their hermitages. He would go to Bihar Sharif near Patna each Friday for congregational prayers, returning to the Rajgir forest afterward. Later, in 782/1381, he was forced to settle down in Bihar Sharif, where he lived throughout the greater part of the reign of Muḥammad ibn Tughluq.[14]

His teachings are embodied in several collections of his letters to his disciples, both '*ulamā*' and Sufis. He also wrote to the state dignitaries and even to Fīrūz Tughluq. One of the collections comprising one hundred letters was compiled in 747/1346–47, and the other, containing 151 letters, was compiled in 769/1367–68.[15] His *Malfūẓāt* (*Discourses*) were also compiled and give an authentic picture of his spiritual contributions to his contemporaries and to posterity. Through Quranic verses, *aḥādīth,* anecdotes and parables from classical Sufi works, he discussed the religious and spiritual duties of Islam and the social and ethical responsibilities of Muslims in a vocabulary enriched by his own contemplative vision of the realities of things. Frequently quoting the Quranic verse "Despair not of the mercy of Allah" (XXXIX, 53), he used to affirm that the divine fire consumed the root of despondency and the young shoots of desperation. Mystical knowledge was the seed of love. All those who penetrated deeply into the realm of mystical knowledge were engulfed by the fire of love and obtained increasingly great delight and distinction from the face of the Beloved and from the sight of the Desired One. Although the shaykh strongly advocated adherence to the *Sharī'ah,* he failed to concede the superiority of the *'ulamā'* over Sufis. He avoided, however, expressing his ecstatic feelings and spiritual experiences and advised his disciples to keep their own knowledge of such experiences secret.[16] He was appalled at the execution by Sultan Fīrūz of his friends and the enraptured Sufis (*majdhūbs*) Shaykh 'Izz Kākū'ī and Shaykh Aḥmad Bihārī. But for the timely intervention of Makhdūm Jahāniyān, he would also have met the same fate.[17]

The number of the shaykh's disciples was quite large; among them Shaykh Muẓaffar Balkhī was most prominent. A network of small *khānqāhs* stretching from Bihar to Bengal and reaching many areas of the Indian subcontinent disseminated the shaykh's spiritual teachings as embodied in his letters.

The Kubrawiyyah of Kashmir

The Kubrawiyyah Order was introduced into Kashmir by Mīr Sayyid 'Alī Hamadānī, who was initiated into it by Shaykh Sharaf al-Dīn Maḥmūd Niẓām al-Dīn Mazdaqānī, a disciple of the great Shaykh 'Alā' al-Dawlah Simnānī. At his *pīr*'s bidding, Mīr Sayyid 'Alī studied under a number of important disciples of Shaykh 'Alā' al-Dawlah, but he was not converted to the view of *waḥdat al-shuhūd* (unity of consciousness), although before the death of the aged shaykh, he went to Simnan and completed his final training with him. He was imbued, however, with the shaykh's missionary fervor and sense of social responsibilities. The Mīr left Simnan with Muḥammad Ashraf Jahāngīr Simnānī (d. *ca.* 840/1436–37), a Kubrawī who, after settling down in Kichawcha in the Sharqi sultanate of Jaunpur in India, founded the Ashrafī branch of the Kubrawī Order. One traveled slightly ahead of the other, shortly before Shaykh 'Alā al-Dawlah's death.

Traveling through Uchh, Mīr Sayyid ʿAlī arrived at Srinagar in 783/1381. He was accompanied by a considerable number of sayyids. Their missionary zeal took the form of temple demolition and the enforced conversion of many Hindus. After a stay in Kashmir of about three years, Sayyid ʿAlī left Srinagar and died *en route* in 786/1385 after having passed through Pakhli near Kunar. His body was taken to Khuttalan, now part of the Soviet Union, where it was buried.[18]

Mīr Sayyid ʿAlī has been credited with the authorship of 170 treatises, generally short in length, of which about fifty have survived. He translated the *Fuṣūṣ al-ḥikam* (*Bezels of Wisdom*) into Persian and wrote a religio-political treatise entitled the *Dhakhīrat al-mulūk* (*Provision of Kings*). The clarity of expression and the force of his arguments in the short treatises dealing with Muslim ethics and spirituality are remarkable. His interpretation of the "oneness of being" is accompanied by a mystical portrayal of the "reality of the perfect man." He identifies the latter with the "Muḥammadan Reality," which acts as a receptable for all of Being's perfections. His treatises entitled the *Akhī* (*Brother*) and the *Futuwwah* (*Spiritual Chivalry*) are designed to arouse devotion in ʿAlī ibn Abī Ṭālib's *futuwwah,* which in turn was based on forgiveness in place of revenge, patience in the time of anger, wishing an enemy well, and preference for the needs of others over one's own. The Mīr believed that spiritual beings whose earthly existence had been completely effaced, who swam in the ocean of *aḥadiyyah* (oneness, unicity) and flew into the realm of *huwiyyah* (Divine Ipseity) belonged to a supernatural category, but those who remained steadfastly dedicated to ordinary people and looked after the comfort of mankind were true members of *futuwwah.*

When Sayyid ʿAlī left Kashmir, only a handful of Persian sayyids were allowed by him to accompany him back to Persia. After 796/1393, the migration of Mīr Sayyid ʿAlī's son, Mīr Sayyid Muḥammad, provided them with much-needed leadership. Sultan Sikandar (788/1386–813/1410), nicknamed *But Shikan* (destroyer of idols), became his disciple, and the sultan's Brahmin vizier, Suhā Bhatta, embraced Islam after instruction by Mīr Muḥammad. Many ancient temples were destroyed and puritanical and discriminatory state laws were introduced for the first time in Kashmir. Mīr Sayyid Hiṣārī, a disciple of Mīr Sayyid ʿAlī who had earlier moved to Kashmir and had lost his influence with the court, was deeply upset with the aggressive evangelism of his *pīr*'s son. Before long he was able to reassert himself at the court and Mīr Sayyid Muḥammad left Kashmir after a stay of some twelve years. By that time, the Kubrawī Order was firmly established there.[19] Their role in converting the Kashmīrī Brahmins to Islam is overestimated, but the devotion to ʿAlī ibn Abī Ṭālib and his descendants inculcated in the Muslims of Kashmir by the Hamadānī Kubrawīs made Kashmīrī spiritual traditions unique in the subcontinent.

Among Mīr Sayyid ʿAlī's disciples was Khwājah Isḥāq al-Khuttalānī, who was executed by the Tīmūrid Sultan Shāhrukh (807/1405–850/1447) in 826/1423 for leading an unsuccessful revolt against the sultan. His impact on the spiritual life of Khuttalan and the Balkh region was most profound. His disciple Sayyid Muḥammad Aḥsā'ī, on whom he bestowed the title *Nūrbakhsh* (Bestower of Light) and whom he considered to be the Mahdī[20] of the Sunni tradition, was hounded from place to place by Shāhrukh. This harassment and persecution helped to make the sayyid famous throughout Persia, Central Asia, and Kashmir. In 869/1464–65 he died at Rayy near Tehran, but his son, Shāh Qāsim Fayḍbakhsh, who lived in the reigns of Sulṭān Ḥusayn Bāyqarā (873/1469–911/1506) of Herat and Shah Ismāʿīl Ṣafawī (907/1501–930/1524) of Persia, transformed the Kubrawī teachings on the devotion to ʿAlī ibn Abī Ṭālib into Ithnā ʿAsharī Shīʿism. His disciple, Mīr Shams al-Dīn ʿIrāqī, introduced Shīʿism into Kashmir. Although Shīʿism was strongly opposed by the Suhrawardī leader Shaykh Ḥamzah Makhdūm (d. 984/1576) and later by the Naqshbandiyyah, the spiritual framework of the Kubrawiyyah in Kashmīr remained deeply rooted in the *awrād* (litanies) of Mīr Sayyid ʿAlī Hamadānī. These were deeply impregnated with the spirit of the invocations to Allah ascribed to ʿAlī ibn Abī Ṭālib's disciple Kumayl ibn Ziyād. The latter's impact on the Kubrawiyyah was indelible.

The Shaṭṭāriyyah

The Shaṭṭāriyyah drew inspiration from works of mystic exegesis on divination ascribed to Imām Jaʿfar al-Ṣādiq (d. 148/765), the sixth Imam of the Shīʿites. Another influence on the order came from mystical stories about the life of Abū Yazīd Basṭāmī. In Ottoman Turkey the order was known as the Basṭāmiyyah and in Persia and Turkey it was known as ʿIshqiyyah. The Indian branch of the order founded by Shah ʿAbd Allāh preferred to call itself the Shaṭṭāriyyah. Shah ʿAbd Allāh moved from Bukhara—where he perfected his mystical training—to India in the early ninth/fifteenth century. The incredible speed with which Sufis trained in this order were able to solve the paradox of Unity in multiplicity prompted Shah ʿAbd Allāh to call the order that of the Shaṭṭārs (those who moved fast). During his travels the shah marched in royal fashion with his disciples dressed in black uniform, holding banners and beating kettledrums. He proclaimed

11. Thẹ meeting of Miyān Mīr and Dārā Shukūh.

that he was engaged in a quest to discover more of the secrets of *waḥdat al-wujūd* from anyone who was more perfect than he. At the same time, others in their turn could learn from his perception. He traveled in northern India as far as Bengal, where the leading Sufi, Shaykh Muḥammad 'Alā', known as Shaykh Qādin, ignored his challenge. Sorely disappointed, the shah retreated to Malwa in central India and settled down in its capital, Mandu, in 846/1442–43; he died there in 890/1485. The local sultans were deeply devoted to the shah, and seekers after spirituality from all over India sat at his feet. Shaykh Qādin also arrived from Bengal and apologized for his earlier rude behavior and enrolled himself among his disciples. The *Laṭā'if-i ghaybiyyah* (*Subtleties of the Invisible World*), of which the shah was the author, outlines the basic framework of Shaṭṭāriyyah teachings and practices. In it, Shah 'Abd Allāh divides Muslim spiritual devotees into three categories: *akhyār* (the chosen ones), *abrār* (the dutiful ones) and *shaṭṭār* (the swift-paced ones). Of these, the Shaṭṭāriyyah were superior to all, for they obtained direct training from the spirits of great saints of the past and thus were able to traverse the path of Sufi ascension rapidly.[21]

Shaykh Qādin's influence made the Shaṭṭārī Order considerably successful in Bengal. His disciple, Shaykh Ẓuhūr Ḥājjī Ḥamīd Huḍūr of Gwalior, lived for a long time in Medina and in his old age returned to Gwalior, where he trained two young boys, Shaykh Muḥammad Phūl and Shaykh Muḥammad Ghawth. He then took both of them to Bihar. At his instigation, Shaykh Muḥammad Ghawth plunged himself into hard ascetic exercises in a cave in Chunar near Banaras. A number of brahmin sages and Nātha siddhas had also made the region their hermitage. Shaykh Muḥammad Ghawth lived there for more than thirteen years.

The Mughal Emperor Humāyūn (937/1530–947/1540 and 962/1555–963/1556) became Shaykh Phūl's disciple. In 946/1539, Humāyūn's brother, Mīrzā Hindāl, killed Shaykh Phūl in Agra for political reasons. Before Humāyūn's exile from Agra in 947/1540, Shaykh Ghawth moved to Gujarat. There the greatest *'ālim* of the region, Shaykh Wajīh al-Dīn Gujarātī (d. 997/1589), became his disciple. Shaykh 'Alī Muttaqī (d. 975/1567), the great Indian scholar of *Ḥadīth,* and some other eminent members of the *'ulamā'* and Sufis resolutely opposed Shaykh Ghawth for the claims he made in his *Risāla-yi mi'rājiyyah* (*The Treatise of Nocturnal Ascent*) that his own mystic ascent enabled him to arrive near Divine Proximity and to hold a conversation with God. Shaykh Wajīh al-Dīn's influence in Gujarat, however, saved his spiritual guide. After Akbar's (963/1556–1014/1605) accession to the throne, the shaykh returned to his *khānqāh* at Gwalior and died there in 970/1563.

The works and disciples of Shaykh Wajīh al-Dīn Gujarātī ensured the popularity of the Shaṭṭārī Order throughout India, and its disciples in Mecca and Medina initiated Sufis from the Malay and Indonesian islands into the order. They, in turn, disseminated the Shaṭṭārī teachings in their homeland. Of all the works written by Shaykh Ghawth, it was his *Jawāhir-i khamsah* (*The Five Substances*) that left the most indelible mark on Sufism on the Indian subcontinent, as well as in Malaya and Indonesia. It was first authored in 929/1522–23, and in 956/1549–50, at the request of his disciples, it was edited and some new material added, superseding the earlier version. Before long it was translated into Arabic and obtained considerable popularity in Arabic-speaking countries. Its third *jawhar* (substance or section), dealing with invocation of the Names of Allah and the mystical importance of Arabic letters, numbers, and rubrics, gained great popularity with those Sufis who were keen to gain supernatural power. Its fourth section discusses the advanced stages of the mystical achievements of the Shaṭṭār, which, according to the contemporary Shaṭṭāriyyah scholar Ghawthī Shaṭṭārī, was the legacy of Imam Jaʿfar al-Ṣādiq and Bāyazīd Basṭāmī. Its fifth section deals with the ontological perfection manifested by the Divine Names, leading to the stage wherein the attributes of the mystics become the theophany of the Divine Attributes.[22]

Shaykh Muḥammad Ghawth retranslated the *Bahr al-ḥayāt* (*The Ocean of Life*), on yogic practices, by Qāḍī Rukn al-Dīn Samarqandī (d. 615/1218). The work, which was originally translated into Arabic from the Sanskrit *Amritkunda,* was designed to integrate more firmly yogic practices and principles with Shaṭṭārī spiritual discipline.

The Qalandariyyah

As mentioned in chapter 10, the founding of Sufi orders synchronized with the movement of itinerant dervishes who did not observe the customary rules of Sufi life and normal social behavior. They considered *khānqāh* life sacrilegious and profane. The Chishtī records portray them as being extremely rude to the Suhrawardī leaders, but somewhat more considerate toward the Chishtiyyah because of their humility. Fakhr al-Dīn ʿIrāqī visited Shaykh Bahāʾ al-Dīn in the company of *qalandars.* Another exception made by Shaykh Bahāʾ al-Dīn was in the case of his most famous disciple, Mīr Sayyid ʿUthmān of Marwand in Sistan, who came to be known as Lal Shahbāz (the Red Falcon). He established his *khānqāh* at Sehwan in Sind at the site of an old Shaivite sanctuary. Incredible miracles are said to have been performed by him, and even his tomb in Sehwan is known for innumerable miracles.[23] Verses said to have been composed by the members of the Sehwan *khānqāh* tend to indicate that they were very deeply devoted to 'Alī ibn Abī Ṭālib and reinvigorated Ḥallājian traditions in their poetry. His disciples developed *bī-shar'* (indifferent to *Sharī'ah*) practices and came to be known as *malangs.* Their annual fair in the month of Shawwāl attracts enormous crowds in Sehwan from all parts of Pakistan.

The Ḥaydarī and Jawāliqī branches of *qalandars* also made a deep impact on Indian spiritual life. Wandering from place to place throughout India, the *qalandars* who sang love songs and walked on burning fire and ate red-hot charcoals presented a staggering spectacle to the urban and rural population of the country. They did not fail, however, to arouse spiritual sensitivity among the Muslim converts, who had not forgotten the siddhas and yogis of their Hindu milieu.

Like the Suhrawardīs, the Chishtīs also initiated the *qalandars* into their orders. One of the most prominent *qalandars* of the Chishtiyyah Order was Shaykh Abū 'Alī Qalandar. His letters explain Sufism and its many controversial aspects. Although a *Dīwān* ascribed to him is apocryphal, some verses and quatrains which appear genuine remind the reader of Aḥmad Ghazzālī and 'Irāqī. He died at Panipat in 724/1324.[24]

The *Majdhūbs* (Enraptured Sufis)

In Sufi traditions, the *malāmatīs* are holy men who deliberately led an outrageous life in order to conceal their spiritual achievements. The *malāmatiyyah,* however, hardly found any respite from their admirers. The same was the case with the *majdhūbs* or enraptured mystics. Many Sufis lived in a state of ecstasy for shorter or longer periods, but some never regained mental stability. Just as there was no external criterion by which to judge a true Sufi or by which to distinguish him from a charlatan, so it was difficult to distinguish a *majdhūb* from a lunatic. In the popular mind, however, *majdhūbs* were supernatural beings who could perform incredible miracles, and both Hindus and Muslims vied with one another in exhibiting devotion to them.

In all decades and in all centuries, there was no dearth of *majdhūbs.* Preposterous stories are told about their spiritual achievements. Biographical notes on some of them are available in even sober hagiological literature, but none could surpass Muḥammad Sa'īd Sarmad in his contribution to the colorful mystical life and exuberance of emotions in poetry. He was an Armenian Jew who came from Kashan but embraced Islam under the influence of his teachers, Mullā Ṣadrā and his contemporary Mīr Findarskī. The *ḥikmat al-ishrāq* and *waḥdat al-wujūd* became the breath of his nostrils. He earned his living as a merchant and amassed a considerable fortune from his overseas trade. In 1042/1632–33 he visited Thatta, where he fell violently in love with a Hindu boy, Abhai Chand by name. In 1044/1634–35, Sarmad went to Lahore and from thence to Hyderabad, Deccan. Around 1064/1654, Sarmad reached Delhi, where Prince Dārā Shukūh became his devotee. The depths of Sarmad's ineffable experience in the mysteries of Divine Love have been articulated in his quatrains of indescribable beauty, although they tend to offend orthodox sentiments.

In 1071/1660–61 Emperor Awrangzeb, in his bid to weed out Dārā Shukūh's influence completely, passed orders to execute Sarmad. When Sarmad was taken to the gallows, the executioner proceeded to cover his eyes, but Sarmad, preventing him from doing so, cast a glance at him and said, smiling, "Come in whatever garb you choose, I recognise you well," and recited the following verse:

> There was an uproar and we opened our eyes from the eternal sleep,
> Saw that the night of wickedness endured, so slept again.
> You have seen kings, dervishes and qalandars,
> Come, see the intoxicated Sarmad in his wretched condition.[25]

Mythical stories were also associated with Sarmad and his quatrains. Both in the history of Sufism and in the popular mind, Sarmad came to occupy the same status that was held by Ḥallāj. Rightly did one of his verses earlier prophesy:

> A long time since the fame of Manṣūr became an ancient relic,
> I will exhibit with my head the gallow and cord.

Sufi Poetry in Indian Languages

Eminent Sufi saints expressed their ideas generally in Persian poetry and prose, but what made Sufism a household word and a mass movement in the Indian subcontinent was the poetry in its regional languages. The Chishtīs, both the eminent leaders in cities and village Sufis, were pioneers in the movement, writing mainly in Hindāwī or Hindi (see chapter 6); later, Sufis in other parts of the country began to give vent to their emotions in touching Hindi poetry.

The Shaṭṭāriyyah wrote both Hindi and Rājasthānī poetry. The Hindi *mathnawī, Madhu-māltī,* which Shah Manjhan Shaṭṭārī (d. 1001/1592–93) composed in 952/1545, reiterates in a most artistic and lyrical style the Sufi and Hindu *bhaktī* (devotional) theory of the self-manifestation of the Absolute.[26] The Shaṭṭārī Sufis, like the Chishtiyyah, freely borrowed symbols and mythological stories from their local Hindu environment, but gave them an Islamic color to delineate their involvement with the splendor of their radiant love for the Divine. The Nātha theory of the unity of being did not differ from the Sufi perception of the *waḥdat al-wujūd*, and the Shaṭṭāriyyah therefore had no difficulty in delving deep into Nātha terminology in order to make their own realization of Reality known to the common people. Nevertheless, they never subscribed to the Hindu belief in the transmigration of the soul. Their main concern was with self-realization through Yoga or love, or both, and this goal was realized within the bounds of Islam, although the poetic frameworks were Hindu or Buddhist.

The Kashmīrī poetry of Shaykh Nūr al-Dīn Rishī (779/1378–842/1439) saw the cross-fertilization of Sufi beliefs with those expressed by Lāl Ded or Lalla, a Kashmīrī Shaivite woman whose Supreme Reality, identified as Shiva, was Eternal, All-Pervading and All-Transcending. Some of Shaykh Nūr al-Dīn's verses are almost identical to those written by Lalla, but those which are attributed only to the shaykh exhibit him as an ardent devotee of the Absolute, trying to reach the Unknowable in the heart by lighting the lamp of love. To him, the repetition of the Islamic profession of faith was incomplete without a valid realization of the reality of the self. He admitted that although eating meat was permitted by the *Sharī'ah*, to him it was cruelty to animals. His disciples invented a distinctive dress for their followers and transformed the teachings of their master into an organized Rishī (ascetical Sufi) movement. The poets and authors of the movement believed they were duty bound to turn Kashmir into a heaven—although they themselves led harshly austere lives—planting fruit trees for the benefit of the common people.

In Bengal, the Ḥusayn Shāhī sultans (897/1494–945/1538) gave considerable encouragement to Bengali literature, but a real flourishing of Bengali Sufi poetry took place mainly from the tenth/sixteenth century on in the Chittagong region and at the Arakanese court. Some works translate the Nātha Panthī literature from Sanskrit into Bengali and try to reconcile them with Sufi *maqāmāt* (stages) and teachings. A distinctive contribution of the Bengali Sufi poets involved the creation of a corpus of mystical and legendary *mathnawīs* on the model of those written in Persian by Niẓāmī, 'Aṭṭār, and Jāmī. Sayyid Sulṭān (957/1550–1058/1648) of Chittagong, a leading Sufi in that region, had obtained a profound mastery over arousing human emotions through the use of the most poignant diction. He composed a number of Bengali *mathnawīs* on themes relating to the life of the Prophet Muḥammad and his family members, borrowing similes and metaphors from the Hindu epics and legends. His mystical poems such as *Gnān*

Chautīsa and *Gnān Pradīp* were believed to have been written in his old age in an attempt to harmonize Hatha-Yoga with Sufism.

The Bengali poets exhibit considerable literary skill and aesthetic taste in depicting their perception of *al-nūr al-muḥammadī* (literally, Muḥammadan Light) or the pre-creation light from which everything was created. In the *Nūr-nāmah* (*Treatise on Light*) or the *Nūr-kandīl* (*Lamp of Light*), Sayyid Murtaḍā (998/1590–1072/1662) passionately makes the Prophet both the cause and the goal of creation. The *ḥadīth, anā Aḥmad bilā mīm* (I am Aḥmad [Muḥammad] without the letter *m,* i.e., Aḥad=One) is represented by many Bengali Sufi poets in Hindu symbols, and some even go to the extent of anthropomorphizing the concept.

The earliest known Ṣufi poets of the Punjab were Bābā Farīd of Pakpattan (see chapter 6 in this volume) and his descendants. Mādho Lāl Ḥusayn (946/1539–1001/1593) was the most colorful of the Punjabi Sufi poets. His verses called *kāfīs* give emotional expression to the doctrine of *waḥdat al-wujūd.* The folktales of Hīr and Rānjhā and Sohnī Mehanwāl are also sung in his poetry. Nawshāh Ganjbakhsh (d. 1064/1654) was deeply influenced by the pioneers of Hindu devotional movements, Kabīr (828/1425–911/1505) and Gurū Nānak (873/1469–946/1539). He wrote many Panjabi *dōhas* (couplets) in which he answered questions earlier posed by Kabīr. Nevertheless, he strongly criticized the Hindu belief in the transmigration of the soul. Sultan Bāhū (d. 1102/1691) was the author of the Punjabi *Sīharfīs* (Golden Alphabets) ending with the exclamation *Hū* (He). Not only were his verses welcome at the *samā'* gatherings but they were—and still are—upon the lips of all sections of the Punjabi community. They deal with the self-manifestation of the Absolute and the preeminence of the life led in spiritual dedication and asceticism. The greatest Sufi poet of the Punjabi language was, however, Mīr Bullhe Shah Qādirī-Shaṭṭārī (1091/1680–1165/1752). His imageries on *waḥdat al-wujūd* are both novel and frank. Around 1180/1766, Wārith Shah, a famous Chishtī Sufi, re-versified the celebrated Punjabi folk story, Hīr-Rānjhā. In it, the yogi Bālnath exercises his spiritual power in collaboration with five *pīrs* (Khwājah Khiḍr, Bābā Farīd Shakarganj, Lāl Shahbāz Qalandar, Shaykh Bahā' al-Dīn Zakariyyā', and Makhdūm Jahāniyān) to bless Rānjhā. The poet repeatedly portrays the *unio mystica* throughout the *mathnawī.*

As was the case in other regions of India, the *samā'* gatherings of Sind reverberated with Sufi music in the Sindhi language. The foremost Sufi poet of Sind was Shah 'Abd al-Laṭīf (1102/1690–91–1165/1752). The melodies of his poetic works called *Risālo* (*The Book*) embodying the folk ballads of Sind are very emotive and stirring. Among the different romantic stories chosen by the Shah to invite Sufis to concentrate on Divine Love is the *Sasui-*

Punhūn. He does not give the details of the story but masterly portrays only some thrilling episodes in order to use them as the background for his mystical perception of quest, separation, and death.

The twelfth/eighteenth century also saw the crystallization of the poetic form of Urdu, spoken both by Hindus and Muslims. The greatest Sufi poets of the period were the Naqshbandī Sufis Khwājah Mīr Dard and Mīrzā Jān-i Jānān Maẓhar. The thirteenth/nineteenth-century poet Mīrzā Asad Allāh Khān Ghālib (1212/1797–1286/1869) did not lead a *khānqāh* life and was known for his gaiety, but his Urdu poetry is marked by a deep spiritual sensitivity. He also wrote profound *ghazals* in Persian. Sir Muhammad Iqbal (1294/1877–1357/1938) also wrote poetry in both Persian and Urdu. He strongly criticized the degenerate Sufism of his own day and considered it a threat to Islamic dynamism and the self (*khwudī*).

The Influence of Sufism on the Indian Subcontinent

Dedicating their whole being to the Absolute, the Sufis in the Indian subcontinent achieved their spiritual goal through intuition, esoteric knowledge, and experience of the mystical world. Theirs was naturally the antithesis of the solely intellectual experience fostered by some of the philosophers. Some Suhrawardī leaders and other dervishes played an important role in the power struggle of the ruling classes and aristocracy and pressured the government into taking a very narrow view of Islam. However, the large number of eminent Sufis whose vision of Islamic spiritual life was broadly based gave moral courage to the people by awakening in them spiritual values and reliance on God during calamities such as drought, floods, and panic due to protracted wars and foreign invasions. The early Chishtiyyah believed that contact with the saintly was the only means by which people would renounce evil or convert to Islam. The social and economic position of the masses of Muslim converts who accepted Islam under a variety of pressures was in fact no better than that of the Hindu masses, because of the dominance of the discriminating ruling classes. Nevertheless, the *khānqāhs* did offer peace and comfort to the thousands of Muslims who crowded the towns. The lack of literary evidence is the most formidable obstacle to the presentation of any pictures of village *khānqāhs,* where the tombs of local *pīrs* and the graves of local martyrs both real and fake offered the sole spiritual comfort to the inhabitants in their sufferings and anguish. The ʿ*urs* (death anniversaries) and other ceremonies celebrated in *khānqāhs* developed into significant cultural institutions and were eagerly awaited by both poor and rich alike.

Not only was Sufi poetry an expression of the mystic love of a thirsty soul seeking an intuitive understanding of God, but it was also an avenue for the outlet of emotions and spiritual feelings which would otherwise never have been expressed because of the fury of the orthodox, social inhibitions, and political repressions. Sufi poetry in Hindi and regional languages opened a fresh avenue for a new spiritual, serene, and colorful way of life. The Nātha Panthī and Vaishnavite symbols did not necessarily make them syncretic, for a number of Sufis who used such symbols enjoyed a reputation for excessively deep devotion to Islam. They were designed to be shared with the experiences of their countrymen whose spirits passionately loved to attain the higher reaches of Reality. Both the Sufi poets of the regional languages and the pioneers of Hindu *bhaktī* (devotional) movements rebelled against all forms of religious formalism, falsehood, hypocrisy, and stupidity and tried to create a world in which spiritual bliss was the all-consuming goal. The devotion of some of the rulers and members of the governing classes to the Sufis went a long way toward making possible the erection of such masterpieces of architecture as the tomb of the Suhrawardī Shaykh Rukn al-Dīn in Multan, the *khānqāh* of Mīr Sayyid ʿAlī Hamadānī in Srinagar (Kashmir), and the tombs of Shaykh Muḥammad Ghawth in Gwalior and Shaykh Salīm Chishtī at Fatehpur Sikri. Even the Mughal miniatures did not neglect the Sufi landscape; some of them integrate Sufi themes with the *bhaktas* (Hindu devotees).

The most serious threat to the survival of Sufism was the presumptuous claims of Sufi charlatans and impostors. The latter exploited Sufi influence to their own advantage. Their poetry and music promoted immoral practices, the use of drugs, and thaumaturgy and was a great threat to a spiritual world view of the genuine Sufis. But genuine Sufism survived this and other threats and has managed to keep alive to this day.

Notes

1. R. C. Zaehner, *Hindu and Muslim Mysticism* (London: Athlone, 1960) 93–134, 198–218; A. J. Arberry, *Revelation and Reason in Islam* (London: Allen & Unwin, 1957) 99–103.
2. L. Massignon, *The Passion of al-Hallāj, Mystic and Martyr of Islam,* trans. H. Mason (4 vols.; Princeton, NJ: Princeton University Press, 1982).
3. Mahdi Husain, *The Reḥla of Ibn Baṭṭūṭa* (Baroda, 1976) 189.
4. J. S. Trimingham, *The Sufi Orders in Islam* (London: Oxford University Press, 1971) 24, 236; F. Meier, ed., *Firdōs al-Murshidiyya: Die Vita des Scheikhs Abū Isḥāq al-Kāzerūnī* (Leipzig: Brockhaus, 1948).
5. ʿAlī ibn ʿUthmān al-Hujwīrī, *The "Kashf al-Maḥjūb," the Oldest Persian Treatise on Sufism by Al-Hujwīrī,* trans. A. Nicholson (London: Luzac, 1911) IX–XII.
6. Ibid., 91.

7. Sayf ibn Muḥammad ibn Ya'qūb Harawī, *Tārīkh-nāma-yi Hirāt* (Calcutta, 1944) 157–58.

8. S. A. A. Rizvi, *A History of Sufism in India* (New Delhi: Munshiram Mansharlal, 1978) 1:206–10.

9. Ḥamīd Qalandar, *Khayr al-majālis* (Aligarh, n.d.) 74–75.

10. Shaykh Ḥamīd al-Dīn Ṣūfī, *Ṭawāli' al-shumūs* (Habibganj Collections, Aligarh Muslim University Library, Aligarh, India) ff. 3b–9b.

11. 'Alī ibn Sa'd ibn Ashraf, *Sirāj al-idāyah* (India Office, London, Delhi Persian Manuscript, 1938) f. 64b.

12. Muḥammad ibn Kabīr, *Afsāna-yi shāhān* (British Library London Manuscript, Rieu I, 234b) ff. 36b–37a.

13. Rizvi, *A History of Sufism in India,* 1:226–28.

14. Ibid., 230–31.

15. See *The Hundred Letters of Sharafuddin Maneri.*

16. Shah Shu'ayb, *Manāqib al-aṣfiyā'* (Lucknow, 1287/1870) 346.

17. Rizvi, *A History of Sufism in India,* 1:231.

18. Ibid., 291–93.

19. Ibid., 296–99.

20. F. Rosenthal, *The Muqaddimah* (London: Routledge & Kegan Paul, 1958) 2:156–90.

21. Ghawthī Shaṭṭārī, *Gulzār-i abrār* (Tashkent, USSR Manuscript) ff. 92a–93a, 165a–166a.

22. Shaykh Muḥammad Ghawth, *Jawāhir-i khamsah* (India Office, London, Manuscript) ff. 202a–206b.

23. 'Abd Allāh Khwēshgī Qaṣūrī, *Ma'ārij al-wilāyah* (Shīrānī Collections, Panjab University, Lahore, Pakistan) f. 542b.

24. 'Abd al-Raḥmān Chishtī, *Mir'āt al-asrār* (British Museum London Manuscript, Rieu I, 359b) ff. 25b–26a.

25. Quoted in Rizvi, *A History of Sufism in India,* 2:475–79.

26. Ibid., 434–37.

13

Sufism in the Malay-Indonesian World

Osman Bin Bakar

Sufism has continued to enjoy a flourishing and influential presence in the Malay world from the beginning of the history of Islam in the region until the present day.[1] But it was during the first few centuries of that history, especially the tenth/sixteenth and eleventh/seventeenth centuries, that Sufism had its greatest and most decisive role in shaping the religious, spiritual, and intellectual landscapes of the Malay archipelago. During this period, Sufism played a central role in the Islamization of the archipelago.[2] This particular historical moment is of great cultural pride to the Malay peoples, for it was through Islam that Malay civilization attained its greatest cultural and intellectual heights or, for that matter, that the intellectual history of the Malays, properly speaking, can be said to have begun.

Through Sufism the intellectual and rational spirit of Islam entered the minds of the people, giving birth to new intellectual and cultural manifestations not seen in pre-Islamic times. Most significantly, the pre-Islamic, mythological world view of the Malays and the language through which that world view was projected underwent a radical transformation. The Malay scholar Syed Muhammad Naquib al-Attas states that the impact of the Islamic *Weltanschauung,* as interpreted predominantly by the Sufis, upon the Malay world view is comparable to that of the Quran upon the Arabs. In both cases, the revolutionary changes in the world view are clearly reflected in the language through which that view is projected, namely, Malay and Arabic.[3]

Without doubt, Sufism's greatest contribution to Malay civilization lies in shaping and crystallizing its intellectual and spiritual milieu during the later phase of the Islamization process, from the ninth/fifteenth century until about the end of the twelfth/eighteenth century. This led to a complete and permanent conversion of the Malays to the Islamic *Weltanschauung.*

In the view of scholars like Professor al-Attas, whose writings have been instrumental in making known to the outside world the contours and dimensions of the Malay intellectual and spiritual universe under Islam, conversion during the earlier phase of the Islamization process had been only partial. Even though there was a faithful conversion and submission to the *Sharī'ah*, many fundamental concepts connected with the central Islamic idea of *tawḥīd* (Divine Unity) were still understood in the light of the old *Weltanschauung*, which appears to be a mixture of an Olympian Greek-type mythology in its decadent stage and popularized versions of Hindu-Buddhist metaphysics. The task of resolving the conceptual overlappings and confusions between the old and new ideas was undertaken later on mainly by the Sufis. Armed, as they were, with both the metaphysical doctrines and the spiritual methods of Sufism, they proved to be the best equipped, intellectually and spiritually, to deal effectively with the problem posed by pre-Islamic Malay mysticism. It was during this period of Sufism's domination that most of the areas in the Malay archipelago were converted to Islam. On this account, the Sufis have been popularly described as the disseminators of Islam in the archipelago.

The role of the Sufis in the propagation of Islam in the Malay archipelago was by no means confined to the later phase of the Islamization process. It is quite clear from historical accounts given in various Malay and Javanese chronicles that Sufis must have participated in the dissemination of Islam right from the beginning of Muslim missionary activity and also during the earlier phase of the Islamization process when jurisprudence and jurists predominated. The characteristics of these first and early propagators of Islam, as described in these accounts, reveal traits peculiar to Sufis. Having briefly referred to the central role played by Sufism in the conversion of the Malay archipelago to Islam and in creating the golden age of Malay civilization, we now take a closer look at this role and its important manifestations in Malay history and culture.

Sufism and the Spread of Islam in the Malay Archipelago

Islam came to the Malay archipelago through trade and missionary activity. Chinese sources mention the establishment of Arab and perhaps other Muslim settlements on the west coast of Sumatra as early as 54/674.[4] This area, which was of strategic importance as far as the trade route between Arabia and China was concerned, served as an important port of call and trading center for Arab and Persian traders. The next major emigration of Muslim traders to the archipelago occurred in 264/878 in the aftermath of the Huang Ch'ao rebellion in South China in which, according to the famous Muslim historian and scientist Abu'l-Ḥasan al-Mas'ūdī (d. 345/956), about one hundred twenty or two hundred thousand traders from the west, the majority of whom were Muslims, were massacred.[5] Muslim survivors of this massacre, who were mainly Arabs and Persians, fled to the archipelago and settled in Kalah on the west coast of the Malay peninsula as well as in San-fo-ch'i (Palembang) in east Sumatra. Other early settlements of Muslim traders mentioned were in Champa in 430/1039 and in Java in 475/1082. Despite the presence of these various early Muslim settlements, however, we know of no significant missionary activity among the Muslims until about the end of the seventh/thirteenth century. This activity increased in momentum in the eighth/fourteenth century and dominated the entire archipelago in the next century.

This highly noticeable rise of Muslim missionary activity in the archipelago beginning from the end of the seventh/thirteenth century calls for some explanation, and several theories have been offered by scholars. There is, first of all, the view given by J. C. van Leur, who, though confessing his inability to assign definite causes to the commencement of intensive propagation of Islam in the eighth/fourteenth century, believes the trade factor to be the primary cause.[6] But several scholars have pointed out that trade could not have been the primary impulse behind this vigorous missionary activity precisely because Islam and trade in the archipelago had been linked together at least from the second/eighth century. Yet, during those intervening centuries, when Muslims profited much from trade with the archipelago and China, no need was felt to propagate Islam in those regions.

Equally implausible is the theory advanced by such scholars as W. F. Wertheim and B. J. Schrieke, who cite the "race" with Christianity at the coming of the Portuguese in the tenth/sixteenth century as the major contributing factor to the spread of Islam.[7] This view is contrary to the fact that the rise of Islamic proselytization activity can be noticed almost two centuries before the arrival of the Portuguese and Christianity. Furthermore, Islam was already a growing power when the Portuguese arrived, and Malacca, captured by the latter in 917/1511, had long been the headquarters for the Muslim missionary penetration into Java. Hence the famous saying: Java was converted in Malacca. The great vigor of Muslim missionary activity in the tenth/sixteenth century, which Schrieke rightly observes, was therefore not the beginning but rather the continuation of a historical process that had started much earlier and was now gaining momentum because of certain internal forces within the community. This historical process is what we have referred to earlier as *Islamization,* and "internal forces" refers mainly to Sufism, since the period cited by Schrieke is precisely that in which Sufism dominates the Islamization process.

In fact, Sufism is the main factor to which many Malay scholars have attributed the rise of missionary zeal from the end of the seventh/thirteenth century on. This view is shared also by a few Western scholars like A. H. Johns, who went so far as to assert categorically that Islam could not and did not take root in the Malay archipelago until the rise of the Sufi orders, and that the quickening tempo of the spread of Islam after the seventh/thirteenth century is, in the main, due to the labors of the Sufi missionaries.[8] The Sufi factor appears to be the most plausible explanation not only because it finds sufficient support in the historical evidence provided by the local Malay and Javanese chronicles, but also because it accords with the general religious and spiritual climate prevailing in the Muslim world after the seventh/thirteenth century. This view is held on the popular level, and there is also the literary evidence furnished by various studies of Malay mystical and religious literature. The most revealing of these is perhaps al-Attas's work on the mystical ideas and teachings of Ḥamzah al-Fanṣūrī, a Malay Sufi poet of the tenth/sixteeth century. This work, which sheds much light on the state of the intellectual and spiritual activity of the Malays during the period from the ninth/fifteenth to the end of the eleventh/seventeenth century, reveals Sufism flourishing on such a scale that it must have significantly influenced the large-scale conversion of the archipelago to Islam, a process that took place during this period.

In the local chronicles as well as in oral traditions, there are references to *faqīrs* (dervishes), *walīs* (saints), and *shaykhs* (masters) among the early propagators of Islam in various parts of the archipelago during the seventh/thirteenth and eighth/fourteenth centuries. These are all technical terms belonging to the vocabulary of Sufism, which even after their adoption into the Malay language and in popular usage continue to retain the specific technical meanings in which they are understood in Sufism, thus suggesting very strongly that these propagators were Sufis. In both the *Sejarah Melayu* (*The Malay Annals*) and the *Hikayat Raja-Raja Pasai* (*The Chronicles of Pasai*), we are told of one Shaykh Ismāʿīl, who was sent to Samudra by the Sharīf of Mecca to spread Islam there in the middle of the seventh/thirteenth century. On the way, his ship called at Ma'abri, the then well-known name for the Coromandel coast, where its ruler, Sultan Muḥammad, abdicated his throne in favor of his son and joined the ship as a *faqīr*. Shaykh Ismāʿīl and the *faqīr* succeeded in converting Perlak and Samudra to Islam. The ruler of the latter kingdom, Merah Silu, adopted the title al-Malik al-Ṣāliḥ (d. 696/1297).

It is further related that the *faqīr* remained in Samudra as a teacher of religion. There is, therefore, a strong possibility that in his capacity as a teacher of religion, the *faqīr* might have introduced some elements of Sufism among these early Malay converts to Islam. It is perhaps in reference to this possibility that the famous Dutch scholar Snouck Hurgronje expressed the view that some form of mysticism was introduced simultaneously into the archipelago with the introduction of Islam.[9]

The Kingdom of Pasai

Perlak and Samudra were soon united under the rule of al-Malik al-Ṣāliḥ to form the kingdom of Pasai, which appears to be the earliest center of Islamic learning in the archipelago. When the famous Muslim traveler Ibn Baṭṭūṭah visited the kingdom in 746/1345–747/1346, he discovered that the then reigning king, al-Malik al-Ẓāhir, probably the elder of the two sons of al-Malik al-Ṣāliḥ, was a lover of religious debates and had surrounded himself with jurists, theologians, and men of learning, several of whom came from as far away as Shiraz and Isfahan in Persia. This shows that by the first half of the eighth/fourteenth century, Malay Muslims had already established religious and intellectual contacts with the rest of the Islamic world. To what extent the influence of Sufism was at work in the religious world of Pasai during this period is still a matter of pure speculation because of the absence of any written records. However, in speaking of this influence, we need to distinguish between Sufism as a spiritual practice or experience and Sufism as an intellectual exposition of doctrines and methods. We know from Islamic history that Sufism in its latter aspect possesses a kind of historical development that is in conformity with the changing needs of the times as well as the "needs" of different types of peoples to whom the exposition of the truths of Sufism was being addressed, whereas Sufism in the former aspect, as a practical realization of Islamic spirituality, knows no development, for it refers to the same reality that is embodied in spiritual methods and practices going back to the Prophet.

As this applies to Malay Sufism, it is reasonable to assume that doctrinal expositions of Sufism had not yet entered into the realms of Malay religious discourses during this period, because the needs for them had not yet arisen. The immediate practical needs of the newly emerging and apparently quite rapidly growing Muslim community were those pertaining to rules and regulations governing individual and collective life, which had now to conform to the dictates of the *Sharī'ah,* irrespective of whether conversion to Islam had been effected by the Sufis. This perhaps partly explains the predominance of jurisprudence and jurists in the royal courts of the Malay kingdoms of this time. As we shall see later, the need for authentic and thorough expositions of Sufi doctrines in the Malay language did not arise until the tenth/sixteenth century. Nevertheless, there is substantial evidence that around the middle of the ninth/fifteenth century some forms of exposition of Sufi doctrines had begun to enter into Malay religious debates and discourses. In speaking, therefore, of the Sufi presence or influence in Pasai in the eighth/fourteenth century, we can only postulate the presence of Sufism as a spiritual realization of the interior life of Islam based on the methods and practices of the Prophet, bearing in mind the earlier presence of Sufis who served as missionaries and teachers of religion.

The Role of Oral Tradition in the Philippines

There are many Filipino Muslims today who claim descent from some of the earliest Muslim missionaries, who were all referred to as *makhdūmīn* (sg. *makhdūm,* "teacher"). These claims are corroborated through the presentation of what Muslim Filipinos call *tarsilas* or *silāsilas* (genealogical trees). The tombs of these *makhdūmīn* are claimed to have existed at different places in the Sulu archipelago, such as Tandu Banak in Sibutu Island, Bud Agad in Jolo, and Lugus Island in Tapul. They are highly revered and have been objects of visits down to the present. This shows how profound is the spiritual and religious influence that these *makhdūmīn* have had on the souls of many Filipino Muslims. These *makhdūmīn* are, in fact, regarded as the first *awliyā'* (saints) in the Philippines. They were credited with having magical powers, and their teachings have been described as being infused with mystical overtones. One of the most famous of these saints was Makhdūm Karīm, whose tomb is believed to be the one at Tandu Banak. He is popularly known as *Tuan Sharīf Awliyā'* (Master of the Saints) on account of his saintly qualities. Sulu traditions relate that he traveled extensively in the region where he effected significant conversions among the local population. These early missionaries to the region which constitutes today the southern Philippines have traits characteristic of Sufis.

The view of the respected Filipino Muslim scholar Cesar Adib Majul is that these *makhdūmīn* were probably Sufis who had fled to the Malay archipelago following the Mongol conquest of Baghdad in 656/1258.[10] If Makhdūm Karīm had indeed arrived in Sulu in the second half or around the middle of the eighth/fourteenth century, as believed by many scholars, then he and others before him must have been quite successful in spreading Islam. Around the turn of that century, Muslims who came from other Malay lands to establish a principality, such as the Sumatran prince Rāja Baguindā 'Alī, found enough support from the local Muslims to realize their political objectives. By the middle of the ninth/fifteenth century,

Sharīf al-Hāshim succeeded in converting to Islam the interior or mountain tribes in Jolo, called the Buranuns. At that time Islam was already a widespread religion in the Sulu archipelago, which made the local chiefs and people receptive to the adoption of Islamic political institutions, specifically the sultanate. Had it not been checked by the Spaniards, who came to colonize and Christianize the Philippine Islands in the second half of the tenth/sixteenth century, the Islamization of the Philippines would probably have been carried to its completion, for by this time Manila was already a Muslim principality ruled by rajahs who were members of the ruling family of Brunei, and the observance of certain Islamic practices had spread as far north as the province of Cagayan.

The Rise of Malacca

In the Malay peninsula itself, it was the rise of Malacca as a powerful and prosperous Muslim kingdom in the ninth/fifteenth century that gave the real impetus to the spread of Islam. Malacca, not long after its foundation and the conversion to Islam of its first ruler, Parameswara, around 817/1414, developed into a center of both commerce and Islamic learning and missionary activity. Al-Attas believes that Sufism must have played a significant role in the Islamization of Malacca and the rest of the peninsula. In support of this view he points to the fact that during the reign of Sultan Manṣūr Shāh (863/1459–882/1477), by which time the Malaccan empire had embraced almost the whole peninsula, the theologians of the kingdom were already formulating such religious questions as whether hell is eternal or not. Their grasp of metaphysical matters, which had been dealt with by the early Sufis, must presuppose a certain level of prior exposure to the doctrinal teachings of Sufism.

It is related in the *Sejarah Melayu* that a certain Sufi shaykh at Mecca by the name of Abū Isḥāq, after completing a book on mysticism entitled *Durr al-manẓūm* (*String of Poetic Pearls*), instructed his disciple Abū Bakr to take the book to Malacca and spread knowledge of it there. Abū Bakr arrived with the book, which dealt with the Essence, Attributes, and Acts of God and was received with great pomp and ceremony and drummed all the way to the Malaccan royal court. Sultan Manṣūr Shāh himself took a keen interest in the study of the book and had it sent to Pasai to Makhdūm Patakan, who was instructed to interpret its inner meanings.

The *Sejarah Melayu* also relates that Manṣūr Shāh sent Tun Bija Wangsa to Pasai to seek a satisfactory answer to the problem of whether those in heaven and hell remain there for all eternity. At first, his messenger received the exoteric answer that this is the case. On his complaining, however, that the people of Malacca already knew this, he was given the esoteric answer that the sufferings of the damned would in the end be turned to pleasure. Some scholars have commented that this answer reflects a teaching of the famous Sufi master, ʿAbd al-Karīm al-Jīlī, in his *al-Insān al-kāmil* (*The Universal Man*), which suggests that perhaps this work was known, at least in Pasai, within a few decades of its author's death, about 832/1428.

There is no doubt, however, that by the time Manṣūr Shāh became sultan of Malacca some forms of exposition of Sufi doctrines had begun to enter into Malay religious debates and discourses. Otherwise, the sultan would not have sought the help of religious scholars in Pasai to interpret the inner meanings of the *Durr al-manẓūm* and Tun Bija Wangsa would not have sought the esoteric answer to the theological problem of the eternity or noneternity of hell. After Manṣūr Shāh, more and more emphasis on Sufism became noticeable. Certain Sufi orders also appear to have been established by this time. For example, Sultan Maḥmūd, who ascended the throne in 893/1488 and whose reign lasted until 917/1511, when Malacca fell into the hands of the Portuguese, is known to have been a disciple of a mystic.

What is of immediate relevance here is the importance of Malacca as the center from which Islamic missionary activity radiated to the extremities of the archipelago and the role of the Sufis associated with it. Mawlānā Abū Bakr, mentioned earlier, appears to be the same Abū Bakr who is one of the best-known missionaries to the Philippines and to whom is attributed the creation of the Sulu sultanate, the introduction of the *Sharīʿah* and the greater dissemination of the Arabic script in the Sulu archipelago. This may be inferred from the claim of Muslim Filipino traditional sources that Abū Bakr originally came from Arabia, stopped in Palembang in Sumatra and arrived in the Sulu region some time at the beginning of the second half of the ninth/fifteenth century, which coincides with the reign of Sultan Manṣūr Shāh. Abū Bakr's importance in the history of Filipino Muslims lies in the fact that he contributed significantly to the further spread and consolidation of Islam in Sulu. This has enabled its people to resist all foreign attempts at subjugating and de-Islamizing them from the time of the Spaniards until today.

The Islamization of Java

It has been claimed that Java was "converted in Malacca." It is, no doubt, true that even before the foundation of Malacca, a significant Muslim missionary movement was already in operation on the east coast of Java around the area of Gresik, being led by a certain Mawlānā Malik Ibrāhīm, who traced his descent to Zayn al-ʿĀbidīn, a great-grandson of the Prophet. He is said to have stayed in Java as a missionary for more than twenty years, until his death in 822/1419, and his tomb in Gresik is still venerated today as that of the first real Muslim missionary to Java. But it is also true that the conversion of many parts of Java is attributed to some of the most famous Javanese Sufi saints who are known to have studied in Malacca. The Javanese chronicle, *Babad Tanah Djawi,* mentions, for example, Sunan Bonang and Santri Giri as having studied in Malacca for a year under Shaykh Walī Lanang. Sunan Bonang is especially famous for having traversed the Javanese countryside, converting Shiva-Buddhist ascetics known as *adjars* to Islam. Walī Lanang himself, whose place of origin was Jedda, is said to have visited and taught in Ampel, which is a little south of Gresik and became around the middle of the ninth/fifteenth century a famous Muslim kingdom as well as a center for the propagation of Islam in Java and neighboring islands. Many of the influential and successful missionaries here were themselves princes who were related in one way or another to the Hindu king of the then mighty kingdom of Majapahit.

On account of this blood relation and the increasing influence which these Muslim princes wielded within the new Muslim community as a result of more and more conversions to Islam, they were appointed by the king of Majapahit as governors of those of his vassal states in east and north Java where mass conversions had taken place. Later, all the Muslim princes with the exception of one Raden Ḥusayn joined a confederacy under the leadership of Raden Patah, a disowned son of the king, to overthrow his father's kingdom. Majapahit fell and Raden Patah became the first Muslim king of Java.

The fall of Majapahit did not, however, bring about the rapid conversion and Islamization of this most populous island of the Malay archipelago. This only confirms the view that, generally speaking, political power has never been the chief instrument of conversion in the archipelago. Even in the case of the Muslim conquest of Majapahit, history records that Raden Patah was more motivated by a desire to avenge his father's cruel treatment of his mother than by religious zeal. The pattern of Islamization is everywhere generally the same: the rise of Muslim states and kingdoms is preceded by mass conversions effected by both foreign and local missionaries, many of whom were Sufis. Thus, after the fall of Majapahit, it took another three centuries for the complete conversion of Java to be realized. The kingdom of Balambangan in the far east of the island, for example, did not finally go over to Islam until late in the twelfth/eighteenth century. In central Java itself, where Hinduism was more deeply rooted, it was not until 1182/1768 that the authority of the Hindu law books, particularly the code of Manu, gave way before a code of laws more in accordance with the spirit of Islamic legislation.

Islam in Sumatra

The conversion of Sumatra was complete by the end of the tenth/sixteenth century with the exception of the Batak country in the interior of the central region of the island, even though it was conquered in 944/1537 by Acheh under its ruler, ʿAlāʾ al-Dīn Riʿāyat Shāh al-Qahhār (d. 976/1568). The Bataks as a people have never been wholly converted to Islam. Acheh must be mentioned together with Pasai and Malacca for its dominant role in the spread of Islam, Islamic theology, and *taṣawwuf* in Java in particular, and the whole of the Malay archipelago in general.

When Malacca fell to the Portuguese, Acheh became its successor as the most important Muslim commercial center in the archipelago as well as a great center of Muslim learning. During the reign of ʿAlāʾ al-Dīn Riʿāyat Shāh (who is not to be confused with the conqueror of the Batak country) from 997/1589 to 1013/1604 and that of Sultan Iskandar Muda from 1016/1607 to 1046/1636, Acheh reached its zenith in military as well as commercial power and witnessed the flourishing of Sufism, which gave birth to the golden age of Malay civilization, particularly insofar as the intensity of its intellectual and spiritual life is concerned. There lived during this period the greatest Malay Sufis, such as Ḥamzah al-Fanṣūrī and Shams al-Dīn al-Sumatrānī, and they were immediately followed by Sufi figures like Nūr al-Dīn al-Rānīrī and ʿAbd al-Raʾūf Singkel. Through their numerous writings and the spread of their respective Sufi orders, they contributed significantly to the Islamization of the Malay archipelago.

This essay does not allow us to go into the details of the spread of Islam in other important islands in the archipelago, like Borneo, the Moluccas, and Celebes. We have dealt only with those areas which are generally recognized and accepted as the key centers of Islam and most profoundly influenced the Islamization of the whole archipelago. It suffices to remark here that the spread and consolidation of Islam in the other islands was also effected by the labors of missionaries provided successively by Pasai, Malacca, and Acheh, the three greatest Islamic religious centers. This took place through a long process of conversion and Islamization, in which the Sufis participated actively.

Sufism and the Appeal of Islam to the Malays

In summing up the role of the Sufis and Sufism in the spread of Islam in the Malay archipelago, we need to stress the point that Sufism, more than any other factor, has greatly facilitated the acceptance of Islam among the Malay people. The general appeal of Sufism among the Malays has something to do with their psychological and spiritual temperaments, which are manifested clearly throughout their religious history in the various forms of what Sir Richard Winstedt calls "deep-seated popular mysticism."[11] In their encounter with Hindu-Buddhist mystics, the Sufi missionaries did not call for the rejection of the existing religious and spiritual doctrines, but sought to reinterpret them in the light of Islamic spiritual teachings as embodied in Sufism. Nor did they insist on the adoption of a new terminology in place of the prevailing ones. In this sense, the coming of Islam to Java, where Hindu-Buddhist mysticism was more deeply rooted, can be seen as effecting a Sufi corrective to the interpretation of the Hindu doctrines according to the Vedānta.

The employment of pre-Islamic Malay-Javanese terms referring to the Hindu doctrines in Javanese Sufi writings led certain scholars to conclude that the Sufi missionaries had deliberately and consciously been forced to hark back to the old Hinduism in order to resolve the conflict between Islam and Javanese Hinduism. Actually, the activity of the Sufis was not an exercise in religious compromise or expediency; rather, it was the question of an ingenious missionary technique devised to bring the Javanese around to the Islamic point of view. At the level of direct, personal spiritual encounter, the effectiveness of the technique is best illustrated by the fact that Javanese history records instances of hundreds of Shiva-Buddha mystics converted to Islam after such encounters with Sufi saints. That effectiveness presupposes in part the condition that there exist common doctrines between Sufism and Shiva-Buddha mysticism. This is indeed so, for otherwise it would not have been possible for the Sufis to read their Islamic meanings into many of the terms employed in the latter form of mysticism.

There are other important characteristics associated with the Sufis which rendered their missionary efforts more fruitful than those of other groups. One of these was their readiness to resort to missionary techniques making use of what would be regarded as familiar mediums, closely and intimately linked with old concepts and the old *Weltanschauung*. The *wayangs* (theaters) were such a medium, for it was through them that the general public had the opportunity to glimpse and "experience" the philosophical-mystical world view envisaged by the poets of Old Javanese literature. In the hands of some of the Sufi missionaries, however, what now filtered through the *wayangs* were the teachings of Islam itself. Sunan Kalijaga's use of the *wayang* to spread Islam in Java is a well-known fact. Thus, whether the Sufis dealt with the poets, the Shiva-Buddha mystics, or the general public, the use of the appropriate missionary techniques in each case made possible significant conversions of the Javanese to Islam.

Another characteristic which is known to have attracted conversions was the Sufis' possession of certain spiritual powers, as manifested, for example, in the healing of the sick. The Malays have termed these supernatural powers *keramat*, which is a corruption of the Arabic *karāmāt*. The affiliations of the Sufi orders with the trade and craft guilds or corporations constitute an additional factor in the success of Sufi missionary work. It is in recognition of the Malays' strong mystical tendencies and their inclinations to what the Sufis could and did offer that A. H. Johns pertinently commented that an "Islam of the Wahhābī type" would have made very little impact on a land like Java.

Contours and Dimensions of Malay Sufism

Numerous Sufi orders found fertile soil in the souls of the Malays and became firmly implanted as an integral component of the Malay religious and spiritual landscape, continuing to this day to cater to the spiritual needs of a sizable segment of the archipelago Muslims. Some of the religious practices of Sufism, in their popularized versions, became assimilated into the common culture of the people. As for the intellectual dimension of Islamic spirituality, its manifestation in the Malay world constitutes the beginning of the literary and intellectual history of that world itself.

For several centuries, Sufism exercised an immense influence on almost every facet of Malay intellectual life. This is hardly surprising considering the fact that the greatest intellectual figures in Malay history have also been the founders and greatest representatives of various Sufi orders of the Malay world. Furthermore, in Islam, intellectual life has frequently been cultivated within the bosom of spiritual realization. In this essay, we will attempt to present a brief survey of the major spiritual and intellectual currents in Malay Sufism as they have shaped and influenced the lives and thoughts of the Malays over the centuries.

Sufi Orders in the Malay World: Their Role and Influence

Because of the lack of historical evidence, the origins and early development of Sufi orders in the Malay archipelago is still problematic. The Sufi order that appears to have been explicitly mentioned for the first time in any of the early writings currently at our disposal is the Qādiriyyah. Ḥamzah al-Fanṣūrī, the famous Malay Sufi poet who lived and flourished most probably in the period preceding and during the reign of Sultan 'Alā' al-Dīn Ri'āyat Shāh of Acheh (997/1589–1013/1604), reveals in one of his *sha'irs* (Arabic *shi'r*, "poetry") that he belonged to the Qādirī Order. He was formally initiated into that order during his stay in Baghdad, where he also received from the shaykh of the Qādirīs his *ijāzah,* that is, the authority to teach and initiate others into the order.

We must, however, consider the strong possibility that some Sufi orders were introduced into the Malay world well before Ḥamzah al-Fanṣūrī's time, perhaps as early as the second half of the ninth/fifteenth century. This possibility is based on several considerations. We know that by this time teachers of Sufism—the *makhdūms*—had attained influential positions and their disciples now included Sultan Maḥmūd Shāh of Malacca. By this time also, all the principal Sufi orders had been founded, and it is generally the case that discipleship in the mystical path is effected through one of these orders. Furthermore, there were close religious contacts between Malacca and Pasai and the rest of the Islamic world, particularly India, Persia, and the Arabian peninsula. The Chishtī Order, which exists in the Malay world, had spread to the whole of the Indian subcontinent by the time its famous saint Muḥammad Gīsūdarāz (d. 825/1422), wrote his *Mir'āj al-'āshiqīn* (*The Ascent of Lovers*) and commented on Ibn 'Arabī's *Fuṣūṣ al-ḥikam* (*Bezels of Wisdom*) and 'Abd al-Qāhir Abū Najīb al-Suhrawardī's *Ādāb al-murīdīn* (*Manners of the Adepts.*). Then there was voluminous trade with Mamlūk Egypt, which, after the fall of Baghdad, became a center for Sufi orders such as the Shādhiliyyah, which became one of the popular orders in the Malay world. This question calls for a more definitive study. It should be added that most of the Sufi orders that spread among the Malays were introduced directly from Mecca after the tenth/sixteenth century.

Among the numerous Sufi orders to have appeared in the archipelago in addition to the Qādiriyyah, Chishtiyyah, and Shādhiliyyah are the Rifā'iyyah, Naqshbandiyyah, Shaṭṭāriyyah and Aḥmadiyyah. The most popular and widespread of these are the Qādiriyyah, Naqshbandiyyah, and Aḥmadiyyah. It is not possible to discuss here in detail all the different rituals and spiritual activities conducted by each of these orders or to discuss their various distinguishing features. We can do no more than provide a few illustrative examples of the kind of role and influence which Malay Sufi orders have enjoyed throughout the centuries of their existence.

The Practices of the Rifā'iyyah Order

The Rifā'ī Order became widespread in the archipelago, particularly in Sumatra and the Malay peninsula, probably through the teachings and efforts of its most famous representative, Nūr al-Dīn ibn ʿAlī ibn Ḥasanjī ibn Muḥammad Ḥamīd al-Rānīrī (d. 1076/1666), who arrived in Acheh in 1047/1637 or even earlier. The famous Shaykh Yūsuf of Macassar also belonged to this order and is said to have studied under al-Rānīrī. One of the most distinctive rituals practiced by this order is what is commonly known in the Malay world as the *dabbūs* ceremony, which the Achehnese in Sumatra sometimes also call the *rapaʿi* performance. It is not known, however, when exactly this ceremony was first introduced to the Malay world. The word *dabbūs* in Arabic means an iron awl. The ceremony is thus named because an iron awl serves as the chief instrument for the infliction of wounds upon the body as part of the ceremony itself, although swords, knives, and sometimes fire are also used. The word *rapaʿi* no doubt derives from the name of the founder of the order, Aḥmad al-Rifāʿī (d. 467/1175), who is believed to have originated these practices while experiencing a state of ecstasy.

Rapaʿi is also the name given to the instrument (tambourine) used to provide the accompanying music to the ceremony. The act of inflicting wounds upon the body is said to demonstrate the power of God and the *karāmāt* of the master of the order, which allow the adept to come out of the ceremony without his body showing any evidence of having been harmed. But the famous Persian Sufi poet, ʿAbd al-Raḥmān Jāmī (d. 898/1492), denied that such practices and a host of other strange performances attributed to the Rifāʿiyyah dervishes, such as eating live snakes, sitting in heated ovens, and riding lions, originated with al-Rifāʿī. "But this is something the Shaykh did not know, nor did his pious companions—we seek refuge from Satan with God!" exclaims Jāmī when speaking of these "aberrations."[12] There is the claim that these practices were introduced into the Rifāʿiyyah after the Mongol invasion.[13]

Whatever the true origin of the *dabbūs* or *rapaʿi* ceremony may be, for the members of the Rifāʿiyyah Order and its admirers in Sumatra, it is linked directly to Aḥmad al-Rifāʿī himself, who is held in high repute in this island. By giving public exhibitions of this mysterious ceremony, the order was able to attract a considerable following, especially among the young. That such public performances were not only possible but widespread indicates the kind of spiritual and religious climate prevailing in the Malay world at the time when Sufism held sway over the spiritual lives of the people. It was not until the rise of exoteric "orthodoxy" and the modernist movement in the late thirteenth/nineteenth century or the beginning of this century that such practices began to disappear—at least from the public scene, though by no means completely. The *dabbūs* ceremony still survives in certain parts of the archipelago, particularly in Sumatra and

Malacca, where it is performed from time to time by members of the Rifāʿiyyah.

The following account of the *dabbūs* or *rapaʿi* ceremony is by R. L. Archer. The description was related to him, so he claims, by members of the Rifāʿiyyah in Padang on the west coast of Sumatra:

> The *dabbūs* performance must be held under the leadership of a true *khalīfah*, i.e., a spiritual successor of the Founder of the Order, in whose name the ceremony is performed; this leader must also have a license from his *guru* (teacher) authorizing him to conduct these otherwise dangerous exercises.
>
> A person who desires to receive instruction in this exercise must bring as a present a bolt of white cloth, three needles and a certain amount of money. These pupils are made up mostly of young men, eighteen to twenty years of age. The instruction is given in a lonely place to which people seldom come. It is necessary that the pupil and the teacher be not disturbed. During the days of training the pupil neither eats nor drinks until he has attained his objective. Some of them hold out as long as twenty days, but in case they are unable to hold out that long, the *khalīfah* orders them to return home. Those who are able to hold out till the completion of the ceremony are regarded as the true pupils of the *khalīfah*'s *dabbūs* and are then prepared to go with him from place to place giving public exhibitions of this mysterious ceremony.
>
> The *dabbūs* exhibition is usually given in the evening after seven o'clock. The *khalīfah* and his pupils gather in a public place and after receiving and returning their respectful salutations they offer praise to their Lord and Muhammad and to the patron saint of their Order, while at the same time they beat loudly on a drum to attract the attention of the people. The recitation of praise prescribed by the master of the Order is supposed to excite holy visions in the minds of the brethren who are favored by Allah's grace; some will see a vision of the founder of the Order, others will by degrees attain to the ecstatic condition to which is attached the quality of invulnerability. Then by turning their weapons upon their own bodies they demonstrate to the witnesses the power of Allah and the excellence of the master of their Order. . . .
>
> The conclusion of the ceremony is a prayer of thanksgiving to Allah for bringing them safely through the exercise. Then a cloth is spread on the ground on which the spectators are invited to throw any gifts of money which they may wish to give as alms. This the *khalīfah* takes as his pay.[14]

It would be wrong to conclude from the above description by Archer that miracles constitute the primary goal of the Rifāʿīs' spiritual activities or that they are determined by purely worldly considerations. From their point of view, as is true also of the other Sufi orders, the real purpose of embarking on the mystical path is to realize an authentic spiritual life at the highest level possible through receiving proper instructions and guidance on methods of invocation (*dhikr*) and meditation (*fikr*) as well as the correct understanding of Islamic doctrines as interpreted by the Sufis. Miracles are viewed as an aspect of God's spiritual gifts to those few whom He favors. They are of secondary importance to the Sufi orders although their positive aspects are duly recognized. This is best illustrated by the fact that in the Sufi orders in the Malay world the prestige and popularity of a particular shaykh before his disciples is never determined primarily by the miracles he is believed to have performed, but by his charisma, the depth of his learning, and the efficacy of his teachings as experienced by the disciples and followers who will propagate them to others.

The positive aspects of miracles associated with the various Sufi orders can be seen in specific historical instances in the past. One such instance is in the spread of Islam in the Malay archipelago itself, which we have mentioned earlier in this article. However, it cannot be denied that there have been many who have joined the various Sufi orders with the hope of possessing some miraculous powers. It is equally true that during the period of spiritual decadence groups and individuals arose in the name of Sufism or mystical teachings, either as offshoots of existing orders and suborders or out of obscurity, and spread false teachings and practices among the Malay people.

General Characteristics of Sufi Practice in the Malay World

Having chosen to discuss an example of a Sufi ritual which has been democratized or popularized by the Malays, as represented by the Rifāʿī Order, we now take a look at some of the general characteristics of the Sufi orders in the Malay world and the scope of spiritual activities that are accessible to anyone who aspires to participate in one of them. The Sufi orders exhibit patterns of authority and general organization similar to what is found elsewhere in the Muslim world. At the beginning of an order, a single shaykh could exercise complete authority over his whole *ṭarīqah* in various parts of the archipelago. An al-Ranīrī or an ʿAbd al-Raʾūf could write and send instructions to his scattered disciples. Today, however, there are many shaykhs in a single order, their leadership being recognized only by members of their respective suborders in particular localities, except in the case of a few whose prestige and popularity have spread to other areas as well. Furthermore, there is no *shaykh al-mashāʾikh* or leader of all the shaykhs. This localization of spiritual authority as invested in the local shaykhs is an indication of both a general decline in the quality of spiritual leadership and a degeneration of organizational discipline.

Another common feature of contemporary Malay Sufi orders is that membership in an order is not exclusive, in the sense that an individual may belong to more than one order at the same time. In reality, however, he is truly attached to only one order. As for the qualification of leadership in a *ṭarīqah,* the emphasis is still, in theory at least, on the possession of deep spiritual insights and sound knowledge in *uṣūl* (principles of religion in general and of Muslim jurisprudence in particular), *fiqh* (jurisprudence) and *taṣawwuf.* In practice, however, it is the element of worship or devotional acts that is emphasized rather than the intellectual element. Thus, quite often the shaykhs are not really very conversant with the doctrines of Sufism, nor are they well versed in the knowledge of *uṣūl* when compared with the earlier Malay Sufis. They have in abundance faith, humility, piety, and sincerity including intellectual honesty. They continue to read, in the presence of their disciples, those texts on Sufi doctrines which they have inherited from the masters of their order before them, but they sincerely acknowledge their failure to rise to the level of intellectual understanding attained by the earlier Malay Sufis. They dare not even discuss some of what they perceive to be the difficult doctrines of Sufism. If they have not inherited the earlier Sufis' understanding of these doctrines, they nonetheless are keeping alive an appreciation of the virtues of possessing such knowledge.

In most of the Sufi orders in the Malay world, the shaykh of an order usually nominates one of his distinguished disciples as a *khalīfah* (representative or vicegerent) to represent him among his disciples or in other places if he is absent because of illness or for some other reason (except death). In the case of a shaykh who has a large following scattered over many distant places, more than one *khalīfah* may be nominated. Only certain powers of the shaykh, however, are invested in his *khalīfah,* who is expected not to introduce any innovations in the teachings of his shaykh. If the *khalīfah* is also to be the successor of his shaykh, then the *ijāzah* to teach and initiate Muslims into his order will be bestowed on him. In those cases in which there is no evident successor at the time of the shaykh's death, the common practice is for the disciples to accept as their new shaykh the person among them who is clearly seen as the shaykh's favorite disciple. The principle of election in finding a successor is no doubt upheld in most of the Sufi orders, but only very rarely is it put into operation, because it is felt that the need for it does not arise.

Traditionally, many shaykhs of Sufi orders have wielded considerable influence within the community in various ways. Especially during the period of Sufi predominance in the eleventh/seventeenth and twelfth/eighteenth centuries, they were at once spiritual leaders and guides for their respective orders, religious and temporal advisers at the royal courts, religious teachers and *imāms* (heads of congregational prayers) in their local communities, and—perhaps even more important from the point of view of the traditional folk—they were medicine men who could cure all kinds of diseases, including psychological ones. Shams al-Dīn al-Sumatrānī, al-Rānīrī, and 'Abd al-Ra'ūf, whose lives and activities span a continuous period of perhaps more than a century, were no doubt the representatives *par excellence* of this category of Sufis. When Sir James Lancaster presented himself at the court of Sultan 'Alā' al-Dīn Ri'āyat Shāh in 1010/1602 to negotiate a treaty of peace and friendship between England and Acheh, his counterpart in that negotiation was al-Sumatrānī, the sultan's spiritual master and the shaykh al-islām of the kingdom, who was described by Lancaster as "the chiefe bishope of the realme."[15] Al-Rānīrī appears to have been an influential court *qāḍī* and so was 'Abd al-Ra'ūf after him. When the news of the conversion to Islam of the people of Kedah in the Malay peninsula reached Acheh at the beginning of the eleventh/seventeenth century, it was Shaykh Nūr al-Dīn, a Sufi teacher from Mecca, who was instructed by the sultan of Acheh to send religious books to Kedah "in order that the faith of Islam may be firmly established and the people fully instructed in their duties and in the rites of the faith."[16]

This general tendency for the earlier Sufi shaykhs to play multiple roles of an influential nature in the life of the community has survived to this day, though it is now visible mainly at the village level, where it is by no means uncommon to find the local shaykh being the most respected and influential figure by virtue of the fact that he caters to his people's spiritual needs, is their *imām* in the prayers, and is also their medicine man. In Indonesia, some of the Sufi orders have taken part in politics and occasionally have tended to become militant. In Sumatra, for example, the Naqshbandīs established a political party known as *Partai Politik Ṭarīqat Islām* (The *Ṭarīqah* of Islam Political Party).

We have also instances when the ruler himself became the *murshid* (spiritual guide) of a Sufi order. This was the case with Engku Ḥājjī Muda Rāja 'Abd Allāh (d. 1274/1858), the ruler of the Malay kingdom of Riau, who was a *murshid* of the Naqshbandī Order and was most instrumental in spreading the order in the Riau region. Many princes of Riau became members of this order and for a time in the history of Riau kingship both spiritual and temporal leadership became united in a single figure. When Rāja 'Abd Allāh died, his nephew Rāja Muḥammad Yūsuf succeeded him as both the ruler of Riau and the *murshid* of the Naqshbandiyyah in the kingdom. Rāja Muḥammad Yūsuf is known to have been a great patron of learning besides being a pious and learned man. He is said to have founded a library at Penyengat Island, which has in its collection, among others, books on Islamic mysticism, philosophy, and science, including Ibn Sīnā's famous *Qānūn*.

Initiation

The first step toward the full realization of spiritual life through participation in the *ṭarīqah* is the pre-initiation spiritual training, which is generally quite severe. The seeker has to undergo certain trials, which are meant to test his capacity for endurance and submission to the shaykh. The training includes strict observance of the obligatory duties prescribed by the *Sharī'ah* as well as fulfilling faithfully other religious duties as may be exacted by the shaykh. These may include periodic retirements to solitude (Arabic *khalwah;* Malay *berkhalwat*), when one is required to meditate upon God and remember Him constantly by reciting His Name repeatedly in the heart, mind, or audibly (*dhikr*), and the suppression of one's carnal desires through fasting. It is only after a period of such training, which varies from one trainee to another depending upon his performance and progress, that the seeker is initiated into the order of his shaykh. This formal initiation ceremony is called the giving of the *bay'ah* (oath of allegiance), which attaches the *murīd* (disciple) to the shaykh and his spiritual chain and is usually held at the completion of a two-*rak'ah* supererogatory prayer, which is performed just after an obligatory prayer.

The ceremony is held either in a congregation in the presence of other disciples or in the presence of the shaykh alone. With this *bay'ah* begins a new phase in the spiritual life of the disciple. He has to perform new duties and obligations which will be added from time to time, and his progress on the spiritual path is observed by the shaykh. In both the Qādirī and Naqshbandī orders, for example, just before the disciple recites the oath of allegiance after the shaykh, the shaykh enumerates the spiritual practices that the disciple must continuously perform and also describes the methods and techniques of their implementation.

Invocations and Litanies

In some orders, alphabetical symbolism plays a role in influencing the quantitative aspect of some of the spiritual practices prescribed by the shaykh for his disciples. Malay Sufis, like their counterparts elsewhere in the Islamic world, attach mystical significance to the Arabic alphabet, each letter of which is known to possess a specific numerical value.

One example of the application to this alphabetical symbolism to spiritual practices is the choice of one of the ninety-nine Names of God, on which a disciple is required to concentrate and meditate in his *wird* (pl. *awrād*, "litany"). Certain calculations are made with regard to the numerical values of the letters contained in the disciple's name and that of his mother, in order to assign to him the Name of God most suitable for the *wird.* For example, if the disciple's name is 'Alī (' *l y*), the total numerical value of the name is 110 ('=70; *l*=30; *y*=10). If his mother's name is Maryam (*m r y m*), its total numerical value is 290 (*m*=40; *r*=200; *y*=10). The total of the two names, 400, is then divided by the number of months in a year; the result is 33 with a remainder of 4. The remainder, 4, is the key to the Name to be chosen for the disciple's *wird.* The fourth Name of God is *al-Malik* (the King). Another example is to be found in the practice of the Qādirī Order, in which the disciple invokes sixty-six times the Name *Allāh,* the figure being the total numerical value of the letters in the word *Allāh* (*A*=1; *l*=30; *h*=5).

Congregational Rites and the Rātib *Ceremony*

In addition to the *dhikr* and *wird* which a disciple performs individually, there are various congregational rites and ceremonies that are held periodically by Malay Sufi orders. The weekly *dhikr* in an assembly is held either in the house of the shaykh or in a convenient mosque or *surau* on Thursday or Friday nights after the prayers.[17] One of the most widely known of these weekly *dhikrs* in the Malay world is that of the Naqshbandiyyah, called the *khattam tawajjuh,* which is performed on Friday after the *'aṣr* (mid-afternoon), the *'ishā'* (night) and the *ṣubḥ* (dawn) prayers. There is also the monthly assembly, usually held at the house of the shaykh, where the *dhikr* peculiar to the order is performed. In this weekly or monthly assembly, the *dhikrs* are sometimes performed to the accompaniment of music, particularly by the Rifā'ī and Shādhilī orders. Also periodically performed are the *rātibs* (Arabic pl. *rawātib*), which are akin to *dhikrs* but into which are incorporated certain forms of poetry known as the *qaṣīdah* (ode) and the *nashīd* (songs of divine love).

There are many types of *rātibs,* each of which traces its origin to a particular *walī* after whom it is usually named. One of the most popular *rātibs* known to have been practiced in the Malay archipelago, especially in the Sumatra of the twelfth/eighteenth century, is the *Rātib Sammān* originated by Shaykh Muḥammad ibn 'Abd al-Karīm al-Sammānī al-Ma'ānī of Medina between the years 1112/1700 and 1163/1750. Shaykh al-Sammānī is said in various sources, both Malay and Arabic, to have belonged to the Shaṭṭāriyyah, the Khalwatiyyah, and the Qādiriyyah. This *rātib,* which still survives in certain parts of the archipelago, is usually performed publicly on such occasions as religious feasts, the fulfillment of vows, and when certain misfortunes like famine and epidemics threaten the community.

The whole ceremony of *Rātib Sammān* usually lasts six or seven hours. The leader of the ceremony and his assistants must be members of a *ṭarīqah* who have been initiated into the art of performing and conducting the *rātib*. As for the rest of the performers, many of them are not members of any particular *ṭarīqah* but are from the audience. They join in at a particular moment of the ceremony to form a circle of devotees around the leader and his companions, chanting the *dhikr* as well as exhibiting various bodily postures and movements in the manner demonstrated by the leader. Without going into detail about this ceremony, we will point out some of its salient features.[18] The *rātib* proper is divided into four parts and is preceded by the offering of salutations and blessings to the Prophet, his Household, and his Companions, and also to ʿAbd al-Qādir al-Jīlānī (d. 561/1166), the founder of the order, and to the celebrated Junayd al-Baghdādī (d. 297/910). Immediately following this offering of salutations and blessings is the chanting of the *dhikr, Lā ilāha ill' Llāh* ("There is no god but God") in six different variations in both tone of voice and tempo. The first three variations are performed in the sitting position and are thus called *rātib duduk* (sitting *rātib*). The other set of variations is performed in the standing position with the stamping of the feet as the body sways from side to side and is thus called *rātib berdiri* (standing *rātib*). With the seventh *dhikr* begins the first part of the *rātib* proper. It is the chanting of Ahum! Ahhhum! . . . Ahum! Ahhhum! . . . accompanied by dancing in a circle, and this first part ends at the tenth *dhikr,* namely, the chanting of Ahil! Ahhhil! . . . Ahil! Ahhhil! . . . . The last *dhikr* in the ceremony is the twenty-third, which by itself constitutes the fourth part of the *rātib*. It is the chanting of ʿAm! Ah! ʿAm! . . . ʿAm! Ah! ʿAm! . . . .

Each of the four parts of the *rātib* thus consists of a set of different kinds of *dhikrs* that are chanted in distinct tones of voice and tempo. Between each *dhikr* of the *rātib* proper as well as of the preceding *rātib duduk* and *rātib berdiri,* the *qaṣīdah* and the *nashīd* are sung by the leader and his companions and by them alone. The *Rātib Sammān* is well known for its dynamism. During the whole performance, the leader and his companions are in constant motion, singing and dancing in peculiar rhythmic movements in the center of the rotating circle of dancing devotees. At the climax of the ceremony, many of the devotees fall into a trance or an ecstasy but are soon revived by the leader and his companions for a short intermission, when the performers are served food and refreshment prepared for the occasion.

In its formal aspect, the ceremony appears to have lost little of its originality through the few centuries of its existence in the Malay world. All the *qaṣīdahs* and the *nashīds* are still sung in the original Arabic except for the last two lines of a verse sung during the chanting of the fifteenth *dhikr,* for which Malay verses are substituted. These two lines exalt and glorify Ḥasan and Ḥusayn, the grandsons of the Prophet, for their martyrdom on the path of God. However, the original meanings embodied in the verses of these *qaṣīdahs* and *nashīds,* which deal mainly with questions of mystical love, have certainly been lost.

In the Malay peninsula, the most well-known *rātibs* are those of the ʻAlawī Order, such as the *rātibs* of al-Ḥaddād, al-ʻAṭṭās and al-ʻIdrūs, and also the *rātib* of Shaykh ʻAbd al-Qādir al-Jīlānī. All these *rātibs* can be performed individually as well as collectively and the performance is open to all Muslims. Earlier in this essay, we referred to the fact that some religious practices of Sufism gradually became assimilated into the common culture of the people. These are *dhikrs* and *rātibs,* which, having gradually become emptied of their spiritual elements, became transformed into games and pastimes of great popularity among the people of the archipelago. Some interesting examples are the *Rātib Sadāti* in Sumatra and the *Dikir Barat* in the Malay peninsula. Similarly, we find today several Malay dances, such as the *hadra* (Arabic *ḥaḍrah,* "presence") and the *gabih,* and important elements of Malay music, particularly the *qaṣīdah* and the *nashīd,* all of which trace their origin to the *samāʻ* (spiritual concert) and *rātibs* of Sufism but are now completely devoid of their original spiritual content and bear no connection with Sufism, save their names and a few formalities. Some of the present-day *qaṣīdahs* and *nashīds* do, however, deal with religious themes, but the message embodied in them pertains mainly to the questions of a Muslim's religious and moral duties and responsibilities and occasionally also to the exemplary lives of the Prophet and his Companions and other great heroes of Islam.

There are other congregational rites in the life of the Malay Sufis through which the general members of the community are endeared to the religious practices of Sufism. One of these is the *ḥōl,* the annual ceremony of the original founder of the order, which for each order occurs at a different time of the year. Many members of that order, from far and near, will congregate at a certain prearranged place of meeting, usually the place where the shaykh lives. The main occasion of the day is the narration of the *manāqib* (excellencies) of the founder of the order. Religious exercises in the form of *dhikrs* and *rātibs,* sometimes with music and dancing of a religious nature, are also performed. The whole ceremony, which includes a special feast, may last for more than one day.

The Impact of Sufi Practices upon the Culture of the Malays

There is no doubt that the Sufi orders have exercised an immense influence on the religious and spiritual lives of the Malay peoples to this day and that Sufism has been a great unifying force. The shaykhs and their orders, by their rites and ceremonies, their traditional and religious feasts, have lifted men above themselves and have tightened the bonds of unity within and between communities. Their *rātibs* and *dhikrs* and religious dances serve not only as outlets for all kinds of emotions but also as integrating factors that unite the participating groups. Generally speaking, the peaceful and nonmilitant character of Malay Sufi orders has influenced the outlook of the Malays with regard to their system of political and social order. Except for one or two incidents, the Malays have never been known to exhibit religious militarism.

In emphasizing the generally positive influence of the Sufi orders, we in no way wish to deny the manifestations of various types of vulgar mysticism brought about by misinterpretations of Sufism and its religious practices. There have also been abuses of Sufism in a variety of ways. But in a society where Sufism flourishes, such negative manifestations are inevitable. In Java, where more excesses have been committed in the name of mysticism than anywhere else in the archipelago and where greater tensions are known to have existed between mysticism and exoteric religious authorities, culminating in such incidents as the execution of Siti Djenar and Sunan Panggung and the condemnation of Shaykh Tjebolek, there are other spiritual manifestations emanating not from Sufism but from the "native source." This is the ancient pre-Islamic and even pre-Hindu and pre-Buddhist Javanese mysticism, of which the core is the concepts of the essential oneness of all existence and the servant's mystical union with the Divine, expressed in Javanese as *manunggal kawula-Gusti*.

When Sufism came to Java, it was able to absorb into its spiritual and intellectual universe the larger part of the Javanese mystical elements, for these were completely in conformity with the teachings contained in the esoteric dimension of Islam. But another segment of the "native" mysticism remained outside Sufism, for even though the majority of its adherents identify themselves with the exoteric or legalistic aspects of Islam, they continue to remain faithful to such ancient views as the incarnation (Arabic *ḥulūl*) of God in the human ego. In its encounter with Sufism, this segment of Javanese mysticism could not help absorbing certain elements of Sufi spirituality. But with the decline of Sufism, it is this segment that has reasserted itself before exoteric Islamic orthodoxy in contemporary Indonesia and manifests itself in what is popularly known as *aliran kebatinan* (mystical sects).[19] Among the most prominent of these *alirans* (sects) are the *Pagujuban Ngesti Tunggal,* which is better known by its abbreviation, *Pangestu,* and which is also known to have an intellectual bent, and the *Susila Budi Dharma* (abbreviated as *Subud*), which is the most internationally known, having disciples scattered all over the world, particularly in Europe.

Famous Malay Sufis, Their Works, and Their Intellectual Influence

Malay intellectual history began with the Islamization of the Malays' world view, which, as mentioned above, was mainly effected by the Sufis. The dominant tendency in the pre-Islamic Malay world view was to underline the aesthetic rather than the intellectual elements of religion.[20] Thus, in spite of centuries of Indian-Hindu influence, there had been no known Javanese translation of the Upanishads or even full expository translations of the Hindu doctrines according to the Vedānta. What was chosen to be translated, first into Javanese and then from Javanese into Malay, was the portions of the *Mahābhārata* and *Bhagavadgītā* that are epical, romantic, or mythological in character. It was these translations that served as the main source for the popular understanding of Hinduism. Whatever few intellectual writings existed, such as Prapanca's most famous work, the *Nāgara Kertāgama,* were criticized by the religious establishment and relegated to the periphery of Javanese civilization. Similarly, from the fourth/tenth century to the fifth/eleventh, Sumatra was a great center of Buddhism and Buddhist philosophy, but again there are no known translations of works of Buddhist theology and philosophy in Malay. The Javanese-Malay genius that was given the fullest freedom of expression was the artistic, as symbolized by the Borobudur, the Chandi Mendut and the Chandi Sewu complexes in Java. When the Sufis came to the archipelago, they understood full well this native genius and exploited it for Islam, even while they were as passionate in introducing the rational and intellectual spirit of Islam in true harmony with Islam's own vocation as a way of knowledge.

By the tenth/sixteenth century, both Malay and Javanese—and particularly the former—emerged through the writings of the Sufis as languages well able to serve as literary vehicles for religious, philosophical, metaphysical, and mystical discourse. In the same manner that Turkish was transformed by the mystical poet, Yūnus Emre (d. 721/1321), into a delightful literary idiom, the Malay language became highly developed as a medium for philosophical and metaphysical concepts and ideas at the hands of the already mentioned al-Fanṣūrī, the greatest intellectual representative of the Malays. This Ibn 'Arabī of the Malay world was the first to set down in Malay all the fundamental aspects of Sufi doctrine. He was also the first to produce systematic speculative writing in Malay. Before al-Fanṣūrī, we know of the existence of no comparable work in the field of Malay literature in general. The early mystical works known to the Malays, such as the *Durr al-manẓūm* mentioned in the *Sejarah Melayu*, and *al-Sayf al-qāṭi'* (*The Sharp Sword*) mentioned in the *Bustān al-salāṭīn* (*The Garden of Kings*) of al-Rānīrī, were not written in the Malay language. Al-Fanṣūrī himself confirmed the view that before him all known works on Sufism were written in Arabic and Persian, for he says in his first book, the *Sharāb al-'āshiqīn* (*The Drink of Lovers*), that he had written it in Malay so that those who did not understand Arabic and Persian might be able to discourse on the subject. Most likely, the *Sharāb* was the earliest book on Sufism in Malay.

As for Sufi writings in Javanese, several scholars have attributed a work to Sunan Bonang, who is said to have lived in Tuban in the northeast of Java about 880/1475–906/1500.[21] The work is entitled *Wirasanin uṣūl sulūk* (*Treatise on The Principles of the Mystical Path*), and it claims to have drawn much of its materials from al-Ghazzālī's *Iḥyā' 'ulūm al-dīn* (*Revivification of the Religious Sciences*). It deals mainly with Sufi ethics and practical issues pertaining to the Path; therefore, it differs significantly from al-Fanṣūrī's writings, which deal mainly with Sufi metaphysics.

Ḥamzah al-Fanṣūrī

Al-Fanṣūrī's writings, which include his three prose works, the *Asrār al-'ārifīn* (*The Secrets of the Gnostics*), the *Sharāb*, and the *Muntahī* (*The Adept*), and his various *sha'irs*, are highly significant in many respects. First of all, from the point of view of Malay literature, he introduced new forms of poetry into the Malay language, namely, the *rubā'ī* and the *sha'ir*.[22] Second, through his coinage of new technical terms and concepts in the Malay language, he enabled that language to be fully equipped to deal with the most profound philosophical and metaphysical doctrines which had been formulated by the classical Sufis. He may not have originated new formulations, but to have been able to expound these doctrines for the first time in the Malay language is significant enough for later Malay intellectuality. This, no doubt, was made possible by al-Fanṣūrī's mastery of the Arabic and Persian languages, as well as his total grasp of Sufi doctrine.

The Sufi who exercised the greatest influence on the intellectual life of al-Fanṣūrī is clearly Muḥyī al-Dīn ibn 'Arabī. But al-Fanṣūrī's writings also reveal his intimate knowledge of the ideas of such Sufis as al-Jīlī (d. 832/1428), al-Basṭāmī (d. 260/874), al-Ḥallāj (d. 310/922), ʿAṭṭār (d. 618/1221), Rūmī (d. 672/1273), Shabistarī (d. 720/1320), Jāmī (d. 898/1492) and many others, including lesser-known Sufis, all of whom he quoted. His writings also reveal much of the religious, spiritual, and intellectual climate in the Malay world of his day. It was a climate in which the representatives of the *Sharīʿah*—the exoteric *ʿulamāʾ*—were actively combating, by means of authoritative writing and polemics as well as administrative measures through the religious authority of the judges (Arabic sg. *qāḍī*), all forms of mysticism that were held in suspicion, for this was the period when pseudo-Sufism made its presence very much felt in the community. Al-Fanṣūrī's writings indicate clearly that he was as much opposed to the activities and ideas of the pseudo-mystics as to the treatment meted out against them by the jurists. He also attacked those jurists who had been interpreting Sufism without having profound knowledge of it, and well-known books on jurisprudence (*fiqh*) such as the *Kitāb maḥallī* and the *Kitāb muḥarrar* became targets of his criticisms.

A good example of the jurists' indulgence in metaphysical discussions beyond their competence was a debate on the nature of the fixed essences or immutable entities (*al-aʿyān al-thābitah*) in Acheh between two pundits who arrived from Mecca in 990/1582, Abu'l-Khayr ibn al-Ḥajar, the author of the above-mentioned *al-Sayf al-qāṭiʿ*, and Muḥammad al-Yamanī. The stage was thus set for an authentic exposition of Sufi doctrines in Malay, and al-Fanṣūrī stepped in to do just that. He remained unsurpassed in the knowledge of these doctrines and he founded the *wujūdiyyah* school, which has generated an endless intellectual debate among the Malays and still survives today in a few traditional circles.

The central doctrine of the *wujūdiyyah* school is that of *waḥdat al-wujūd* (transcendent unity of being). Al-Fanṣūrī's treatment of this doctrine is nothing more than an admirably rendered Malay reproduction and exposition of the teachings of Ibn ʿArabī. In his writings, al-Fanṣūrī employs many analogies to describe the concept of the transcendent unity of being. But his favorite analogy is that of the fathomless ocean and the waves, because it alone conveys not only the sense of transcendence (*tanzīh*) and immanence (*tashbīh*) but also a synthesis of both. Furthermore, it alone evokes a picture that is not static, but dynamic in maintaining that God's Being and the being of the Universe are one and the same essentially like waves and the water of the ocean. Al-Fanṣūrī means *essential* identification as opposed to *substantial* identity and continuity. Thus he writes in the *Muntahī*, quoting a famous Arabic poem by the *Fuṣūṣ* commentator al-Jandī (d. *ca.* 700/1300):

The sea is the sea, as it was before,
The "new" are waves and rivers;
Let not the forms that resemble them veil thee,
From Him who takes shape within them, for they
  are curtains.
But the waves exist together with the eternal sea.
As the hemistich says:
  The sea is eternal: when it heaves
  One speaks of "waves," but in reality they are the sea,
for sea and waves are one. As God Most Exalted says:
"God embraces everything" (Quran, XLI, 54).

Al-Fanṣūrī's key phrase in the above description is *pada ḥaqīqatnya* ("in reality, essentially"). Other doctrines discussed by al-Fanṣūrī in his various writings include that of the ontological "descents" of the Absolute, the scheme of which follows closely that of Ibn 'Arabī and Jīlī; the doctrine of creative emanation, which he says is not opposed to the theological idea of the *creatio ex nihilo* but in fact explains its meaning; the relation between the Divine Qualities and the Divine Essence; the doctrine of the Universal Man (*al-insān al-kāmil*), and the concept of *fanā'* (extinction) and its relation to *ma'rifah* (gnosis) and *ikhtiyār* (freedom).

Al-Sumatrānī

After al-Fanṣūrī, these doctrines were further elaborated and debated by many Malay Sufis and theologians, the most famous being al-Sumatrānī, al-Rānīrī, and 'Abd al-Ra'ūf. All three lived in the eleventh/seventeenth century, which was the most prolific period of Malay writings on Sufism and theology. Al-Sumatrānī (d. 1039/1630), whose works and teachings were first made known to the outside world by several Dutch scholars,[23] is no doubt the greatest exponent of the *wujūdiyyah* school after al-Fanṣūrī. It appears that both al-Fanṣūrī and al-Sumatrānī enjoyed the protection and patronage of their respective sultans in carrying out their intellectual activities in the face of strong opposition from the exoteric *'ulamā'*. There is a poem which al-Fanṣūrī composed either under the order of the then sultan, 'Alā' al-Dīn Ri'āyat Shāh, or as his own dedication to the sultan. In this poem, al-Fanṣūrī describes his patron, who was known also by the titles Shah 'Ālam and Sayyid al-Mukammal, as the saintly king. A stanza reads:

Shah 'Ālam the just king,
The Pole whose perfection is complete;
The saint of God who is eminently united with God,
The gnostic king, the most excellent.[24]

We have previously mentioned that al-Sumatrānī was the *shaykh al-islām* of the kingdom of Acheh and also the spiritual master of the then sultan, Iskandar Muda. When the shaykh died, his disciples remained in the sultan's favor and continued to control the spiritual life in Acheh, which meant that the climate was rather unhealthy for an exponent of legalistic Islam. For this reason, al-Rānīrī, the greatest and most famous critic of the *wujūdiyyah* of al-Fanṣūrī and al-Sumatrānī, chose not to criticize them openly until 1045/1636, when the sultan was succeeded by Iskandar Thānī, a man of a different spiritual temperament.

Al-Rānīrī

Al-Rānīrī (d. 1076/1666), of Malay-Indian blood, was a thinker of considerable worth and a prolific writer of famous books and treatises.[25] His most well-known works are the *Ḥujjat al-ṣiddīq li daf' al-zindīq* (*Proofs of the Truthful in Refuting the Heretics*), the *Bustān al-salāṭīn* (*Garden of Kings*), and the *Tibyān fī ma'rifat al-adyān* (*An Exposition of the Understanding of Religions*). A major portion of his works is, however, devoted to refuting al-Fanṣūrī and al-Sumatrānī, whom he branded as heretics and whose writings he considers to be replete with "pantheistic" tendencies. As a consequence of al-Rānīrī's destructive attacks against the *wujūdiyyah*, most of the works of al-Fanṣūrī and al-Sumatrānī were thrown to the flames by their opponents.

Al-Rānīrī's main accusations against al-Fanṣūrī in particular may be summarized as follows: (1) that al-Fanṣūrī's belief is "pantheistic" in the sense that God's essence is completely immanent in the world; (2) that, like the philosophers, al-Fanṣūrī believes that the world is eternal, the Quran is created and God is Simple Being. In his detailed study of al-Rānīrī's refutations, al-Attas clearly shows that none of the above accusations has any validity.[26] Considering the fact that the original works of al-Fanṣūrī and al-Sumatrānī were available to al-Rānīrī, al-Attas was led to the conclusion that, apart from bias and personal interest, al-Rānīrī's criticisms arose out of his lack of comprehension of the Sufi doctrines as well as his lack of mastery of the Malay language. This is not to deny, however, that al-Rānīrī was fully justified in his efforts to cleanse the minds of the people of the Malay world from the corrupting influence of the heretical members of the *wujūdiyyah*, who had in fact grown in number during al-Rānīrī's time.

'Abd al-Ra'ūf

The last great Malay intellectual figure of the eleventh/seventeenth century, 'Abd al-Ra'ūf of Singkel (d. 1104/1693), has survived in popular esteem as a saint. Several of his works are no longer extant.[27] A prolific writer, ʿAbd al-Raʾūf was the first Malay mystic to introduce the Shaṭṭārī Order into the Malay archipelago, an order that spread first in Sumatra and then in Java and the Malay peninsula. He is credited with the first complete Malay translation and commentary on the Quran, based on the famous work of al-Bayḍāwī. As regards his mystical views, his writings imply a rejection of the "heresies" of al-Fanṣūrī and al-Sumatrānī, though he has never been found to criticize their views explicitly.

Later Sufi Figures

The profusion of Sufi writings which also saw al-Rānīrī's translation into Malay of al-Taftāzānī's famous *Sharḥ al-ʿaqāʾid al-nasafiyyah* (*A Commentary upon the Creed of al-Nasafī*) and the translation of the popular *Tāj al-salāṭīn* (*The Crown of Kings*) in 1012/1603,[28] began to decline beginning in the twelfth/eighteenth century, although works on Sufism continued to be translated, paraphrased, and summarized right up to the end of the thirteenth/nineteenth century. Among later figures who were also influential in their own times, one can mention ʿAbd al-Ṣamad of Palembang, who translated and commented on parts of al-Ghazzālī's *Iḥyāʾ ʿulūm al-dīn* in a work that became known as *Sayr al-sālikīn* (*Progress of Travelers on the Path*); Shaykh Muḥammad Sammān previously mentioned; Dāʾūd ibn ʿAbd Allāh ibn Idrīs of Patani; and Kemas Fakhr al-Dīn of Palembang. Another significant translation is that of Ibn ʿAṭāʾ Allāh's *Kitāb al-ḥikam* (*Aphorisms*), dated 1252/1836; it is on the basis of this Malay translation that we have the first English translation of this famous book.[29]

For about a century, under the influence of modernism and Sufism's own general decadence, the Malays' intellectual and spiritual heritage bequeathed by the Sufis has survived only in small traditional circles. Of late, there appears to be a revival of interest among various groups, including the modern educated elites. Be that as it may, Sufism remains an integral aspect of Malay religious and cultural life and a source of spirituality to this day.

Notes

1. By the Malay world or the Malay archipelago we mean that whole region which has been the home of people of the Malay racial stock and whose *lingua franca* today and in the past, amid an ocean of innumerable local languages and dialects, is Malay. It embraces the present-day Brunei, Indonesia, Malaysia, Singapore, South Thailand, and the Philippines.

2. See S. M. N. al-Attas, *Preliminary Statement on a General Theory of the Islamization of the Malay-Indonesian Archipelago* (Kuala Lumpur: Dewan Bahasa dan Pustaka, 1969).

3. S. M. N. al-Attas, *The Mysticism of Ḥamzah Fanṣūrī* (Kuala Lumpur: University of Malaya Press, 1970) 191.

4. See T. W. Arnold, *The Preaching of Islam* (Lahore: Ashraf Publication, 1979) 368.

5. F. Hirth and W. W. Rickhill, trans., *Chau Ju-Kua: His Works on the Chinese and Arab Trade in the Twelfth and Thirteenth Centuries, entitled Chu-fan-chï* (St. Petersburg: Imperial Academy of Sciences, 1911) 18.

6. J. C. van Leur, *Indonesian Trade and Society* (The Hague: W. van Hoeve, 1955) 168–69.

7. For Wertheim's views, see *Indonesie* 4/1 (1950) 88–89; Schrieke's view is expounded in his *Indonesian Sociological Studies* (The Hague: W. van Hoeve, 1955–57) vol. 2.

8. A. H. Johns, "Sufism as a Category in Indonesian Literature and History," *Journal of South East Asian History* 2 (1961) 23.

9. C. Snouck Hurgronje, *The Achehnese* (Leiden: Brill, 1906) 9–10.

10. Cesar Adib Majul, "The Muslims in the Philippines: An Historical Perspective," in *The Muslim Filipinos,* ed. P. G. Gowing and R. D. McAwis (Manila: Solidaridad Publishing House, 1974) 3.

11. R. Winstedt, *The Malays: A Cultural History* (London: Routledge & Kegan Paul, 1956) 38.

12. ʿAbd al-Raḥmān Jāmī, *Nafaḥāt al-uns,* quoted by A. Schimmel, *Mystical Dimensions of Islam* (Chapel Hill: University of North Carolina Press, 1975) 248–49.

13. H. A. R. Gibb and J. H. Kramers, eds., *Shorter Encyclopedia of Islam,* 476.

14. R. L. Archer, "Muhammadan Mysticism in Sumatra," *Journal of Malaysian Branch, Royal Asiatic Society* (*JMBRAS*) 15 (1937) 108–9.

15. See S. M. N. al-Attas, "Rānīrī and the Wujūdiyyah of 17th Century Acheh," *Monographs of MBRAS* 3 (1966) 8–9.

16. Arnold, *The Preaching of Islam,* 379.

17. The *surau,* a specially built house for the purpose of performing religious functions and exercises other than the Friday congregational prayer, is an important religious institution especially in the Malay peninsula. In the past in particular, the *surau* often played the role of the *zāwiyahs* of the Sufis in other parts of the Muslim world. For a study of the origin of this institution, see R. A. Kern, "The Origin of the Malay Surau," *JMBRAS* 29/1 (1956) 179–81.

18. For a detailed description, see S. M. N. al-Attas, *Some Aspects of Sufism as Understood and Practiced among the Malays* (Singapore: Malaysian Sociological Research Institute Ltd., 1963) chap. 7.

19. See N. Mulder, *Mysticism and Everyday Life in Contemporary Java* (Singapore: Singapore University Press, 1978).

20. This is the conclusion reached by such respected scholars as Sutan Takdir Alisjahbana and Naguib al-Attas. See Alisjahbana, *Values as Integrating Forces in Personality, Society and Culture* (Kuala Lumpur: University of Malaya Press, 1966); idem, *Indonesia's Social and Cultural Revolution* (Kuala Lumpur: Oxford University Press, 1966); and al-Attas, *The Mysticism of Ḥamzah Fanṣūrī,* 187–90.

21. This work has been translated into English by G. W. J. Drewes; see his *The Admonitions of Seh Bari* (The Hague: Koniklijk Instituut, 1969).

22. See S. M. N. al-Attas, *The Origin of the Malay Shaʿir* (Kuala Lumpur: Dewan Bahasa dan Pustaka, 1968); also his *The Mysticism of Ḥamzah Fanṣūrī,* 184.

23. See, e.g., C. A. O. van Nieuwenhuijze, *Shamsu'l-Din van Pasai* (Leiden: Brill, 1954).

24. Al-Attas, *The Mysticism of Ḥamzah Fanṣūrī,* 12.

25. On the life, works, and main teachings of this figure, see, e.g., P. Voorhoeve, *Twee Maleise Geschriften van Nūruddīn ar-Rānīrī* (Uitgaven van de Stichting De Goeje 16; Leiden: Brill, 1955); see also Voorhoeve's list of al-Rānīrī's works in *Bijdragen tot de taal, land- en volkenkunde von Nederlandsch-Indie* 111 (1955) and 115 (1959); al-Attas, "Rānīrī and the Wujūdiyyah of 17th Century Acheh"; R. Winstedt, "A History of Classical Malay Literature," *JMBRAS* 31/3 (1958) 119–21; and especially the major work of al-Attas, *A Commentary on the Ḥujjat al-Ṣiddīq of Nūr al-Dīn al-Rānīrī* (Kuala Lumpur: Ministry of Culture, 1986). This latter work contains a translation and study of al-Rānīrī's major work.

26. Al-Attas, "Rānīrī and the Wujūdiyyah of 17th Century Acheh."

27. On this figure and the spread of the Shaṭṭāriyyah in Java, see D. A. Rinkes, *Abdoerraeof van Singkel* (Heerenveen: Hepkema, 1909).

28. Winstedt believes that this work, which was translated by A. Marre into French in 1878, is of Persian origin, reaching the Malays through an Indian source ("A History of Classical Malay Literature," 114–16). A Malay scholar, Khalid Hussain, has raised the possibility that this work was originally composed in Malay, but his discussion lacks scholarly proofs and argumentations. See his introduction to Bukhayr al-Jawharī, *Tāj al-salāṭīn* (Kuala Lumpur: Dewan Bahasa dan Pustaka, 1966).

29. The translation was made by R. L. Archer; see his "Muhammadan Mysticism in Sumatra," 21–89.

14

Sufism in Africa

ABDUR-RAHMAN IBRAHIM DOI

Sufism and the Spread of Islam in Africa

QUIET HOLY MEN AND TEACHERS had casual contact with parts of Africa long before the final establishment of Islam. The peaceful Muslim missionaries and merchant princes had departed before the final Islamization of these territories and had left gently enough to be forgotten by the inhabitants. Many of the early traders were also self-styled missionaries. Whenever they went on a caravan journey and halted for trade or for rest, they prayed in congregation, an act that greatly influenced the local population. Slowly and gradually, as local Africans became interested, the traders took along with them teachers and holy men, who volunteered to teach Islam to the local people. These holy men and Sufis taught them the tenets of Islam, showed them by their practice the performance of rituals and used their *barakah* (spiritual and mystical power) in settling secular and religious affairs. Some of these early missionaries dedicated their lives to this cause and spent years in foreign lands despite untold hardships. "As participators in a written culture whose mysteries were only available directly to the literate, these sturdy protagonists of Islam came to exercise a remarkable effect in the communities upon which they impinged."[1] They adopted these lands as their homes and often married there and became part of these countries. They offered guidance to the local people in every sort of situation and whenever necessary pointed out the difference between pure Islamic and local syncretic practices.

Islam and Sufi tendencies entered Africa at the same time, and their spread was simultaneous. The Sufis, whether as individual preachers or members of organized *ṭarīqahs,* were the leaders in the task of conversion among the local population and the superficially Islamized tribes. Sir Hamilton Gibb describes later developments:

> The most successful missions were often those of co-nationals of the tribesmen, uncouth, illiterate and crude though many of them were. They laid the foundations upon which in later generations the refining influences of orthodox law and theology could be brought to bear. It was mainly due to them [the Sufi preachers] that through successive centuries the religious frontiers of Islam were steadily extended in Africa, in India and Indonesia, across Central Asia into Turkestan and China, and in parts of South-eastern Europe.[2]

Sufism began its spread rapidly in Africa in the north. It entered the Maghrib through Spain, and by the seventh/thirteenth century, it was spreading rapidly, and Sufi masters had started founding *zāwiyahs.* By the ninth/fifteenth century, Sufi orders came into existence displaying the salient features that have characterized them ever since.[3] After the Sufi *ṭarīqahs* or orders were formed, Sufi *zāwiyahs, tekkes,* and *ribāṭs* were founded by each brotherhood. Such *ribāṭs,* says Trimingham, were fortified frontier posts whose guards were often effective propagators of Islam.[4]

The Sufi Orders

There are a number of Sufi orders or brotherhoods to which the majority of African Muslims are linked. The missionaries were sent out by such orders to spread Islam in non-Muslim areas. The *ribāṭ* or *zāwiyah* included school and offered food and lodging to the wayfarer. "In Africa," says A. S. Tritton, "it was a centre of civilization."[5] Later, the brotherhoods became jealous of one another, and a keen competition started in their spread and propagation of Islam. Those who became the followers of a particular Sufi order gave their affection and veneration to one shaykh or spiritual mentor. These spiritual leaders of the Sufi orders trained small bands of devoted disciples in the study of Islamic scriptures and legal traditions as well as in the methods of praying and devotion. They preached that salvation came through action, holding fast to the moral code of Islam, and enthusiasm for the spread of the religion. All the members of the order were considered equal and had to obey the code of conduct formulated by the spiritual master of the order. The *ṭarīqahs* acted on the Prophetic advice that this world is the sewing field for the next world; one should work hard here to reap the harvest there.

The Sufi orders carried out various reform movements, the main idea of which was to return to the purity and spirituality of Islam as it was in the time of the Prophet. The Sufi orders usually claim a spiritual genealogy going back to the Companions (*ṣaḥābah*) of the Prophet and then to the Prophet himself. This legitimates the claim that a follower of a Sufi order should possess religious virtue above that of ordinary men.

The strict disciplinary and reform movement carried out in a *ribāṭ* can be seen from the activities of an early fifth/eleventh-century *ribāṭ* constructed somewhere on the Atlantic coast of Mauritania.[6] The primary aim was to teach the tenets of Islam to the semi-"pagan" tribesmen, who were converted to a nominal Islam. The leader of the *ribāṭ* was a strict disciplinarian named ʿAbd Allāh ibn Yāsīn, who launched his reform mission among the Berber tribes of the Maghrib—the Goddala, Sanhaja, and Lamtuma—from 430/1038–39 to 450/1058–59. According to Ibn Abī Zarʿ, he launched his movement among people "who did not pray, who did not utter Allah's name and hardly knew the *shahādah*, who were enslaved by ignorance and withdrew from Him to follow their passions."[7] ʿAbd Allāh ibn Yāsīn was soon surrounded in the *ribāṭ* by a large number of people who became his spiritual disciples and then began to preach Islam to the Berbers. This reform movement is known as the Almoravid or al-Murābiṭūn movement (since it began from the *ribāṭ*).

Al-Bakrī has described ʿAbd Allāh's rigorous rules about ritual practices. Lateness in offering prayers was punishable by twenty lashes, omission of the *sajjādah* (prayer carpet) was punishable by five lashes and raising one's voice in the mosque was punishable by as many lashes as the disciplinarians thought fit.[8] ʿAbd Allāh ibn Yāsīn finally lost his life in a *jihād* against the heretic Barghawata sect, whose confused teaching included a new Quran of eighty *sūrahs*, fasting in the month of Rajab instead of Ramaḍān, celebration of ʿĪd al-Aḍḥā on the eleventh of Muḥarram, Thursday as a day of congregational prayer, and not eating eggs, fish, or animal heads.[9]

Sufism of the marabouts characterized Islam in Senegambia very early. It remains an important factor in the religious life of the people even today. The Mauritanian marabouts introduced Islam to many areas south of the Senegal River.[10] Today most West African Muslims are affiliated with one of the major Sufi orders. The spiritual teacher is the marabout and his spiritual disciple is the *talibe* (*ṭālib*), who receives guidance in religious exercises.

There is no need to go into details concerning the spread of the Sufi orders into North Africa and the Maghrib, since this is another subject. Here we will only have space to look at one of the most important recent orders, the Sanūsiyyah. At the end of the chapter, a list is given of many of the African orders, showing the period when they came into existence. We will examine the spread and growth of the orders in East Africa, eastern Sudan, and West Africa in some detail.

In the eastern Sudan, the Sufi influence came mainly from the Hijaz during the Fung period, which began in 906/1500. There are more than twenty different orders of the Sufis in this region, the most prominent among them being the Shādhiliyyah and the Khatmiyyah, which is otherwise known as the Mirghāniyyah *ṭarīqah.* In the Sudan Republic, the Khatmiyyah Order is most prominent, especially among the descendants and the followers of Muḥammad Aḥmad, the Mahdi of the Sudan from 1259/1843 to 1302/1885, although the Mahdi himself was the spiritual master of the Sammāniyyah Order.

In the northeastern Sudan and the Horn of Africa, the most prominent *ṭarīqah* is the Qādiriyyah, which was introduced in Harar in Ethiopia by Sharīf Abū Bakr ibn ʿAbd Allāh al-ʿAydarūs, who died in 915/1255 in Aden. Another very prominent *ṭarīqah* is the Aḥmadiyyah, founded by the most learned reformer of Mecca, Sayyid Aḥmad ibn Idrīs al-Fāsī (1173/1760–1253/1837). The famous Muslim *mujāhid* Shaykh ʿAbdille Ḥassan (Shaykh ʿAbd Allāh Ḥasan), a pious Somali learned man, was an ardent follower of this *ṭarīqah.* It was he who led his *jihād* at the beginning of the present century against Christian colonization and encroachment upon the Muslim Somali lowlands and the antagonism of the Christian people of the highlands of Ethiopia.

The Spread of Sufism in East Africa

The Sufi orders that spread in East Africa are the same as are found in other parts of the Islamic world. The most popular is the Qādirī Order of Shaykh ʿAbd al-Qādir al-Jīlānī, which was introduced into Zanzibar from a place called Barawa on the Somali coast. Sayyid ʿUmar Akullatain (al-Qullatayn) preached it there for the first time. He lies buried in Welezo, which is situated about four miles from Zanzibar. The Qādiriyyah is a prominent order in Lindi.

The other prominent Sufi order in East Africa is the Shādhiliyyah. The Sufi shaykh who devoted himself to spread the teachings of the Shādhilī Order was Sayyid Muḥammad ibn Shaykh, who lived in the Comoro Islands and died in 1338/1920. In Kilwa, the Shādhiliyyah Order is the most prominent.

The Rifāʿiyyah Order has spread on the coast and in Zanzibar. The Rifāʿī practices are extremely difficult; as mentioned in the previous chapters, they include swallowing fire and using sharp instruments to pierce parts of the body. The members of the order use drums and tambourines while reciting the *dhikr* and songs of praise for Allah, the Prophet, and Shaykh Aḥmad al-Rifāʿī.

Similarly, the 'Aydarūsiyyah *ṭarīqah,* founded by Abū Bakr ibn 'Abd Allāh al-'Aydarūs and the Ḥaddādiyyah, founded by 'Abd Allāh ibn 'Alawī ibn Muḥammad ibn Aḥmad al-Ḥaddād (d. 1132/1720), are also followed by some people, especially in Lamn and Zanzibar. The 'Aydarūsiyyah and the Ḥaddādiyyah orders are offshoots of the 'Alawiyyah *ṭarīqah,* founded by Muḥammad ibn 'Alī ibn Muḥammad (d. 653/1255). The Dandarāwiyyah *ṭarīqah* founded by Aḥmad al-Dandarāwī is also followed in Zanzibar, northern Kenya, Somalia, and the Comoro Islands. But, on the whole, the Qādiriyyah has the largest following in East Africa, and the Shādhiliyyah is the strongest in Uganda and Zanzibar, followed by the Qādiriyyah.

In East Africa Sufism influenced the coastal areas first and then spread into the interior, though not very successfully. Tombs of Sufi saints are to be found on the coast and the islands, for example, at Lamu. Swahili women pay visits to these tombs (*ziyārah*). The most recent tomb of a saint is that of Ṣāliḥ ibn 'Abd Allāh, who died in 1354/1935 and was a founder of Ribāṭ Riyāḍāt al-Lamu. As can be seen in some other parts of the Islamic world, flowers are placed on the tomb, and the annual *'urs* celebration takes place with many songs of praise and *dhikr.* The tomb of Shaha Mshaham ibn Hishām (d. 1000/1592), who was a Shirazi ruler of Mombasa, is also a celebrated shrine. Another tomb where *ziyārah* is made in Mombasa is that of Shaykh Jundānī in the Jundānī Mosque. There is also Shaykh Faqīhī Manṣūrū's tomb in the town of Taka, which is visited by the local people in large numbers.

Sufism in West Africa

Sufi orders spread in West Africa through the Berbers of North Africa, who placed great importance on the tombs of holy men, such that in some areas their attitude can be described virtually as saint worship. But there are two important differences in West Africa: (a) saint worship is rarely found, with the exception of the Wolof people, who venerate the tomb of Aḥmad Bāmbā at Touba; (b) there are not as many Sufi orders. The two orders which have spread are the Qādiriyyah and the Tijāniyyah. A negligible group of people follow the Shādhiliyyah *ṭarīqah* in western Guinea, as a result of being influenced during their *ḥajj* travel and also through contacts with North African Muslims. Similarly, at one time the 'Arūsiyyah *ṭarīqah* was introduced into the Chad region by the Tripolitarian tribe of Awlād Sulaymān, but their members also changed to the Tijāniyyah.[11] But adherents of the Tijāniyyah and Qādiriyyah can be found in all the countries of West Africa.

The Qādiriyyah Order

The Qādiriyyah was the first to enter West Africa. It was through the influence of ʿUmar al-Shaykh (864/1460–960/1553), who belonged to the Kunta tribe, that it was first brought to the western Sudan. He came in contact with the Qādiriyyah masters during the *ḥajj* and became initiated into the order.[12] ʿUmar sent his disciples to preach Islam throughout the Sahara, the Niger buckle, and Hausaland. One of his most active successors was al-Mukhtār ibn Aḥmad (1142/1729–1226/1811), who gave a boost to Qādirī teachings among the black Africans. He founded a *zāwiyah* in Azawad, which is situated north of Timbuktu. It was from this center that the Qādirī Order spread far and wide and influenced great leaders enabling them to launch their reform movements.

Two such reformists who launched *jihāds* and revolutionized their people were Shehu ʿUthmān Dan Fodio of Nigeria and Shaykh Ḥamadu of Masina. It was because of the influence from the Azawad *zāwiyah* that Shaykh Sidya al-Kabīr (1194/1780–1285/1868) of the Awlad Birri and his grandson Sidya Bābā (1286/1869–1342/1924) were able to influence the Moorish tribes in Mauritania and the Wolofs in Senegal. Then there appeared a number of branches of the Qādiriyyah: the Lisīdiyyah led by Sidya Bābā (d. 1342/1924), the Fāḍiliyyah of Muḥammad Fāḍil (d. 1276/1860), and the Murīdiyyah of Aḥmadou Bāmbā (d. 1345/1927). These branches were geared to the spiritual needs of black Africans. The most famous of these is the Murīdiyyah, which commands a large following and has spread very fast among the Wolofs, who are mainly agriculturists, and the "pagans" of Senegal. With its center at the Touna Mosque, special emphasis is placed on agriculture. The leaders of the *ṭarīqah* have encouraged collective farming. The present leader is Shaykh Falilu Mbake, who is revered by all the disciples of the *ṭarīqah.*

Another illustrious Qādirī shaykh was Shehu ʿUthmān Dan Fodio, who launched a famous *jihād* for reforming his followers. His influence spread far beyond the present northern states of Nigeria to the Middle Niger and Zerma. The Qādirī influence became so powerful at one stage that the leaders of the *ṭarīqah* were instrumental in forming new states in Fouta Jallon in 1137/1725, Fouta Toro in 1190/1776, Masina in 1225/1810, and the Sokoto caliphate of Nigeria in 1219/1804. At present, this influence has diminished a great deal and people have changed and are still changing in favor of the Tijāniyyah, which has emerged as the dominant Sufi order in West Africa today.

The Tijāniyyah Order

The Tijāniyyah Order, founded by Shaykh Aḥmad ibn Muḥammad al-Tijānī (1150/1737–1230/1815), was widely accepted almost immediately after its birth. The dynamic shaykh ʻAlī ibn ʻĪsā (d. 1260/1844) sent missionaries from his *zāwiyat al-timāsin* along with the trading caravans, and soon *zāwiyahs* were established in Kano, Bornu, and Waday.

The order gained a large number of followers through the efforts of ʻUmar ibn Saʻīd al-Fūtī. In the thirteenth/nineteenth century the order emerged as both a religious and a political force south of the Sahara. In North Africa, particularly in the Maghrib, the resurgence of the Sufi orders was partly due to the French colonial domination, since the orders became an instrument used by the Muslim rulers to resist the political expansion of the French and English empires in the Muslim states. The French referred to al-Ḥajj ʻUmar ibn Saʻīd al-Fūtī as "Le Faux Prophet" and a dangerous Muslim fanatic, because he succeeded in rousing people against their colonial expansion. The Tijāniyyah became the most vigorous opponents of France and "many early French administrators feared the passion that Tijani Marabouts were able to arouse in their followers."[13]

Al-Ḥājj ʻUmar Tāl's association with the Tijāniyyah proved to be the turning point in the history of the order. Born in Fouta Toro in 1212/1797, al-Ḥājj ʻUmar was the son of a marabout. Around 1235/1820 he went on pilgrimage to Mecca and became a disciple of the Tijāniyyah Order. On his return from the pilgrimage, he helped to spread the order by going on missions to the courts of the Muslim rulers of West Africa, visiting Islamic centers like Kanem, Sokoto, Fouta Toro, and Fouta Jallon. Al-Ḥājj ʻUmar was also a great scholar and wrote *Jawāhir al-maʻānī* (*Jewels of Meaning*), which is considered to be an important source to this day by the Tijānī shaykhs.

The Tijānī Order was introduced in Nigeria by al-Ḥājj ʻUmar when he returned from his pilgrimage and stayed for some time in Bornu with al-Kāminī. He then came to Sokoto, where he spent several years in the company of Sultan Muḥammad Bello, the son of Shehu ʻUthmān Dan Fodio, and also married the daughter of Muḥammad Bello. The Qādiriyyah were dominant in the Sokoto caliphate, but gradually the Tijāniyyah Order came to be preferred by the educated youth. The Tijāniyyah have a much broader-based following than the Qādiriyyah, whose membership is restricted to the elite. The Tijānī leaders tour West African countries and appoint new *muqaddams* in various areas, and in this way the Tijāniyyah continue to spread. Shaykh Sidi ibn ʻUmar al-Tijānī of the Maghre visited various countries in West Africa and appointed new Tijāniyyah *muqaddams* in the northern and southern parts of Nigeria. Shaykh Ibrāhīm Niasse of Kaolak also pays visits to the countries of West Africa. Muslims flock to see him, because seeing him personally is believed to be a great source of spiritual blessing. Some people travel hundreds of miles from the hinterland of the countries to visit him, become initiated into the order, and listen to his exhortations. In the East Central State of Nigeria, which happens to be a Christian majority area inhabited by the Ibos, there is an Ibo Muslim leader and a *muqaddam* of the Tijāniyyah, who, after his conversion from Christianity to Islam, renamed himself after Shaykh Ibrāhīm Niasse of Kaolak, calling himself Shaykh Ibrāhīm Niasse Nwagui. He has established various Muslim schools in and around Afikpo and Engugu-Ezike and has also set up a Muslim dispensary and built mosques. The new Ibo converts to Islam follow the Tijāniyyah Order. Shaykh Ibrāhīm Nwagui is at present engaged in the translation of the Quran into the Ibo language.

The Shādhiliyyah Order

Although this order has spread in other parts of Africa, it has very little influence in West Africa. It was first brought there by a Pulo Muslim, ʿAlī al-Ṣūfī from Fouta Jallon, during his visit to Fez. His spiritual disciples founded *zāwiyahs* at Gomba, N'dama, and Jawiya. The Shādhiliyyah exerted some degree of influence in Fouta Jallon until they were superseded when al-Ḥājj ʿUmar Tāl began to spread the Tijānī Order. The Shādhiliyyah followers then changed to the Tijāniyyah.

The Degeneration of Sufi Orders in Africa

Signs of degeneration have crept into African Sufism in a number of ways. For example, it was common for disciples to devote themselves to the service of their shaykh and exalt him above shaykhs of other orders, but some people went so far as to say that one must follow the shaykh and forget the rest, which gave rise to various lapses in the religious observances of Islam. Belief in the great Sufis, who are usually referred to as the friends of God (*awliyāʾ Allāh*), has often become so exaggerated that people believe that all good flows from them and that it is only through their mediation that God will be pleased with them. They go to the tombs of such shaykhs, lay wreaths, pour milk on the tomb, circumambulate it as one does at the *Kaʿbah,* and slaughter goats, rams, and fowl at their tombs if they feel that their wishes have been fulfilled. This veneration for the shaykh sometimes gives the impression of saint worship. At times, people begin to bow down almost in prostration before the tombs and seek help from the saints rather than from God.

The New Trends: Attempts at Reform

It is in such circumstances that the echoes of the pronouncements of Ibn Jawzī and Ibn Taymiyyah are heard in the present time in parts of Africa, with an added boost from the Wahhābī movement. As in North African countries, northeastern Africa, and the Horn, modernist opinion is often strongly opposed to the veneration of saints and the exaggerated regard in which some holy men are traditionally held.[14] In East Africa, for example, the *Matwas* have begun to oppose saint worship, because it leads consciously or unconsciously to *shirk* (polytheism). This was the reason they vehemently opposed the building of the mausoleum on the tomb of Sultan Sa'īd.

The reformers also consider some of the Tijāniyyah practices as *al-bid'at al-sayyi'ah* (bad innovations). On Friday afternoons, the Tijāniyyah followers sit in a circle, spread a white cloth in the middle, and begin to recite the litanies under the guidance of the *muqaddam*. They believe that during their chantings, the Prophet Muḥammad comes and sits on the white cloth. Similarly, during the recitation of the *mawlidī* (birthday), when the reciter makes the statement that "our Prophet was born," the gathering stands up as a sign of respect for the Prophet, since they believe that the Prophet himself comes personally on that occasion. Then they recite: "O Prophet *al-salām*^{u} *'alaykum*." This practice, which is common in the Indo-Pakistan subcontinent, seems to have made a strong impact on the Muslims of East Africa.

The Sanūsiyyah Order

In the thirteenth/nineteenth century the Sanūsiyyah Order was founded in Cyrenaica by Muḥammad ibn 'Alī al-Sanūsī al-Khaṭṭābī al-Idrīsī al-Ḥasanī (1201/1787–1275/1859) and quickly became popular.[15] The founder of the *ṭarīqah* revolutionized the social structure of Libya, contributing to the making of modern, independent Libya.

Sayyid Muḥammad ibn 'Alī al-Sanūsī was born at Tursh in the Algerian town of Mostaghanem. He was a scion of the famous Idrīsī family and was also a descendant of the fourth caliph of Islam, 'Alī, through his eldest son Ḥasan, the grandson of the Prophet Muḥammad. His father died when he was still young, and he was brought up by his mother. He attended school first in his native place, studying under Abū Ra's (d. 1238/1823) and Belghandūz (d. 1244/1829). Then he went to the Qarawiyyīn University at

Fez in 1236/1821. He spent eight years at the university, learned Quranic exegesis, *Ḥadīth* and jurisprudence and came into contact with several of the *'ulamā'* and the Sufi fraternities of Morocco. His academic achievements won him a teaching position at the university. He returned to Algeria in 1244/1829 with his growing fame as a learned and pious man and a Sufi. He was accompanied by his first disciples and traveled through the Sahara, Tunisia, Tripolitania, and Cyrenaica preaching Islam. He appealed for a greater Islamic unity and told the people to do away with devilish innovations in their beliefs and practices and to return to the religion of the Prophet, stripped of later additions and irrelevant details.

Sayyid Muḥammad left Fez for a journey to the east and stopped in Cairo, where he spent some time among the scholars of Al-Azhar University. He then proceeded to the Hijaz for a pilgrimage and stayed there teaching, meditating, and studying the conditions of Islamic society. He was grieved at what he found and resolved to dedicate his life to helping people rediscover themselves.

During his stay in the Hijaz, Sayyid Muḥammad met his most powerful supporter, Amīr Muḥammad Sharīf, the ruler of Waday. It was during this period that he also met the famous theologian and Sufi Aḥmad ibn Idrīs al-Fāsī, the spiritual master of the Moroccan Khaḍiriyyah *ṭarīqah.* In him, Sanūsī found a teacher with similar ideas. He became a close friend of al-Fāsī and went to Yemen in his company on a missionary journey. Al-Fāsī died there, but before his death he instructed that his disciples should henceforth follow the teachings of Sanūsī, who soon established a *zāwiyah* and college near Mecca. Around 1256/1840, he finally decided to return home to Algeria but was not able to because of the French occupation. He then went to Cyrenaica.

The Grand Sanūsī established his first *zāwiyah* in 1259/1843 in a place known as Zāwiyat al-Bayḍā'. It served as a mosque, a school, a guesthouse, and if need be a fort. Within a short period, the surrounding areas were dotted with many such *zāwiyahs.* They were of similar structure, situated at a six hours' walking distance from each other, and always located in important and strategic places. Regular congregations assembled in the *zāwiyahs* every Friday and were attended by the local people. From the pulpit of the *zāwiyah* mosques, people were exhorted to adhere to the fundamentals of Islam and to consider the wider Islamic society. The *zāwiyahs* served as community centers under an elder who was also responsible to make peace in local disputes. Each *zāwiyah* had an attached school. The adjoining land was cultivated by the local people, providing for the *zāwiyah*'s expenses. The novices of the *zāwiyahs* were called the *ikhwān* or "brethren."

Under the inspired leadership of Sanūsī, the movement spread to Chad, Central Africa, and the Hijaz. But the order had a special importance for Libya, proving to be a religious, cultural, and political movement. It had a far-reaching effect on the struggle against colonialism, first in Central Africa under the leadership of Sayyid al-Mahdī, the father of King Idrīs, and then against the Italians in Libya from 1329/1911 up to their final departure during the Second World War.

The Grand Sanūsī had a rare combination of gifts, being at once a scholar, mystic, and man of action. The order preached greater devotion to and understanding of Islam within the context of a life of action illuminated by mystical experience. The Grand Sanūsī urged his followers to go back to the Quran and the *Sunnah* of the Prophet, keeping away from the practice of the later ages.

After a few years, Sanūsī again went to Mecca and preached to the pilgrims who came from different parts of the Islamic world. The Ikhwān, or the Sanūsī's followers, were so much inspired by the teachings of their master that they became the living ambassadors of the Sanūsiyyah *ṭarīqah,* traveling from place to place and founding new *zāwiyahs.* Sanūsī returned to Cyrenaica in the year 1269/1853, and in 1271/1855 he moved the center of his *ṭarīqah* from al-Bayḍā' to the remote oasis of Jaghbub, about 180 miles south of Tobruk. In Jaghbub he created a thriving community of his followers on the brink of the Sahara desert. He built an Islamic university on the pattern of al-Azhar of Cairo and other North African seats of Islamic learning. He collected a large number of great scholars and built a library that contained eight thousand volumes and one thousand manuscripts. He trained three hundred scholars of high caliber who were filled with the desire to reform Islamic society from its roots and to spread the message of Islam in Central Africa and the lands adjoining the Sahara. The new headquarters of the Sanūsiyyah was located on an important trade route and became a center for the growing Sanūsī influence in Egypt, Sudan, and Libya, far from political interference by the Europeans and the Turks.

The Grand Sanūsī died in Jaghbub in the year 1275/1859 after he had laid the firm foundations of the Sanūsiyyah movement. He is buried there in a great tomb which the Sanūsīs visit with reverence even today. The success of the Sanūsiyyah movement can be judged by the fact that when Sayyid Muḥammad al-Mahdī, the successor of the Grand Sanūsī, took over the leadership of the order in 1275/1859, the Sanūsiyyah had 146 *zāwiyahs.*

Conclusion

Sufism has played the central role throughout Islamic history in the propagation and preservation of Islam and its culture in Africa. It has affected all aspects of Islamic life in Africa, from architecture to politics. But most of all, Sufism has made possible the training of generations of devout and saintly men and women, who have been models of spiritual nobility and wisdom. Such figures have been loved and followed across the continent and over the centuries by millions of Africans who have accepted the call of Islam. To this day the spirituality taught by Sufism remains a living reality across the length and breadth of Africa, the majority of whose inhabitants are now Muslims.

Appendix
Some of the Sufi Orders in Africa Today

The *ṭarīqah*	The period when the *ṭarīqah* began its impact	Where it is followed
The Qādiriyyah	At the time of ʿAbd al-Qādir al-Jīlānī (d. 561/1166)	Throughout Africa
The Shādhiliyyah	Abu'l-Ḥasan al-Shādhilī of Tunis (d. 648/1250)	Mainly in Morocco, Tunisia, Algeria, and Uganda
The Sammāniyyah (a branch of the Shādhiliyyah)	thirteenth/nineteenth century	Egypt, Sudan
The Rifāʿiyyah	570/1175	In most of Africa
The ʿAlawiyyah	653/1255	
The Aḥmadiyyah	Sayyid Aḥmad al-Badawī (d. 675/1276)	Egypt
The Burhāniyyah	Ibrāhīm al-Dasūqī (d. 676/1277)	Egypt
The Jazūliyyah (a branch of the Shādhiliyyah)	869/1465	Morocco
The ʿĪsawiyyah	Muḥammad ibn ʿĪsā (d. 930/1523)	Morocco, Algeria, and Tunisia
The Tijāniyyah	1196/1782	North and West Africa
The Sanūsiyyah	1253/1837	Libya

The Darqāwiyyah	1238/1823	Algeria, Morocco
The Madaniyyah (a branch of the Darqāwā)	thirteenth/nineteenth century	Tripolitania
The ʻAydarūsiyyah	915/1509	Lamu and Zanzibar
The ʻAlawiyyah (a branch of the Darqāwiyyah)	Shaykh Aḥmad al-ʻAlawī, 1337/1919	Algeria
ʻAmmāriyyah (a branch of the Qādiriyyah)	thirteenth/nineteenth century	Algeria, Tunisia
ʻArūsiyyah (a branch of the Qādiriyyah)	ʻAbd al-ʻAbbās ibn ʻArūs (d. 864/1460)	Tripolitania
Awamiriyyah (a branch of the ʻĪsawiyyah)	thirteenth/nineteenth century	Tunisia
Bakkā'iyyah (a branch of the Qādiriyyah)	911/1505	Sudan
Būʻaliyyah (a branch of the Qādiriyyah)	thirteenth/nineteenth century	Egypt, Algeria
Ismāʻīliyyah	thirteenth/nineteenth century	Nubian order of Kurdufan
Mashīshiyyah	Ibn Mashīsh (d. 623/1226)	Morocco
Yūsufiyyah (a branch of the Shādhiliyyah)	tenth/sixteenth century	Maghrib
Khatmiyyah or Mirghaniyya (Nubian branch of the Idrīsiyyah)	1269/1853	Sudan
The Murīdiyyah (a branch of the Qādiriyyah)	Aḥmadou Bāmbā (d. 1345/1927)	Senegal
Ḥaddādiyyah	–	Uganda

Notes

1. I. M. Lewis, *Islam in Tropical Africa* (London: Oxford University Press, 1966) 27.
2. H. A. R. Gibb, *Mohammedanism* (London: Oxford University Press, 1964) 14.
3. See J. S. Trimingham, *A History of Islam in West Africa* (London: Oxford University Press, 1968) 158.
4. Ibid., 23 n. 2.
5. A. S. Tritton, *Islam* (London: Hutchinson's University Library, 1962) 97.
6. Trimingham, *History of Islam*, 23.
7. Ibn Abī Zar' al-Fāsī, *Roudh el Kartas: Histoire des souverains du Maghreb*, trans. A. Beaumier (Paris: Imprimerie impériale, 1860) 170.
8. Al-Bakrī, *Description de l'Afrique septentrionale*, trans. and ed. Baron MacGuckin de Slane (Paris: Geuthner, 1913) 169–70.
9. Ibid., 134–41, 204.
10. M. A. Klein, *Islam and Imperialism in Senegal* (Stanford: Stanford University Press, 1968) 63.
11. Trimingham, *History of Islam*, 91.
12. Trimingham, *The Sufi Orders in Islam*, 88.
13. Klein, *Islam and Imperialism in Senegal*, 66; see also J. M. Abun-Nasr, *The Tijāniyya* (London: Oxford University Press, 1965).
14. Lewis, *Islam in Tropical Africa*, 9.
15. On the Sanūsiyyah Order, see N. Ziadeh, *Sanūsīyah: A Study of a Revivalist Movement in Islam* (Leiden: Brill, 1958).

15

Spiritual Chivalry

Seyyed Hossein Nasr

It is not possible to discuss Islamic spirituality without dealing with that spiritual reality which is called *futuwwah* in Arabic and *jawānmardī* in Persian and which can be rendered into English as "mystical youth" or spiritual chivalry. Both the Arabic and Persian terms (*fatā* in Arabic and *jawān* in Persian) refer to youth or the Latin *juvenis* but have acquired a meaning related much more to the youth associated with the eternal spring of the life of the Spirit than to physical young age. To possess *futuwwah* or *jawānmardī* is to be embellished with the characteristics of courage and generosity associated with a chivalry transposed onto the highest level of meaning from the realm of external action to that of the spiritual life, without, however, excluding the world of external action. Therefore, their translation as "spiritual chivalry" evokes more than any other expression this basic Islamic concept, whose reality has been manifested in so many domains, from the activity of the guilds in the bazaars to those of knights on the battlefield, from the world of Sufi contemplatives to that of sultans and viziers.[1] Much of the spiritual substance of the Muslim soul has been molded over the centuries by *futuwwah* and *jawānmardī*, and to this day a traditional Muslim looks with awe, reverence, and trust upon a person who manifests this "spiritual chivalry."

The Origin of *Futuwwah*

There has been a great debate concerning the origin of *futuwwah*. Some believe that the pre-Islamic Persian institution of *'ayyārī* became combined with Sufism to create *futuwwah*. (The term *'ayyār* means in general "keen of intelligence" and "brisk," but it was connected more particularly with organized groups that often rose up against the central authority of the caliph and his governors in various Persian provinces.) Others believe that just as there existed among the pre-Islamic Arabs the virtue of *muruwwah* (manliness), which consisted of courage (*shajā'ah*) and generosity (*sakhāwah*), so did the corresponding virtue develop among the sedentary people during the Islamic period under the heading of *futuwwah.* Yet others consider *futuwwah* to be a branch of Sufism with its own peculiar characteristics.[2] The traditional sources, especially those of the followers of *futuwwah,* consider the founder of this spiritual chivalry to be the father of monotheism, Abraham himself. The term *fatā* or youth is used in the Quran concerning Abraham in the following verse: "They said: We heard a youth (*fatā*) make mention of them, who is called Abraham" (XXI, 60). This is in reference to Abraham's breaking of idols. The celebrated Khurasani Sufi Imam Abu'l-Qāsim al-Qushayrī says in his *Risālah* (*Treatise*): "The *fatā* is he who breaks an idol. And the idol of each man is his ego."[3]

The Quran (XVIII, 13) also refers to the Seven Sleepers of the Cave (*aṣḥāb al-kahf*) as young men (*fityān*), and they too have been considered as people of *futuwwah* in later Islamic works on the subject. Considering the "ecumenical" significance of the Seven Sleepers, who belong to the whole monotheistic family,[4] and the role of Abraham as the father of monotheism, it is easy to see why *futuwwah* always possessed an "ecumenical" character. Before modern times, the followers of spiritual chivalry, whether they were Jews, Christians, or Muslims, formed a brotherhood that went beyond confessional boundaries. The *Gottesfreunde* mentioned in Rhenish mysticism bear a striking similarity to the *awliyā' Allāh,* the "friends of God" of mystical *futuwwah,* and the ideal of the followers of *futuwwah* is very similar to what one finds in the poetry of Wolfram von Eschenbach.[5] Abraham, who separated himself from the seductions of this world to seek the One God, remains the father of this spiritual chivalry common to Islam and the traditional West.[6]

"Abraham made this group embark upon the ship of the *ṭarīqah,* the mystic path. He cast the ship upon the full sea of the *ḥaqīqah,* the metaphysical truth, and made it land at the island of *futuwwah,* where the group established its domicile."[7]

Abraham was therefore the initiator of the cycle of *futuwwah,* which, according to later authors such as Wā'iẓ Kāshifī, was transmitted like prophecy (*nubuwwah*) itself. Abraham passed it to Ishmael and Isaac, Isaac to Jacob, and Jacob to Joseph, one of the chief exemplars of *futuwwah.* Then it was transmitted to Christianity and finally Islam. The Prophet of Islam received through the "Muḥammadan Light" the truth and power of *futuwwah,* which he transmitted to 'Alī, who henceforth became the supreme source of *futuwwah* in Islam for both Sunnis and Shi'ites. In one of the later treatises on *futuwwah* by 'Abd al-Razzāq Kāshānī entitled *Tuḥfat al-ikhwān fī khaṣā'iṣ al-fityān* (*The Gift of Brothers concerning the Characteristics of Spiritual Chivalry*), the cycles of prophecy and *futuwwah* are compared as follows:[8]

prophecy (*nubuwwah*)	origin	- Adam
	pole	- Ibraham
	seal	- Muḥammad

futuwwah	origin	- Abraham
	pole	- 'Alī
	seal	- Twelfth Imam al-Mahdī

The History of *Futuwwah*

There is no doubt that historically *futuwwah* was at first closely associated with Shi'ism and also Persia. After 'Alī, it was Salmān al-Fārsī who was revered as the master of *futuwwah* and after him Abū Muslim Khurāsānī, the famous Persian general who brought about the downfall of the Umayyads. *Futuwwah* remained closely bound to the Shi'ite idea of *walāyah* or initiatic and spiritual power. Throughout the centuries, those devoted to the Twelfth Imam have been considered as *jawānmards* and *fatās par excellence*, as those knights who carry out the ultimate battle of good against evil and of the spirit against that externalization which stultifies and eclipses spiritual reality. Even after the sixth/twelfth century, when *futuwwah* spread to Sunni circles in Iraq, Syria, and Egypt, it retained its attachment to 'Alī, while in Ottoman Turkey it continued to possess a strong Shi'ite color until the rule of Sultan Selim, when Shi'ism in general became ever more curtailed in the Ottoman world.

The utterance *lā fatā illā 'Alī lā sayf illā dhul'-fiqār* (there is no *fatā* except 'Alī and no sword except *dhu'l-fiqār* [the famous double-bladed sword of 'Alī]) has been traditionally attributed to the archangel Gabriel, who transmitted it to the Prophet. This celebrated saying has echoed over the centuries throughout the Islamic world and is especially revered in the Shi'ite world but is not confined to it. The personality of 'Alī, at once sage and knight, contemplative and protector of laborers and craftsmen, has continued to dominate through the centuries over the horizon of *futuwwah* as it has over much of Sufism.

During the Umayyad period, *futuwwah* gained many adherents among the non-Arabs and especially Persians who had embraced Islam (the *mawālī*). It is known that Salmān, 'Alī's close associate, had contacts with the class of craftsmen in Iraq as did Abū Muslim, around whom an extensive literature grew during later centuries when he became one of the heroes of *futuwwah*. Despite the decadence of certain forms of *futuwwah* in the third/ninth and fourth/tenth centuries, authentic *futuwwah* became integrated into Sufism and references began to appear in Sufi texts to this distinct form of spiritual chivalry. In his *Ṭabaqāt al-ṣūfiyyah* (*The Classes of Sufis*), Sulamī, who is the author of the first work on *futuwwah,* considers many of the great figures of Sufism, such as Ma'rūf al-Karkhī, Abū Turāb al-Nakhshabī and Abū 'Abbās al-Dīnawarī to have belonged to the tradition of *futuwwah.*[9] After this early period, references to *futuwwah* and *jawānmardī* become even more common in Sufi writers, especially those who were Persian, such as Qushayrī and Maybudī in his voluminous Quranic commentary the *Kashf al-asrār* (*Unveiling of Secrets*), while such famous poets as 'Unṣurī and Firdawsī and such prose writers as 'Unṣur al-Ma'ālī Kā'ūs ibn Iskandar, author of the *Qābūs-nāmah* (*Book Dedicated to Qābūs*) extolled the virtues of spiritual chivalry. These references become more common among later Sufi writers such as Rūmī, leading to the period from the seventh/tenth century to the ninth/twelfth, when most of the famous *Futuwwat-nāmahs* (treatises on spiritual chivalry) were written, the most extensive being the *Futuwwat-namā-yi sulṭānī* (*The Royal Book on Futuwwah*) by the ninth/fifteenth-century scholar and Sufi, Ḥusayn Wā'iẓ-i Kāshifī Sabziwārī.[10]

During the last phase of the rule of the Abbasids, the caliph al-Nāṣir li-Dīni'Llāh (d. 622/1225) transformed *futuwwah* into a chivalric initiation and instituted an organized order of knights who were bound together by the rites drawn from chivalry. This order was destroyed in Iraq as a consequence of the Mongol invasion but survived for some time in Mamluk Egypt and Syria and to some extent in Ottoman Turkey.

It was, however, the guild form of *futuwwah* which came to replace knightly *futuwwah* from the eighth/fourteenth century but which also remained closely associated with Nāṣirian *futuwwah.* In its popular manifestation, this type of guild *futuwwah* continued to be associated with Shi'ite circles in Anatolia as was also the case later in India, where the *Kasb-nāmahs* (*Books of Sustenance*) had a distinctly Shi'ite color. These guilds survived in the Ottoman world up to the thirteenth/nineteenth century, each guild having its own *fütüwwet-nāme,* the most important of which was *Fütüwwet-nāme-i kebir* (*The Great Book of Futuwwah*) of Sayyid Meḥmed al-Raḍawī, from the tenth/sixteenth century.[11] The guilds even continue to survive to this day here and there in Syria, Persia itself, Muslim India, and other regions of the Islamic world wherever traditional methods of craftsmanship and trade are still practiced.

Knightly *futuwwah* also left its mark on traditional sports such as wrestling, where in Persia the *zūr-khānah* (literally, "house of strength") survives to this day as its offshoot. The *zūr-khānah,* with its "sacred pit," guide or *murshid,* initiation, emphasis on moral virtue as well as the building and strengthening of the body, represents an important survival of knightly *futuwwah.* Over the centuries a whole class of men has appeared in society possessing proverbial physical strength combined with moral virtue, especially generosity and courage, which are so much emphasized in *futuwwah.*[12] They have been the protectors of society against both the oppression of rulers and internal aggression from thieves and ruffians. One of these wrestler knights, Pahlawān Maḥmūd Khwārazmī (d. 722/1322), known as Pūriyā-yi Walī, is one of Persia's national heroes. A great wrestler and fighter, he was also an accomplished Sufi and poet to whom the treatise *Kanz al-ḥaqā'iq* (*Treasure of Truths*) is attributed. To this day young wrestlers in the *zūr-khānah* swear by his name, and he embodies the combination of strength with humility, courage, and generosity which has characterized this type of *futuwwah* or *jawānmardī* over the centuries.

The Content of the *Futuwwat-nāmahs:* The Goal of *Futuwwah*, Initiation, Relation to the Crafts and Professions

The *Books of Futuwwah* written between the seventh/thirteenth and the ninth/fifteenth century by such figures as 'Abd al-Razzāq Kāshānī, Shams al-Dīn Āmulī, Shihāb al-Dīn 'Umar Suhrawardī, and Wā'iẓ-i Kāshifī reveal much about the goal and purpose of *futuwwah,* the rites associated with it, and the link between *futuwwah* and various crafts and guilds. As an example, one can consider Kāshānī's *Tuḥfat al-ikhwān fī khaṣā'iṣ al-fityān.*[13] According to the author, the fundamental concept associated with *futuwwah* is *fiṭrah* or man's primordial nature. Despite being cast into this world of chaos and darkness, man continues to bear within himself that *fiṭrah* with which he was created. The *fiṭrah* is a light that shines at the center of man's being even if it has now become covered by the veils of passion and forgetfulness. *Futuwwah* creates a condition in the soul that allows the spirit of man's *fiṭrah* to triumph over the darkness of this world and to conquer man's fallen nature rather than remaining within him in a state of potency. The goal of *futuwwah* is to make possible the transfer of the light of *fiṭrah* from potentiality to actuality. The greatest battle of the veritable knight is this struggle to make possible the reconquest of our nature by the light of *fiṭrah.* Spiritual chivalry on the highest level is the art by means of which we become ourselves and gain full awareness of our primordial nature.

In the first chapter of his work, Kāshānī deals with the stages of *futuwwah.* It begins with *muruwwah,* which is close to the Western medieval notion of *courtoisie.* Its higher stage is *walāyah,* in the Shi'ite sense of spiritual initiation, which Kāshānī identifies as return to one's *fiṭrah.* Repentance, which is the beginning of every spiritual quest, is none other than the primordial purity (*ṭahārah*) of man, and *futuwwah* or *jawānmardī* none other than the return to the condition of *alast,* that is, the primordial covenant made between God and man when, according to the Quran, God asks man "Am I not your Lord?" (*alast*^{u} *bi-rabbikum*) and man replies "Yea!" (*balā*) (VII, 172). The third level above *futuwwah* is *risālah* or prophecy, which is at once the source of both *walāyah* and *futuwwah.* Without revelation man cannot actualize the light of his primordial nature in himself, although that nature resides at the center of his being.

The second chapter of Kāshānī's treatise treats the subject of *walāyah* (Persian *walāyat*), revealing why it is so central and why it is the link between prophecy and *futuwwah, walāyah* being the perfection (*kamāl*) of *futuwwah.* Abraham was the first person in whom *futuwwah* and *walāyah* became manifested at the same time. It is he who broke the idols in the name of the One God.

The third chapter deals with the roots of *futuwwah* and the conditions for entering into its fold. There is a clear indication in Kāshānī of the initiatic rites associated with *futuwwah.* The rites involve the drinking of water and salt, which the Prophet had offered to 'Alī and Salmān. Then it involves the wearing of a pair of pants (*sarāwāl*) under one's dress like the one worn by 'Alī. Finally, it involves the wearing of a belt as the Prophet had put on a belt around 'Alī's waist. Each of these rites is symbolic of a spiritual reality. Water symbolizes gnosis and wisdom, salt justice, the pants decency and continence, and the belt courage and honor. There is an initiatic transmission from master to disciple actualized through rites that resemble the Sufi initiation as far as transmission of initiatic power is concerned, but the forms of these rites differ.

In the fourth chapter the author turns to the foundations and meaning of *futuwwah,* the foundation being none other than the purification of the soul, which alone can make possible the actualization of the light of man's primordial nature or *fiṭrah.* Kāshānī then proceeds to discuss the virtues of *futuwwah* which are central to the understanding of its reality.

The Virtues according to *Futuwwah*

Kāshānī's enumeration and description of the virtues of spiritual chivalry reveal how central the virtues are to the whole of *futuwwah,* just as they are to Sufism, for in both cases the reality involved is not words or thoughts but being and actions which affect and modify one's mode of being. The virtues enumerated by Kāshānī, as by other masters of *futuwwah* in one form or another, are as follows:

1. repentance (*tawbah*). This involves inner transformation and return to one's origins.

2. generosity (*sakhā*). This is the highest level of *muruwwah* and consists of three degrees: the first involves objectivity and generosity without expectation of return; the second is beneficence and the giving of oneself and one's property through preference and freely; and the third is the giving of one's wealth in helping one's friends and allowing them to share in what one possesses.

3. humility (*tawāḍu'*). This is to make one's ego subservient to the intellect at the moment of action.

4. peace (*amn*). This is to have inner certitude and tranquillity of mind, and it is not possible without the light of faith (*īmān*) in one's heart.

5. truthfulness (*ṣidq*). *Ṣidq* is the basis of wisdom, and the *jawānmard* is the person who is always truthful and whose outward and private actions do not contradict each other.

6. guidance (*hidāyat*). This is to follow the path that leads to salvation, and it implies being firm in moving forward; at this stage guidance implies "vision through the heart" and gaining the knowledge of certainty (*'ilm al-yaqīn*).

7. counsel (*naṣīḥat*). This is the origin of the light of justice and the result of inner equilibrium bestowed by God.

8. faithfulness (*wafā*). This is to remain faithful to one's word, and on the highest level it refers to fulfilling the pre-eternal covenant made between God and man.

Kāshānī then mentions the calamities (*āfāt*) that can harm *futuwwat.* Foremost among these is pride, which always remains a danger, necessitating control of the carnal soul (*nafs*) at all times.

Finally, the author delineates the differences between *fatā, mutafattī,* and *mudda'ī.* Here he distinguishes between the real spiritual knight (*fatā*) or possessor of *futuwwah,* the person who claims such a state without being faithful to its principles (*mutafattī*), and the pretender (*mudda'ī*) who joins the circle of spiritual knights without having ever walked upon their path or learned of their inner states.

The author concludes his treatise by summarizing the virtues and their importance and emphasizes again the significance of generosity and hospitality.

Virtue, then, lies at the heart of *futuwwah,* for it alone can transform the soul and embellish it. Through popular forms of *futuwwah,* certain virtues were inculcated among different groups and classes of traditional Islamic society, and on the highest level the virtues of *futuwwah* became synonymous with those of Sufism.

Futuwwah and the Guilds

As mentioned already, *futuwwah* became the spirit and guiding principle of many of the guilds in Persia, Anatolia, Syria, and other regions of the Islamic world. Through it, the activities of the artisan were integrated into the religious life and the outward activity of craftsmen became the support for the "inner work," much like the activity of medieval Western architects and craftsmen. There are several treatises in Persian, Arabic, and Turkish that bear testimony to the role of *futuwwah* in making possible the spiritual integration of traditional activities in the realm of the arts and crafts, which from the Islamic point of view are one and the same.[14] Such treatises exist for example for the guild of blacksmiths and textile makers.

The *Futuwwat-nāmah* of the textile makers (*chītsāzān*) is particularly significant in clarifying the relation between the guilds and *futuwwah*.[15] According to this treatise, every action in making and painting the textile has a symbolic significance. The chief of the guild of textile makers was the sixth Shi'ite Imam, Ja'far al-Ṣādiq, and it was Gabriel who first taught mankind how to dye cloth. The treatise insists that it is necessary to have a master (*ustād*) and that only through the spiritual instructions transmitted by the chain of *futuwwah* can spirit be breathed into the labor of the craftsman and significance be bestowed upon it.

Through *futuwwah,* Islamic spirituality penetrated into the everyday activities of Islamic society, and art became integrated into the spiritual dimension of Islam, not only theoretically but also in practice. No full understanding of Islamic spirituality is possible without the comprehension of the role of spiritual chivalry in transforming the soul of those who in turn transformed and ennobled matter in that universal activity which is art in its traditional sense and before it became confined to a special class of human beings within modern Western society.

Rūmī and Sincerity of Action

In one of the most famous episodes in the *Mathnawī,* Rūmī has summarized in immortal Persian poetry what lies at the heart of *futuwwah,* namely, selfless generosity, courage, and detached action combined with sincerity (*ikhlāṣ*) and dedicated to God. The account involves the battle between 'Alī, the pole of *futuwwah,* and a warrior who had engaged him upon the battlefield:

Learn how to act sincerely [*ikhlāṣ*] from 'Alī: know that the Lion of God ('Alī) was purged of (all) deceit.

In fighting against the infidels he got the upper hand of (vanquished) a certain knight, and quickly drew a sword and made haste (to slay him).

He spat on the face of 'Alī, the pride of every prophet and every saint;

He spat on the countenance before which the face of the moon bows low in the place of worship.

'Alī at once threw his sword away and relaxed (his efforts) in fighting him.

That champion was astounded by this act and by his showing forgiveness and mercy without occasion.

He said, "You lifted your keen sword against me: why have you flung it aside and spared me?

What did you see that was better than combat with me, so that you have become slack in hunting me down?

What did you see, so that such anger as yours abated, and so that such a lightning flashed and (then) recoiled? . . .

In bravery you are the Lion of the Lord: in generosity who indeed knows who (what) you are?

In generosity you are (like) Moses' cloud in the desert, whence came the dishes of food and bread incomparable." . . .

He ['Alī] said, "I am wielding the sword for God's sake, I am the servant of God, I am not under the command of the body.

I am the Lion of God, I am not the lion of passion: my deed bears witness to my religion.

In war I am (manifesting the truth of) *thou didst not throw when thou threwest:* I am (but) as the sword, and the wielder is the (Divine) Sun.

I have removed the baggage of self out of the way, I have deemed (what is) other than God to be non-existence.

I am a shadow, the Sun is my lord; I am the chamberlain, I am not the curtain (which prevents approach) to Him.

I am filled with the pearls of union, like a (jewelled) sword: in battle I make (men) living, not slain.

Blood does not cover the sheen of my sword: how should the wind sweep away my clouds?

I am not a straw, I am a mountain of forbearance and patience and justice: how should the fierce wind carry off the mountain?"[16]

Ibn 'Arabī and *Futuwwah*

The highest meaning of *futuwwah* is to be found in the writings of Ibn 'Arabī, who integrated this particular strand of spirituality along with so many other currents into the vast synthesis for which he is so well known. Ibn 'Arabī had already encountered a number of masters of *futuwwah* while he was in Andalusia. In his *Rūḥ al-quds* (*Sacred Spirit*) he writes concerning Abū Muḥammad ibn Ibrāhīm al-Malāqī al-Fakhkhār, "This man, who was known as the 'ship-caulker' (al-Qalafāt), was a companion of Abū al-Rabīʿ al-Kafīf and others and a friend of Ibrāhīm b. Ṭarīf. He followed the way of Chivalry (*futuwwah*) and showed all the signs of doing so."[17]

Ibn ʿArabī devoted three chapters of his magnum opus *al-Futūḥāt al-makkiyyah* (*The Meccan Revelation*) to the subject of *futuwwah* and also discusses this theme in his other works. For example, in his *Ḥilyat al-abdāl* (*The Ornament of the Abdāl*) he mentions not only the following of the *Sharīʿah* but also the acquisition of virtues (*makārim al-akhlāq*), among which he mentions explicitly *zuhd* (asceticism) and *futuwwah* as indispensable for spiritual progress.[18] It is, however, in the *Futūḥāt* that Ibn ʿArabī delves into the deepest mysteries of *futuwwah*. In the first chapter of this monumental work he describes the meeting with the mysterious youth (*fatā*) to whose encounter he attributes the creation of the whole work. It is this dazzling figure who reveals to him the mystery of the *Kaʿbah* of Divine Lordship.

> We may roughly distinguish four moments in this prelude. The first moment is constituted by the processional and the encounter before the Black Stone; it culminates in the declaration in which the Youth states who he is. The recognition of the mystic meaning of the Kaʿba, emerging through its stone walls, goes hand in hand with the mystic's encounter with his own celestial pleroma in the person of the Youth. The Youth commands him: "Behold the secret of the Temple before it escapes; you will see what pride it derives from those who revolve in processional around its stones, looking at them from beneath its veils and coverings." And indeed the mystic sees it take on life. Gaining awareness of the Youth's rank, of his position dominating the where and the when, of the meaning of his "descent," he addresses him in the world of Apparitions (of Idea-Images, *ʿālam al-mithāl*): "I kissed his right hand and wiped the sweat of Revelation from his forehead. I said to him: "Look at him who aspires to live in your company and desires ardently to enjoy your friendship." For all answer he gave me to understand by a sign and an enigma that such was his fundamental nature that he conversed with no one except in symbols. "When you have learned, experienced, and understood my discourse in symbols, you will know that one does not apprehend or learn it as one apprehends and learns the eloquence of orators. . . ." I said to him: "O messenger of good tidings! That is an immense benefit. Teach me your vocabulary, initiate me into the movements one must give to the key that opens your secrets, for I should like to converse by night with you, I should like to make a pact with you." Again, he who is thus introduced as the eternal Companion, the celestial *paredros*, answers only by a sign. But then I understood. The reality of his beauty was unveiled to me, and I was overwhelmed with love. I fainted and he took hold of me. When I recovered from my faint, still trembling with fear, he knew that I had understood who he was. He threw away his traveler's staff and halted (that is, ceased to be the evanescent one, he who escapes). . . . I said to him: "Impart to me some of your secrets that I may be among the number of your doctors." He said to me: "Note well

the articulations of my nature, the ordering of my structure. What you ask me you will find etched in myself, for I am not someone who speaks words or to whom words are spoken. My knowledge extends only to myself, and my essence (my person) is no other than my Names. I am Knowledge, the Known and the Knower. I am Wisdom, the work of wisdom and the Sage (or: I am *Sophia, philosophy* and the *philosopher*)."[19]

Who is this figure who is at once the knower and the known and whom Ibn ʿArabī describes with such paradoxical characteristics as "being neither alive nor dead" and "contained in all things and containing all things," the being from whose nature "all that is written in this book" is drawn?[20] This youth, the reality of *futuwwah,* is none other than Ibn ʿArabī's own reality in the world of eternity, his being *in divinis.*

Certain *ḥadīths* of the Prophet refer to the inhabitants of paradise as beardless youths, and Ibn ʿArabī himself quotes a *ḥadīth* according to which, "I have seen my Lord in the form of a beardless youth."[21] The meeting with the *fatā* before the *Kaʿbah* is therefore nothing other than Ibn ʿArabī's encounter with his Lord. For those who, like Abraham, have been able to break the idol of their passions, it is possible to meet the *fatā* who is the source of all spiritual chivalry. In meeting with one's celestial reality man participates in that mystical youth which is none other than the youthfulness of the eternal spring of the life of the Spirit. From that youth there emanates the spiritual chivalry which has affected the mores and wonts of numerous knights and rulers, craftsmen, and artisans. But on the highest level, this eternal youth enables man to realize supreme knowledge and to become aware that he *is* himself only when he realizes himself *in divinis.* The highest form of spiritual chivalry is therefore to break the yoke of servitude to our lower nature in order to be worthy of encountering that celestial youth, that *fatā,* who *is* who we are, have been and will be eternally and in whom alone are we truly ourselves, immortalized in the proximity of the Divine Self.

Notes

1. This translation has been used by H. Corbin in his numerous important studies of the subject, such as *En Islam iranien* (Paris: Gallimard, 1972) vol. 4, Livre VII, entitled "Le Douzième Imam et la chevalrie spirituelle" (pp. 390ff.); and his *L'Homme et son ange: Initiation et chevalrie spirituelle* (Paris: Fayard, 1983) chap. 3, entitled "Juvénilité et chevalrie en Islam iranien" (pp. 207ff.).

2. There is a vast literature on *futuwwah* in European languages as well as in Arabic and Persian. Some of the most important essays on the subject have been assembled and rendered into Persian by E. Naraghi in his *Āʾīn-i jawānmardī* (Tehran: Chāpkhāna-yi Katībah, 1363 A.H.S.). For a bibliography of works in European languages, see the article "*futuwwa*" by F. Taeschner in the *New Encyclopedia of Islam.* The best study in

Arabic is still that of A. ʿAfīfī, *al-Malāmah wa'l-ṣūfiyyah wa ahl al-futuwwah* (Cairo, 1945).

3. Quoted by M. Chodkiewicz in his introduction to Ibn al-Ḥusayn al-Sulamī, *The Book of Sufi Chivalry (Futuwwah),* trans. Sheikh Tosun Bayrak al-Jerrahi al-Halveti (New York: Inner Traditions International, 1983) 21.

4. The late L. Massignon carried out many studies on the *aṣḥāb al-kahf* to bring out their significance as a bridge between the three monotheistic religions. See his *Opera Minora,* ed. Y. Moubarac (Paris: Presses universitaires de France, 1969).

5. See Corbin, *L'Homme et son ange,* 218–19.

6. The later texts of *futuwwah* identify Seth as the person with whom *futuwwah* became a spiritual path (*ṭarīqah*) and whose dress was the cape or *khirqah.* But at the time of Abraham this *khirqah* became "too heavy" to bear and so Abraham found a new way, which was that of *futuwwah* as it came to be known in later periods.

7. Corbin, *L'Homme,* 219.

8. See M. Ṣarrāf, ed., *Rasā'il-i jawānmardān* (Tehran and Paris: A. Maisonneuve, 1973); see also Naraghi, *Ā'īn-i jawānmardī,* 20.

9. See A. Zarrīnkūb, *Justijū dar taṣawwuf-i Īrān* (Tehran: Amīr Kabīr, 1357 A.H.) chap. 14; and S. Nafisi, *Sarchashma-yi taṣawwuf dar Īrān* (Tehran: Librairie Foroughi, 1965) 130ff. Ibn Miʿmār Ḥanbalī is the earliest Sufi figure associated with *futuwwah.*

10. Edited for the first time by M. J. Maḥjūb (Tehran: Bunyād-i farhang-i Īrān, 1350 A.H.) with an extensive introduction by the editor on the history of *futuwwah.*

11. See F. Taeschner, "*Futuwwa,*" in *New Encyclopedia of Islam,* where the *futuwwāt* in the Ottoman world are discussed in detail. Each guild, such as that of smiths, leather workers, or textile makers, possessed its own *futuwwat-nāmah* relating its artistic practices to spiritual principles. See also Yasar Nuri Ozturk, *The Eye of the Heart* (Istanbul: Redhouse Press, 1988) chap. 8.

12. On the *zūr-khānah,* see Partaw Bayḍā'ī Kāshānī, "Ta'thīr-i ā'īn-i jawānmardī dar warzishhā-yi bāstānī," in Naraghi, *Ā'īn-i jawānmardī,* 142–48.

13. The text is given by Ṣarrāf in his *Rasā'il.*

14. This has been treated amply by T. Burckhardt in many of his works, such as *The Art of Islam,* trans. P. Hobson (London: Festival of the World of Islam, 1976); and *Mirror of the Intellect,* trans. W. Stoddart, (Albany: State University of New York Press, 1987).

15. See Ṣarrāf, *Rasā'il.*

16. R. A. Nicholson, *The Mathnawī of Jalāluddīn Rūmī* (London: Luzac, 1982) 2:202–5.

17. See Ibn ʿArabī, *Sufis of Andalusia,* trans. R. W. J. Austin (London: Allen & Unwin, 1971) 129. In the same work he also mentions another master of *futuwwah,* Abu'l-Ḥasan al-Qanawī, whom he met in Andalusia.

18. See C. Addas, *Ibn ʿArabī ou La quête du Soufre Rouge* (Paris: Gallimard, 1989) 199.

19. H. Corbin, *Creative Imagination in the Ṣūfism of Ibn ʿArabī,* trans. R. Manheim (Princeton: Princeton University Press, 1969) 383–85.

20. See Chodkiewicz, introduction to Ibn al-Ḥusayn al-Sulamī, *The Book of Sufi Chivalry,* 23.

21. Ibid., 28.

Part Two

ISLAMIC LITERATURE AS MIRROR OF ISLAMIC SPIRITUALITY

16

Arabic Literature

Safa Khulusi

THE SPIRITUALITY OF ISLAM, as reflected in Arabic literature, can be viewed from four angles: (1) the Quran and *Ḥadīth,* (2) the Platonic love of the early Umayyads, (3) Shīʿism, and (4) Sufism. All these have played major roles in imparting spirituality to Arabic literature.

The Quran and *Ḥadīth*

Islamic spirituality in Arabic literature begins with the Noble Quran, as it marks the beginning of a new era, separating Jāhiliyyah or "Age of Ignorance" from the new faith. The Quran, destined to influence the daily life of Muslims for the following fourteen centuries and after, supplanted the "concrete" gods with the transcendent One who neither begets nor is begotten. As A. J. Arberry rightly states, the Quran "ranks amongst the greatest masterpieces of mankind."[1] In M. Pickthall's words, "it is an inimitable symphony, the very sounds of which move men to tears and ecstasy."[2]

Its stylistic inimitability came to be viewed as a standard for good literary taste. There is no great Muslim writer, poet, or spiritual figure of any category who has not come, one way or another, under the influence of the Quran.[3] Both the Quran and the *Ḥadīth* have studded the daily speech of the Arabs in particular and the Muslims in general with illuminating quotations. Certain parts of the Quran verge on pure poetry, for example, *sūrah* 94, which is in iambic meter. Rendered into English in the same meter, it runs thus:

> Enlarged thy heart for thee, have We not?
> And have stripped thy burden from thy back?
> Stripped the galling burden from thy back;
> And have We not raised thy name for thee?
> There comes with thy trouble ease also,
> Comes with thy trouble ease also,

And when thou hast finished, worship;
For thy Lord with zeal enquire.[4]

The meter and prosody of the verses of the Quran are well known and have been studied by some of the literary authorities of the Arabic language from the earliest Islamic centuries to the present.[5]

The *Ḥadīth* is complementary to the Quran. As far as the spiritual influence of *Ḥadīth* upon Arabic literature is concerned, however, it is significant especially to draw attention to the presence of a special body of *Ḥadīth,* known as *ḥadīth qudsī* or "Divine Saying," in which God speaks in the first person. This body of sayings falls between the Quran and the ordinary speech of the Prophet. The following is a good example of the *ḥadīth qudsī,* especially since it illustrates the central practice of *dhikr:* "God Most High said, I am the Companion of him who recollects Me and I am with My servant when he makes mention of Me and his lips move with the mention of My Name."[6] Such traditions had profound influence on Arabic literature.

The Platonic Love of the Early Umayyads: The 'Udhrī Love Lyrics of Hijaz and Najd

This kind of love is linked with Sufism and Divine Love. The great Arab mystic Ibn ʿArabī declares in the well-known poem: "We have a pattern in Bishr, the lover of Hind and her sister, and in Qays and Lubna, and in Mayya and Ghaylan." Then he goes on to comment on this verse: "Love, qua love, is one and the same reality to those Arab lovers and to me; but the objects of our love are different, for they loved a phenomenon, whereas I love the real."[7]

'Udhrī love, as it was called, was unknown in Arabia before the advent of Islam. It spread like wildfire among the Banū 'Udhrah, a clan of Banū Quḍāʿah, in Wādī al-Qurā, north of Hijaz and also spilled over into Najd. It is said that at one time there were no fewer than thirty youths, in one locality alone, on the brink of death for no reason other than ungratified pure Platonic love. The Banū 'Āmir became celebrated in this genre of literature. There is no explanation of this phenomenon other than that Islam purified the soul and condemned illicit sexual relations. This 'Udhrī love was a pristine Islamized bedouin love that was far removed from the polluted urban sexuality. It was unknown to town dwellers, who enjoyed sensual love as portrayed by the poetry of al-Aḥwaṣ and al-ʿArajī. It was more akin to the love of the mystic Rābiʿat al-ʿAdawiyyah. It remained a youthful love even in old age, if the lover was destined to live that long without going insane like Qays (Majnūn), the mad lover of Laylā. The love story of Laylā and Majnūn is an allegory with Shī'ite embellishments. Qays represents the Shī'ite claim to the caliphate, Laylā and her relentless father who caused all his sufferings, the Umayyads. This is clearly illustrated by Aḥmad Shawqī, in his versified version of the romance.[8]

Some of the 'Udhrī lovers were celebrated ascetics, such as 'Abd al-Raḥmān ibn Abī 'Ammār al-Jushamī, 'Urwah ibn 'Udhaynah, and 'Ubayd Allāh ibn 'Abd Allāh ibn 'Utbah. 'Abd al-Raḥmān was one of the Meccan ascetics and was therefore nicknamed al-Quss, the priest. He fell in love with a songstress, Sallāmah by name, so he was ultimately called Sallāmah al-Quss, linking his name with hers.[9] 'Urwah ibn 'Udhaynah was one of the theologians of Medina and a narrator of Prophetic traditions.[10] It is interesting to note that he used to set his own poems to music.

All the Platonic love romances bear a close resemblance to Sufi love lines: "The tales of Majnūn and Laylā, Yūsuf and Zulaykhā, the Moth and the Candle, the Nightingale and the Rose are shadow-pictures of the soul's passionate longing to be re-united with God."[11]

Shī'ism

I have sought elsewhere to provide the answer to the question of the influence of Shī'ism upon Arabic literature.[12] The answer is complex, and it is possible here to deal only briefly with a number of Shī'ite poets and writers who reflect Shī'ite spirituality in Arabic literature. Of these al-Farazdaq, Kuthayyir, and al-Kumayt are good examples.

Al-Farazdaq was a staunch supporter of the 'Alīds. His poem in praise of Zayn al-'Ābidīn (39/659–94/713), the fourth Shī'ite Imam and 'Alī's grandson, is a laudable masterpiece. It is related that both the caliph 'Abd al-Malik ibn Marwān and Zayn al-'Ābidīn were on pilgrimage to Mecca when the caliph noticed that large crowds were paying respect to a person other than himself.[13] Enraged, he pointed to him angrily and asked, "Who is that?" Being within hearing distance, al-Farazdaq replied, extemporizing his famous ode:

> This is the man whose footsteps are familiar to the hard rocks of Mecca. The Sacred House knows him, so does the firm covenant and oath, as well as the Holy Sanctuary. This is the son of Fāṭimah, if you do not know him! His grandfather was the Seal of the prophets.

For this offensive answer, al-Farazdaq was cast into a dungeon.

Kuthayyir was a representative of the Kaysanite sect, whereas al-Kumayt was a representative of the Zaydīs.[14] Kuthayyir believed that the slaying of al-Ḥusayn in Karbala' was not an ordinary death, but a *ghaybah* or occultation, and so was the death of his half brother Muḥammad ibn al-Ḥanafiyyah, who vanished in Mount Radwa, where he is sustained with honey and water.[15] This idea of the "Concealed Imam" penetrates Shī'ite literature throughout.

Al-Kumayt became famous for his *Hāshimiyyāt*, which introduced a new genre into the spirituality of Arabic literature, namely, "emotional Shī'ism" and the versification of Shī'ite "polemics" (*adab al-ḥajāj*), which had been confined to prose until this time. He tried to substantiate the rightful claim of the 'Alīds to the caliphate by constantly referring to the Noble Quran and *Ḥadīth*.

Shī'ism gave rise to the elegies of the great martyr al-Ḥusayn, which acquired the designation of *adab al-ṭaff*, the literature of al-Ṭaff, after the name of the district where he was slain. It is characterized by its melancholic grief and tenderness. Indeed, by and large, Shī'ite literature is soft and tender, so much so that it became proverbial for its gentleness as echoed in the saying, "More tender than a Shī'ite woman's tears crying over 'Alī ibn Abī Ṭālib!"

Another outcome of Shī'ite spirituality is the celebrated book *Nahj al-balāghah* (*The Path of Eloquence*). In beauty of diction and style, it comes next to the Quran. Whatever critics may say about the authenticity of the book, there still remains a substantial part that can be safely ascribed to the Imam 'Alī himself. It was compiled by the well-known Shī'ite poet al-Sharīf al-Raḍī (d. 453/1016) or, according to some, by his brother al-Murtaḍā. The intense emotions displayed in the *Nahj*, especially in 'Alī's speech after his return from the battle of Ṣiffīn,[16] make one realize how glorious the failure of a leader can be, especially if he is surrounded with a halo of sanctity and also romance, uttering apologetic statements that are at once charming and full of rhetorical appeal.[17]

The book consists of speeches, sermons, maxims, and wise sayings.

> The exaltation and passionate conviction of the born preacher is felt in these homilies. 'Alī clothes his thoughts in a graceful, aphoristic form, his epistles and sermons are expressive, laconic and combine charity of thought with vivid and striking imagery. To these should be added his superb stylistic mastery as a preacher, his range of epithets and metaphors, literary examples, virtuosity in the use of rhymed prose, and musical cadence.[18]

Sufism or the Religion of Love and Beauty

In Sufism, Islamic spirituality in Arabic literature reaches an apex unparalleled by any other literary category.[19] Indeed, the three categories

12. The lover Majnūn in the wilderness.

previously discussed merged into Sufism, forming one forceful spiritual current. It must be mentioned here that woman Sufis were by no means lacking. For example, there was Nafīsah, the daughter of al-Ḥasan, who died in Cairo in 208/823. The celebrated Imam Shāfiʿī used to visit her and perform the *tarāwīḥ,* the late evening prayers of Ramaḍān, in her mosque. ʿĀʾishah (d. 145/762 in Egypt), the daughter of the sixth Shīʿite Imam, Jaʿfar al-Ṣādiq, used to address God in the tone of a coquettish lover: "By Thy might and glory I swear, if Thou castest me into Hell, I will hold my testimony of unity in my right hand and go round amongst the inmates of Hell and tell them, 'I testified to His unity, yet He tortured me.'"[20]

But outstanding among women—and, indeed, among men as well—was Rābiʿat al-ʿAdawiyyah (95/714–185/801), whose heart was so full of the love of God that there was no room for the love of the Prophet or the hatred of Satan. Some of her verses are constantly remembered when people speak of love for God.

> Two ways I love Thee: selfishly,
> And next, as worthy is of Thee.
> 'Tis selfish love that I do naught
> Save think of Thee with every thought;
> 'Tis purest love when Thou dost raise
> The veil to my adoring gaze.
> Not mine the praise in that or this,
> Thine is the praise in both, I wis.[21]

Rābiʿah excelled not only in verse but also in prosodic prayers. Since her repentance from her early sinful life, she remained burning in the fire of Divine Love till her death at the age of eighty-seven.

With the advent of the third Islamic century, the Sufis began to give less expression to their antinomian or paradoxal trends. Al-Junayd al-Baghdādī (d. 296/906) began to speak of the path of sobriety and the reconciliation of Law (*Sharīʿah*) and the Truth (*Ḥaqīqah*). It was al-Ghazzālī (d. 505/1111), however, who reconciled exoteric Islam with Sufism and rendered the latter a recognized way of thinking. He achieved this task despite the fact that a Sufi like al-Ḥallāj (d. 310/922) went to the extreme of expressing his inner union with God when he declared, "*al-Ḥaqq^u fi jubbatī*" ("the Truth is in my gown"). Again, "*Anaʾl-Ḥaqq waʾl-Ḥaqq^u huwaʾ-Llāh!*" ("I am the Truth and the Truth is God"), the famous utterance which led to his execution. Al-Ḥallāj was one of the major Sufi poets of the Arabic language, and this gem of Sufi spirituality is attributed to him: "I am He whom I love, and He whom I love is I; we are two spirits dwelling in one body. If thou seest me, thou seest Him; and if thou seest Him, thou seest us both."[22]

On his way to crucifixion, al-Ḥallāj was seen dragging himself along proudly in his chains and singing these verses:

> My boon-companion is not to be charged with oppression. He gave me to drink from what he was drinking just as a noble host would do for his guest; but after several rounds of drink, he ordered the sword and the executioner's leather cloth to be brought along. Such is the fate of him who drinks with a monster on a summer day![23]

Most of al-Ḥallāj's writings have been lost, but the *Dīwān* and the *Kitāb al-tawāsīn* (*Book of T's and S's*) survive as testaments to his great poetical skills.[24]

Most of the Sufis were Persians and non-Arabs, but the Arabs produced one of the greatest Sufis of all times, Muḥyī al-Dīn ibn 'Arabī, who was also one of the greatest Arab Sufi poets. His *Tarjumān al-ashwāq* has come to be appreciated also in the West.[25] There he sings:

> Before now I used to reject my friend, unless his faith was close to mine, but then my heart became capable of every form: It is a pasture for gazelles and a convent for Christian monks, and a temple for idols, and the pilgrims to the Ka'bah, and the tables of the Torah and the book of the Quran. I follow the religion of Love, whichever way its caravan may proceed. Indeed, Love is my religion and faith.[26]

M. Asín Palacios, among others, believes that Dante's Sufi tendencies and his depiction of the Unseen World are derived from Ibn 'Arabī with little adaptation,[27] and Ibn 'Arabī's influence of both a gnostic and a literary nature upon later Sufism remains immense.

The Arabs also produced a great Sufi poet in the person of 'Umar ibn al-Fāriḍ (576/1180–631/1234), the contemporary of Ibn 'Arabī and 'Umar al-Suhrawardī and the author of the famous *al-Tā'iyyat al-kubrā wa'l-tā'iyyat al-ṣughrā* (*The Greater and Lesser Odes Rhyming in 'T'*). The following are lines from one of his ecstatic mystical songs:

> Lo! in his face commingled
> Is every charm and grace;
> The whole of Beauty singled
> Into a perfect face
> Beholding Him would cry,
> "There is no God but He, and He is the Most High!"[28]

Ibn al-Fāriḍ was born and died in Cairo,[29] and lived in the so-called Valley of the Poor (Wādī al-mustaḍ'afīn) in al-Muqattam, in that city and for some time in Hijaz. He composed numerous poems that have become well known. In his bacchic and amorous odes (*al-Khamriyyah*) he wields all the vocabulary of love to express his adoration of God:

Remembering the Beloved, wine we drank
Which drunk had made us ere the wine's creation...
They tell me: "Thou hast drunk iniquity."
Not so, I have but drunk what not to drink
Would be for me iniquitous indeed.[30]

Nor did Arabic literature cease to reflect Islamic spirituality after the classical age of Ibn 'Arabī and Ibn al-Fāriḍ. Throughout the centuries that followed, the deepest yearnings of the soul for God have continued to be reflected in Arabic poetry and prose as witnessed by the *dīwāns* of Sufi masters such as Shaykh al-'Alawī and Shaykh Ḥabīb in recent times and also in many works of prose which echo the longing of the soul for God and concern for man's spiritual life on earth.

Notes

1. A. J. Arberry, *The Quran Interpreted* (London: Oxford University Press, 1975) x. On the significance of the Quran, see S. H. Nasr, "The Quran as the Foundation of Islamic Spirituality," in *Islamic Spirituality: Foundations,* ed. S. H. Nasr (World Spirituality 19; New York: Crossroad, 1987) 3–10.
2. M. Pickthall, *The Meaning of the Glorious Quran* (Karachi: Taj, 1973) 3.
3. P. K. Hitti, *History of the Arabs, From the Earliest Times to the Present* (London: Macmillan, 1964) 127.
4. J. C. Archer, *Mystical Elements in Mohammad* (New Haven: Yale University Press, 1926) 21.
5. See, e.g., 'Abbās Maḥmūd al-'Aqqād, *al-Lughat al-shā'irah, mazāyā al-fann wa'l-ta'bīr fi'l-lughat al-'arabiyyah* (*The Poetic Language: The Artistic and Expressive Characteristics of Arabic*) (Cairo, 1960) 33-34.
6. This is known in Arabic as *dhikr,* which is at once the remembering, invoking, and mentioning of the Name of God. On the *ḥadīth qudsī,* see W. Graham, *Divine Word and Prophetic Word in Early Islam* (The Hague: Mouton, 1975).
7. R. A. Nicholson, *The Mystics of Islam* (London: G. Bell & Sons, 1914) 105.
8. A. J. Arberry, *"Majnūn Laylā," Shawki's Poetical Drama,* translated into English verse (Cairo, 1933).
9. *Aghānī,* ed. De Sacy, vol. 21, 105; Ibn Qutaybah *al-Shi'r wa'l-shu'arā',* vol. 2, 560; Marzubānī, *al-Muwashshaḥ,* 211.
10. *Aghānī,* ed. Dār al-Kutub, 11/204; *al-Shi'r wa'l-shu'arā',* 1/416; al-Qālī, *Amālī,* 1/86.
11. Nicholson, *Mystics of Islam,* 116–17.
12. S. A. Khulusi, *Shī'ism and its Influences on Arabic Literature* (Ph.D. diss., 1947; Senate House Library, University of London).
13. 'Abd al-Malik al-Marwān (25/646–96/715) is the fourth Umayyad caliph, and Zayn al-'Ābidīn (39/659–94/713) is the son of the martyr al-Ḥusayn. He is one of the Imams of the Twelvers, known also as 'Alī al-Aṣghar (the Younger 'Alī). See his *The Psalms of Islam,* trans. W. Chittick (London: Muhammadi Trust, 1988).
14. Shawqī Ḍayf, *Ta'rīkh al-adab al-'arabī:* vol. 2, *al-'Aṣr al-islāmī* (Cairo, 1963) 315.
15. Ibid., 323.

16. *Nahj al-balāghah,* ed. Muḥammad ʻAbduh (Cairo, n.d.) 1:22.
17. S. A. Khulusi, "The Authenticity of *Nahj al-Balāghah,*" *The Islamic Review* (October, 1950) 34.
18. I. M. Filshtinsky, *Arabic Literature* (Moscow: USSR Academy of Sciences, Institute of the Peoples of Asia, Moscow, 1966) 81.
19. On earlier Arab Sufi poetry, see M. Lings, "Mystical Poetry," in *ʻAbbasid Belles-Lettres,* ed. J. Ashtiany et al. (Cambridge History of Arabic Literature; Cambridge: Cambridge University Press, 1990) 235–64.
20. Aḥmad Tawfīq al-ʻAyyāḍ, *at-Taṣawwuf al-islāmī, ta'rīkhuh*^{u} *wa madārisuh*^{u} *wa ṭabīʻatuh*^{u} *wa āthāruh*^{u} (Cairo, 1970) 53–54.
21. R. A. Nicholson, *A Literary History of the Arabs* (Cambridge: Cambridge University Press, 1921) 234; for the Arabic text, see al-Ghazzālī, *Iḥyā' ʻulūm al-dīn* (Cairo, 1289 A.H.) 4:298; see also ʻAbd al-Raḥmān Badawī, *Shahīdat al-ʻishq al-ilāhī, Rābiʻat al-ʻAdawiyyah* (Cairo, n.d.) 64, 73, 110, 119, 123, 162.
22. Nicholson, *Mystics of Islam,* 151.
23. ʻAyyāḍ, *al-Taṣawwuf al-islāmī,* 88.
24. Ed. L. Massignon (Paris: Geuthner, 1913); see also ʻAyyāḍ, *al-Taṣawwuf al-islāmī,* 80.
25. See chapter 3 of this volume, by William Chittick.
26. ʻAbbās Maḥmūd al-ʻAqqād, *Āthār al-ʻarab fi'l-ḥaḍrat al-awrūbiyyah* (2nd ed.; Cairo: Dār al-Maʻārif, 1963) 98.
27. Ibid. See M. Asín Palacios *La escatologia musulmana en la Divina Comedia* (Madrid: Libros Hiperión, 1984); idem, *El Islam cristianizado* (Madrid: Libros Hiperión, 1981).
28. Nicholson, *Literary History,* 397.
29. F. Totel, *al-Munjid fi'l-adab wa'l-ʻulūm, Muʻjam li-aʻlām al-sharq wa'l-gharb* (Beirut, 1956) 379. For the "Odes of Ibn al-Fāriḍ," see Nicholson, *Studies in Islamic Mysticism,* 162–266. See also A. J. Arberry, *The Mystical Poems of Ibn al-Fāriḍ* (London: E. Walker, 1952); and M. Lings, "The Wine-Song (al-Khamriyyah) of ʻUmar Ibn al-Fāriḍ," *Studies in Comparative Religion* (Summer-Autumn, 1980) 131–32.
30. Lings, "The Wine-Song," 131, 133.

17

Persian Literature

S. H. Nasr and J. Matini

Persia and Islam

The current Persian language and the literature written in it were born from the wedding between Islam and the soul of the Persian people, who embraced this religion after the destruction of the Sassanid empire by the Arab armies in the first/seventh century and the subsequent conquest of Persia. Without doubt, Islam affected deeply all facets of life of the Persians from the social and political to the artistic and religious and even its language, which it helped to mold in its present form. It is significant to note, however, that in contrast to lands west, where the domination of Islam brought with it also Arabization to the extent that lands from Egypt to Morocco speak Arabic to this day, in Persia Islam spread without the Persians becoming Arab as had Egyptians and Syrians. On the contrary, the Persian language developed from the earlier Pahlavi and Dari languages of Sassanid Iran but became deeply infused with the vocabulary of Quranic Arabic and used a modified form of the Arabic alphabet.

The Persians did not become Arab, but they developed Persian into a major Islamic language while also making major contributions to Arabic. In fact, Persian is the only language in the Islamic world besides Arabic to become universal and to be used by others beyond the borders of the land of its native speakers. When one speaks of the Persian language or Persian literature, one is speaking not only of the language and literature of the inhabitants of the Iranian Plateau but of a language and literature that were shared for a millennium between Muslims from China to Iraq and even farther west within the Ottoman Empire. But the center of cultivation of this language and literature has remained, of course, Persia itself.

The Religious Background for Persian Islamic Literature

Before dealing with the so-called Islamic *genres* of Persian literature, it is necessary to recall briefly the Islamic background of such literature in Persia. It must be remembered that during most of its history Persians were predominantly Sunnis, mostly of the Shāfiʿī and Ḥanbalī schools, and yet Persia was the major center of both Twelve-Imam Shīʿism, which became finally predominant with the Safavids, and Ismāʿīlism, at least as far as its intellectual aspects were concerned. Moreover, Persia was also a major center of Sufism. As mentioned earlier in this volume, many of the greatest of the early Sufis, such as Bāyazīd Basṭāmī, Ḥallāj, Tirmidhī and Qushayrī, were Persians, as were the founders of several major Sufi orders such as the Qādiriyyah, Suhrawardiyyah and Mawlawiyyah.

Finally, Persia has been one of the main centers of the Islamic transmitted and intellectual sciences. Some of the greatest scholars of *Ḥadīth* such as Bukhārī and Muslim, came from the Persian cultural world,[1] as did some of the major Quranic commentators such as Zamakhsharī and Bayḍāwī. Among the founders of the Sunni schools of law, one of them, Abū Ḥanīfah, was Persian, whereas both Muʿtazilite and Ashʿarite *Kalām* found some of their greatest exponents in that land. As for the "intellectual" sciences, it need hardly be mentioned that the majority of Islamic philosophers, such as Ibn Sīnā and Suhrawardī, were Persians, as were many of the most illustrious scientists such as Khayyām and Naṣīr al-Dīn Ṭūsī.

There were periods of harmony and eras of discord between various schools of thought in Persia. But in nearly every century, Persia remained a major center for nearly the whole spectrum of Islamic thought, from legal studies to Sufism, and it was like an intellectual and spiritual microcosm of the entire Islamic world. This situation left a profound mark on Persian literature, which became the vehicle for most schools of Islamic thought and spirituality and exercised an influence in the rest of the Islamic world far beyond Persia's geographical borders.

Islamic Persian literature falls under three major categories: (1) literature dealing with wisdom and morality, (2) works of religious inspiration, and (3) Persian Sufi literature.

Wisdom Literature and Literature of Religious Inspiration

Most of Persian poetry from the third/fourth century on contains moral advice or practical wisdom including the national epic of the Persians, the

Shāh-nāmah (*Book of Kings*) of Firdawsī, and the famous *Rubāʿiyyāt* (*Quatrains*) of Khayyām. The peak of this tradition was, however, reached in the seventh/thirteenth century in the *Gulistān* (*Rose Garden*) and *Būstān* (*Garden*) of Saʿdī, the most eloquent writer of the Persian language. Such works, which also include the poetry of Khāqānī Shīrwānī and Niẓāmī Ganjawī, are replete with references to the Quran and *Ḥadīth* and became guides for the moral life of many generations of Persians, Turks, and Indians.

Works of religious inspiration which reflect Islamic spirituality in its aspect of piety also form an important literary category going back to Kisāʾī Marwazī in the fourth/tenth century and reaching one of its early peaks with Nāṣir-i Khusraw.

Nāṣir-i Khusraw (d. *ca.* 470/1077) is one of the greatest authors of Persian poetry of a highly didactic, religious, and ethical nature. Originally of lukewarm Twelve-Imam Shīʿite persuasion, he underwent a transformation after a dream in midlife and became an ardent Ismāʿīlī, whereupon his poetry gained a more sermonizing tone. He composed a large *dīwān* of 11,047 verses, which is replete with moral advice, admonishment, and philosophical expositions. The *Dīwān* is one of the masterpieces of the Persian language and has remained of great popularity among scholars of Persian to this day.[2] Nāṣir-i Khusraw also wrote a number of important prose works, of which the most important is *Jāmiʿ al-ḥikmatayn* (*The Sum of Two Wisdoms*), written, like his other works, in Persian and dealing with Ismāʿīlī philosophy and cosmology. The writings of Nāṣir-i Khusraw possess a universality which made him a major figure of Persian literature, appreciated not only by Ismāʿīlīs but by all Persian speaking Muslims, Sunni and Shīʿite alike.

It should be emphasized that religious literature in Persian deals not only with Shīʿite themes but Sunni ones as well. In fact, most religious works in the Persian language are of a Sunni background and inspiration, and some of them, like early renditions of the Quran into Persian and Ghazzālī's *Kīmiyā-yi saʿādat* (*Alchemy of Happiness*), are of a high literary quality. But there is no doubt that religious works of Shīʿite inspiration became more prevalent after the Mongol invasion and especially with the advent of the Safavids in the tenth/sixteenth century. A well-known independent book written during the period just preceding the Safavids about the calamities befalling the Prophet and his family, especially the martyrs of Karbalāʾ, is the *Rawḍat al-shuhadāʾ* (*The Garden of Martyrs*) by Kamāl al-Dīn Ḥusayn Sabziwārī, known as Kāshifī (d. 910/1504). Although such books as *Maqtal* or *Maqtal-nāmah* (*Book on the Place of Martyrdom*) concerning the martyrdom of religious personages had been written earlier, none had the universal appeal of *Rawḍat al-shuhadā'*.[3]

Toward the end of the reign of the Timurids and the beginning of the Safavid era, other poets such as Amīr Shāhī Sabziwārī, Faghānī Shīrāzī, Amīr Ḥājj Ḥusayn Junābādī, Ahlī Shīrāzī, and Lisānī Shīrāzī also became famous for their poems in praise of the Prophet and his family. Under the Safavids, no poet could be found who did not write at least one poem in praise of the Prophet and the Imams. Shah Tahmāsb once told Muḥtasham Kāshānī, who had composed a poem praising him, that if he expected any reward from him he should write poetry in praise of the Prophet and his family. The same policy was followed by Shah 'Abbās and other Safavid rulers. It was such a policy that induced Ḥayratī Tūnī (d. 961/1554) to compose forty thousand verses in praise of the Prophet and his family. He also composed a poem about the battles and miracles of the Prophet and the Imams known as *Shāh-nāmah* (*The Book of Kings* or *The Book of Miracles*).

Other such poems were composed during the tenth/sixteenth, eleventh/seventeenth, and twelfth/eighteenth centuries, the most important of which was the *Dawāzdah-band* (*Twelve Verses*) by Muḥtasham Kāshānī, who is the most famous religious poet during this period and in fact the most outstanding poet of eulogies in the Persian language.

Religious poetry of this kind continued to be written during the Qajar and Pahlavi periods, but with the advent of modernism, the appeal of this kind of poetry decreased in modern educated circles. It continued, however, on the popular level, and a number of works of this genre have been composed during this century.

Persian Sufi Literature

Persian Sufi literature, especially poetry, is like a cultural miracle in the bosom of Islamic civilization. It is a vast ocean which has succeeded in expressing the most inward and spiritual dimensions of Islam in a most universal language that has spread far and wide beyond the geographical confines of Persia itself. Much of Asia was Islamized through Persian Sufi poetry, and in many a Muslim home as far east as Bengal the only book found besides the Quran used to be the *Dīwān* of Ḥāfiẓ. Ottoman sultans wrote Persian poetry inspired by Persian Sufi poets, and to this day simple *tonga* drivers in Lahore or shopkeepers in Kashmir can still recite Persian Sufi poetry. One of the greatest of the Persian Sufi poets, Jalāl al-Dīn Rūmī, became also the spiritual pole of the Turks, and Konya, where he is buried, remains the religious and spiritual center of Turkey. It was through the translation of Ḥāfiẓ and Shabistarī in the middle of the thirteenth/nineteenth century into German and later English that the attention of some of the most sensitive and perceptive European and American minds such as Goethe, Rückert, and Emerson turned toward the spiritual treasures of Islam.

Sufi literature in Persian is so extensive and diversified that it is not possible to enumerate and describe fully even all its peaks nor to talk of some of its less sublime expressions. It includes a vast literature composed in a period of over a millennium not only by Persians—including those now living in Afghanistan, Tajikistan, Soviet Azerbaijan etc., which were part of the Persian world—but also by Persian-speaking Indians and Turks. It includes Quranic commentaries, didactic metaphysical works and ethical treatises all in prose as well as a wide range of poetry embracing all the classical forms from the quatrain (*rubāʿī*) to the rhyming couplet (*mathnawī*) to the sonnetlike *ghazal*. But the greatest masterpieces of this literature appeared as poetry and because of their great beauty and spiritual quality left their imprint on the whole of Persian culture and were also instrumental in the birth of mystical literature in several languages of the Indian subcontinent.[4]

The Earliest Persian Works of Sufism

The first important Sufi treatise in Persian is the *Kashf al-maḥjūb* (*The Unveiling of the Veiled*) by Abu'l-Ḥasan ibn ʿUthmān Hujwīrī (d. 465/1071).[5] Over the centuries, this work has remained one of the most authoritative and popular books on Sufism. Following soon after Hujwīrī's famous opus were two books translated from Arabic into Persian and considered as important Persian sources on Sufism. One of them, *al-Taʿarruf li madhhab al-taṣawwuf* (*Introduction to the School of the Sufis*) by Abū Bakr ibn Abī Isḥāq Bukhārī Kalābādhī (d. 380/990), was rendered into Persian with a detailed commentary by Imam Abū Ibrāhīm Ismāʿīl Bukhārī (d. 434/1043).[6] This vast work is of great literary quality and is a synthesis of Sufi knowledge and practice. The other work is the Persian translation of the *Risālat al-qushayriyyah* written by Imam Abu'l-Qāsim Qushayrī (376/986–465/1073). The work, rendered into Persian by one of the author's students, is a masterpiece of Persian prose.[7]

Traditionally Abū Saʿīd Abi'l-Khayr (357/967–440/1049), a famous Sufi of Khurasan, is said to have been the first Persian Sufi poet, although some now believe that the poems attributed to him were by his teacher Bishr ibn Yāsīn.[8] Two treatises written a century after him—the *Asrār al-tawḥīd*

13. Khwājah ʿAbd Allāh Anṣārī and his disciples.

(*Secrets of Unity*),[9] by one of his grandchildren, Muḥammad ibn Munawwar, and *Ḥālāt wa sukhanān-i Shaykh Abū Sa'īd* (*The States and Sayings of Abū Sa'īd*)—bear testimony to his significance as a Sufi and also to the literary influence of his work. The quatrains attributed to him have resonated in Sufi circles over the centuries.[10] Abū Sa'īd's contemporary, Bābā Ṭāhir, also composed some of the earliest Sufi quatrains of the Persian language, impregnated, like those attributed to Abū Sa'īd, with intense love and yearning for God.

The works of Khwājah 'Abd Allāh Anṣārī (396/1006–481/1089) mark a watershed in Persian Sufi literature. He wrote prose works which often contain his own verses as well. His prose style is itself quite poetical, often written in rhythmical prose (*musajja'*), as seen in his most famous opus, the *Munājāt* (*Supplications*), which is among the most popular works of the Persian language. The work appeals directly to the heart and expresses the deepest spiritual attitudes in simple language as can be seen in this prayer:

> O God
> Take me by the hand, for I have nothing to
> present to Thee.
> Accept me, for I am unable to flee.
> Open a door, for Thou openest all doors.
> Show the way, for Thou showest all ways.
> I give my hand to no helper,
> for all are transitory:
> only Thou abidest forever.[11]

Anṣārī composed a number of other treatises, including *Naṣā'iḥ* (*Advice*), *Zād al-'ārifīn* (*Provisions of Gnostics*), *Risāla-yi dil wa jān* (*Treatise on the Heart and Soul*), *Kanz al-sālikīn* (*Treasure of the Travelers upon the Path*) and *Maḥabbat-nāmah* (*The Book on Love*). He also rendered the *Ṭabaqāt al-ṣūfiyyah* (*The Classes of Sufis*) of Sulamī from Arabic into the Persian dialect of Herat. Anṣārī's prose is well balanced, direct, and yet musical and poetic. His work displays a reverential fear of God combined with repose and a keen sense of yearning for God before Whom man is nothing.

Sufi Prose Literature in the Fifth/Eleventh and Sixth/Twelfth Centuries

One of the foremost figures of Sufism, Abū Ḥāmid Muḥammad Ghazzālī (450/1058–505/1111), who hailed from Tus in Khurasan, is not only of great significance in the history of Sufism because he made Sufism acceptable in Sunni Sharī'ite circles; he is also of importance in Persian Sufi literature because of a number of important Sufi tracts, especially the *Kīmīyā-yi sa'ādat*, which he wrote as a Persian summary of his own *magnum opus* of Sufi ethics, the *Iḥyā' 'ulūm al-dīn* (*Revivification of the Sciences of Religion*).[12] The *Kīmīyā-yi sa'ādat* is a masterpiece of Persian prose and a major text treating various facets of Sufism, especially its ethical and practical teachings.

Abū Ḥāmid's brother, Aḥmad Ghazzālī (d. 520/1126) is also of great importance in the history of Persian Sufi literature. Besides being an outstanding Sufi master who trained many disciples, Aḥmad Ghazzālī wrote a number of Persian treatises and even some quatrains. Among these works, the *Sawāniḥ fi'l-'ishq* (*Inspirations from the World of Pure Spirits*) occupies a unique position[13] and represents a new genre of Sufi literature in which Sufi gnosis is presented in the dress of love and longing and in a language of great poetic beauty. Aḥmad Ghazzālī belongs to that family of Persian *fedele d'amore*, to use the terminology of Henry Corbin,[14] whose members have sung of the love of the Beloved and set out in quest of the union that at once illuminates and liberates. The *Sawāniḥ* was followed by Suhrawardī's *Risālah fī ḥaqīqah al-'ishq* (*Treatise on the Reality of Love*), Rūzbihān Baqlī, the patron saint of Shiraz's *'Abhar al-'āshiqīn* (*The Jasmine of Lovers*), Fakhr al-Dīn 'Irāqī's *Lama'āt* (*Divine Flashes*) and 'Abd al-Raḥmān Jāmī's *Lawāmi'* (*Flashing Lights*). All of these treatises were written in Persian poetic prose and represent great literary masterpieces while also depicting the teachings of Sufism in such a manner that gnosis is presented in the language of love, which ranges from love for the beauty of forms to the love of the Beauty of the Face of the Beloved, that absolute inebriating and liberating beauty which is itself formless.

Gradually in the sixth/twelfth-century Sufi metaphysics began to be formulated in Persian beginning with the works of 'Ayn al-Quḍāt Hamadānī, who, accused of heresy, was put to death at the age of thirty-three in 525/1131. In his letters, his two major works *Tamhīdāt* (*Dispositions*) and *Zubdat al-ḥaqā'iq* (*The Best of Truths*) as well as his last work written in prison before his death, the *Shakwa'l-gharīb* (*Complaint of the Stranger*), 'Ayn al-Quḍāt has left some of the most moving works of Sufism, a corpus which left a deep mark upon many a later Sufi.[15]

One of the figures who was to follow in many ways the life of 'Ayn al-Quḍāt and who was to meet with the same tragic end was Shaykh al-ishrāq Shihāb al-Dīn Suhrawardī, the founder of the school of illumination (*ishrāq*), who was killed in Aleppo in 587/1191.[16] Besides being one of the greatest of Islamic philosophers, writing such major philosophical and theosophical works as the *Ḥikmat al-ishrāq* (*Theosophy of the Orient of Light*), Suhrawardī wrote a number of Sufi treatises in Persian which are among the masterpieces of Persian prose and represent the peak of the art of visionary recitals commenced by Ibn Sīnā.[17] The mystical prose of Suhrawardī has never been surpassed in the annals of Persian literature in its combining of symbolic representation of metaphysical truths with beauty and vividness of language.

Sanā'ī, 'Aṭṭār, Rūmī

Persian Sufi poetry reached the peak of its maturity in the sixth/twelfth and seventh/thirteenth centuries with Sanā'ī, 'Aṭṭār, and Rūmī. Sanā'ī (d. between 525/1131 and 545/1150) spent much of his life, like many other poets of his era, praising various rulers. But after making a pilgrimage to the House of God, he became an ascetic and retired from courtly life. During this period he completed the *Ḥadīqat al-ḥaqīqah* (*The Garden of Truth*), which is the first Sufi *mathnawī* in the Persian language.[18]

The *Ḥadīqah* had an extensive impact upon later Persian literature. One can see its direct effect upon such works as the *Tuḥfat al-'irāqayn* (*The Gift of Two Iraqs*) by Khāqānī and the *Makhzan al-asrār* (*The Storehouse of Secrets*) by Niẓāmī. The two outstanding later Sufi poets, 'Aṭṭār and Rūmī, also paid a great deal of attention to it.

Sanā'ī's style in the *Ḥadīqah* and also in his other poems written after his initiation into Sufism is new and distinguished. It is a style in which he was able to combine religious beliefs and gnostic themes. The poems of Sanā'ī during this period are full of gnostic knowledge and truths and replete with religious thoughts, admonition against worldliness, sermons, and educational examples. During this period, his poems were greatly affected both directly and indirectly by the verses of the Quran and the *Ḥadīth.* He even composed a *qaṣīdah* in which the second part of the second verse is taken directly from Quranic verses.[19]

The path tread by Sanā'ī was followed in a most masterful manner by Farīd al-Dīn 'Aṭṭār, one of the supreme Sufi poets, some of whose poems have never been surpassed in the annals of Persian Sufi literature. 'Aṭṭār was a druggist, as the literal meaning of his name *'aṭṭār* reveals, and he traveled widely in the region from Transoxiana to Mecca, meeting many Sufi masters. He became an accomplished Sufi with unparalleled poetic powers. Rūmī could say of him, "Not in a hundred years does there appear an 'Aṭṭār." During his later life, 'Aṭṭār continued to practice as a druggist in his native city of Nayshapur, where he was probably killed during the Mongol invasion in 618/1221.

The great troubadour of Nayshapur wrote a famous prose work on the life of Muslim saints entitled *Tadhkirat al-awliyā'* (*Memorial of Saints*), which contains a moving description of the life and death of Ḥallāj, but the main body of his works consists of poetry which poured forth profusely from his pen. In fact, it has been said that he wrote 114 poetic works corresponding to the chapters (*sūrahs*) of the Quran. This seems to be an exaggeration, but it points to his voluminous output. In his *Khusraw-nāmah* (*Treatise Dedicated to Khusraw*) he himself mentions that his critics called him the "one of abundant speech" (*bisyār-gūy*) but adds that he composed in quantity because of the wealth of meaning and truth within his being which had to be expressed.

Besides a *dīwān* of *ghazals*, *qaṣīdahs*, and *rubāʿiyyāt*, ten *mathnawīs* have survived whose attribution to ʿAṭṭār is certain, such as *Muṣībat-nāmah* (*The Book of Tribulation*) and *Ilāhī-nāmah* (*The Book of the Divine*). But his most important *mathnawī* is the *Manṭiq al-ṭayr* (*Conference of the Birds*), which in some forty-six hundred verses describes the journey of thirty birds (*sī murgh*) through the seven mountains and valleys of cosmic existence to the top of the cosmic mountain Qāf, where they finally encounter the Sīmurgh, the symbol of the Divine. After having endured the great hardship of the journey, they have difficulty in gaining access to His Presence. When finally allowed to behold that Presence, they realize that the *sī murgh* are identical with the Sīmurgh, that the self is none other than the Self. In some of the most powerful and moving verses of Persian poetry, ʿAṭṭār describes this union which is the end of all spiritual wayfaring:

> To be consumed by the light of the presence
> of the Sīmurgh is to realize that,
> I know not whether I am Thou or Thou art I;
> I have disappeared in Thee and duality
> hath perished.[20]

ʿAṭṭār died in the Mongol invasion, but Bahāʾ al-Dīn Walad, who belonged to the same Kubrawiyyah branch of Sufism as ʿAṭṭār, left his homeland of Khurasan before the Mongol onslaught for safer lands west. The author of the *Kitāb al-maʿārif* (*The Book of Divine Knowledge*), Bahāʾ al-Dīn Walad is said to have visited ʿAṭṭār on his way to Mecca. It was then, according to traditional sources, that he presented his young son Jalāl al-Dīn to the venerable poet, the son who was destined to surpass ʿAṭṭār as the foremost of all Sufi poets and one of the greatest of all Muslim saints.

Jalāl al-Dīn Muḥammad Balkhī, known also as Mawlānā, "our master," or Rūmī, brought the tradition of Persian Sufi poetry to its peak.[21] Trained in the religious and Sufi sciences by his father, Jalāl al-Dīn became a celebrated religious teacher in Konya with over a thousand students and led the life of a sober and quiet teacher until his encounter with the mysterious wandering Sufi Shams al-Dīn Tabrīzī. The meeting of these two stars in the firmament of Islamic spirituality transformed the life of Jalāl al-Dīn. He gave up all worldly activity and even his scholarly life, spending all his time with Shams until the latter's mysterious disappearance. After this event, Jalāl al-Dīn spent the rest of his life in the training of Sufi disciples and the founding of the Mawlawiyyah Order, characterized by the famous whirling dance the inspiration for which Mawlānā received from Heaven. He was so celebrated in the later period of his life that even the governor of Anatolia, Mu'īn al-Dīn Parwānah, had become his disciple. When he died, the stepson of Ibn 'Arabī and the foremost expositor of his teachings in the East, Ṣadr al-Dīn Qunawī, led the prayer of the dead and Jalāl al-Dīn's body was buried in Konya in a place which remains to this day a site of pilgrimage.

The encounter of Rūmī and Shams not only changed Rūmī's life outwardly; it also created a tidal wave which henceforth poured forth verses of heavenly beauty. He composed twenty-six thousand verses of poetry in *mathnawī* form, which became known henceforth as the *Mathnawī*, a work of unparalleled breadth and depth which Jāmī called "the Quran in the Persian language." The work is in fact an esoteric commentary on the Quran and a compendium of the esoteric sciences expressed in the language of symbols and parables in a deceivingly simple form although some of the verses of the *Mathnawī* are quite enigmatic. There is no work in Persian Sufi literature that investigates the heights and depths of the human soul, the meaning of existence, the nature of God, man, and the universe, and the enigmas of the unity of the Truth and the diversity of revealed forms in poetic language of such power and beauty. No wonder that the work became rapidly the mainstay of the spiritual culture of Persian-speaking people and is quoted to this day not only by mystics but also by religious teachers, not only by poets but also by military leaders and rulers. Moreover, the *Mathnawī* inspired many works in other languages from Turkish to Sindhi and even whole schools of music to chant its hypnotic verses. R. A. Nicholson, who spent a lifetime in translating all its six books into English, called Rūmī the greatest mystical poet who ever lived.

The very first verses of the preludium to the work announce in symbolic language the theme of the *Mathnawī:*

> Hearken to this Reed forlorn,
> Breathing ever since 'twas torn
> From its rushy bed, a strain
> Of impassioned love and pain.[22]

The "strain" of the reed cut off from its bed is the longing of the human soul separated from its Source. These verses guide the soul to return to that Original Abode, for which it always longs and to which it will finally return. The strain of the flute or reed which also characterizes the music of the Mawlawī Order conjures up nostalgia for our original homeland,

14. The tomb of Khwājah ʿAbd Allāh Anṣārī in Herat, Afghanistan.

nostalgia that is most deeply felt by those who are pulled by the attraction of Heaven in this life and for whom Rūmī remains the supreme guide.

Jalāl al-Dīn was also to write many quatrains as well as the famous prose work *Fīhi mā fīhi,* which contains his intimate discourses. But his great masterpiece after the *Mathnawī* is the monumental *Dīwān-i Shams,* also called the *Dīwān-i kabīr,* which consists of 36,360 verses. In contrast to the *Mathnawī,* which is didactic in nature and reveals the meaning of the Quran and *Ḥadīth* as well as drawing from nearly all the Islamic sciences and schools of thought, the *Dīwān-i Shams* is a work of an ecstatic nature written in a highly musical and poetic form and revealing through its very rhythm and music something of the ecstasy of Divine Love and Union with the Beloved. The inner power of spiritual attraction erupts and rends asunder linguistic forms, creating a poetry of unique spiritual power and hypnotic quality.[23]

After Rūmī, the landscape of Persian Sufi literature was never the same again. It seems that a whole ocean had been created and wherever one looked one could see this boundless ocean on the horizon. No Sufi literature was henceforth created in the eastern lands of Islam without being influenced by the incomparable creative genius combined with sanctity of Jalāl al-Dīn Rūmī, whose verses have been chanted by "*Mathnawī*-chanters" (*Mathnawī khwāns*) in inns for simple believers as well as recited and meditated upon by the greatest sages and seers who have followed in the wake of this supreme mystical poet of the Persian language.

The Poets Inspired by Ibn 'Arabī's School

The dissemination of the teachings of Ibn 'Arabī in the Persian world not only produced a large number of prose works on Sufi metaphysics in both Persian and Arabic, such as Jandī's commentary upon the *Fuṣūṣ al-ḥikam* (*Bezels of Wisdom*)—not to speak of Ṣadr al-Dīn Qunawī's own works; it also led to the appearance of several major Sufi poets whose writings were directly inspired by the teachings of the Murcian sage who was to die in Damascus. One of these poets, who was a companion of Ibn 'Arabī, was Awḥad al-Dīn Kirmānī (d. 635/1238), a shaykh of the Suhrawardiyyah Order who composed poems expressing what later became known as the doctrine of *waḥdat al-wujūd.* He was also one of the foremost expositors of the Sufi doctrine of beauty, expressed in many of his quatrains, which were his "heart's witness" (*shāhid-i dil*).[24]

Another major poet who was also an expositor of the doctrine of *waḥdat al-wujūd* and at the same time one of the most eloquent of the Persian *fedeli d'amore* was Fakhr al-Dīn 'Irāqī (610/1213–688/1289), who belongs both to the school of Ibn 'Arabī and to the poetical tradition of 'Aṭṭār and Rūmī.

'Irāqī is famous not only for his *Lama'āt*, which is among the classics of Persian Sufi prose, but also for his love-intoxicated poems.[25] His *Dīwān* became famous not only in Persia but also in India and became an integral part of Sufi love poetry which was often chanted with musical accompaniment.

In the eighth/fourteenth century, there appeared in Persian poetry one of the most perfect and eloquent summaries of the purest form of Sufi gnosis, by Shaykh Maḥmūd Shabistarī (687/1288–720/1320, and, according to some, d. 737/1337). In answer to seventeen questions on different aspects of Sufi doctrine and practice sent by the Khurasani Sufi Sayyid Ḥusayn Hirawī, Shabistarī composed a *mathnawī* of 993 verses entitled *Gulshan-i rāz* (*The Garden of Divine Mysteries*). These poems of celestial beauty and inspiration became immediately famous throughout the Persian-speaking world, and the work has remained to this day among the most famous in the annals of Sufism. It has inspired numerous commentaries, of which the most extensive is that of Muḥammad Lāhījī, whose commentary is itself among the most extensive Persian prose works on Sufism. The work has also been emulated over the centuries, the last well-known example being the *Gulshan-i rāz-i jadīd* (*The New Garden of Divine Mysteries*) by Muḥammad Iqbāl. But the original *Gulshān-i rāz* remains unique in its sublimity and beauty, matching the works of 'Aṭṭār, Rūmī, and Ḥāfiẓ in its depth of meaning and poetic power. Its very first line is one of the most famous verses of Sufi poetry:

> In the Name of Him who taught the soul to meditate,
> Who illumined the heart with the light of the soul.

No wonder that this *summa* of Sufism was one of the first works of Sufism to be translated into a European language and that it has been translated several times into English.[26]

One could also mention many other poets from the centuries immediately following the spread of the teachings of Ibn 'Arabī, such as Shams al-Dīn Maghribī, one of the most daring formulators of the doctrines of *waḥdat al-wujūd*, whose verses have been particularly popular among the Sufis themselves.

The Poets of Shiraz: Sa'dī and Ḥāfiẓ

One would imagine that after Rūmī the possibilities of the Persian language to express the realities and experiences of Sufism in poetry would have been exhausted, but such was not the case. In the seventh/thirteenth and eighth/fourteenth centuries two poets of Shiraz, Sa'dī and Ḥāfiẓ, brought Persian to the height of its formal perfection and left behind works that have had the profoundest literary and spiritual effect on people as far away as Turkey and Bengal.

Saʿdī (*ca.* 580/1184 to between 691/1292 and 695/1296), as already mentioned, was primarily a moralist, but he was also a Sufi of the Suhrawardiyyah Order. In his *Dīwān,* his *Būstān,* and the fourth chapter of the *Gulistān* are to be found many profound verses and phrases dealing with the spiritual life. Saʿdī brought to perfection the writing of Persian, and for centuries his *Gulistān,* a prose work replete with poetry, has been the standard for the perfect style of writing Persian. He has also acted as a moral teacher and the mirror in which the ethos of not only his own Persian society but Islamic society as a whole has been reflected.

Saʿdī was followed a century later by Shams al-Dīn Muḥammad Ḥāfiẓ (literally, "memorizer of the Quran") (d. 791/1389), who is the supreme poet of the Persian language, the master with whom the genius of Persian poetic expression reaches its peak. He is the master alchemist, whose rhymes and rhythms transmute the soul and open it unto the invisible world, for which he was the most eloquent of spokesmen. He was called and is known to this day as *lisān al-ghayb* (the Tongue of the Invisible World) and *tarjumān al-asrār* (Interpreter of Divine Mysteries). Ḥāfiẓ created the most perfect Persian poetry in the *ghazal* form and left behind a *dīwān* that became the most widely cherished book of poetry throughout Asia, inspiring not only countless Muslim poets but even Hindu ones such as Tagore, who confessed that Ḥāfiẓ was the source of his inspiration.

Ḥāfiẓ was not only a poet but also a scholar knowledgeable in the religious sciences, literature, philosophy, and in Sufism, to which he was devoted. He had an extraordinary talent to combine the profoundest thoughts with the most delicate poetic images. In his poetry one observes the final and most perfect wedding between exalted spirituality and vivid sensuality. He speaks of the Divine Names and Qualities while describing the hair of the beloved moving gently in the morning breeze. He alludes to the most esoteric of Sufi doctrines while emphasizing the importance of the *Sharīʿah,* in which he was an authority. In his work the exoteric and the esoteric, the outward and the inward, the worldly and the otherworldly, the spiritual and the sensual are woven together in a poetry which is itself a vehicle that carries man to the exalted proximity of the Divine Empyrean.

Ḥāfiẓ remains the most untranslatable of all Persian poets because the meaning of his verses is so perfectly molded with the formal expression of the Persian language with its particular prosody, symbolic imagery, and music that it is hardly possible to disentangle the meaning in order to express it in another language and medium. Many have translated Ḥāfiẓ, and some in a masterly fashion, but that alchemy which transmutes the soul of the reader or hearer of the verses in Persian has hardly ever been transmitted to another language. In a celebrated *ghazal* engraved on his tombstone, he says:

> Though I be old, clasp me one night to thy breast,
> And I, when the dawn shall come to awaken me,
> With the flash of youth on my cheek from thy bosom
>   will rise.
> Rise up! Let mine eyes delight in thy stately grace!
> Thou art the goal to which all men's endeavor
>   has pressed,
> And thou the idol of Ḥāfiẓ's worship; thy face,
> From the world and life shall bid him come forth
>   and arise![27]

Something of the beauty of Ḥāfiẓ's thought and the richness of his symbolic imagery can be seen in the translation, but not that rhapsodic music which in the original Persian moves the soul and carries the sensitive hearer of these words to the "Garden of Divine Proximity" Itself.

The uniqueness of Ḥāfiẓ's language lies in the fact that he explains accurately the delicate meanings of gnosis and wisdom in a nearly miraculous language, which is combined with the fruit of his subtle poetic imagination and piercing thoughts. Many factors have combined to make Ḥāfiẓ's poetry of universal appeal. According to Muḥammad Gulandām, Ḥāfiẓ's friend and classmate, even during his lifetime his poetry had already spread to Turkey, India, Iraq, and Azerbaijan, and no Sufi gathering was complete without a recitation of his poems.

It has been said that Ḥāfiẓ continued to study the Quran and its traditional methods of recitation and commentaries throughout his life. This poet, who knew the whole of the Quran by heart, often cites the Word of God in his poems and in fact refers to this point in one of his verses:

> I have never seen better poetry than thine, O Ḥāfiẓ—
> By the Quran which thou carriest in thy breast.[28]

No wonder that wherever the Persian language spread the divine poetry of Ḥāfiẓ became synonymous with the highest literary expression of Islamic spirituality.

Jāmī, the Seal of Persian Poets

ʿAbd al-Raḥmān Jāmī (817/1414–898/1492), who was given the honorary title of Seal of Poets (*khātam al-shuʿarā*ʾ), was at once an advanced Sufi of the Naqshbandiyyah Order, an authority in the gnostic teachings of the school of Ibn ʿArabī,[29] a great scholar and theologian, and one of the foremost poets of the Persian language. In him the Sufi traditions of Ibn ʿArabī and Rūmī became in a sense united. Although as a general rule he did not guide disciples upon the Path, Jāmī was deeply respected in his own lifetime as an undisputed authority in Sufism, and his poetry gained fame from Turkey to the Malay world almost immediately after its composition.

Jāmī wrote both prose and poetic works of great literary quality. His prose works include such gnostic treatises as the *Ashiʿʿat al-lamaʿāt* (*Rays of Divine Flashes*), which is a commentary on ʿIrāqī's *Lamaʿāt* and deals with the whole cycle of gnosis in the language of love. His *Lawāʾiḥ* (*Gleaming Lights*) is a short and masterly summary of Ibn ʿArabī's doctrines, while his *Naqd al-nuṣūṣ fī sharḥ naqsh al-fuṣūṣ* (*Selected Texts to Comment the "Imprint of the Fuṣūṣ"*) is one of the major commentaries on Ibn ʿArabī's works. Jāmī is also the author of one of the most important histories of Sufism, the *Nafaḥāt al-uns* (*Breaths of Familiarity*), which became an authoritative reference book from the time of its composition.

In poetry Jāmī followed the dramatic and romantic tradition of Niẓāmī and composed several romances, but he transformed them into openly Sufi poetic works. He also followed the poetic tradition of Jalāl al-Dīn Rūmī. His most famous poetic work is the *Haft Awrang* (*The Seven Thrones*), which consists of seven *mathnawīs*, including *Salāmān wa Absāl* (*Salāmān and Absāl*), *Yūsuf wa Zulaykhā* (*Joseph and Potiphar's Wife*), and *Laylī wa Majnūn* (*Laylī and Majnūn*), in which human love is transformed into the vehicle and symbol of Divine Love. The very name of Laylī symbolizes the beauty of the dark night—hence the Divine Essence, which is obscure because of its excess of light. The Beloved is loved with such intensity by the traveler upon the Path, or Majnūn, that the love kills, obliterates, and annihilates him. There is a transformation of metaphorical love (*ʿishq-i majāzī*) into real love (*ʿishq-i ḥaqīqī*) through a poetic art that echoes the lyrics of Niẓāmī, the stories of the *Mathnawī*, the commentaries upon the Quran, and folk stories about mythical lovers.

Jāmī's poetical works also include the *Bahāristān* (*Spring-land*), written on the model of Saʿdī's *Gulistān* and the famous *Dīwān*, which the author compiled in three different volumes. Jāmī even translated forty *ḥadīths* of the Prophet into Persian quatrains. Moreover, because of his great love for the Arabic Sufi poetry of ʿUmar ibn al-Fāriḍ, Jāmī translated and commented on the Egyptian poet's *Qaṣīdah mīmiyyah* (*Qaṣīdah Ending with the Letter "M"*) in his *Lawāmiʿ* (*Flashing Lights*). He wrote also a commentary on the first seventy-five verses of the *Tāʾiyyah* (*Qaṣīdah Ending with the Letter "T"*).

Altogether Jāmī left behind an imposing edifice of Sufi works in both

15. The Sufi poet Farīd al-Dīn ʿAṭṭār and his disciples.

prose and poetry, which were to have a wide appeal and influence. In a sense he represents a grand synthesis of many currents of Persian literature. It is not therefore accidental that he was honored with the title of *khātam al-shu'arā'* or Seal of the Poets.

Sufi Poetry after Jāmī

Although he was the "seal," Jāmī did not terminate activity in the field of Persian Sufi literature. From the tenth/sixteenth century on, the "Indian style" or *sabk-i hindī* with its ornate language became prevalent not only in India but also in Persia itself. Some of the great representatives of this style such as Ṣā'ib-i Tabrīzī composed many verses inspired by Sufi literature. Moreover, the tenth/sixteenth century was witness to the simple and appealing *mathnawīs* of Shaykh Bahā' al-Dīn 'Āmilī such as *Nān wa ḥalwā* (*Bread and Sweetmeat*), which spread the teachings of Sufism in a more popular manner. To this day a great deal of Sufi ethics is transmitted by traditional storytellers and bards in coffeehouses throughout Persia through the chanting of Shaykh Bahā' al-Dīn's *mathnawīs.*

During the Qajar period, Sufi masters especially of the Nimatullāhī Order continued to compose Sufi poetry. Among them Nūr 'Alī Shāh, Mushtāq 'Alī Shāh, and Ṣafī 'Alī Shāh became especially known as poets.[30] The poems of Ṣafī 'Alī Shāh, who lived at the end of the Qajar period, became popular even among the general public. Many of the well-known poets of this period also continued to write in the classical Sufi poetical tradition. One of the most famous among them, Hātif Iṣfahānī, is particularly known for his *tarjī'-bands* (strophic poems), which resonate with Sufi doctrines, especially the transcendent unity of religions to which Rūmī and Ḥāfiẓ also refer in many of their verses.

During this period also certain of the philosophers who themselves had strong mystical tendencies composed noteworthy poems of a metaphysical and mystical nature. Foremost among this group was Ḥājjī Mullā Hādī Sabziwārī, who continued the tradition of the Safavid gnostics Mīr Dāmād and Mullā Ṣadrā, and two students of Mullā Ṣadrā, 'Abd al-Razzāq Lāhījī, and Fayḍ Kāshānī, all of whom left behind a notable body of poetry devoted to mystical themes.

Even during this century, despite the turning of many poets to modern subjects, Persian Sufi poetry has continued to be composed not only by the Nimatullāhī masters and disciples such as Javad Nurbakhsh but also by members of other orders, especially the Dhahabiyyah, as well as by such notable authorities in the history and doctrines of Sufism as Hādī Ḥā'irī, Jalāl Humā'ī, and Badī' al-Zamān Furūzānfar. Sufism has had such a profound influence on Persian literature that its world view and its language and imagery continue to be vivid realities even amid the modernization and secularization of language and thought and the externalization of the teachings of religion which have been carried out in different circles of Persian society during the past century.[31]

Sufism and the Other Iranian Languages

Persian is the best known and most widely used of the Iranian languages, but there are other languages of this family that have also served over the centuries as vehicles for the expression of Islamic spirituality. Languages such as Kurdish, Baluchi, Simnani, and the like are rich in folk Sufi poetry, and Kurdish and Baluchi are especially significant. Baluchi Sufi poetry has been mostly the product of the Qādirīs of that area, who in their gatherings recite to this day not only classical Persian poetry but also Baluchi poems modeled mostly on the Persian.

Kurdish too has produced a sizable mystical literature, much of it preserved only orally. Most Sufi poetry in this language is related to the Naqshbandiyyah and Qādiriyyah, but there is also a class of Kurdish literature related to the *Ahl-i ḥaqq* ("People of the Truth"), which represents a peculiar expression of Sufism. This "Kurdish esoterism" as some of its followers and disciples have called it,[32] has produced a literature of much mystical and cosmological interest that has remained dear to the heart of the Kurdish people.

The main spiritual theme of these literatures remains close to themes found in Persian Sufi literature. The wedding between the Quranic revelation and the soul of the Persian people created a vast mystical literature that is unmatched in its diversity and depth and has had an impact on numerous literary traditions from Malay to Turkish. In the peaks of this Sufi literature is to be found that perfect wedding between form and spiritual content which marks the greatest masterpieces of traditional and sacred art. To quote Rūmī's son, Sultan Walad:

> These words are the ladder to heaven.
> Whoever ascends them reaches the roof,
> Not the roof which is the blue sky,
> But the roof which is beyond all the celestial orbs.

Notes

1. See S. H. Nasr and M. Mutahhari, "The Religious Sciences," in *The Cambridge History of Iran* (Cambridge: University Press, 1975) 4:464–80.

2. Dh. Ṣafā, *Tārīkh-i adabiyyāt dar Īrān* (Tehran: Intishārāt-i Ibn-i Sīnā, 1347 A.H.S.) 2:448–52, 455; see also *Nāṣir-i Khusraw: Forty Poems from the Divan,* trans. P. Wilson and G. Aavani (Tehran: Imperial Iranian Academy of Philosophy, 1977).

3. Works associated with Shī'ite mourning became an important literary genre. See S. Humāyūnī, *Ta'ziyah wa ta'ziyah-khwānī* (Tehran: Festival of Arts Series, 1354 A.HS.).

4. See A. Schimmel, *As Through a Veil: Mystical Poetry in Islam* (New York: Columbia University Press, 1982) 135ff.

5. Muḥammad Taqī Bahār, *Sabk-shināsī* (Tehran: Wizārat-i Farhang, 1321 A.H.S.–) 2:187. Trans. by R. A. Nicholson as *The Kashf al-Maḥjūb: The Oldest Persian Treatise on Sufism.*

6. Ṣafā, *Tārīkh-i adabiyyāt,* 1:628. Kalābādhī's work has been translated into English by A. J. Arberry as *The Doctrine of the Sufis* (Cambridge: University Press, 1935).

7. Abu'l-Qāsim Qushayrī, *Tarjama-yi risāla-yi qushayriyyah,* ed. B. Furūzānfar (Tehran: BTNK, 1345/1967) 71.

8. See F. Meier, *Abū Sa'īd-i Abū'l-Ḫair: Wirklichkeit und Legende* (Leiden: Brill, 1976).

9. Ṣafā, *Tārīkh-i adabiyyāt,* 1:604.

10. R. A. Nicholson, *Studies in Islamic Mysticism* (Cambridge: University Press, 1921).

11. See Kwaja Abdullah Ansari, *Intimate Conversations,* trans. W. Thackston (New York: Paulist Press, 1978) 204. Translation slightly revised.

12. Many "books" of this major work have been rendered into English and other European languages. A summary of the whole work is contained in G. H. Bousquet, *Iḥyā' ouloum ed-din; ou Vivication des sciences de la foi* (Paris: M. Besson, 1955). See also H. Ritter, *Das Elixir der Glückseligkeit* (Jena: E. Dieterichs, 1923); and W. Montgomery Watt, *Faith and Practice of Al-Ghazali* (London: Allen & Unwin, 1953).

13. See Aḥmad Ghazzālī, *Sawāniḥ-Inspirations from the World of Pure Spirits,* trans. N. Pourjavady (London: KPI, 1986). See also N. Pourjavady, *Sulṭān-i ṭarīqat* (Tehran: Intishārāt-i Āgāh, 1358 A.H.S.).

14. Corbin has devoted many pages in his writings to the Persian *fedeli d'amore.* See his *En Islam iranien* (Paris: Gallimard, 1972) vol. 3, which has for its subtitle *Les fidèles d'amour.* Corbin has also translated the title of the *'Abhar al-'āshiqin* of Rūzbihān Baqlī Shīrāzī in his edition of the work (with M. Mo'in) as *Le Jasmin des Fidèles d'amour* (Tehran and Paris: A. Maisonneuve, 1958).

15. The major works of 'Ayn al-Quḍāt have been edited by A. 'Uṣayrān as follows: *Tamhīdāt* (Tehran: Tehran University Press, 1962); and *Zubdat al-ḥaqā'iq* (Tehran: Tehran University Press, 1962). See also A. J. Arberry, *A Sufi Martyr* (London: Allen & Unwin, 1969), which is a translation of *Shakwa'l-gharīb.*

16. See chapter 22 of this volume.

17. The Persian works of Suhrawardī were edited critically for the first time by S. H. Nasr as Suhrawardī, *Oeuvre philosophique et mystique,* vol. 3 (Tehran: Imperial Iranian Academy of Philosophy, 1977) and translated by H. Corbin as *L'Arcange empourpré* (Paris: Fayard, 1976). See also W. Thackston, *The Mystical and Visionary Treatises of Suhrawardī* (Trowbridge: The Octagon Press, 1982).

18. See Sanā'ī, *The Enclosed Garden of the Truth,* trans. J. Stephenson (New York: Samuel Weiser, 1975).

19. Ṣafā, *Tārīkh-i adabiyyāt,* 2:978–82.

20. See S. H. Nasr, *Islamic Art and Spirituality* (Albany: State University of New York Press, 1987) 110. On 'Aṭṭār, see also B. Furūzānfar, *Sharḥ-i aḥwāl wa naqd wa*

taḥlīl-i āthār-i Shaykh Farīd al-Dīn Muḥammad-i 'Aṭṭār-i Nayshābūrī (Tehran: Chāpkhāna-yi Dānishgāh-i Tihrān, 1340 A.H.S.).

21. Since chapter 5 of this work is devoted to Rūmī and the Mawlawiyyah Order, his biography will not be repeated here; only the literary aspect of his works will be treated.

22. R. A. Nicholson, *Rumi: Poet and Mystic* (London: Allen & Unwin, 1978) 31.

23. There are translations of selections of the *Dīwān* by R. A. Nicholson, A. J. Arberry, and W. Chittick, but the whole of the *Dīwān* has not yet been translated. See R. A. Nicholson, *Selected Poems from the Divani Shamsi Tabrizi* (Cambridge: University Press, 1898); A. J. Arberry, *Mystical Poems of Rumi I* (Chicago: University of Chicago Press, 1968) and *II* (Boulder: Westview Press, 1979); and W. C. Chittick, *The Sufi Path of Love: The Spiritual Teachings of Rumi* (Albany: State University of New York Press, 1983).

24. See Kirmānī, *Heart's Witness*, trans. B. M. Weischer and P. L. Wilson (Tehran: Imperial Iranian Academy of Philosophy, 1978).

25. Fakhruddīn 'Iraqī, *Divine Flashes*, trans. W. C. Chittick and P. L. Wilson (New York: Paulist Press, 1982) 71.

26. It was one of the first Sufi works to be translated into a European language (by J. von Hammer-Purgstall, who rendered it, albeit imperfectly, into German). Its first complete English translation (by E. Whinfield, *Gulshan-i rāz: The Mystic Rose Garden* [London: Trubner, 1880]) has been followed by several less complete translations during this century, such as *The Secret Garden*, trans. J. Pasha (London: The Octagon Press, 1977); and *The Secret Rose Garden*, trans. F. Lederer (Grand Rapids: Phanes Press, 1985).

27. Translation by G. Bell, quoted in E. G. Browne, *A History of Persian Literature* (Cambridge: University Press, 1920) 3:310.

28. Ṣafā, *Tārīkh-i adabiyyāt*, 3:1064–82.

29. See chapter 3 of this volume, by W. Chittick, on Ibn 'Arabī and his school. On Jāmī himself, see the edition of W. Chittick of Jāmī, *Naqd al-nuṣūṣ fī sharḥ naqsh al-fuṣūṣ* (Tehran: Imperial Iranian Academy of Philosophy, 1977) English and Persian introductions.

30. On the masters of this order, see chapter 7 in this volume, by J. Nurbakhsh, on the Nimatullāhī Order. J. Nurbakhsh, the present master of the order, is himself an accomplished Sufi poet. See also M. De Miras, *La Méthode spirituelle d'un maître du soufisme iranien: Nūr 'Alī-Shāh* (Paris: Courrier du Livre, 1973).

31. All that has been said about Persia applies *mutatis mutandis* to Afghanistan, whose earlier literary history up to the thirteenth/nineteenth century was the same as that of Persia, for the two countries were one until that time. From the thirteenth/nineteenth century on, Sufi poetry connected mostly with the Naqshbandiyyah and Qādiriyyah Orders has continued to flourish, and Afghanistan has continued to enjoy a rich poetic tradition to this day.

32. See Nūr 'Alī Shāh Ilāhī, *L'Esotérisme kurde: Aperçus sur le secret gnostique des fidèles de vérité*, trans. M. Mokri (Paris: Albin Michel, 1965).

18

Turkish Literature

GÖNÜL A. TEKIN

THERE ARE TWO MAJOR sources that have nourished and stimulated religious expression in the Turkish literature that began to develop in Anatolia in the seventh/thirteenth century. The first is certainly the formal dimension of Islam itself. Conceptions of God, man, the universe, and other principal doctrines of Islam became the subject of these religious literary works, and important events and personalities in Islamic history inspired major literary figures throughout the centuries. The other source was the inner dimension of Islam or Sufism, which influenced every genre of Turkish literature, both religious and seemingly nonreligious.

Since Sufi thought is based on love and is related directly to absolute values and to human feelings and emotions, we find Sufi influences in both the *dīwān* or high society literature and the folk literature. In the *dīwān* literature, ideas and images drawn from Sufism were used mostly as a part of the poet's vocabulary in rhetorical and prosodical devices, or as intellectual modes of expression. This poetry was not meant to move audiences or to put them into a state of ecstasy. Sufi poetry, which flourished in *tekkes* (and for this reason we shall refer to it as *tekke* poetry), has a totally different impact, because it is addressed directly to the emotions. It inevitably arouses in the listener an excitement and an enthusiasm. Because of its massive appeal in Turkey, we can say that to examine it is to examine the values that make up the very essence of the soul of the Turkish nation. What follows is, therefore, a survey of *tekke* poetry, in which are preserved the forms and aesthetics of Turkish folk literature.

Even though the *tekke* poets belong to various Sufi orders which differ somewhat from one another, it is Sufism that served as the unifying principle, and its vocabulary was frequently embellished with elements drawn from ancient Turkish customs and beliefs. From the time they began to arise in Anatolia in the early sixth/twelfth century, *tekke* poets addressed themselves directly to a wide audience, creating a rich mystical literature consisting primarily of poems designed for chanting accompanied by musical instruments. *Tekke* poets for the most part used the syllabic meter and quatrains typical of Turkish poetry, occasionally combined with elements of the prosody found throughout Islamic literatures. These features served to create a literature that is called in its own right Turkish folk literature.

Tekke poetry, however, differs from *dīwān* and folk literature in its religious and philosophical views. During the seventh/thirteenth century in Anatolia, wandering poets chanted their mystical religious poetry; they did not belong to the palace or the army but were attached to a shaykh or a *tekke.* The same tradition was carried on into the eighth/fourteenth and ninth/fifteenth centuries by dervishes. These poems were called *ilāhīs* (from the word *ilāh,* meaning "divinity"), that is, hymns or mystical songs that were primarily designed to propagate the views of the Sufi orders. It is interesting to note that we find this type of vocal music only in Anatolia, not in any other Islamic country. This religious literature was fully developed by the second half of the ninth/fifteenth century within the Baktāshī Order, which was already established at this time. The dervish poets of the Baktāshiyyah called their songs *nefes* (breath), and the poets themselves were called *'āshiqs,* or lovers, because they chanted of their love for God. Later, in the tenth/sixteenth century, this term was used to refer to any poet who chanted either religious or secular songs accompanied by a stringed instrument called a *sāz;* thus the poetry was known as *sāz* poetry. This "secular" stringed-instrument literature or sāz poetry imitated the prosodical elements, style, and poetical images of *tekke* literature. Because its poets also adopted the title of the mystical *tekke* poets, namely, *'āshiq,* *sāz* poetry came to be known as *'āshiq* literature.

The literature of the *tekke* flourished by using elements both from *dīwān* prosody and folk literature, thus separating itself from *'āshiq* literature, especially in the cities, within the *tekkes* of the great orders such as those of the Qādiriyyah, Khalwatiyyah, and Mawlawiyyah. However, in the villages and in the countryside, where Shī'ite-oriented orders such as the 'Alawiyyah flourished, the illiterate *tekke* poets have survived up until recent time, keeping the features specific to their orders combined with those of the *'āshiqs.* As a result of this, it became at one point impossible to distinguish the 'Alawī-Qizilbāsh poets from the *'āshiqs* as the representatives of "secular" folk literature.

Aḥmad Yesevi

The very first representative of Turkish Sufi literature is Aḥmad Yesevi (Yasawī) (d. 561/1166) from West Turkestan. In order to teach the basics of orthodox Islam to the eastern Turks, Yesevi composed innumerable quatrains in the eastern Turkish dialect using prosodical elements derived from folk literature. His poetry is of a didactical-mystical nature. If we compare him to those later Anatolian Turkish poets of the seventh/thirteenth and eighth/fourteenth centuries, we find Yesevi to be quite rigid in his orthodoxy, lacking in poetical brilliance, and full of religious advice and parables. In contrast, the later Anatolian poets seem to embrace the whole of existence as seen in their ecstatic poetry, which insists that the ultimate goal of existence is the experience of Divine Love. Despite his dry and rigid style of poetry, Yesevi's influence was widespread throughout all of Turkey. One of the geographical areas where his influence was felt was Anatolia. In the first decades of the seventh/thirteenth century, when the Mongol armies invaded the territories of western Asia, a mass migration of merchants, academicians, artisans, and religious scholars into Anatolia took place. Among them were also dervishes of the Yasawiyyah Order from West Turkestan, and it was because of these dervishes that the legends and customs of the Yesevis spread throughout Seljuq Anatolia. Finally, when the Baktāshiyyah Order was fully developed and established in the ninth/fifteenth century, Yesevi occupied a very important and prestigious place in the Baktāshī tradition, which indicates the importance of the Yasawiyyah Order in the formation of the Turkish orders in Anatolia.

Tekke Poetry: Yūnus Emre

The founder of the Sufi *tekke* poetry of the Anatolian Turks is Yūnus Emre (d. 720/1320), who adapted the ancient Central Asian Turkish prosodical forms brought to Anatolia by Yesevi dervishes. In his own thought, Yūnus Emre is the spiritual product of the diverse cultural strands of the medieval Seljuq Anatolia.

The sources about Emre's life are few and contradictory. He was born around 638/1240 in the northwest corner of central Anatolia. He traveled to Azerbaijan and visited Konya, Damascus, and other cities in Anatolia and Syria. His educational background appears to have been not that of a rigidly defined school curriculum. Rather, his training seems to have been rooted in the mystical philosophy of the Sufi *tekkes.*

Yūnus Emre's poetry focuses frequently on the theme of death, which is the starting point of his meditations. He writes vividly about tombs and graveyards, where viziers, teachers, young and old lie buried. The material world and our bodies are doomed to perish.

> When the day comes, 'Azrā'īl [the angel of death] will take our souls, and no one can save us. They will put us on a wooden horse and bring us to the

graveyard. They will lower us into the grave, and we will be seen no more. For three days they will carry out all the ritual ceremonies, and then we will be forgotten.[1]

Yūnus Emre laments the temporality of human existence as expressed in the lines, "I wish you would not drink death's wine. What should I do with you, my life?" Yūnus Emre felt compassion for all the dead, especially the young. "One thing is painful to me, to see the young die, cut down like an unripened crop!" But he was also the poet of resurrection after death (*baʿth baʿd al-mawt*) and with high spirits greets the world, which springs to life again in spring: "This world is as a young bride dressed in bright red and green—look on and on, you can't have enough of that lass."

Yūnus Emre recognized that there is a continuum in life which he called "the eternal change," which has nothing to do with the material world. As a Sufi, he knew that one can grasp this "eternal change," that is, the only unchanging phenomenon in life, that which is "permanent, and everlasting," only through the human heart, because the heart is the mirror of God. Therefore in his poetry the sacredness of the human heart has a very special place: "If you break a true believer's heart once, it's no prayer to God—this obeisance, all of the world's seventy-two nations, cannot wash the dirt off your hands and face." Man is considered to be the center of the universe and therefore, as the Prophet has said, "He who knows himself knows his God" (*man ʿarafa nafsahu—faqad ʿarafa rabbahu*). Thus, after having found God in himself, in his heart, Yūnus Emre became intoxicated with this love and with help overcame the fear of death:

Now I have found my own true self within.
It has happened—I saw God Almighty,
I had qualms about what might happen then.

According to the Sufis, God became manifest from the state of non-existence because He wanted to be known, and therefore the whole of existence is coming into being continuously. Thus, every being has something of the divine in it. Yūnus Emre says: "Wherever I looked, it was God I saw!"

Yūnus Emre, as a *waḥdat al-wujūd* Sufi, openly attacked the exoteric scholars who were opposed to esoterism. He said to them that true knowledge cannot be acquired in theological schools. One can reach God only through true love. Yūnus Emre was always against the concept of a solely vigilant and vengeful God. He ridiculed such a conception of God in certain famous stanzas which influenced the poets of the following centuries so much that almost every poet imitates them.[2]

In addition to these poems, Yūnus Emre composed *shaṭḥiyyah,* or paradoxical statements, which are difficult to interpret because semantically and logically they do not appear to make any sense. However, when approached with the attitude that behind every external appearance there is a hidden meaning, they become clearer. In fact, throughout the centuries following Emre's life, numerous commentaries were written upon them.[3]

In thought and technique, Yūnus Emre did not create anything new and original. What then are the qualities that make his poetry unique in the field of Turkish Islamic literature? Scholars have generally agreed that Yūnus Emre's genius lay in conveying complex Sufi concepts to a wide range of people by addressing them in the vernacular using traditional prosody. No Turkish poet before him was able to accomplish this. Aḥmad Yesevi also used Turkish prosodic elements, but his dry and lifeless quatrains did not have the moving lyrical ecstasy that dominates Yūnus Emre's poetry.

The "Yūnus-Style"

The seventh/thirteenth century was the beginning of the formative period of Anatolian Turkish literature. It was at this time that Yūnus Emre laid the foundation of Anatolian literary Turkish and created the famous "Yūnus-style," which has been imitated ever since. As A. Schimmel has said, "In this respect Yūnus Emre stands in the same line with the great mystical preachers and poets not only of Islam but also of Christianity and Hinduism."[4] Even today, Yūnus Emre's poems are widely known. A shepherd in the remote countryside, a schoolboy in a village, an intellectual from Istanbul, all will know some of his poems by heart along with their melody.

One of the characteristics of the Yūnus-style is the personification of that which is inanimate, the observation of the correspondence between human emotions and the world of nature, leading finally to the identification of the human being with nature, with the world of creation. In the following poem, nature is filled with emotions like a man; Yūnus himself resembles a flowing stream, a blowing wind:

> I am dust on your path, you would have me
>   lower, are you
> These black mountains that threaten me
>   with their breast of stone?
> And you, clustering clouds
>   on the snowbound heights,

Will you loosen your hair and weep
  for one so alone?[5]

Again:

Now and then like the winds I blow,
Now and then like the roads I go,
Now and then like the floods I flow,
Come see what love has done to me.[6]

Another characteristic of the Yūnus-style is seen in certain poems which imitate the Islamic litany (*dhikr*), which is a chant wherein a dervish continuously repeats words such as "*Allāh*" or "*Hū*," often bringing about an ecstasy in which he feels himself united with God. Indeed, Yūnus Emre grasped the mysterious power of the *dhikr* by repeating a "refrain," which creates a musical and ecstatic effect, calling his Creator together with the fishes, birds, stones, mountains, and with the entire natural world, which remembers God constantly in its own language:

With the mountains with the stones
Will I call Thee, Lord, O Lord!
With the birds in early dawn
Will I call Thee, Lord, O Lord![7]

The Yūnus-style became so influential and popular that throughout the centuries numerous poets adopted the very name Yūnus, which resulted in collections of poems belonging to various poets using the same style. It is one of the difficult tasks of comparative philosophy and literature to separate the real Yūnus Emre's poems from those written by others. There have been, nevertheless, successful attempts at editing Yūnus Emre's poetry, and numerous poems of his have been rendered into Western languages.

The form that the Sufi religious life took on, beginning in the seventh/thirteenth century in Anatolia, continued in two directions after the establishment of the Ottoman Empire. On the one hand, several Sunni orders developed in accordance with the official religious policy of the Ottomans; on the other hand, the orders with Shīʿite tendencies could survive only by joining the Baktāshī Order and continuing their existence in a different form. Since those Baktashī (sometimes also Qizilbāsh Baktāshī) orders did not follow the official religious policy of the Ottoman Empire, they revolted every time the empire had political and economical difficulties and were therefore often persecuted.

Both types of orders played a great role in the sociopolitical structure of the Ottoman Empire and in the religious life of the people. They composed manuals, teaching their rules and regulations, along with their perspective, and spread the legends and miracles of their shaykhs. They emphasized most of all the use of poetry to disseminate their teachings. In this way Sufi *tekkes* became literary centers. Poetry and music were essentials in their regular ceremonies. Talented shaykhs followed the style of Yūnus Emre in their literary creations, in part out of necessity, because the people whom they were addressing adored Yūnus Emre and his style. In all the *tekkes* except the Mawlawī and Naqshbandī *tekkes*, Emre's poems were chanted with music. These poems became so powerfully influential that he became known as *lisān al-ghayb* (The Tongue of the Invisible). No matter how much a shaykh wanted to distance himself from this influence, he had to follow the Yūnus-style, which had become an almost sacred tradition.

Because Ḥājjī Bayrām-i Walī, a famous shaykh of the ninth/fifteenth century used the Yūnus-style in his poetry, both types of orders began to appropriate Yūnus Emre. He found his way into the hearts of the secular *sāz* (stringed instrument) or *'āshiq* poets also. Yūnus Emre also deeply influenced the classical *dīwān* Sufi poets, for example, his contemporary 'Āshiq Pāshā (d. 733/1332), who composed as a counterpart of Mawlānā's *Mathnawī-i ma'nawī* a *mathnawī* called *Gharīb-nāmah* (*The Book of the Stranger*) in Turkish.

Because of limitations of space we will describe briefly here those *tekke* poets inspired by Yūnus Emre in three groups: Sunni Sufi poetry, Malāmī-Hamzāwī poetry, and 'Alawī-Baktāshī (Qizilbāsh) poetry.

Sunni Sufi Poetry

In the eighth/fourteenth century we find the earliest of Yūnus Emre's followers, his contemporary, Sa'īd Emre, who was a scholar, and Emre's son Ismā'īl Emre, who also imitated his father. In the ninth/fifteenth century there were numerous poets who called themselves Yūnus. Outstanding among them was the famous shaykh Emir Sulṭān (d. 832/1429), who lived in Bursa and belonged to the Nūrbakhshiyyah, a branch of the Khalwatiyyah. The most influential shaykh of that time was Ḥājjī Bayrām-i Walī (d. 833/1430). Of his many poems only four have survived, but they clearly reflect the Yūnus-style. In fact, it is related that he used to sing Emre's poems while he was washing his laundry. The most talented poet of this period was certainly Eshrefoghlu 'Abd Allāh Rūmī (otherwise known as Ibn al-Ashraf or Ashraf-zādah, d. 873/1469). He spent some time studying theology, but he abandoned it and after long years serving as a novice, founded in Iznik the Ashrafī Order, a branch of the Qādiriyyah.

He was the most successful poet in the use of the Yūnus-style. His *dīwān* has been printed several times.

Another important poet was Ummī Kamāl (d. 880/1475). The sources give contradicting information on his life. He joined Khwājah 'Alī, the grandson of Shaykh Ṣafī al-Dīn, the founder of the Ṣafawī Order in Ardabil. However, there are no traces of Shī'ism in his poetry. Kamāl stresses that the greatest holy war (*ghazāh*) is the battle with the *nafs* or carnal soul. As was the case with many of Emre's poems, some of Kamāl's poems are also inspired by *dhikr*. Ummī Kamāl was not only an ecstatic *tekke* poet of the *waḥdat al-wujūd* school of the Anatolian Turks; his poetry also traveled over the Crimea to the Qazan Turks, to the Bashgirds, and to the Uzbeks.

Other *tekke* poets of this century include Shaykh 'Umar Rawshanī (d. 891/1486), whose poetry was dry and didactic, and Shaykh Wafā' from Konya (d. 896/1491), who also composed music.

Besides the poems and songs that were composed primarily to propagate the religious views of the Sufi orders, there were also some didactic works written in *mathnawī* form with *'arūḍ* meter. The topics of these works are religion and Sufism, and they are related to *tekke* literature. *Faraḥ-nāmah* (*Treatise of Joy*) was written by Khatiboghlu in 828/1425. It contains one hundred traditions and some relevant short stories concerned mainly with the teachings of Sharī'ite Islam. The same author translated the *Maqālāt-i ḥājjī Baktāsh-i Walī* from Arabic into Turkish in verse form. In 828/1425 Shaykh Alwān Shīrāzī translated Maḥmūd Shabistarī's famous *Gulshan-i rāz* from Persian with substantial additions. This translation in *mathnawī* form contributed to the Turkish Sufi technical vocabulary. *Khiḍr-nāmah* (*Treatise of Khiḍr*) was composed in *mathnawī* form in 881/1476 by Shaykh Maḥmūd Dād Sulṭān (d. 900/1495). It describes the career of a dervish as he journeys through the material and spiritual worlds. In this book dervishes appear not only as those who have a personal experience of Divine Love, but as popular religious heros. It is highly significant and interesting that in this book Ḥājjī Baktāsh-i Walī is described as a holy hero marching in front of the Ottoman army. Another *mathnawī* by Shaykh 'Abd al-Raḥīm (written in 864/1460), the *Waḥdat-nāmah* (*Treatise of Unity*) treats the story of Manṣūr al-Ḥallāj as a legend using a sensitive and moving style, in order to explain *waḥdat al-wujūd* and Divine Love. *Tekke* poetry continued in the following centuries with such figures as Ibrāhīm Gulshanī (d. 940/1534), Shaykh Muḥammad Muḥyī al-Dīn Uftāde (d. 989/1581), and Niyāzī Miṣrī (d. 1105/1694).

In the centuries following the eleventh/seventeenth, many educated *tekke* poets carried on the dissemination of conservative orthodox Islamic views, although it was not a time of originality and creative brilliance. Perhaps only two poets are worth mentioning: Maḥwī ʿĪsā (d. 1127/1715) and Sizāʾī Ḥasan (d. 1152/1739). Both belonged to the Gulshaniyyah.

Malāmī-Ḥamzāwī Poetry

The Malāmī-Hamzāwīs developed a unique poetry drawn from Sunni *tekke* poetry, combining it, however, with more esoteric views. The late historian of Turkish *tekke* poetry, Abdulbaki Gölpinarli, writes:

> Malāmī-Ḥamzāwī poetry differs at first sight from the Baktāshī poetry. Even though the poets of this school adopted a Shīʿite perspective and demonstrate veneration for the *Ahl al-bayt,* they do not write with any trace of *tabarrā* (detesting the adversaries of ʿAlī's family). They do not employ satire and irony, but they seem to have a fondness for composing *shaṭḥiyyāt.* They are very serious Sufis, but they are not ascetics, they are wise. They combine love with knowledge. Their literary source is definitely Yūnus Emre.[8]

This style of poetry originated with a famous *dīwān* poet named Duqaqin-zāde Aḥmad Sarbān (d. 964/1557), whose writings contain both esoteric and exoteric elements. When he died, he was the shaykh of the *tekke* in Hayrabolu near Tekirdag, and his successor was Vize ʿAlāʾ al-Dīn, whose penname was Qayghusuz (d. 970/1563). His successors, men such as Oghlan Shaykh Ibrāhīm Efendī (d. 1066/1656), Ṣunʿ Allah ibn Aḥmad ibn Bashīr Ghaybī (d. 1072/1662), Emīr ʿUthmān Hāshimī (d. 1003/1595), Lamakānī (d. 1034/1625), and Idrīs Mukhtefī (d. 1024/1615), all carried on this literary tradition of combining Islamic Persian prosody with earlier Turkish forms and meters.

Qayghusuz distinguishes himself from those Malāmī-Ḥamzāwī poets who came after him in that he is a poet who composed his poems mostly in pure Turkish and using Turkish syllabic meter. His successors preferred the *ʿarūḍ* meter. Qayghusuz was a typical folk poet: his rhymes are free and sometimes half. The classical *dīwān* poetry did not influence him. Those poems written in syllabic meter have the quatrain form, a Turkish form also used by him in those poems composed in *ʿarūḍ.*

The last spiritual pole (*quṭb*) of the Malāmī-Ḥamzāwī *tekke,* Sütçü Bashīr Āghā, and forty of his novices were killed in 1072/1662. After that catastrophe, the members of the *tekke* went underground. This also brought the expansion of Malāmī-Ḥamzāwī literature to an end.

ʿAlawī-Baktāshī Poetry

The Baktāshī *bābās* (their leaders are called *bābā,* instead of *shaykh* or *pīr*) came always from among the simple people, that is, from the lower classes.

Therefore, the Baktāshī poets always addressed the masses using pure Turkish and entirely Turkish prosody. Their poetry was always intended to be chanted with music. The poems were called *nefes* and were full of jokes and witticisms. They drew upon Sufism as their source but always expressed themselves in very simple terms. They gave first place to an elaborate treatment of ʿAlī and the *ahl al-bayt,* including *tabarrā* and *tawallā*. Views such as the trinity of Allah–Muḥammad–ʿAlī, and the equation of Ḥājjī Baktāsh-i Walī (d. 668/1270) with ʿAlī and Muḥammad, were contrary to Islamic orthodoxy. Some of them even went so far as to divinize ʿAlī and to give him precedence over the Prophet.

The love of God appears to become more and more corporeal in this genre of poetry, and the poets emphasize human values so much that man becomes the center of everything. We know very little about Ḥājjī Baktāsh Walī, the founder of this order. He came to Anatolia from Khorasan and settled in the small village of Suluca Karahoyuk, which later became known as Haci Bektaş (Ḥājjī Baktāsh). He was the novice of Bābā Ilyās and Bābā Isḥāq. Because he was also of the Bābā'īs, his teachings were a combination of *waḥdat al-wujūd* and Turkish beliefs and traditions. To this order later came Bālim Sulṭān's reformations, related to the organization of the order, and the influences of the Ḥurūfiyyah and the Shīʿī-ʿAlawī views of Khaṭā'ī.

Qayghusuz Abdāl (d. in the ninth/fifteenth century) is the first and most important representative of Baktāshī literature. There is contradictory information concerning his life. He established his *tekke* in Egypt. His ideological background is identified with the Bābā'īs, and he is a good imitator of Yūnus Emre, emphasizing subtle irony, satirical humor, and wit. These characteristics later became the dominant elements in Baktāshī poetry.

Historically, the Baktāshī Order was organized in the ninth/fifteenth century and was officially adopted by the Ottomans as the spiritual core of the army, that is, of the Janissary corps. At the time, when the Janissary corps was established by Sultan Murād I (d. 791/1389), a certificate from a religious leader was necessary in order to establish an official institution. For the Janissary corps this happened to be from the Baktāshiyyah *tekke.* In these formative years, Baktāshī *bābās* always lived among the Janissary soldiers. The *bābās* were the representatives of Ḥājjī Baktāsh, and the soldiers were called his sons; thus, every young man who joined the Janissary corps took an oath of loyalty to Ḥājjī Baktāsh Walī. They took Yūnus Emre as the model for their poetry, because, as we have seen, Yūnus Emre was also a novice both of Bābā Isḥāq and Ḥājjī Baktāsh Walī. Taking advantage of the political importance the Baktāshīs enjoyed, the Ḥurūfīs, who held extremist views, entered into the Baktāshī Order and spread throughout the Ottoman lands. According to their perspective, the Quran is manifest wholly in man, and therefore all the letters of the Arabic alphabet can be found in man's face. Through this view they brought about an understanding of man different from that of other Sufis. Man is not only the reflection of Divine Beauty, but he is Divine Beauty Itself; he "is" God; he "is" the Truth.

It was the powerful Ḥurūfī poet, Nasīmī (d. 806/1404), who greatly influenced most of the Turkish poets and most of the orders, especially the Baktāshiyyah in Anatolia, and nourished them spirituality. In addition to the influence of the Ḥurūfī perspective felt especially through the poems of Nasīmī, Shah Ismā'īl Ṣafawī (d. 930/1524) was also very successful in spreading his 'Alawī-Bāṭinī ideas among the Qizilbash Baktāshīs in Anatolia through his religious and mystical poems written under the pen name Khaṭā'ī. The already existing Shī'ite and esoteric views among the Baktāshīs were nourished by the 'Alawī-Bāṭinī perspective as found in the poetry of Khaṭā'ī, although Khaṭā'ī himself was a Twelve-Imam Shī'ite. As a result, the "trinity" of God–Muḥammad–'Alī, *ḥulūl* or the incarnation of God, "transmigration" (*tanāsukh*), tawallā, and *tabarrā* became dominant themes in Baktāshī poetry. Furthermore, Khaṭā'ī's influence combined and merged with the Ḥurūfīs' veneration of man and brought about the veneration of 'Alī. With those elements brought in by Khaṭā'ī, the development of Baktāshī poetry (now called 'Alawī-Baktāshī poetry) was completed and took on the form in which we know it now.

After Khaṭā'ī there were many 'Alawī-Baktāshī poets, but here we will deal with only one of them, Pīr Sulṭān Abdāl. As a Turkoman coming from Khurasan, Pīr Sulṭān Abdāl found himself in Anatolia in the midst of the socioreligious conflict between Sunni and 'Alawī Islam. In his early youth, he joined an 'Alawī *tekke* and received a general education. He became a leader of the 'Alawīs thanks to his powerful and provocative poetry. The rebellion against the Sunni Ottomans grew, provoked by Shī'ite Iran under Shah Ṭahmāsb (930/1524–995/1578). Finally he was captured and, upon the order of the Ottoman vizier, Khiḍr Pāshā, executed in Sivas in 967/1560.

His tragic death had a tremendous impact on the 'Alawī-Baktāshī-Qizilbāsh population of Anatolia, and numerous legends sprang up around his personality. His *nefes* were chanted in the Baktāshī and 'Alawī *tekkes.* Moreover, Abdāl's poems are chanted not only by the 'Alawīs but also by the Sunni-Orthodox Muslims. Even today in the twentieth century, poems by Abdāl are quoted by modern Turkish novelists.

After Abdāl there were many other 'Alawī-Baktāshī poets, although none of them was of his caliber. To name a few: in the eleventh/seventeenth century, Dervish Aḥmad, Qul Budala, Qul Muṣṭafā, Taslīm Abdāl, Qul Nasīmī, Shamsī, and Yamīnī; in the twelfth/eighteenth century, 'Azbī, Kātib, and Kalbī Ṭāhir; and in the thirteenth/nineteenth century, Sham'ī, Walī, Ramzī, Wahbī, Zaḥmī, and Sayrānī. Especially at the beginning of the fourteenth/twentieth century, Adīb Kharābī was one of the most eminent representatives of this genre of literature.

Although today there are many Baktāshī poets in Turkey, these poets continue to treat the same topics in the same style, so that this type of literature is slowly dying out. The socioeconomic and cultural changes that Turkey has been experiencing for quite some time have also contributed to this end.

Notes

1. These and the other selections of Emre's poetry that follow are among his well-known verses translated by this author into English.
2. For example:

   O God, if Thou wouldst ever question me,
   This would be my outright answer to Thee:

   True, I sinned–brutalized my own being,
   But what have I done against Thee, my King?

   Did I make myself? I'm Thy creation.
   Why drench me in sin, Benevolent One?
3. For these ecstatic sayings of the Sufis and their significance, see C. Ernst, *Words of Ecstasy* (Albany: State University of New York Press, 1983).
4. A. Schimmel, in *Yunus Emre and His Mystical Poetry*, ed. T. S. Halman (Bloomington: Indiana University Press, 1981) 62.
5. N. Menemencioglu, *The Penguin Book of Turkish Verse* (London: Penguin Books) 126.
6. T. S. Halman, in *Yunus Emre and His Mystical Poetry*, 162.
7. A. Schimmel, *Mystical Dimensions of Islam* (Chapel Hill: University of North Carolina Press, 1975) 331.
8. A. Gölpinarli, *Yunus Emre ve Tasavvuf* (Istanbul, 1961) 241.

19

Indo-Muslim Spirituality and Literature

Annemarie Schimmel

Islamic Spirituality in India

The first reaction the word "India" evokes in a Westerner's mind is probably the Taj Mahal, for the Taj has come to be considered the embodiment of Indian beauty. If one is interested in the history of religion, one may perhaps think of the Vedic Upanishads, regarded as the highest expression of wisdom ever since their Latin translation by Anquetil-Dupérron appeared in 1801. But few persons would know that the Taj Mahal is a work of Islamic art and that the Persian translation of the Upanishads on which Anquetil-Dupérron based his work was made by Dārā Shikoh, the mystically minded heir apparent of the Mughal Empire, who was executed for heresy by his younger brother Aurangzeb in 1069/1659. Both princes were from among the fourteen children whom Mumtāz Maḥal, in whose memory the Taj is built, bore to her husband Shāhjahān, the fifth of the Mughal rulers from the House of Tīmūr in India.

The Muslim share in Indian spirituality has generally been overlooked, and even Islamicists are rarely aware of the immense wealth of the mystical and, in fact, the whole religious heritage of Indian Islam. Yet the history of this heritage begins as early as 92/711, when a small contingent of Arabs under Muḥammad ibn al-Qāsim conquered Sind, the southern part of present-day Pakistan, extending Muslim rule to Multan. The new province had to deal with a great number of Buddhist and Hindu citizens who were treated by Muḥammad as *ahl al-kitāb* (people of the book), like the Christians and Jews in the Near East.

The Influence of Ḥallāj

Sind and Multan became a way station through which Indian mathematics, astronomy, and medicine reached the central parts of the Muslim world. The study of religious literature seems to have been popular among the Muslim scholars in the first capitals of Sind and was enhanced by those who emigrated thence to Baghdad and other central places. Although almost nothing is known about the religious life of the population, one may surmise the existence of a certain interest in mystical thought. The first name of a mystic connected, at least in part, with Sind, is that of al-Ḥusayn ibn Manṣūr al-Ḥallāj, who wandered through Gujarat, Sind, and probably Kashmir shortly after 287/900 "to call people to God." Ḥallāj's mystical experience, which involves a very personal relationship with God, can be considered the first climax of mystical life in early Islam, and he had to pay with his life for his daring interpretation of the essential love between man and God. He thus became the arch-martyr of mystical Islam (d. 309/922). One does not know what Ḥallāj preached to the slim Muslim population of the Indus Valley; one does not even know exactly whether or not he had relations with the Karmathians, who at the time of his visit began to rule in the Multan area. The government in Baghdad later accused him of being in contact with these "archenemies" of the Abbasid caliphate.

It is fascinating to see that the name of "Manṣūr" Ḥallāj became in later centuries the favorite mystical symbol in the western part of India (partly also in Bengal and the Deccan). Perhaps this phenomenon can be explained by the constant influx of Persian mystical poetry, in which the martyr mystic and his utterance *ana'l-ḥaqq*, "I am the Creative Truth," are mentioned time and again. Yet, as much as his name is known all over the Muslim world, in no other tradition does he appear so frequently as in the Indo-Muslim one—and here in Sindhi and Punjabi verse. The folk poets, interpreting him as the representative of *waḥdat al-wujūd* (the unity of being), sang in his name the most ecstatic verses, in which they claimed to have reached a stage where only *al-Ḥaqq*, the Divine Reality, was left and nothing else mattered, a stage where there is no difference left between Manṣūr and his judge, between Moses and Pharaoh, between Abū Ḥanīfah and Hanuman. Or else the folk poets who had sipped from the "wine of Manṣūr" would see in him the prototype of the lover who, intoxicated, had revealed the secret of union between the human lover and the Divine Beloved and was therefore liable of execution: for the secret of love must never be divulged to the noninitiated. They would sing in ever-new verses of the happy moment when Ḥallāj experienced the nuptials of death, when "the gallows became his bridal bed," faithful to the tradition of Sufism, according to which "death is beautiful because it is a bridge leading from the lover to the Beloved," faithful also to Ḥallāj's oft-repeated verse *uqtulūnī yā thiqātī:*

> Kill me, O my trustworthy friends,
> For in my being killed there is my life.

Verses of this kind are attested from the tenth/sixteenth century in popular literature, but they may have been used earlier. The imagery, repetitive and similar in almost all Indian vernaculars used by the Muslims, percolated even into the *gināns,* the mystical songs of the Ismāʿīlī community in the areas of Gujarat and Sind. It is as though the spiritual seeds that Ḥallāj planted in the Indus Valley around 287/900 bore fruit after a long time.[1]

Hujwīrī, the first of the Sufis who settled in northwest India after the Muslim conquests in the beginning of the fifth/eleventh century, has also written a book about Ḥallāj. It is lost, but we owe to him also the first comprehensive theoretical work on Sufism in Persian, the indispensable *Kashf al-maḥjūb.* His piety endeared him to the people of Lahore, where he settled and is buried (d. *ca.* 463/1071); to this day they tenderly call him Dātā Ganj Bakhsh, and for centuries it was customary for those Sufis who entered India from the northwest first to pay a visit to his shrine in order to take permission to proceed further into the country.

Chishtī Literature

Chishtī literature flowered in Delhi in the circle of Niẓām al-Dīn Awliyā'. Among his devotees, Amīr Khusraw and Ḥasan Sijzī were the two leading Persian poets of his time. Amīr Khusraw, the "Parrot of India" (d. 725/1325), is credited with the invention of several musical instruments and with the shaping of the Hindustani musical tradition. Since musical sessions (*qawwālī*) became a typical aspect of the religious life in Chishtī *dargāhs,* Amīr Khusraw's participation in such sessions may have led him to invent new forms and styles. His own charming lyrical poetry is still a favorite with the *qawwāls* of Indo-Pakistan. Although he emulated many earlier forms of Persian literature and especially the poetry of Niẓāmī, he also invented new types of Persian narrative poetry and is credited with some Hindi verses and riddles. Ḥasan Sijzī also composed delightful verses, but is mainly remembered because he collected his aging master's words, beginning from 717/1317, and continued this work for years, later under Niẓām al-Dīn's supervision. Thus, he gave the literature of the subcontinent the genre of *malfūẓāt* ("sayings"), a genre that became popular among Sufis and offers insights not only into the thought process and teaching methods of mystical teachers but also into the problems of the people who frequented the master to ask for help.

The Qādiriyyah

The Qādiriyyah reached India in the eighth/fourteenth century and had many eminent representatives in that land, for example, Miyān Mīr, who was called "the flute of love" by Iqbal, and Dārā Shikoh, who is of significance from both a mystical and a literary point of view. Dārā Shikoh, a typical representative of *waḥdat al-wujūd,* had tried to bridge the gap between Islam and Hinduism and to reach a "confluence of the two oceans" (Quran XVIII, 65). He thought (as many historians of religion after him did) that the deepest wisdom of the Vedic Upanishads and of the Quran was the same; in fact, the Upanishads were for him the "book that is hidden" (Quran LVI, 78), to which the Quran alludes. Therefore he set out to translate fifty Upanishads into Persian, with the help of some pandits.[2] This translation was even less popular than the attempts of his great grandfather Akbar, who had several Hindu epics translated into Persian to make the Muslims acquainted with the thoughts of their Hindu neighbors—attempts that met with the strong aversion of most Muslims.

Sufism and the Growth of Indigenous Literature in the Subcontinent

The writings of Bāyazīd Anṣārī, the founder of the Rawshanā'iyyah Order, usher in the growth of Pashto literature, and this brings us to an important aspect of Sufism in India, that is, the Sufis' role in the development of the indigenous languages. From the seventh/thirteenth century, sentences in Indian languages are preserved in the biographies of Sufi saints. It soon became incumbent upon them to preach in an idiom that not only the elite but also the masses could understand. The small Muslim elite was conversant with Arabic, the language of the Quran, and with Persian, the language of higher civilization and official correspondence, but in order to reach beyond them, the Sufis had to revert to indigenous languages. Around 800/1398 several mystics in Bengal, in the Deccan, and in north India expressed the view that the local languages are necessary vehicles for preaching the Truth. In the ninth/fifteenth century Muslim Bengali poetry appeared, in which the mystical veneration of the Prophet played an important role. At the same time, the first mystical treatises in Dakhni Urdu were composed.

With Bāyazīd Anṣārī, Pashto began to grow into an expressive literary language. His contemporaries Qāḍī Qāḍān in Sind (d. 958/1551) and Mādho Lāl Ḥusayn in Lahore (d. 1001/1593) expressed their longing for the Divine Beloved in short, touching verses in their mother tongues, Sindhi and Punjabi, respectively. They used, as most Sufis in the vernaculars did, Indian poetical forms.

These poets were able to express the deepest secrets of the heart in words that even a child could understand, because they took their imagery from the daily life of farmers and housewives, from spinning and fishing, from desert travel or life near the powerful streams. Early Dakhni Urdu poetry uses the same devices. Thus, in the spinning songs the soul is admonished to "spin" continuously, that is, to remember the name of the Lord uninterruptedly, until at Doomsday she will bring "fine yarn" or be dressed in a beautiful garment of religious activities, while the lazy soul is exposed naked. Besides adopting these images, the mystical poets utilized the traditional folktales as bases for their instruction. The heroines of the tales of Sind and the Punjab are transformed into symbols of the soul who has to undergo endless trials and tribulations and has to wander on difficult paths through hills and dales until she is finally united in death with her Beloved. The heartrending verses of Sindhi poets, mainly Shah ʿAbd al-Laṭīf Bhitai (d. 1165/1752), tell these stories, which grew out of the classical Sufi teaching that "dying to oneself" is the prerequisite of eternal life in loving union. This mystical poetry helped Sufi ideas to percolate into all strata of society and to color the people's outlook. The poetry of the Pathans is more indebted to the austere ascetic verse of early Sufis such as Sanāʾī of Ghazna and tends to highlight the transcendence of God, the Lord of the universe, rather than His immanence or His role as the eternal Beloved to whom everything craves to return. In the mystical poetry in Bengal, Vedantic thought, Vaishnavite love mysticism, and Sufi teachings are sometimes blended in a strange way. All of Sufi poetry is singable and thus forms an important ingredient of cultural life.

Syncretistic trends are also found in the Ismāʿīlī literature. The Ismāʿīlīs, represented in the subcontinent from the late third/ninth century (the Karmathians in Multan), and more actively from *ca.* 495/1102, carried out their conversion activities in the areas of Sind and Gujarat, skillfully using Hindu terminology (ʿAlī as the tenth *avatar*, etc.) to find the ears of the Hindus. Cruelly persecuted in early centuries, the Ismāʿīlīs later often assumed Sufi attitudes, and thus their religious literature (the poetical *gināns*) closely resembles Sufi poetry in the languages of Indo-Pakistan, especially Sindhi and Gujarati. Imagery and themes are the same, with the difference that the longed-for beloved of the maiden soul is not God but the Imam.

In Sunni literature, again, one finds also the Prophet Muḥammad, or the *ḥaqīqah muḥammadiyyah,* as the friend of the soul for whom she craves, whom she wants to visit (in Medina), and who may appear as the "rain of grace" to quicken the dead hearts and bless both the country and the individual soul that devotes her love to him. No one can appreciate Indian Islam properly without recognizing the central role of the Prophet in high and popular piety, whether it is expressed in the Sufi way that finally leads to the union with the *ḥaqīqah muḥammadiyyah,* or in popular songs that implore his help and express the Muslims' deep loving trust in him, God's most beloved creature and intercessor at Doomsday, or whether he constitutes the "beautiful model" (Quran XXX, 21) for his followers. His person becomes central in the revivalist movements of the twelfth/eighteenth and thirteenth/nineteenth centuries and is the axis around whom the attempts at building a modern Islamic society revolve.

The days of Akbar seemed to bring a rapprochement between at least some aspects of Hinduism and Sufi thought, but this process was viewed with mistrust by many. Their spokesman became Shaykh Aḥmad Sirhindī (d. 1033/1624), who was the leading figure in the struggle against "intoxicated" Sufism and, as a good Naqshbandī, tried to implement his religious ideals in society.[3] He began his career with attacks against the Twelve-Imam Shī'ites, who waxed strong at the Mughal court and elsewhere as a consequence of the uninterrupted influx of poets, painters, calligraphers, and also adventurers from Safavid Persia into India. In involved sentences he called the Muslims to regain their strength against the Hindus, who he believed should not play such an important political role. Jahāngīr considered the letters which Aḥmad Sirhindī sent out to be "a bundle of absurdities" and imprisoned him for some time, but his followers hailed him as the *mujaddid-i alf-i thānī,* the Renovator of the second millennium after the *hijrah.* (The year 1000 A.H./1592 had just been reached in Akbar's reign, and certain chiliastic motives may have determined some of Akbar's religious attitude.) Aḥmad Sirhindī has often been regarded as the protagonist of the Two-Nations Theory of the fourteenth/twentieth century. He certainly exerted a far-reaching influence on an important segment of Indian, particularly north Indian, Muslim intelligentsia, and his enormous self-consciousness led him to claim to be the *qayyūm,* the being upon whom the well-being of the world rests. The great reformers of the twelfth/eighteenth century, for example, Shah Walī Allāh, Maẓhar Jān-i Jānān and Mīr Dard (to whom Urdu owes its only truly mystical verse) were all affiliated to his *ṭarīqah,* even though they also had some other affiliations (double or triple initiation became quite common among the Indian Muslims).

Aḥmad's ideas seem to have influenced at least partly Aurangzeb and strengthened his intention to overcome his brother, Dārā, and it appears as if an age-old conflict, visible through the entire history of Muslim India, manifested itself most dramatically in the struggle of these two sons of Shāhjahān. One faction of the Muslims—and here particularly the *ashrāf,* Muslims of non-Indian origin (*sayyids,* Persian *mīrzās,* Turkish officers, Pathans, etc.)—felt that their real loyalty belonged to places outside India, especially to the heartland of Islam. They did not regard themselves as parts of "Indian" culture but rather longed for the central sanctuary in Mecca and for the Prophet's last resting place in Medina. In no other literature is the Prophet called so often with surnames pertaining to his Arabic origin (Makkī, Madinī, Abṭaḥī, etc.) as in Indo-Persian and vernacular songs. Aurangzeb appears as the embodiment of the "Mecca-centered" approach out of which most of the reform movements of the thirteenth/nineteenth century emerged, whereas Dārā Shikoh hoped for the other solution of the problem of Muslim identity in India, namely, the reconciliation with spiritual Hinduism. These two conflicting trends finally manifested themselves in partition in 1947.

There was, however, one figure to whom all Muslims in India were indebted and whose verse largely shaped Indo-Muslim poetical and mystical thought. That is Mawlānā Rūmī. His *Mathnawī* was recited by the Brahmins in Bengal in the ninth/fifteenth century and influenced Shah ʿAbd al-Laṭīf in Sind, who modeled his *Risālō* after it. It moved Aurangzeb to tears and was, in excerpts, calligraphed by Dārā Shikoh. Rūmī's influence on the spirituality of Indo-Pakistan cannot be overrated and would deserve a detailed study. It was also Rūmī who appeared in the present century as the spiritual guide of that Muslim thinker and poet who expressed the hopes, sorrows, and problems of the Indian Muslims most eloquently, namely, Muhammad Iqbal, in whose work the different aspects of Indian Islam seem to find once more a thought-provoking poetical and philosophical expression.[4]

Notes

1. For this development, see A. Schimmel, "The Martyr-mystic Ḥallāj in Sindhi Folk-poetry," *Numen* 9 (1963) 161–200.

2. These works were rendered into Persian under the title *Sirr-i akbar* (*The Great Secret*), ed. J. Nāʾīnī (Tehran: Tābān Press, 1961). Sanskrit religious and mystical literature rendered into Persian constitutes an important literary category which needs to be considered in any complete study of the mystical literature associated with the Muslims of the subcontinent.

3. See K. A. Nizami, "The Naqshbandiyyah Order" (chap. 8) and S. A. Rizvi, "Sufism in the Indian Subcontinent" (chap. 12) in this volume.

4. A survey of Rūmī's influence in Indo-Pakistan is found in A. Schimmel, *The Triumphal Sun* (London: East West Publications, Fine Books, 1978) the last chapter, entitled "Mawlānā Rūmī's influence in East and West."

20

Malay Literature

Baharudin Ahmad

The Malay Language

When both Malaysia and Indonesia chose Malay as their national language, right after both nations gained their independence, the choice should not be considered as having been made out of sheer chauvinistic and nationalistic interest. Malay is not only the language of 140 million people of Southeast Asia, but it has also proved itself to be the only possible carrier of the systematic and objective knowledge of Islam in that part of the Muslim world. The same choice was made earlier by Sufi saints when they first came to introduce and propagate Islam in the Malay-Indonesian world. By then, possibly in the sixth/twelfth century or even earlier, Malay was already used as the *lingua franca* but was yet to gain the status of a carrier of spiritual and religious discourses.

The Malay language was of such a nature that it allowed itself to be developed and nurtured by the teachings of the Quran and Islamic metaphysical doctrines. By means of new terminologies that were blended with the new world view, the semantic content of the Malay language was systematized.[1]

This language had undergone many developments before it was used as a vehicle for Islamic metaphysical and philosophical literature. Arab and other missionaries must have introduced the letters of the Arabic alphabet as written symbols of the Malay language.[2] The second contribution, made by the Sufi saints and missionaries, was the introduction and propagation of Islamic learning and literature, especially in the field of *taṣawwuf* (Sufism) and *kalām* (theology). In line with the language used in Sufi discourses, the Sufi literature from the Arab world and Persia was introduced to the Malay world. Some works were translated, and others were taught in their original language.

Traces of the teaching of most classical Muslim scholars and Sufis can be found in the writings of Malay Sufi thinkers after the seventh/thirteenth century. Various terms, together with the meaning and relations between them, were brought into Malay and helped to develop the language as a vehicle for religious and scholarly thought. Moreover, the Malays themselves formulated terms that refer to spiritual and nonspiritual meanings within the same act.[3] Ḥamzah al-Fanṣūrī, the eleventh/seventeenth-century Malay Sufi thinker and poet, refers to God's will (*irādah*) to create the world with the word *hendak* instead of *mahu.*[4] In terms of knowledge, the Malay language differentiates between *tahu* (to know), *faham* (to understand), and *kenal* (to know definitely).

Malay and the Islamic Intellectual Tradition

Transformation of meaning from the horizontal to the vertical dimension of reality through differentiation of the semantic content of Malay words marks a historic change, which was aimed at the formulation of a systematic language for philosophical discourse through the medium of literature. Before the coming of Islam, myths were used to indicate the higher reality of man. Aesthetic expression in literature was dominant and encompassed human thought without providing any abstract language to accommodate the intellectual aspects of the human mind.

The Sufi saints in the Malay-Indonesia world did not eliminate at once all the folk and mythical elements in Malay literature when they introduced Sufi treatises to the masses. However, through gradual stages, the importance of the *hikayats* decreased, while the esoteric teachings of Islam began to take their place. The Malays, through the gradual process of Islamization, first through the introduction of the *Sharī'ah* (the Divine Law) and later, *taṣawasuf* (especially Sufi metaphysics), realized the distinction between popular entertaining readings and formal literature. The term *hikayat* generally constituted the aesthetic reading meant for entertainment, whereas *kitab* is a term given to serious formal literature.

Ḥikāyat Muḥammad al-Ḥanafiyyah, the first chapter of the *Bustān al-salāṭīn* (*The Garden of Kings*), and *Ḥikāyat nūr Muḥammad* emphasize the perfection of the Prophet in a semihistorical way. The *Ḥikāyat nūr Muḥammad* no doubt uses allegorical presentations to show that the Prophet is the source of creation and the Perfect Man. We can trace the teachings of Sa'dī, Rūmī, al-Jīlī, and 'Aṭṭār here, mixed with other Persian influences, to formulate a symbolic prose story of creation.

The content of this *hikayat* is very much in agreement with Sufism. According to the Sufis, *al-nūr al-muḥammadī* (the Metaphysical Light of Muḥammad) is the Primordial Muḥammad, the Perfect Man for whose sake the world was created. Muḥammad, in our *hikayat,* kisses the earth, because the earth allows itself to be dominated and enslaved. Only as a result of this willingness could the world come into being with the perfection that characterizes the whole of creation. The bodily Muḥammad, which belongs to the four *'anāṣir,* has been described by Rūmī as a veil that covers the One, the Eternal,[5] and 'Aṭṭār describes the two *m*'s in the name of Muḥammad as the origin of the two worlds.[6]

The theory of creation in Islamic literature is as old as the teaching of Islam itself. A large number of *ḥadīths* of the Prophet concern this theory. In Islamic literature we can trace the theory of creation in the poems of Ibn al-Fāriḍ, Sanā'ī, Rūmī, and 'Aṭṭār. In the circle of Malay *hikayat* or stories, the *Ḥikayat nūr Muḥammad* is a work in which this theory is more fully developed compared with other *hikayats.*

The imagery used in *Ḥikāyat nūr Muḥammad* and *Ḥikāyat Nabī Bercukur* shows the influence of Persian literature on Malay literature. However, this imagery no doubt exists in the Quran itself, where the images of light and the tree are used in certain verses that deal with more esoteric events and with higher realities. In the famous "Light Verse," God declared Himself to be the light of the Heavens and the earth (Quran XXXIV, 25).

The symbol of the bird (*al-ṭayr*) is one of the most universal symbols used to represent the human spirit. In the Quran, Solomon is said to have inherited from David the wisdom through which he was able to understand the language of the birds (*'ullimnā manṭiq al-ṭayr*) (Quran XXVII, 15). In the native Malay myth, the bird is known as *Kur,* or spirit, whereas in Nordic legends man understands the language of the birds once he overcomes the dragon, which represents the evil soul.[7] In 'Aṭṭār's *Manṭiq al-ṭayr* each bird represents a level of the human soul, and the Simurgh (the mythical bird) represents the Universal Spirit, that which is also known as the Reality of Muḥammad, who always guides man even from his starting point to reach his inner reality.[8] *Ḥikāyat nūr Muḥammad* conveys the idea of creation and knowledge through the symbol of the bird, which represents the Reality of Muḥammad, making it possible for the Malays to share the universal symbol of the bird in their literary tradition.

Besides the symbols that we have discussed above, the Malays also use the symbol of the white pearl (*mutiara putih*) to represent the origin of creation. Shaykh Nūr al-Dīn al-Rānirī in his first chapter of *Bustān al-salāṭīn* narrates his cosmological doctrine by using the white pearl as a symbol of the first creation of God from which the whole cosmos was then created.[9] This symbolism reminds us of Sanā'ī's white pearl in the heart of the shell. In the *Sejarah Melayu* or the *Malay Annal,* in chapter 20, it is related that a certain Sufi shaykh at Mecca, Ibn Isḥāq by name, had written a book or *kitab* entitled *al-Durr al-manẓūm* (*Poetic Pearl*). This book of Sufism, which discussed the *Dhāt* (Essence) and the nature of the Divine Qualities or *ṣifāt,* was brought to Malacca and was discussed at the court of the sultan as early as the ninth/fifteenth century.[10]

Through their content it is evident that as early as the ninth/fifteenth century the teachings of Ibn ʿArabī and al-Jīlī had reached Malacca and Pasai and have been known to the Malay world since then. Besides *Durr al-manẓūm,* another *kitab* is also known to have been used in ninth/fifteenth-century Malacca: it is called *al-Sayf al-qāṭiʿ* (*The Sharp Sword*).

Both of the *kitabs* we have mentioned spread the teachings of Sufism to the local Malays. By the eleventh/seventeenth century the local Malays produced scholarly works of their own. Ḥamzah Fanṣūrī is probably the first local scholar who exposed Islamic mystical teaching in the most systematic and scholarly structure.[11] The student of and main commentator on Ḥamzah, Shams al-Dīn al-Sūmātrānī, wrote mostly in prose. At least two major works of Shams al-Dīn are known: *Dhikir da'irah* (*The Circle of Invocation*) and *Mi'rāt al-muḥaqqiqīn* (*Mirror of Verifiers*).[12] Ḥamzah and Shams al-Dīn both belonged to Ibn ʿArabī's school of thought. The main themes of their writing concerned *waḥdat al-wujūd* and *al-insān al-kāmil,* which are also the two most important themes in Sufism. However, the arrival of Shaykh Nūr al-Dīn al-Rānirī, a Gujarati theologian, to the court of Acheh after Shams al-Dīn presented a fierce challenge to Ḥamzah's teaching.[13] Shaykh Nūr al-Dīn attacked Ḥamzah's teaching as al-Ghazzālī had attacked the Peripatetic philosophers before him.[14]

Malay Sufi Literary Figures

The *Kitāb al-ḥikam* (*Aphorisms*) of Ibn ʿAṭā' Allāh al-Iskandarī was translated by Shaykh Abdul Malek. The translation is called *Hikam Melayu* or *The Malay Ḥikam,*[15] and both a translation and a commentary on the original *Ḥikam* of Ibn ʿAṭā' Allāh are found in the *Malay Ḥikam.*[16]

ʿAbd al-Ra'ūf Singkel was a popular Sufi saint who translated the Noble Quran into Malay. ʿAbd al-Ra'ūf also wrote a *kitab* on *fiqh* (jurisprudence) entitled *Mir'āt al-ṭullāb* (*Mirror of the Seekers*).[17]

Shaykh ʿAbd al-Ṣamad of Palembang, who is known as the main expositor of Imam al-Ghazzālī in the Malay-Indonesian world, translated al-Ghazzālī's *Bidāyat al-hidāyah* (*The Beginning of Guidance*) into Maylay. The *Iḥyā'* of al-Ghazzālī became known in Maylay literature in the twelfth/eighteenth century, when ʿAbd al-Ṣamad translated and abridged this magnum opus of al-Ghazzālī, which is known among the Malays as *Siyar al-sālikīn* (*The

Way of Seekers).[18] In the thirteenth/nineteenth century, Shaykh Dā'ūd al-Fatānī wrote mainly on *fiqh* and *taṣawwuf.* He is known also as a systematizer of the *i'tiqād* (foundation of beliefs) in a treatise entitled *al-Durr al-thamīn* (*The Precious Jewel*).[19]

The coming of Western power to the Malay region affected the spread of Islamic mystical teachings. However, we still can name a few figures who, despite the influence of the West, continued in the struggle to propagate the traditional Malay civilization. One of them is Ḥājjī Muḥammad Yūsuf, known to the local people as Tok Kenali. Through his student Ḥājjī Nik 'Abd Allāh, the teaching of Shah Walī Allāh of Delhi came to be known in the Malaysian peninsula.[20]

Ḥamzah Fanṣūrī

Ḥamzah Fanṣūrī wrote on the all-pervasiveness of the Creator in a manner that is very similar to the writings of Jāmī.[21] He compared God's all-pervasiveness to the light of the sun, which shines on the Ka'bah and the temple alike.[22]

To Ḥamzah Fanṣūrī God is all-pervading in the universe and in all living creatures, but man, because of his state and limited knowledge, cannot comprehend God.[23] The imagery used by Ḥamzah to show the relation between the creature and the Creator is that of the wave and the ocean: the wave is but part of the ocean but the ocean is not the wave.

According to Ḥamzah, when God wanted Himself to be known, He created His first creation, which is known as *al-ta'ayyun al-awwal* or First Determination.[24]

> The first determination is the existence of "Oneness";
> This reality is the *rūḥ iḍāfī* (the added Spirit):
> The principle of the whole created order,
> Its name is the Muḥammadan Reality.[25]

According to Naguib al-Attas, Ḥamzah applies the doctrine of *waḥdat al-wujūd* to the whole of creation in its essential reality. This unity of being consists of stages, each stage having its own limited reality.

The *rūḥ iḍāfī* or *al-ḥaqīqat al-muḥammadiyyah* is the station of *waḥdah* (the First Determination), whereas *rūḥ insānī,* that is, the human spirit, is the station of *wāḥidiyyah.* Both are eternal and created—eternal in comparison to the external world and being created in comparison to the Divine Innermost Essence.[26] A Malay proverb considers the external world to be the manifestation of the internal world; whatever is manifested is actually the "Hidden Treasure" of the Innermost Essence. The Reality of man is described by Ḥamzah thus:

> Man is indeed too lofty,
> His Reality is the Compassionate, the Eternal.
> *Aḥsan*^{u} *taqwīm*^{in} (His inner constitution) is divine,
> The seat of the One called "Praise be to Me."[27]

Man is a double-faced mirror, an intermediary being (*barzakh*) situated between the worlds of spirit and corporeality. In his imagery of the "Primordial Fish" Ḥamzah says:

> Its body is in the form of man;
> Swim and swim in the Ocean of Permanence.[28]

Man must realize the multiplicity of forms as being, in reality, aspects of the One. In a Malay mystical treatise, probably belonging to the Ḥamzah school of Sufism, the *sālik* (traveler) is asked to forget the aspect of "many beings" and affirm the Oneness of Being as the only Reality. "He is now as He was, that is to say there is no being other than that of God, for the many beings that are to be seen, merely manifest His being which is the One (True Being)."[29]

Amir Hamzah's Literary Achievement

Among contemporaries, the most noteworthy is Amir Hamzah, a twentieth-century Malay-Indonesian poet who writes both in the form *pantun* and freestyle modern poetry.[30] Throughout his two anthologies, *Buah Rindu* (*Fruits of Longing*) and *Nyanyi Sunyi* (*Song of Solitude*), Amir Hamzah shows us his masterly genius in using Malay as a medium for poetry and the striking vividness of his inclination toward metaphysical and spiritual teachings.

Amir Hamzah was described by A. Teeuw as "the only 'modern' Malay poet who reverts to 'the traditional' mystically-tinged religious Malay poetry,' which in its turn can be traced back directly or indirectly to the great mystics of Islam (Djalāluddīn Rūmī, Ibn 'Arabī)."[31] Amir was born in 1329/1911 to the royal family of Langkat. His father was the Bendahara Paduka Radja or the prime minister of the sultanate of Langkat, in northern Sumatra. His father, who was also a Sufi, is said to have had a lively interest in Malay literature and used to hold *shair* and *hikayat* recitations probably at the court of Langkat. In this way Amir was exposed to the traditional Malay literature in his young days. A. Teeuw mentions that his "Malay spirit" could be traced in his poem "Hang Tuah," which tells a story of how the traditional Malay culture hero, Hang Tuah, tried to stop the attack of the Portuguese on Malacca, but failed because of old age.[32]

When he was fourteen, Amir went to Java and fell in love with a Javanese girl. So deep was his love that when he was summoned to return to Sumatra to take charge at the Deli Court, Amir showed some resistance. Most critics, for example, Ali Sjahbana and Zubir Usman, mention that his later spiritual struggle was the result of his failure in love, which caused him to turn to God for comfort and satisfaction. However, I suggest here the possibility that Amir's struggle, even at the very beginning of his journey into spiritual love, was a struggle to know the Truth.[33] To Amir, horizontal (or human) love is part of the true and ultimate Divine Love which is the source of all love, human and divine.

In his early poems, Amir shows us that his is longing for a true love. *Buah Rindu* (*Fruits of Longing*) was written early in Amir's career as a poet, and his *Nyanyi Sunyi* (*Song of Solitude*), which was written later, shows a more vivid and clearer picture of his spiritual journey to love. Even in *Buah Rindu,* Amir asks God: "What is the Permanent, that which will never change?" Amir's realization came early in his life, during his young days in Java. To the young Amir, human love would always end unfruitfully. To the mature Amir, human love is but a fruit of the Divine Love which is its Root. Amir surrendered his happiness and tried to smile at all of God's "play" in His drama of love, which comes and goes at His pleasure. In Amir's own words:

> Laughter have I presented,
> Our love you have ended.
> What more do you expect, my love,
> From me, in this state of misery. . . .[34]

In another verse:

> Kamadewi! Aren't you asking for my life instead?[35]

Amir realized at one point that all human love must be vanquished because it is impermanent. The true love is that for the Beloved, the Source of all love. In his poem *Barangkali* (*May Be*), Amir calls upon his Beloved, whom he describes as the One Who "sleeps" in his heart and Who is All-Pervasive in creation, to wake up and dance, to open His eyes of pearls, to make the world dance together with Him.

God is the One behind all the "Divine Play" who does what He wishes, whenever He wants to, and at whatever risk it might entail for man. Amir realized that the world of multiplicity is not for him. He has to leave it to its multiplicity and fly to his Beloved. In *Do'a* (*Prayer*) he considers his meeting with the Beloved in his spiritual self, while his bodily self has surrendered to the Divine Will.

Amir finally realized that there are two "selves" within him, the heavenly, which is pure, and the earthly, which is defiled. He knew that Pure Love never tortured him; it was simply he who tortured himself because his love was mixed with lowly elements. Amir ended his *Nyanyi Sunyi* (*Song of Solitude*) with the poems *Inṣāf* (*Realization*) and *Rela* (*Surrender*), which describe his final realization. Even though his Beloved is veiled to him by the earthly elements, the time will come when the Beloved will wed him, and they will flow together eternally. This perfect wedding took place during the Indonesian Revolution. In early 1946, during the massacre in Deli, Amir was killed. A. Teeuw described his death as "a sad symbol of the irreconcilability of the Malay past with the Indonesian future."[36] Amir lived like Rūmī's reed, loved like Niẓāmī's Majnūn, and died like Suhrawardī Maqtūl. His life and works remain as witness in our own day and age of the influence of Islamic spirituality upon Malay literature, which goes back to the birth of this literature as a vehicle for the teachings of Islam and especially its inner dimension contained in Sufism.

Notes

1. S. M. N. al-Attas, *The Mysticism of Ḥamzah Fanṣūrī* (Kuala Lumpur: University of Malaya Press, 1970) chaps. 3 and 4. See also his *Islam Dalam Sejarah Dan Kebudayaan Melayu* (Kuala Lumpur: National University of Malaysia Publication, 1972) 41.

2. S. M. N. al-Attas, *Preliminary Statement on a General Theory of the Islamization of the Malay-Indonesian Archipelago* (Kuala Lumpur: Dewan Bahasa dan Pustaka, 1969) 27.

3. S. M. N. al-Attas, *Al-Rānirī and Wujūdiyyah of Seventeenth Century Acheh* (Monograph of the Malaysian Branch of the Royal Asiatic Society 3; Singapore, 1966) 57–59.

4. Ibid.; see also al-Attas, *The Mysticism of Ḥamzah Fanṣūrī*, chap. 4.

5. See A. Schimmel, *As Through a Veil: Mystical Poetry in Islam* (New York: Columbia University Press, 1982) 194.

6. Ibid., 193.

7. R. Guénon, "The Language of the Birds," in *The Sword of Gnosis*, ed. J. Needleman (Baltimore: Penguin Books, 1974) 299.

8. S. H. Nasr, *Islamic Art and Spirituality* (Albany: State University of New York Press, 1987) 89–113; see also his *Three Muslim Sages* (Cambridge, MA: Harvard University Press, 1964) especially on Ibn Sīnā's oriental philosophy.

9. Nūr al-Dīn al-Rānirī, *Bustān al-salāṭīn*, chap. 1 in *Kitab Tajul Muluk* (Penang: Sulaiman al-Maari, n.d.).

10. See R. O. Winstedt, *A History of Classical Malay Literature* (Kuala Lumpur: Oxford University Press, 1969) 135–36.

11. Ḥamzah Fanṣūrī was very much influenced by Ibn 'Arabī, 'Abd al-Karīm al-Jīlī, and 'Abd al-Raḥmān Jāmī. His prose works include *Asrār al-'ārifīn* (*The Secret of the Gnostics*), *Sharāb al-'āshiqīn* (*The Drink of Lovers*), and *al-Muntahī* (*The Final End*). His

poetical works include *Shi'r fī bayān 'ilm al-sulūk wa'l-tawḥīd* (*The Shair on Knowledge of Spiritual Progress and Unity*), *Shair Perahu* (*The Shair of the Boat*), and *Shair Dagang* (*The Shair of Travellers*). See S. M. N. al-Attas, *The Mysticism of Ḥamzah Fanṣūrī*, xiii–xiv.

12. Winstedt, *Classical Malay Literature,* 143–44.

13. Ibid., 145.

14. On Nūr al-Dīn al-Rānirī, see S. M. N. al-Attas, *A Commentary on the Ḥujjat al-Ṣiddīq of Nūr al-Dīn al-Rānirī* (Kuala Lumpur: Ministry of Culture, Malaysia, 1988).

15. Shaykh 'Abd al-Malik 'Abd Allāh, *Kitab Hikam Melayu* (Penang and Singapore: Alharamain, n.d.).

16. Winstedt, *Classical Malay Literature,* 153.

17. Shaykh 'Abd al-Ra'ūf Singkel, *Mir'āt al-ṭullāb* (Acheh: Universitas Syiah Kuala, 1978).

18. Winstedt, *Classical Malay Literature,* 152–53.

19. Most of the treatises on *taṣawwuf* are being reproduced by Sulaiman al-Maari Press in Penang and Singapore. They are widely read by the Malays up to the present.

20. A. H. Johns, "From Coastal Settlement to Islamic School and City: The Islamization of Sumatra, the Malay Peninsula and Java," *Hamdard Islamicus* 4/4 (1981) 25.

21. See al-Attas, *Rānirī and Wujūdiyyah,* 46.

22. Ibid.

23. Ibid.

24. See al-Attas, *The Mysticism of Ḥamzah Fanṣūrī,* 68–69.

25. Ibid., 492 (Ḥamzah's *Syair*). The English translation of this verse and other verses of Ḥamzah's poetry were taken from al-Attas's translations, with slight modifications.

26. Al-Attas, *The Mysticism of Ḥamzah Fanṣūrī,* 66–110.

27. Ibid., 495.

28. Ibid., 501; see also al-Attas, *Rānirī and the Wujūdiyyah,* concerning Ḥamzah's metaphysical teaching.

29. A. H. Johns, "Malay Sufism," *Journal of the Malaysian Branch of the Royal Asiatic Society* 30/2 (August 1957) 58.

30. A. Teeuw, *Modern Indonesian Literature* (The Hague: Nijhoff, 1967) 97–98.

31. Ibid., 99.

32. Ibid.

33. Our meeting with his daughter Teuku Tahurah revealed the fact that Amir practiced *taṣawwuf* from the time that he was a young boy at the court of Langkat.

34. Amir Hamzah, *Buah Rindu* (Kuala Lumpur: Bi-Karya, 1963) 5–42. The English translation of Amir's poems were taken from A. Teeuw, with slight modifications (*Modern Indonesian Literature*).

35. Amir Hamzah, *Buah Rindu,* 42.

36. Teeuw, *Modern Indonesian Literature,* 105.

21

Berber, Swahili, and Other African Languages

JAN KNAPPERT

IN THIS ARTICLE there is space only to describe briefly the Islamic literatures of the "great" traditions, such as Berber, Fulani, Hausa, and Swahili cultures, but there are many other literatures such as that of the city of Harar or Somali and Songhay which must be passed over or mentioned only briefly. Nearly all these languages have a written tradition in Arabic script and are related in their ethos to Arabic and other literature of the Islamic people.

There has been a great deal of uncertainty about the origins of the themes of the Islamic literatures in Africa, and even today only some of the answers have been found. When M. Hiskett and I discovered how close Swahili and Hausa Islamic literatures were in spite of three thousand miles separating the two nations, we decided to hold a conference. At this meeting in 1968, C. Seydou and A. J. Drewes revealed very similar themes in Fulfulde and Amharic Islamic literatures respectively. Drewes later added his data on Gurage and Harari, and J. Bynon found some literary pieces in Berber (e.g., the legend of Yūsuf in verse). In the Somali and Mandinka areas, on the other hand, as B. W. Andrzejewsky and G. Innes have demonstrated, the Islamic literature in Arabic is all written, whereas the literary products in the Somali and Mandinka languages are not written but are oral. Nor are they really Islamic in essence: Mandinka and Somali verse traditions are basically secular; that is, they do not deal with Islamic subjects such as the prophets, the saints, or the holy wars. Nevertheless, in an Islamic culture (both the Somali and Mandinka peoples have been Muslims for centuries) all literature is necessarily full of Islamic concepts, since Islamic thinking permeates all aspects of daily life. In almost every Swahili song some hidden Islamic thought may be detected.

It was finally P. Cachia who solved part of the puzzle of the origins, by pointing out in a paper read at the same conference, that there are two

Arabic literatures, an official literature and a popular one. It had been evident to all insiders for some time that the "high" Arabic literature did not contain the genres, the themes, or the ambience of the popular literatures of Africa. Arabic literature as it is known to scholars is the literature of an elite. The popular literature, composed in the vulgar dialects, is more varied, more expressive of the concerns of the masses, though its appeal is by no means confined to the uneducated. Moreover, among its composers are not only "men of the people" but also several scholars who have written works in classical Arabic as well as in the colloquial languages. It should be pointed out that this popular literature in "vulgar" Arabic is not exclusively oral. On the contrary, many printed editions in paperback, some containing only a few pages, can be obtained in bookshops in Egypt or Morocco. Many of these texts are in verse, like the ones that Enno Littmann collected and the ones that Edward Lane describes. They include many long poems about the same traditional subjects that one meets in the African literatures, though the majority are in vulgar or semiclassical Arabic prose, interspersed with verses. This popular literature includes also some major prose works like the Romance of the Banū Hilāl and Sayf ibn Dhī Yazan. A large body of this popular literature in Egypt owes its existence to the Sufi orders, whose authors compose in it to propagate their ideas. The long narrative ballads are recited by a professional performer called a *mawwāl* in Egypt, who accompanies himself on a *rabābah* or rebek, in coffeehouses or in marketplaces, but preferably at a *mawlid,* a feast in honor of a saint, of which there are over a hundred every year. Most popular as material for these ballads are the Quranic legends of Adam and Eve, Abraham and Nimrod, Moses and Pharaoh, Joseph, etc. Yet a comparison between these Egyptian ballads and the Swahili long-verse narratives on the same themes brings out many differences in treatment and numerous distinctive details in the story. None of the Swahili epics is based on any of the known Arabic versions.

The theme of death, the angel Azrael, and God's immutable decree to end a person's life, is one of the commonest in popular literature of all the Islamic countries. Especially among the common people, many legends circulate of famous kings and tyrants of the past, like Pharaoh, Solomon, Nimrod, Alexander the Great, Khosroes (al-Kisrā), Anūshīrawān, and other kings whose names are known from Nigeria to Indonesia. A very popular theme in Egypt and North Africa is the wealth of the pharaohs, the immense treasures they had to leave behind when they suddenly died, treasures that were many centuries later discovered by lucky young men who decipher the inscription on the tomb: "You who found this, remember that I too was once alive. . . ."

In some cases of African Islamic literatures, versified translations of the same Arabic poem have been found in many languages, for example, the *Burdah* of al-Būṣīrī, which is popular in both Fulani and Swahili. The Fulani work *Miradj-Nemah* has a Persian title, so that the question arises how it originally arrived in West Africa, and from where. In Swahili, there are half a dozen poetic versions of the *mi'rāj;* none has been traced to its origin. Popular religious poetry like this, including that describing the scenes of paradise, is perhaps frowned upon by the scholars but tolerated because it certainly helps to spread Islamic ideas in general in the broadest layers of the people. We find descripions of paradise as royal gardens with glittering palaces, and horseback riding is the chief amusement in both Fulani and Swahili poetry.

Another important theme is that of the genesis of the world. There are poems describing God's creation of the earth composed in the Fulani and Swahili languages. Although separated by some three thousand miles across the continent of Africa, these poems have a remarkable similarity and offer a unique opportunity to compare and appreciate the cultural closeness of the two literatures. Islam was the moving force that inspired poets of both languages as well as many others located geographically between them. Islam taught the poets to visualize the creation as an immense manifestation of God's power and His wish to show humanity the beauty of His works.

Berber Literature

There is no single Berber language, since the Berber tribes were scattered by the Arab invasions after 50/670 and lost their national coherence. There are five main groupings: (1) in the east, the Luwata (Levatians), to which belong the Awriga (to whom we owe the name Africa), Awraba, Hawwara, and Nafzawa, extending over Cyrenaica, Tripolitania, Djerid, and Aures; (2) in the west, the Sanhaja in scattered groups, the Kutama in Little Kabylia, the Zwara in Great Kabylia, the Ghumara in the Rif, the Masmuda on the Atlantic coast of Morocco, the Gezula (Djazula) in the High Atlas, the Lemta in southern Morocco, the Ifren between the rivers Chelif, and Moulouya along the coast of Oran Province; (3) inland from Tripolitania along Djebel Amour to south Morocco, the Zanara; (4) in Mauritania, the Zenaga, chief among them the Trarza; (5) in the western Sahara, the Touareg, who transhume in the vast area between the ancient trading centers of Timbuctoo, Zinder, Ghadames, Ouargla, El Ghardaia, Figuig, Tafilalet, and as far west as the Wadi Dades.

Since ancient times, the Berbers have possessed a script that is called Tifinagh by them, a word that may derive from the Phoenician; it is called

"Libyan" in Western literature, since it was first discovered in the Libyan inscriptions. Over a thousand "Libyan" inscriptions of the pre-Islamic period have been discovered, but even though the script is known, the language has not been deciphered. The same is true of the inscriptions in Latin letters.

The Berber dialects are extremely complicated in their mutual phonetic and morphological relationships. In total there are more than four thousand local idioms, because each village and each nomadic community has its own speech. Folk literature could be collected in every single one of these communities. Numerous collections have been published in various dialects with mainly French translations. These comprise folktales, legends of the saints, songs, proverbs, and riddles.[1]

Berber literature has been written in the Arabic script (with additional diacritic points for its adaptation to the extra Berber consonants) mainly for the purpose of teaching Islamic subjects to students. Perhaps the most important work is *The Ocean of Tears,* an adaptation in verse of the Arabic *Baḥr al-dumūʿ* by al-Khalīl.[2] There are some other interesting and fairly long religious poems, including a few Berber versifications of Islamic texts that are universally popular in the world of Islam, for example, the *Legend of Yūsuf,* the biblical Joseph, and the *Burdah* of al-Būṣīrī. The most interesting creators of Berber literature are the *imdyazen* (plural of *amdyaz).*[3] They travel about the country and, like the troubadours, celebrate important events, sing the praises of likely patrons and discharge their scorn at those who disappoint them. These products of oral art are secular and ephemeral. Most interesting for the folklorist are the innumerable fairy tales which display an unusually rich variety of motifs, clearly the result of the Berbers' being at the receiving end of both the European and Oriental traditions of storytelling.

Of all the Berber dialects, Shilha, Shuluh, or Chleuh in western Morocco seems to have developed more literature than the others. More remote than its cousins, shielded by the Sous mountains, looking out toward the ocean, the Chleuh, though Islamized, were less affected by the impact of Arabic as a literary language. The most famous of their authors is Mohammed-ou-Ali-ou-Ibrahim, who flourished in the early twelfth/eighteenth century. All his surviving works are didactic treatises on the doctrine of Islam. One is entitled *al-Ḥawḍ,* after the name of a pond at the entrance of paradise where those who drink will be completely purified from sin. It is a translation from the Arabic work *al-Mukhtaṣar* by Sidi Khālī, in 960 rather monotonous verses, covering the Attributes of God, ablutions, prayers, funeral rites, fasting, and pilgrimage. No grace, only rules—hardly a subject for poetry. It is useful, but not beautiful. ʿAlī's second work on theology was entitled *Baḥr al-dumūʿ* (*The Ocean of Tears*), an Islamic catechism for advanced students, entirely in verse in a strongly Arabicized Berber.

Of the many beautiful Berber songs only a few lines can be quoted here. In the following song, a religious man of the people comments on the public display of wealth:

O cloth what makes you proud?	You clothe the lepers.
O pearl what makes you proud?	The harlots wear you.
Fortress what makes you proud?	The heathens built you.
Fountain what makes you proud?	The camels drink you.

There are many poems about love and a few gems about friendship. It is not suggested here that "the Friend" refers to the Divine Proximity or spiritual reality, even though a great deal of *taṣawwuf* literature exists in Arabic in North Africa.

When your heart is broken, who will heal it,
if not the presence of your friend, his soothing words?
If your heart has no one to console it
it is like exile. Who is happy without friends?
To be betrayed by one who was a friend is bitter.
To see one's friend shed tears of hopelessness is bitter.
To be without a friend in loneliness is bitter.
To suffer for your best friend's sorrow, that is bitter.

Ifni

Ifni is a small region between Morocco and Mauritania on the Atlantic coast. It was a Spanish province for many centuries. It is inhabited by the Ait Bamran, who belong to the Chelha subdivision of the Berbers, whose language is spoken in a large part of southern Morocco. Arcadio Palacin has described a special kind of traditional song (*cancion*) which is sung by a professional bard (*rais,* literally, "chief"), probably because these bards sometimes conduct companies of dancing boys. The songs that the *rais* sings resemble in structure the Persian and Urdu *ghazal,* of which there are a few examples in Swahili. It consists of a string of stanzas of the same prosodic scheme, sung in the same tune but dealing with different subjects—romantic, religious, or lyrical. Even the songs with narrative themes contain stanzas that are philosophical or lyrical digressions from the main theme. We are concerned here only with the religious-Islamic aspects of Ifni poetry, for example:

Whither O faithless world, have the good people gone?
From those you treat with grace, expect only contempt.
For only God is grateful; only He will last.
His grace is medicine for healthy men and sick.
Whatever we may eat, we eat it by His grace.
Whatever clothes we wear, we wear them by His grace.
Whatever alms we give 'tis only by His grace.
Thus friends, be free of care, He is your warranty.

Zenaga

Zenaga (or Znaga, Zanagha, Sanhaja) is a Berber language spoken in western Mauritania. It seems to be rapidly losing ground to Hassaniyyah, which is the most westerly dialect of Arabic.[4] The Senaga have always been nomads by necessity, because their country is very arid, and they are extremely conservative and proud of their ancient culture. They were of old divided into the following subtribes: Tajakani, Midlish, Lamtuna, Mashduf (Massufa), Idaw'ish, Malata, Hawd, and Banu Dayman. Although they were Islamized well before 390/1000, they attribute their scholastic and literary tradition to the Almoravids: *Murābiṭ* or *Zuwāyā* is the name sometimes used for this early Sufi literature, although Norris, the chief authority on Mauritanian languages and literatures, is in no doubt that the original Zenaga literature is much older. Unfortunately, however, it is all lost, and no manuscripts survive from before 1111/1700, in spite of a dry climate which should be kind to manuscripts. Perhaps war was the cause of the destruction of this ancient and refined literature, for, as the Mauritanian poet says:

War when it starts is like a lovely maid
with her enticing hair a loosened braid,
promising power, prize and perfumed nights
thus she seduces many foolish knights
eager to conquer the deceitful wench;
their end is the embrace of fire, smoke and stench.[5]

Harari

Harari or Adare is the language of the ancient town of Harar in eastern Ethiopia, near the border of Djibouti, the country that faces the corner of Arabia. From that corner, Islam was carried into Africa at an early stage of its history, and Harar is one of the oldest Islamic cities south of Egypt. It was an independent Islamic state for many centuries, but it was conquered by Menelik II, the emperor of Ethiopia, who made it a duchy in his empire. Harari is one of the five Semitic languages of Ethiopia, and it is the only one that regularly uses Arabic script. Almost all of the literature of Harar is written on manuscripts, of which there must be several thousand in the city. Two European scholars have worked on this literature, Enrico Cerulli and A. J. Drewes. They have examined numerous manuscripts which are mainly in Arabic; only a few are older than ca. 1060/1650. The chief prose work is the *Kitāb al-farā'iḍ* (*The Book of Obligations*), in Harari, which Cerulli edited. It contains the basic doctrinal and moral precepts of Islam. Much of the poetry in Harari is liturgical, called *zikri,* and is intended to be recited during nocturnal prayer meetings, often under the supervision of the local leaders of the Qādiriyyah. Following is an excerpt from the almost six hundred lines of the *zikri* of 'Abd al-Malik.

O Prophet may God's blessing be upon you,
we seek our refuge with you from our problems.
You are a medicine for all diseases.
Praying to God for you will be salvation.

O Prophet whom the Lord of light created
from light that is more radiant than sunshine.
O Prophet who revealed the hidden knowledge,
whose name was first of all the names God mentioned.

O God admit the people who have studied
and love the humble servants who implore Thee.
Open for us the shining gate of mercy,
as Thou hast showered mercy on Thy Prophet.

O Prophet who hast filled our hearts with splendor,
pray God for us that He may give us blessing.
His blessings have no end and no beginning.
May you guide us towards the gate of Heaven.[6]

Fulani

The name Fulani was originally Hausa; it is the plural indicating the people who call themselves Fulbe (sg. Pullo). The French call them Peul and their language Poular; various branches of the nation are called Toucouleur (Tuculor), Fula, etc. The Fulbe call their language Fulfulde and are very proud of it. Indeed, its intricate structure has exercised the minds of some of Europe's most prominent linguists, such as Meinhof, Klingenheben, Gaden, Labouret, and Arnott.

Fulfulde belongs to the west Atlantic family of languages, and its origin must be sought in the extreme west of Africa. From there the Fulani spread out toward the east along the savannah belt of West Africa, so that they are now well established as far east as Cameroun. They are cattle owners, and thus a large part of their oral literature centers on their herds and their herding work. It is not known when this eastward movement in search of fresh grass began, but it has certainly taken the Fulani several centuries. At some stage during their wanderings they were Islamized, perhaps as early as the late Middle Ages, although the process called Islamization must be seen as a long evolution from adopting a few semi-Islamic customs, such as wearing talismans made from folded-up chapters of the Quran, to instituting religious schools where the Quran is properly taught and interpreted. It was only in the mid-twelfth/eighteenth century that reform movements began in earnest, usually preceded by a *jihād*, which resulted in solidly Islamizing the Fulani and most of the peoples they conquered. The central leader of the Fulani at the close of the century was ʿUthmān ibn Fūdī, better known by his Hausa name Usman dan Fodio (Fulfulde: Usman bii Fooduye). He styled himself *almami* (= *imām*) of the region which comprised most of what is now northern Nigeria and surrounding districts. Finally he was recognized as caliph and established his capital at Sokoto. In addition to ruler and general, he was also scholar and author, writing Islamic works in both Arabic and his native Fulfulde. This Islamic empire lasted for about a century, until 1321/1903, when the British occupied Sokoto, and the modern period of history began.

The oldest texts in Fulfulde that we possess were written by the reformists of the late twelfth/eighteenth century, prominent among whom were ʿUthmān himself and his brother ʿAbd Allāh, who, being more intellectually inclined than his warrior brother, devoted himself to study and may have been the inventor of Fulfulde literary forms. It was a well-tried principle in Islamic scholarly circles that works on doctrine and duties had to be composed in verse in the vernacular, so that local preachers could memorize them and recite them before their illiterate audiences in the villages.

One of the first poets to use Fulfulde, writing in Arabic script, was the famous scholar Muhammadu Tukur, an older contemporary of Usman dan Fodio. He is still revered as a saint in Zamfara, southeast of Sokoto, where he was born. He lies buried in the same region, in the village of Matuzzigi.

Although manuscripts exist in Arabic script of most Fulani poems, singing them is still a living oral tradition among the Fulani. Many mendicant men and women, often blind, call at the houses of the well-to-do in the towns and, when admitted to the courtyard, sing these pious songs for a modest fee. Another group of singers is the professionals. They can be invited to recite their repertoire on the occasion of special celebrations, for example, when a boy has completed his studies at the Quranic school or on the eve of ʻĀshūrā, the 10th of Muḥarram. Many people will come to listen, standing in the dark street or sitting on mats on the veranda or in the yard of the "concession," that is, the compound. All the songs are religious and are preceded by a prayer and an invocation of God and His Prophet. Many of these songs are *waṣiyyah* or *waʻẓ*—sermons, admonitory verses in which the listeners are warned against the tricks and temptations of this world, against association with nonbelievers, against negligence in prayer or fasting. Other aspects of the *Sunnah* are also enjoined, including the pilgrimage to Mecca, which is depicted in glowing colors. The prophets of the past (e.g., al-Khaḍir or al-Khiḍr) as well as the "messiah" of the future, al-Mahdī, are also celebrated. The Last Judgment, which will take place after the Resurrection, and the punishments of hell for those who were sinners during their lives, are described in terrifying detail. Finally, the road to paradise is described, along which the Blessed Prophet leads his faithful believers toward the joyful gates of paradise. Of all the songs sung by these singers, both the mendicants and the professionals, the *Busarau* (*The Bringers of Good Tidings*), which comprises 1,250 couplets, is by far the most famous.[7]

Unfortunately, this beautiful literature is in danger of extinction. Some of the most renowned singers have already died or are too old to perform, and the younger generation shows little interest in learning the difficult art of this melodious recitation. The same sad reports have come from East Africa concerning Swahili manuscripts, many of which are lost forever. Yet this literature is still for many Muslims the highest expression of their deepest feelings of devotion to God and His Prophet.

Another poet of the early period is Tierno Mouhammadou Samba Mombeya (1179/1765–1266/1850), whose best-known work, *Oogirde Malal* (*The Source of Eternal Happiness*), is a versified exposition of *fiqh*, an abridged textbook of Islamic duties, in a rigid meter of eleven syllables in the line. It is not composed in an easily accessible language, because it contains too many Arabic words. It has to be studied by aspiring young scholars under the guidance of an Islamic teacher.

Other great poets of the Fouta Djallon area of Guinea were Tierno Aliyyu Buuba Ndiyang (1261/1845–1345/1927) and his grandnephew Mahmuudu Bun Tierno Umar Pereejo Daara Labe. They belonged to two great families of scholars and poets who were linked by marriage, many of whose members excelled in piety. The *Burdah* of al-Būṣīrī was translated into Fulfulde by Shaykh Abou Saidou Sa'adou, abridged in twenty-three couplets. Praises in honor of the Prophet are frequently recited (or, rather, cantillated) during vigils that may last until dawn. Following is a sample of one stanza:

> More shining than all pearls or rubies is Muḥammad.
> More beauty than all gold or silver has Muḥammad.
> More splendor than all moonshine or sunlight has
> Muḥammad.
> More sweetness than the purest honey has Muḥammad.
> More quenching for the thirst than water is Muḥammad.[8]

The Tijāniyyah and Fulfunde Literature

Of the greatest importance for Fulfulde literature is the influence of the Tijānī movement, founded by Abu'l-'Abbās Aḥmad ibn Muḥammad al-Tijānī in 1195/1781. Born in Algeria, he studied in the centers of learning and Sufism of his time in Fes, Tunis, Cairo, and Medina. In a dream the Blessed Prophet appeared to him and instructed him to found a new order. This he did in his native Ain Mahdi, where his new *ṭarīqah* became so successful that it disquieted the Ottoman governor of Oran. Tijānī died in 1230/1815, bequeathing to his disciples Sidi al-Ḥājj 'Alī al-Harāzimī and Sidi Muḥammad ibn al-Mashrī al-Sayhī written instructions for the organization of his new order and full details for the religious rituals and practices of his followers. In this he had worked eclectically, selecting the best from the existing *ṭarīqahs* but taking care that nothing would be too hard for his followers who had little education. This may be one of the reasons why his teachings had such a phenomenal success in West Africa. His work *Jawāhir al-ma'ānī* (*Jewels of Meaning*) became the breviary of the order. His disciple Muḥammad al-Ḥāfiẓ al-Bājī was sent by the master to teach faith in Senegal and to create the apex of the hierarchy upon which the order would depend for its survival. Soon the Tijāniyyah spread eastward and became well known even in Nigeria. The basis of the hierarchical structure of the order is the inspiration which the founder received from the Blessed Prophet and which radiates *barakah* full of beneficent strength, a sort of fluid energy that can heal the sick and give insight to men who wander in dark error. Through the ramifications of the order, from the first disciples and their assistants down to the broad layers of the laymen followers, this *barakah* spreads by God's permission to whomever He wishes to cure or enlighten.

Numerous tales are told of miracles that have been witnessed by many. This is one explanation for the success of the order.

The first great religious leader of the Western Fulani was no doubt ʿUmar Seydu ibn Tierno Seydu Usman Tall, best known as al-Ḥājj ʿUmar. He was born in 1212/1797 in Halwar near Guede, thirty miles from Podor. He studied with ʿAbd al-Karīm, the grand master of the Tijānī, in Fouta Djalon. Traveling east, passing Sokoto and Fezzan, he arrived in Medina, where he visited Shaykh Muḥammad al-Ghālī, who was then caliph general of the Tijānī Order. Then al-Ghālī had a dream in which al-Tijānī appeared to him and instructed him to make ʿUmar Seydu his caliph (deputy) over all the black African countries (*khalīfat al-sūdān*). This he did, and ʿUmar Seydu traveled back to Sokoto, where he preached the Tijāniyyah doctrine. Soon he gathered numerous followers around him and even earned the confidence of the sultan of Sokoto, the famous Muḥammad Bello. After further peregrinations, ʿUmar Seydu, now called al-Ḥājj ʿUmar, settled in Dinguiraye (Guinea) above the Tinkisso River, where there is still a famous mosque. Here in 1268/1852 he heard a divine voice commanding him to "sweep the lands," that is, to cleanse the earth of paganism. From that moment on, the scholar and mystic became a general. After numerous victorious battles his fortune changed; he had to take refuge in a cave fifteen miles southwest from Bandiagara, where pilgrims still come to pray. His body was never found, and his followers are convinced he was the Mahdi.

Hausa

Hausa is spoken by some thirty million people in northern Nigeria, southern Niger, and elsewhere. To the west it is widespread in Ghana; toward the east it is used as a commercial language as far as the Sudan, where many Hausa speakers have settled.[9]

Praise songs for Hausa rulers of the late Middle Ages are still remembered. These lines are strongly reminiscent of praise songs in other African languages, especially when animal images are used:

> Male elephant Lord of the town,
> Abdulla, like a bull hippopotamus.[10]

The style, tenor, and content of these songs evidently precede the inception of the proper Islamic tradition, which Hiskett calls the Reform Tradition.[11] Ever since Islam was first introduced in Hausaland ca. 905/1500, it coexisted with the "heathen" practices of the older Hausa religion. This mutual toleration continued for about three centuries, during which the Muslim community gradually grew from a few scattered households to a sizable minority. It was toward the end of the twelfth/eighteenth century that Hausa scholars under the protection of Usman dan Fodio, who later established his capital at Sokoto, began to write admonitory verse and rhymed sermons in Hausa. Initially these writings fulminated against heathen practices among the Hausa populace and later also against the corruption and venality of the upper classes, the Fulani bureaucracy who had become Hausa-speaking. Thus, the Hausa writers used the same weapon against their oppressors that the latter had once used against the slack Hausa Muslims: the ideal of absolute righteousness in submission to the all-seeing God.

Hausa Islamic literature, according to Hiskett, is classifiable according to the following eight categories: (1) *waazu* and *zuhudi,* describing death and resurrection, the interrogation in the grave, divine reward and punishment on Judgment Day; (2) *madih an-Nabii,* panegyric to the Prophet and sometimes to other saints; (3) *tauhidi,* didactic and mnemonic verse setting out the Attributes of God and the basic principles of Muslim theology; (4) *fikihi,* didactic and mnemonic verse dealing with the precepts of Islamic law and personal duties (prayers, ablution, inheritance, etc.); (5) *sira,* the biography of the Prophet Muḥammad, including his campaigns and his miracles (best known in this category is the *Wakar Sira* by ʿAbd Allāh Muḥammad); (6) *tarihi,* history (there are several versified chronicles in Hausa); (7) *ilmin nujumi,* astrology, or *hisabi,* calculation of auspicious days (there are numerous works on the subject, which proves its popularity in Nigeria); (8) minor compositions, for example, political verse; *addua* "invocation" (much of this category is secular rather than Islamic).

It might be of interest to note that all these categories exist also in Swahili literature, though their relative importance is different. In Swahili there are only a few chronicles, and all the works on astrology are in Arabic. There is, however, a very important subcategory of the Swahili *qaṣīdahs:* the *mawlidi,* panegyrics sung at the Prophet's birthday during the week following the 12th Rabīʿ al-Awwal. However, in this *mawlid* literature, all the conventional praises that Hiskett mentions in this Hausa category (2 above) are repeated. The palace of the Persian king caved in when Muḥammad was born, while the sacred fires of the Magi were extinguished; old and shriveled goats gave milk when the Prophet touched them, etc.

Some of the most prominent Hausa poets of the thirteenth/nineteenth century were ʿAbd Allāh ibn Muḥammad (1180/1766–ca. 1244/1829), the younger brother of the Shehu Usman dan Fodio, who also made verse in Fulfulde. ʿAbd Allāh ibn Muḥammad wrote mainly *waʿẓ,* and a long poem on the life of the Prophet Muḥammad is also extant. His niece, Asma bint Shehu, daughter of Usman dan Fodio, also wrote poetry in the Islamic tradition, including "Ode to the Messenger of God" and "Poem of the

Wandering," a long poem describing her father's eventful life. Asim Degel of Kano also wrote a long epic poem describing the life of the Blessed Prophet and his battles, composed ca. 1261/1845. Muhammadu Tukur was a contemporary of Shehu Usman dan Fodio; he too wrote in Fulfulde as well as in Hausa and is still revered as a saint by pilgrims at his shrine in Matuzzigi. He is best known for his poem about hell. Buhari dan Gidado was the son of Gigado dan Laima, vizier to Sultan Bello. His mystic poem, the "Song of Buhari," was composed shortly after 1310/1893. Following is stanza 10:

> I pray to the Glorious, He is sufficient for me,
> The debt that I owe, He pays for me,
> For what I have desired, outwardly and inwardly,
> I repent, O God, forgive me.
> For the sake of the Shehu, the Light of my time,
> Usuman.[12]

Of great interest both for historians and Islamologists are the rhymed chronicles in Hausa. The "Song of Bagauda," which purports to begin in the fifth/eleventh century and is full of allusions to Islamic mythical concepts, is especially important:

> King Sulayman married the world.
> She behaved with the submissiveness of a bride
> but he heeded not.[13]

Swahili

Of all the Islamic literatures of Africa, the Swahili contribution is by far the most extensive, even though numerically the Swahili come well behind the Berber, Fulani, Galla, Hausa, Mande, and Somali nations. Swahili literature is also the oldest: the first datable text gives us 1062/1652 as a starting point for written Swahili literature. There are some oral traditions that go back even farther, but they are not Islamic.[14] The history of Swahili literature is closely linked to the typical shape of their homeland: the Swahili coast, between Mogadishu and Mozambique, is a thousand miles long and only some forty miles wide. The poetic activity was the fruit of the commercial towns, which all date from the Middle Ages: Barawa, Kisimaiu, Siu, Pate, Lamu, Malindi, Mombasa, Tanga, Bagamoyo, Dar es Salaam, Kilwa, Mikindani, and Zanzibar. Commercial ties with the Islamic Middle East existed from the early second/eighth century on, mainly with the port towns along the Persian Gulf, the Red Sea, and the south Arabian coast, later also with the towns on the west coast of India.

Although the Swahili coast was open to trading links with the Indian Ocean countries and islands (Madagascar, the Seychelles, the Comores, the Maldives, Socotra), the history of the Swahili literature is not well known, even during and after the Portuguese occupation (903/1498–1141/1729). Re-Islamized from this latter date on, the Swahili towns flourished, and so did their literature, especially the Islamic epic, the *qaṣīdahs* (hymns to the Prophet) and the *Waadhi* or admonitions to the believers. The tradition of writing Islamic poetry continued through the thirteenth/nineteenth century and is alive today. Muslim scholars write hymns and prayers (*du'ā*) to be sung in the mosque. Especially popular is the celebration of the Prophet's nativity, a week during which special hymns (*mawlidi*) are recited. Some of the finest lyrical verse are the elegies (*rithaa*) and the farewell songs for the *ḥājjīs*. Many secular songs contain allusions to aspects of Islamic life or cosmology. Other subjects are dealt with in prose (law, history, *tawḥīd*) or in verse (*fiqh*). Wedding songs still composed and sung to send off bridal couples include prayers sung to God that He may give them long life, happiness, and healthy children. Proverbs and gnomic epigrams contain aspects of Islamic philosophy. Swahili tales show strong influence of the Middle East and India, and Swahili literature in general is one of the important African literatures mirroring Islamic spirituality.

Notes

1. For the latter, see J. Bynon, "Riddle-Telling among the Berbers of Central Morocco," *African Language Studies* 7 (1966) 80–104, with complete bibliography. Concerning the history of the Berbers, see the well-condensed articles of C. Pellat and G. Yver in the *Encyclopedia of Islam,* 1:1173–78, with extensive bibliographies.
2. See *L'Océan des pleurs,* ed. B. Stricker (Leiden: Brill, 1960).
3. See A. Roux in *Memoires Henri Basset* (Paris: E. Leroux, 1928) 2:237–42.
4. See H. Norris, *Shingiti Folk Literature and Song* (Oxford: Oxford Library of African Literature, 1968).
5. Free translation, after H. Norris.
6. Free translation, after A. J. Drewes.
7. See J. Haafkens, *Chants musulmans en peul* (Leiden: Brill, 1983) 9.
8. Free translation, after C. Seydou ("Essai d'etude stylistique de poemes peuls du Fouta-Djallon," *Bulletin d'IFAN* 29/1–2 [1967] 191–233).
9. For an account of Hausa Islamic literature, see M. Hiskett, *History of Hausa Islamic Verse* (London: School of Oriental and African Studies, 1975).
10. Ibid., 3.
11. Ibid., 12.
12. Ibid., 77.
13. Ibid., 141.
14. See J. Knappert, *Four Centuries of Swahili Verse* (Singapore: Heinemann, 1979) chaps. 3 and 4. For the dating, see Knappert, "The Hamziya Deciphered," *African Language Studies* 9 (1968) 55.

Part Three

THE SPIRITUAL MESSAGE OF ISLAMIC ART AND THOUGHT

22

Theology, Philosophy, and Spirituality

S. H. Nasr

The Significance of *Kalām* in Islamic History

EVERY INTEGRAL RELIGION has within it intellectual dimensions that may be called theological, philosophical, and gnostic—if this latter term is understood as referring to a knowledge that illuminates and liberates. Islam is no exception to this principle and has developed within its bosom all three types of intellectual activity, each possessing a millennial tradition with numerous illustrious representatives. The relative significance of each dimension is, however, not the same in Islam and Christianity, nor do the categories correspond exactly to schools into which their names are translated in a European language such as English.

In the Islamic intellectual universe, there exists first of all *al-ma'rifah* or *al-'irfān* (gnosis). Then there is *falsafah,* which is itself derived from the Greek *philo-sophia* and corresponds to philosophy in the older sense of the term, before it became limited to its positivistic definition. This school in turn became transformed for the most part in later centuries into *al-ḥikmat al-ilāhiyyah* (literally, *theo-sophia*). Finally, there is *kalām,* usually translated as theology, whose propagators, the *mutakallimūn,* were referred to by Thomas Aquinas as the *loquentes.* The significance of these intellectual dimensions is not the same as corresponding perspectives in the West. This is especially true of *kalām,* which does not at all occupy the same central role in Islamic thought as theology does in Christianity. Furthermore, the Islamic schools have interacted with each other in a totally different manner from what one observes in the Christian West. Gnosis has played a more central role in the Islamic tradition than it has in the West, and the destiny of philosophy has been very different in the two worlds despite their close affinity in the European Middle Ages. As for theology, it has continued to harbor over the centuries the profoundest religious and spiritual impulses of Christianity, whereas in Islam it has always been more peripheral—although much that is considered to be theology in the West is to be found in Islamic philosophy.

In Christianity not only has theology attempted to provide a rational defense for the faith, but it has also sought to provide access to the highest realms of the life of the spirit, as one finds in the mystical theology of Dionysius the Areopagite or, in the Protestant context, in the *Theologica Germanica* of Martin Luther. Such has never been the case in Islam, where *kalām*, which means literally "word," continued to be "the science that bears responsibility of solidly establishing religious beliefs by giving proofs and dispelling doubts."[1] The deepest spiritual and intellectual expressions of Islam are not to be found in works of *kalām*. Yet this science is important for the understanding of certain aspects of Islamic thought and must be treated in any work seeking to deal with the manifestations of Islamic spirituality.

Early Kalām

Traditionally, ʿAlī ibn Abī Ṭālib, the cousin and son-in-law of the Prophet, is credited with having established the science of *kalām*, and his *Nahj al-balāghah* (*Path of Eloquence*) contains the first rational proofs of the unity of God, following upon the wake of the Quran and the *Ḥadīth*. Already in the first Islamic century, the early community was confronted with such problems and questions as the relation between faith and works, who is saved, the nature of the Quran, and the legitimacy of political authority, all of which became crystallized later into the structure and concerns of *kalām*. Moreover, the debates held in Syria and Iraq between Muslims and followers of other religions—especially Christians, Mazdaeans, and Manichaeans, all of whom had developed philosophical and theological arguments for the defense of the tenets of their faith—caused the Muslims to seek to develop a rational edifice of their own for the protection and defense of Islam. This response to the theology of other religions is particularly true for the case of Christianity, whose theology directly challenged the young faith of Islam to construct its own theological edifice. Greco-Alexandrian philosophy, which early Christian thinkers had already encountered and with which Muslims were also becoming acquainted was also an important factor in the formation of the early schools of *kalām*.

The rapid spread of Islam had brought diverse groups within the fold of the Islamic community and necessitated a clear definition of the creed to prevent various kinds of error. Because of the emphasis of Islam upon the Divine Law and its practice, these creeds are not as important as the *credo* in traditional Christianity, but they are nonetheless of significance for an understanding of the early theological concerns of the Islamic community. These creeds include the *Fiqh al-akbar* ("The Great Knowledge") and the *Waṣiyyah* ("Testament") either by or based upon the teachings of Imam Abū Ḥanīfah (d. 150/767), who was also the founder of one of the major Sunni schools of Law. These creeds emphasize above all else the unity of God and His power over human life. They usually also emphasize the importance of gaining knowledge of God to the extent possible. There were later theologians who insisted that every Muslim must know as many proofs for the existence of God as he is able to master.

The Mu'tazilites

The first systematic school of *kalām* grew out of the bosom of the circle of traditional scholars of the Quran and *Ḥadīth* in the second/eighth century and came to be known as the Mu'tazilite. Its founder, Wāṣil ibn 'Aṭā' (d. 131/748), is said to have been a student of the famous scholar of *Ḥadīth* and Sufism in Basra, Ḥasan al-Baṣrī, but he separated from his master and established his own circle in that city.

The Mu'tazilites, who were seen as the freethinkers and rationalists of Islam by early Western Islamicists, dominated the theological scene in Iraq for more than a century and developed an imposing theological edifice based on emphasis on the use of reason and the importance of human free will. The outstanding Mu'tazilites were either from Basra, for example, Abu'l-Hudhayl al-'Allāf (d. 226/840), Abū Isḥāq al-Naẓẓām (d. 231/845), and the famous literary figure 'Amr ibn Baḥr al-Jāḥiẓ (d. 255/869); or from Baghdad, among whose leaders were Bishr ibn al-Mu'tamir (d. 210/825) and Abū 'Alī al-Jubbā'ī (d. 303/915). After al-Ma'mūn, early in the third/ninth century, the fortunes of the Mu'tazilites began to wane, and soon they were replaced as the dominant school of *kalām* by the Ash'arites. They did not completely die out, however, but continued to survive for another two centuries in various parts of the heartland of the Islamic world, as can be seen in the vast Mu'tazilite encyclopedia of the Persian theologian Qāḍī 'Abd al-Jabbār, composed in the fifth/eleventh century. Their school survived even longer in the Yemen, where their teachings became adopted by the Zaydīs of that land.[2]

In the history of Islamic thought the Mu'tazilites came to be known for five principles or affirmations (*al-uṣūl al-khamsah*), which in fact summarize their basic teachings. These are unity (*al-tawḥīd*), justice (*al-'adl*), the promise and the threat (*al-wa'd wa'l-wa'īd*), in-between position in relation to a Muslim who commits a sin (*al-manzilah bayn al-manzilatayn*), and exhorting to perform the good and forbidding to commit evil (*al-amr bi'l-ma'rūf wa'l-nahy 'an al-munkar*).

The Mu'tazilites possessed a rationalistic concept of the unity of God, and as a result they emphasized God's transcendence in such a manner as to reduce God almost to an abstract idea. In an atmosphere in which a great deal of debate was taking place concerning the meaning of God's Attributes and Qualities as mentioned in the Quran, they sought to avoid all possible anthropomorphism. As a result, they claimed that man cannot understand the real meaning of such Divine Attributes as Hearing or Seeing and that such Attributes have no reality of their own. Rather, they are identical with the Divine Essence. They also denied the possibility of knowledge of God's Nature. In denying any reality to Attributes, the Mu'tazilites also denied the eternity of the Quran as the Word of God. This view became their most famous and contested thesis because of its sociopolitical implications.

The Mu'tazilites also emphasized justice to the extent that they became known as the "people of unity and justice." Justice for them meant that God, being All-Wise, must have a purpose in the creation of the universe and that there is objective justice and good and evil in God's creation even if one puts aside the teachings of the Divine Law (*al-Sharī'ah*) concerning good and evil. Because God is just and good and cannot go against His Nature, He must always act for the best and is just. Furthermore, God does not will evil. Rather, evil is created by human beings, who have been given by God the freedom to act in either a good or an evil manner. They are therefore responsible for their actions and will be rewarded or punished by God accordingly.

The third principle, *al-wa'd wa'l-wa'īd,* which means literally "promise and threat," refers to the ultimate fate of various classes of people, namely, the believers (*mu'minūn*), those who are nominally Muslims but who have committed sin (*fāsiqūn*) and those who are unbelievers (*kuffār*). The Mu'tazilites had a severe view of sin and condemned both sinners and infidels to the punishment of hell. For the Mu'tazilites, faith (*īmān*) was not only the assertion of the unity of God and consent to the truth of religion with the heart. It was also the avoidance of any grievous sins.

A major problem that confronted the early Islamic community was the question of who was saved and who was a Muslim. Was the sole condition faith, or was it necessary also to practice the tenets of the religion and avoid what was forbidden by the *Sharī'ah?* Amid this debate, the Mu'tazilites had to express their position clearly, which they did in the fourth of their five principles, one that follows directly from the principle of promise and threat. Their "in-between" position for sinners, *al-manzilah bayn al-manzilatayn,* asserts that the Muslim sinner (*fāsiq*) occupies a position between the believer and the unbeliever and is still a member of the Islamic community in this world although condemned to damnation in the world to come.

Finally, the Mu'tazilites emphasized the principle of *al-amr bi'l-ma'rūf wa'l-nahy 'an al-munkar.* This well-known Islamic principle, emphasized also by several other schools, asserts that man not only must exhort others to perform the good but also must forbid people from committing evil. It implies an active attitude toward the establishment of a religious order and a morality that is not simply a matter of private conscience but involves Islamic society as a whole.

The Mu'tazilites were the first group of Muslim thinkers to apply rational arguments systematically to various questions of religion and even natural philosophy. They also knew some of the tenets of Greek thought, which was being translated into Arabic at the time of their intellectual activity in Baghdad in the third/ninth century and had a share in the introduction of Hellenic and Hellenistic thought into the Islamic intellectual world. Most of the Mu'tazilites devoted themselves to purely theological and politico-theological questions, and all were concerned with ethics. They in fact developed a "rational ethics," for which they became well known in later Islamic history.[3] A few were also interested in physics or natural philosophy, chief among them al-Naẓẓām, who developed the theory of leap (*ṭafrah*) to explain the possibility of motion over a space that is infinitely divisible. He is known also for the theory of latency and manifestation (*kumūn wa burūz*), according to which God created everything at once in a state of latency and then gradually various forms from minerals to animals became actualized or manifested. Abu'l-Hudhayl al-'Allāf developed the theory of atomism, which became central in Ash'arite theology. It is above all for the development of a rational theology that the Mu'tazilites are known in the history of Islamic thought. In this way, they influenced not only later Sunni theological thought but also Shī'ite thought and Islamic philosophy.

Al-Ash'arī and Early Ash'arism

During the third/ninth century, following Ma'mūn's policy of making Mu'tazilism compulsory and introducing a test of faith in these doctrines (*miḥnah*), a strong reaction set in against the "rationalist" *kalām* of the Mu'tazilites. The strict followers of the *Ḥadīth* and the jurisprudents (*fuqahā'*), especially the followers of Imam Aḥmad ibn Ḥanbal, opposed all rational proofs of the tenets of the faith. Muslims were asked to accept the doctrines of the faith without asking how (*bilā kayf*), but this extreme reaction against the rationalist tendencies of the Mu'tazilite *kalām* could not last indefinitely. The emphasis of the Quran on the use of the intellect (*al-'aql*) necessitated the creation of a theology that would use rational arguments and be at the same time orthodox and acceptable to the Islamic community at large. It was to this task that Abu'l-Ḥasan al-Ash'arī addressed himself, founding a new theological school which became the most widespread in the Sunni world. This school has come to be known in the West as that of orthodox theology, although the term orthodox in Islam has levels and nuances of meaning beyond the confines of Ash'arism.

Abu'l-Ḥasan al-Ash'arī was born in Basra around 260/873 and died in Baghdad around 330/941. During his younger days, he was a student of the famous Basrean Mu'tazilite al-Jubbā'ī, but at the age of forty, possibly as the result of a dream of the Prophet, he turned against Mu'tazilite teachings and sought to return to the authentic teachings of the Quran. He went to the mosque of Basra and stated:

> He who knows me, knows who I am, and he who does not know me, let him know that I am Abu'l-Hasan 'Alī al-Ash'arī, that I used to maintain that the Quran is created, that eyes of men shall not see God, and that the creatures create their actions. Lo! I repent that I have been a Mu'tazilite. I renounce these opinions and I take the engagement to refute the Mu'tazilites and expose their infancy and turpitude.[4]

Following this public statement made at the age of forty, al-Ash'arī set out to develop a theology that used reason in the defense of the tenets of the faith and remained loyal to the *dicta* of revelation while making use of dialectic. He composed more than ninety works, many of which have survived. Among the most famous are *al-Ibānah 'an uṣūl al-diyānah* (*Elucidation Concerning the Principles of Religion*), in which he sought to draw to his side the extreme "traditionalists," who were opposed to the use of dialectic in matters of religion; *Kitāb al-luma'* (*The Book of Light*), which contains the principles of Ash'arite *kalām;* and *Maqālāt al-islāmiyyīn* (*Doctrines of the Muslims*), a later work, which sets out to describe the views of various theological schools and sects.[5]

Al-Ash'arī sought to charter an intermediate course between two extremes: that of Mu'tazilite rationalists, who made revelation subservient to reason, and that of "externalists" of different persuasions, who rejected the role of reason completely and remained satisfied with the purely external meaning of the verses of the Quran and the teachings of the *Ḥadīth.* One of the great Ash'arite theologians of later centuries, al-Juwaynī, stated in fact that al-Ash'arī was not really a theologian (*muktakallim*) but a reconciler of the two extreme views prevalent in Islamic society at his time.

To combat the extreme views of the day, al-Ash'arī held, against the view of the Mu'tazilites, that the Divine Attributes were real but added that they were not like human attributes as claimed by the anthropomorphists. He believed that on the Day of Judgment man could see God, but without there being an incarnation (*ḥulūl*) of God in a human or nonhuman form. He believed that the Quran was uncreated and eternal; yet its ink and paper, individual letters and words were created. Again in contrast to the Mu'tazilites and their extreme opponents on this matter (the Murji'ites), al-Ash'arī believed that the Muslim who sins is in God's Hands and can be forgiven by God and go to paradise or he can be punished in hell for a temporary period. Also against the view of Mu'tazilites, who believed that the Prophet could not intercede for Muslims before God, and the extreme Shi'ites, who believed that the Prophet and 'Alī could intercede for Muslims on their own, al-Ash'arī held that the Prophet could intercede on behalf of a sinner but with God's permission.

Altogether, al-Ash'arī sought to create a moderate position in nearly all the theological issues that were being debated at that time. He made reason subservient to revelation and negated the free will of man in favor of a voluntarism which deprives man of his creative free will and emphasizes the omnipotence of God in a way that goes beyond even the text of the Quran. In the Sacred Book, on the one hand, God's omnipotence and omniscience are constantly emphasized, and, on the other, human beings are held responsible for their actions. In emphasizing the doctrine of voluntarism, al-Ash'arī in a sense reduced the Divine Nature to the Divine Will and conceived of God as an All-Powerful Will rather than the Supreme Reality which *is* and also wills.[6]

Ash'arism is concerned not only with specifically religious issues but also with epistemology and the philosophy of nature. The most salient feature of Ash'arism in this domain is the justly famous atomism, which has also come to be known as occasionalism, a doctrine that was refuted explicitly by Thomas Aquinas.[7] Developed mostly by his student Abū Bakr al-Bāqillānī, who was the most important of the early Ash'arites after the founder of the school, this thoroughgoing atomism takes away from the created world and all things in it their specific nature. All things are composed of atoms (*juz' lā yatajazzā*, literally, the part that cannot be further divided), which are themselves without extension. Space is likewise composed of discontinuous points, and time of discontinuous moments. There is no causality. Fire does not burn because it is in its nature to do so but because God has willed it. Tomorrow He could will otherwise and as a result fire would cease to burn. There is no such thing as the nature of fire. What in fact appears to us as cause and effect—for example, fire causing a piece of cotton to burn—is nothing but a habit of the mind (*'ādah*), because we have seen fire being brought near a piece of cotton and the cotton then being in flames.[8] God is the only cause; it is His Will that makes fire burn the cotton. Miracles are in fact nothing other than the breaking of this habit of mind (literally, *khāriq al-'ādah,* which is one of the Arabic terms for miracles).

Ash'arism dissolves all horizontal causes in the vertical cause which is God's Will. It thereby reduces the whole universe to a number of atoms moving in a discontinuous time and space in a world where nothing possesses any specific nature. No wonder then that Ash'arism was strongly opposed to Islamic philosophy, which sought to know the cause of things leading finally to the Ultimate Cause. Ash'arism did not contribute to the flowering of Islamic science, because most Islamic scientists were also philosophers and very few were *mutakallim* or Ash'arite theologians.

Māturīdism and Ṭaḥāwism

Several other contemporaries of al-Ash'arī sought, like him, to formulate a theology that would be acceptable to the majority of Muslims, among them Abū Ja'far al-Ṭaḥāwī from Egypt (d. 321/933) and Abū Manṣūr al-Māturīdī (d. 337/944) from what is now known as Central Asia. The former was a great scholar of *Ḥadīth* and *fiqh* and developed a more "dogmatic" theology. The latter was given more to "speculative" theology; both were Ḥanafīs and sought to follow the theological as well as juridical views of Imam Abū Ḥanīfah. This is especially true of al-Ṭaḥāwī, whose theology is in reality another version of the theological thought of Imam Abū Ḥanīfah. Al-Māturīdī held a position in many ways close to that of al-Ash'arī but with more value placed on reason than his contemporary would allow. For example, he considered it incumbent upon all human beings to seek to know God whether they followed the Divine Law or not, whereas al-Ash'arī believed that it was as a result of following the injunctions of the *Sharī'ah* that man was required to seek to know God. For a whole century, Ash'arism remained popular only among the Shāfi'ites, while Māturīdism and to some extent Ṭaḥāwism held sway among the Ḥanafīs. But finally Ash'arism triumphed over its rivals, mostly thanks to the work of the later Ash'arites, especially al-Ghazzālī, although not all the theological works of al-Ghazzālī can be considered as Ash'arite. It became widespread in Persia and other eastern lands of the Islamic world as well as in the Maghrib, where Ash'arite teachings became influential under the Almohads, whose founder, Ibn Tumart, was a disciple of al-Ghazzālī.

Later Ash'arism

It was the later Ash'arites or the people whom Ibn Khaldūn called the theologians of the *via nova*,[9] who opened a new chapter in the history of *kalām* and made possible its spread throughout the Islamic world. These "later theologians" (*muta'akhirrūn*) include Imam al-Ḥaramayn al-Juwaynī (d. 478/1085), the author of the classical work of Ash'arism, *Kitāb al-irshād* (*The Book of Guidance*); his student Abū Ḥāmid Muḥammad al-Ghazzālī (d. 505/1111), the most celebrated of all Muslim theologians and an outstanding figure in the history of Sufism, who wrote numerous theological works, especially *al-Iqtiṣād fi'l-i'tiqād* (*The Just Mean in Belief*), which is of a more specifically Ash'arite nature than his other works; and Abu'l-Fatḥ al-Shahristānī (d. 548/1153), the author of *Nihāyat al-iqdām* (*The Extremity of Action or Summa Philosophiae*). This later Ash'arism, which became more and more philosophical during later centuries, reached the peak of its development through Fakhr al-Dīn al-Rāzī (d. 606/1209), perhaps the most learned of all Ash'arite theologians,[10] with the *Sharḥ al-mawāqif* (*Commentary upon the Stations*), the commentary being by Mīr Sayyid Sharīf al-Jurjānī (d. 816/1413) and the text by 'Aḍud al-Dīn al-Ījī (d. 756/1355). This work, which marks the peak of philosophical *kalām*, is taught to this day in such centers of Islamic learning as al-Azhar, along with the works of Sa'd al-Dīn al-Taftāzānī (d. 791/1389), who represented a competing school of *kalām* that was more opposed to Islamic philosophy while seeking itself to deal with the issues of philosophy.

There were other notable Ash'arite theologians of the later period, for example, Muḥammad al-Sanūsī (d. ca. 895/1490), whose short "creed," *al-Sanūsiyyah*, is popular to this day; Jalāl al-Dīn Dawānī (d. 907/1501), at once theologian and philosopher, who is said to have embraced Twelve-Imam Shi'ism toward the end of his life; and many other figures whose summaries and commentaries have been studied over the centuries. But the peak of this philosophical Ash'arite *kalām* was reached in the ninth/fifteenth century, and the later authors represent for the most part the continuation of the teachings of the earlier masters. The most important development in the later centuries was the wedding of Ash'arism and Sufism that is found among so many of the later Ash'arites including al-Sanūsī.

Kalām in the Modern World

Until the last century, many manuals of Ash'arite *kalām* continued to appear summarizing the earlier classics, for example, the manual *Jawharat al-tawḥīd* (*The Substance of Unity*) by the thirteenth/nineteenth-century Egyptian scholar al-Bājūrī. But it was also at this time that a number of

Sunni thinkers inaugurated the modernist period in the Islamic world and some sought to resuscitate *kalām* as a way of reviving Islamic religious thought. Foremost among these modern scholars of *kalām* was Muḥammad ʿAbduh (d. 1323/1905), who in his *Risālat al-tawḥīd* (*The Treatise of Unity*) delineated the "new theology" which paid greater attention to the use of reason and revived certain Muʿtazilite theses. His path was followed by several later Egyptian scholars, including the early fourteenth/twentieth-century figure Shaykh Muṣṭafā ʿAbd al-Rāziq (d. 1366/1947), who, like ʿAbduh, became a rector of al-Azhar University. Similar attempts to formulate a modern *kalām* were carried out in India by such well-known modernist thinkers as Sayyid Ahmad Khan (d. 1316/1898) and Syed Ameer Ali (d. 1347/1928). Even Muḥammad Iqbāl (d. 1357/1938), although more a philosopher than a *mutakallim*, could be included in this group if one considers his *Reconstruction of Religious Thought in Islam*. To what extent these and similar works reflect Islamic spirituality is another matter. Whatever one's view might be of these tendencies, one can say with certitude that they reflect more the concern for an apologetic defense of Islam and the accommodation of modernity than the expression of Islamic spirituality.

The Message of Ashʿarism

When one ponders the message of Ashʿarism and its spiritual significance, one becomes aware of the central concern of this school—to bring the reality of God into the everyday world by making intelligence subservient to the Will of God. It also reduces man to that aspect of his being which is in obedience to God because it is determined by God, not the aspect of man as a free being with a freedom which is granted to him by God by virtue of his being created in "His form" and as a creature who is the central reflection of God's Names and Qualities.

> Omnipotentialism [of the Ashʿarite school], which in practice denies the human mind all capacity to understand Divine motives, and which refers our intelligence to Revelation alone, has the function of suggesting that it is "God alone who knows," but it does this arbitrarily *ab extra* and forgets that, if it is indeed God who is always the thinker, then He is also the thinker in us and in pure intellection or inspiration. . . . But Ashʿarism thinks only of one thing: to make the immensity of God concretely present in the world; and it is perfectly realistic in its presentiment that for the average man the acceptance of higher truths passes through the will and not through the Intellect, and that consequently it is the will that must receive the shock; this shock, both crushing and sacramental, is provided precisely by all but blind omnipotentialism.[11]

Ash'arite voluntarism or omnipotentialism possesses a positive aspect, although against the reality of human intelligence and freedom and impervious to God's Nature, which is Pure Goodness, while emphasizing His will. It emphasizes the presence of God in the day-to-day life of man and the assertion of His Will in the running of the world that surrounds man. To achieve this end fully, the Ash'arites posited the previously mentioned atomism or occasionalism, which reduces the reality of the phenomenal world to nothingness and holds that the world is annihilated and recreated at every moment thereby reasserting the dominance of God's Will over all things and at all moments. This atomistic doctrine, which stood opposed to the view of the Islamic metaphysicians, philosophers, and scientists, follows nevertheless a direction in a sense totally opposed to that of modern science, which since the scientific revolution has accepted only "horizontal" causes in the explanation of phenomena, denying all "vertical" causes. In contrast, Ash'arism denies all "horizontal" causes and helped to create an ambience in which a secular science such as that of the seventeenth century could not possibly have taken root.

> In summary, the purpose of this doctrine—or this atomism or occasionalism—is to remind us constantly that God is present and active in all things, and to suggest to us that this world here below would only be a discontinuous chaos were it not for the Divine Presence. Regarded in this way, Ash'arite atomism is a reminder of the Divine Presence, or an introduction of the transcendent—of the marvelous, one might say—into everyday life. Man must feel that faith is something other than ordinary logic and that it sees things in terms of God and not in terms of the world; and by this fact, the believer is himself not entirely of this world, his faith is not a "natural" thought, but a "supernatural" assent; what is divinely true seems absurd to unbelievers, who follow only an earth-bound process of thought. According to this perspective, the unbeliever thinks in a horizontal direction, according to the "straight path"; and this divine transparency of earthly things—since the Divine Cause is everywhere and since it alone is really present—confers on faith a sort of concrete and sacramental mystery, in short, an element of the marvelous which makes of the believer a being marked by the supernatural. From the point of view of metaphysics, this is an unnecessary luxury, since the intellect has resources other than pious absurdity; but from the theological point of view it doubtless marks a victory. In a word, if unbelief in the form of atheistic scientism admits only physical causes and denies the transcendent causality which works in them, Ash'arism has replied in advance, and has done so radically, by denying physical causes; it is like a surgical operation or a preventive war. The Renaissance certainly could not have hatched in an Asharite climate.[12]

Ash'arite atomism also possesses a metaphysical significance beyond its immediate theological meaning. There is at once continuity and discontinuity between the Divine Principle and its manifestations. The Ash'arites emphasize this discontinuity, whereas the Islamic philosophers in general accentuate the continuity. This discontinuity is not only of cosmological significance. It also reflects, on the level of cosmic reality, the discontinuity between the Supreme Principle as Beyond-Being and Being as the immediate Principle of cosmic reality. Ash'arite atomism also echoes on the theological level a discontinuity or atomism that is to be seen in the Arabic language itself, in which one observes an intuitive leap from one idea to another or even from the subject to the predicate, whereas Indo-European languages possess a plasticity and continuous flow that is reflected also in the metaphysical expositions of people who think in such languages. A metaphysical treatise in Arabic by an Arab gnostic like Ibn 'Arabī is like a series of discontinuous bolts of lightning striking a mountaintop, whereas—to use an example within the citadel of Islam—the Persian metaphysicians like Mullā Ṣadrā present a more systematic and flowing exposition of metaphysics as if pouring honey from a jar.

It is remarkable that despite its "anti-intellectualism" Ash'arism not only became the prevalent *kalām* in the Sunni world but also became combined in certain circumstances with Sufism, at whose heart lies the gnosis which is illuminative knowledge actualized with the help of revelation through the immanent intellect whose symbol is the heart. One need only think of al-Ghazzālī, who was more responsible than any other figure for the spread of Ash'arism beyond its early confines in the Arab East although, as mentioned already, not all of his theological works are of an Ash'arite character. This great theologian was not only an eminent Sufi but also one who wrote many luminous pages concerning intellection through the heart and the cultivation of *al-ma'rifah* or Divine Knowledge. Many a later Sufi figure, including several of the important figures of North African Sufism, was to continue this wedding between Ash'arism and Sufism. Yet, many other Sufi masters and authorities of Islamic gnosis stood against Ash'arism and criticized its limitations severely, as did the Islamic philosophers, many of whom during later centuries did not believe that Ash'arism possessed the intellectual requirements necessary for dealing with the questions of God's Names and Qualities or other problems related to *theo-logia* in the original sense of this term.

Ash'arism, while not ceasing to oppose both the Islamic philosophers and certain types of Sufi metaphysics, nevertheless continued to discuss the basic philosophical and metaphysical issues dealt with by its adversaries. Its later treatises deal with such questions as being and non-being, necessity and contingency, the relation of the one to the many, substance and accidents—all of which were treated also by Islamic philosophers. Ash'arism also deals with the "science of God" (*ilāhiyyāt*), which is so amply treated in works of theoretical Sufism such as those of Ibn ʿArabī and Ṣadr al-Dīn al-Qunawī. Ashʿarism thus became one of several major schools of Islamic thought vying with the theosophers and gnostics, who dealt with matters of more direct spiritual concern than the Ashʿarites. Ashʿarism nevertheless provided a rational defense of the tenets of the faith and created a climate in which religious truths were real and the Will of God reigned supreme. For those who wanted to know God as well as obey His will, Ashʿarism appeared either as an impediment or, at best, the walls of the city of Divine Knowledge; they protected the city, and one had to pass beyond them in order to reach the treasures of the city itself, the city to which the Prophet referred when he said, "I am the city of knowledge and ʿAlī is its gate."

Shīʿite Kalām

In addition to Sunni *kalām*, there developed in Islam other schools of *kalām* associated with the Ismāʿīlīs and Twelve-Imam Shīʿites. As for the Zaydīs, the third school of Shīʿism, they adopted more or less Muʿtazilite *kalām* as a result of which this form of *kalām* lasted in Yemen, the home of Zaydī Shīʿism, long after it had ceased to exist as a notable school of thought elsewhere in the Islamic world. Ismāʿīlī thought, both philosophical and theological, developed early in the history of Islam, and the two remained close to each other. Some of the earlier Ismāʿīlī thinkers, for example, Ḥamīd al-Dīn al-Kirmānī (d. ca. 408/1017) and Nāṣir-i Khusraw (d. between 465/1072 and 470/1077), were more philosophers than theologians. Others, including Abū Ḥātim al-Rāzī (d. 322/933) and al-Muʾayyid bi'Llāh al-Shīrāzī (d. 470/1077), were more theologians than philosophers. But both groups dealt with the major themes of Ismāʿīlī thought, such as the meta-ontological status of the "unknowable" God or *Deus absconditus*, the celestial archetype of Adam, the relation between the function of prophecy (*nubuwwah*) and initiatic power (*wilāyah*), and esoteric hermeneutics (*taʾwīl*).[13]

Twelve-Imam Shīʿite *kalām*, however, developed much later. The early concern of Twelve-Imam Shīʿite thinkers was mostly *Ḥadīth*, Quranic commentary, and jurisprudence, although earlier Shīʿite thinkers, including Shaykh al-Mufīd (d. 413/1022), must also be considered as theologians. It was, however, only in the seventh/thirteenth century that the first systematic treatise on Twelve-Imam Shīʿite *kalām* was written by none other than the celebrated mathematician and philosopher, Naṣīr al-Dīn al-Ṭūsī (d. 672/1273). This is probably the only instance in history in which the major theological text of a religious community was composed by a scientist of the order of Naṣīr al-Dīn. The work of Ṭūsī entitled *Tajrīd al-iʿtiqād* (*Catharsis of Doctrines*) became rapidly the standard theological text, and more than a hundred commentaries came to be written on it before this century. Perhaps the most notable commentary is the *Kashf al-murād* (*The Unveiling of the Desired*) by Jamāl al-Dīn ʿAllāmah al-Ḥillī (d. 726/1326), who is the most notable Shīʿite *mutakallim* after Ṭūsī.

In studying this major opus, one can see clearly how Twelve-Imam Shīʿite *kalām* differs in its concerns from Ashʿarism. The work begins with a discussion of being and non-being and modes and grades of being. It develops an elaborate ontology that reminds one more of the ontology of Ibn Sīnā than the atomism of al-Ashʿarī.[14] The work then proceeds to a discussion of quiddity or essence, which complements that of existence. Finally, the first section of the work turns to the relation between cause and effect and the discussion of causality in general. Again, in this basic issue, the work confirms the reality of horizontal causality in direct opposition to the Ashʿarite view.

The second section (*maqṣad*) of the work turns to the discussion of substance and accidents. Once again in contrast to Ashʿarism, the *Tajrīd* rejects all forms of atomism and asserts along with Ibn Sīnā that a body can be divided *ad infinitum* potentially but that such a division can never be actualized. Ṭūsī also confirms the reality of substances that are free of all potentiality and entanglement in matter and are immortal. These substances include both the intellect (*al-ʿaql*) and the human soul (*nafs*), which for Shīʿite *kalām* is an immortal substance and not a perishable configuration of atoms as in Ashʿarism. Ashʿarism does not accept a reality for the soul independent of the body but believes that the soul is recreated by God at the Day of Judgment along with the resurrection of the body.

It is only in the third *maqṣad* that Ṭūsī turns to theology properly speaking, in contrast to general metaphysics, with which he is occupied in the first two sections of the book. In the third, fourth, and fifth sections he turns to God, prophecy, and imamology respectively, dealing with general Islamic doctrines first and turning to the specifically Shīʿite doctrines concerning the Imam only in the fifth *maqṣad.* Finally, in the sixth and last section, he turns to questions of eschatology (*al-maʿād*), explaining both the metaphysical and theological meaning of general Islamic eschatological doctrines and the theological meaning of specific Islamic images and symbols used in the explanation of complex posthumous realities. This manner of treating theological subjects became a model for many a later treatise, and many theologians and philosophers began to distinguish between *al-ilāhiyyāt bi maʿnaʾl-ʿāmm* (metaphysics in its general sense, corresponding to the first two sections of Ṭūsī's work) and *al-ilāhiyyāt bi maʿnaʾl-khāṣṣ* (theology dealing with the nature of God, prophecy, and other specifically religious issues).

From the time of Ṭūsī to the Safavid period in the tenth/sixteenth century, a number of Shīʿite scholars of *kalām* appeared, some of whom, like Sayyid Ḥaydar Āmulī (d. after 787/1385), were also Sufis. Others, including Jalāl al-Dīn Dawānī, who was first a Sunni theologian and later turned to Shīʿism, were at once theologians and philosophers. During the Safavid period, Islamic philosophy associated with the School of Isfahan eclipsed *kalām*. But strangely enough, during the latter part of Safavid rule, the most famous students of the greatest of Safavid philosophers, Ṣadr al-Dīn Shīrāzī (d. 1050/1640)—Mullā Muḥsin Fayḍ Kāshānī (d. 1091/1680) and ʿAbd al-Razzāq Lāhījī (d. 1071/1660)—were more scholars of *kalām* than philosophers. This is especially true of Lāhījī, the author of *Gawhar-murād* (*The Sought Jewel*) and *Kitāb al-mashāriq* (*The Book of Orients*), which are two of the most important later texts of Shīʿite *kalām*. This tradition continued into the Qajar and even the Pahlavi period, but the main arena of Shīʿite thought became dominated more by philosophy or theosophy (*ḥikmah*) on the one hand and the science of the principles of jurisprudence (*ʿilm al-uṣūl*) on the other—not to speak of jurisprudence itself. To understand fully later Shīʿite *kalām*, it is necessary to turn not only to texts of *kalām* following the tradition of Ṭūsī, but also to those major works of theosophy (*al-ḥikmat al-ilāhiyyah*) which deal with all the traditional problems of *kalām* and claim to possess the intellectual means necessary to deal with these problems more than did the *mutakallimūn* themselves.

Islamic Philosophy: Its Meaning and Significance in the Islamic Intellectual Tradition

In the Islamic perspective, the intellect (*al-ʿaql*) and the spirit (*al-rūḥ*) are closely related and are two faces of the same reality. Islamic spirituality is inseparable from intellectuality as traditionally understood, and those who have been concerned with the intellect in the Islamic cultural citadel and those concerned with the world of the spirit form a single family with profound affinities with each other. This fact is certainly true of the Islamic philosophers who have been considered by most Western scholars of Islam as well as anti-intellectualist elements within the Islamic world to be peripheral and outside of the main current of Islamic intellectual life. In reality, however, Islamic philosophy constitutes an important component of the Islamic intellectual tradition, and the Islamic philosophers belong to the same spiritual universe as the gnostics (*ʿurafāʾ*) among the Sufis.

Furthermore, Islamic philosophy has played an important role in the development of *kalām,* not to speak of the Islamic sciences such as mathematics, astronomy, and medicine, which have been inseparable from Islamic philosophy throughout their history.[15]

To understand the significance of Islamic philosophy, it is necessary to go beyond the prevalent Western view, according to which Islamic philosophy began with al-Kindī and terminated with Ibn Rushd (the famous Latin Averroes) with Ibn Khaldūn representing an interesting postscript.[16] Moreover, one must understand this philosophy as Islamic and not Arabic philosophy, for, although some of its great representatives such as al-Kindī and Ibn Rushd were Arabs, the majority, including such major figures as Ibn Sīnā, Suhrawardī, and Mullā Ṣadrā, were Persian. Especially during the later centuries, the main home of Islamic philosophy was Persia and adjacent areas of the Islamic world such as Muslim India, which had close links with Persian culture. This philosophy is also Islamic not only because different Muslim peoples cultivated it but because it is related by its roots, dominating concepts, and determining world view to the Islamic revelation, which also molded the mind and soul of those intellectual figures who developed this philosophy.

Some figures within the Islamic world wrote works on philosophy, for example, Muḥammad ibn Zakariyyā' al-Rāzī (d. ca. 320/932), but their philosophy was not Islamic in this sense of being related in its principles to the Islamic revelation and functioning in a universe in which revelation looms as a blinding reality upon the horizon. The main tradition of philosophy from al-Kindī and al-Fārābī to Shāh Walī Allāh of Delhi and Sabziwārī, however, was Islamic in that it was integrally related to the principles of the Islamic revelation and an organic part of the Islamic intellectual universe.[17] Moreover, this philosophical tradition did not die eight centuries ago with Ibn Rushd but has continued as a living tradition to this day.[18] To understand Islamic spirituality fully, one must gain some knowledge of this long philosophical tradition, which may be called "prophetic philosophy,"[19] although a full discussion of this tradition requires a separate volume and lies outside the scope of an encyclopedia devoted to spirituality as such and not to philosophy.

Early Peripatetic (Mashshā'ī) Philosophy

The best-known school of Islamic philosophy, the *mashshā'ī* or Peripatetic, which is a synthesis of the tenets of the Islamic revelation, Aristotelianism, and Neoplatonism of both the Athenian and Alexandrian schools, was founded in the third/ninth century in the rich intellectual climate of

Baghdad by Abū Ya'qūb al-Kindī (d. ca. 260/873). The so-called philosopher of the Arabs was a prolific author who composed over two hundred treatises, in which he dealt with the sciences as well as philosophy, beginning a trend that characterizes the whole class of Muslim sages who were philosopher-scientists and not only philosophers.[20] His main concern was the discovery of the truth wherever it might be. In a famous statement that has been repeated often over the centuries and characterizes all Islamic philosophy, he said:

> We should not be ashamed to acknowledge truth and to assimilate it from whatever source it comes to us, even if it is brought to us by former generations and foreign peoples. For him who seeks the truth there is nothing of higher value than truth itself; it never cheapens or abases him who reaches for it, but ennobles and honours him.[21]

It was this universal conception of truth that has always characterized Islamic philosophy—a truth, however, that is not bound by the limits of reason. Rather, it is the illimitable Truth reached by the intellect which al-Kindī, like other Islamic philosophers, distinguished clearly from reason as the analytical faculty of the mind. This intellect is like an instrument of inner revelation for which the macrocosmic revelation provides an objective cadre. The Islamic philosophers considered the call of the truth to be the highest call of philosophy, but this did not mean the subservience of revelation to reason, as some have contended. Rather, it meant to reach the truth at the heart of revelation through the use of the intellect, which, in its macrocosmic manifestation usually identified with the archangel of revelation, Gabriel, is the instrument of revelation itself. The treatise of al-Kindī on the intellect known as *De intellectu* in the Latin West points to the significance that the doctrine of the intellect was to have for later Islamic philosophers and even many Latin scholastics.

Al-Kindī was also deeply interested in the relation between religion and philosophy or faith and reason. In his classification of the sciences, he sought to create harmony between divine and human knowledge and wrote the first chapter in the long history of the relation between faith and reason which occupied nearly all Islamic philosophers for the next millennium. Al-Kindī also helped create the Arabic philosophical terminology that soon became a powerful vehicle for the expression of Islamic philosophy. Much of the translation of Greek philosophical works was made in Baghdad during his lifetime. He knew in fact some of the translators, and it is said that the summary of the *Enneads* of Plotinus, which came to be known to Muslims as the *Theology of Aristotle,* was translated for him by Ibn al-Nā'imah al-Ḥimṣī. In any case, one of the major achievements of al-Kindī was the molding of the Arabic language as a vehicle for the expression of philosophy, as one sees in his celebrated treatise *Fi'l-falsafat al-ūlā* (*On Metaphysics*). Although some of the terminology used by him was rejected by later philosophers writing in Arabic, he remained a pioneer in the creation of Arabic philosophic vocabulary and the father of Islamic philosophy. He was the first devout Muslim who knew Greco-Alexandrian philosophy well and sought to create a philosophical system in which this philosophy was integrated into the Islamic world view with its emphasis on the unity of God and the reality of revelation.

Al-Kindī's immediate students were mostly scientists, and his real successor as the next major figure in early *mashshā'ī* philosophy did not appear until a generation later in Khurasan. He was Abū Naṣr al-Fārābī (d. 339/950), who was born and raised in Farab in Central Asia in a family of Turkish background living within a Persian cultural milieu. He was already a famous philosopher when he came to Baghdad for a short period at midlife only to migrate once again westward to settle in Damascus, where he spent the rest of his life. At once a logician and musician, metaphysician and political thinker, al-Fārābī formulated *mashshā'ī* philosophy in the form it was to take in later Islamic history.

Al-Fārābī was attracted to the spiritual life from an early age and was a practicing Sufi. He was also one of the greatest theoreticians of music in Islam and a composer some of whose compositions can still be heard in the repertory of Sufi music in India. Yet, he was an acute logician who commented on all the logical works of Aristotle. He also composed *Fī iḥṣā' al-'ulūm* (*On the Enumeration of the Sciences*), which classified and categorized the sciences and left a deep impact on later Islamic thought. It was entitled *De Scientiis* in the West. Al-Fārābī in fact came to be known as the "Second Teacher" (*al-mu'allim al-thānī*) not because he taught philosophy or the sciences but because he was the first to enumerate and delineate clearly the sciences in the context of Islamic civilization, as Aristotle, the first teacher, had done for the Greek sciences.[22]

Al-Fārābī knew Aristotle well and in fact wrote commentaries not only on the Stagirite's logical writings but also on his cosmological works. Al-Fārābī's commentary on the *Metaphysics* exercised a great influence on Ibn Sīnā. But al-Fārābī was not interested so much in pure Aristotelianism as in synthesizing the teachings of Aristotle and Plato and the Neoplatonists within the universal perspective of Islam. This intellectual effort is seen most of all in his *Kitāb al-jam' bayn ra'yay al-ḥakīmayn Aflāṭūn al-ilāhī wa Arisṭū* (*The Book of Accord between the Ideas of the Divine Plato and Aristotle*).

Al-Fārābī was also the founder of Islamic political philosophy in which he sought to harmonize the idea of the philosopher-king of Plato with the idea of the prophet in monotheistic traditions. His definitive masterpiece, *Kitāb ārā' ahl al-madīnat al-fāḍilah* (*The Book of the Opinions of the Citizens of the Virtuous City*), influenced not only later political philosophical thinkers such as Ibn Rushd but the *mutakillimūn* as well. This major opus was supplemented by several works on practical philosophy and ethics, including *Kitāb taḥṣīl al-sa'ādah* (*The Book of the Attainment of Happiness*), which established al-Fārābī once and for all as the prime authority in this domain of philosophy in Islam.

From the spiritual point of view, the *Fuṣūṣ al-ḥikmah* (*Bezels of Wisdom*) of al-Fārābī, sometimes attributed to Ibn Sīnā, is of particular significance. Besides being rich in technical vocabulary,[23] this work represents the first important synthesis between speculative philosophy and gnosis in Islam. Many commentaries have been written on it, and it is taught to this day in Persia as a text of both philosophy and gnosis.[24] The work reflects the mind and soul of al-Fārābī, in whom critical philosophical analysis was combined with intellectual synthesis and in whose perspective both the musical and logical dimensions of reality were combined without any contradiction, both issuing from that *coincidentia oppositorum* which is realized in gnosis alone.

Al-Fārābī's most famous immediate student was Yaḥyā ibn 'Adī, a Christian theologian, but his real successor in the field of Islamic philosophy was Abū 'Alī Sīnā (the Latin Avicenna), who lived two generations after him. Between these two giants of Islamic thought there stand a number of figures who are of some importance in the development of *mashshā'ī* philosophy. In Baghdad, the imposing figure was Yaḥyā ibn 'Adī's student Abū Sulaymān al-Sijistānī (d. 371/981), who was most of all a logician. His circle drew to itself philosophers as well as men of letters such as Abū Ḥayyān al-Tawḥīdī (d. 399/1009).[25] Meanwhile the locus of philosophical activity was shifting to an ever-greater degree to Khurasan, where the most significant figure preceding Ibn Sīnā was Abu'l-Ḥasan al-'Āmirī (d. 381/992), known for his works on ethics as well as the philosophical defense of Islam, particularly in his *al-I'lām bi manāqib al-islām* (*Declaration of the Virtues of Islam*), which is unique in *mashshā'ī* literature for its manner of defense of the Islamic religion.

Al-'Āmirī trained a number of scholars and philosophers, including Ibn Muskūyah (usually pronounced Miskawayh) (d. 421/1030), known especially for his major work on philosophical ethics, the *Tadhhīb al-akhlāq* (*Purification of Morals*) and a doxography entitled *Jāwīdān-khirad* in Persian or *al-Ḥikmat al-khālidah* in Arabic (*Eternal Wisdom* or *Philosophia Perennis*). This book marks a genre of philosophical writing in which sayings of sages of antiquity—not only Greek but also Indian and Persian—were assembled to point to the permanence and universality of the truth asserted in its final form in the Islamic revelation and developed by Islamic philosophers. This type of writing continued during later centuries with such figures as Ibn al-Fātik, who lived in Egypt in the fifth/eleventh century, Shams al-Dīn Shahrazūrī (d. ca. 680/1281), who was a commentator of Suhrawardī, and the Safavid philosopher Quṭb al-Dīn Ashkiwarī and pointed to the significance of the idea of the *philosophia perennis* among Islamic philosophers long before Steuco and Leibnitz wrote of it and made it famous in the West.[26]

Islamic Peripatetic or *mashshā'ī* philosophy reached its peak with Ibn Sīnā, who is perhaps the greatest and certainly the most influential Islamic philosopher and in a sense the father of specifically medieval philosophy to the extent that this philosophy is concerned basically with being. This incredible intellectual figure, who was at once a philosopher and the most famous physician of the period the West calls the Middle Ages, was a Persian born in Bukhara in 370/980. He wandered most of his life in various Persian cities, especially Rayy, Isfahan, and Hamadan, and finally died from colic in the latter city in 428/1037 at a relatively young age.[27] Despite a tumultuous life marked by externally unsettled conditions in Persia, Ibn Sīnā composed more than two hundred works, including the monumental *Kitāb al-shifā'* (*The Book of Healing*), which is an encyclopedia of Peripatetic philosophy and science. He also wrote *al-Qānūn fi'l-ṭibb* (*The Canon of Medicine*), which is the most celebrated single work in the history of medicine. His philosophical works include also the *al-Najāt* (*Salvation*), *al-Mabda' wa'l-ma'ād* (*The Beginning and the End*), his last philosophical masterpiece, *al-Ishārāt wa'l-tanbīhāt* (*Directives and Remarks*), and a number of visionary recitals that concern his "Oriental Philosophy."

In his *mashshā'ī* works crowned by the *Shifā'*, Ibn Sīnā created that final synthesis of Islam with Aristotelian and Neoplatonic philosophy which became a permanent intellectual dimension in the Islamic world and survives as a living philosophical school to this day. Toward the end of his life, however, he criticized *mashshā'ī* philosophy including his own as being the common philosophy meant for everyone, while pointing to the philosophy that he considered to be for the intellectual elite, which he called "Oriental Philosophy" (*al-ḥikmat al-mashriqiyyah*). This philosophy is oriental because it is related to the world of light and not because of the geographic Orient. It is based on the illumination of the soul as well as ratiocination and sees the cosmos as a crypt through which the true philosopher must journey with the help of the guide, who is none other than the Divine Intellect. The language of this philosophy is eminently symbolic rather than discursive. It points to a path that was to be followed fully and to its ultimate end a century and a half after Ibn Sīnā by the founder of the School of Illumination (*al-ishrāq*), Shihāb al-Dīn Suhrawardī.[28] Ibn Sīnā was therefore at once the elaborator of the most complete and enduring version of *mashshā'ī* philosophy and himself the guide to the threshhold of that philosophy or theosophy of illumination which marked the indissolvable union between philosophy and spirituality.

After Ibn Sīnā, *mashshā'ī* philosophy became temporarily eclipsed in the eastern lands of Islam as a result of the attacks of Ash'arism against it. Journeying to the western lands of Islam, it experienced a period of marked activity. Some of the students of Ibn Sīnā such as Bahmanyār ibn Marzbān (d. 458/1066), the author of *Kitāb al-taḥṣīl* (*The Book of Attainment*), continued the teachings of the master well into the fifth/eleventh century. Moreover, the few important philosophers of the sixth/twelfth century, such as Abu'l-Barakāt al-Baghdādī (d. ca. 560/1164), whose *Kitāb al-mu'tabar* (*The Book of What Is Established by Personal Reflection*) contains important ideas in the domain of physics as well as epistemology, and 'Umar Khayyām (d. ca. 526/1132), at once poet, metaphysician, and mathematician, were deeply influenced by and indebted to Ibn Sīnā.[29]

Avicennan Ontology and Cosmology

The philosophy of Ibn Sīnā, which marks the peak of Islamic Peripatetic philosophy, is based on ontology, and Ibn Sīnā has been called the "philosopher of being" and the founder of what is characteristically medieval philosophy whether it be Jewish, Christian, or Islamic.[30] For Aristotle, existence is a "block without fissure," whereas for the Islamic philosophers, God is Pure Being and transcends the chain of being and the order of cosmic existence while the existence of the world is contingent. To distinguish Pure Being from the existence of the world, Ibn Sīnā made the fundamental distinction between necessity (*wujūb*), contingency (*imkān*), and impossibility (*imtinā'*). The Necessary Being is that reality which must be and cannot not be, the reality whose nonexistence would imply contradiction. There is only one such reality, and that is the Necessary Being (*wājib al-wujūd*) which is the God revealed in monotheistic religions. Impossible being (*mumtani' al-wujūd*) is that quiddity which cannot exist objectively, for that would imply contradiction. All beings apart from the Necessary Being are contingent beings (*mumkin al-wujūd*); considered as quiddities they could exist or not exist. This distinction is one of the most fundamental in the whole history of philosophy. It influenced deeply all later Islamic philosophy and even theology. It also traveled to the West to become one of the key concepts of philosophy. This basic distinction was itself related to the basic distinction between existence (*wujūd*) and quiddity (*māhiyyah*), which is also central to medieval ontology.[31]

The contemplation by the Necessary Being of Itself generates the First Intellect; and the First Intellect's contemplation of the Necessary Being as well as of itself as contingent being and as necessitated by the Necessary Being (*al-wājib bi'l-ghayr*) leads to the generation of the Second Intellect, the Soul of the First Sphere and the First Sphere. The process continues in this manner until the Tenth Intellect and the Ninth Sphere and its Soul are generated. This Ninth Sphere is the sphere of the Moon in accordance with the nine heavens of Ptolemaic astronomy as modified by Muslim astronomers. Below that level stand the spheres of the four elements governed by the Tenth Intellect, which is the "giver of forms" (*wāhib al-ṣuwar*) for all the existents in the sublunar region.[32]

The sublunar region is also organized in a hierarchical order consisting of the three kingdoms crowned by man, who represents the point of return to the Origin. By means of knowledge, he can ascend through the levels of cosmic manifestation to gain union with the Active Intellect (*al-'aql al-fa''āl*). His mind ascends from the state of potentiality to actuality in which it becomes *intellectus in actu*. The universe consists of a vast hierarchy beginning with the ten Intellects which emanate from each other and ultimately from the Necessary Being. Below them stand the sublunar beings stretching from the *materia prima* to man, in whom the arc of ascent commences, terminating with the return to the purely intelligible world. The universe is generated through contemplation and returns to its origin through knowledge. The world is not created in time because time is a condition of the world, but it is not eternal in the sense that God is eternal. There is, rather, a basic distinction between the world and God, for God is the Necessary Being in need of nothing but Itself while all existents are contingent in themselves, gain their existence from the Necessary Being, and remain in utter poverty in their own essence. The Avicennan universe is one that preserves the transcendence of God through the radical distinction between necessity and contingency and at the same time emphasizes the emanation of the levels of cosmic existence from the Necessary Being as a result of the very nature of the Origin which generates the universe like the sun which radiates light by its very nature.

Ismā'īlī and Hermetico-Pythagorean Philosophy

During the early centuries of Islamic history, Islamic philosophy was not confined to the *mashshā'ī* school, which is the best known of the early schools and is usually considered to be synonymous with Islamic philosophy as such. Even before al-Kindī, one can observe the beginning of Ismā'īlī philosophy, which was to have a long and fecund history. In this tradition, philosophy is identified with the inner truth of religion and possesses an esoteric character. As a result, Ismā'īlism became not only a congenial ground for the development of philosophy but an impetus for the growth and cultivation of a distinct philosophical tradition which, while dealing with basic Islamic themes such as unity (*al-tawḥīd*) and the reality of a sacred book, differed in many ways from Islamic Peripatetic philosophy.

The earliest text of this school dates back to the second/eighth century and is known as the *Umm al-kitāb* (*The Archetypal Book*). It purports to be the record of a conversation held between Imam Muḥammad al-Bāqir (d. 115/733), the fifth Shī'ite Imam, and three of his disciples and reflects Shī'ite gnosis in its earliest forms of elaboration. The work emphasizes the esoteric science of letters (*al-jafr*) so prevalent in early Shī'ite circles and expounds a cosmology based on the number five and reminiscent of certain Manichaean cosmological schemes.

The systematic elaboration of Ismā'īlī philosophy came two centuries later with such figures as Abū Ya'qūb al-Sijistānī (who died sometime after 360/971), the author of the *Kashf al-maḥjūb* (*Unveiling of the Veiled*), Ḥamīd al-Dīn al-Kirmānī, whose *Rāḥat al-'aql* (*Repose of the Intellect*) is the most systematic work of this early school of Ismā'īlī philosophy, and the works of the greatest Ismā'īlī philosopher, Nāṣir-i Khusraw. This celebrated Persian poet and philosopher wrote all his philosophical works in Persian rather than Arabic.[33] His most important opus is the *Jāmi' al-ḥikmatayn* (*The Sum of Two Wisdoms*), in which he compares and contrasts the philosophy derived from the Islamic revelation with Greek philosophy.

Ismā'īlī philosophy continued to flourish in both Persia and Yemen even after the downfall of the Fāṭimids in Egypt. In Persia, Ḥasan al-Ṣabbāḥ declared the "Grand Resurrection" in the mountain fortress of Alamut in 557/1162 and established the new Ismā'īlī Order in the formidable fortresses of northern Persia. Consequently, a new period of Ismā'īlī history began, during which Ismā'īlism and Sufism came closer together. In fact, certain Sufis such as the poets Sanā'ī and 'Aṭṭār as well as Qāsim-i Anwār (d. 837/1434) are claimed by the Ismā'īlīs as their own. The Ismā'īlīs even wrote commentaries on certain major Sufi works such as the *Gulshan-i rāz* (*Rose Garden of Divine Mysteries*) of Shabistarī. Also during this period important Ismā'īlī philosophical tracts were composed in prose, mostly in Persian, such as the well-known *Taṣawwurāt* (*Notions*), attributed to Naṣīr al-Dīn al-Ṭūsī, and the tradition continued well into the tenth/sixteenth century.

In Yemen, a form of Ismāʿīlism that was closer to the Fāṭimids continued, culminating in the works of the nineteenth "missionary" (*dāʿī*) of the Yemen, Sayyidnā Idrīs ʿImād al-Dīn (d. 872/1468). Interesting enough, this branch of Ismāʿīlism was finally to make its home in India along with the continuation of the Alamut tradition, which has become known since the last century as the Āghā-Khānid. The Yemeni authors followed by and large the theses presented in the earlier classical philosophical works of Ḥamīd al-Dīn and Nāṣir-i Khusraw, whereas the tradition of Alamut represented more the close link between imamology and mystical experience, between Ismāʿīlī theosophy and Sufi metaphysics.

While Ismāʿīlī philosophy was developing, a number of works of Hermetic and Neo-Pythagorean inspiration appeared that have been claimed by some to be of Ismāʿīlī inspiration and by others to belong more generally to Shīʿite circles—in fact to Islamic esoterism itself. The Hermetic corpus was translated into Arabic and was known to both alchemists and many philosophers.[34] Jābir ibn Ḥayyān, who lived in the second/eighth century and is the father of Islamic alchemy, whote many philosophical works that are of Hermetic inspiration. This was to continue among later alchemists such as Abu'l-Qāsim al-ʿIrāqī, ʿIzz al-Dīn al-Jaldakī, and Abū Maslamah al-Majrīṭī.[35] One must remember that both the *Turba Philosophorum* and the *Picatrix* were translated into Latin from Arabic and that there is a copious Islamic Hermetic literature of considerable philosophical importance. On the one hand, the visionary recitals of Ibn Sīnā reflect Hermetic prototypes, whereas the works of Suhrawardī are replete with references to Hermes and Hermeticism. On the other hand, one can see Hermetic themes in the works of many Sufis from Dhu'l-Nūn al-Miṣrī to Ibn ʿArabī.

Neo-Pythagorean philosophy too found a place in the Islamic intellectual citadel early in the history of Islam. The concern with the symbolism of numbers in early Shīʿite and Sufi circles points to this fact, and in the fourth/tenth century there appeared a major work entitled the *Rasāʾil ikhwān al-ṣafāʾ* (*Epistles of the Brethren of Purity*), which contains an elaborate summary of philosophy, cosmology, and the natural sciences bound together by the unifying thread of Pythagorean mathematical symbolism.[36] Although this work is also claimed by many scholars to be of Ismāʿīlī origin, it issued from a more general Shīʿite background and wielded an influence reaching nearly all sectors of Islamic intellectual life, including such a figure as al-Ghazzālī, who had read the work. Islamic spirituality has an inner link with what has been called "Abrahamic Pythagoreanism," as seen in the sacred art of Islam. This inner link has manifested itself in many forms in philosophical expositions throughout Islamic history and among numerous philosophers and is far from being confined to the Brethren of Purity. Furthermore, one can see its manifestation not only in the eastern lands of Islam but also in Andalusia in the works of Ibn al-Sīd of Badajoz (d. 521/1127), whose works, especially the *Kitāb al-ḥadā'iq* (*The Book of Circles*), are concerned with mathematical symbolism.

The metaphysics expounded by the classical Ismāʿīlī philosophers such as al-Sijistānī, Ḥamīd al-Dīn al-Kirmānī, and Nāṣir-i Khusraw and followed for the most part by the later Yemeni school is based not on Being, as is the case with Ibn Sīnā and his followers, but on the Supreme Principle or Originator (*al-Mubdiʿ*) which is Supra-Being, beyond all categories and delimitations including even being. It lies even beyond the negation of being. Being is the first act of *al-Mubdiʿ*, the command stated in the Quran when God says, "But His command, when He intendeth a thing is only that he saith into it: Be! and it is" (XXXVI, 81). This *kun* or *Esto* is the origin of the chain of being, of all realms of existence. It is the One (*al-wāḥid*), and the Originator or *al-Mubdiʿ* is the maker of oneness (*al-muwaḥḥid*), which is also called the Mystery of mysteries (*ghayb al-ghuyūb*). The Supreme Principle has the function of "monadizing" and unifying all beings, and unity or *al-tawḥīd* "then takes on an aspect of monadology. At the same time that it disengages this Unifying Principle from all the *ones* which it unifies, it is by them and through them that it affirms It."[37]

The first being, which is called also the "First Originated" (*al-mubdaʿ al-awwal*), is the Word of God (*Kalām Allāh*) and the First Intellect. From it emanate the beings in the hierarchy of existence according to the basic Ismāʿīlī concept of limit or degree (*ḥadd*). Each being has a *ḥadd* by virtue of which it is delimited (*maḥdūd*) in a hierarchy of beings or "monads" unified by virtue of the unifying act of the Originator. This hierarchy stretches from the celestial pleroma created by the imperative *kun* and called the World of Origination (*ʿālam al-ibdāʿ*) or the World of Divine Command (*ʿālam al-amr*) to the world of creation (*ʿālam al-khalq*). According to the earlier Ismāʿīlī philosophers, followed by the Yemeni school, emanation of lower states of being (*inbiʿāth*) commences with the First Intellect. The relation of all the lower levels of being reflects the rapport between the first limit (*al-ḥadd*) and the first delimited (*al-maḥdūd*), namely, the First Intellect and the Second Intellect which proceeds from it and has its limit in it. This dual relationship is referred to by the Ismāʿīlīs as *sābiq* (that which comes before) and *tālī* (that which follows) and is considered to correspond to the Pen (*al-qalam*) and the Guarded Tablet (*al-lawḥ al-maḥfūẓ*) of Quranic cosmology. This archetypal relationship is reflected in the lower states of being and has its counterpart on earth in the rapport between the prophet (*al-nabī*) and his inheritor (*al-waṣī*), who is the Imam.

In the procession of the Intellect, the Third Intellect is the Celestial Adam (*al-Ādam al-rūḥānī*), who is the archetype of humanity. The Celestial Adam, however, refuses to see the *ḥadd* which defines his horizon as leading through hierarchy to the Originator and thereby seeks to reach the Originator directly. He falls as a result into the worst metaphysical idolatry of setting himself up as the Absolute. He finally awakens from this stupor and realizes his error, but as a result he has already passed by the procession of the Celestial Intellects and finds himself as the Tenth Intellect. This drama in heaven is the origin of time. Celestial Adam must now redeem himself with the help of the Seven Intellects separating him from his original station and degree. These Intellects are called the "Seven Cherubim," and they indicate the distance of his fall. Time is in a sense "retarded eternity," and henceforth the number seven becomes the archetypal number governing the unfolding of time.

The Ismāʿīlīs have a cyclic view of history dominated by the number seven. There are seven cycles, each with its own prophet followed by his Imam. Within Islam, it was after the sixth Shīʿite Imam, Jaʿfar al-Ṣādiq, that the Ismāʿīlīs parted from the main branch of Shīʿism, considering Ismāʿīl as their seventh Imam. The number seven has henceforth continued to be of major significance in their sacred history as well as in their cosmology.

It must be recalled that Ismāʿīlī philosophy is based on the principle of *ta'wīl* or esoteric hermeneutic interpretation. Everything has an outward (*al-ẓāhir*) and an inward (*al-bāṭin*) aspect, and *ta'wīl* is the process of going from the outward to the inward. In the domain of religion, the outward is represented by the prophet and the inward by the imam. The role of philosophy is precisely to make possible the discovery of the inward or the esoteric. Its language is therefore eminently symbolic, and its function ultimately esoteric. In the context of Ismāʿīlism, philosophy became synonymous with the truth (*al-ḥaqīqah*) lying at the heart of religion, which establishes rites and practices on the exoteric level with the ultimate aim of leading man to that knowledge which the Ismāʿīlī philosophers and theosophers considered to have been expounded in their works for the intellectual elite among their community.[38]

Islamic Philosophy in the Western Lands of Islam

Islamic philosophy had a shorter life in the western lands of Islam than in the East, but even in that faraway region of the Islamic world–and especially in Andalusia–there appeared many illustrious Islamic philosophers who left an indelible mark on Western philosophy while creating an important chapter in the history of Islamic philosophy itself. The founder of this chapter in the history of Islamic thought was Ibn Masarrah (d. 319/931), the mysterious founder of the school of Almeria, who was both mystic and philosopher and who led a group of disciples in the Cordovan Sierra until his death. His works are for the most part lost, and only two, *Kitāb al-tabṣirah* (*The Book of Penetrating Explanations*) containing the key to his metaphysical teachings, and the *Kitāb al-ḥurūf* (*The Book of Letters*) dealing with "mystical algebra," are known to have circulated among his disciples. His influence was nevertheless immense, and his teachings have been reconstituted by M. Asín Palacios, thanks to many later references to him.[39]

At the heart of Ibn Masarrah's teachings stands a cosmology named after Empedocles and often referred to as pseudo-Empedoclean and insistence on the esoteric character of philosophy and even psychology. His doctrines emphasized the absolute simplicity and ineffability of the absolute Being, the emanation of the levels of existence, the hierarchization of souls, and their emanation from the Universal Soul. The so-called pseudo-Empedoclean cosmology is especially interesting because of its vast influence on later Andalusian Sufism, from Ibn al-ʿArīf and Ibn Barrajān to Ibn ʿArabī, as well as on later Islamic philosophers such as Mullā Ṣadrā and also Jewish philosophers such as Solomon ben Gabirol. Empedocles was seen by Ibn Masarrah as the first of the great Greek philosophers, followed by Pythagoras, Socrates, Plato, and Aristotle. Empedocles was viewed almost as a prophet who had received his teachings from Heaven. The cosmology attributed to him is based on the theory of hierarchic emanation of five substances: the *materia prima* (which is the first of intelligible realities and is not understood in the same way as the Aristotelian *materia prima*), the Intellect, the Soul, Nature, and *materia secunda.* The *materia prima* is "intelligible matter" existing in actuality and the first emanation of the Divine, while the Divine Principle Itself is above this schema, much like the Originator (*al-Mubdiʿ*) of the Ismāʿīlīs. Ibn Masarrah also mentions the well-known Empedoclean theory of the two cosmic energies, namely, love and discord, which he, however, interprets in a very different manner by using the term *qahr* (which means dominion or victory and has an astrological color) rather than discord. What was basic to Ibn Masarrah's teachings, however, was the idea of "intelligible matter," which stood opposed to the teachings of both the Aristotelians and the Neoplatonists and is seen elaborated later by Ibn ʿArabī, who speaks of "spiritual matter."

One of the major early intellectual figures of Islamic Spain was Abū Muḥammand ʿAlī ibn Ḥazm (d. 454/1063). At once jurist, moralist, historian, theologian, and philosopher, he represents a remarkable intellectual presence in the Cordova of the fifth/eleventh century. He was a Ẓāhirite in jurisprudence and a theologian of note who remained sharply critical of the Ash'arites. His vast literary output, marked often by seething attacks on his opponents, touches on many branches of Islamic learning including comparative religion and philosophy.[40] His *Kitāb al-fiṣal fi'l-milal wa'l-ahwā' wa'l-niḥal* (*The Book of Critical Detailed Examination of Religions, Sects, and Philosophical Schools*) is considered by many to be one of the first works in the field of comparative religion, along with the *Taḥqīq mā li'l-hind* (*India*) of al-Bīrūnī. Ibn Ḥazm's *Ṭawq al-ḥimāmah* (*The Ring of the Dove*), translated many times into European languages, is the most famous Islamic treatise on Platonic love.[41] In this beautifully written work, Ibn Ḥazm follows upon the wake of earlier Muslim Platonists such as the Persian philosopher Muḥammad ibn Dā'ūd al-Iṣfahānī (d. 297/909) and echoes the teachings of Plato in the *Phaedrus.* The beauty of the soul attracts it to a beautiful object, and, as a result of the existence in the beautiful object of something corresponding to the nature of the soul, love is created. One finds in Ibn Ḥazm a full development of Platonic love, which marks him as a notable philosopher in addition to being a jurist and theologian and makes him a congenial companion of the *fedeli d'amore* among the Sufis despite certain differences of perspective.

The first major follower of eastern *mashshā'ī* philosophy in Spain was Abū Bakr ibn Bājjah, the famous Latin Avempace, who had a great influence on Ibn Rushd and Albert the Great as well as on many Jewish philosophers. Originally from northern Spain, he led a difficult life in a Spain torn by local wars; he settled in Fez in Morocco, where he became vizier and was finally imprisoned and died in 533/1138. Ibn Bājjah was an accomplished physician, astronomer, physicist, and natural historian as well as philosopher, but his work remained incomplete and much of it perished. He is, however, quoted extensively by later authorities, and one can surmise from these sources his importance in the anti-Ptolemaic astronomy and cosmology being developed in Spain in the sixth/twelfth century as well as his crucial role in the history of the critique of the Aristotelian theory of projectile motion.

As far as the spiritual significance of his work is concerned, one must turn to his major opus the *Tadbīr al-mutawaḥḥid* (*Regimen of the Solitary*) which is one of the most significant works of Islamic philosophy in the Maghrib.[42] In this work, the author speaks of the perfect state which is created not by external transformations, reforms, or revolutions but by the inner transformation of those individuals who have become inwardly united with the Active Intellect (*al-'aql al-fa''āl*) and whose intellects are completely in act. These individuals are solitary figures, strangers, and exiles in a world that is comprised for the most part of human beings who cannot raise their gaze to the realm of the purely intelligible. Ibn Bājjah opposed explicitly the Ghazzālian type of mysticism and proposed a more intellectual and detached form of mystical contemplation. Yet in many ways he belongs to the same family as Sufi gnostics, and his *Tadbīr* is reminiscent of the *Occidental Exile* of Suhrawardī and the *gharīb* or stranger to the world emphasized in so many Sufi works. Unfortunately, this major opus was never completed, and we do not know how Ibn Bājjah envisaged the termination and completion of the actualization of the intellect in the solitary figure who becomes inwardly united with the Active Intellect which is at the same time the Holy Spirit.

If Ibn Bājjah was particularly drawn to the teachings of al-Fārābī, his successor upon the philosophical scene in Spain, Abū Bakr Muḥammad ibn Ṭufayl of Cadiz, was especially attracted to Ibn Sīnā. Ibn Ṭufayl was also a physician and scientist as well as a philosopher, and, like Ibn Bājjah, he even became vizier in Morocco, where he died in 580/1185. He was also a friend of Ibn Rushd and asked the great commentator to undertake a study and an analysis of the works of Aristotle. He was known as Abubacer in the Latin West, but his major opus, *Ḥayy ibn Yaqẓān* (*Living Son of the Awake*), did not become known to the scholastics. It was translated into Hebrew and later in the seventeenth century into Latin as *Philosophus autodidactus*, a work that had much influence on later European literature and is in fact considered by some to be the source of inspiration for the Robinson Crusoe story as well as certain forms of seventeenth-century mysticism concerned with the inner light. This major philosophical romance takes its title from the earlier work of Ibn Sīnā but seeks a path toward inner illumination in a manner similar to that of Suhrawardī, who was Ibn Ṭufayl's contemporary. It is of interest to note that at the beginning of his work Ibn Ṭufayl refers to the "Oriental Philosophy" which Ibn Sīnā was seeking in his later works and which Suhrawardī restored.

In Ibn Ṭufayl's "initiatic romance," the names in the Avicennan recitals are retained but their function changes. Ḥayy ibn Yaqẓān himself is the hero of the story rather than the Active Intellect. He appears in a mysterious manner through spontaneous generation from a matter that is made spiritually active by the Active Intellect. He is helped and brought up by a gazelle as a result of the sympathy (*sym-pathia*) which relates all living beings together. As he grows up, he begins to attain knowledge first of the physical world, then of the heavens, the angels, the creative Demiurge, and finally of the Divine Principle and the universal theophany. Upon reaching the highest form of knowledge, he is joined by Absāl from a nearby island where he had been instructed in religion and theology. After mastering Ḥayy's language, Absāl discovers to his astonishment that all he had learned about religion is confirmed by Ḥayy in its purest form. Together they try to educate the people of the nearby island from which Absāl had come but few understand what they say.

Far from being a treatise on naturalism denying revelation, as some have claimed,[43] *Ḥayy ibn Yaqẓān* is a work that seeks to unveil within man the significance of the intellect whose illumination of the mind is like an inner revelation that cannot but confirm the truths of the outer revelation. Ḥayy *is* the solitary of Ibn Bājjah, whose inner experience to reach the truth through the intellect—a truth that is then confirmed to be in accord with the religious truths learned by Absāl—points to one of the major messages of much of Islamic philosophy. That message is the inner accord between philosophy and religion and the esoteric role of philosophy as the inner dimension of the truths expounded by revealed religion for a whole human collectivity. The eminently symbolic language of *Ḥayy ibn Yaqẓān* also indicates the esoteric character of veritable philosophy, whose meaning cannot be exhausted by the outer meaning of its language and mode of exposition.

It is in the light of this background that one must examine the attempt of the most celebrated of the Islamic philosophers of Spain, Abu'l-Walīd ibn Rushd, to reconcile religion and philosophy. The philosopher who became a central intellectual figure in the Latin West under the name of Averroes was born in Cordova in 520/1126, where he was to become the chief judge (*qāḍī*) later in life. But the political situation of Andalusia changed and Ibn Rushd fell from political favor. He spent the last part of his life in Marrakesh, where he died in 595/1198.

This greatest speculative philosopher of the Maghrib was to have two distinct destinies. In the West he became known as the commentator par excellence of Aristotle: hence the words of Dante, "Averroìs che'l gran comento feo" (*Divine Comedy,* Inferno; iv, 144). It was through his eyes that the West saw Aristotle, and by mistake he became known as the author of the double truth theory and the inspiration for a politicized Averroism. He even came to be known as the symbol of a rationalism opposed to religious faith, a view that continued into the modern period, as seen by the classical work of the nineteenth-century French rationalist E. Renan.[44] Averroes became a major figure in Western intellectual history, and in fact most of his works have survived not in the original Arabic but in Hebrew and Latin. As a result, there came into being a distinct school known as Latin Averroism.[45]

The Muslim Ibn Rushd was quite a different figure. Besides seeking to present the pure teachings of Aristotle, his main aim was to harmonize religion and philosophy. But his real thesis was not "double truth" but recourse to *ta'wīl*, which is so important for the understanding of the whole Islamic philosophical tradition. According to this doctrine, there are not two contradictory truths but a single truth which is presented in the form of religion and, through *ta'wīl*, results in philosophical knowledge. Religion is for everyone, whereas philosophy is only for those who possess the necessary intellectual faculties. Yet, the truth reached by one group is not contradictory to the truth discovered by the other. The principle of *ta'wīl* permits the harmony between religion and philosophy.[46] The whole thrust of the philosophy of Ibn Rushd, who was at once a pious Muslim and an authority in the *Sharīʿah* and a great philosopher, was to harmonize faith and reason.

One of Ibn Rushd's most important works was his response to al-Ghazzālī's attack against the philosophers contained in the latter's *Tahāfut al-falāsifah.* Ibn Rushd took up the challenge of defending Islamic philosophy and sought to respond to al-Ghazzālī point by point in his *Tahāfut al-tahāfut* (*Incoherence of the Incoherence*), which is one of the major works of Islamic philosophy.[47] This work did not have the influence of al-Ghazzālī's attack, but it did not go without a further response by later Islamic thinkers.

Ibn Rushd revived Aristotle, but he did not have the influence of the Peripatetic Ibn Sīnā, whom he criticized in many ways. Ibn Rushd was especially opposed to Ibn Sīnā's theory of emanation and emphasis on the soul of the spheres as well as his doctrine of the intellect and the relation of the soul with the Active Intellect. The result of Ibn Rushd's critique was the banishment of the angels, of the *Anima caelestis,* from the cosmos. The influence of Averroes in the West could not but help in the secularization of the cosmos, preparing the ground for the rise of a totally secularized knowledge of the natural order. Islamic philosophy itself, however, chose another path. It revived Avicennan philosophy rather than following Ibn Rushd and turned to the Orient of Light through the works of Suhrawardī and set out on a path whose first steps had been explored by Ibn Sīnā himself.

With the death of Ibn Rushd something died—but not Islamic philosophy, as has been claimed by Western students of the Islamic philosophic tradition for seven centuries. Philosophy began a new phase of its life in Persia and other eastern lands of Islam, while its sun set in the Maghrib. But even in the western lands of Islam, there appeared at least one other major philosophical figure, ʿAbd al-Ḥaqq ibn Sabʿīn, who hailed from Murcia, spent the middle part of his life in North Africa and Egypt, and lived the last period of his life in Mecca, where he died ca. 669/1270. He had definitely pro-Shīʿite tendencies and expounded openly the doctrine of "the transcendent unity of being," which caused him to fall into difficulty with exoteric religious authorities both in the Maghrib and Egypt. Even in Mecca, where he was supported by the ruler, he was attacked from many quarters, and the circumstances of his death remain a mystery. Some have said that he was forced to commit suicide, others that he committed suicide before the Kaʿbah to experience the ecstasy of union,[48] and still others that he was poisoned.

Ibn Sabʿīn was at once a philosopher and a Sufi and a follower of the Shawdhiyyah Order, which went back to the Andalusian Sufi from Seville Abū ʿAbd Allāh al-Shawdhī and was characterized by its mixing of philosophy and Sufism. Ibn Sabʿīn had an extensive knowledge of both traditions. He knew well the early classical Sufis of Baghdad and Khurasan such as al-Junayd, al-Ḥallāj, Bāyazīd, and al-Ghazzālī as well as the earlier Andalusian masters such as Ibn Masarrah, Ibn Qasī, and Ibn ʿArabī, who like him was born in Murcia, traveled to North Africa and Egypt, and lived for some time in Mecca. But Ibn Sabʿīn is not a direct follower of the School of Ibn ʿArabī, some of whose later representatives he was to meet in Egypt.

Ibn Sabʿīn also knew well both the eastern philosophers such as al-Fārābī and Ibn Sīnā and the Andalusian ones such as Ibn Bājjah, Ibn Ṭufayl, and Ibn Rushd. He even knew Suhrawardī, whom he, however, classified with the Peripatetics and criticized severely along with nearly all the earlier philosophers and many of the earlier Sufis. Ibn Sabʿīn was a follower of the doctrine of "absolute Unity" according to which there is only the Being of God and nothing else. He criticized the earlier Islamic thinkers for not having reached the level of this "absolute Unity." He is in fact probably the first person to use the term *waḥdat al-wujūd.*

It is also of interest to note that Ibn Sabʿīn had extensive knowledge of Judaism, Christianity, and even Hinduism and Zoroastrianism as well as Greek philosophy including Hermeticism. He was furthermore considered a master in the "hidden sciences,"[49] especially the science of the inner meaning of letters and words. His highly difficult writings often contain "kabbalistic" sentences whose meaning cannot be understood save through recourse to these sciences. These writings include also treatises on the hidden sciences as well as works devoted to philosophy and practical Sufism.

Many of Ibn Sabʿīn's works are lost, but a few survive and bear witness to the depth and fecundity of his thought. The most significant of his philosophical works is the *Budd al-ʿārif* (*The Object of Worship of the Gnostic*), which starts with logic and terminates with metaphysics and must be considered the synthesis of his metaphysical teachings.[50] But his most influential work as far as the Western world is concerned is *Ajwibah yamāniyyah 'an as'ilat al-ṣiqilliyyah* (*Yemeni Answers to Sicilian Questions*), which consists of answers to four philosophical questions sent by Emperor Frederick II. The work was translated into Latin and became well known in scholastic circles.

Ibn Sab'īn must be considered along with Suhrawardī and Ibn 'Arabī as a master of Islamic spirituality who combined the purification of the soul with the perfection of the intellectual faculties, who created a synthesis between spiritual life and speculative thought, between Sufism and philosophy. As the last great representative of the Maghribī-Andalusian school of Islamic philosophy, Ibn Sab'īn embodies that synthesis between the practical spiritual life and intellectual doctrine that one finds in Ibn Masarrah, who stands at the origin of this school.[51] The West may have seen in the Islamic philosophy of Spain a pure Aristotelian rationalism with which it was fascinated but which it feared. In the light of the integral tradition of Islamic philosophy, however, it is this synthesis between practical Sufism and philosophy as metaphysics and gnosis which represents the central message of this school. The journey of Ibn Sab'īn to the East and his death in the holy city of Mecca, the heartland of Islam, is itself symbolic of the wedding of that knowledge which transforms and illuminates and the spiritual practice which opens the heart to the reception of such a knowledge. If with the journey of Ibn Sab'īn, the light of this type of philosophy became dimmed in Andalusia, it shone already brightly in the eastern lands of Islam thanks to the teachings of the master of the School of Illumination, Suhrawardī, whose commentators and students were Ibn Sab'īn's contemporaries.

Suhrawardī and the School of Illumination (al-Ishrāq)

The complete harmonization of spirituality and philosophy in Islam was achieved in the School of Illumination (*al-ishrāq*) founded by Shaykh al-ishrāq Shihāb al-Dīn Suhrawardī. Born in the small village of Suhraward[52] in Western Persia in 549/1153, he studied in Zanjan and Isfahan, where he completed his formal education in the religious and philosophical sciences and entered into Sufism. He then set out for Anatolia and settled in Aleppo, where as a result of the opposition of certain jurists he met his death at a young age in 587/1191. Suhrawardī was a great mystic and philosopher and the restorer within the bosom of Islam of the perennial philosophy, which he called *al-ḥikmat al-'atīqah,* the *philosophia priscorium* referred to by certain Renaissance philosophers, whose origin he considered to be divine. He saw veritable philosophy—or one should rather say theosophy, if this word is understood in its original sense and as still used by Jakob Boehme—

as resulting from the wedding between the training of the theoretical intellect through philosophy and the purification of the heart through Sufism. The means of attaining supreme knowledge he considered to be illumination, which at once transforms one's being and bestows knowledge.[53]

During his short and tragic life, Suhrawardī wrote more than forty treatises, the doctrinal ones almost all in Arabic and the symbolic or visionary recitals almost all in Persian. Both his Arabic and Persian works are among the literary masterpieces of Islamic philosophy. His doctrinal writings, which begin with an elaboration and gradual transformation of Avicennian Peripatetic philosophy, culminate in the *Ḥikmat al-ishrāq* (*The Theosophy of the Orient of Light*), which is one of the most important works in the tradition of Islamic philosophy.[54] His recitals include some of the most beautiful prose writings of the Persian language, including such masterpieces as *Fī ḥaqīqat al-ʿishq* (*On the Reality of Love*) and *Āwāz-i par-i Jibraʾīl* (*The Chant of the Wing of Gabriel*).[55] Few Islamic philosophers were able to combine metaphysics of the highest order with a poetic prose of almost incomparable richness and literary quality.

Suhrawardī integrated Platonism and Mazdaean angelology in the matrix of Islamic gnosis. He believed that there existed in antiquity two traditions of wisdom (*al-ḥikmah*), both of divine origin. One of these reached Pythagoras, Plato, and other Greek philosophers and created the authentic Greek philosophical tradition which terminated with Aristotle. The other was disseminated among the sages of ancient Persia whom he calls the *khusrawāniyyūn*, or sages who were followers of the Persian philosopher-king Kay Khusraw. Finally, these traditions became united in Suhrawardī. Like many Islamic philosophers, he identified Hermes with the prophet Idrīs, who was given the title Father of Philosophers (*wālid al-ḥukamāʾ*) and was considered to be the recipient of the celestial wisdom which was the origin of philosophy. It was finally in Islam, the last and primordial religion, that this primordial tradition became restored by Suhrawardī as the school of Illumination (*al-ishrāq*).

The Master of Illumination insisted that there existed from the beginning an "eternal dough" (*al-khamīrat al-azaliyyah*), which is none other than eternal wisdom or *sophia perennis.* It is hidden in the very substance of man ready to be "leavened" and actualized through intellectual training and inner purification.[56] It is this "eternal dough" which was actualized and transmitted by the Pythagoreans and Plato to the Sufis Dhu'l-Nūn al-Miṣrī and Sahl al-Tustarī and through the Persian sages to Bāyazīd al-Basṭāmī and Manṣūr al-Ḥallāj and which was restored in its full glory by Suhrawardī, who combined the inner knowledge of these masters with the intellectual discipline of such philosophers as al-Fārābī and Ibn Sīnā. Suhrawardī, however, never mentions historical chains connecting him to this long tradition of wisdom but insists that the real means of attainment of this knowledge is through God and His revealed Book. That is why he bases himself so much on the Quran and is the first major Muslim philosopher to quote the Quran extensively in his philosophical writings.

Suhrawardī created a vast philosophical synthesis, which draws from many sources and especially the nearly six centuries of Islamic thought before him. But this synthesis is unified by a metaphysics and an epistemology that are able to relate all the different strands of thought to each other in a unified pattern. What is most significant from the point of view of spirituality is the insistence of *ishrāqī* philosophy on the organic nexus between intellectual activity and inner purification. Henceforth in the Islamic world, wherever philosophy survived, it was seen as lived wisdom. The philosopher or *ḥakīm* was expected to be not only a person possessing cerebral knowledge but a saintly person transformed by his knowledge. Philosophy as a mental activity divorced from spiritual realization and the inner life ceased to be accepted as a legitimate intellectual category, and Islamic philosophy became henceforth what *sophia* has always been in Oriental traditions, namely, a wisdom lived and experienced as well as thought and reasoned.

Although as a result of his violent death Suhrawardī and his doctrines were not visible for a generation, the teachings of the School of Illumination reappeared in the middle part of the seventh/thirteenth century in the major commentary by Muḥammad al-Shahrazūrī (d. sometime after 687/1288) on the *Ḥikmat al-ishrāq.* This was followed by the second major commentary on this work by Quṭb al-Dīn al-Shīrāzī (d. 710/1311). The latter must be considered one of the major intellectual figures of Islam, at once physicist and astronomer, authority in logic and medicine, commentator on Ibn Sīnā and Suhrawardī.[57] His *Durrat al-tāj* (*Jewel of the Crown*), which is a vast philosophical encyclopedia mostly along Peripatetic lines, is well known, as is his commentary on the *Canon of Medicine* of Ibn Sīnā and several major astronomical treatises. But Quṭb al-Dīn al-Shīrāzī's most enduring philosophical work is his commentary on the *Ḥikmat al-ishrāq,* which resuscitated the teachings of Suhrawardī and is read and studied in Persia and Muslim India to this day. After him a long line of *ishrāqī* philosophers appeared in both Persia and the Indian subcontinent, where the influence of Suhrawardī has been very extensive. Suhrawardī established a new and at the same time primordial intellectual dimension in Islam, which became a permanent aspect of the Islamic intellectual scene and survives to this day.

What Is Ishrāqī Philosophy?

Ishrāqī philosophy—or theosophy, to be more precise—is based on the metaphysics of light. The origin and source of all things is the Light of lights (*nūr al-anwār*), which is infinite and absolute Light above and beyond all the rays which it emanates. All levels of reality, however, are also degrees and levels of light distinguished from each other by their degrees of intensity and weakness and by nothing other than light. There is, in fact, nothing in the whole universe but light. From the Light of lights there issues a vertical or longitudinal hierarchy of lights which comprises the levels of universal existence and a horizontal or latitudinal order which contains the archetypes (sg. *rabb al-naw*ʿ) or Platonic ideas of all that appears here below as objects and things. These lights are none other than what in the language of religion are called angels. Suhrawardī gives names of Mazdaean angels as well as Islamic ones to these lights and brings out the central role of the angels in cosmology as well as in epistemology and soteriology.[58]

The word *ishrāq* in Arabic itself means at once illumination and the first light of the early morning as it shines from the east (*sharq*). The Orient is not only the geographical east but the origin of light, of reality. *Ishrāqī* philosophy is both "Oriental"and "illuminative." It illuminates because it is Oriental and is Oriental because it is illuminative. It is the knowledge with the help of which man can orient himself in the universe and finally reach that Orient which is his original abode, while in the shadow and darkness of terrestrial existence man lives in the "occident" of the world of being no matter where he lives geographically. The spiritual or illuminated man who is aware of his "Oriental" origin, is therefore a stranger and an exile in this world, as described in one of Suhrawardī's most eloquent symbolic recitals *Qiṣṣat al-ghurbat al-gharbiyyah* (*The Story of the Occidental Exile*). It is through reminiscence of his original abode that man begins to have a nostalgia for his veritable home and with the help of illuminative knowledge that he is able to reach that abode. Illuminative knowledge, which is made possible by contact with the angelic orders, transforms man's being and saves him. The angel is the instrument of illumination and hence salvation. Man has descended from the world of the "signeurial lights" and it is by returning to this world and reunifying with his angelic "alter-ego" that man finds his wholeness once again.

Ishrāqī philosophy depicts in an eminently symbolic language a vast universe based on the symbolism of light and the "Orient," which breaks the boundaries of Aristotelian cosmology as well as the confines of *ratio* defined by the Aristotelians. Suhrawardī was able to create an essentialistic metaphysics of light and a cosmology of rarely paralleled grandeur and beauty which "orients" the veritable seeker through the cosmic crypt and guides him to the realm of pure light which is none other than the Orient of being. In this journey, which is at once philosophical and spiritual, man is led by a knowledge which is itself light according to the saying of the Prophet who said *al-ʿilm*^{u} *nūr*^{un} (knowledge is light). That is why this philosophy, according to Suhrawardī's last will and testament at the end of his *Ḥikmat al-ishrāq*, is not to be taught to everyone. It is for those whose minds have been trained by rigorous philosophical training and whose hearts have been purified through inner effort to subdue that interior dragon which is the carnal soul. For such people, the teachings of *ishrāq* reveal an inner knowledge which is none other than the eternal wisdom or *sophia perennis* which illuminates and transforms, obliterates and resurrects until man reaches the pleroma of the world of lights and the original abode from which he began his cosmic wayfaring.

Between Suhrawardī and the School of Isfahan

The period stretching from the seventh/thirteenth to the tenth/sixteenth century is characterized by the ever-greater rapprochement between various schools of Islamic philosophy as Persia becomes the main arena for activity in Islamic philosophy. Early in this period, Ibn Sīnā's philosophy was resurrected by Naṣīr al-Dīn al-Ṭūsī, who is one of the foremost Islamic *mashshāʾī* philosophers. His commentary on the *Ishārāt wa'l-tanbīhāt* and his response to the criticisms of Fakhr al-Dīn al-Rāzī against Ibn Sīnā had a much greater influence on later Islamic philosophy than the *Tahāfut al-tahāfut* of Ibn Rushd. Ṭūsī was the leading light of a whole circle of philosophers including not only the already mentioned Quṭb al-Dīn al-Shīrāzī, but also Dabīrān-i Kātibī Qazwīnī (d. 675/1276) the author of the *Ḥikmat al-ʿayn* (*Wisdom from the Source*). Another well-known Peripatetic philosopher of the same period who needs to be mentioned is Athīr al-Dīn Abharī (d. 663/1264), whose *Hidāyat al-ḥikmah* (*Guide of Philosophy*) became popular during later centuries, especially with the commentary of Mullā Ṣadrā.

Perhaps the most distinctive philosopher of this period who is said to have also been related to Naṣīr al-Dīn was Afḍal al-Dīn Kāshānī (d. ca. 610/1213) known also as Bābā Afḍal. An eminent Sufi whose tomb is a locus of pilgrimage to this day, Bābā Afḍal was a brilliant logician and metaphysician. He wrote a number of works in Persian which rank along with the Persian treatises of Suhrawardī as among outstanding masterpieces of Persian philosophical prose.[59] His works represent yet another wedding between Sufism and philosophy, and they are based on a self-knowledge or autology that leads from the knowledge of the self to the Self according to the prophetic *ḥadīth, man ʿarafa nafsahu faqad ʿarafa rabbahu* (he who knows himself know his Lord).

Parallel with the revival of Peripatetic philosophy by Ṭūsī and *ishrāqī* theosophy by his colleague at Maraghah, Quṭb al-Dīn Shīrāzī, theoretical Sufism of the school of Ibn ʿArabī spread rapidly in the East,[60] while philosophical *kalām* was developing greatly. During the next three centuries important philosophers appeared who tried to synthesize these various schools of thought. Some, like Dawānī, were at once scholars of *kalām* and *ishrāqīs.* Others, like the Dashtakī family of Shiraz, were followers of Ibn Sīnā and Suhrawardī. Still others, like Ibn Turkah Iṣfahānī (d. ca. 835/1432), who is a major figure of this period, was an *ishrāqī* interpreter of Peripatetic philosophy and a gnostic of the School of Ibn ʿArabī. These figures prepared the ground for the grand synthesis between the four schools of *ishrāq, mashshāʾ, ʿirfān,* and *kalām,* which, however, was not achieved until the Safavid period with the establishment of what has become known as the School of Isfahan.

Mullā Ṣadrā and the School of Isfahan

Three centuries of the drawing together of the various schools of Islamic thought culminated in the Safavid period in Persia with the School of Isfahan, associated with the Safavid capital which was its center. The most important figure of this school was Ṣadr al-Dīn Shīrāzī, known as Mullā Ṣadrā, but the founder was Mīr Dāmād (d. 1041/1631), theologian, philosopher, mystic, and poet.[61] A rigorous philosopher who taught the philosophy of Ibn Sīnā, which he interpreted in an *ishrāqī* manner, he was also a mystic who wrote of his ecstatic experiences and a fine poet who used the pen name *ishrāq.* Concerned most of all with the question of time, which he discussed extensively in his masterpiece, the *Qabasāt* (*Firebrands*), he represents the beginning of that synthesis of the schools of philosophy, theology, and gnosis which characterizes later Islamic philosophy.

Mīr Dāmād had a number of notable contemporaries on the philosophical scene. His friend in Isfahan Shaykh Bahāʾ al-Dīn al-ʿĀmilī (d. 1030/1622) was a scientist, jurisprudent, theologian, architect, and poet and was of great importance in the intellectual life of the age of Mīr Dāmād. His other notable contemporary, Mīr Abu'l-Qāsim Findiriskī (d. 1050/1641) was more important from the philosophical point of view. This remarkable figure taught the works of Ibn Sīnā in Isfahan while spending much of his time in India, where he encountered Hindu pundits and yogis. He wrote little, but what he did write is of unusual significance. His works include a metaphysical study of human society, *Risālay-i ṣinā'iyyah* (*Treatise on the Arts*); a work on alchemy; a celebrated poem summarizing his metaphysical views; and a commentary on the *Yoga-Vasiśtha* based on the Persian translation of Niẓām al-Dīn Panīpātī.[62]

Islamic translations and studies of Hindu metaphysical and philosophical texts are remarkable intellectual and spiritual events pointing to contact between the Abrahamic and Indian spiritual worlds before modern times. This tradition goes back to al-Bīrūnī's Arabic translation of the *Patañjali Yoga* followed by numerous translations into Persian over the centuries of the *Rāmāyaṇa*, the *Mahābhārata*, the *Bhagavad-Gītā*, and also the Upanishads.[63] Not only the Muslims of India but also Persian Muslims were aware of the Hindu intellectual universe. It is, nevertheless, most remarkable that a man like Mīr Findiriskī should teach the *Shifā'* of Ibn Sīnā in Isfahan and comment on texts of yoga in India. This is proof of the fact that he breathed in an intellectual universe that stood not only geographically but also spiritually between the Mediterranean Sea and the Ganges River. He was the master of a philosophy which had also been studied by the medieval schoolmen and which in the West had developed in the direction of a nominalism and finally a skepticism that stood at the very antipode of Mīr Findiriskī's world view. How difficult it is to imagine his European contemporaries being interested seriously in Hindu metaphysics and—even if this were to be the case—to combine this interest with the love for St. Thomas and St. Bonaventure! The parting of ways in the intellectual destinies of Islam and the West can be seen in the distance that separates the masters of the School of Isfahan from their contemporary Renaissance and seventeenth-century European philosophers.

Nowhere is this difference to be seen more starkly than in the writings of Mullā Ṣadrā, the foremost figure of the School of Isfahan, whom many consider to be the greatest of all Muslim metaphysicians. This remarkable figure was born in Shiraz about 979/1571, studied with Mīr Dāmād and other masters of the day in Isfahan, then retired for some ten years to a village near Qum, and finally returned to Shiraz, where he spent the last thirty years of his life writing and training students who came to him from as far away as North Africa and Tibet. He died in Basra in 1050/1640 while returning from his seventh pilgrimage on foot to Mecca.[64]

Mullā Ṣadrā incorporates that Suhrawardian ideal according to which the perfect philosopher or theosopher (*ḥakīm muta'allih*) must have undergone both intellectual training and inner purification. Later Islamic philosophy in fact bestowed the title of *Ṣadr al-muta'allihīn* upon Mullā Ṣadrā, meaning foremost among theosophers. Indeed, he does represent the perfection of this Suhrawardian norm. A master dialectitian and logician as well as a visionary and seer, Mullā Ṣadrā created a perfect harmony between the poles of ratiocination and mystical perception. Through the intellect wed to revelation he reached a *coincidentia oppositorum,* which embraces the rigor of logic and the immediacy of spiritual unveiling. Like the *Ḥikmat al-ishrāq,* which begins with logic and ends with mystical ecstasy, Mullā Ṣadrā wove a pattern of thought that is logical and immersed in the ocean of the light of gnosis. He called this synthesis—which he considered to be based specifically on the three grand paths to the truth open to man, namely, revelation (*waḥy* or *shar'*), intellection (*'aql*), and mystical unveiling (*kashf*)—*al-ḥikmat al-muta'āliyah* or the transcendent theosophy. His synthesis represented a new intellectual perspective in Islamic philosophy, a perspective which has had numerous followers especially in Persia and India but also in Iraq and certain other Arab lands over the centuries.

Mullā Ṣadrā composed some fifty books, almost all in Arabic, of which the most important is *al-Asfār al-arba'ah* (*The Four Journeys*), which remains the most advanced text of traditional Islamic philosophy in the *madrasahs* to this day. It includes not only his own metaphysical and cosmological views and the most extensive treatment of eschatology found in any Islamic philosophical text; it also deals with the views of various schools of thought both Islamic and pre-Islamic. It is a veritable philosophical encyclopedia in which the influence of the Avicennan school, of Suhrawardī and Ibn 'Arabī, and of *kalām* both Sunni and Shī'ite is clearly discernible. But above and beyond these sources one can detect in this work, as in Mullā Ṣadrā's other writings, the great influence of the Quran and the sayings of the Prophet and the Shī'ite Imams. His Quranic commentaries such as the *Asrār al-āyāt* (*The Secrets of the Verses of the Quran*) are the most important contributions made to Quranic studies by an Islamic philosopher, and his commentary on the Shī'ite collection of *Ḥadīth,* the *Uṣūl al-kāfī* of Kulaynī, is one of his philosophical masterpieces. But these works also reveal the central significance of the Quran as the source of philosophical meditation for Islamic philosophers and of the sayings of the Prophet and the Imams as sources of inspiration for later Islamic philosophy.[65] Among Mullā Ṣadrā's major achievements is the creation of a perfect harmony between faith and reason or religion and philosophy and the achievement of the goal of some nine centuries of Islamic theology and philosophy.

No other Islamic philosopher has dealt in depth with matters of faith ranging from the basis of ethics to eschatological imagery depicted in the Quran and *Ḥadīth* as has Mullā Ṣadrā. Nor have any of the philosophers dealt as thoroughly as he with all the questions which concerned the scholars of *kalām*. In fact, Mullā Ṣadrā claims that the *mutakallimūn* did not possess the divine knowledge (*al-ma'rifah*) necessary to deal with the questions they were treating and that therefore their activity was illegitimate. It was for the *ḥukamā-yi ilāhī* (literally, "the theosophers") to deal with such questions and to provide the answers for the enigmas and complex problems contained in religious teachings. Much of what Christians understand by theology would find its counterpart in Islamic thought in the writings of Mullā Ṣadrā rather than the Ash'arites, except that his is a "theology" always immersed in the light of divine knowledge, of gnosis, and not only of rational arguments concerning the tenets of the faith. Mullā Ṣadrā's "transcendent theosophy" is in fact philosophy, theology, and gnosis and draws from all these schools as they developed during the earlier centuries of Islamic intellectual history.

In his youth Mullā Ṣadrā followed the "essentialist metaphysics" of Suhrawardī, but as a result of a spiritual experience combined with intellectual vision he brought about what Corbin has called "a revolution in Islamic philosophy" and formulated the "existential metaphysics" by which he has come to be known. This metaphysical edifice, which is incomprehensible without a knowledge of Avicennan ontology and Suhrawardian cosmology and noetics, is based on the unity (*waḥdah*), principiality (*aṣālah*), and gradation (*tashkīk*) of being (*wujūd*). There is only one reality, which participates in grades and levels. The reality of each thing comes from its *wujūd* and not its quiddity or essence (*māhiyyah*).[66] The quiddities are nothing but limitations imposed on *wujūd*, which extends in a hierarchy from the dust to the Divine Throne. God Himself is the Absolute Being (*al-wujūd al-muṭlaq*) who is the origin of all realms of existence and yet transcendent vis-à-vis the chain of being. Moreover, there is unity of all being not so much in the general *waḥdat al-wujūd* sense according to which there is only One Being, God, and nothing else even exists. Rather, Mullā Ṣadrā speaks of a unity that is more similar to the unity between the sun and the rays that emanate from it.

This vast ocean of being—or rather becoming—moreover, is in constant movement toward its Divine Origin in what Mullā Ṣadrā calls transsubstantial motion (*al-ḥarakat al-jawhariyyah*). He has the vision of a cosmos in constant becoming moving toward its entelechy or perfection (*kamāl*). This movement must not, however, be construed in an evolutionary sense, for Mullā Ṣadrā asserts categorically the reality of the Platonic ideas or the immutable archetypes of all things existing in the world below. The higher states of being do not belong to a future time. They are real and present here and now to be realized by man, who forms the vertical axis of cosmic existence.

This vertical progression in the scales of being is achieved most of all through knowledge. Knowledge transforms the being of the knower, as from another point of view knowledge depends on the mode of the knower. Mullā Ṣadrā points to the principle of the identity of the intellect and the intelligible (*ittiḥād al-ʿāqil waʾl-maʿqūl*) to emphasize the inner link between knowing and being. In fact, in the supreme form of knowledge, being is knowledge and knowledge being, as the dichotomy between the object and the subject is transcended.

In ascending the scales of being, man not only traverses the physical and spiritual or intelligible realms of reality but also the realm between the two, which Islamic metaphysicians have called the "world of imagination."[67] Mullā Ṣadrā insists on the reality of this world both macrocosmically and microcosmically and insists on its survival after man's death. He provides an ontological status for a realm spoken of already by Suhrawardī in its microcosmic aspect and emphasized greatly by Ibn ʿArabī, who speaks of the creative power of imagination.[68] It was, however, Mullā Ṣadrā who treated this world in a thoroughly metaphysical and cosmological manner, bringing out its significance in both the descending and the ascending arcs of universal existence.

It is in fact in this intermediate realm that eschatological events referred to in the Quran and *Ḥadīth* take place.[69] Mullā Ṣadrā dealt extensively with this issue in many of his works. Not only did he devote independent treatises to this subject, such as the *Risālah fiʾl-ḥashr* (*Treatise on Resurrection*), but also the extensive fourth "journey" or *safar* of his masterpiece, the *Asfār al-arbaʿah,* is devoted to the soul (*nafs*) and its journey from the womb to its resurrection in the Divine Presence. No Islamic philosopher has ever dealt with the vast ocean of the soul and its posthumous development with such thoroughness as Mullā Ṣadrā. Those who search for an Islamic counterpart to the major treatises on eschatology found in other religions such as Hinduism and Buddhism must turn to later Islamic philosophy, especially the teachings of Mullā Ṣadrā and his students. They bring out the inner meaning of the teachings of the Quran, *Ḥadīth,* the sayings of the Shīʿite Imams concerning eschatology, and also of such earlier Sufis as Ibn ʿArabī, who also wrote extensively on the subject.

Mullā Ṣadrā created a vast metaphysical synthesis in which strands from many earlier schools of Islamic thought were woven together in a rich tapestry of many hues and shades, dominated by the unity of Ṣadrian ontology and metaphysics. In Mullā Ṣadrā one finds not only peaceful coexistence, but complementarity and harmony between the tenets of faith or revelation, intellection, and mystical vision or unveiling. This last major school of Islamic philosophy achieved in a sense the final elaboration of the synthesis of modes of knowledge toward which Islamic philosophy had been moving since its earliest patriarchs such as al-Kindī began to philosophize in a world dominated by the reality of prophetic revelation and characterized by the inalienable wedding between the intellect as the instrument of inner illumination and the reasoning faculty of the human mind.

Islamic Philosophy after Mullā Ṣadrā

Mullā Ṣadrā has remained the dominating figure in the continuing tradition of Islamic philosophy to this day, although his school was not the only one to have followers during the succeeding centuries. Avicennan and Suhrawardian schools flourished side by side with that of Mullā Ṣadrā, marking a rich and varied philosophical life which did not by any means die out but has rather witnessed a renaissance during the past few decades, especially in Persia.[70] Mullā Ṣadrā's most famous immediate students, for example, 'Abd al-Razzāq Lāhījī (d. 1072/1661) and Mullā Muḥsin Fayḍ Kāshānī (d. 1091/1680), devoted themselves mostly to the purely religious sciences such as *Ḥadīth* or to *kalām* and pure gnosis and did not write on the "transcendent theosophy," mostly because of opposition to Mullā Ṣadrā among some of the exoteric *'ulamā'*.[71] But they were well versed in this school of thought and trained a number of students who kept the tradition alive. One of them, Qāḍī Sa'īd Qummī (d. 1103/1692), is known both for his philosophical writings, including his commentary on the *Enneads* of Plotinus, and for his explanation of the inner meaning of the Islamic acts of worship, to which he devoted one of his major works, the *Asrār al-'ibādāt* (*The Mysteries of the Acts of Worship*).[72]

It was, however, the little-known figure Mullā Muḥammad Ṣādiq Ardistānī (d. 1134/1721) who served as the bridge between the school of Mullā Ṣadrā in the Safavid era and its revival during the Qajar period. Because the oral tradition is very important in the transmission of traditional Islamic philosophy, the chain of masters and students linking later generations of philosophers to the earlier authorities is of much significance.[73] In the case of the school of Mullā Ṣadrā, the link of transmission goes through Ardistānī, who was exiled from Isfahan at the end of the Safavid period and took refuge in Qum during the period of turmoil marking the transition from the Safavids to the Afsharids and the Zands.

It was not until the Qajar period and the early thirteenth/nineteenth century that the school of Mullā Ṣadrā was revived fully again in Isfahan by Mullā Ismā'īl Khājū'ī (d. 1173/1760) and Mullā 'Alī Nūrī (d. 1246/1830), who is especially significant as the great commentator upon the *Asfār* and as the one who taught Mullā Ṣadrā's philosophy to some three generations of students stretching over a period of seventy years. The Qajar period was also witness to a number of other well-known philosophers such as Mullā 'Alī Zunūzī (d. 1307/1890), who in his *Badāyi' al-ḥikam* (*Marvels of Wisdom*) sought to provide Islamic answers to certain of the Kantian antinomies presented to him by a Persian student who had returned from Europe. He is perhaps the most creative philosopher of the period.[74]

The most celebrated philosopher of the day, however, was Ḥājjī Mullā Hādī Sabziwārī (d. 1289/1878), a great saint, philosopher, and poet. He wrote the *Sharḥ al-manẓūmah* (*Commentary upon the Rhyming Composition*), which summarizes the principles of Mullā Ṣadrā's philosophy, and numerous other philosophical and gnostic works in both Arabic and Persian, including a commentary on the *Mathnawī* of Rūmī.[75] He was also known as a revered saintly figure throughout Persia, and even the king went to visit him in his home in Sabziwar in Khurasan.

During the Qajar period Tehran gradually became the center for the study of Islamic philosophy, and most of the outstanding masters of the later Qajar and the Pahlavi periods such as Mīrzā Mahdī Āshtiyānī (d. 1373/1953), Sayyid Muḥammad Kāẓim 'Aṣṣār (d. 1394/1975), and Sayyid Abu'l-Ḥasan Qazwīnī (d. 1394/1975) taught in Tehran. After the Second World War, Qum also became an important center for the teaching of Islamic philosophy, thanks mostly to 'Allāmah Sayyid Muḥammad Ḥusayn Ṭabāṭabā'ī (d. 1402/1981), whose *Uṣūl-i falsafah wa rawish-i ri'ālism* (*The Principles of Philosophy and the Method of Realism*) is the most important philosophical response issuing from the background of Ṣadrian metaphysics to Marxism.[76] These and other masters in turn trained a number of students such as Murtaḍā Muṭahharī (d. 1399/1979), Sayyid Jalāl al-Dīn Āshtiyānī, and Mahdī Ḥā'irī Yazdī, who have kept this tradition alive to this day.[77] In fact, starting in the 1950s there occurred a revival of interest in Islamic philosophy in Persia revolving around the figure of Mullā Ṣadrā, a renaissance that continues to this day as this later Islamic philosophical tradition encounters the challenges of Western thought, begins a dialogue with other schools of thought within the Islamic world, and becomes better known as a living intellectual tradition in the West.[78]

Of course, Persia has not been the only land in which Islamic philosophy has survived during later centuries, although it has definitely been the main arena for activity in Islamic philosophy. The school of Mullā Ṣadrā spread rapidly into India soon after his death, and although the history of Islamic philosophy in the Indian subcontinent has yet to be written, one can see the presence of Mullā Ṣadrā's thought in the writings of most of the outstanding intellectual figures of the subcontinent such as Shāh Walī Allāh of Delhi. His metaphysics bears the unmistakable mark of the "transcendent theosophy," as does his attempt at synthesizing the various strands of Islamic thought.

Likewise in Iraq, the Islamic philosophical tradition continued to flourish and has not ceased to this day, as can be seen in the works of Muḥammad Bāqir al-Ṣadr (d. 1400/1980).[79] The revival of Islamic philosophy in Egypt and other Arab countries goes back to Jamāl al-Dīn Astrābādī, known as al-Afghānī (d. 1315/1897), who began to teach it while at al-Azhar in Cairo during the late thirteenth/nineteenth century. He also originally belonged to the school of Mullā Ṣadrā, whose works he had studied while in Tehran.

It was the destiny of Islamic philosophy to become finally wed to gnosis in the bosom of the revealed truth of Islam. When one studies later Islamic philosophers, one realizes immediately this wedding between ratiocination and inner illumination, between intellection and spiritual experience, between rational thought and sanctity. This final union characterizes the ultimate nature and destiny of Islamic philosophy, which, besides its great importance in the domains of logic, mathematics, and the natural sciences, has always been concerned with the supreme science and that knowledge which is inseparable from inner realization. That is why Islamic philosophy has been and remains to this day an important element in the vast and multidimensional universe of Islamic spirituality.

Notes

1. This is the definition given by ʿAḍud al-Dīn al-Ījī, one of the later masters of the science of *kalām,* in his *Mawāfiq* (*Stations*) (translated in the article of G. C. Anawati entitled "Kalām" in the new *Encyclopedia of Religion* [New York: Macmillan, 1987] 8:231).

2. On the Muʿtazilites, see J. van Ess, "Muʿtazilah," in the *Encyclopedia of Religion,* 10:220–29; W. Montgomery Watt, *The Formative Period of Islamic Thought* (Edinburgh: Edinburgh University Press, 1973); A. Nader, *Le Système philosophique des muʿtazila* (Beirut: Editions Les Lettres Orientales, 1956); and R. Frank, *The Metaphysics of Created Being According to Abuʾl-Hudhayl al-ʿAllāf* (Istanbul: Nederlands Historisch-Archaeologisch Institut in Het Nabije Oosten, 1966); idem, *Beings and their Attributes* (Albany: State University of New York Press, 1978). On Islamic *kalām* as a whole, see M. Horten, *Die philosophischen Systeme der spekulativen Theologen in Islam* (Bonn: F. Cohen, 1912); H. A. Wolfson, *The Philosophy of the Kalam* (Cambridge, MA: Harvard University Press, 1976); L. Gardet and G. C. Anawati, *Introduction à la théologie musulmane,* vol. 1 (Paris: J. Vrin, 1970); J. Windrow Sweetman, *Islam and Christian Theology* (2 vols.; London: Lutterworth, 1945).

3. See G. Hourani, *Islamic Rationalism: The Ethics of ʿAbd al-Jabbār* (London: Oxford University Press, 1971).

4. Trans. M. Abdul Hye in his "Ash'arism," in *A History of Muslim Philosophy,* ed. M. M. Sharif (Wiesbaden: Harrassowitz, 1963) 1:223.

5. This work is one of the most exhaustive among a whole class of writings in Islam, usually called *firaq* or "sects" literature associated with the names of al-Nawbakhtī, al-Baghdādī, Ibn Ḥazm, al-Shahristānī and others. Al-Ash'arī's work is among the most thorough and detailed work in this category of religious writings usually composed by scholars of *kalām.*

6. On the metaphysical critique of Ash'arite voluntarism, see F. Schuon, *Christianity/Islam: Essays on Esoteric Ecumenism,* trans. G. Polit (Bloomington, IN: World Wisdom Books, 1981) 203ff.

Many studies and translations have been made of al-Ash'arī. See, e.g., W. C. Klein, *The Elucidation of Islam's Foundation* (New Haven: American Oriental Society, 1940), which contains a translation of *al-Ibānah;* R. J. McCarthy, *The Theology of al-Ash'arī* (Beirut: Imprimerie Catholique, 1953), which contains a study of al-Ash'arī and the translation of two of his creeds; D. Gimaret, *La Doctrine d'al-Ash'ari* (Paris: Les Editions du Cerf, 1990); and D. B. Macdonald, *Development of Muslim Theology: Jurisprudence of Constitutional Theory* (New York: Charles Scribner's Sons, 1926).

7. On Ash'arite atomism and occasionalism, see the still valuable work of S. Pines, *Beiträge zur islamischen Atomenlehre* (Berlin: A. Heine, 1936); and M. Fakhry, *Islamic Occasionalism* (London: Allen & Unwin, 1958). Ash'arite atomism was not new in Islam in the sense that certain Mu'tazilites had already developed such a theory. But it became much more elaborated than before by the Ash'arites and was made a cornerstone of their theological system.

8. The Islamic philosophers refuted this view strongly, as seen in the arguments offered by Averroes in his *Incoherence of the Incoherence* against al-Ghazzālī on this issue. See S. H. Nasr, *Science and Civilization in Islam* (Cambridge: Islamic Texts Society, 1987) 307ff. It is of interest to note that David Hume used the same argument as the Ash'arites to refute causality and even mentioned the example of fire and cotton given by al-Ghazzālī and referred to by Averroes. Needless to say, Hume did not reach the same conclusion as the Ash'arites, because he did not see the Divine Will as the cause of all things.

9. This is the translation of *kalām al-muta'akhkhirīn* given by G. C. Anawati in his article on *kalām* (new *Encyclopedia of Religion* 8:238).

10. He was well versed in Islamic philosophy as well as in medicine, astronomy, and even the "hidden sciences" (*al-'ulūm al-gharībah* or *khafiyyah*). See S. H. Nasr, "Fakhr al-Dīn al-Rāzi," in *A History of Muslim Philosophy,* ed. M. M. Sharif, 1:642–56. On later Islamic theology, see also Horten, *Die philosophischen Systeme;* J. van Ess, *Die Erkenntniss Lehre des 'Aḍudaddin al-Īcī* (Wiesbaden: Harrassowitz, 1966); and Gardet and Anawati, *Introduction à la théologie musulmane* 1:76ff.

11. F. Schuon, *Christianity/Islam,* 221.

12. Ibid., 220–21.

13. Some of these ideas have been treated already by A. Nanji in his article "Ismā'īlism" in the previous volume of this encyclopedia on Islam, *Islamic Spirituality: Foundations* (ed. S. H. Nasr; World Spirituality 19; New York: Crossroad, 1987) 179–98. See also H. Corbin (with S. H. Nasr and O. Yahya) *Histoire de la philosophie islamique* (Paris: Gallimard, 1964) 110ff.

14. See *Kashf al-murād fi sharḥ tajrīd al-i'tiqād,* trans. and commented upon by Abu'l-Ḥasan Sha'rānī (Tehran: Kitābfurūshī-yi islāmiyyah, 1351 A.H. solar). On Shī'ite theology, especially of the earlier period before it became systematized by Ṭūsī, see W.

Madelung, *Religious Schools and Sects in Medieval Islam* (London: Variorum Reprints, 1985) VII–XV.

15. We have elsewhere elaborated these issues relating to the significance of Islamic philosophy in Islam; see S. H. Nasr, "The Meaning and Role of Philosophy in Islam," *Studia Islamica* 36 (1973) 57–80.

16. This view survived from the Latin philosophers to constitute the framework for modern works on Islamic philosophy, including the classical books of S. Munk, T. De Boer, G. Quadri, and many others. Even more recent writers with such breadth and depth of scholarship as H. Wolfson were interested primarily in early Islamic philosophy. Likewise, works dealing with the history of Western philosophy—whether they specialize in the Middle Ages, as in the case of E. Gilson, or treat the whole of Western philosophy, as in the case of F. Coplestone, B. Russell, and others—usually have a small chapter about "Arab philosophy" to provide the missing link between the philosophy of antiquity and Latin scholasticism, but there is no interest in Islamic philosophy itself.

17. Certain Pakistani and Indian scholars writing in English distinguish between Muslim and Islamic: the former concerns whatever is created or cultivated by Muslims even if not related to the religion of Islam, and the latter concerns what is related directly to the Islamic revelation. They then refer to Islamic philosophy as Muslim philosophy. Even if this distinction between Muslim and Islamic be accepted, most of the philosophy cultivated by Muslims should be called Islamic rather than Muslim because, whatever its origin, the philosophy in question was digested and integrated into the Islamic intellectual universe if that universe is seen in its total breadth and depth and not only in a sectarian manner or from a purely juridical point of view.

18. Early in this century, gradually a number of works began to be devoted to post–Ibn Rushdian Islamic philosophy, as seen in several works of M. Horten such as *Die philosophischen Ansuchten von Râzî und Tûsî* (Bonn: Hanstein, 1910) and his works on Mullā Ṣadrā; see also the well-known early opus of M. Iqbal, *The Development of Metaphysics in Persia* (London: Luzac, 1908). But these works remained incomplete and often contained blatant errors. It was only after the Second World War that, thanks to the pioneering work of H. Corbin followed by others such as S. H. Nasr and T. Izutsu, later Islamic philosophy became gradually known in the West—although even to this day the error of limiting Islamic philosophy to its first phase of development up to Ibn Rushd continues in many quarters. Concerning Corbin and his significance as a scholar of Islamic thought, see *Mélanges offerts à Henry Corbin,* ed. S. H. Nasr (Tehran: Imperial Iranian Academy of Philosophy and Tehran University, 1977); and *L'Herne–Henry Corbin* (Paris: Edition de l'Herne, 1981). See also H. Corbin, *En Islam iranien* (4 vols.; Paris: Gallimard, 1971–72); idem (with S. H. Nasr and O. Yahya), *Histoire de la philosophie islamique;* S. H. Nasr, *Three Muslim Sages* (Delmar, NY: Caravan Books, 1975) and several essays on later Islamic philosophy in *A History of Muslim Philosophy,* ed. M. M. Sharif. T. Izutsu has devoted a number of important studies to Sabziwārī and Mīrzā Mahdī Āshtiyānī; see, e.g., *The Metaphysics of Sabzavari* (Delmar, NY: Caravan Books, 1977). M. Fakhry in his *A History of Islamic Philosophy* (New York: Columbia University Press, 1983) devoted a few pages to later Islamic philosophy, but most of the work follows earlier models of Western scholarship on Islamic philosophy.

It is of some interest to note that a major work in Spanish by M. Cruz Hernández (*Historia del pensamiento en el mundo islámico* [2 vols.; Madrid: Alianza Editorial, 1981]) gives serious consideration to later Islamic philosophy, and Corbin's *Histoire de la philosophie islamique,* which has been translated into most of the important European languages, does not as yet have an English translation.

19. The term *philosophie prophétique* was used quite correctly by Corbin to describe Islamic philosophy, which functions in a universe dominated by the presence of a revealed book that is not only the source of religious law and ethics but also the fountainhead of knowledge and a means of access to the truth.

20. See Nasr, *Three Muslim Sages,* chap. 1.

21. Translated by R. Walzer in his "Islamic Philosophy," in *The History of Philosophy, Eastern and Western,* ed. S. Radhakrishnan (London: Allen & Unwin, 1953) 2:131.

22. The title "teacher" (*mu'allim*), which was also to be used later by Thomas Aquinas and other scholastics, is not of Greek origin. It is Islamic and refers in this context to the function of defining and classifying the sciences. See S. H. Nasr, "Why was al-Fārābī called the Second Teacher?" trans. M. Amin Razavi, *Islamic Culture* 59/4 (1985) 357–64.

23. Al-Fārābī was particularly interested in the question of the relation of words to their meaning, as seen in his important opus *Kitāb al-ḥurūf* (*The Book of Letters*) (ed. M. Mahdi; Beirut: Dār El-Machreq, 1969). Arabic philosophical vocabulary owes its final crystallization to him more than to anyone else.

24. One of great masters of traditional Islamic philosophy in Persia during this century, Mahdī Ilāhī Qumsha'ī, taught this text with two levels of meaning, one philosophical (*falsafī*) and one gnostic (*'irfānī*). See his *Ḥikmat-i ilāhī khāṣṣ wa 'āmm* (Tehran: Mu'assasa-yi maṭbū'āt-i islāmī, 1345 A.H. solar) 2:1–232.

25. For a description of the climate of Baghdad and the teachings of al-Sijistānī, see J. L. Kramer, *Philosophy in the Renaissance of Islam: Abū Sulaymān Al-Sijistānī and his Circle* (Leiden: Brill, 1986).

26. The term was actually used before Leibnitz by Agostino Steuco, who lived in the sixteenth century. It is interesting to note that Steuco used the term *antiqua* as well as *perennis,* the former corresponding to Suhrawardī's *al-ḥikmat al-'atīqah* or *philosophia antiqua.*

27. There is a vast literature on Ibn Sīnā in Islamic as well as European languages. As far as the spiritual significance of his philosophy is concerned, see H. Corbin, *Avicenna and the Visionary Recital,* trans. W. Trask (Princeton, NJ: Princeton University Press, 1960); S. H. Nasr, *Three Muslim Sages,* I; idem, *An Introduction to Islamic Cosmological Doctrines* (Cambridge, MA: Harvard University Press, 1964; London: Thames & Hudson, 1987) 177ff., which also contains an extensive bibliography of primary and secondary sources concerning him.

28. For the significance of the "Oriental Philosophy" of Ibn Sīnā, see Corbin, *Avicenna,* 271ff.; and Nasr, *Islamic Cosmological Doctrines,* 185–91.

29. It is important to note that this gnostic, often misconstrued in the West as a hedonist, translated the sermon of Ibn Sīnā on Divine Unity (*al-tawḥīd*) from Arabic to Persian.

30. A. M. Goichon, "L'Unité de la pensée avicenienne," *Archives Internationales d'Histoire des Sciences* 20–21 (1952) 290ff.

31. See Nasr, *Islamic Cosmological Doctrines,* 198ff.

32. This scheme is described in the *Shifā'* of Ibn Sīnā. See Avicenne, *La Métaphysique du Shifā',* vol. 2, trans. G. C. Anawati (Paris: J. Vrin, 1985) 137ff. It is summarized in Nasr, *Islamic Cosmological Doctrines,* 202ff.; see also A. Davidson, "Alfarabi and Avicenna on the Active Intellect," *Viator: Medieval and Renaissance Studies* 3 (1972) 134–54.

33. Persian was an important language for this whole philosophical tradition. Even the *Umm al-kitāb* has reached us in an archaic Persian translation rather than Arabic; see *Ummu'l-Kitāb,* ed. and trans. P. Filippani Ronconi (Naples: Istituto Universitario Orientale, 1966).

34. See S. H. Nasr, *Islamic Life and Thought* (Albany: State University of New York Press, 1981) 102ff. ("Hermes and Hermetic Writings in the Islamic World").

35. On Islamic alchemy and its philosophy, see H. Corbin, *L'Alchimie comme art hiératique,* ed. P. Lory (Paris: Edition L'Herne, 1986); P. Lory, *Alchimie et mystique en terre d'Islam* (Paris: Verdier, 1989); P. Kraus, *Jābir ibn Ḥayyān* (Paris: Les Belles Lettres, 1986); Nasr, *Science and Civilization in Islam,* 242–82.

36. See Nasr, *Islamic Cosmological Doctrines,* Part 1; see also I. R. Netton, *Muslim Neoplatonists: An Introduction to the Thought of the Brethren of Purity* (London: Allen & Unwin, 1982).

37. Corbin et al., *Histoire de la philosophie islamique,* 119; see also W. Madelung, "Aspects of Ismāʿīlī Theology: The Prophetic Chain and the God beyond Being," in *Ismāʿīlī Contributions to Islamic Culture,* ed. S. H. Nasr (Tehran: Imperial Iranian Academy of Philosophy, 1977) 51–65.

38. It is important to remember that many important Ismāʿīlī philosophical and theosophical treatises were kept hidden from the public at large and did not become publicly available until recently.

39. See M. Asín Palacios, *Ibn Masarra y su escuela: Origenes de la filosofía hispano-musulmana* (Madrid: Imprenta Ibérica, 1914); translated somewhat imperfectly by E. Douglas and H. Yoder as *The Mystical Philosophy of Ibn Masarra and His Followers* (Leiden: Brill, 1978). On Islamic philosophy in Spain, see M. Cruz Hernández, *Historia del pensamiento en el mundo islámico;* see also T. Burckhardt, *Moorish Culture in Spain,* trans. A. Jaffe (London: Allen & Unwin, 1972) chap. 9, which treats the spiritual significance of Islamic philosophy in Spain.

A number of scholars such as S. M. Stern have criticized and refuted Asín's views concerning "Empedoclean cosmology" without their views altering appreciably the description of the thought of Ibn Masarrah as reconstructed by Asín and others who have followed him.

40. There are numerous works devoted to Ibn Ḥazm, especially in Spanish. See M. Asín Palacios, *El cordobes Aben hazam: Primer historiador de las ideas religiosas* (Madrid: Imprentas de Estanislao Maestre, 1924); idem, *Abenhazam de Cordoba y su historia critica de las ideas religiosas* (6 vols.; Madrid: Ediciones Turner, 1984).

41. See *The Ring of the Dove: A Treatise on the Art of Arab Love,* trans. A. J. Arberry (London: Luzac, 1953).

42. See M. Asín Palacios, *El régimen del solitario* (Madrid and Granada: Imprentas de la Escuela de Estudios Arabes de Granada y Fransisco Roman Camacho, 1946). See also D. M. Dunlop, "Ibn Bājjah's *Tadbīru'l-Mutawaḥḥid (Rule of the Solitary),*" *Journal of the Royal Asiatic Society* 40 (1945) 61–81.

43. This is an interpretation given to the text by many scholars in the West over the centuries. For the latest example of this interpretation, see S. S. Hawi, *Islamic Naturalism and Mysticism, a Philosophic Study of Ibn Tufayl's Hayy bin Yaqzān* (Leiden: Brill, 1974). See also Ibn Ṭufayl, *Ḥayy ibn Yaqẓān,* trans. L. E. Goodman (Los Angeles: University of California Press, 1983).

44. In his *Averroès et l'averroisme* (Paris: Michel Levy Frères, 1861), Renan makes of Averroes a "freethinker" opposed to the submission of reason to faith and the ancestor of modern rationalism and skepticism. There is an extensive European literature on

Averroes; see, e.g., O. Leeman, *Averroes and His Philosophy* (London: Oxford University Press, 1988).

45. The Latin translations followed Hebrew ones and go back to the seventh/thirteenth century and the efforts of Michael Scot. The Latin texts of Averroes's commentaries on Aristotle are being published by the Mediaeval Academy of America in the series *Corpus philosophorum medii aevi corpus commentariorum Averrois in Aristotelem.*

46. See G. Hourani, *Averroes, On the Harmony of Religion and Philosophy* (London: Luzac, 1961). This is the translation of the *Faṣl al-maqāl,* Ibn Rushd's most important treatise on the relation between philosophy and religion.

47. See S. van den Bergh, *Averroes' Tahāfut al-tahāfut ("The Incoherence of the Incoherence")* (2 vols.; Oxford: Oxford University Press, 1954).

48. This seems most unlikely, because Ibn Sab'īn was a pious Muslim who followed the *Sharī'ah,* which forbids suicide. All of these views are discussed by A. al-Taftazānī in his *Ibn Sab'īn wa falsafatuhu'l-ṣūfiyyah* (Beirut: Dār al-Kutub al-Lubnānī, 1973). This is by far the most thorough and detailed study of Ibn Sab'īn, who has not been studied extensively in the West. For references in Western languages, see Corbin et al., *Histoire de la philosophie islamique,* 2:366–68; Cruz Hernández, *Historia,* 2:249–57.

49. See chap. 23 in this volume, "The Hidden Sciences in Islam," by Jean Canteins.

50. This is one of the few works of Ibn Sab'īn to have been studied and translated into a Western language. See E. Lator, "Ibn Sab'īn de Murcia y su 'Budd al-'Ārif,'" *Revista al-Andalus* 9/2 (1944) 371–417.

51. Cruz Hernández refers to the school represented by Ibn Sab'īn as "*gnosofia*" (*Historia,* 2:249). This school, sometimes referred to as the Sab'iyyah, was represented after Ibn Sab'īn by the great Sufi poet al-Shūstarī, who was a student of Ibn Sab'īn.

52. This village in the Zagros mountains south of Zanjan is also the original home of the Suhrawardī family of Sufis, to whom Shaykh al-ishrāq was not, however, related.

53. On Suhrawardī, his life, and works, see Corbin, *En Islam iranien,* vol. 2; Nasr, *Three Muslim Sages,* chap. 2; idem, "Suhrawardi," in *A History of Muslim Philosophy,* ed. M. M. Sharif, 2:372–98; Corbin, *Histoire de la philosophie islamique,* 284ff.

54. See Suhrawardī, *Le Livre de la sagesse orientale,* trans. H. Corbin; ed. C. Jambet (Paris: Verdier, 1986).

55. The beautiful recitals of Suhrawardī have been translated into elegant French by H. Corbin as *L'Archange empourprée* (Paris: Fayard, 1976); they have also been translated much less successfully into English by W. Thackston as *The Mystical and Visionary Treatises of Suhrawardi* (London: Octagon Press, 1982).

56. See Suhrawardī, *Opera Metaphysica et Mystica,* vol. 1, ed. H. Corbin (Tehran and Paris: A. Maisonneuve, 1976) 503; see also G. Dayyānī, *Shu'ā'-i andīshah wa shuhūd-i falsafa-yi Suhrawardī* (Tehran: Intishārāt-i ḥikmat, 1364 A.H. solar).

57. See S. H. Nasr, "Quṭb al-Dīn Shīrāzī," in *Dictionary of Scientific Biography,* ed. C. Gillespie (New York: Charles Scribner's Sons, 1976) 247–53.

58. For an explanation of the complex angelology of Suhrawardī, which is discussed in many of his works, especially the *Ḥikmat al-ishrāq,* see Corbin, *Les Motifs zoroastriens dans la philosophie de Sohrawardî,* vol. 3 (Tehran: Société d'Iranologie, 1946); see also Nasr, "Suhrawardi," in *A History of Muslim Philosophy,* ed. M. M. Sharif, 2:383–91.

59. All of his extant works have been critically edited and published by M. Minovi and Y. Mahdavi in the *Muṣannafāt* (2 vols.; Tehran: Tehran University Press, 1952–58). On this remarkable figure, see S. H. Nasr, "Afḍal al-Dīn Kāshānī and the Philosophical World of Khwājah Naṣīr al-Dīn Ṭūsī," in *Islamic Theology and Philosophy: Studies in Honor of George F. Hourani,* ed. M. E. Marmura (Albany: State University of New

York Press, 1983) 249–64; and W. Chittick, "Bābā Afżal al-Dīn Kāšānī, *Encyclopedia Iranica,* 3:285–91.

60. See chap. 3 in this volume, "Ibn 'Arabī and His School," by W. C. Chittick.

61. See H. Corbin, "La confession extatique de Mîr Dâmâd," in *Mélanges Massignon* (Damascus: Institut français de Damas, 1956) 1:331ff.; Corbin, *En Islam iranien,* 4:9–53; also S. H. Nasr, "The School of Isfahan," in *The History of Muslim Philosophy,* ed. M. M. Sharif, 2:904–32. For a general survey of philosophy and theology during the Safavid period, see S. H. Nasr, "Spiritual Movements, Philosophy and Theology in the Safavid Period," in *The Cambridge History of Iran,* vol. 1, ed. P. Jackson and L. Lockhart (Cambridge: University Press, 1986) 656–97.

62. On 'Āmilī and Mīr Findiriskī, see Nasr, "The School of Isfahan," in *The History of Muslim Philosophy,* ed. M. M. Sharif, 2:909–14, 922–26; also Nasr, "Mīr Findiriskī," in the new *Encyclopedia of Islam.*

63. By Dārā Shukūh (Shikoh), to which reference was made in chap. 19 of this volume. See D. Shayegan, *Hindouisme et soufisme* (Paris: La Différence, 1979).

64. During the last few decades, Mullā Ṣadrā has finally become known in the West, and there are a few works in European languages that analyze many aspects of his thought, although much still needs to be done in this field. See M. Horten, *Das philosophische System von Schirázi (1640†)* Strassburg: K. J. Trübner, 1913); H. Corbin, *En Islam iranien,* 4:54–122; Corbin's French introduction to Mullā Ṣadrā's *Le Livre des pénétrations métaphysiques* (Paris: Verdier, 1988); S. H. Nasr, *The Transcendent Theosophy of Sadr al-Din Shirazi* (Tehran: Imperial Iranian Academy of Philosophy, 1978); idem, "Ṣadr al-Dīn Shīrāzi," in *A History of Muslim Philosophy,* ed. M. M. Sharif, 2:932–61; and F. Rahman, *The Philosophy of Mulla Sadra* (Albany: State University of New York Press, 1976), which gives a somewhat overrationalistic interpretation of Mullā Ṣadrā. Only one of Mullā Ṣadrā's works is available in English: *Wisdom of the Throne,* trans. J. Morris (Princeton, NJ: Princeton University Press, 1981). There is an extensive literature on him written mostly in Persian; see the introduction of S. H. Nasr to Mullā Ṣadrā's *Si aṣl* (Tehran: Tehran University Press, 1961).

65. Although the synthesis achieved by Mullā Ṣadrā was carried out within the Shī'ite universe of Safavid Persia, his philosophy cannot be confined only to the Shī'ite world. Many of his followers in India were Sunni, and his *Asfār* was translated into Urdu not by a Shī'ite but by a Sunni Indian scholar.

66. On *wujūd* and *māhiyyah* in Islamic philosophy and the question of principiality (*aṣālah*), see S. H. Nasr, "*Wujūd* and *māhiyyah* in Islamic Philosophy," *International Philosophical Quarterly* 29 (1989) 409–28; also T. Izutsu, *The Fundamental Structure of Sabzawari's Metaphysics* (Tehran: McGill University Institute of Islamic Studies, Tehran Branch, 1968).

67. To prevent any confusion with the current, popular meaning of this term, and following Corbin, perhaps one should refer to it as the "imaginal world" or the *mundus imaginalis.*

68. See H. Corbin, *Creative Imagination in the Ṣūfism of Ibn 'Arabī* (Princeton, NJ: Princeton University Press, 1969); and the major study of Ibn 'Arabī's metaphysics by W. Chittick, *The Sufi Path of Knowledge* (Albany: State University of New York Press, 1989). See also chap. 3 in this volume.

69. These are discussed in the previous volume in this series; see W. C. Chittick, "Eschatology," in *Islamic Spirituality: Foundations,* 378–409.

70. The extensive philosophical activity of the period stretching from Mīr Dāmād and Mullā Ṣadrā on can be gauged in part by the vast anthology of the philosophy of this era planned and prepared by H. Corbin and S. J. Āshtiyānī in seven volumes, of

which only four appeared, the project having come to a standstill after Corbin's death. See *Anthologie de la philosophie iranienne* (4 vols.; Paris and Tehran: A. Maisonneuve, 1972–78); see also Corbin, *La Philosophie iranienne islamique aux XVII et XVIII siècles* (Paris: Buchet/Chastel, 1981), which contains Corbin's French prolegomena to the Arabic and Persian volumes. The four existing volumes, which cover the time span up to the Qajar period, bear witness to the remarkable philosophical activity during a period when, according to the Western historiography of Islamic philosophy, philosophical activity was supposed to have come to an end in the Islamic world.

71. It is of interest to note that both Lāhījī and Fayḍ Kāshānī were also fine poets and composed *dīwāns* replete with metaphysical poetry.

72. See H. Corbin, *En Islam iranien,* 4:72ff.

73. It is mostly thanks to the efforts of S. J. Āshtiyānī that the history of the transmission of the teachings of Mullā Ṣadrā has come to be known. See his Persian introduction to *Sharḥ risālat al-mashā'ir* of Mullā Ṣadrā by Mullā Muḥammad Ja'far Lāhījānī (Mashhad: Mashhad University Press, 1964) 37ff.

74. On this period, see Corbin, *Histoire de la philosophie islamique,* 476ff.

75. On Sabziwārī, see S. H. Nasr, "Sabziwāri," in *A History of Muslim Philosophy,* ed. M. M. Sharif, 2:1543–56; and M. Mohaghegh and T. Izutsu, *The Metaphysics of Sabzavari* (Delmar, NY: Caravan Books, 1977). See also the introduction of S. J. Āshiyānī to his edition of Sabziwārī, *Rasā'il* (Mashhad: Mashhad University Press, 1970) and the English preface of S. H. Nasr.

76. On Ṭabāṭabā'ī, see the introduction of S. H. Nasr to Ṭabāṭabā'ī's *Shi'ite Islam* (Albany: State University of New York Press, 1975). On Islamic philosophy in Persia during this century, see the Persian introduction of S. J. Āshtiyānī to Mullā Ṣadrā, *al-Shawāhid al-rubūbiyyah* (Mashhad: Mashhad University Press, 1967) 124–44; and S. H. Nasr, *Islamic Philosophy in Contemporary Persia: A Survey of Activity during the Past Two Decades* (Salt Lake City: Middle East Center, University of Utah, 1972).

77. Among these well-known contemporary philosophers, Muṭahharī was given more to social thought than the others, although he did also write on logic and metaphysics. Several of his works have been rendered into English during the past few years. See, e.g., his *Fundamentals of Islamic Thought,* trans. R. Campbell (Berkeley: Mizan Press, 1985). Āshtiyānī has devoted a lifetime to editing and commenting on classical texts of later Islamic philosophy and gnosis, although he has also written independent works on these subjects. Ḥā'irī alone among the class of originally traditionally trained philosophers also knows Western philosophy well and has spent years in Western universities studying and even teaching both Islamic and Western philosophy and has written a number of major works on Islamic philosophy in confrontation with and in relation to Western philosophy. One of these works, *Epistemology in Islamic Philosophy,* has been translated into English and is to be published soon.

78. See Corbin, "The Force of Traditional Philosophy in Iran Today," *Studies in Comparative Religion* 2 (Winter 1968) 12–26.

79. Like 'Allāmah Ṭabāṭabā'ī, he sought to provide an Islamic response to the challenges of Western philosophy; see his *Our Philosophy,* trans. S. Inati, with preface by S. H. Nasr (London: Muhammadi Trust, 1987).

23

The Hidden Sciences in Islam

JEAN CANTEINS

WE PROPOSE, IN THIS CHAPTER, to bring to light the spiritual significance of the "hidden sciences," but not to delve into these sciences, for that would not be possible in the space allotted. These sciences are represented in most traditions under the names alchemy, astrology, etc., and some authors, such as P. Ruska and J. Kraus, have made known the essentials of the Islamic domain in such a way that it is not at all a *terra incognita.* The Islamic specificity of these sciences does not differentiate them a great deal from their Occidental or Far Eastern equivalents. The terminology is not an obstacle inasmuch as one makes use of the Greek, which the Arabic copies to a large extent in this domain.

By "hidden sciences" (*al-'ulūm al-khafiyyah*) must be understood diverse traditional sciences that for reasons intrinsic (esoteric sciences taught by means of the oral tradition) or extrinsic (sciences that modernism has relegated to the rank of out-of-date disciplines and has placed in obsolescence, with the result that what one can know of them—especially of the texts that are incomprehensible for want of the necessary deciphering or because of ignorant scribes—is presented as a degraded residue and in many cases as practically unusable) do not figure in the programs of universities and are not made the subjects of official instruction.

That is not to say, however, that these sciences do not make up or no longer make up part of the patrimony of Islam. The magisterial transmission has not entirely ceased, even though today it resembles a clandestine teaching nourishing a subterranean current that is difficult to discern. It must be remembered that Sufism no longer has an official status in a number of Muslim countries; although it is not overtly prohibited, it has only an officious character in those lands. The Sufi milieus have been the conservatories of an authentic tradition of certain of these sciences, and although this tradition is no longer integral, it is not fossilized. This presence and perennity relative to the interiority and to the protective shelter of Sufism are explained by the congruence of finalities, but pertain as well without doubt to the fact that these sciences offer the appropriate means of expressing esoteric truths—and whoever says esoterism says "polysemy"—which modern sciences, with their unequivocal stance, are lacking. Indeed, Sufism has an elaborate terminology that is sufficient in itself, but the act of signifying is a demanding process. One must understand that the Sufi authors—and not the least of them—had utilized the resources of these sciences in order to expose certain views with the desired precision, tonality, or suggestive profundity. We think here most particularly of the science of letters (*al-jafr*). This sacred science—characteristic of the Semitic world—is considered to be the key to all the other sciences, and for this reason we give it preference.

In Islam as elsewhere, these sciences, inasmuch as they are manifestations of suprarational thought, appear to be experiencing a rebirth of interest in them. It is deplorable that the literature to which they give rise resorts too often to occultism, but what is important, and is to be stressed, is the significance of the "return swing of the pendulum" which this rebirth marks. Taking into account the extreme richness of the Arab and Persian patrimony in these matters, it is not utopian to look for the flourishing of these forms of "analogous thought," which are, in the final analysis, the sciences called "hidden." Every "analogist" will rejoice in this.

The Science of Letters

The science of letters, which rests on a sacred language, has necessarily a metaphysical foundation. This consists in comparing the universe to a book in which the letters are "Immutable Essences." From these Divine Essences or Ideas results the Book of the World, which is compared to the Logos. This Book is still called the "cosmogonic Quran" (*al-qur'ān al-takwīnī*), as opposed to the Quran *composed* of a collection of revealed verses (*al-qur'ān al-tadwīnī*). This "genesis" of the cosmos takes as its basis the celebrated *ḥadīth* "I was a Hidden Treasure [*kanz*, a word with the same initial letter as *kun*, "Be!", the creative command, as Ibn 'Arabī remarked] and I desired to be known; therefore, I created the world." This "Hidden Treasure" corresponds, in the process under consideration and in conformity with scriptural symbolism, to the formless and primordial point prior to the emanation, properly speaking, of the letters of the alphabet.[1] Limiting oneself to the Islamic domain (because one encounters parallel formulations in Philo of Alexandria, the gnostic Marcos, and many others), one finds this doctrine mentioned in the celebrated mystical poem the *Gulshan-i rāz* (*The Rose Garden of Divine Mysteries*) of Shabistarī. "For the one whose soul is the place of theophany, the whole of the universe is the Book of God Most High. The accidents are His vowels and the substance His consonants" (verses 200–209). Paraphrasing the Ikhwān al-Safā', Y. Marquet was able to write in a more elaborate manner:

> The Universe is the Book written by the Pen . . . on the Tablet . . . or, if one wishes, they are the Forms which by virtue of Divine Will the Universal Intellect furnishes to the Universal Soul. The lines bursting forth from this Book preserve its content: "It is through them that the emanation of their powers will be made" on that which is above (the celestial sphere). In fact, beginning with these lines and emanating from them, the simple and luminous spiritual "things" will be formed which will be found in the echelons subordinate to the Universal Soul. Then each of these lines will be established at a rank from which it will not depart; they will remain ordered in their respective places like those of a real book. . . .[2]

The best summation, however, is given us by Ibn 'Arabī in terms that will allow us to dispense with other quotations:

> The Universe is a vast book; the characters of this book are all written, in principle, with the same ink and transcribed on to the eternal Table by the Divine Pen; all are transcribed simultaneously and inseparably; for that reason the essential phenomena hidden in the "Secret of Secrets" were given the name of "transcendent letters." And these transcendent letters, that is to say, all creatures, after having been virtually condensed in the Divine Omniscience, were carried down on the Divine Breath to the lower lines and composed and formed the manifested Universe."[3]

The science of letters rests on an esoteric usage and interpretation of letters of the Arabic alphabet considered triply as ideophonic (preponderance of sonoral symbolism), ideographic (preponderance of graphic or "hieroglyphic" symbolism), and arithmologic (each letter having a numerical value in such a way that the science of letters does not go without a science of numbers).[4]

Abū Isḥāq Qūhistānī has characterized the importance of the science of letters by saying that it is the "root of all the other sciences."[5] One could say schematically that the science of letters involves the following: (1) divine and metaphysical or metacosmic symbolism; (2) universal or macrocosmic symbolism by virtue of correspondences between letters and "astrological" givens (celestial spheres, planets, zodiacal signs, lunar mansions, etc.), on the one hand, and "physical" givens (elements, "natures," etc.), on the other; (3) human and individual or microcosmic symbolism by virtue of physiological correspondences (organs of the body, "temperaments," etc.), from which comes its correlation with chirognomy etc.

Its particular status has been defined well by Tirmidhī:

> All the sciences are contained in the letters of the alphabet, for the beginning of science is indeed the Divine Names from which come forth the creation and governance of the world. . . . Now the Divine Names themselves precede the letters and return to the letters. This hidden treasure of science is known to the saints alone whose intelligences receive understanding from God and whose hearts are attached to God and are ravished by His Divinity, there where the veil is lifted before the letters and the attributes. . . .[6]

Like "knowledge of the virtues of numbers and names," the science of letters is designated by the term *sīmiyā'*, but the "magical" or divinatory applications by which *sīmiyā'* is most known have caused them to be discredited—with good reason. We will not treat them here, except by this brief allusion. These applications are for the most part in a degenerate state, as seen in the "art of talismans" (amulets, pentangles, magic squares), geomancy (*'ilm al-raml*), and the mysterious and scholarly onomatomancy (*zā'irajah*). Ibn Khaldūn himself speaks of this subject in a fashion so confusing that it is necessary to renounce it despite the efforts of V. Monteil (*Muqaddimah,* III) to penetrate its mysteries. In order summarily to situate it, one may say that it probably inspired the Art of Combination of Ramon Lull.[7]

The Arabic term *sīmiyā'* is derived from the Greek *sēmeion,* "sign." Insofar as it is a "science of signs," the science of letters is capable of intermixing with semiological sciences—although the ends and the means differ radically. It is remarkable in this respect that the science of letters—without awaiting de Saussure and the others—recognized in the alphabet, beyond the linguistic instrument which it obviously is, another system of codes with an incomparable plasticity in the resources of indefinite combinations. One can apply to it in all appropriateness the term "metalanguage," as employed in its discipline by modern authors.

The science of letters intends in effect to go beyond the purely "phenomenal" understanding of things by attaching itself to the "noumenal" content. In other words, it intends to uncover behind the contingent fact, the corresponding archetype, and this is an additional reason for according it a privileged position.

Furthermore, the search for the archetype and symbolic transparency goes through a structural understanding. These relations to certain currents of contemporary thought are mentioned here in order to suggest modern "readings" of this ancient science of letters and to show that those considered it to be out-of-date were anxious gravediggers and for the most part gave proof only of their prejudice and profane spirit—not to mention a lack of culture.

When one speaks of the science of letters in Arabic (and the same is true for Hebrew), one generally has in mind only the consonants, the only letters which these languages include in their alphabets. The vowels are considered to be accessory sonoral modalities, "stamps" that have as their object the "coloring" of the consonants with a fixed sonority. The consequence of this is that in the Arabic context—contrary to that which occurs, for example, in the Greek context, where the seven vowels play a preponderant role—the science of letters has, with rare exceptions, neglected vowels.

In order to understand this attitude, it is helpful to specify that for the Semite in general the consonant-vowel relationship reflects the relationship between the Essence and the attributes (*dhāt/ṣifāt*). The consonant (*ḥarf*, pl. *ḥurūf*, from which comes the phrase *'ilm al-ḥurūf* to designate this science) is to the vowel (*ḥarakah*, "motion") what "substance" (*jawhar*) is to "accident" (*'araḍ*). In terms of metalinguistics, the sum total of the consonants represents sound as such, taken in its invariable multiplicity in conformity with the diffraction of the Word from which a particular language arose. Vowels represent only accessory "modifications" or "alterations" proper to the syntax (declensions, conjugations, etc.) of this language. Thus considered, the consonant is a pure given (Niffarī goes so far as to make of it a hypostatic entity); the vowel a practical given.

Far from wishing to take a stance opposed to that of tradition, but because vowels are open to an interesting interpretation, we begin with the vowels. In Arabic there are three "vocalizations": *a*, *u*, and *i*, called respectively *fatḥah*, *ḍammah*, and *kasrah*. They are noted (optionally) by conventional signs of very summary orthography: primitively by a dot, like the Hebrew vowel points, placed either above (*a*), at the same level (*u*), or below (*i*) the consonant to be vocalized. Later on, they were denoted with the signs in use today: an oblique stroke above the consonant (*a*), a comma also above (*u*), and an oblique stroke below (*i*).

On the last syllable of words, vocalization has an "inflecting" function, the cases and moods being determined by the "timbre" of this syllable. This has led to the use of the same name for inflection and vowel: the vocalization *u* (nominative and indicative) is called "raised" or ascendant; the vocalization *i* (indirect case) is called "lowered" or descendant; and, between the two, the vocalization *a* (direct and subjunctive cases) is called "planed" or intermediate. The position of the vocalic signs, nouns and qualifiers (to which it would be necessary to add the locations of articulation: *a* [the throat], *i* [the palate], and *u* [the lips]) thus defines three cohesive tendencies which "qualify" the consonantic entity in a manner analogous to the three *guṇas* of the Hindu tradition.

This structuring of being (the whole of the alphabetic corpus insofar as it is a symbol of the whole of Reality) is still more evident with *alif, wāw,* and *yā'*, which, although consonants, act also as *matres lectionis*—that is, they serve to render the three corresponding long vowels *ā, ū,* and *ī.* In this function they have a hybrid status—neither vowel nor consonant, a fact that has brought about the exegesis of grammarians. They say that the *a* with *alif* is characterized by "sublimation," the *i* with *yā'* by "precipitation," and the *u* with *wāw* by the intermediary state. Sublimation and precipitation come under the classification of alchemical terminology; as for the intermediate state, *i'tirāḍ,*[8] it implies a completely different context. *I'tirāḍ* connotes the word *'arḍ* ("width"), which in its Sufi sense means "amplitude," that is, all amplification in the horizontal dimension of a given "state of being" taken as the point of reference or "horizon." The dimension of "amplitude" induces the complementary dimension of "exaltation," polarized in the vertical according to the two inverse meanings of "height" (for *a*) and of "depth" (for *i*). This structural trinity expresses a diversification. Diversification can be of a metaphysical order: it concerns "movements or orientations of the Spirit": descending movement by the (apparent) distance from the Principle, which measures the depth of the possible horizontal movement, of which the amplitude measures the expansion, and, finally, ascending movement of "return" toward the Principle or height. It can be of an ontological order, as in the reference mentioned above. It can also be of a ritual order, and from there derives a Sufi perspective.

The exegesis of the three basic postures of prayer assumes a truly initiative coloring. In the *Fuṣūṣ al-ḥikam* (*Bezels of Wisdom*), Ibn 'Arabī explains them from two points of view. Existentially, prayer includes three movements: an ascending movement, corresponding to the standing position of the supplicant; a horizontal movement, corresponding to the inclined position; and a descending movement, corresponding to the prostrate position. Principially (in this case, Ibn 'Arabī says, it concerns the prayer that God "prays upon us"), the three movements concern the "creative movements" (Ibn 'Arabī employs the expression "existentiating theophanies") of God to know: the "intentional" (descending) movement toward the world here below in order to manifest it, the (ascending) movement toward the upper world, and the horizontal movement. Thus the master of Islamic theosophy presents the gripping idea of a symmetry between divine service (*'ibādah*) and the creation of the world (*ibdā'*), the attitudes of the supplicant imitating in an individual mode the "gestures" which God the Creator accomplished in a universal mode.

More simply, Ismā'īl Ḥaqqī, Ibn 'Arabī's Ottoman commentator, breaks down the prayers by considering the orthographic symbolism not only of the three *matres lectionis* but of the ternary *alif, lām, mīm,* one of the set of initial letters figuring at the head of several *sūrahs* of the Quran of which we will speak later. Such a view ended by becoming in some way a common ground, since it was equally enunciated with regard to the three letters comprising the Name Allah: *alif, lām, hā,* upon which Ismāʿīlī gnosis did not hesitate to graft an exegesis for which the key is given by the structure of the cross. We will content ourselves by mentioning the existence of such an exceptional—indeed, even paradoxical—correspondence in Islam by reason of the proscription of this symbol by Muslim exoterism. We cannot treat here the facts contained in a highly questionable work in which R. von Sebottendorf has exposed a so-called method of spiritual realization which he supposedly learned of in Turkey at the beginning of this century. It concerns pseudo-alchemical lucubrations, which we mention here only in view of a possible correspondence between the ternary *a–i–u* and the ternary Mercury–Sulfur–Salt.

In conclusion we note the eminent structural properties of vowels. We have presented Arabic vocalization as a trinity, and in doing so we have passed over in silence a fourth modality: the absence of "motion." This state is marked by the *sukūn,* the sign of "rest" or of "quiescence" of the consonant. This fourth modality—which is phonetically conceivable only in relation to the three others for which it is, so to speak, the "empty" counterpart—is systematically neglected by the symbolic. But it does have a place in a quadripartite vision of things. To keep to the symbolism of the prayers, we emphasize that the *sukūn* takes into account an attitude that was not considered: the seated position, at once a time of "pause" or of immobility between two movements and a synthesis of the three other attitudes of the supplicant. Furthermore, the coming to the fore of a vocalic "fourth term" orients the exegesis toward quaternary correspondences (elements, "natures," directions, etc.). An example of this is the application presented by the appendix of the *Kitāb al-tadhkirah* (*The Book of Memorial*) of Dā'ūd al-Anṭākī, in which the twenty-eight letters of the Arabic alphabet are differentiated into four series of seven letters according to the double criterion of "timbre" and "nature": *a*=warm, *sukūn*=cold, *u*=dry, and *i*=humid. Being aware of the esoteric preoccupations of Anṭākī and of the disciple who was the author of the appendix, one is able to foresee the speculations, particularly alchemical ones, of which such a cleavage is capable.

The Letters of the Alphabet

The letters of the alphabet, the essential signs and providential instruments of the Sacred Science, are twenty-eight in number. The number twenty-eight, congruent with four and seven (28 = 4 x 7, and 28 is the "Pythagorean sum" of 7), immediately suggests a relation with the lunar mansions. There result from it diverse cross-references of a cosmological order, to which we will make allusion later on. The connection between the number of letters and the lunar mansions is sufficiently remarkable that it is emphasized and exploited. Thus Tirmidhī (*Khatm al-awliyā'*, question 142) states that the number of letters was primordially set at twenty-eight owing to the number of lunar mansions. Ibn 'Arabī was to make this point more explicitly by "localizing" in the moon—the intermediary between heaven and earth—the "prophetic" residence of Adam and by specifying that the manifestation *par excellence* of the mediating function of the heavenly body is the differentiation of the *unique* primordial sun (in the manner of Adam as the "*unique* man") in articulated language.

As can be foreseen from its reference to the duration of a lunar cycle, the number twenty-eight, the total of the letters, was considered to be composed of two equal halves of fourteen letters each, based on the model of the waxing and waning phases of the moon, estimated at fourteen days each. There are numerous other divisions made by grammarians as well as by exegetes, but it is not a question of expanding the above. The most remarkable among them is that which divides the alphabet into "luminous" letters and "obscure" letters. In the correspondence to the lunar cycle, it is the invisible mansions of the southern hemisphere that are identified with the fourteen "luminous" letters (namely: *a, ḥ, r, l, q, y, s, ṣ, ṭ, k, m, n,* and *h*) "since their spiritual light corresponds to the hidden light of these mansions." As for the visible mansions of the northern hemisphere, they correspond to the fourteen "obscure" letters, namely, the remaining letters of the alphabet. A long tradition, from Ibn Sīnā to the Ikhwān al-Ṣafā', from Jābir to the Pseudo-Majrīṭī, has echoed this point of view. This is shown by a characteristic passage of the *Ghayāt al-ḥakīm* (*The Goal of the Sage,* known in the Middle Ages under the Latinized title of *Picatrix*):

> If the letters are 28 in number, the reason for this is that this number is a perfect individual made up of a spirit and a body. There are 14 (luminous) letters which are found at the beginning of the *sūrahs* of the Quran. They represent the spirit and just as the spirit is hidden, so the secret of these letters is hidden as well. It is at the same time the number of the invisible stations of the moon. On the other hand, the other letters (called obscure) which never figure at the beginning of the *sūrahs* represent the body and correspond to the visible stations of the moon. . . . There is the mystery of the Quran.[9]

The luminous letters are found at the beginning of twenty-nine *sūrahs* of the Quran, isolated or in a group as initial letters (their number varying from one to five). Scholars of Arabic and orientalists have been wondering for centuries about the presence and role of these initial letters without reaching the least consensus concerning them. By all appearances verse III,7, dealing with passages of the Quran having more than one meaning (*mutashābihāt*), applies to these letters: "And no one *knows the interpretation* [of these passages] *except God and those rooted in Science.*" Such is the "reading" made by the Sufis of this verse by extending to "*those rooted in Science*" the capacity of understanding and interpretation of the stated passages. As Tirmidhī wrote: "In the *Fawātiḥ* of the suras, there is an allusion to the meaning of the sura, known only to the Sages of God on His earth . . . men whose hearts have reached His essential solitude from which they have received this knowledge, that of the consonants of the alphabet."[10] Although dealing with such a subject is a delicate matter, we risk doing so with the hope not of giving an exhaustive explanation of it—such a thing is humanly impossible—but of suggesting an appropriate approach to the subject.

The initial letters are a theophany of the Uncreated in the created. The Quran, the scriptural manifestation of the uncreated Divine Word, belongs as the Book to the created order. The uncreated Word is not able to be expressed without recourse to the created letter. The letter is not the Word but its reflection. The Revelation is a superhuman effort at the transmutation of the Uncreated into the created. In the course of this process, the coagulation of the Word into a spoken and written sacred language—here Arabic—was left in suspense at certain points in the Quran where the divine impact is conserved, so to speak, in a state of the least crystallization, of the least literary hardening.

The initial letters take into account this state of "undifferentiation." They are not vocalized and, since they cannot be articulated, are not given to "recitation." With regard to manifestation, the initial letters are therefore imperfect or incomplete (=*non finis*). They have an apophatic dimension that distinguishes them from the rest of the Book. The Quran can be *recited* in all the verses wherein the Muḥammadan receptacle contained integrally the Divine Message; it can, on the contrary, be only *spelled*—as by someone who does not understand what he is reading—there where the earthly and human receptacle was in some way less sealed off. The Prophet gave a sonoral vestment, clear and comprehensible, to the inaudible Word of God except in the initial letters where the Word remained relatively "naked" and was received as so many broken peals of the primordial Sound.

The initial letters are the part of the Book that has kept something of the celestial state in which was found the Revelation before its descent into Muḥammad. It is that to which the tradition refers when it emphasizes that the initial letters concern the Divine Science transmitted directly to Muḥammad in a time span (so brief) during which no archangel was able to serve as intermediary or interpreter between God and the Prophet. On this subject it is reported that when Gabriel *descended* with *khy*'*ṣ* (the initial letters of the nineteenth *sūrah*), to each letter that he enumerated, the Prophet added, "I know." Finally Gabriel exclaimed, saying, "How dost thou know something which I myself do not know?"

If one considers them more specifically in the framework of the mystery of the Revelation, the initial letters are the mediating boundary between the Divine Word and the Quran as the Book for the believers. They are an intermediary stage accidentally or providentially (according to the appreciation of the above-mentioned mystery) interposed between the Principle (God, the Divine Name, etc.) and the manifestation: that is, this same Divine Name developed, differentiated in conformity with the economy of the Message revealed to men and in the form of the Book—from whence comes the name *sūrah* (literally, "order," "ordered"), therefore, a group of *ordered* "sayings."

Letters of the Alphabet and Human Hands

Considered as the filigree of the alphabet, the numbers 28 and 14 are the symbolic values of the whole and of the half. We have just seen how the Quranic initial letters concern one half—implicitly preeminent—of the alphabet. From these speculations one can extract a highly affirmed dichotomy between the two halves (of the letters) concerned. This tendency is particularly aided and shaped by chirognomy. It can be observed that each hand, made up of five fingers, includes fourteen phalanxes (the name of the hand, *yad,* equals 14); the two hands therefore total twenty-eight phalanxes, being as letters of the alphabet in such a manner that one can imagine them to be distributed as if they were in the "crucible" of the printer.

The distribution between the two hands would consequently have to divide the alphabet into letters of the right hand and letters of the left hand. Where this distribution would lead can easily be conceived from the fact that there is a difference of value attached from time immemorial to the right (of good augur) and to the left (of bad augur).[11] Without going so far as do some rather Manichaean interpretations, let us note that the preceding distinction between luminous and obscure letters is congruent with that of the letters of the right hand and the left hand. The right and the left correspond respectively to the south and the north and are applied consequently to the southern and northern hemispheres of the lunar mansions.

From the point of view of chirognomy, the left hand points to "nature," the sum total of the traits that define what is innate. It is related to the *passive* aspect as well as to the *past.* It is the part of predestination. The right hand points to what is acquired, the total of the modifications brought to heredity. What is acquired, in permanent becoming, comes to complete and correct the givens of the left hand, relatively immutable. The right hand is related to the active aspect; it is the hand of the future.

The remarkable numerical coincidence between the phalanxes and the letters potentializes the presence of Divine Names in the articulations of the two hands. The initiatic symbolism of the "union of the hands," at the time of the linking of the disciple to the spiritual master, confirms this idea of the theophoric hand. In brief, all this occurs as if the "union of the hands" had as its aim to awaken the sacred letters of the Name from sleep in the articulations and *to articulate* them (we stress the coincidence which the vocabulary notes between the act of elocution and the movement of the fingers) in the hand, albeit in a nonsonoral manner—therefore in a solely potential fashion, which then remains for the disciple to actualize. Since the hands make up the sum total of the letters, the composition of all of the Names is found therein in full force.

The Kabbala has made clear the appropriateness of this by distributing the Name YHVH expanded into twenty-eight letters upon the phalanxes of the *two hands.* If such a disposition is not possible without distortions or expedients with regard to the Name *Allāh,* it is so with the Name *Huwa* expanded into fourteen letters on *one hand,* and this would be done in order to relate it to the mystery according to which, in the union of the hands at the time of the initiatic pact, the two hands which the master places above the hand of the disciple are like "two right hands" (and not one left hand and one right hand in conformity with physiology). The anatomical bipolarization inherent in the profane human state is thus symbolically annulled and transcended. Because of the "union of the hands" (this expression is synonymous with "invocation"), the distribution and therefore the division of the letters between those of the right (hand) and those of the left (hand) become meaningless when the Sacred Name is recomposed.[12]

To this incursion into chirognomy from the angle of the science of letters one could add another facet. It is said that the principal lines of the hand sketch a figure that has the form of the number 18 (١٨) on the right hand and 81 (٨١), the inverse, on the left hand. The total, 99, is the number of the Divine Names—we mean the innumerable essential Divine Qualities leading back to a canonically determined series of soteriological and criteriological Names mentioned in the Quran. To these ninety-nine traditional Names must be added *Allāh,* which makes them one hundred.

This fact brings about the appearance of a new relation between the science of the hand (*ʿilm al-kaff, kaff,* another name for hand = 100) and the science of letters and names, a relation made particularly evident by the fact that the Muslim rosary is made up of 99 + 1 elements concretely: ninety-nine beads plus the hundredth one, which is of a larger size; it is a structure remarkably congruent with that of the Names.

Conjointly with this projection of the twenty-eight letters in terms of the microcosm of the structural properties of the two hands, there exists a representation comparatively macrocosmic–indeed, metacosmic–of these letters on a celestial "sphere" or rather on a group of concentric "spheres" whose hierarchy and arrangement were expounded by Ibn ʿArabī in the order of his "theory" of the "Divine Breath" (*nafas al-Raḥmān*). This cannot be explained in detail here, but it involves different levels of reality *woven* upon the twenty-eight letters of the alphabet.

Schematically one can distinguish a divine level, a suprahuman or universal level, and a human level, represented respectively by the Divine Names, the cosmic degrees, and the twenty-eight letters of the alphabet. The letters are arranged following the order of phonetic emanation such as was established by the grammarian Sībawayh. Ibn ʿArabī contented himself with combining *alif* and *hamzah* to obtain the number 28, necessary to the "economy" of the exposition. The sequence that develops, beginning with the most internalized phonemes, the gutturals, through the most externalized, the labials–that is, from *hāʾ* to *mīm*–is framed by *alif* as the first degree (corresponding to the breaking of silence, to the sonoral eruption of *hamzah*) and by *wāw* as the final degree.

The Breath of the Compassionate and the Letters of the Alphabet

The theory starts with the idea of an expansion (what Ibn ʿArabī calls breadth) from a unique and primordial Reality. In conformity with the sonoral symbolism, from the Divine Breath proceed first of all the Names or Qualities, before even the creation of the world. At their "request," the Breath intervenes determining all of the "cosmic degrees," as a kind of easing or "relaxation" forming emanation into a hierarchy from the manifestation of the First Intellect to the creation of man.

These twenty-eight cosmic degrees are distributed into four quarters of seven. The first quarter, which is principial, extends according to an ascending progression from the vernal equinox to the summer solstice marked by the Throne and the polar letter *qāf*. The two succeeding, or intermediary quarters, extend from the summer solstice to the winter solstice, thus

Illustration A

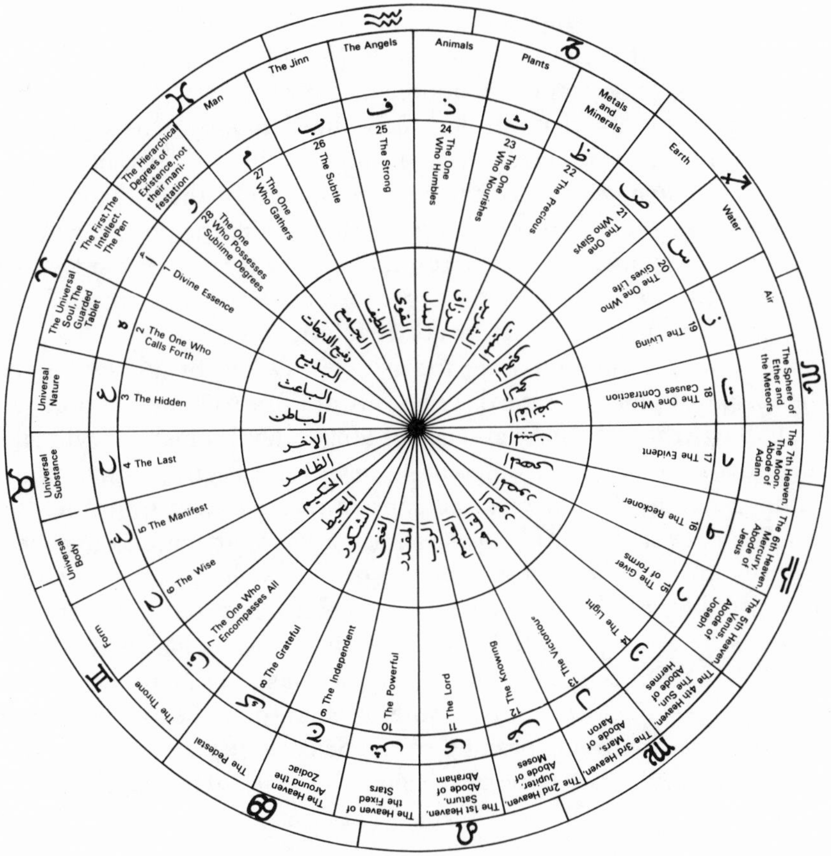

---

following a descending progression. They symbolize the whole of the formal world, which ends with the degree of the earth; they have for a center the sun and the letter *nūn* (the fourteenth letter linking the two halves of the phoneme series) situated at the autumnal equinox. The fourth quarter, once again ascending, ends with man (the letter *mīm*). The final degree (the letter *wāw*) accounts for the possibility of reintegration of all emanation in the initial degree (the letter *alif*).

Reintegration does not mean reunion. The cycle is not closed again exactly upon itself; the end is not rejoined by the beginning. Emanation proceeds in open spirals and not in closed circles. If it did not, parallel cyclical processes such as those of the sun and the moon would come to an end at the same time, with the result that their evolutionary relationship would cease and they would no longer have a *raison d'être*—or, to paraphrase the *sūrah Yā' Sīn*, "nor doth the night outstrip the day" (Quran XXXVI, 39).[13] This unequal superposition of sequences (which makes, for example, each of the "signs" of the Zodiac [*burūj*] to cover seven thirds of the lunar mansion) explains the nonrepetition of the cycles and rhythms, and it is upon this law that astrology is founded and, by extension, all the secondary divinatory sciences. Other examples could be given of this nonrepetition, the *sine qua non* of the continuum and of the diversity of the manifested. Let us cite, for the astronomical domain, the precession of the equinoxes, from which results the current time lag between the signs of the zodiac and the twelve corresponding constellations, the reestablishment taking place at the end of each major revolution.

For a good representation of the theory of the Divine Breath we will refer to the accompanying synoptic diagram (Illustration A), which is borrowed from T. Burckhardt.[14] In the absence of longer development, it will allow a view of the whole of the different "spheres" and degrees in question.

In this diagram, the *alif* must be considered separately from the other letters. We have said that, like *hamzah,* it marks the irruption of sound. It is the principle of sonoral manifestation of which all the other letters are differentiated symbols. It is necessary, therefore, to consider that the sequence of letters begins with *hā'* and ends with *wāw,* bringing out the two letters of the Divine Name *Huwa.* In the Sufi milieu, this Name has as much prestige as the Name *Allāh,* if not more. It is not possible to deal with the science of letters without speaking of the Science of Names. This can be treated only briefly in the present chapter; we will leave aside the esoteric expansions upon the "Supreme Name," *al-ism al-aʿẓam,* to which it ordinarily leads.[15]

Illustration B

The Science of Names

In order to bear in mind certain subtle interferences and structural considerations, we will take as our point of departure the Name *Allāh.* In brief, it can be said that the expanded form of this Name is the (first) *shahādah–lā ilāha illa'Llāh* (there is no divinity but God)–and that the shortened form is *Huwa*–He. The Name *Allāh* is represented in traditional calligraphy in the accompanying illustration. It is a tetragram composed of *alif, lām, lām,* and *hā'*. As a tetragram, it would necessarily be written *Allh.* This could be grating; therefore, the form is *Allāh.* Three letters alone compose it: *alif, lām,* and *hā'*. *Alif* is a vertical line and represents the masculine, active principle (or injunctive, from the point of view of the symbolism of sonoral energy); this meaning is reinforced by the dot above it, of which it is a sort of vertical projection.[16] Its numerical value, 1, is in fact the symbol of Unity. The last letter, *hā'*, which is approximately a circle, represents the feminine, passive principle, and this meaning is reinforced by the crown (in the geometric sense of the term) above it. Between the initial rectitude of *alif* and the final, completely encircled form of *hā'*, the two *lāms* constitute an intermediary stage assuring a sort of written transition.

We have just made allusion to the two signs, the dot and the crown which come above the *alif* and the *hā'*. The most plausible explanation is that the dot recalls a potential *hamzah* systematically left in an unmanifested state from a sonoral as well as a graphic point of view, and that the crown is the stylization of a miniature *hā'* added to indicate that the final *hā'* of the Name is a radical letter forming part of the tetragram and not an accessory letter (such as the indication of the feminine, for example). The dot and the crown are proportioned in such a way that they can interlock one into another and be fitted so precisely that they blend together in forming a single circle. Their coincidence makes clear the coincidence of the extremes, *alif* and *hā'*. This means that the Name *Allāh* cannot but join the essential aspect–the dot–and the substantial aspect–the crown; the two determinations of Being naturally supported by the polar letters *alif* and *hā'*. This coincidence can be considered the result of two inverse processes: the involutive or centripetal process in the case of the conjunction of the dot in the crown converging toward the unique Point (*stricto sensu* a circle, an "aggrandized dot"–if one can be allowed this geometric heresy), which is none other than the Name; and the evolutive or centrifugal process in the case of the separation of the dot from the crown diverging from the primordial Point, which is none other than the Name. They proceed from the Name and end there; the Name is at once their beginning and their end. They develop outside of it and are resolved in it, reciprocally annulling each other in the immutable heart of the Name, the place of the intersection of all the processes located not only outside of time and space but still more outside of all contingency.

The specificity of the *shahādah* appears in the turn of the phrase which Arabic syntax calls *istithnā* ("exception"), denoted by the particle *illā* (=*in lā*, "if it is not") the transcendent content of which is hidden in the internal structure of the formula. In brief, several connections based on reflection (in the optic sense) and symmetry (the "balance," Jābir would say) articulate the *shahādah* and reveal in it the complex interior equilibrium which the traditional distinction takes into account only imperfectly, in an unequivocal manner, in the "negative" clause: *lā ilāha* (the initial *lā*, the particle of negation) and the "positive" clause: *Allāh* (the initial *al*, the definite article and beginning of *Allāh* › *al-ilāh*).[17] The *shahādah* makes it evident that the Name *Allāh*, the symbol of the Universal Being as much as it is an affirmation, contains in an implicit or subjacent manner the symbol of the absolute indetermination of Non-Being (the negative particle buried within the word *al-ilah* decomposed and recomposed in *lā* and *ilāh:*

ilāh

lā

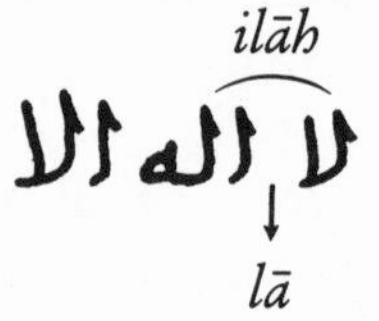

As the Name *Allāh* includes four letters, the *shahādah* includes four words, and these words are composed exclusively of the same letters as the Name: *alif, lām, hā'*. We will note only the connection of the last letter of the Name and the last word of the formula: *Hā'* and *Allāh*. Just as the formula concludes with the Name *Allāh*, the Name concludes in its turn with the letter *hā'* by a kind of common convergence of the formula and the Name toward the same letter. *Hā'* marks a kind of ending; it is identified with exhalation (the most profound sound), with the last breath of the dying. *Hā'* thus makes a counterpart to the initial *alif* of *Allāh* (comparable to the first cry). An expression of Ipseity, *hā'* prolongs indefinitely sound and breath in the self. It can be said that *hā'* is, in a concentrated form, the Name *Huwa* inserted into *Allāh*, as *Allāh* is itself inserted into the *shahādah*. Inversely, it can be said that the Name *Huwa* is expanded in the Name of four letters, *Allāh*, itself expanded in a formula of four words, the *shahādah*. One finds oneself in the presence of a series of successive interconnections which Arabic orthography makes particularly clear:

$$\left[\left[\left[\text{o}\right]\ \text{الله}\right]\qquad\text{لا اله الا}\right]$$

The inherent nature of *Huwa* (we propose this form by analogy with that of *Allāh*) in *Allāh* explains the rather enigmatic presence of the crown above its final letter. It can be added here that it is a question of a "signature" (in the Boehmian sense of the word) of Self, precisely of the "*huwa*-ness" of *Allāh,* that is to say, of its connection with the absolute and universal Ipseity. It is this which several Sufis have recalled by showing the inherent nature and the permanence—or perennity—of *Huwa* in *Allāh.* In effect, by successive amputations of the Name one obtains *LLH* (*lillāh,* "to *Allāh*"), *LH* (*lahu,* "to Him") and finally *H* (*hū,* "He"), these being so many states of the Divinity whose enumeration expresses a progressive "reduction" to Ipseity: the *Huwiyyah,* an abstract term beginning with *Huwa* and equivalent to the scholastic term "aseity."

Ritually, one observes this "reduction" in the *ḥaḍrah* or danced *dhikr.* The Name *Allāh,* at first clearly articulated, loses the first syllable and then is progressively reduced to a strongly exhaled breath like a death rattle. At this stage there is no longer conscious articulation; the final phoneme *hā'* itself disappears, diluted and mixed with the vital breath which escapes every act of will. The dancer no longer articulates; it cannot even be said that he "breathes" the Name. Rather, he is "breathed" by It: the Self has then absorbed the self.

The Divine Name *Huwa* is formed of the two letters *hā'* and *wāw* whose respective numerical values, 5 and 6, are traditionally those of the Earth and Heaven or, on the human plane, of the feminine and the masculine. Their total, 11, is the number of hierogamy, the number of the androgyne. The "Pythagorean sum" of 11, 66, is at once the number of the Name *Allāh* (1+30+30+5) and of the original couple, Adam and Eve (Ādam wa Ḥawā: 45+6+15). This situates *Huwa* at the intersection of two axes, that of sacred onomastics and that of primordial androgyny. The Earth and Heaven can still be symbolized by two so-called "magic" circles having respectively as center *hā'* or the number 5 and *wāw* or the number 6. These expanded circles have respectively as their total value the numbers 45 and 54, the sum of which, 99, is related, as we have already seen, to the totality of the Divine Names—another testimony, from the angle of arithmology, of the synthetic quality of *Huwa.*

Remarks concerning Alchemy

Throughout these pages we have had the occasion to evoke diverse aspects relating to astrology, alchemy, etc. We have taken the side of approaching these sciences through the specifically Semitic perspective of the science of letters considered, let us remember, from an epistemological point of view, as the key science. By comparison, the other sciences result from borrowings from and adaptations of foreign currents and particularly from Alexandrian Hermeticism.[18] They would imply, therefore, from the point of view of methodology, a completely different approach. It is not possible to treat each of these sciences in depth; however, some complementary considerations on alchemy can find a place here.

The alchemy of which we speak here is not reducible to a sort of craftsmanship of metals and to laboratory work centered on the art of fire. (*Mutatis mutandis,* the activities of the blacksmith, potter, glassblower, etc. are not without connection to those of the alchemist.) Rather, it concerns a "mysticism" that utilizes the metallurgical process (physical and chemical) as symbolic support and interprets it, systematically, through analogy, in a spiritual perspective. For a Westerner the image that is most suggestive of this "way" is without doubt that of the alchemist in prayer (*oraison*) in his "lab-oratory," as the Latin adage *laborare orare* states. In the Islamic context an equivalent connotation is expressed in the declaration of ʿAlī that alchemy is the sister of prophecy.

In such a perspective alchemical transmutation concerns not metals but the soul. The quest and the long "operative" process—common ground of the treatises on alchemy—are nothing other than the struggle to realize the Self, the Eternal Being, through the self. It is to this difficult "work" (in the full alchemical sense of the word) upon oneself that the "transmutation" of lead into gold applies, symbol of the primordial state (Arabic *fiṭrah*). Such a "transmutation" cannot occur spiritually without the direction of a master—the veritable human catalyst equivalent to what alchemy has designated as the "Philosopher's Stone."

There would be nothing in particular therein, and the "alchemical way" would not be distinguishable from other "mysticisms," if its means for attaining the goal common to all the ways were not completely original. Alchemy has recourse to no metaphysical, theological—indeed ethical—argument. Its method is essentially cosmological: the human soul in order to bear perfection is treated as a "substance" which supposes a profound knowledge of the analogies between "metallic" (exterior) and psychic (interior) domains. Furthermore, its objective character identifies alchemy as a path of gnosis rather than as a path of love. The formulation of alchemical treatises—the written part being the tip of the iceberg; the oral part, fundamentally, being invisible and, so to say, lost—rather insists on the Zen *koan,* logically incomprehensible (that is not to say, as do the profane, an unreadable and literally contraditory lucubration). The alchemist expresses himself through symbols. All of his language is in code. This coding has not failed to utilize the science of letters, and only a few rare initiates of the Great Art are capable of "reading" without misinterpretation; the majority form part of what has been called the "glassblowers."

We have evoked speculations concerning the four elements: earth, water, air, fire. It must be understood that this does not concern, for the alchemist, what scientists designate by these names but rather "qualities" or modalities through which the *materia prima* is capable of manifesting and differentiating itself. The process that alchemy "performs" for the Earth, astrology performs similarly for Heaven—starting from the astral givens. The two sciences stem from the same perspective, and their paths, which are complementary, closely interfere. The four elements—without forgetting the four "natures," hot, cold, dry, humid, from which they emanate—correspond to the states of the soul. Let us imagine them placed on a wheel or a "sphere." All "art" (Arabic *ṣināʿah*) is to escape from the permanent process of transformations (coagulation, dissolution, etc.) and to reach the hub, the point where all movement ceases and wherein it is said that water becomes fire, fire water, earth air, and air solid. In this immobile center, this mysterious quintessence is comprehensible and *a fortiori* realizable only from a metaphysical point of view: this is an alchemy that is pure spirituality.

In order to arrive at this end—or "completion"—alchemy proceeds through the "bodies," and among them the couple Mercury-Sulfur is the object of very special consideration. They can best be compared to the couple Yin/Yang, the Taoist symbol of the two complementary principles. Mercury is the feminine principle; Sulfur the masculine principle. Islamic esoterism has identified Sulfur with the "Divine Command" or "Order," to the original *kun* through which the world, by means of the Divine Will, was brought forth from chaos and formed an "ordered" whole. (This is the meaning of the Greek *kosmos,* generally translated by the Arabic *kawn,* "that which exists.") Mercury represents the "Universal Nature," *ṭabīʿat*

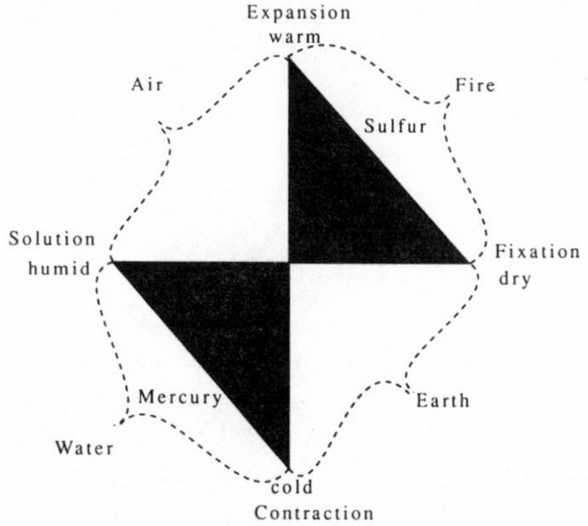

al-kull, the passive and plastic counterpart of the preceding. From the hierogamy of Sulfur and Mercury—corresponding in the microcosmic realm to the couple spirit/soul—Salt naturally issues, corresponding to the body. This hierogamy is sometimes imagined in the form of the two protagonists: Man and Woman (the King and the Queen, the Father and the Mother, etc. of which the treatises speak), sometimes also in the form of an androgynous entity (the "Rebis of alchemy"). All these aspects are found structured in the preceding diagram.

The Alchemy of Happiness

We do not wish to conclude this chapter without taking into account the text of Ibn ʿArabī which comprises chapter 167 of the *Futūḥāt al-makkiyyah* (*The Meccan Revelations*). The title of this chapter, "Of the Knowledge of the Alchemy of Happiness" (*kīmiyāʾ al-saʿādah*) and Its Secrets," is by itself strongly evocative of spiritual alchemy. The hermeneutics of the Existentiating Divine Command, *kun,* to which Ibn ʿArabī surrendered himself, "sets off the demiurgic properties of the letters which make up [this imperative]" and attest to "the truly divine nature of spiritual alchemy which the 'Science of Letters' uses. It is precisely this miraculous science which Jesus owns. . . . Like the demiurge which animates and organizes a preexistent matter, Jesus the Alchemist borrows a lump of clay with which to fashion the bird into which he then breathes the Spirit of Life[19] because Jesus is the Spirit of God."[20] It is with this remarkable parable concerning Jesus in whose person and function Ibn ʿArabī brings together the science of letters and "demiurgy" (to be understood as "the alchemical science of the production of beings," in brief, spiritual alchemy), that we will conclude this all too brief outline, hoping that we have given to the reader the desire to delve deeper into this spiritual Reality. This is achieved especially through a "transparent" vision of things, that is, by a personal meditation on what is beyond the senses, whether it be a question of letters or of the world of appearances.

Translated by Katherine O'Brien

Notes

1. Here is, for example, the way in which Ibn ʿAṭāʾ Allāh describes the formation of *alif,* the first letter, by means of emanation from the Point: "When the Point willed to be named *alif* . . . it extended itself . . . and descended . . . and became this *alif* . . . ." And in a still more suggestive fashion: "It is said that the first thing that Allah created was a Point which He looked at . . . the Point melted [for fear under the Divine Gaze]

and flowed downward in the form of *alif*" (*Traité sur le nom Allāh,* trans. M. Gloton [Paris: Les Deux Océans, 1981] 137–38).

2. Y. Marquet, "Imâmat, Résurrection et Hiérarchie selon les Ikhwân al-Ṣafâ'" *Revue des études islamiques* 30 (1962) 49ff.

3. Quoted by R. Guénon in his *Symbolism of the Cross,* trans. A. Macnab (London: Luzac, 1975) 68.

4. Being unable to deal with this science, let us cite on this subject this formula from al-Būnī: "Numbers symbolize the spiritual world and letters symbolize the corporeal world." He develops this some pages further along as follows: "Know that the secrets of God and the objects of His Science, the subtle and the gross realities, the reality of on-high and of the here-below, and those of the angelic world are of two kinds, numbers and letters. The secrets of the letters are in the numbers and the theophanies of the numbers are in the letters. Numbers are the realities of on-high due to spiritual entities and letters belong to the circles of the material and angelic realities. Numbers are the secret of words and letters the secret of actions. Numbers are the World of the Pedestal" (*Shams al-ma'ārif al kubrā* [Cairo, n.d.] 1:78). Because they are quantitative and qualitative symbols, numbers are the keys to the comprehension of the intelligible world; like letters, they have as their end an arrangement that considers reality essentially in its connections with harmony (proportions and music). In this regard this "science" is a direct descendant of the Pythagorean tradition.

5. Abū Isḥāq Quhistānī, *Haft bāb-i pīr,* trans. V. Ivanow (Bombay: Ismaili Society, 1959) 60.

6. From al-Tirmidhī's *Nawādir al-usūl (*MS).

7. See Ibn Khaldūn, *Discours sur l'histoire universelle (al-Muqaddima),* trans. V. Monteil (Paris: Sindbad, 1967); and D. Urvoy, *Penser l'Islam* (Paris: J. Vrin, 1980) 9, 111, 162–64.

8. The current meaning of the verbal noun *i'tirāḍ* is opposition, incidence, insertion. In his quotation, M. M. Bravman (*Materialien und untersuchungen zu den phonetischen Lehren der Araber* [Dissertation, Göttingen, 1934]) translates this word by *mittenhindurchgehen,* "that which comes in the middle"; the adverb *hindurch,* giving the idea of "something which is crosswise," is expressed in the root *'araḍa.*

9. See al-Majrīṭī, *Ghāyat al-ḥakīm,* quoted in H. Corbin, *L'Alchimie comme art hiératique,* ed. P. Lory (Paris: Edition de l'Herne, 1986) 175.

10. From the *Nawādir al-uṣūl,* quoted by L. Massignon in *The Passion of al-Hallāj, Mystic and Martyr of Islam,* trans. H. Mason (4 vols.; Princeton, NJ: Princeton University Press, 1982) 3:95–96.

11. See Quran LVI, 7–14, on the "Companions of the Right" and of "the Left."

12. In this idea of "recomposition" of a lost, unknown, and secret Name is implied the tradition of the Supreme Name of which the reality and the pronunciation would be known to only a few initiates. It concerns a persistent esoteric tradition found throughout the whole Semitic world.

13. One can see in the passage from the Quran referred to here a synthesis of what came before. The complete verse is as follows: "It is not for the sun to overtake the moon, nor doth the night outstrip the day. They float each in an orbit."

14. T. Burckhardt, *Mystical Astrology according to Ibn 'Arabī,* trans. B. Rauf (Gloucestershire: Beshara Publications, 1977) 32-33.

15. See n. 12.

16. See n. 1.

17. I am following here the economy of diverse graphic equations found in my essay "Lo specchio della *Shahâda,*" *Conoscenza Religiosa* 4 (October–December 1980) 317–56.

18. One of the oldest mentions of the *Emerald Table*, the epitome of the Hermetic Revelation, is found in Jābir ibn Ḥayyān, at the end of the *Kitāb sirr al-khalīqah* (*The Book of the Secret of Creation*).

19. Cf. Quran III, 49: "I have come to you with a sign from my Lord [It is Jesus who is speaking]. I am going, for you, to create from clay a type of bird; I breathe into it and it becomes a bird with the permission of God. . . ." This passage refers to a miracle related particularly in the *Gospel of Childhood.*

20. S. Ruspoli, *L'Alchimie du bonheur parfait* (Paris: L'Ile Verte, 1981) 65–68.

24

Sacred Music and Dance in Islam

Jean-Louis Michon

A Controversial Question

"O Lord! Make us see things as they are!" asked the Prophet when addressing himself to his Lord.[1] The same prayer was to be repeated later over and over by devout Muslims desiring to judge objectively a more or less ambiguous situation. These words are therefore well placed at the beginning of an essay on the art of music such as it was and such as it is still practiced in the countries of *dār al-islām*. Few subjects have been debated or have raised as many contradictory emotions and opinions as the statute (*ḥukm*) of music vis-à-vis religious law and at the heart of Islamic society. In fact, the debate is not yet over and, no doubt, never will be because it concerns a domain in which it seems that Providence wanted to give Muslims the greatest possible freedom of choice and of appreciation. No Quranic prescription explicitly aims at music. The *Sunnah,* the "customs" of the Prophet, cites only anecdotal elements, none of which constitutes a peremptory argument either for or against musical practice. The third source of Islamic Law, the opinion of doctors of the Law, spokesmen recognized by social consensus, varies extremely ranging from a categorical condemnation of music to its panegyric while passing through various degrees of acceptance and reservation.

To understand how such divergent positions could have arisen and been expressed in the same context on the subject of Islamic thought and ethics, it is useful to refer to their interpreters who knew how to take into consideration ideas at once metaphysical, philosophical, or theosophical as well as the imperative of the Muslim ethic, both individual and social. To this category belong the Ikhwān al-Ṣafā', the Brethren of Purity, whose vast encyclopedia of philosophy, science, and art, compiled in the fourth/tenth century, contains a precious epistle on music.[2]

Like the Greek philosophers, the Ikhwān recognized in terrestrial music the echo of the music of the spheres, "inhabited by the angels of God and by the elite of his servants." Thus, "the rhythm produced by the motion of the musician evokes for certain souls residing in the world of generation and corruption the felicity of the world of the spheres, in the same way that the rhythms produced by the motion of the spheres and the stars evoke for souls who are there the beatitude of the world of the spirit." By reason of the law of harmony, which reigns over all the levels of existence, linking them according to an order at once hierarchical and analogical, "the beings produced by secondary reactions imitate in their modalities the first beings which are their causes . . . from which it must be deduced that the notes of terrestrial music necessarily imitate those of celestial music." Like Pythagoras, who "heard, thanks to the purity of the substance of his soul and the wisdom of his heart, the music produced by the rotation of the spheres and the stars" and who "was the first to have spoken of this science," other philosophers such as Nichomacus, Ptolemy, and Euclid, had "the habit of singing accompanied by percussive instruments which produced chords from words and measured verses that were composed for exhortation to the spiritual life and described the delights of the world of the spirit, the pleasure and the happiness of its inhabitants." Later came the Muslim conquerors, who, when given the signal to attack, recited certain verses of the Quran or declaimed Arabic or Persian poems describing the paradisal delights reserved for those who died while fighting on the path of God. Returning to music, in inventing the principles of its melodies and the constitution of its rhythms, the sages had no goal except "to soften hardened hearts, to wake the negligent souls from their sleep of forgetfulness and the misguided spirits from their slumber of ignorance, to make them desire their spiritual world, their luminous place and their journey of life, to make them leave the world of generation and corruption, to save them from submersion in the ocean of the material world and to deliver them from the prison of nature."

How, under these circumstances, can it be explained that music could become an object of reprobation? Because, explain the Ikhwān, even if it is good in itself, music can be turned aside from its natural and legitimate ends. "As for the reason for the interdiction of music in certain laws of the prophets . . . it relates to the fact that people do not use music for the purpose assigned it by the philosophers, but for the purpose of diversion, for sport, for the incitation to enjoy the pleasures of this lower world." Thus, that which can become reprehensible is not music itself but the use to which certain people put it. "Be watchful while listening to music, that the appetites of the animal soul do not push you toward the splendor of nature. Nature will lead you astray from the paths of salvation and prevent you from discourse with the superior soul."[3] The warning issued by the Ikhwān goes along with the teaching given a century earlier by the Sufi Dhu'l-Nūn the Egyptian (d. 246/861): "Listening (*al-samā'*) is a divine influence which stirs the heart to see Allāh; those who listen to it spiritually attain to Allāh, and those who listen to it sensually fall into heresy."[4] In the same way, Hujwīrī wrote in his *Kashf al-maḥjūb* (*The Unveiling of the Veiled*), the first treatise on Sufism written in Persian, "Listening to sweet sounds produces an effervescence of the substance moulded in man; true, if the substance be true, false, if the substance be false."[5]

Such was, generally speaking, the attitude of the philosophers and theoreticians of music, as well as that of the majority of Sufis and a good number of canonists. Aware of the benefits of the art of music, they did not show themselves less circumspect about its utilization, distinguishing between noble and vulgar genres, between sensual melodies, "useful" melodies, etc.[6]

However, numerous jurists went much further and, seeing the evil usage that could be made of the practice of music, concluded that music itself was evil or, at least, that it involved more disadvantages than advantages and had, therefore, to be banned from society. Poetry that was sung and the use of instruments gave rise, they said, to corrupting excitations of the soul, which turned one aside from religious duties, encouraged one to seek out sensual satisfactions and bad company, pushed one into drunkenness and debauchery. Such jurists went so far as to say that the public singer, even if he sings the Quran to arouse pleasure in his listeners, could not be heard as a legal witness. They also maintained that it was lawful to break musical instruments.[7]

For the jurist and moralist Ibn Abi'l-Dunyā (d. 281/894), who wrote a short treatise entitled *Dhamm al-malāhī* (*Censure of Instruments of Diversion*),[8] singing and music were condemnable distractions of the same type as the games of chess and backgammon. Later, the Ḥanbalite jurist Ibn al-Jawzī (d. 597/1200) was to show himself to be just as severe vis-à-vis music, which the evil human nature, "the soul which incites to evil" (*al-nafs al-ammārah bi'l-sū'*) according to the Quran XII, 53) has a tendency to seize upon in order to anchor man in sensuality. "The spiritual concert (*al-samā'*) includes two things," he wrote in his *Talbīs Iblīs* (*The Dissimulation of the Devil*). "In the first place, it leads the heart away from reflection upon the power of God and from assiduity in His service. In the second place, it encourages enjoyment of the pleasures of this world. . . ." Furthermore:

> Music makes man forget moderation and it troubles his mind. This implies that man, when he is excited, commits things which he judges reprehensible

> in others when he is in his normal state. He makes movements with his head, claps his hands, strikes the ground with his feet and commits acts similar to those of the insane. Music leads one to this; its action appears to be like that of wine, because it clouds the mind. This is why it is necessary to prohibit it.[9]

Ibn al-Jawzī admits, however, that there are certain musical genres in which the emotional element does not enter and which, therefore, are legal, such as songs of pilgrims to Mecca, songs of fighters for the faith, and songs of camel drivers. He recognized also that in the epoch in which Ibn Ḥanbal lived (third/ninth century), poems were sung that exalted only religious feeling, which consequently escaped interdiction. But such times, according to him, are over and the innovations introduced since then in music and poetry are such that these arts can only have a deleterious influence.

The Philosopher-Musicologists

Although arguments of this nature must be regarded as permissible on the part of the jurists, who are concerned above all with the moral health of the man of the community and the collectivity, these arguments did not apply to seekers of Truth, to those who had sufficiently refined themselves so as not to fall into the trap of sensuality. For them music occupied an important place in the hierarchy of the arts and the sciences, and they practiced it as a discipline capable of elevating man above the gross world, of making him participate in the universal harmony. Such seekers were numerous and with abundant talent in the Islamic world, which, thanks to them, can pride itself on an extremely fecund tradition on the level of theory as well as that of the practice of vocal and instrumental music.

Among the theoreticians who thought and wrote about music, two clearly distinguishable schools can be recognized which sometimes converged but, more often, went along their separate paths, drawing on their own sources and applying different methods of investigation. They are, on one side, the philosophers, *falāsifah, ḥukamā'* (pl. of *ḥakīm,* "sage") and, on the other side, the mystics, *ṣūfiyyah* (pl. of *ṣūfī*), *'ārifūn, 'urafā'* (pl. of *'ārif,* "gnostic").

To the first group are linked the great thinkers whose names are forever inseparable from the history of Islamic philosophy, names such as Ya'qūb al-Kindī, Abū Bakr al-Rāzī (Rhazes), Abū Naṣr al-Fārābī, whose *Kitāb al-mūsiqa'l-kabīr* (*Grand Book of Music*) achieved considerable fame, Ibn Sīnā (Avicenna), Ibn Bājjah (Avempace), and Ṣafī al-Dīn (d. 629/1293).[10] If they inherited the legacy of ancient Greece and renewed the Pythagorean, Aristotelian, Platonic, and Neoplatonic discourse, they imprinted upon it a unique and profoundly original mark, enriching it not only with numerous scientific developments but with the whole school of thought based on the

Quranic revelation.[11] The Ikhwān al-Ṣafā', previously mentioned, also belonged to this group. Their "Epistle on Music" opens as follows:

> After having completed the study of the theoretical spiritual arts which are of a scientific genre, and the study of the corporeal, practical arts which are of an artistic genre, . . . we propose in the present epistle entitled "Music" to study the art which is made up of both the corporeal and the spiritual. It is the art of harmony (*ta'līf*) which can be defined by the function of proportions.[12]

Two ideas occur at the onset, the first being that music is composed of corporeal and spiritual elements, the second that it is based on proportions. Because of its dual composition, the art of music possesses the special power of freeing matter in order to spiritualize it, and of materializing the spiritual in order to render it perceptible. This power comes also from the fact that music is a science of proportions, as the Ikhwān explain in another epistle (the sixth) in which, after having shown by examples how number, proportion, and numerical relationship are applied to all phenomena they add, "All these examples demonstrate the nobility of the science of proportion which is music. This science is necessary for all the arts. Nevertheless, if it is connected with the name of music, it is because music offers the best illustration of harmony."[13]

That which, according to the Ikhwān, characterizes music and distinguishes it from other arts is that the substance upon which it works—the soul of the listeners—like the elements it employs—notes and rhythms—are of a subtle nature and not corporeal. "Music leaves in the souls of those who listen to it diverse impressions similar to those left by the work of the artisan in the matter which is the substratum of his art." The Ikhwān cite many examples of emotional states which melodies are capable of inspiring in man, such as regret and repentance for past mistakes, courage in battle, relief from suffering and joyful excitation. Animals themselves are roused by hearing music; the camel quickens its step upon hearing the song of the camel driver; the horse drinks more willingly when its master whistles a tune; the gazelle allows itself to be approached at night by the hunter who hums a melody.

"Music (*ghinā'*)," exclaimed also Ibn Khurdādhbih (d. ca. 300/912), who was raised in Baghdad by the inspired Isḥāq al-Mawṣilī,[14] when beginning a speech delivered at the court of the caliph al-Mu'tamid, his protector and friend, "sharpens the intellect, softens the disposition, and agitates the soul. It gives cheer and courage to the heart, and high-mindedness to the debased. . . . It is to be preferred to speech, as health would be to sickness. . . ."[15]

Not only does music stir the soul and the emotions; it "descends" into the body and from there comes its power to move the body and make it dance. From there also come the therapeutic applications to which the classical treatises refer, notably those of al-Kindī and Ibn Sīnā. Besides this, it "rises" as far as the spirit because it is itself a vibration of supernatural origin like the *kun,* the primordial *fiat lux* from which, from nothingness, from silence, from darkness, existence was brought forth. Thus the remark of Ibn Zaylah (d. 440/1048), a disciple of Ibn Sīnā: "Sound produces an influence on the soul in two directions. One is on account of its special composition (i.e., its physical content); the other on account of its being similar to the soul (i.e., its spiritual content)."[16]

Because of its power of animation (*ta'thīr*), the *ethos* of the Greeks, music—and it is this power that gives it the highest title of nobility for the theosophical Ikhwān as for the Sufis—can set souls in flights that are measured in proportion to the receptacle in which they are produced:

> Know, my brethren, that the effects imprinted by the rhythms and melodies (*naghamāt*) of the musician in the souls of listeners are of different types. In the same way, the pleasure which souls draw from these rhythms and melodies and the manner in which they enjoy them are variable and diverse. All that depends on the degree which each soul occupies in the domain of gnosis (*al-ma'ārif*) and on the nature of the good actions which make up the permanent object of his love. Therefore, each soul, while listening to descriptions which correspond to the object of his desires and to melodies which are in accord with the object of his delight, rejoices, is exalted and delights in the image that music makes of his beloved. . . .[17]

The Ikhwān conclude their epistle with a justification of the most beautiful and the most perfect music, which is none other than the psalmody of sacred texts:

> Tradition teaches that the sweetest melody which the inhabitants of paradise have at their disposal and the most beautiful song they hear is the discourse of God—great be His praise. It is thus that the Word of God Most High states, "The greeting which [will welcome them] there will be peace!" (Quran X, 10–11). And the end of their invocation will be: "Praise to Allāh, Lord of the worlds." It is said that Moses—peace be upon him—upon hearing the words of his Lord, was overcome with joy, with happiness and with rapture to the point of being unable to contain himself. He was overwhelmed by emotion, transported while listening to this serene melody and from that point on regarded all rhythms, all melodies, and all songs as insignificant.[18]

Sufis and the Spiritual Concert (*al-samā'*)

To listen to music is therefore, in the final analysis, to open oneself to an influence, to a vibration of suprahuman origin "made sound" in order to awaken in us the echoes of a primordial state and to arouse in the heart a longing for union with its own Essence. Abū Ḥāmid al-Ghazzālī writes at the beginning of the long chapter of *Iḥyā' 'ulūm al-dīn* (*The Revival of the Sciences of Religion*), which he consecrates to the laws governing the spiritual concert (*al-samā'*):

> Hearts and inmost thoughts, song and ecstasy, are treasuries of secrets and mines of jewels. Infolded in them are their jewels like as fire is infolded in iron and stone, and concealed like as water is concealed under dust and loam. There is no way to the extracting of their hidden things save by the flint and steel of listening to music and singing, and there is no entrance to the heart save by the antechamber of the ears. So musical tones, measured and pleasing, bring forth what is in it and make evident its beauties and defects. For when the heart is moved there is made evident that only which it contains like as a vessel drips only what is in it. And listening to music and singing is for the heart a true touchstone and a speaking standard; whenever the soul of the music and singing reaches the heart, then there stirs in the heart that which in it preponderates.[19]

For the man in whom the desire for the good and the beautiful predominates, him who has an ear made for listening to music, it becomes a privileged tool for self-knowledge and interior improvement. Manifesting the latent possibilities of an individual, it permits him to observe, by their movements and their reciprocal interactions, the potentialities of which he was not aware until that moment. A discrimination operates in him, which makes him perceive in his inmost heart, with an acuity in proportion to the quality of the music and to his own receptive capacity, clear and obscure zones of aspirations toward the absolute light, in alternation often with emotional attractions. That this age-old doctrine, already taught by the sages of antiquity and raised up by generations of Sufis to the rank of a veritable alchemy of the soul, has been transmitted and maintained through to the present time, I have only a very simple, but significant fact as proof. It is a sentence in Turkish that the father of a contemporary musician who specialized in the songs of Sufi brotherhoods[20] inscribed on the tambourine with which his son accompanied himself. It says: *Aşikin aşkini fasikin fiskini arttirir bir alettir* ("this instrument augments the love of the lover, the hypocrisy of the hypocrite").

The use of the spiritual concert (*al-samā'*) as a technique for spiritual realization must necessarily surround itself with conditions and precautions that will guarantee its efficacy and avoid the strayings and the misguidings of the *nafs*. These conditions are generally the same as those demanded of the candidates of the initiatic path (*ṭarīqah*): moral and spiritual qualifications of the disciple and the acceptance of him by the master (*shaykh, pīr*), obedience to the *shaykh,* service to the *fuqarā',* strict observance of ritual practices particular to the order, as well as those of the *Sharī'ah.* More especially, at the time of participation in sessions of spiritual concert (*samā'*), dervishes are enjoined to remain as sober as possible and to exteriorize their emotion only when it becomes an ecstatic rapture of an intensity so great that it exceeds all control. Referring to the example of the Prophet, who, at the time of the first appearances of the archangel of the Revelation, did not succeed in mastering his emotion, Hujwīrī excused the beginners who, in *samā',* show excitement. He insisted that the states provoked by listening be spontaneous:

> As long as *samā'* does not reveal its strength, it is essential not to force it, but the moment it becomes powerful, it must not be resisted. It is necessary to follow the "moment" in whatever it indicates: if it excites you, excite yourself; if it keeps you tranquil, keep yourself tranquil. . . . It is necessary that he who participates in *samā'* have sufficient discernment to be capable of receiving the divine influence and to recognize in it its true value so that, when this influence takes hold of his heart, he does not endeavour to chase it out and, when its power has abated, he does not endeavour to recapture it.[21]

Abū Ḥamid al-Ghazzālī, in the *Iḥyā',* expressed a similar opinion:

> That the participant remain seated, his head lowered as if he were deep in meditation, avoiding clapping his hands, dancing and making any other movement designed to artificially induce ecstasy or to make a display of it. . . . But when ecstasy takes hold of him and causes him to make movements independent of his will, he is to be excused and must not be blamed.

However, the same master admits that it is certainly not blameworthy to imitate the attitudes and movements of an ecstatic if the intention is not to make a display of a state that one has not attained, but rather to put oneself into a frame of mind receptive to grace.

> Know that ecstasy (*wajd*) is divided into that which itself attacks and that which is forced, and that is called affecting ecstasy (*tawājud*). Of this forced affecting of ecstasy there is that which is blameworthy, and it is what aims at hypocrisy and at the manifesting of the Glorious States in spite of being destitute of them. And of it there is that which is praiseworthy, and it leads to the invoking of the Glorious States and the gaining of them for oneself and bringing them to oneself by device. And therefore the Apostle of God commanded him who did not weep at the reading of the Qur'an that he should force weeping and mourning; for the beginning of these States is sometimes forced while their ends thereafter are true.[22]

Summarizing the teachings of numerous masters of Sufism in his glossary of technical terms, Ibn 'Ajībah describes four successive degrees of approach toward ecstasy.[23] First, the "seeking out of ecstasy" (*tawājud*):

> One affects the appearances of ecstatic emotion (*wajd*) and one uses them methodically; thus one employs dance (*raqṣ*), rhythmic movements, etc. This seeking out is only admissible among the *fuqarā'* who have made vows of total renunciation. For them, there is nothing wrong in simulating ecstasy and in repeating its gestures in order to respond to an inner call (*ḥāl*). . . . It is, certainly, the station of the weak but the strong practice it nevertheless, either in order to sustain and encourage the weaker ones, or because they find a sweetness in it. . . . Myself, when I participated in a session of spiritual concert with our Shaykh al-Būzīdī, I saw him sway from right to left. One of the disciples of Mawlāy al-'Arabī al-Darqāwī told me that his master would not stop dancing until the end of the concert. . . .

In the second place comes "ecstatic emotion" (*wajd*) through which must be heard "that which befalls the heart and takes hold of it unexpectedly, without the man having any part in it. It can be an ardent and anxious desire or a troubling fear. . . ."

Third, "one speaks of 'ecstatic meeting' (*wijdān*) when the sweetness of the presence is prolonged, accompanied most frequently by intoxication and stupor."

Finally:

> If the meeting lasts until the stupor and hinderances dissipate and the faculties of meditation and insight are purified, it becomes ecstasy (*wujūd*), the station to which Junayd[24] alluded in this verse:
>
> "My ecstasy is that I remove myself from existence,
> by the grace of him who shows to me the Presence."
> (*wujūdī an aghība 'an al-wujūd*
> *bimā yabdū 'alayya mina'l-shuhūd*).[25]

The Elements of the Spiritual Concert

The animating power of music comes, we have seen, from that which it is in essence, a manifestation of the Divine Word, a language that reminds man of the state in which, before creation, he was still united with the Universal Soul, radiated from the original light, which reminds him of that instant in pre-eternity when, according to a Quranic saying frequently cited by the Sufis (VII, 172) the Lord asked souls: "Am I not your Lord?" They answered: "Yea!" It is the memory of this primordial covenant (*al-mīthāq al-awwal*) and the nostalgia for it that music evokes in hearts entrapped in earthly attachments.

There is in music an interpenetration of two aspects inherent in the Supreme Being, Allah. One is the aspect of Majesty (*al-jalāl*), which translates into rhythm, and the other the aspect of Beauty (*al-jamāl*), which renders the melody. The drum announces the arrival and the presence of the all-powerful King. It is the sign of transcendence, of the discontinuity which separates us, the impoverished, the dependent, from Him, the Highest, subsisting in Himself, while the human voice and the flute sing of the Immanence, the inexhaustible Wealth (*al-ghinā'*) that no human imagination will ever be able to comprehend but whose every manifestation, mode, or station (*maqām*) is capable of becoming a grace and a blessing for the believer.

Instruments

Each of the elements of the spiritual concert is invested with a symbolic value and becomes an aid in recollection, in remembrance (*dhikr*) for those who are attentive to the language of signs. Aḥmad Ghazzālī, who taught Sufism approximately a century and a half before Rūmī, states:

> The saints of Allah apply the forms to the realities (*ma'ānī*) on account of their abandoning the ranks of the forms and their moving in the ranks of the branches of gnosis. So among them the tambourine is a reference to the cycle of existing things (*dā'irat al-akwān*); the skin which is fitted on to it is a reference to the Absolute Being; the striking which takes place on the tambourine is a reference to the descent of the divine visitations from the innermost arcana within the Absolute Being to bring forth the things pertaining to the essence from the interior to the exterior. . . . And the breath of the musician is the form of the rank of the Truth (Exalted and holy is He!), since it is He who sets them in motion, brings them into existence, and enriches them. And the voice of the singer is a reference to the divine life which comes down from the innermost arcana to the levels of the spirits, the hearts, and the consciences (*asrār*). The flute (*qaṣab*) is a reference to the human essence, and the nine holes are a reference to the openings in the outer frame (*ẓāhir*), which are nine, viz. the ears, the nostrils, the eyes the mouth and the private parts. And the breath which penetrates the flute is a reference to the light of Allah penetrating the reed of man's essence. And the dancing is a reference to the circling of the spirit round the cycle of existing things in order to receive the effects of the unveilings and revelations; and this is the state of the gnostic. The whirling is a reference to the spirit's standing with Allah in its inner nature (*sirr*) and being (*wujūd*), the circling of its look and thought, and its penetrating the ranks of existing things; and this is the state of the assured one. And his leaping up is a reference to his being drawn from the human station to the unitive station and to existing things acquiring from him spiritual effects and illuminative helps.[26]

In this passage, Aḥmad Ghazzālī makes no mention of stringed instruments. That is because he, like his brother, considered them to be forbidden "by general consensus" by reason of the frequent use that was made of them in the first centuries of Islam by effeminates (*mukhannathūn*) for evenings of entertainment hardly compatible with the concerns of men of God. This ostracism, however, was not universal and only reflected the uncertainties which, even in mystical circles, existed in the matter of musical practice. It did not prevent the lute, the *tanbūr* (pandore), the *rabāb* (rebec) and the *qānūn* (zither) from finding their place next to the drums and the reed flute (*nay*) in the oratorios of several Sufi orders such as the Mawlawīs ("whirling dervishes") and the Baktashīs of Turkey, the Chishtīs of India, and, much later (mid-thirteenth/nineteenth century), the Shādhilīs-Ḥarrāqīs of Morocco, who adopted for their sessions of remembrance the instruments of the Andalusian *nawbah.*

In fact, these instruments have always been held in the highest esteem by musicologists, who have based scholarly studies concerning the groupinqs and divisions of notes on them. It must be remembered that al-Fārābī, among others, was himself such a marvelous lutist that he was able, according to his contemporaries, to hold his listeners in rapt attention or to put them to sleep, to make them laugh or cry and to inspire in them feelings in concordance with his own "moments." Such performances are, moreover, consistent with the theory of the tuning of the lute, formulated by al-Kindī among others, according to which the four strings of the instrument correspond to other micro- and macrocosmic quaternaries such as the "animal tendencies" (gentleness, cowardice, intelligence, courage), the "faculties of the soul" (memorative, attentive, imaginative, cognitive), the elements (water, earth, air, fire), the seasons, and the signs of the zodiac.[27]

Melodic Modes

The effect that Islamic music, whether vocal or instrumental, has on the soul is directly connected with its modal structure, which, technically speaking, is without doubt its fundamental characteristic. In contrast to Western music, which has only two modes, the major and the minor, Oriental modes are quite numerous: the contemporary Arab, Turkish, and Persian musicians list them most often as numbering either thirty-two or twenty-four, twelve of which are very common, whereas during the classical epoch, a hundred were used.[28]

A mode (Arabic *maqām;*[29] Turkish *makām;* Persian *dastgāh* or *āwāz*) is a type of melody that is expressed by a series of well-defined sounds. It is a series (*sullam*) corresponding approximately to a Western scale, which does not have to use the same notes for ascending and descending to the octave. Each mode carries a specific name, which denotes, for example, its geographic origin such as *ḥijāz, nahāwand, ʿirāqī* or the position of its dominant note on the lute: *dugāh* (second position, or A), *sigāh* (third position, or B) or suggests the state of the soul or the cosmic phenomenon that the mode is supposed to translate into music: *faraḥfazā,* "the joyous"; *nesīm,* "the breeze"; *ṣabā,* "the morning wind," bringer of longing; *zemzeme,* "the murmur." It is said that the musicians in former times had a precise knowledge of the virtues of the *maqāms* and performed them in accordance with this knowledge, exactly as still occurs in Pakistan and northern India, where the system of *rāgas* obeys rules very similar to those of Persian, Turkish, and Arabic modes. It is thus that they played certain melodies only during certain seasons or at certain hours of the day or on special occasions in conjunction with the places and the ceremonies for which one wished to create a propitious ambience, a spiritual or emotional aura. In the opinion of specialists of Turkish music, "The emancipation of music, its detachment from the complex base of human activities, has certainly taken from *makâm* much of its original character, but a portion remains alive, even if it is unconscious. Musicians recognize a *makâm* right from the first notes. . . . Therefore the *makâm* always exerts an influence, but only long practice permits one to feel it."[30]

In the mystical perspective, the exploration of a *maqām* by a performer who, on the one hand, humbly adapts himself to the model or preexisting pattern which makes up the mode and, on the other hand, improvises a series of melodic passages, of grace notes, and of vocalizations around the essential notes constitutes a true spiritual discipline. It demands as its basic condition *faqr,* detachment or interior emptiness, and in compensation brings the unveiling of a state (*ḥāl*) or rather a contemplative station, that is, in Sufi terminology, a *maqām,* a term which rejoins—and this is not an accident—that of the musicians. Lifted up on the wings of the melody, the musician is able to progress from *maqām* to *maqām,* up to the extreme limits of joy and plenitude, carrying along in his wake those listeners whose hearts are open.

Rhythm

The rhythmic structures—*uṣūl* (from *aṣl,* "root") or *īqāʿāt* (sg. *īqāʿ*)—serve the function of sustaining the melody while providing it with divisions, a temporal framework, and sometimes also a profound and majestic sonorous base. They produce periods of equal duration which, like the meters of prosody, are composed of beats now uneven, broken, and precipitous. The blows themselves are of two kinds, muffled and clear, and their infinitely varied combinations evoke the game of complementary principles such as

16. The master in the sacred dance of the Mawlawīs from Turkey.

heat and cold, dry and humid, active and passive, in the sustenance and renewal of cosmic harmony.

The effect of rhythm on the human soul is thus described by a contemporary scholar of the sciences and sacred art of Islam:

> The rhythm, the meter of the music changes the relation of man with ordinary time—which is the most important characteristic of the life of this world. Persian music possesses extremely fast and regular rhythms in which there are no beats or any form of temporal determination. In the first instance man is united with the pulsation of cosmic life, which in the human individual is always present in the form of the beating of the heart. Man's life and the life of the cosmos become one, the microcosm is united to the macrocosm. . . . In the second case, which transcends all rhythm and temporal distinction, man is suddenly cut off from the world of time; he feels himself situated face to face with eternity and for a moment benefits from the joy of extinction (*fanā'*) and permanence (*baqā'*).[31]

The Human Voice

Among the Arabs as among the ancient Semites, music was an exclusively vocal art, designated by the word *ghinā'*, "song," which for a long time served to signify it, before being supplanted by the term *mūsīqā,* derived from Greek.[32] In pre-Islamic Arabia, it was in sung verses that the soothsayers and magicians rendered their oracles and uttered their incantations. Even if bards and professional singers (*qā'ināt*) played several instruments, these served above all to introduce or to accompany the sung poems.

The advent of Islam did not change at all the attraction exercised by vocal music, and song and poetry stayed in honor during the lifetime of the Prophet as well as after it. It is told, for example, how the Prophet admitted the presence of singers among his wives or how, while traveling, he asked some of his Companions to sing the *ḥudā'*, poems that punctuate the march of the caravans.[33] When the chronicler al-Iṣfahānī reports, in the twenty volumes of his *Kitāb al-aghānī* (*Book of Songs*), composed in the third/tenth century, the acts and gestures of the successive generations of musicians up to the Abbasid caliphate, it is all the cultural life of Arabia and the Near East, before and after Islamization, which he brings to life before our eyes.

For the philosopher and musicologist al-Fārābī, only the human voice is capable of attaining to perfect music, that is, to that which reunites the three virtues of the art of music: the ability to bring pleasure and calm, that of provoking certain emotions and certain sentiments, and that of speaking to the imagination and of inspiring ideas.[34] "Instrumental music sometimes possesses certain of these qualities," concludes al-Fārābī, implying by this that it never possesses them all; and he expresses thus a consensus that has always generally prevailed in the world of Islam. When, in a rare exception, an instrument such as the *nay*, the reed flute of the Mawlawī dervishes, itself also attains by all evidence to the "perfect music," the initiated will explain that this is because it is itself a voice, a breath, that of the human soul which traverses the body, the microcosm purified by love.

Quranic Psalmody

That which makes the human voice the most appropriate instrument for the perfect music is above all its aptitude to convey the Divine Word. "God has never sent a prophet without giving him a beautiful voice," declared the Prophet, and the history of the Quranic revelation illustrates the pertinence of this remark. Brought to men "in a clear, Arabic tongue" (according to Quran XXVI, 195), the Divine Message had to be proclaimed clearly. "Chant the Quran very distinctly!" was the command given to the Prophet (Quran LXXIII, 4); and he himself, in a *ḥadīth,* recommended to the faithful, "Embellish your voices with the Quran, and embellish the Quran with your voices," meaning that there exists a veritable consubstantiality between the Divine Word and the human voice. To read, to recite the Quran, is in effect and in the most direct way, to let oneself be penetrated by the Divine Word, to become imbued with its significance and its vibration; it is, for each believer, to approach the Divine, to live in the Presence, to taste the Names and the Qualities before, perhaps, having a presentiment of the Essence.

The Quran cannot be compared to any other literary production; likewise, psalmody, which constitutes the first sacred art of Islam, is necessarily distinguished from all other musical expression. Its unique character is reflected in its terminology, since the terms by which it is designated borrow nothing from musical vocabulary, terms such as *qirā'ah* (reading), *tartīl* or *tilāwah* (psalmody), *tajwīd* (from the root *jwd,* "embellish"), but never *ghinā'* (song, vocal music). It should not include any element of individual creation apt to denature an intangible text, and the only concern of the reciter should be to efface himself before the Divine Model and to conform himself to it as thoroughly as possible.

It is said that psalmody obeys precise rules which, if they vary in detail according to different schools, nevertheless rest on common principles.[35] In the first place, given that the Divine Book contains in itself its own rhythm, its reading never allows for any instrument of accompaniment. It is incumbent upon the reciter to render the rhythmic structure perceptible by giving a correct pronunciation, by respecting the lengthening of vowels, by redoubling of consonants, by making the traditional pauses and breaks–

these latter having the special function of retaining the attention, of letting the imagination work, and of facilitating the assimilation of the meaning of the verses.

As for the melodic element, it can be totally dismissed, as one of the juridical schools of Sunnism, that of Imam Mālik, wished, without losing any of the vibratory effect. It suffices to listen to the collective reading as it is practiced in the mosques of Morocco to be convinced of the power of penetration of a recitation done *recto tono.* Most generally, however, the systems of reading teach a kind of more or less rapid cantillation, the modulation of which spans a variable but generally narrow register, and which underlines and embellishes the syllables and the words by means of melismas and vocalizations so as to engrave them more easily on the human substance.

"Recite the Quran following the melodies and the intonations of the Arabs," the Prophet was to advise.[36] That this injunction was generally followed is demonstrated by the undeniable kinship that exists among all the styles of psalmody in the Muslim world. It is true that in the course of its expansion in space, the art of psalmody has absorbed a number of melodic elements present in the local milieu, and it is that which gives birth to easily recognizable, characteristic styles. All these styles, however, bear the indelible stamp of Islam; they incorporate a unique sonorous substance which itself has served as a vehicle of the Quranic message.

Pslamody is practiced on all occasions, individually or collectively. It is for each believer the means *par excellence* of remembering God and of meditating on His Qualities and blessings following His injunction,

> Surely in the creation of the heavens and earth and in the alternation of night and day there are signs for men possessed of minds who remember God, standing and sitting and on their sides, and reflect upon the creation of the heavens and the earth: "Our Lord, Thou has not created this for vanity. Glory be to Thee! Guard us against the chastisement of the Fire!" (Quran III, 190–91)

Taught to children from the earliest age, psalmody not only impresses on them the spiritual and moral teachings of Islam, but it acts on the very fibers of their sensibility and, through the alchemy of the Word, works a transmutation which restores to the human creature something of its primordial sacredness.

Musical Genres

In each of the great ethnolinguistic sectors of the Muslim world—the Arab, the Persian, the Turkish, the Indo-Pakistani (without mentioning here the Malays and Chinese, who, because of their distance, have been less permeated by the artistic models of Islam except as it concerns the liturgical arts, the recitation of the Quran and calligraphy)—the coexistence of three musical genres can be seen: (1) a liturgical and devotional ritual music, (2) a classical music of an intellectual nature, and (3) a popular music. The first genre—in addition to Quranic psalmody, whose exceptional importance has just been underlined—includes the call to prayer; the songs dedicated to the praises of the Prophet and those which, among the Shīʿites, commemorate the martyred Imams; and finally the multiple forms of the spiritual concert (*samāʿ*) with or without dance practiced by mystical circles. The classical genre is the music of the cities, the princely courts, the men of letters and dignitaries, which is meant especially to give birth to diverse nuances of aesthetic emotion (*ṭarab*). This music rests on the same technical base as the previous one and shows itself capable, if played with the desired intention and in the proper context, of opening the doors of mystical experience to the listeners. The popular music aims at marking the seasonal rhythms and at celebrating occasions for rejoicing and for mourning. It allows itself in many instances to be penetrated by Islam and opens to the common people exceptional possibilities for going beyond themselves.

Since, strictly speaking, only the first of these categories relates directly to the sacred domain, it is this music in particular that will be discussed in the following sections. Among the classical and popular forms of music only those which, adopted by the mystics, found their way into the *zāwiyahs, tekkes,* and *sama-khanehs* will be examined. This being said, we will perhaps succeed in evoking the immense richness of the sonorous heritage of Islam and in inspiring the reader to seek out musical experiences which no description is capable of replacing.

The Call to Prayer (*adhān*)

Instituted by the Prophet at the very beginning of the *hijrah,* the call to prayer is perhaps, among the exterior signs of Islam, the most powerful symbol of the influence of the realm of the Divine upon the world of man. Chanted five times each day, every day of the year, the *adhān* marks time and fills it. Issued from the tops of minarets toward the four cardinal points, it traverses and fills space, thus affirming the sacred character of these two dimensions in which human existence unfolds. By the proclamation of the *takbīr,* the formula *Allāh*[u] *akbar,* "God is infinitely great," and by the *shahādah,* it places the entire universe under the sign of transcendence. It also likens prayer to "joy" (*al-falāḥ*), enjoining the faithful to interrupt their ordinary chores or pleasures for a moment of consecration, a veritable preparation for and prelude to the beatitude that awaits the believers in the hereafter.

Like psalmody, the *adhān* uses modes of cantillation that can vary according to the region, but the same homogeneous structure appears in all these modes. Those who are charged with giving the call, the muezzins, are chosen not only for their beautiful voices but also for their human qualities and their piety. Sometimes they also perform the functions of the imam of a mosque, and most of them participate as singers (*munshid*) at religious festivals and spiritual gatherings of the initiated circles.

Praises upon the Prophet (*amdāḥ nabawiyyah*)

The second great source of knowledge after the Quran is the Prophet Muḥammad, whose teachings, transmitted in the collections of *Ḥadīth,* and whose deeds, related in the *Sīrah,* make up the prophetic "custom," the *Sunnah.* If Quranic psalmody was able to give birth to different forms of modulated recitation, the person of the Prophet, for its part, has given rise to a great wealth of literary compositions and devotional songs. The importance of these litanies is linked in Islamic mysticism to the doctrine of the Perfect Man, *al-insān al-kāmil,* for Muḥammad, if he is a man, is not a man like others. He is, according to a Sufi saying, "like a diamond among stones." He is also called "the best of created beings" or "the evident prototype," meaning by this that he is the summation of the entire creation, a universal model. To offer prayer upon the prophet is thus to pray for the salvation of all beings and is also to pray for the rediscovery of one's own primordial nature, to pray for one's own deliverance. Moreover, mystical gatherings almost always begin with praises upon the Prophet. In the Syrian *zāwiyahs* of the Qādirī or Shādhilī orders for example, the gatherings open with a song, performed as a solo, of the *Mawlidiyyah* of Shaykh Barzanjī (d. 1190/1766). The words are notably the following:

> Our Lord Muḥammad was always smiling, affable; he never showed the least brutality, the least violence in his words or in his criticisms; he never made a show of his desires and he abstained from judging others and speaking ill of them. When he spoke, his companions kept silent as if a bird had perched on their heads; never did they raise their voices in argument, and when they spoke, it was he who was silent.

Another poem also very popular among the Sufis of North Africa and the Middle East is the *Burdah,* the "Cloak," composed in Egypt by Muḥammad al-Būṣīrī (d. 694/1296), a work whose title recalls a miraculous healing. Being stricken by paralysis and moribund, in a dream Shaykh al-Būṣīrī saw the Prophet, who enveloped him in his cloak. Upon awakening, he found himself cured and able to move, and he carried the poem within him. It needed only to be transcribed. For seven centuries, it has been taken up in chorus by generations of *fuqarā'*. Rhyming in *mī*, including 162 verses, it lends itself admirably to quick rhythmic variations and, always sung in unison, possesses a great emotional charge.

In Turkey, the meetings of the whirling dervishes, the Mawlawīs, also open with a song in praise of the Prophet, the *naat-i sherīf* by the composer Itrī (1050/1640–1123/1711), whose solemnity, reminiscent of Byzantine psalmody, plunges those attending into a state of recollection which prepares them to perform the whirling dance. It says:

> O Beloved of God, incomparable Envoy . . .
> preferred among all the creatures, Light of our eyes . . .
> Thou knowest the weakness of nations,
> Thou art the guide for the infirm,
> the guardian of the garden of prophecy,
> the springtime of gnosis,
> Thou art the rose garden of religious law and
> its most beautiful flower.

These examples, which could be multiplied, illustrate the way that Islam, while keeping itself from anything appearing as a divinization of the intermediary, recognized Muḥammad as an ever-present spiritual guide, able to help the seeker through his influence and his intercession to approach the Lord of the worlds. This manner of recognition, moreover, was not reserved solely for the Prophet, but includes, in Sufism, several categories of saints living or dead and, in Shī'ite Islam, the Imams and certain of their representatives.

Ecstatic Dance

Numerous Sufi orders practice various forms of "dance" accompanied by instrumental, vocal, or simply rhythmic background music. It is thus, at least in Western languages, that these corporeal exercises are named, although the Sufis themselves, cautious to avoid any confusion with the forms of entertainment that accompany popular or worldly merrymaking, generally avoid using the Arabic word *raqṣ*, which properly signifies "dance," and substitute other conventional expressions. In the classical treatises of Sufism,[37] dance is commonly designated by the term *samā'*, which, of course, applies to the totality of the spiritual concert but, taken in this limited sense, makes felt once again the central importance certain orders of dervishes accord physical movements in the context of their mystical gatherings. In addition, the Sufis often speak of *ḥaḍrah,* "presence," to designate ecstatic dance, suggesting by this, on the one hand, that the Prophet himself, together with the angels, attends the assembly of the *fuqarā'* and, on the other hand, that the rhythmic movement that animates the participants is made by a suprahuman power lent to man, so that it is not man who dances but God who makes him dance. They speak also, especially in the Maghrib, of *'imārah,* "plenitude," since he who, by the honesty of his intention and the strength of the collective dance empties himself of selfish thoughts and desires, receives in compensation an abundance of blessings.

The dance of the Sufis has nothing in common with either that which the word "dance" signifies in the West, or even with the traditional forms of Oriental and Far Eastern sacred dance, such as that of the Brahmanic temples or the Shinto sanctuaries, for example, where the protagonists mime and play the parts of supernatural powers. Nor is it a representation, since in principle only the actors take part in it, spectators not being admitted to gatherings except in exceptional cases, such as that of relatives or sympathizers wishing to benefit from the blessed ambience which issues from the gathering.

The movements that make up a *ḥaḍrah* differ according to the brotherhood but can be reduced to a few fairly simple motions. According to the explanations given by the Sufis, in the beginning of the dance there is usually a spontaneous movement, of the same nature as that elicited by the arrival of good news. It is thus that the words of the Prophet addressed to certain of his Companions would have caused physical expressions of overflowing joy, which, imitated by other Companions and repeated from generation to generation, would be at the base of the *ḥaḍrah.* An ecstasy of Abū Bakr was to give birth to the whirling dance practiced by the first group of Sufis before becoming the preferred rite of the Mawlawīs. Another of Ja'far ibn Abī Ṭālib was to be carried on in the leaps into the air to which numerous brotherhoods of *fuqarā'* give themselves over, particularly the Qādirī or Shādhilī orders.[38] Other movements such as the rapid lowering of the upper part of the body passing from a vertical position to a horizontal one and then returning quickly to the vertical in an increasingly rapid rhythm, or the rotation of the head alternatively to the right and to the left derive without doubt from the motions of the canonical prayer while at the same time appear linked to the punctuations of the Semitic speech, which provoke a spontaneous rocking of the body during Quranic psalmody or Judaic prayer.

Sacred dance, like music itself, grafted certain ethnic elements that the Sufis adopted onto the ancient Arabo-Semitic base, already enriched by the coming of Islam. These elements responded to the Sufis' own concerns. Rhythms of African singers (*griots*) entered into the Moroccan brotherhoods—the ʿĪsawiyyah, for example—by way of converted black slaves;[39] fragments of shamanistic ritual were integrated, it is said, into the *samāʿ* of the whirling dervishes;[40] breathing techniques were taken from Christian or Hindu monks, etc. The mystic path, by the same definition, has no borders, and the identical end sought by the seekers of God justifies the sharing of their means.

Whatever their methods, the dances of the dervishes all concur in the same goal, which identifies itself with other Sufi practices and is summed up in the single word *dhikr* (recollection, remembrance of the Divine), ending in the effacement of the creature and in his being taken over by the Being who knows no limits. Sometimes this "state of being" or "ecstasy" (*wijdān, wujūd*) already exists at the beginning of the dance, and this dance then is only the incoercible, spontaneous, and exterior manifestation of an interior state. Sometimes the dance appears like an "effort of seeking" (*tawājud*), which, according to the predisposition of the dancer, may or may not lead to a veritable ecstatic experience.[41] In all the cases, the ideas of spontaneity, simplicity, and absence of affectation reappear constantly in the teaching of the masters, who stress their importance in the validity of the *samāʿ* and its efficacy. Wishing to exculpate themselves and their disciples from the accusation of hypocrisy hurled by the exoteric scholars who accuse them of feigning ecstasy, certain masters went so far as to say that the dance should begin only when one or more dervishes had already entered into a state of rapture and become incapable of controlling themselves. At this moment their "brothers" had the duty of rising and joining them in the ecstatic dance. Most often, however, it is the enthusiasm of the dervish itself, his desire to give himself to God that is taken as the criterion of sincerity and, for the dervish, constitutes the authorization to throw body and soul into the *samāʿ* and with the help of Grace to reach the desired goal, the extinction of self, the inner illumination.

Because of its collective character, which is necessarily noisy and—especially in the case of the Mawlawīs—spectacular, the ecstatic dance has been not only criticized but in numerous instances forbidden by religious or secular authorities. It continues, however, in numerous Sufi orders such as the Rifāʿiyyah and Saʿdiyyah in Syria and Egypt and the Qādiriyyah and Shādhiliyyah which span all of the Muslim world. But it often clothes itself in more discreet forms or dissimulates itself with more or less success under the aspect of cultural or folkloric manifestations as in the case of the Mawlawīs in Turkey or the ʿĪsawiyyah of the Maghrib.[42]

The *Qawwālī* of India and Pakistan

The mystical songs known as *qawwālī* (from the Arabic root *qwl,* "to say") were popularized in India with the Chishtiyyah during the seventh/thirteenth–eighth/fourteenth centuries. This is attributed sometimes to the patronage of Shaykh Muʿīn al-Dīn Chishtī himself, the founder of the order (d. 633/1236), sometimes to that of the Sufi poet Amīr Khusraw (d. 726/1325), whose tomb in Delhi adjoins that of Niẓām al-Dīn Awliyāʾ (d. 726/1325), the fourth great master of the Chishti Order, and remains to this day the preferred meeting place of the *qawwāl* (*qawwālī* singers). In this sanctuary throughout the year one can hear the dervishes singing their religious hymns and poems while accompanying themselves on drums. On holidays real concerts are organized in which eight to ten singers accompanied by various instruments participate; their instruments include the Japanese zither (*jaisho koto*), clarinet, a drum shaped like a cask (*dholak*), the violin (*sarāngi*) and a small manual harmonium imported from Europe in the last century.

The lyrics of the songs, sometimes in Urdu and Persian, sometimes in Hindi, are borrowed from the repertoire of the figurative type of Sufi poetry in which evocations of terrestrial beauty such as the garden with its flowers and perfumes, wine, taverns and cupbearers, the face of the beloved and the sighs of the lover elevate the soul toward contemplation of celestial realities and lead it back to its true existence. Repetitive formulas drawn from the Quran such as *huwa'Llāh* ("He is God") often separate the stanzas of the poems and are taken up as a refrain in unison by the audience. Certain poems are, as in the Shādhilī or Mawlawī *samāʿ*, praises upon the Prophet or his Companions and the saints who came after them. Others are connected with the Arabic tradition, and especially the Persian love song (*ghazal*). Here in the ambience of Sufi brotherhoods is a musical art which, while expressing itself at a popular level, is particularly rich through its permeation by the rhythms and melodic modes (*rāgas*) of Hindustani music.

The Music of the Kurds, "The Faithful to the Truth"

In Iranian Kurdistan (especially the province of Kirmanshah) and in other regions where Kurdish communities are fairly numerous such as Iraq,

Turkey, Azerbaijan, and even India, Pakistan, and Afghanistan, there exists a Shīʿite sect of an esoteric nature, the Ahl-i Ḥaqq or "The Faithful to the Truth," for whom music plays an important role during their ritual assemblies. The importance given to listening to music rests in doctrinal and theosophical considerations that are heavily influenced by Ismāʿīlism and close to Sufism. These are that music awakens the aspiration of the believer and links him again to the Beloved, God (*Yār*), with whom an alliance was sealed in preeternity.[43]

Technically speaking, the principal characteristic of this music is the almost exclusive use that it makes of *ṭanbūr,* a type of long-necked mandolin having two, sometimes three, metallic strings and sixteen frets which when touched with the fingertips give one low sound and one high-pitched sound. The high-pitched sound is used especially for performing solos, the low sound for accompanying song.

Each spiritual guide (*pīr*) should be a musician and, while playing the melodies transmitted by the tradition (certain among them dating, it is said, from the fifth/eleventh century), he renews the Primordial Pact in the manner in which the Angel Gabriel, Pīr-Binyānūn, celebrated it first with the angels and later with their earthly manifestations.

The assembly (*jam*ʿ) includes a series of chanted recitations during which the chanter (*kalām-khwān*), accompanying himself on the *ṭanbūr,* sings religious poems whose refrain is taken up in chorus by those in attendance, who at times clap their hands to mark the rhythm. They often return to the invocation "My beginning and my end are *yār*" in order "to attract the heart' s attention to the Divine Principle." One of the remarkable traits of this music is that it has kept many characteristics of the ancient Persian tradition, that which the court musicians practiced and which, following several periods of persecution, especially in the late Safavid period, was completely lost. That is why at the present time Iranian musicians and Western musicologists are very interested in the twelve melodic modes (*dastgāh*) as well as in the sacred songs and hymns that continue to resonate throughout the rural sanctuaries of the Ahl-i Ḥaqq, poems such as this, whose first verse invites the faithful to the mystical union:

> The Eternal Hunter, O my soul,
> has cast the net of the Pact, O my soul. . . .

Religious Music of Shīʿite Iran

Among the genres of music which are practiced in contemporary Iran, certain ones show a devotional efficacy and an incontestable mystical resonance. These are first of all the ceremonial musical styles associated with the great Shīʿite mourning period (*ʿazādārī*), which commemorates the Karbalāʾ massacre in which Imam Ḥusayn and the members of his family were martyred in 61/680.

These events are recalled in the singing of poems, especially those composed at the beginning of the eleventh/seventeenth century by Ḥusayn Wāʿiẓ Kāshifī in his *Garden (Rawḍah) of the Martyrs.* This collection of poems became so popular that the word *rawḍah* serves to designate all the gatherings, whether held in a mosque or in a private home, during which the martyrdom of the Imams is evoked. The *rawḍah khwāns,* the singers specializing in the recitation of these poems, are held in high esteem by the population.

The processions of penitents and flagellants that take place between the 1st and the 10th of Muḥarram, the first month of the Muslim year, are accompanied by songs and exclamations modulated to the rhythm of the march and are used by the men to punctuate the blows of their fists to their chests and backs.

Finally, the theatrical presentations retrace the same tragic events. These are the *taʿziyahs,* the sacred dramas that are enacted, at least since the eighteenth century, in the open air in a location that has been specially arranged (*takiyyah*). This place includes an elevated stage surrounded by an open space for the actors and their props. The performance lasts well into the night and includes processions accompanied by songs and the sounds of trumpets, with rhythms maintained by drums and cymbals. The cries of "Ḥusayn, Ḥusayn" return again and again, arousing echoes and tears in the crowd.

Each sequence of the drama is sung in a mode (*dastgāh*) that corresponds to the character of the scene and the person represented.[44] One finds here, therefore, the example of a classical music that was popularized and, in the case of the music of the Ahl-i Ḥaqq, later became an instructional tool and a source of inspiration for numerous court musicians, particularly in the Qājār period.

Equally specific to Persia is the music of the *zūrkhānah,* sessions of martial training where the participants wield clubs and heavy chains, spurred on by lyrical songs and powerful rhythms. These sessions take place in a school where corporeal discipline serves the ideal of chivalry such as it was incarnated in the past by Rustam, the hero of the *Shāh-nāmah* (*Book of Kings*), and by ʿAlī, son-in-law of the Prophet and the first of the series of Shīʿite Imams, whose courage earned him the epithet "the Lion of God."

17. The dance of the Mawlawīs from Turkey.

Spiritual Concert of Classical Music

Throughout the entire Islamic world very close threads have been woven between the mystical path and the principal expressions of classical music, this music having shown itself capable, as the Ikhwān al-Ṣafā' had affirmed, not only of arousing aesthetic emotion (*ṭarab*) but of putting the soul into communication with spiritual realities. The distinction between sacred music, devoted to worship, and profane music was often abolished, and music "for entertainment," with its inseparable constituent of sung poetry, was retained in literary and artistic circles as well as in mystical gatherings. Because of the diverse levels of interpretation to which the majority of Oriental poetic compositions lend themselves, with their metaphorical and allegorical language, numerous Sufi musicians did not hesitate, following the example of the *qawwāls* of India in singing *ghazals,* to introduce into their concerts "profane" poems charged for them with a supraterrestrial resonance. Inversely, musicians with a particular mystical calling appreciated—if not for the profundity of their symbolism, at least for their evocative power and their formal beauty—the works of Sufi poets such as *The Great tā'iyyah* and the *Khamriyyah* (*Praise of Wine*) of the Egyptian 'Umar ibn al-Fāriḍ in Arabic, the pieces from the *dīwāns* of Ḥāfiz, of Jāmī or of Rūmī in Persian and, in Turkish, those of Yūnus Emre and Ismail Hakki. Thus a breath of spirituality was made to penetrate by means of music as far as the interior of the princely courts and the noble residences of the cities.

The association between Sufi groups and classical musicians was a quasi-permanent characteristic of Islamic society, and it continues to the present day. The importance of this can perhaps be illustrated by some examples taken from the great cultural regions of the Islamic world.

Arabo-Andalusian Music

In the Arabic-speaking world, a constant progression toward "the perfection of musical knowledge"—to use the title of a musicological treatise previously cited[45]—was carried on during the initial three or four centuries of the *hijrah.* From the mid-second/eighth century, at the end of the Umayyad caliphate of Damascus, there was a formal Arabic music which, being an elaborated version of the popular old recitative, was slowly enriched by Persian and Hellenistic elements borrowed from the new city environments. To ancient poetic meters were added new rhythmic formulas furnished by the quatrain. The melody had assimilated, in adapting to the Arabic taste, the modal system of the Byzantines and Persians. Finally, to the popular instruments, the reed flute and the single stringed *rabāb*, were added the *'ūd* (lute), the *qānūn* (zither), and the three-stringed *kamānchah*, as well as several percussion instruments such as the standing drum (*duff*). From that time on, this music had only to reach its full expansion, which came during the long reign of the Abbasids, from 132/750 to 656/1258.

Then suddenly came the Mongol invasion, the destruction of Baghdad, and the end of the great epoch of Arabo-Islamic civilization. Some musicians no doubt survived the disaster and continued to transmit their art even in Baghdad and in various Oriental cities. However, it would hardly be possible today to form any kind of precise notion of what this ancient music was in its plenitude, such as it was analyzed by an Ibn Misjāḥ, an Isḥāq al-Mawṣilī, al-Kindī, al-Fārābī and their followers if, several centuries before the Mongol invasion, a branch of this art had not been transplanted from Baghdad to the land of Andalusia and had not prospered marvelously there before being taken up in North Africa, where it has been perpetuated to the present day. The creator of this act of transplanting was a musician of genius, Zaryāb, who, after having studied with Isḥāq al-Mawṣilī in Baghdad, found himself forced to emigrate to Cordova in order to escape the jealousy of his master. Received with full honors at the court of the caliph 'Abd al-Raḥmān II in 206/821, Zaryāb developed there an original musical style that was based on the canons of classical music. Relying on the correspondences established by al-Kindī between the four strings of the lute: first (*zīr*, C), second (*mathnā*, G), third (*mathlath*, D), fourth (*bam*, A), the cosmic qualities (cold-humid; hot-dry), the colors (yellow, red, white, black), and the human temperaments (bilious, sanguine, phlegmatic, melancholic), he went very far in the knowledge and utilization of the psycho-physiological effect of musical modes. He added a fifth string to the lute to represent the soul, and he elaborated a musical style called the *nawbah*, a style thoroughly imbued with these symbolic perceptions.

A *nawbah*, which could be translated approximately as "suite," contains four (five in Morocco) melodic and rhythmic movements (*dawr*) performed with song and orchestra in an order fixed by Zaryāb that never varied. The order was (1) free recitative (*nashīd*), (2) moderato movement (*basīṭ*), (3) rapid passages (*muḥarrakāt*) and (4) a lively finale (*hazajāt*). There currently exist eleven *nawbahs*, each of which is performed in a particular musical mode (*maqām*; called *ṭba'*, pl. *ṭubū'*, in Morocco) such as the major mode (*raṣd*), which expresses pride; the mode of lovers (*ushshāq*), which is that of joy and is played in the morning; the *mayā*, which evokes the sadness of separation and is played in the evening; or the *ramelmayā*, reserved for the praise upon the Prophet.[46]

Still today, a concert of Andalusian music, whether in a light style (*kalām al-hazl*) or a serious style (*kalām al-jadd*), whether its recitatives are borrowed from classical prosody (*kalām mawzūn*) or popular poetry (*kalām malḥūn*), or whether, as often happens, it alternates pieces of different styles, has always a soothing and purifying effect on the souls of the listeners. All vulgarity is excluded, and the numerous allusions and conventional but always efficacious images with which it is punctuated—the Beloved, the night (*Laylā*) whose presence is awaited with hope and longing, the garden and its flowers, its fruits and its streams of nectar, the frequently mentioned Friend of God (the Prophet Muḥammad) and that of God Himself, named by his "Beautiful Names"—are a constant call to return to the source of Beauty expressed in the music. This is why—in Fez, for example—since the epoch in which the Meridian sultans patronized the Andalusian musicians, the authorities and the dignitaries of the city have never ceased to encourage the practice of an art that was felt to be completely compatible with their religious sentiments.

In the Maghrib, despite the rule most usually followed, forms of *samā'* derived directly from Andalusian music and using its instruments—the lute, the *rabāb*, the drum, and the flute—found favor in the eyes of certain Sufi masters in the cities that excluded from the religious context the performance of instrumental music. In Tetuan particularly, a city that was a refuge of Andalusian artistic traditions from the time of the final exodus of the Muslims from Spain in the ninth/fifteenth and eleventh/seventeenth centuries, an eminently "orthodox" Sufi order can be found, the Ḥarrāqiyyah, founded around 1261/1845 by Muḥammad al-Ḥarrāq, a disciple of Mawlāy al-'Arabī al-Darqāwī. This order uses the instruments and the melodies of the *nawbah* to prepare the participants for the performance of the sacred dance (*'imārah*) by having them listen to a series of pieces. The dance itself is also sustained by a chorus of singers (*munshidūn*) and beats of the drum.

Persian Music

Heir to the rich Sassanid tradition, then impregnated with Islamic influences—first Arab and later Turkish and Indian—the music of Persia managed to preserve its personality and its own characteristics throughout the centuries. Its efficacy as a transmuting agent of the soul and the conditions in which it is licit to have recourse therein has perhaps never been explained as explicitly as by the Sufi Rūzbihān Baqlī of Shiraz (d. 606/1209), master of theology, music, and poetry, of whom it could be said that he was "one of the *fedeli d'amore* of Islam."[47] All of his written works—

treatises, commentaries, and poems—are exhortations to return to the Divine Source, which calls to man, issuing from Itself, by means of the voice of the Quranic Word and that of spiritual music, the *samāʿ*.

> Sometimes He says, "You are myself," and sometimes He says, "I am you." . . . Sometimes, He rejects him and sometimes He grants him peace in divine intimacy. . . . Sometimes He throws him into complete slavery, and sometimes He plunges him into the essence of Lordship. Sometimes He makes him drunken from the Beauty of God, sometimes He belittles him before His Majesty. . . . All that happens during the *samāʿ* and still much more.[48]

It is the same message that Jalāl al-Dīn Rūmī delivers in his *Mathnawī:*

> The believers say that the effects of
>   paradise will make every ugly voice beautiful.
> We were all part of Adam and heard those
>   melodies in paradise.
> Though water and clay have covered us with doubt,
>   we still remember something of those sounds. . .
> Sounds and songs strengthen the images within the mind
>   or rather, turn them into Forms.[49]

That the Persians were particularly gifted in composing, performing, and listening to music with a spiritual intention is confirmed by numerous historical testimonies. In the contemporary period, despite certain signs of degeneration and ruptures that are no doubt irreparable, there are musicians to whom it is given to enter into a sublime mystical state (*ḥāl*) and from it to communicate with their listeners. In this state, the artist "plays with an extraordinary facility of performance. His sonority changes. The musical phrase surrenders its secret to him. . . ."[50] According to another contemporary observer, even if the hardening manifested by the official Shīʿite circles toward the Sufi orders, which began near the end of the Safavid period, has more or less discouraged the use of music in mystical gatherings, the content of this music has nonetheless preserved its spiritual connotations and efficacy: "there always exists among traditional musicians a certain sense of the sacred." Thus for the master Davāmī, the ninety-year-old depository of a very vast and difficult repertoire, "it is indispensable to have first a knowledge of the hereafter (*irtibāt-i maʿnawī*) before being able to practice music," this knowledge (*ʿirfān*) itself implying a purification of the external senses and the internal faculties which make man become like a mirror.[51]

Judging by my personal experience, listening to a concert of Persian classical music demands of the listener the same meditative disposition and leads him along the same paths and toward the same experiences as an evening of Andalusian music. Even if the resonances of the voices and instruments are different—those of Iran having the advantage of sweetness and of femininity—the melodic and rhythmic structures show so many affinities that one feels oneself transported into the same realm. It is that of the twelve fundamental modes (*āwāz*), which subdivide into modal figures (*gūshah*) arranged according to an order (*radīf*) established by the greatest masters and in part immutable. It is a world where quality does not consist of innovation and of displays of virtuosity but rather of exposition with fidelity, embellishing with appropriate ornamentation and improvisation the various sequences or figures of the chosen mode. The concert thus takes on the aspect of a gathering of friends where a theme is solemnly introduced and developed, then debated during an exchange of questions and responses, before being meditated upon in a collective spirit in order finally to culminate in the exaltation of a discovery that fills all the listeners with joy.

Turkish Music

The same remarks, or similar ones, could be applied to the classical music of Turkey. It not only is heir to the Arab, Byzantine, and Persian melodic modes but also is the bearer of sounds and rhythms that came from the steppes of Asia and were for centuries strongly permeated with mystical concerns. In Turkey, perhaps more than in any other Islamic region, the great religious orders—Mawlawīs, Baktāshīs, Khalwatīs—made much use of music in their ceremonies. The first of these orders particularly trained a large number of singers and instrumentalists who, while remaining affiliated with the order, became musicians attached to the court of the sultans such as the *dede* (dervish) Ismail, one of the great masters of classical music, much in favor during the reign of Selim III (1203/1789–1222/1807). Some 150 compositions have been handed down from him to us.

Performing and listening to a *peşrev,* or "prelude"—one of the most characteristic forms of Turkish classical music—constitutes an exercise of concentration for the musician and, for the listener, an invitation to contemplative reflection. Composed of four parts (*hane,* "house"), each one followed by a refrain (*teslím*) that forms the key for the melodic construction, the *peşrev* is played in one or more modes (*makām*). During its unfoldment, always slow and restrained, accelerating slightly only in the finale, each musician restricts himself to embellishing the fundamental melody at the appropriate places, adding there the conventional grace notes: the *taşil bezek* or "petrified decoration"—a term that designates also the arabesques of architectural decoration—and, at the desired moment, to interrupting the combined movement to perform a solo improvisation (*taksīm*). During the sessions of *samā'* of the whirling dervishes, where the *peşrev* has its place, the *taksīm* is always given to the player of the *nay*, the reed flute, this voice of the soul in love with the Absolute:

> It is necessary to have heard a *nay* played in a large resonant hall; it is necessary to have seen at the same time the dance of the dervishes, in all its solemnity to realize the profound inner emotion which is released.[52]

The *nay*, however, is not restricted to the dervishes. Whether it accompanies vocal ensembles or is integrated into complete instrumental ensembles—including the zither (*qānūn*), the ordinary lute, the *ṭambūr* (a lute with a very long neck allowing the division of the octave by twenty-four frets), the violin (*kamānchah*) of two or three strings and percussive instruments—it punctuates most classical concerts with its nostalgic calls.

Hindustani Music

Between Hindus and Muslims in northern India a remarkable synthesis has taken place in the realm of the art of music that began with the growth of Islam on the Indian subcontinent in the sixth/twelfth and seventh/thirteenth centuries. The first artisans of this meeting were, as we have seen in relation to the singers of *qawwālīs*, the masters and the members of the Chishtī Order, who by the radiance of their faith brought about conversions to Islam by the score—indeed, by the hundreds of thousands. Practicing *samā'* as a method of spiritual realization (Mu'īn al-Dīn Chishtī, the founder of the order, considered that "song is the sustenance and the support of the soul"[53]), these Sufis contributed by introducing a number of Islamic elements into Indian classical music, and they borrowed extensively from the very rich melodic and rhythmic repertoire of India.

In order for such an interpenetration to be possible, it was necessary that the theoretical and practical foundations of the two musical universes thus brought into contact—the Arabo-Persian and the Indian—be compatible, if not identical. To the theory of "influence" (*ta'thīr*)—that is, the *ethos* of the ancient Greeks thereafter Arabized and applied to the Arabo-Persian musical modes—corresponds Hindu *bhava*, the nature of the emotion connected to a *rāga* (the musical mode of India). *Bhava* engenders the *rasa*, the flavor or state of the soul (Arabic *dhawq*, *ḥāl*) particular to this mode. The classification of *rāgas* and of their effects and macro- and microcosmic relationships surpassed in subtlety even that of the Muslim musicologists. All the conditions were therefore assembled for fruitful reciprocal relations, which often had as a theater the princely courts. These courts included that of the sultan of Delhi, 'Alā' al-Dīn Khiljī, where the Sufi poet, musician, and composer of Turkish origin Amīr Khusraw inaugurated the style of highly modulated "imaginative" song (*khayāl*) and popularized the Persian love poem (*ghazal*), and the court of the great Mughals, especially of the emperor Akbar, where Hindu and Muslim musicians brought to perfection such noble styles as the *dhrupad*, which is constructed on rhythmic poems of four verses; the *dhamar*, still more rhythmic; and the *tappā* with its delicate ornamentation.[54]

Even today, the performers of Hindustani music are recruited from among Hindu as well as Muslim families, the latter being able to pride themselves on having contributed to the transmission through generations of musicians of one of the most beautiful musical traditions humanity has ever known. Considering that according to Indian doctrine, "he who is expert in the science of modal intervals and scales and who knows the rhythms, travels easily on the path of deliverance,"[55] and that "at the time of *samā'*, the Sufis hear another sound, from God's Throne,"[56] one cannot doubt that this music was an effective means of reaching inner perfection for the members of the two religious communities.

> Music is not only the first art brought by Śiva into the world, the art through which the *asrār-i alast* or the mystery of the primordial covenant between man and God in that preeternal dawn of the day of cosmic manifestation is revealed; but it is also the key to the understanding of the harmony that pervades the cosmos. It is the handmaid of wisdom itself.[57]

Popular Music

In all the regions penetrated by Islam, numerous forms of popular music were allowed to exist or to expand alongside the strictly religious music and the great classical currents. To take an inventory would not be possible in these pages, but we shall cite some cases in which popular music is used for the mystical quest. Sometimes it is a music with a classical structure that is popularized by adopting the vernacular language and local instruments. Thus the *griha* of the Maghrib, sung in various Arabic dialects—Moroccan, Algerian, or Tunisian—continues the tradition of pre-Islamic ballads (*qaṣīdas*) based on the airs of *nawbahs*. The Moroccan, Tunisian, and Libyan *malḥūn* is a dialectized Andalusian music. Both serve to perform innumerable pieces of poetry or rhymed prose composed in dialects of Arabic by Sufi masters.

Throughout the expanse of the *dār al-islām*, non-Arab ethnic groups integrated Islamic formulas into their repertoires. The Atlas Berbers sing the *ahellel* (Arabic *tahlīl*), which is none other than the profession of faith, *lā ilāha illa'Llāh.* The Moorish women of the western Sahara dance the *guedra,* the ancient rite of communication with the fecundating forces, while the chorus of men introduces the names of the Prophet and the One God into its rhythmic breathing.

A final example, taken from the folklore of Morocco, illustrates the very frequent situations in which the music of a village, connected to the cult of a saint, regularly animates religious ceremonies and feasts. The village of Jahjuka, located in the region of Jbala, not far from Ksar el-Kebir, possesses a troupe of clarinetists and drummers whose origin goes back to the time when, twelve centuries ago, the village was founded by the saint Sidi Aḥmad Sharq and his companion, a musician named Muḥammad al-'Aṭṭār, of Oriental origin. Each Friday, the musicians march through the village to the tomb of the saint, where the faithful come to ask for healing of diseases of the body and soul. The high-pitched sound of the *ghaitas* and the intense rhythm of the drums puts the listeners in a state of trance, which opens for them the blessed influence (*barakah*) of the saint while facilitating its therapeutic action.[58]

Epilogue

From each of the areas of classical music as well as from popular music flow strong and enduring testimonies showing that these styles of music, like those that serve more explicitly as a vehicle for the words of the Quranic revelation—the litanies of the pious or the hymns of the mystics—are an echo of the Beyond, an open path to the liberation of the soul and to its return to the lost homeland, toward the infinite Silence which is the origin of all sounds just as the infinitesimal point is the origin of space and the nonmeasurable instant is the principle of temporality. Providential instrument of the unification of multiplicity, the traditional music of Islam aids man in realizing by a path of beauty that "in truth we belong to God and in truth to Him we will return" (Quran II, 156).

Translated by Katherine O'Brien

Notes

1. *Arinā'l-ashyā' kamā hiya; ḥadīth* cited by Fakhr al-Dīn al-Rāzī in his *Great Commentary* on the Quran (*Mafātiḥ al-ghayb*) with respect to the verse XVII, 85: "They will question thee concerning the Spirit . . ." (*Al-Tafsīr al-kabīr* [2nd ed.; Tehran, n.d.) vols.

21–22, 37. Also cited by Hujwīrī in his *Kashf al-maḥjūb* (see n. 5 below) with respect specifically to the contradictory opinions concerning the spiritual concert (*al-samāʻ*).

2. The complete work includes fifty-one (or fifty-two) "Epistles" (*rasāʼil*), of which the one treating music is the fifth. See "L'épître sur la musique des Ikhwān al-ṣafāʼ," translation and annotation by A. Shiloah, *Revue des études islamiques* 31 (1964) 125–62; 33 (1966) 159–93. The passages cited hereafter are found on pp. 155–58 (1964).

3. Shiloah, *Revue des études islamiques* 33 (1966) 185. In the same way, F. Schuon writes, "while listening to beautiful music, the guilty will feel innocent. But the contemplative, on the contrary, while listening to the same music, will forget himself while fathoming the essences" (*Sur les traces de la religion pérenne* [Paris: Le Courier du Livre, 1982] 66–67).

4. Cited by H. G. Farmer, *A History of Arabian Music* (London: Luzac, 1929; repr. 1973) 36.

5. This work dates to the second half of the fifth/eleventh century, according to R. A. Nicholson, who gave an English translation of it in the E. J. W. Gibb Memorial Series, vol. 17 (London: Luzac, 1911; repr. 1959).

6. As by Ibn ʻAlī al-Kātib, who cites al-Fārābī. See A. Shiloah, *La Perfection des connaissances musicales* (Paris: Geuthner, 1972) 65–68.

7. On this see especially Farmer, *History*, chap. 2 ("Islam and Music"); J. Robson (see n. 8 below); and M. Molé (see n. 9 below).

8. A translation was made of this by J. Robson, *Tracts on Listening to Music*, Oriental Translation Fund n.s. 34, R.A.S. (London: Royal Asiatic Society, 1938). It is followed by the translation of the treatise entitled *Bawāriq al-ilmāʻ*, attributed to the Sufi Aḥmad al-Ghazzālī surnamed Majd al-Dīn (d. 520/1126), brother of the celebrated Abū Ḥāmid al-Ghazzālī (Algazel), author of the *Iḥyāʼ*. In contrast to Ibn Abiʼl-Dunyā, the author supports the legality of music and exalts the virtues of the spiritual concert. In his introduction to these two treatises (pp. 1–13), J. Robson summarizes well the arguments employed by the defenders of these antithetical positions.

9. Cited by M. Molé, in *Les Danses sacrées* (Paris: Seuil, 1963) 164 ("La Danse extatique en Islam"). This study contains abundant documentation, drawn from original and often little-known sources, on the arguments for and against the use of music and dance in the mystical path.

10. On all these philosophers, who wrote extensively on musical theory, see *The Encyclopaedia of Islam*, vols. 1, 2; see also the bibliography of this chapter under Erlanger and Farmer.

11. For a better understanding of the Greco-Islamic affinities and their influence on musical science, see the works of H. G. Farmer, especially *The Sources of Arabian Music* (Glasgow: Glasgow Bibliographical Society, 1939), which includes the writings of Arabic authors. See also P. Kraus, *Jābir ibn Ḥayyān: Contribution à l'histoire des idées scientifiques dans Islam, Jābir et la science grecque* (Paris: Les Belles Lettres, 1986); Y. Marquet, "Imāmat, résurrection et hiérarchie selon les Ikhwān aṣ-Ṣafāʼ," in *Revue des études islamiques* 29 (1962) 49–142; E. Werner and J. Sonne, "The Philosophy and Theory of Music in Judeo-Arabic Literature," in *Hebrew Union College Annual* 16 (1941) 251–319; 17 (1942–43) 511–72, wherein the three chapters concerning music are translated from the *Kitāb ādāb al-falāsifah* of Ḥunayn ibn Isḥāq.

12. *Revue des études islamiques* 31 (1964) 126–27 (see n. 2 above).

13. Ibid.

14. Singer/composer, theoretician and historian as well as jurist (150/767–236/850), Isḥāq al-Mawṣilī played a considerable role in the transmission of an Arabo-Persian musical art that was highly refined under the Abbasid caliphate. His father, Ibrāhīm

(124/742–188/804) was himself a consummate musician. A regular guest of Hārūn al-Rashīd, he owned the most richly endowed music school of Baghdad (see Farmer, *History,* 124–26).

15. Cited by Farmer, *History,* 156.

16. Cited by G. H. Farmer, "The Religious Music of Islam," *Journal of the Royal Asiatic Society* (1952) 60–65. See also in M. M. Sharif, ed., *A History of Muslim Philosophy* (Wiesbaden: Harrassowitz, 1963) 2:1126 (chap. 57, "Music"). Chapter 58 in this last work contains a good summary of musical theories that were expressed at different epochs and in different regions of the Islamic world, such as the influence exercised by Islamic music in other cultural domains.

17. Shiloah, *Revue des études islamiques* 33 (1966) 192–93.

18. Ibid.

19. It is the eighth book of the "quarter" of the *Iḥyā'* dealing with the "social customs" (*'ādāt*). It has been translated into English by E. B. Macdonald, *Journal of the Royal Asiatic Society* (1901) 195–252, 705–46; (1902) 1–28, where the passage cited appears on p. 199.

20. This concerns Nezih Uzel, who has given several recitals in Europe and made recordings of Sufi music together with Kudsi Erguner, a player of the *nay,* the reed flute precious to the Mawlawīs.

21. *Kashf al-maḥjūb;* cited by Molé in *Danses sacrées,* 192.

22. Trans. E. B. Macdonald, *Journal of the Royal Asiatic Society* (1901) 730–31. The *ḥadīth* to which Ghazzālī alluded states: "If ye weep not, try to weep," and it is often cited to justify certain Sufi practices, such as the sacred dance (see M. Lings, *A Sufi Saint of the Twentieth Century, Shaikh Aḥmad Al-'Alawī* [Berkeley: University of California Press, 1971] 92–93.

23. Aḥmad ibn 'Ajībah (1160/1747–1224/1809), his master Muḥammad al-Būzīdī (d. 1229/1814), and his master Mawlāy al-'Arabī al-Darqāwī (d. 1238/1823) belong to the great initiatic line of the Shādhilī, who, in Morocco, gave rise to numerous ramifications such as the Darqāwī Order, founded by the last named of these three masters.

24. The "master of the circle" of the Sufis, who taught and died in Baghdad in 298/911.

25. J.-L. Michon, *Le Soufi marocain Aḥmad Ibn 'Ajība et son Mi'rāj, Glossaire de la mystique musulmane* (Paris: J. Vrin, 1973) 241–42.

26. *Bawāriq* (see n. 8 above). Cited by Molé, *Les Danses sacrées,* 205–6; and Robson, *Tracts,* 98–99.

27. On the subject of these correspondences, which the Arabs systematized starting with Greek sources but which also had roots in the ancient Semites, see H. G. Farmer, *Sa'adyah Gaon on the Influence of Music* (London: A. Probsthain, 1943) 9.

28. On the theory of *maqām,* see in particular R. Erlanger, *La Musique arabe* (Paris: P. Geuthner, 1949) vol. 5; on its current practice in the diverse areas of the Arabo-Muslim world, see S. Jargy, *La Musique arabe* (Paris: Que sais-je? 1971) 49–69.

29. The most anciently used term was *ṣawt,* literally, "the voice," which clearly marks the principally vocal character of the Arabo-Islamic music during its first period. Later, authors spoke of *ṭarīqah,* "way," "manner of acting," a term that has also fallen into disuse.

30. K. Reinhard and U. Reinhard, *Les Traditions musicales–Turquie* (Paris: Buchet-Chastel, 1969) 69–70.

31. S. H. Nasr, "The Influence of Sufism on Traditional Persian Music," in *Islamic Art and Spirituality,* 163–74.

32. *Encyclopaedia of Islam,* vol. 1, under "Mūsīḳī."

33. Farmer, *History,* 25.

34. Erlanger, *La musique arabe,* 1:14–16.

35. There are seven or, according to certain classifications, ten readings of the Quran which all go back to the second/eighth century and are drawn from the prophetic tradition. They are as follows: (1) the school of Medina, founded by Nāfi' (d. 169/785), whose principal disciple was the Imam Mālik, spread into Egypt, Tunisia, Sicily, Algeria, and Spain; (2) the school of Mecca, founded by Ibn Kathīr (d. 120/738); (3) the school of Basra, founded by Ibn al-'Alā' (d. 154/771); (4) the school of Damascus, founded by Ibn 'Amīr (d. 118/736) and still widely practiced in Syria; (5) the school of Kufa, which itself is made up of three branches—(a) the school of 'Aṣim al-Asadī (d. 128/745), which spread throughout the Muslim world and today is firmly implanted in Egypt, thanks to the recent editions of the Quran; (6=b) the school of Ḥamzah al-Ijlī (d. 156/772), propagated in Morocco; and (7=c) the school of Kisā'ī (d. 189/805), of which Ibn Ḥanbal was a zealous defender and which is still popular in Eastern Arabia and in Iraq. See Muḥammad Ṭāhir al-Khaṭṭāt, *Ta'rīkh al-qur'ān,* (Cairo, 1372/1953) 108; and Si Hamza Boubakeur, "La psalmodie coranique," in *Encyclopédie des musiques sacrées* (Paris: Labergerie, 1968).

36. *Ḥadīth* cited by Boubakeur, "Psalmodie," in *Encyclopédie des musiques sacrées,* 1:388.

37. Such as the *Risālah* (*Epistle*) of al-Qushayrī (d. 465/1072) and, by the same author, a short treatise on the conditions and the modalities of *samā'* (*aḥkām al-samā'*). See *al-Risā'il al-qushayriyyah,* ed. F. Muḥammad Ḥasan (Beirut, n.d.); reprinted by the same editor (Karachi, 1964) 50–63. See also the *'Awārif al-ma'ārif* of 'Umar al-Suhrawardī, which contains a very interesting chapter on the *ādāb al-samā'*, a French translation of which was made by E. Blochet, *Etudes sur l'ésotérisme musulman* (Louvain, 1910).

38. We have already seen the explanation of the symbolism of these gestures given by Aḥmad Ghazzālī in his *Bawāriq.* The two great "styles" of the mystical gathering which they incorporate are described in greater detail in our chapter "The Spiritual Practices of Sufism" in *Islamic Spirituality: Foundations,* 265–93.

39. See J.-L. Michon, "'Īsawiyya," in *The Encyclopaedia of Islam,* vol. 2.

40. See M. Köprülüzade, "Influence du chamanisme turcomongol sur les ordres mystiques musulmans," *Mémoire Institut de Turcologie Université Stamboul,* N.S.I., 1929.

41. The question of the relationships between *dhikr* and *samā'* and the primacy which, depending on the period and the school, was given to one or the other of these two is examined by F. Meier, "Der Derwischtanz," *Etudes Asiatiques* 8/1–4 (1954) 107–36.

42. For a more detailed inventory of these brotherhoods, see L. Massignon and V. Monteil, *Annuaire du monde musulman* (1954); and J. Spencer Trimingham, *The Sufi Orders in Islam.*

43. The sect has been thoroughly studied by Mohammad Mokri, who sets the number of its adherents at approximately five hundred thousand. See the essay by him, *Journal asiatique* (1956) 391–422; (1962) 369–433. See also *L'Esotérisme kurde;* and "La musique sacrée des kurdes," in *Encyclopédie des musiques sacrées,* 1:441–53.

44. Some examples with musical transcriptions are given by N. Caron, "La musique chiite en Iran," in *Encyclopédie des musiques sacrées,* 1:430–40.

45. Shiloah, *La Perfection des connaissances musicales.*

46. On the *nawbah* and music of the Maghrib in general, see J. Rouanet, "La musique

arabe" and "La musique maghrébine" in A. Lavignac and L. de la Laurencie, *Encyclopédie de la musique et dictionnaire du Conservatoire* (Paris: C. Delagrave, 1921–31); and P. Garcia Barriuso, *La musica hispano-musulmana en Marruecos* (Madrid: Instituto de Estudios Africanos, 1950).

47. H. Corbin, *En Islam iranien,* 2:9–146; cited by S. H. Nasr, "L'Islam e la Musica secondo Ruzbahan Baqli, santo patrono di Sciraz," in *Sufi, musiche et cerimonie dell'Islam* (Milano: Centro di Ricerca per il Teatro, 4, 1981).

48. Rūzbihān Baqlī of Shiraz, *Risalat al-quds* (Tehran, 1351) 54; cited by J. During, "Revelation and Spiritual Audition in Islam," in *The World of Music–Sacred Music, Journal of the International Institute for Comparative Music Studies and Documentation* 24/3 (1982) 68–84.

49. Cited by W. Chittick in *The Sufi Path of Love: The Spiritual Teachings of Rumi,* 326.

50. N. Caron and D. Safvate, *Iran–Les traditions musicales* (Paris: Buchet-Chastel, 1966) 232.

51. J. During, "Eléments spirituels dans la musique traditionelle iranienne contemporaine," *Sophia Perennis* 1/2 (1975) 129–54.

52. K. Reinhard and U. Reinhard, *Turquie–Les traditions musicales,* 105.

53. Cited by J. Sharif, *Islam in India* (London: Curzon Press, 1972) 289.

54. Concerning these different styles, see A. Daniélou, *Northern Indian Music* (2 vols.; London and Calcutta: C. Johnson, 1949–1954). The spiritual value of Indian music and the vigor that the music of Mughal India experienced under the influence of Islam have been analyzed in depth by L. Aubert, "Aperçus sur la signification de la musique indienne," *Revue musicale de la Suisse romande* 34/2 (1981) 50–61.

55. *Yājnavalkya Smriti,* cited by W. N. Perry, *A Treasury of Traditional Wisdom* (London: Allen & Unwin, 1971) 685.

56. Rūmī, *Dīwān,* 11163, trans. W. Chittick, *Sufi Path of Love,* 328.

57. S. H. Nasr, "Traditional Art as Fountain of Knowledge and Grace," in *Knowledge and the Sacred,* The Gifford Lectures (Edinburgh: Edinburgh University Press, 1981) 272.

58. To meet the requirements for the production of a documentary film, ethnomusicological research was conducted in the summer of 1982 in the village of Jahjuka by Philip D. Schuyler, who was then Assistant Professor of Music, Columbia University, New York, who kindly showed me his notes and the synopsis of his film.

25

The Spirituality of Islamic Art*

TITUS BURCKHARDT

In one of the halls of the Alhambra, there is a basin of water to which an Arabic poem inscribed on the wall refers:

> The water of the basin in my center is
> like the soul of a believer who rests in
> the remembrance of God.

THE ART OF ISLAM, without doubt, is essentially a contemplative art. This means that it expresses above all a state of the soul that is open toward the interior, toward an encounter with the Divine Presence. We can say equally that it is directly concerned with a sacred art or the absence, in its most typical works, of any individual impulse; the artist is effaced in the work or in the tradition which guarantees its legitimacy.

The essence of art is beauty. Beauty is at once very much interior and very much exterior. It attaches itself to the appearances of things and at the same time rejoins in its qualitative limitlessness the Divine Being Itself, since it penetrates beyond all duality, such as that of creator and creature, unfathomable plenitude in unity and unity in diversity. It is like a bridge that goes from the tangible world toward God. Beauty includes in its character illusion and seduction only to the degree to which it is disordered and limited by human subjectivity; it is then as if mixed with foreign tendencies. For an art to be contemplative it must reflect beauty objectively, therefore, without overtaxing it. We do not speak of sentiments but of emotions and vanities. This calls for certain clarifications. A work of art does not depend, in its contemplative capacity, on social circumstances; that

*This is the last work of Titus Burckhardt, written several weeks before his death with instructions to the editor of this volume for the adaption of certain of its passages from his previous writings.

such and such a monarch or such and such a rich merchant has a church or a mosque built in order to derive glory personally therefrom clearly does not diminish the validity of the implied sacred art. Human vanity corrupts art only insofar as it corrupts the vision itself of the artist. Either the very style of the art is the impression of an individual or collective emotion—as in Greek art of the classical period, in which man is emotionally divinized—or the subject of the art is vain, or the artistic methods are tributaries of illusion, such as occurs in the naturalist art of the West—without speaking of the total and exasperated subjectivism of the Western art of our times.

It is easy to see that Islamic art avoids all these tendencies. Its serenity is not disturbed by any emotion. Individualism does not drag it into its traps; never does it seek to create illusions, and its beauty is all the less subjective in that it manifests itself in a quasi-abstract aspect. One could even say, without risk of false generalization, that Islamic art has no other content. It is so because Islamic art is above all, as is all Islamic spirituality, a witness to (*shahādah*) or a contemplation of (*mushāhadah*) Divine Unity. On the level of forms, Unity manifests itself the most directly as beauty. That is why the consciousness of Unity and the love of beauty are closely linked in Islamic gnosis. All Sufi poetry exalts beauty; for the contemplative whose vision is no longer disturbed by emotion and vanity, beauty, where it manifests itself, is the very face of God: "Wherever ye turn, there is the Face of God" (Quran II, 115). "We will show them Our signs upon the horizons and within themselves, until they know that it is the truth" (Quran XLI, 53). "He is the First and the Last, the Outward and the Inward" (Quran LVII, 3).

Since the majority of men are subject to emotional illusions, it is not upon beauty but upon law and virtue that religious instruction must insist. The doctrine of beauty, which is implicitly contained in the Quran, is necessarily the appanage of esoterism. Is it conceivable that this irradiation of pure and impersonal beauty which is Islamic art could have been produced without it?

The Ka'bah

It seems natural and even inevitable to begin a study of Islamic art with a brief description of the Ka'bah, which is a proof of the timeless character of the great Semitic tradition from which Islam is descended. The Ka'bah is in effect the spiritual center of Islam—the origin and the center—toward which all believers turn while they recite the prescribed prayers and toward which all mosques are oriented. The Ka'bah is the sole irreplaceable object in the religion of Islam. If it is not a work of art in the proper sense of the term—being no more than a simple cube of masonry—it belongs rather to what might be termed "proto-art," whose spiritual dimension corresponds to myth or revelation, depending on the point of view. This means that the inherent symbolism of the Ka'bah, in its shape and the rites associated with it, contains in embryo everything expressed by the sacred art of Islam.

The Ka'bah's role as the liturgical center of the Muslim world is bound up with the fact that it demonstrates Islam's link with the Abrahamic tradition and thereby with the origin of all the monotheist religions. According to the Quran, the Ka'bah was built by Abraham and his son Ishmael, and it was Abraham who established the yearly pilgrimage to this sanctuary. Center and origin are two aspects of one and the same spiritual reality or, one could say, the two fundamental options of every spirituality.

For the generality of Muslims, to pray facing the Ka'bah—or facing Mecca, which comes to the same thing—expresses a priori a choice: by this gesture, the Muslim is distinguished both from the Jews, who pray facing Jerusalem, and the Christians, who "orientate" themselves literally by facing the sunrise. He elects to join the "religion of the center," which is like the tree of which the other Semitic religions are the branches. "Abraham was neither Jew nor Christian," says the Quran, "but detached (*ḥanīf*) and submitting (*muslim*) . . ." (III, 67). The impact of these words is that the faith of Abraham—who is here the very typification of a Muslim—is free from the specializations and limitations represented, in Muslim eyes, by the Jewish concept of a people chosen to the exclusion of all others, and by the Christian dogma of a unique savior, the Son of God.

Let us note that the Quranic account of the building of the Ka'bah by Abraham does not stress his role as ancestor of the Arabs—his descendants through Ishmael and Hagar—but his function as the apostle of pure and universal monotheism that Islam purposes to renew. Whatever the historical basis of this account, it is inconceivable that the Prophet should have invented it for more or less political motives, apart from questions of sincerity. The pre-Islamic Arabs were obsessed with genealogy, which is, in any case, a characteristic of nomads, and would never have accepted the "interpolation" of a hitherto unknown ancestor. If the Bible makes no reference to a sanctuary founded by Abraham and Ishmael in Arabia, this is because it had no cause to refer to a sanctuary placed outside the land and destiny of Israel. It nevertheless recognized the spiritual destiny of the Ishmaelites by including them in God's promise to Abraham. Let us note finally—without straying too far from our subject—that it is typical of a divine "geometry," which is both strict and unforeseeable, to make use of an Abrahamic sanctuary lost in the desert and forgotten by the great religious communities of the time, in order to have a starting point for renewing monotheism of a Semitic complexion.

The eminently archaic form of the Mecca sanctuary accords well with the Abrahamic origin attributed to it. It has, indeed, been destroyed and rebuilt frequently, but the very name Ka'bah, which means "cube," is a warrant that its shape has not been essentially modified; it is slightly irregular, being twelve meters long, ten meters broad, and about sixteen meters high. The building is traditionally covered with a "vesture" (*kiswah*), which is changed yearly and has since the Abbasid period been made of shimmering black cloth embroidered with gold lettering, which bespeaks in striking fashion the abstract and mysterious aspect of the edifice. The custom of "clothing" the sanctuary was apparently introduced by an ancient Himyarite king and seems to be part of an extremely venerable Semitic tradition that is alien in style to the Greco-Roman world: to "clothe" a house is, in a way, to treat it as a living body or as an ark bearing a spiritual influence, and that is how the Arabs understood it. The celebrated black stone is enclosed not in the center of the Ka'bah but in an outer wall close to its meridian angle. It is a meteorite, a stone fallen from heaven, and the Prophet did no more than confirm its sacred character. Finally, let us mention the outer precinct, roughly circular, of the *ḥaram,* which forms part of the sanctuary.

The Ka'bah is the only Islamic sanctuary that can be compared to a temple. It is commonly called the "house of God" (*bayt Allāh*), and it has in fact the character of a "divine dwelling"–paradoxical as this may seem in an Islamic climate, where the idea of Divine Transcendence outweighs everything. But God "dwells," as it were, in the ungraspable center of the world, as He "dwells" in the innermost center of man. It will be recalled that the Holy of Holies in the Temple at Jerusalem, which was likewise a divine "habitation," had the shape of a cube, like the Ka'bah. The Holy of Holies, or *dĕbîr,* contained the Ark of the Covenant, whereas the interior of the Ka'bah is empty; it contains only a curtain, which oral tradition calls the "Curtain of Divine Mercy" (*Raḥmah*).

The cube is linked to the idea of the center, because it is a crystalline synthesis of the whole of space, each face of the cube corresponding to one of the primary directions–namely, the zenith, the nadir, and the four cardinal points. Let us remember, even so, that the positioning of the Ka'bah does not entirely correspond to this scheme, because it is the four corners, and not the sides of the Ka'bah, that face the cardinal points, doubtless because the cardinal points mean, in the Arab concept, the four "corner pillars" (*arkān*) of the universe.

The center of the terrestrial world is the point intersected by the "axis" of heaven: the rite of circumambulation (*ṭawāf*) around the Ka'bah, which is to be found in one form or another in the majority of ancient sanctuaries, is then seen to reproduce the rotation of heaven around its polar axis.

Naturally, these are not the interpretations attributed by orthodox exegesis to the ritual elements, but they are inherent *a priori* in a view of things shared by all the religions of antiquity. The "axial" character of the Ka'bah is, however, affirmed by a well-known Muslim legend according to which the "ancient house" first built by Adam, then destroyed by the flood, and rebuilt by Abraham is situated at the lower extremity of an axis that traverses all the heavens. At the level of each heavenly world, another sanctuary, frequented by angels, marks this same axis. The supreme prototype of each of these sanctuaries is God's Throne, around which circulates the chorus of the heavenly spirits. It would be more exact to say that they circulate within it, since the Divine Throne encloses all creation.

This legend bears clear witness to the relationship that exists between ritual "orientation" and Islam as submission or abandonment (*islām*) to the Divine Purpose. The fact of turning in prayer to a single point, ungraspable as such but situated on earth and analogous in its singleness to the center of every world, speaks eloquently of the integration of human will in the Universal Will: "and to God are all things returned" (Quran III, 108). At the same time, there is a difference between this symbolism and that of Christian worship, where the point of orientation is that part of the sky where the sun, the image of Christ reborn, rises at Easter. This means that all oriented churches have parallel axes, whereas the axes of all the mosques in the world converge. The convergence of all the gestures of adoration upon a single point becomes apparent, however, only in the proximity of the Ka'bah, when the believers bow down in common paryer from all sides toward the center. There is perhaps no more immediate and tangible expression of Islam.

The liturgy of Islam is linked to the Ka'bah in two different but complementary modes, one static and the other dynamic. The first mode means that every place on earth is directly attached to the Meccan center, and it is in this sense that the Prophet said, "God has blessed my community by giving them the face of the whole world as a sanctuary." The center of this unique sanctuary is the Ka'bah, and the believer who prays in the universal sanctuary finds that all distance is momentarily abolished. The second mode, which is dynamic in nature, is made manifest in the pilgrimage, which every Muslim must make at least once in his lifetime, if he is able. There is an aspect of divestment in the pilgrimage, and this ordinarily transmits itself to the entire Islamic ambience. At the same time, its impact on the believer is that of a dramatic recapitulation of his *islām:* arriving at the threshold of the sacred area surrounding Mecca, the pilgrim divests himself of all his clothing, purifies himself with water from head to toe, and garbs himself in two pieces of seamless cloth, one around his waist and the other over one shoulder. It is in this "consecrated" state (*iḥrām*) that he approaches the Ka'bah to accomplish the rite of circumambulation (*ṭawāf*), ceaselessly invoking God. Only after this visit to the "House of God" does he set out for the various places associated with sacred history and complete his peregrination by sacrificing a ram in memory of Abraham's sacrifice.

We shall see later how these two modes of adoration, static and dynamic, are reflected at different levels in the world of Islam. In the present context we wish to show only one thing, namely, that the Muslim soul and thereby Islamic art are grounded in a world that is closer to that of the Old Testament patriarchs than to the Greco-Roman universe, to which Islam had to turn for the first elements of its art. Let us not forget that Islam was born in a "no man's land" between two great civilizations, the Byzantine and the Persian, which were at the same time empires disputing Arabia, and which Islam had to fight and overcome for its own survival. Compared with these two worlds, both of which had artistic heritages tending toward naturalism and rationalism, the Ka'bah and its associated rites are like an anchor cast into a timeless deep.

When the Prophet had conquered Mecca, he went first to the sacred enclosure and performed the circumambulation of the Ka'bah on camelback. The pagan Arabs had surrounded this area with a girdle of 360 idols, one for each day of the lunar year. Touching these idols with his riding stick, the Prophet overturned them one after another, while reciting the verse from the Quran, "Truth has come; vanity has vanished; in truth vanity is evanescent" (XVII, 33). He was then handed the key of the Ka'bah and went in. The inner walls were adorned with paintings executed by a Byzantine artist on the orders of the Ka'bah's pagan masters; they portrayed scenes from the life of Abraham and certain idolatrous customs. There was also a representation of the Holy Virgin and Child. Protecting this icon of the Holy Virgin with both hands, the Prophet ordered that all the others be effaced. The icon of the Virgin was later destroyed by a fire. This traditional story demonstrates the meaning and the scale of what is erroneously called "Islamic iconoclasm," which we would rather call "aniconism." If the Ka'bah is the heart of man, the idols that inhabited it represent the passions, which invest the heart and impede the remembrance of God. Therefore, the destruction of idols—and, by extension, the putting aside of every image likely to become an idol—is the clearest possible parable for Islam of the "one thing necessary," which is the purification of the heart for the sake of *tawḥīd*, the bearing of witness or the awareness that "there is no divinity save God."

Arab Art, Islamic Art

One may well ask whether the term "Arab art" corresponds to a well-defined reality, because Arab art before Islam is represented by only scarce remains. Arab art born under the sky of Islam is confused—and one wonders to what degree—with Islamic art itself. Art historians never fail to stress that the first Islamic monuments were not built by the Arabs, who lacked adequate technical means, but by levies of Syrian, Persian, and Greek craftsmen and that Islamic art was gradually enriched by the artistic heritage of the sedentary populations of the Near East as these were taken into Islam. Despite this, it is still legitimate to speak of Arab art, for the simple reason that Islam itself, if it is not limited to a "racial phenomenon"—and history is there to prove the point—does nonetheless comprise Arab elements in its formal expression, the foremost of which is the Arabic language. In becoming the sacred language of Islam, Arabic determined to a greater or a lesser degree the "style of thinking" of all the Muslim peoples. Certain typically Arab attitudes of soul, spiritually enhanced by the *Sunnah* of the Prophet, entered into the psychic economy of the entire Muslim world and are reflected in its art. It would, indeed, be impossible to confine the manifestations of Islam to Arabism; on the contrary, it is Arabism that is expanded and, as it were, transfigured by Islam.

In order to grasp the nature of Islamic Arab art—the Muslim will naturally stress the first part of this term, and the non-Muslim the second—one must take account of the marriage between a spiritual message with an absolute content and a certain racial inheritance which, for that very reason, no longer belongs to a racially defined collectivity but becomes a "mode of expression" that can, in principle, be used universally. Moreover, Islamic-Arab art is not the only great religious art to be born from such a marriage. Buddhist art, for example, whose area of expression is chiefly confined to Mongol nations, nevertheless preserves certain typically Indian traits, particularly in its iconography, which is of the greatest importance to it. In a far more restricted context, Gothic art, of German-Latin lineage, provides an example of a "style" so widespread that it became identified with the Christian art of the West.

Without Islam, the Arab thrust of the first/seventh century—even supposing it to have been possible without the religious impulse—would have been no more than an episode in the history of the Middle East. Decadent as they may have been, the great sedentary civilizations would have made short work of absorbing these hordes of bedouin Arabs, and the nomadic invaders of the cultivated lands would have finished, as is generally the case, by accepting the customs and forms of expression of the sedentary people.

But exactly the opposite happened in the case of Islam, at least in a certain regard. It was the Arabs, nomads for the most part, who imposed on the sedentary peoples they conquered their forms of thought and expression by imposing their language on them. In fact, the outstanding and somehow refulgent manifestation of the Arab genius is language, including writing. It was this language that not only preserved the ethnic heritage of the Arabs outside Arabia but caused it to radiate far beyond its racial homeland. It was by the mediation of the Arabic language that the essential Arab genius was effectively communicated to Islamic civilization as a whole.

The extraordinary normative power of the Arabic language derives from its role as a sacred language as well as from its archaic nature, both factors being connected. It is its archaic quality that predestined Arabic for its role as a sacred language, and it was the Quranic revelation that, as it were, actualized its primordial substance. Archaism, in the linguistic order, is not synonymous with simplicity of structure. Much to the contrary, languages generally grow poorer with the passing of time by gradually losing the richness of their vocabulary, the ease with which they can diversify various aspects of one and the same idea, and their power of synthesis, which is the ability to express many things with few words. In order to make up for this impoverishment, modern languages have become more complicated on the rhetorical level; while perhaps gaining in surface precision, they have not done so with regard to content. Language historians are astonished by the fact that Arabic was able to retain a morphology attested as early as the Code of Hammurabi (nineteenth to eighteenth century before the Christian era) and a phonetic system that preserves, with the exception of a single sound, the extremely rich sound range disclosed by the most ancient Semitic alphabets, even though there was no "literary tradition" to bridge the gap between the far-off age of the patriarchs and the time when the Quranic revelation would establish the language for all time.

The explanation of this perennial quality of Arabic is to be found simply in the conserving role of nomadism. It is in towns that languages decay by becoming worn out, like the things and institutions they designate. Nomads, who live to some extent outside time, conserve their language better; it is, moreover, the only treasure they can carry around with them in their pastoral existence. The nomad is a jealous guardian of his linguistic heritage, his poetry, and his rhetorical art. But his inheritance in the way of visual art cannot be rich. Architecture presupposes stability, and the same is broadly true of sculpture and painting. Nomadic art in general is limited to simple, yet striking, graphic formulas, ornamental motifs, and heraldic emblems and symbols.

It would be tempting to say that the Arab does not so much see things as hear them, but that would be a false generalization. It is true, nevertheless, that the need for artistic exteriorization is, in the Arab, largely absorbed by the cultivation of his language with its fascinating phonetic range and almost unlimited possibilities of expression. If the term contemplative be taken to describe the type of man who contemplates rather than acts and whose mind loves to repose in the being of things, then the Arab, who possesses a dynamic mentality and an analytical intelligence, is no contemplative. But contemplation is not limited to simply static modes; it can pursue unity through rhythm, which is like a reflection of the eternal present in the flow of time. That the Arab is in fact contemplative is proved by Islam and confirmed by Arab art.

Plastic examples illustrating these tendencies leap to the eye. The arabesque in particular, with its both regular and indefinite unfolding, is the most direct expression of rhythm in the visual order. It is true that its most perfect forms are inconceivable without the artistic contribution of the nomads of Central Asia; it was, however, in an Arab milieu that it flowered most resplendently. Another element that is typical of Islamic art, whose development goes side by side with Arab domination, is interlacement. It first appears in all its perfection in the form of sculptured trelliswork on the windows of mosques and palaces. In order to appreciate the geometrical play of interlacement, it is not enough simply to look at it head on; it must be "read," by letting the eye follow the flow of intertwining and compensating forces. Interlacement exists already in the pavement mosaics of late antiquity, but it is rudimentary and naturalistic in conception, without any of the complexity and rhythmic precision of Arab-Muslim interlacing work. These examples belong to abstract art, which is itself characteristic of the Arab genius. Contrary to what is customarily believed, the average Arab does not by any means possess an "extravagant imagination." Whenever such imagination is found in Arabic literature—for example, in the *Tales of the Thousand and One Nights*—it comes from some non-Arab source (Persian and Indian in this case); only the art of storytelling is Arab. The creative spirit of the Arabs is a priori logical and rhetorical, then rhythmic and incantational. The luxuriance of typically Arab poetry lies in mental and verbal arabesque and not in the profusion of images evoked.

Islam rejects portraiture for theological reasons. The Semitic nomads had no figurative tradition—the pre-Islamic Arabs imported most of their idols from abroad—and the image never became a natural and transparent means of expression for the Arabs. Verbal reality eclipsed the reality of static vision: compared with the word forever "in act," whose root is anchored in the primordiality of sound, a painted or carved image seemed like a disquieting congealment of the spirit. For the pagan Arabs, it smacked of magic.

The Arabic language is not wholly dynamic. True, its base is the action-verb, but it possesses likewise a static—or, more exactly, a timeless—ground that corresponds to "being" and reveals itself particularly in the so-called nominal sentence, where the noun and its predicates are juxtaposed without a copula. This permits a thought to be expressed in lapidary fashion and without any consideration of time. The Arabic language is such that a whole doctrine can be condensed into a short and concise formula of diamantine clarity. This means of expression is realized in all its fullness only in the Quran; yet it is part of the Arab genius nonetheless and is reflected in Arab-Islamic art. This art is not only rhythmical; it is also crystalline.

The conciseness of the Arabic sentence does not, quite clearly, limit the profundity of the meaning; neither does it facilitate synthesis on the descriptive level. An Arab will rarely assemble a number of conditions or circumstances in a single sentence; he prefers to string together a series of brief phrases. In this respect, an agglutinative language like Turkish, which belongs to the family of Mongol languages, is less austere and more flexible than Arabic. When it comes to describing a situation or a landscape, Turkish is frankly superior to Arabic. The same applies to Persian, which is an Indo-European language close to Gothic. However, both languages have borrowed not only their theological terminology but also their philosophical and scientific terms from Arabic. The opposite extreme to Arabic is a language like Chinese, which is ruled by a static vision of things and which groups the elements of a thought around generic images, as is shown by the ideographic nature of Chinese script.

The Turks, like the Arabs, were originally nomads, but their languages reveal vastly different mental types. Arabs are incisive and dynamic in their thought processes; Turks are all-embracing. In the general framework of Islamic art, the Turkish genius reveals itself by a certain power of synthesis—one might almost say, by a totalitarian spirit. The Turks have a plastic or sculptural gift that the Arabs do not have. Their works always proceed out of an all-enveloping concept, as if hewn from a single block. Persian art is distinguished by its sense of hierarchical gradations. Persian architecture is perfectly articulated, without ever being "functional" in the modern sense of the term. For Persians, Unity manifests itself above all as harmony. Moreover, Persians are by nature and by culture people who see things, but see with lyrical eyes; their artistic activity is as if animated by an inner melody. It is said proverbially in the East that "Arabic is the language of God, but Persian is the language of paradise," and this describes very well the difference that exists, for example, between a distinctively Arab type of architecture, like that of the Maghrib, where crystalline geometry of forms proclaims the unitary principle, and Persian architecture, with its blue domes and floral decoration. The Arab architect is not afraid of monotony; he will build pillar upon pillar and arcade upon arcade and dominate repetition by rhythmic alternation and the qualitative perfection of each element.

The language of the Quran is omnipresent in the world of Islam. The entire life of a Muslim is filled with Quranic formulas, prayers, litanies, and invocations in Arabic, the elements of which are drawn from the Sacred Book; innumerable inscriptions bear witness to this. It could be said that this ubiquity of the Quran works like a spiritual vibration—there is no better term to describe an influence that is both spiritual and sonorous—and this vibration necessarily determines the modes and measures of Islamic art. The plastic art of Islam is, therefore, in a certain way, the reflection of the word of the Quran.

It is assuredly very difficult to grasp the principle by which this art is linked to the text of the Quran, not on the narrative plane of the text, which plays no part in the customary art of Islam, but on the level of formal structures, since the Quran obeys no laws of composition, neither in the strangely disconnected linking together of its themes, nor in its verbal presentation, which evades all the rules of meter. Its rhythm, powerful and penetrating as it is, follows no fixed measure; entirely unpredictable, it maintains at times an insistent rhyme like the beat of a drum and then suddenly modifies its breadth and pace, shifting its cadences in a manner as unexpected as it is striking. To affirm that the Quran is Arabic verse because it includes passages with a uniform rhyme like the Bedouin *rajaz* would be mistaken; but to deny that these uniformities and abrupt breaks correspond to profound realities in the Arab soul would be equally so. Arab art—poetry and music as well as the plastic arts—loves to repeat certain forms and to introduce sudden and unforeseen variants against this repetitive background. Art is played out in accordance with easily fathomable rules; the waves of sacred speech may sometimes fall in regular patterns, although they arise out of a whole formless ocean. In the same way, the state of inner harmony engendered by the words and sonorous enchantment of the Quran is situated on a plane different from, for example, perfect poetry. The Quran does not satisfy; it gives and at the same time takes away. It expands the soul by lending it wings, then lays it low and leaves it naked; for the believer, it is both comforting and purifying, like a rainstorm. Purely human art does not possess this virtue. That is to say, there is no such thing as a Quranic style that can simply be transposed into art, but there does exist a state of soul that is sustained by the recitation of the Quran and favors certain formal manifestations while precluding others. The diapason of the Quran never fails to join intoxicating nostalgia to extreme sobriety; it is a radiation of the Divine Sun upon the human desert. It is to these poles that the fluid and flamboyant rhythm of the arabesque and the abstract and crystalline character of architecture in some way correspond.

But the most profound link between Islamic art and the Quran is of another kind: it lies not in the form of the Quran but in its *ḥaqīqah*, its formless essence, and more particularly in the notion of *tawḥīd* (unity or union) with its contemplative implications. Islamic art, by which we mean the entirety of plastic arts in Islam, is essentially the projection into the visual order of certain aspects or dimensions of Divine Unity.

Calligraphy

In sacred inscriptions the Arabic letters combine fluently with arabesques, especially with plant motifs, which are thus brought into closer relationship with the Asiatic symbolism of the tree of the world; the leaves of this tree correspond to the words of the Sacred Book. Arabic calligraphy contains within itself alone decorative possibilities of inexhaustible richness. Its modalities vary between the monumental Kufic script, with its rectilinear forms and vertical breaks, and the *naskhī*, with its line as fluid and as serpentine as it could be. The richness of the Arabic script comes from the fact that it has fully developed its two "dimensions": the vertical, which confers on the letters their hieratic dignity, and the horizontal, which links them together in a continuous flow. As in the symbolism of weaving, the vertical lines, analogous to the "warp" of the fabric, correspond to the permanent essences of things. It is by the vertical that the unalterable character of each letter is affirmed. The horizontal, analogous to the "weft," expresses becoming or the matter that links one thing to another. The significance of this is particularly evident in Arabic calligraphy, where the vertical strokes transcend and regulate the undulating flow of the connecting strokes.

Arabic is written from right to left; this is as much as to say that the writing runs back from the field of action toward the heart. Among all the phonetic scripts of Semitic origin, Arabic writing has the least visual resemblance to Hebrew writing. Hebrew is static like the stone of the Tables of the Law, while at the same time it is full of the latent fire of the Divine Presence. Arabic manifests Unity by the breadth of its rhythm: the broader the rhythm, the more its unity becomes evident.

The friezes of inscriptions crowning the inner walls of a hall of prayer or surrounding the *miḥrāb* recall to the believer, as much by their rhythm and their hieratic form as by their meaning, the majestic and forceful current of the Quranic language.

The Arabesque

In the arabesque, the typical creation of Islam, geometrical genius meets nomadic genius. The arabesque is a sort of dialectic of ornament, in which logic is allied to a living continuity of rhythm. It has two basic elements, the interlacement and the plant motif. The former is essentially a derivative of geometrical speculation, and the latter represents a sort of graphic formulation of rhythm, expressed in spiraloid designs, which may possibly be derived not so much from plant forms as from a purely linear symbolism. Ornaments with spiraloid designs—heraldic animals and vines—are also found in the art of Asiatic nomads; the art of the Scythians is a striking example.

The elements of Islamic decorative art are drawn from the rich archaic heritage that was common to all the peoples of Asia as well as to those of the Near East and northern Europe. It came to the surface again as soon as Hellenism, with its essentially anthropomorphic art, had gone into retreat. Christian medieval art picked up this same heritage, brought to it by the folklore of immigrant peoples from Asia and by insular art, both Celtic and Saxon, itself one of the most astonishing syntheses of prehistoric motifs. But this heritage was soon obscured and diluted in the Christian world by the influence of Greco-Roman models, assimilated by Christianity. The Islamic spirit has a much more direct affinity with this vast current of archaic forms, for they are in implicit correspondence with its conscious return toward a primordial order, toward the "primordial religion" (*dīn al-fiṭrah*). Islam assimilates these archaic elements and reduces them to their most abstract and most generalized formulations. It levels them out in a certain sense and thereby eliminates any magical qualities they may have possessed. In return, it endows them with a fresh intellectual lucidity—one might almost say, with a spiritual elegance.

Let us not forget the art of the carpet, particularly that of the knotted rug, which is most probably of nomadic origin. Its formal repertoire is in a way parallel to that of the arabesque and is a vehicle also of an archaic heritage. Through the art of the carpet, the nomadic life has set foot into every Islamic dwelling.

The Alchemy of Light

The artist who wishes to express the idea of the "unity of being" or the "unity of the real" (*waḥdat al-wujūd*) has actually three means at his disposal: geometry or, more precisely, the infinity inherent in regular geometric figures; rhythm, which is revealed in the temporal order and also indirectly in space; and light, which is to visible forms what Being is to limited existences. Light is, in fact, itself indivisible; its nature is not altered by its refraction into colors nor diminished by its gradation into clarity and darkness. In the same way, nothingness does not itself exist except by its illusory opposition to Being; so also darkness is visible only by contrast with light, to the extent that light makes shadows appear.

"God is the light of the heavens and the earth," says the Quran (XXIV, 35). The Divine Light brings things out from the darkness of nothing. In the symbolical order in question, to be visible signifies to exist. Just as shadow adds nothing to light, things are real only to the extent that they share in the light of Being. There is no more perfect symbol of the Divine Unity than light. For this reason, the Muslim artist seeks to transform the very stuff he is fashioning into a vibration of light. It is to this end that he covers the interior surfaces of a mosque or palace—and occasionally the outer ones—with mosaics in ceramic tiles. This lining is often confined to the lower part of the walls, as if to dispel their heaviness. It is for the same purpose that the artist transforms other surfaces into perforated reliefs to filter the light. *Muqarnas,* "stalactites," also serve to trap light and diffuse it with the most subtle gradations.

Colors reveal the interior richness of light. Light viewed directly is blinding; it is through the harmony of colors that we divine its true nature, which bears every visual phenomenon within itself.

Among the examples of Islamic architecture under the sway of the sovereignty of light, the Alhambra at Granada occupies the first rank. The Court of Lions in particular sets the example of stone transformed into a vibration of light; the lambrequins of the arcades, the friezes in *muqarnas,* the delicacy of the columns that seem to defy gravity, the scintillation of the roofs in green tilework, and even the water-jets of the fountain all contribute to this impression.

We have compared this art to alchemy,[1] the well-known theme of which is the transmutation of lead into gold. Lead is the base metallic substance, shapeless and opaque, whereas gold, the solar metal, is in some way light made corporeal. In the spiritual order, alchemy is none other than the art of transmuting bodily consciousness into spirit: "body must be made spirit," say the alchemists, "for spirit to become body." By analogy, we will say of alchemy, in the manner in which it appears to us here, that it transforms stone into light, which in its turn transforms stone into crystal.

Aniconism (Iconoclasm)

Islamic aniconism, although differing within various ethnic milieus, is often blamed by orientalists for a certain poverty of art. If this is true, it must not, however, be forgotten that this poverty, which is more exactly a sobriety, can easily be transmuted into "poverty of the Spirit." Furthermore, a sacred art is not necessarily made of images, even in the broadest sense of the term. It may be no more than a silent exteriorization of a contemplative state, and in this case it reflects no ideas but transforms the surroundings qualitatively, by having them share in an equilibrium whose center of gravity is the unseen. That such is the nature of Islamic art is easily verified. Its object is, above all, man's environment—hence the dominant role of architecture—and its quality is essentially contemplative. By precluding every image that invites man to fix his mind on something outside himself and to project his soul onto an "individualizing" form, it creates a void. In this respect, the function of Islamic art is analogous to that of virgin nature, especially the desert, which is likewise favorable to contemplation. Yet in another respect the order created by art opposes the chaos of virgin nature.

It is instructive to compare Islam's attitude to images with that of the Greek Orthodox Church. The Byzantine Church is known to have gone through an iconoclast crisis, perhaps influenced by the example of Islam. Certainly, the church was moved to reconsider defining the role of the sacred image, the icon, and the Seventh Ecumenical Council, in confirming the victory of the venerators of images, justified its decision in the following words: "God Himself is beyond all possible description or representation, but since the Divine Word took human nature upon itself, which it 'reintegrated into its original form by infusing it with Divine Beauty,' God can and must be adored through the human image of Christ." This is no more than an application of the dogma of Divine Incarnation, and it shows how far this way of seeing things is from the viewpoint of Islam. Nevertheless, the two perspectives have a common basis in the notion of man's theomorphic nature.

The Persian Miniature

In the Seljuq period, figurative themes of a Turco-Mongol character are somewhat apparent in all the minor arts, in both Iran and Iraq. The true

Persian miniature, however, which is indisputably the most perfect figurative art on the soil of Islam, did not come into the world until after the conquest of Persia by the Mongols—more precisely, under the rule of the Il-Khanids. It is modeled on Chinese painting, with its perfect blend of calligraphy and illustration. Following this model, the reduction of space to a plane surface and the coordination of human figures and landscape were all retained in the Persian miniature. But the bold and delicate strokes of the Chinese brush gave way to the precise and continuous line drawn by the calamus in the true manner of Arabic calligraphy, and the contoured surfaces were filled with unbroken colors. The link between writing and image remains fundamental to the Persian miniature, which belongs, as a whole, to the art of the book. All the famous miniaturists were calligraphers before becoming painters. We said earlier that the art of writing somehow takes the place of the art of icons in Islam; it was by way of the art of the book that drawing finally came together with writing.

What gives the miniature its almost unique kind of beauty is not so much the scenes it portrays as the nobility and simplicity of the poetical atmosphere that pervades them. This atmosphere occasionally confers upon the Persian miniature a kind of Edenic reverberation. This is profoundly significant, for one of its basic themes is that of the transfigured landscape, symbolizing both the earthly paradise and the "heavenly land," an unshadowed landscape, in which each object is made of exceedingly precious substance and where every tree and flower is unique of its kind, like the plants that Dante situates in the earthly paradise, on the mountain of purgatory, and whose seeds are borne by the perpetual wind that plays upon the mountaintop to produce all the vegetation on earth.

This symbolic landscape is essentially distinct from that suggested by Chinese painting. Unlike the latter, it is not undefined; it does not appear to be emerging from the void, the undifferentiated origin of all things. It is like a well-ordered cosmos, occasionally encased in a crystalline architecture that encloses it like a magic casing and sets the scenes without making them too material.

In general terms, the Persian miniature—and we are here considering it in its best phases—does not seek to portray the outward world as it commonly presents itself to the senses, with all its disharmonies and accidentalities. It is indirectly describing the "immutable essences" (*al-a'yān al-thābitah*) of things. It is this generic quality that the art of the miniature seeks to grasp. If the "immutable essences" of things, their archetypes, cannot be apprehended because they are beyond form, they are nonetheless reflected in the contemplative imagination. Hence the dream quality—not one of idle reverie—that pertains to the most beautiful miniatures: it is a clear and translucent dream as if illumined from within.

All normal painting is, moreover, dependent on intuition to take sense experience and draw out from it those traits that are typical of a particular thing or being and transcribe them in elements that are suited to two-dimensional space, namely, line and colored surfaces. The Oriental artist would never dream of attempting to convey the entire appearance of things; he is deeply persuaded of the vanity of such an endeavor and, in this sense, the almost childlike naïveté of his works is no less than wisdom.

The Mosque

The Islamic hall of prayer, unlike a church or a temple, has no center toward which worship is directed. The grouping of the faithful around a center, so characteristic of Christian communities, can only be witnessed in Islam at the time of the pilgrimage to Mecca, in the collective prayer around the Ka'bah. In every other place believers turn in their prayers toward that distant center, external to the walls of the mosque. But the Ka'bah itself does not represent a sacramental center comparable to the Christian altar, nor does it contain any symbol that could be an immediate support to worship, for it is empty. Its emptiness reveals an essential feature of the spiritual attitude of Islam. Whereas Christian piety is eager to concentrate on a concrete center—the "Incarnate Word" being a center, both in space and in time, and the eucharistic sacrament no less so—a Muslim's awareness of the Divine Presence is based on a feeling of limitlessness. Muslims reject all objectification of the Divine, except that which presents itself in the form of limitless space.

Nonetheless, a concentric plan is not alien to Islamic architecture, for such is the plan of a mausoleum roofed with a cupola. The prototype of this plan is found in Byzantine as well as in Asiatic art, where it symbolizes the union of heaven and earth. The rectangular body of the building corresponds to the earth, and the spherical cupola to heaven. Islamic art has assimilated this type while reducing it to its purest and clearest formulation; between the cubical body and the more or less ogival cupola, an octagonal "drum" is usually inserted. The eminently perfect and intelligible form of such a building can dominate the indeterminate spaciousness of an entire desert landscape. As the mausoleum of a saint, it is effectively a spiritual center of the world.

The assimilation of Byzantine models by Islamic art is exemplified with special clarity in the Turkish variations on the theme of the Hagia Sophia. As is well known, the Hagia Sophia consists of an immense central dome flanked by two half-cupolas, which in their turn are amplified by several vaulted apses. The whole covers a space more extensive in the direction of one axis than the other. The proportions of the resulting environment are highly elusive and seem to be indefinite, owing to the absence of conspicuous articulations. Muslim architects like Sinan, who took up the theme of a central cupola amplified by adjacent cupolas, found new solutions more strictly geometrical in conception. The Selimiye mosque at Edirna is a notably characteristic example. Its huge dome rests on an octagon with walls alternately flat and curved into apses, which results in a system of plane and curved facets with clearly defined angles between them. This transformation of the plan of the Hagia Sophia is comparable to the cutting of a precious stone, made more regular and more brilliant by polishing.

Seen from inside, the cupola of a mosque of this type does not hover in indefiniteness, but neither does it weigh upon its pillars. Nothing expresses effort in Islamic architecture; there is no tension, nor any antithesis between heaven and earth.

> There is none of that sensation of a heaven descending from above, as in the Hagia Sophia, nor the ascending tendency of a Gothic cathedral. The culminating point in the Islamic prayer is the moment when the forehead of the believer prostrated on the rug touches the floor, that mirror-like surface which abolishes the contrast of height and depth and makes space a homogeneous unity with no particular tendency. It is by its immobility that the atmosphere of a mosque is distinguished from all things ephemeral. Here infinity is not attained by a transformation from one side of a dialectical antithesis to the other; in this architecture the beyond is not merely a goal, it is lived here and now, in a freedom exempt from all tendencies; there is a repose free from all aspiration; its omnipresence is incorporated in the edifice so like a diamond.[2]

The exterior of Turkish mosques is characterized by the contrast between the hemisphere of the dome, more in evidence than in the Hagia Sophia, and the needles of the minarets: a synthesis of repose and vigilance, of submission and active witness.

Art to the Muslim is a "proof of the Divine Existence" only to the extent that it is beautiful without showing the marks of a subjective individualistic inspiration. Its beauty must be impersonal, like that of the starry sky. Islamic art does indeed attain to a kind of perfection that seems to be independent of its author; his triumphs and his failures disappear before the universal character of the forms.

Wherever Islam has assimilated a preexisting type of architecture, in Byzantine countries as well as in Persia and in India, subsequent development has been in the direction of a geometrical precision having a qualitative character—not quantitative nor mechanical—which is attested to by the elegance of its solutions of architectural problems. It is in India that the contrast between the indigenous architecture and the artistic ideals of the Muslim conquerors is without doubt most marked. Hindu architecture is at once lapidary and complex, elementary and rich, like a sacred mountain with mysterious caverns. Islamic architecture leans toward clarity and sobriety. Wherever Islamic art appropriates incidental elements from Hindu architecture, it subordinates their native power to the unity and the lightness of the whole. There are some Islamic buildings in India that are numbered among the most perfect in existence; no architecture has ever surpassed them.

But Islamic architecture is most faithful to its particular genius in the Maghrib, the west of the Muslim world. Here, in Algeria, in Morocco, and in Andalusia, it realizes the state of crystalline perfection that turns the interior of a mosque—or of a palace—into an oasis of freshness, a world filled with a limpid and almost unworldly beatitude.

A mosque generally comprises a court with a fountain, where the faithful can make their ablutions before accomplishing their prayers. The fountain is often protected by a small cupola shaped like a baldaquin. The court with a fountain in the middle, as well as the enclosed garden watered by four runnels rising in its center, are made in the likeness of paradise, for the Quran speaks of the gardens of Beatitude, where springs of water flow, one or two in each garden, and where celestial virgins dwell. It is in the nature of Paradise (*jannah*) to be hidden and secret; it corresponds to the interior world, the innermost soul. This is the world which the Islamic house must imitate, with its inner court surrounded with walls on all four sides or with an enclosed garden furnished with a well or fountain. The house is the sacratum (*ḥaram*) of the family, where woman reigns and man is but a guest. Its square shape is in conformity with the Islamic law of marriage, which allows a man to marry up to four wives on condition that he offer the same advantages to each. The Islamic house is completely closed to the outer world. Family life is withdrawn from the general social life; it is only open above, to the sky, which is reflected beneath in the fountain of the court.

The *Miḥrāb*

The *miḥrāb* is the niche oriented toward Mecca and is the place where the imam who recites the ritual prayer stands in front of the rows of believers who repeat his gestures. The primary function of this niche is acoustic, to echo the words directed toward it; but at the same time its form is reminiscent of that of a choir or an apse, the "holy of holies," the general shape of which it reproduces on a smaller scale. This analogy is confirmed in the field of symbolism by the presence of the lamp hung in front of the niche of prayer. The lamp recalls the "niche of light" of which it is said in the Quran: "God is the light of the heavens and of the earth. His light is like a niche in which there is a lamp; the lamp is in a glass, which is like a shining star . . ." (XXIV, 35). Here is something like a meeting point between the symbolism of the mosque and of the Christian church, as well as of the Jewish temple and perhaps of the Parsee temple. To return, however, to the acoustic function of the prayer niche: it is by virtue of its reverberation of the Divine Word during the prayer that the *miḥrāb* is a symbol of the Presence of God, and for that reason the symbolism of the lamp becomes purely accessory or, one might say, "liturgical." The miracle of Islam is the Divine Word directly revealed in the Quran and "actualized" by ritual recitation. This makes it possible to situate Islamic iconoclasm very precisely: the Divine Word must remain a verbal expression, and as such instantaneous and immaterial, in the likeness of the act of creation. Thus alone will it keep its evocative power pure, without being subject to that attrition which the use of tangible materials instills, so to speak, in the very nature of the plastic arts and into the forms handed on through them from generation to generation. Being manifested in time but not in space, speech is outside the ambit of the changes brought about by time in spatial things; nomads know this well, living as they do not by images but by speech. This point of view and the manner of its expression are natural to peoples in migration and particularly to Semitic nomads. Islam transposes them into the spiritual order, conferring in return on the human environment, particularly on architecture, an aspect of sobriety and intellectual transparency, as a reminder that everything is an expression of the Divine Truth.

Art and Craft

It remains for us to say what is the notion of art in Islamic art itself. From this point of view, art cannot be dissociated either from artisanal technique (*ṣanʿah*), which is its material basis, or from science (*ʿilm*), which confers upon it its logical and symbolic content. In fact, the Arabic word for "art"—*fann*—includes at once the sense of technique and that of science. In the traditional framework that is of interest to us here, technique will always be artisanal and science will always have, at least implicitly, a character of wisdom (*ḥikmah*), which links its rational ideas to universal principles.

The Prophet said: "God has prescribed perfection upon all things." (We could also translate the word *iḥsān* as "beauty" [*Inna'Llāha kataba'l-iḥsānᵃ 'ala kullⁱ shay'*].) The perfection or the beauty of a thing resides in that it "praises God"; in other words, it is perfect or beautiful by the fact that it reflects a Divine Quality. One cannot achieve perfection, such as it may be, without knowing the very nature of a thing and in what manner it can be enhanced in order to offer a mirror to a universal and Divine Quality.

If we take architecture as an example, its artisanal base is the craft of the master mason with all that is implied of technical experience, whereas the science that governs it is geometry. This geometry is not limited to its more or less quantitative aspects, as it is in the case of modern architecture, but it will always include a qualitative aspect, which is manifested most directly by the laws of proportion thanks to which an edifice acquires its quasi-organic unity. The principle of qualitative unity inherent in the proportion is expressed directly elsewhere by the fact that the perfect proportion flows from the circle. Often all the measurements of an architectonic whole are derived from the division of a directive circle by a regularly inscribed figure. The circle itself will not necessarily figure in the work; it will nevertheless determine the form in a subtle manner by communicating to it something of its nature, which is at once indivisible and inexhaustible.

That which is true for architecture is equally valuable for all other traditional arts and crafts: the least artisanal work, such as woodwork, pottery, weaving, and so forth includes, beyond its material technique, a certain transmitted science, sometimes reduced to some very simple rules but always bearing an aspect of wisdom, which the artisan will more or less penetrate, according to the degree of his contemplative intelligence and his experience. In conformity with the Islamic perspective, the implicitly suprahuman and sacred content of a craft is generally attributed to such or such pre-Islamic prophet, who was to have instituted it by virtue of a Divine Revelation. Thus, certain fundamental crafts are attributed to Seth, the third son of Adam.

In this same perspective are also found the organization of craftsmen into guilds and the often initiatic form of the latter. As the craft guilds normally formed military contingents charged with the defense of the cities, and since the "holy war," the protection of the community of believers by means of arms, is a duty occasionally incumbent upon every Muslim, the initiations grafted onto this order of things often includes a symbolism at once artisanal and knightly. Such a symbol was to be found in the case of the medieval brotherhoods known by the name *futuwwah,* this term signifying courage and magnanimity.[3] Furthermore, such craft guilds from one region could be more or less interdependent on certain *ṭuruq* or Sufi "paths," and these links sometimes still exist to this day. Often, but not always, they are explained by the fact that the founding saint of a *ṭarīqah*—of a "path"—had himself practiced such a craft. One finds an analogous history, be it more indirect, in the Christian guilds and their patron saints.

Independently of a particular artisanal initiation, every normal craft—that is, every activity having a function for the individual who practices it as well as for society—can be the support of a contemplative work, as is indicated in certain sayings of the Prophet, such as those which say that God loves to see His servant practice a manual craft (*ḥirfah*). Since there is no better action than the remembrance (*dhikr*) of God, according to the sayings of the Prophet himself, a craft can be good only to the degree to which it aids in this remembrance, directly or indirectly. It is that, most precisely, which marks the border beyond which the development of a traditional civilization such as that of Islam cannot go without destroying itself. In return, one can be certain that the perfume of serene beatitude and of morning freshness which certain works of Islamic art have exhaled for centuries, is only the trace of the "remembrance of God" in the heart and on the lips of the craftsmen who have created them.

By considering the internal hierarchy of traditional art, a hierarchy made of craft, science, and contemplative wisdom, one understands that a traditional art can be destroyed from above or from below, depending on the case: Christian art was destroyed from "above," starting with the so-called Renaissance, through the loss and systematic negation of spiritual principles, whereas Islamic art has disappeared gradually following the destruction of its artisanal bases.

Translated and adapted by Katherine O'Brien

Notes

1. T. Burckhardt, *Moorish Culture in Spain* (London: Allen & Unwin, 1972) 205ff.
2. U. Vogt-Göknil, *Turkische Moscheen* (Zurich: Origo-Verlag, 1953).
3. See chap. 15 in this volume, "Spiritual Chivalry," by S. H. Nasr.

Bibliography

Because of lack of space, only works in European languages have been cited. Editions of works in Islamic languages are usually found in the bibliographies of works cited below. The bibliography of the previous volume, *Islamic Spirituality: Foundations,* should also be consulted. Full publication information is given only in the first citation of a work.

Reference Works

Encyclopedia of Islam. Old and new editions. Leiden: Brill.

Massignon, L. *The Passion of al-Ḥallāj.* 4 vols. Trans. H. Mason. Princeton: Princeton University Press, 1982.

Pearson, J. D. *Index Islamicus.* Cambridge: Heffer, 1958–.

Schimmel, A. *Mystical Dimensions of Islam.* Chapel Hill, NC: The University of North Carolina Press, 1975.

Part One
Sufism

Abu-Rabi', I. M. "Al-Azhar Sufism in Modern Egypt: The Sufi Thought." *Islamic Quarterly* 30 (1988) 207–35.

Addas, C. *Ibn 'Arabî ou La quête du Soufre rouge.* Paris: Gallimard, 1989.

Affifi, A. *The Mystical Philosophy of Muḥyîd-Dîn Ibn al-'Arabî.* Cambridge: Cambridge University Press, 1939.

Ahmad, A. *Studies in Islamic Culture in the Indian Environment.* Oxford: Clarendon Press, 1964.

Aini, M. A. *Un Grand saint de l'Islam. Abd al-Kadir Guilânî.* Paris: P. Geuthner, 1938.

Algar, H. "Kubrā, Shaykh Abu'l-Djannāb Aḥmad b. 'Umar Nadjm al-Dīn." *Encyclopaedia of Islam.* 2nd ed. vol. 5, 300–301.

——. "Some Notes on the Naqshbandī Ṭarīqat in Bosnia." *Die Welt des Islam* 13 (1971) 168–203.

——. "'The Naqshbandī Order': A Preliminary Survey of its History and Significance." *Studia Islamica* 44 (1976) 123–97.

Arasteh, R. *Rumi the Persian: Rebirth in Creativity and Love.* Lahore: Sh. Muhammad Ashraf, 1965.

Arberry, A. J., trans. *Discourses of Rumi.* London: John Murray, 1961.

——. *Mystical Poems of Rumi.* First Selection. Chicago: University of Chicago Press, 1968.

——. *Mystical Poems of Rumi.* Second Selection. Boulder: Westview Press, 1979.

Asín Palacios, M. *El Islam cristianizado.* Madrid: Editorial Plutarco, 1931. French translation as *L'Islam christianisé: Etude sur le Soufisme d'Ibn 'Arabî de Murcie.* Paris: Guy Trédaniel, 1982.

——. *Saint John of the Cross and Islam.* Trans. H. W. Yoder and E. H. Douglas. New York: Vantage Press, 1981.

Ateş, A. "Ibn al-'Arabī." *Encyclopedia of Islam.* 2nd ed. vol. 3. 707–11.

Al-Attas, S. M. M. *The Mysticism of Ḥamzah Fansūrī.* Kuala Lumpur: University of Malaya Press, 1970.

Aubin, J., ed. *Materiaux pour la biographie de Shāh Ni'matullāh Walī Kirmānī.* Tehran: Institut Franco-Iranien, 1983 reprint.

Austin, R. W. *Sufis of Andalusia.* Translated from the Arabic of Ibn al-'Arabī. Berkeley: University of California Press, 1971.

Balyānī, Awḥad al-Dīn. *Epitre sur l'unicité absolue.* Trans. M. Chodkiewicz. Paris: Les Deux Oceans, 1982.

Baljon, J. M. *A Mystical Interpretation of Prophetic Tales by an Indian Muslim: Shāh Walī Allāh's Ta'wīl al-aḥādīth.* Leiden: Brill, 1973.

Bayrak al-Jerrahi al-Halveti, Sheikh Tosun. *The Most Beautiful Names.* Putney, VT: Threshold Books, 1985.

Begg, Mirza Wahid al-Din, *The Holy Biography of Hazrat Khwāja Mu'īn ad-Dīn Chishtī.* Ajmer, 1960.

Birge, J. K. *The Bektashi Order of Dervishes.* London: Luzac, 1937.

Bradford, M. *Muslim Brotherhoods in Nineteenth-Century Africa.* Cambridge: Cambridge University Press, 1976.

Braune, W. *Die Futūḥ al-Ǧaib des Abdul Qādir.* Berlin: W. de Gruyter, 1933.

Brown, J. P. *The Darvishes or Oriental Spiritualism.* Oxford: Oxford University Press, 1927.

Brunschvig, R. *La Berbérie orientale sous les Ḥafsides des origines à la fin du XV siècle.* 2 vols. Paris: A. Maisonneuve, 1940–47.

Burckhardt, T. *An Introduction to Sufism.* Trans. D. M. Matheson. London: Crucible, 1990.

——. *Mystical Astrology according to Ibn 'Arabi.* Gloucestershire: Beshara Publications, 1977.

——. *Letters of a Sufi Master.* Bedfont, Middlesex: Perennial Books, 1987.

Cahen, C. "*Futuwwa,*" *Encyclopaedia of Islam.* 2nd ed. vol. 2, 961–65.

Chatelier A. L. *Les Confréries musulmanes du Hedjaz.* Paris: 1887.

Chelkowski, P., ed. *The Scholar and the Saint: al-Bīrūnī/Rūmī.* New York: New York University Press, 1975.

Chittick, W. C. "Belief and Transformation: The Sufi Teachings of Ibn al-'Arabī." *The American Theosophist* 74/5 (1986) 181–92.

——. "The Five Divine Presences: From al-Qūnawī to al-Qayṣarī." *The Muslim World* 72 (1982) 107–28.

——. "Mysticism vs. Philosophy in Earlier Islamic History: The al-Ṭūsī, al-Qūnawī Correspondence." *Religious Studies* 17 (1981) 87–104.

——. "Rūmī and *waḥdat al-wujūd*," *The Heritage of Rūmī*. Ed. A. Banani and G. Sabagh. Cambridge: Cambridge University Press, forthcoming.

——. *The Sufi Path of Love: The Spiritual Teachings of Rūmī.* Albany: State University of New York Press, 1983.

——. *The Sufi Path of Knowledge: Ibn al-'Arabī's Metaphysics of Imagination.* Albany: State University of New York Press, 1989.

Chodkiewicz, M. *Le Sceau des saints, prophétie et sainteté dans la doctrine d'Ibn 'Arabî.* Paris: Gallimard, 1986.

Corbin, H. *Creative Imagination in the Sufism of Ibn 'Arabī.* Trans. R. Mannheim. Princeton: Princeton University Press, 1977.

——. *Spiritual Body and Celestial Earth.* Trans. N. Pearson. Princeton: Princeton University Press, 1977.

——. *Temple and Contemplation.* Trans. Ph. Sherrard. London: KPI, 1986.

——. *The Man of Light in Iranian Sufism.* Trans. N. Pearson. Boulder and London, 1978.

——. "L'intériorisation du sens en herméneutique soufie iranienne." *Eranos-Jahrbuch* 26 (1957) 57–187.

——. *L'Homme et son ange–Initiation et chevalrie spirituelle.* Paris: Fayard: 1983.

——. *En Islam iranien.* vol. 4. Paris: Gallimard, 1971.

Daly, M., ed. *Al Majdhubiyya and Al Mikashfiyya: Two Sufi Tariqas in the Sudan.* Khartoum: University of Khartoum Press, 1985.

Depont, O., and X. Coppolani. *Les Confréries religieuses musulmanes.* Algiers: A. Jourdan, 1897.

Dermenghem, E. *Le Culte des saints dans l'Islam maghrebin.* Paris: Gallimard, 1954.

Douglas, E. H. "Al-Shādhilī, a North African Sufi, according to Ibn Sabbāgh." *Muslim World* 38 (1948) 257–79.

Eaton, R. M. *Sufis of Bijapur–1300–1700.* Princeton: Princeton University Press, 1978.

Faruqi, B. A. *The Mujaddid's Conception of Tawḥīd.* Lahore: Sh. Muhammad Ashraf, 1940.

Friedmann, Y. *Shaykh Aḥmad Sirhindī: An Outline of His Thought and a Study of His Image in the Eyes of Posterity.* Montreal and London: McGill–Queen's University Press, 1971.

Gilsenan, M. *Saint and Sufi in Modern Egypt.* Oxford: Clarendon Press, 1973.

Gramlich, R. *Die schiitischen Derwischorden Irans. Erster Teil: Die Affiliationen.* Wiesbaden: Abhandlungen für die Kunde des Morgenlandes, 1965.

Grousset, R., et al. *L'Ame de l'Iran.* Paris: Albin Michel, 1990.

Haqq, Enamul. *Muslim Bengali Literature.* Karachi, 1957.

Al-Hujwīrī, 'Alī ibn 'Uthmān. *Kashf al-maḥjūb.* Trans. R. A. Nicholson. London: Luzac, 1911.

Ibn 'Arabī. *Fuṣūṣ al-ḥikam.* Trans. R. W. J. Austin [*Ibn al-'Arabī: The Bezels of Wisdom*]. Ramsey, NJ: Paulist Press, 1981. Trans. A. A. al-Tarjumana [*The Seals of Wisdom–Muḥyiddīn Ibn al-'Arabī*]. Norwich: Diwan Press, 1980. Partial French translation by T. Burckhardt, rendered into English by A. Culme-Seymour [*The Wisdom of the Prophets*]. Gloucestershire: Beshara Publications, 1975.

——. *al-Futūḥāt al-makkiyyah.* Introduced by M. Chodkiewicz; selections translated by W. C. Chittick, C. Chodkiewicz, D. Gril, and J. Morris [*Les Illuminations de la Mecque/The Meccan Illuminations*]. Paris: Sindbad, 1988.

——. *Shajarat al-kawn.* Trans. by A. Jeffrey ["Ibn al-'Arabī's *Shajarat al-kawn*"] *Studia Islamica* 10 (1959) 43–77; 11 (1960) 113–60.

——. *Tarjumān al-ashwāq.* Ed. and trans. R. A. Nicholson. London: Oriental Theosophical Publishing House, 1978.

Ibn al-'Arīf, Aḥmad. *Maḥāsin al-majālis.* Trans. W. Elliott and K. Abdulla. England: Avebury Publishing Company, 1980.

Ibn al-Ḥusayn al-Sulamī. *The Book of Sufi Chivalry (Futuwwah).* Trans. Sheikh Tosun Bayrak. New York: Inner Traditions, 1983.

Ibn 'Aṭā' Allāh, Aḥmad. *Kitāb al-ḥikam.* Trans. V. Danner as *Sufi Aphorisms.* Leiden: Brill, 1973; New York: Paulist Press, 1978.

Ikram, Sheikh Muhammad. *Muslim Rule in India and Pakistan.* Lahore, 1966.

'Irāqī, Fakhr al-Dīn. *Fakhruddīn 'Irāqī: Divine Flashes.* Trans. W. C. Chittick and P. L. Wilson. Classics of Western Spirituality. New York: Paulist Press, 1982.

Izutsu, T. *Sufism and Taoism.* Los Angeles: University of California Press, 1983. First edition as *A Comparative Study of the Key Philosophical Concepts in Taoism and Sufism.* Tokyo: Keio University, 1966.

Jāmī, 'Abd al-Raḥmān. *Lawā'iḥ: A Treatise on Sufism.* Trans. E. H. Whinfield and M. M. Kazwini. London: Oriental Translation Fund, 1906. Reprinted with an introduction by S. H. Nasr. London: The Theosophical Publishing House, 1978.

al-Jazā'irī, Amīr 'Abd al-Qādir. *Al-Mawāqif.* Partial trans. M. Chodkiewicz [*Ecrits spirituels*]. Paris: Editions du Seuil, 1982.

al-Jīlī, 'Abd al-Karīm. *Al-Insān al-kāmil.* Partial trans. T. Burckhardt. [*De l'Homme universel*]. Lyon: P. Derain, 1953.

Jong, F. de. *Ṭuruq and Ṭuruq-Linked Institutions in Nineteenth Century Egypt: A Historical Study in Organizational Dimensions of Islamic Mysticism.* Leiden: Brill, 1978.

Kāzerūnī, Abū Isḥāq. *Firdaus al-murshidiyah: Die Vita des Scheichs Abū Isḥāq al-Kāzerūnī.* Leipzig, 1948.

Khan, H. Y. *L'Inde mystique au moyen âge.* Paris: A. Maisonneuve, 1929.

——. *Glimpses of Medieval Indian Culture.* Bombay: Asia Publishing House, 1957.

Khan, Khaja. *Studies in Tasawwuf.* Madras: Hogarth Press, 1923.

Kubrā, Najm al-Dīn. *Fawā'iḥ al-jamāl wa fawātiḥ al-jalāl.* Ed. with a lengthy study in German by F. Meier. Wiesbaden, 1957.

Landolt, H. "Der Briefwechsel zwischen Kāšānī und Simnānī über *Waḥdat al-wuǧūd.*" *Der Islam* 50 (1973) 29–83.

——. "Two Types of Mystical Thought in Muslim Iran: An Essay on Suhrawardī, Shaykh al-ishrāq and 'Aynulqużāt-i Hamadānī." *Muslim World* 68 (1978) 187–204.

Lings, M. *A Sufi Saint of the Twentieth Century: Shaikh Aḥmad al-'Alawī.* Berkeley: University of California Press, 1975.

Mackeen, A. M. M. "The Early History of Sufism in the Maghrib Prior to Al-Shādhilī (d. 656/1258)." *Journal of the American Oriental Society* 91 (1971) 398–408.

——. "The Rise of al-Shādhilī (d. 656/1258)." *Journal of the American Oriental Society* 91 (1971) 477–86.

Martin, B. *Muslim Brotherhoods in Nineteenth-Century Africa.* Cambridge: Cambridge University Press, 1976.

Massignon, L. "Salmān Pāk and the Spiritual Beginnings of Iranian Sufism." Pp. 93–110 in *Testimonies and Reflections.* Ed. and trans. H. Mason. Notre Dame: Notre Dame University Press, 1989.

McPherson, J. W. *The Moulids of Egypt.* Cambridge: Cambridge University Press, 1970.

Meier, F. *Bahā'-i Walad: Grundzuge seines Lebens und seiner Mystik.* Leiden: Brill, 1989.

Meyerovitch, E. de Vitray. *Mystique et poésie en Islam: Djalâl-uddîn Rûmî et l'ordre des derviches tourneurs.* Paris: Desclée de Brouwer, 1972.

Mir Qutb al-Din Angha. *Destination: Eternity.* Trans. N. Angha. San Raphael, CA: Multidisciplinary Publications, 1975.

Mir Valiuddin. *Contemplative Disciplines in Sufism.* London: East-West Publications, 1980.

Molé, M. "Les Kubrawīya entre sunnisme et chiisme aux huitième et neuvième siècles de l'Hégire." *Revue des Etudes Islamiques* 29 (1961) 61–142.

——. "Professions de foi de deux Kubrawīs: 'Alī-i Hamadānī et Muḥammad Nūrbaḫš." *Bulletin d'Etudes Orientales* 17 (1961–1962) 133–204.

——. "La version persane du traité de dix principes de Najm al-Dīn Kobrā, par 'Alī b. Shihāb al-Dīn Hamadānī." *Farhang-i Īrān-Zamīn* 6 (1958) 38–51.

——. *Les Mystiques musulmanes.* Paris: Presses Universitaires de France, 1965.

——. "Autour de Bahā' al-Dīn Naqshband." *Revue des Etudes Islamiques* 27 (1959) 35–66.

Morris, J. W. "Ibn 'Arabī and his Interpreters." *Journal of the American Oriental Society* 106 (1986) 539–51, 733–56; 107 (1987) 101–19.

Mujeeb, M. *The Indian Muslims.* Montreal and London: Allen & Unwin, 1969.

Nasr, S. H. *Three Muslim Sages.* Delmar, NY: Caravan Books, 1975.

——. *Sufi Essays.* Albany: State University Press of New York, 1972.

——. *Islamic Art and Spirituality.* Albany: State University Press of New York, 1987.

——, ed. *Mélanges offerts à Henry Corbin.* Wisdom of Persia Series 9. Tehran, 1977.

——. "Sufism" in *Cambridge History of Iran.* vol. 4. Ed. R. N. Frye. Cambridge: Cambridge University Press, 1975, 442–63.

——. "Spiritual Movements, Philosophy and Theology in the Safavid Period" in *Cambridge History of Iran.* vol. 6. Ed. P. Jackson and L. Lockhart. Cambridge: Cambridge University Press, 1986, 656–97.

Nasafi, A. *Le Livre de l'homme parfait.* Trans. I. de Gastines. Paris: Fayard, 1984.

Nicholson, R. A. *Studies in Islamic Mysticism.* Cambridge: Cambridge University Press, 1978.

Nizami, K. A. "Naqshbandī influence on Mughal Rulers and Politics." *Islamic Culture* 39 (1965) 41–52.

——. *The Life and Times of Shaikh Farīd Ganj-i Shakar.* Aligarh: Department of History, Muslim University, 1958.

Nizami, A. K. *Studies in Medieval Indian History and Culture.* Allahabad: Kitab Mahad, 1966.

Nûr 'Alî Shâh Ilâhî. *L'Esotérisme kurde: Aperçus sur le secret gnostique des Fidèles de vérité.* Paris: Albin Michel, 1965.

Nurbakhsh, J. *In the Paradise of the Sufis.* New York: Khaniqahi Nimatullahi Publications, 1979.

——. *In the Tavern of Ruin: Seven Essays on Sufism.* New York: Khaniqahi Nimatullahi Publications, 1978.

——. *Masters of the Path: A History of the Masters of the Nimatullahi Sufi Order.* New York: Khaniqahi Nimatullahi Publications, 1980.

——. *Divani Nurbaksh: Sufi Poetry.* New York: Khaniqahi Nimatullahi Publications, 1980.

——. *Sufi Symbolism I (The Nurbakhsh Encyclopedia of Sufi Terminology).* Part I: The Esoteric Symbolism of the Parts of the Beloved's Body. Part II: Sufi Symbolism of Wine, Music, Mystical Audition, and Convivial Gatherings. London: Khaniqahi Nimatullahi Publications, 1984.

——. *Sufi Symbolism II.* London: Khaniqahi Nimatullahi Publications, 1987.

Nwyia, P. *Ibn 'Abbād de Rondā (1332–1390).* Beirut: Imprimerie Catholique, 1961.

——. *Ibn 'Aṭā' Allāh (m. 709/1309) et la naissance de la confrérie šāḏilite.* Beirut: Dar el-Machreq, 1972.

Nyberg, H. S. *Kleinere Schriften des Ibn al-'Arabî.* Leiden: Brill, 1919.

Padwick, C. *Muslim Devotions.* London: S.P.C.K., 1961.

Rice, C. *The Persian Sufis.* London: Allen & Unwin, 1964.

Rinn, L. *Marabouts et Khouan.* Paris: A. Jourdan, 1884.

Rizvi, S. A. A. *A History of Sufism in India.* New Delhi: Munshiram Manoharlal. I, 1978; II, 1983.

——. *A Socio-Intellectual History of the Isnā 'Asharī Shī'īs in India.* Canberra: Ma'rifat Publishing House, 1986.

Rose, H. A. "Some Problems in Naqshbandī History." *The Indian Antiquary* 52 (1923) 203–11.

Rosenthal, F. "Ibn 'Arabi between 'Philosophy' and 'Mysticism,'" *Oriens* 31 (1988) 1–35.

Rūmī. *Fīhi mā fīhi.* Trans. A. J. Arberry [*Discourses of Rūmī*]. London: John Murray, 1961.

——. *The Mathnawī of Jalālu'ddīn Rūmī.* Ed. and trans. R. A. Nicholson. 8 volumes. London: Luzac, 1925–1940.

——. *More Tales from the Masnavi.* Trans. A. J. Arberry. London: Allen & Unwin, 1968.

——. *The Rubā'īyāt of Jalāl al-Dīn Rūmī.* Trans. A. J. Arberry. London: E. Walker, 1949.

Ṣarrāf, M., ed. *Traités des companions–chevaliers.* Paris: A. Maisonneuve, 1973.

Schuon, F. *Sufism: Veil and Quintessence.* Trans. W. Stoddart. Bloomington: World Wisdom Books, 1981.

Schimmel, A. *Islam in the Indian Sub-continent.* Leiden: Brill, 1980.

——. *The Triumphal Sun: A Study of the Works of Jalāloddīn Rūmī.* London: Fine Books, 1978.

Sells, M. A. "Ibn 'Arabī's Garden Among the Flames: a Reevaluation." *History of Religions* 23 (1984) 287–315.

Shah, Iqbal Ali. *Islamic Sufism.* London: Rider, 1933.

Shah Walī Allāh. *Ta'wīl al-aḥādīth.* Trans. G. N. Jalbani. Lahore: Sh. Muhammad Ashraf, 1977.

——. *Sufism and the Islamic Tradition.* Trans. G. N. Jalbani. London: The Octagon Press, 1980.

Sharif, M. M., ed. *A History of Muslim Philosophy.* vol. 1. Wiesbaden: O. Harrassowitz, 1963.

Shayegan, D. *Hindouisme et soufisme.* Paris: Edition de la Difference, 1979.

Sobhan, J. A. *Sufism, Its Saint and Shrines.* Lucknow: Lucknow Publishing House, 1960.

Sorley, H. T. *Shah Abdul Latif of Bhit: His Poetry, Life, and Times.* London: Oxford University Press, 1966.

Taeschner, F. *Zunfte und Brüderschaften in Islam.* Zurich and Munich: Artemis, 1979.

——. "*Futuwwa*" in the *Encyclopaedia of Islam.* 2nd ed. vol. 2, 922–69.

Takeshita, M. *Ibn 'Arabī's Theory of the Perfect Man and its Place in the History of Islamic Thought.* Tokyo: Institute for the Study of Languages and Cultures of Asia and Africa, 1987.

Teufel, J. K. *Eine Lebensbeschreibung des Scheichs 'Alī-i Hamadānī (gestorben 1385): die Xulāṣat ul-manāğib des Maulānā Nūrud-dīn Ča'far-i Badaxšī.* Leiden: Brill, 1962.

Yahia, O. *Histoire et classification de l'oeuvre d'Ibn 'Arabî.* Damascus: Institut Français de Damas, 1964.

Part Two
Islamic Literature as Mirror of Islamic Spirituality

Abdul Ghani, M. *A History of Persian Language and Literature at the Mogul Court.* 3 vols. Allahabad: The Indian Press, 1972.

Andrzejewski, B. W. "Sheikh Hussen of Bali in Galla Oral Traditions." Pp. 463–80 in *IV Congresso Internazionale di Studi Etiopici.* Rome: Accademia Nazionale dei Lincei, 1974.

——. "Islamic Oral Traditions in Africa: Lives of Muslim Saints." Paper, SOAS, 9 March, 1970.

——, and I. M. Lewis. *Somali Poetry.* London: Clarendon Press, 1964.

Arberry, A. J. *Classical Persian Literature.* London: Allen & Unwin, 1958.

Archer, J. C. *Mystical Elements in Mohammed.* New Haven: Yale University Press, 1926.

Arnott, D. W., and I. Mukoshy. *Aspects of Fulani Poetry.* mimeo. paper, London: SOAS, 1968.

Ashtiany, J., et al., eds. *ʿAbbāsid Belles Lettres.* Cambridge: Cambridge University Press, 1989.

Al-Attas, S. M. N. "Rānirī and the Wujūdiyyah of 17th Century Acheh." *Monographs of the Malaysian Branch of the Royal Asiatic Society,* 3. Singapore, 1966.

——. *The Mysticism of Ḥamzah Fanṣūrī.*

——. *A Commentary on the Ḥujjat al-Ṣaddīq of Nūr al-Dīn al-Rānirī.* Kuala Lumpur: Ministry of Culture, Malaysia, 1986.

Basset, H. *Essai sur la littérature des Berbères.* Algiers: J. Carbonel, 1920.

Beeston, A. F. et al., eds. *Arabic Literature to the End of the Umayyad Period.* Cambridge: Cambridge University Press, 1984.

Birge, J. K. "Yunus Emre: Turkey's Great Poet of the People." *The MacDonald Presentation Volume.* Princeton: Princeton University Press, 1933.

Browne, E. G. *A Literary History of Persia,* 4 vols. Cambridge: Cambridge University Press, 1957.

Cerulli, E. *Studi Etiopici.* Rome: Instituto per l'Oriente, 1936.

Chelkowski, P., ed. *Taʿziyeh: Ritual and Drama in Iran.* New York: New York University Press, 1979.

Corbin, H. *En Islam iranien.*

——. "Mystique et humeur chez Sohrawardī." Ed. M. Mohaghegh and H. Landolt. Pp. 13–38 in *Collected Papers on Islamic Philosophy and Mysticism.* Tehran: Tehran University Press, 1971.

Dalby, D. P. *Dichtungen in der Lamu Mundart des Suaheli.* Hamburg, 1940.

Dermenghem, E. *Les Plus beaux textes arabes.* Paris: La Colombe, 1951.

Drewes, A. J. *Classical Arabic in Central Ethiopia.* Leiden: Brill, 1976.

Filshtinsky, I. N. *Arabic Literature.* Moscow: USSR Academy of Sciences, Institute of Peoples of Asia, 1966.

Gerard, A. *African Language Literatures: An Introduction to the Literary History of Sub-Saharan Africa.* Harlow: Longman, 1981.

Gibb, H. A. R. *Introduction to Arabic Literature.* London: Oxford University Press, 1926.

Grahame, B. T. *A History of Urdu Literature.* London: Oxford University Press, 1932.

Gramlich, R. *Gedanken über die Liebe.* Wiesbaden: Steiner, 1977.

Gray, R., ed. *The Cambridge History of Africa,* vols. 4–5. Cambridge: Cambridge University Press, 1975–76.

Haafkens, J. *Chants musulmans en Peul.* Leiden: Brill, 1983.

Halman, T. S. *The Humanist Poetry of Yunus Emre.* Publications of the R. C. D. Cultural Institute 39. Istanbul: Istanbul Matbaasi, 92 (pp. 43-83: poems in English).

——, ed. *Yunus Emre and His Mystical Poetry.* Indiana University Turkish Studies 2. Bloomington, IN: Indiana University Press, 1981.

Hiskett, M. *A History of Hausa Islamic Verse.* London: SOAS, 1975.

Ibn ʿArabī. *The Tarjumān al-ashwāq.* Ed. and trans. R. A. Nicholson.

Ibn al-Fāriḍ. *The Mystical Poems of Ibn al-Fāriḍ.* Trans. and annotated A. J. Arberry. Dublin: Chester Beatty Monographs, 1956.

Innes, G. *Sunjata. Three Mandinka Versions.* London: SOAS, 1974.

Johns, A. H. "Malay Sufism." *Journal of the Malayan Branch Royal Asiatic Society* 30 (1957) 1–108.

Knappert, J. *Swahili Islamic Poetry.* 3 vols. Leiden: Brill, 1971.

——. *Traditional Swahili Poetry.* Leiden: Brill, 1976.

Lawrence, B. *Notes from a Distant Flute.* Tehran: Imperial Iranian Academy of Philosophy, 1977.

——. *The Rose and the Rock.* Durham, NC: Duke University Press, 1979.

Lings, M. *A Sufi Saint of the Twentieth Century.*

Menemencioğlu, N. *The Penguin Book of Turkish Verse.* Harmondsworth: Penguin Books, 1978.

Nasr, S. H. *Islamic Art and Spirituality.*

Nicholson, R. A. "Mysticism in Persian Poetry." *Proceedings of the Iran Society* 1 (1936–1938) 60–69.

——. *A Literary History of the Arabs.* London: Cambridge University Press, 1969.

——. *Studies in Islamic Mysticism.*

——. *Studies in Islamic Poetry.* Cambridge: Cambridge University Press, 1921.

Nizami, K. A. *The Life and Times of Shaikh Farid Ganj-i Shakar.*

Norris, H. T. *Saharan Myth and Saga.* Oxford: Clarendon Press, 1972.

Pagliaro, A., and A. Bausani. *Storia della letteratura persiana.* Milan: Nuova Accademia Editrice, 1960.

Palmer, E. H. *Oriental Mysticism.* London: Luzac, 1938.

Ritter, H. *Das Meer der Seele: Gott, Welt und Mensch in den Geschichten Farīduddīn ʿAṭṭārs.* Leiden: Brill, 1955.

Rypka, J. *History of Iranian Literature.* Trans. P. van Popta-Hope. Dordrecht: D. Reidel, 1968.
Sadiq, M. *A History of Urdu Literature.* London: Oxford University Press, 1964.
Schimmel, A. *As Through a Veil.* New York: Columbia University Press, 1982.
——. "The Influence of Sufism on Indo-Muslim Poetry." Pp. 181–210 in *Anagogic Qualities of Literature.* Ed. J. P. Strelka. Philadelphia: University of Pennsylvania Press, 1971.
——. *Islam in the Indian Subcontinent.* Leiden: Brill, 1980.
——. *Pain and Grace.* Leiden: Brill, 1976.
Smith, M. *Teachings from the Mystics of Islam.* London: Luzac, 1950.
Teeuw, A. *Modern Indonesian Literature.* Hague: Martinus Nijhoff, 1967.
Waheed Mirza. *The Life and Works of Amīr Khusrau.* Lahore: University of Panjab Press, 1975.
Wilson, P. L., and N. Pourjavady, trans. *The Drunken Universe–An Anthology of Persian Sufi Poetry.* Grand Rapids: Phanes Press, 1987.
Winstedt, R. O. *A History of Classical Malay Literature.* Kuala Lumpur: Oxford University Press, 1969.

Part Three
Theology, Philosophy, and Spirituality

Asín Palacios, M. *The Mystical Philosophy of Ibn Masarra and His Followers.* Trans. E. H. Douglas and H. W. Yoder. Leiden: Brill, 1978.
Bello, I. *The Medieval Islamic Controversy Between Philosophy and Orthodoxy.* Leiden: Brill, 1989.
Corbin, H. *La Philosophie iranienne islamique aux XVII et XVIII siècles.* Paris: Buchet-Chastel, 1981.
——. *Shihāboddīn Yaḥyā Sohravardī Shaykh al-ishrāq: L'Archange empourpré.* Paris: Fayard, 1976.
——. *Philosophie iranienne et philosophie comparée.* Tehran: Imperial Iranian Academy of Philosophy, 1977.
——. *En Islam iranien,* vols. 2 and 4.
—— (in collaboration with S. H. Nasr and O. Yahya). *Histoire de la philosophie islamique,* Paris: Gallimard, 1986.
——. *Avicenna and the Visionary Recital.* Trans. W. Trask. Irving, TX: University of Dallas, 1980.
Cruz Hernández, M. *Historia del pensamiento en el mundo islámico,* 2 vols. Madrid: Alianza Editorial, 1981.
Fakhry, M. *A History of Islamic Philosophy.* New York: Columbia University Press, 1983.
Gimaret, D. *La Doctrine d'al-Ash'ari.* Paris: Les Editions du Cerf, 1990.

Izutsu, T. *The Concept and Reality of Existence.* Tokyo: The Keio Institute of Cultural and Linguistic Studies, 1971.
——. *Unicité de l'existence et création perpetuelle en mystique islamique.* Trans. M.-C. Groundry. Paris: Deux Oceans, 1980.
Kogan, B. S. *Averroes and the Metaphysics of Causation.* Albany: State University of New York Press, 1985.
Morris, J., trans. *The Wisdom of the Throne: An Introduction to the Philosophy of Mullā Ṣadrā.* Princeton: Princeton University Press, 1981.
Nasr, S. H. *Islamic Life and Thought.* Albany: State University of New York Press, 1981.
——. *Three Muslim Sages.*
——. *Traditional Islam in the Modern World.* London: KPI, 1990.
Peters, J. R. *God's Created Speech.* Leiden: Brill, 1976.
Sharif, M. M. *A History of Muslim Philosophy.* 2 vols. Wiesbaden: O. Harrassowitz, 1963–66.
Van Ess, J. *Die Erkenntniss Lehre des 'Aḍudaddīn al-Īcī.* Wiesbaden: O. Harrassowitz, 1966.
Wolfson, H. A. *Studies in the History and Philosophy of Religion.* 2 vols. Cambridge: Harvard University Press, 1979.

The Spiritual Significance of the Hidden Sciences

Burckhardt, T. *Introduction to Sufism.*
——. *Alchemy.* Trans. W. Stoddart. London: Stuart and Watkins, 1967.
Canteins, J. *La Voie des lettres.* Paris: A. Maisonneuve et Larose, 1981.
——. *Miroir de la shahâda.* Paris: A. Maisonneuve et Larose, 1989.
——. *Phonèmes et archétypes.* Paris: A. Maisonneuve et Larose, 1972.
Dornseiff, F. *Das Alphabet in Mystik und Magie.* Leipzig: Teubner, 1925.
Guénon, R. "La Science des Lettres." *Les Etudes Traditionnelles* 36 (1931).
——. "The Mysteries of the Letter Nûn." Pp. 166–68 in *Art and Thought Issued in Honor of A. K. Coomaraswamy.* Ed. B. Iyer. London: Luzac, 1947.
——. "Notes sur l'angélologie de l'alphabet arabe." *Les Etudes Traditionnelles* 43 (1938) 324–27.
Massignon L. "L'arithmologie dans la pensée islamique primitive." *Archeion* 14 (1932) 370–71.
——. "La philosophie orientale d'Ibn Sînâ et son alphabet philosophique." *Mémorial Avicenne.* Cairo: Institut Français d'Archéologie Orientale du Caire, 1952. 4:1–18.
Nasr, S. H. *Introduction to Islamic Cosmological Doctrines.* Cambridge: Harvard University Press, 1964.
Schuon, F. *Comprendre l'Islam.* Paris: Gallimard, 1961.
Urvoy, D. *Penser l'Islam.* Paris: J. Vrin, 1980.

Music and Sacred Dance

A bibliography arranged alphabetically by author's name which numbers more than 500 titles was compiled by J. Jenkins and P. R. Olsen in *Music and Musical Instruments in the World of Islam*, London: World of Islam Festival, 1976, 90–100.

As to the importance of the sources to which they give access, the following authors and works in particular should be mentioned:

Erlanger, R. L. *La Musique arabe.* 4 vols. Paris: P. Geuthner, 1930–1939.

Farmer, H. G. *A History of Arabian Music to the XIIIth Century.* London: Luzac, 1929 (repr. 1973).

——. *Historical Facts for the Arabian Musical Influence.* London: W. Reeves, 1930.

——. *Studies on Oriental Musical Instruments.* London: H. Reeves, 1931; Glasgow, 1939.

——. *The Sources of Arabian Music.* Leiden: Brill, 1965.

Discography

There exists a large number of recordings of Islamic music on long-playing records. Some indicative lists, although already outdated, are given in the works of the collection "Musical Traditions" published by the International Institute for Comparative Music Studies, particularly:

Inde du Nord, by A. Daniélou. Paris, 1966.

La musique arabe, by H. H. Touma. Paris, 1977.

Iran, by N. Caron and D. Safvate. Paris, 1966.

Turquie, by K. and U. Reinhard. Paris, 1969.

The same institute compiled the "'UNESCO Collections of Traditional Music," whose sections "Middle East" and "Indian Continent" contain a number of irreplacable documents. Information concerning these may be obtained from the International Counsel of Music (UNESCO) in Paris, or at the offices of the Institute in Berlin or Venice.

The recent series of "Musiques traditionnelles vivantes" produced by Radio-France includes excellent performances of Arabic, Turkish, and Iranian music. Among them are:

II "Musiques rituelles et religieuses": "Turquie, musique soufi," by N. Uzel and K. Erguner, December, 1980.

III "Musiques savantes," "Iran," in several volumes, 1979, 1980.

The collection "Arabesques," produced in Paris by J. C. Chabrier specializes in performances of *taqsīm* by various soloists.

Cassettes of "Sufi music" are produced by the Mevlana Association in Paris.

Spirituality of Islamic Art

Ardalan, N., and L. Bakhtiar. *The Sense of Unity: The Sufi Tradition in Persian Architecture.* Chicago: University of Chicago Press, 1973.

Burckhardt, T. *The Art of Islam.* Trans. P. Hobson. London: Festival of The World of Islam, 1976.

——. *Mirror of the Intellect.* Ed. and trans. W. Stoddart. Albany: State University of New York Press, 1987.

——. *Fes–Stadt des Islam.* Olten and Freiburg: Urs Graf Verlag, 1960.

——. *Sacred Art–East and West.* Trans. Lord Northbourne. Bedfont, Middlesex: Perennial Books, 1967.

——. *Moorish Culture in Spain.* Trans. Alisa Jaffa. New York: McGraw-Hill, 1972.

Coomaraswamy, A. K. *I. Selected Papers–Traditional Art and Symbolism.* Ed. Roger Lipsey. Princeton: Princeton University Press, 1977.

Critchlow, K. *Islamic Patterns.* New York: Schocken Books, 1976.

Lings, M. *The Quranic Art of Calligraphy and Illumination.* London: Festival of the World of Islam, 1976.

Michon, J. L. "From the Koranic Revelation to Islamic Art." Pp. 219–31 in *Religion of the Heart: Essays Presented to Frithjof Schuon on his Eightieth Birthday.* Ed. S. H. Nasr and W. Stoddart. Washington, DC: Foundation for Traditional Studies, 1990.

Nasr, S. H. *Islamic Art and Spirituality.*

Schimmel, A. *Islamic Calligraphy.* Leiden: Brill, 1970.

——. *Calligraphy and Islamic Culture.* New York: New York University Press, 1984.

Schuon, F. *Spiritual Perspectives and Human Facts.* Trans. P. N. Townsend. Bedfont, Middlesex: Perennial Books, 1987.

Contributors

SEYYED HOSSEIN NASR is University Professor of Islamic Studies at George Washington University and a former professor at Tehran University and Temple University and president of the Iranian Academy of Philosophy. He is the author of *Ideals and Realities of Islam, Sufi Essays, Knowledge and the Sacred* (the 1981 Gifford lectures), and *Traditional Islam in the Modern World.*

BAHARUDIN AHMAD is a Malay scholar and lecturer in the humanities at the University of Science of Malaysia and a specialist in Malay Sufi literature. He is the editor of a volume on Sufi literature in Malay and translator into Malay of S. H. Nasr (ed.), *Philosophy, Literature and Fine Arts.*

OSMAN BAKAR is a Malay scholar, associate professor of the philosophy of science at the University of Malaya and a specialist in the Malay intellectual tradition. He is the author of several essays on the Islamic philosophy of science and Sufism and of *Al-Fārābī: Life, Works and Significance.* He has also edited *Critique of Evolutionary Theory.*

TITUS BURCKHARDT was a Swiss metaphysician and expert on traditional art who devoted a lifetime to traditional studies in general and Islamic subjects in particular. He is the author of several major translations of Sufi classics and books on traditional art and culture including *Sacred Art: East and West, Moorish Culture in Islam, Art of Islam,* and *Mirror of the Intellect.*

JEAN CANTEINS is a French scholar who has devoted a lifetime to the study of the traditional sciences and especially the science of letters in Islam as well as in other traditions. He is the author of *Phonèmes et archétype, La Voie des lettres,* and *Miroir de la shahāda.*

WILLIAM C. CHITTICK is assistant professor of religious studies at the State University of New York at Stony Brook and a former assistant professor at Aryamehr University in Tehran. He is a specialist in Sufism, and his works include *The Sufi Path of Love: The Spiritual Teachings of Rumi, The Sufi Path of Knowledge,* and a translation of Fakhr al-Dīn 'Irāqī, *Divine Flashes.*

VICTOR DANNER is professor of religion and Islamic studies at Indiana University. An authority on Sufism, he is the translator of *Ibn 'Aṭā'illāh's Sufi Aphorisms* and the author of *The Islamic Tradition.*

ABDUR-RAHMAN IBRAHIM DOI was professor in Islamics and director of the Centre for Islamic Legal Studies at the Ahmadu Bello University in Nigeria. A specialist in Islamic Law, he is the author of *Introduction to the Quran, The Cardinal Principles of Islam, Islam in Nigeria,* and numerous other books and articles on Islam, especially in its African context. He now teaches at the International Islamic University in Malaysia.

SHEMS FRIEDLANDER is an American artist and devotee of Sufism who has traveled extensively in Turkey and written on Sufism. His books include *The Whirling Dervishes* and *When You Hear Hoofbeats Think of a Zebra.*

SAFA ABDUL AZIZ KHULUSI is an Iraqi scholar of Arabic literature who was professor of the University of Baghdad and who has also lectured at Yale, the University of Chicago, and the University of Bath. He is the author of many works in Arabic and the translator into Arabic of Nicholson's *A Literary History of the Arabs.* He has also published short stories, poems, and a novel. His English works include *Islam Our Choice.*

JAN KNAPPERT is a Dutch scholar who has traveled widely in Africa and was professor of the languages and literatures of Africa at the University of London and at Louvain. He is the author of numerous works on the literature of Africa including *Swahili Islamic Poetry, Four Centuries of Swahili Verse,* and *Epic Poetry in Swahili and Other African Languages.*

JALAL MATINI is an Iranian Scholar of Persian literature who was formerly professor of Ferdowsi University in Mashhad and is now editor of the Persian literary journal *Iranshenasi.* He is the author and editor of many works in Persian dealing with the earlier periods of Persian literature.

JEAN-LOUIS MICHON is a French scholar who specializes in Islam in North Africa, Islamic art, and Sufism. He has participated in several UNESCO projects on Islamic art and is the author of many works on Sufism and art, including *Le Soufi marocain Aḥmad ibn ʿAǧība et son miʿrāǧ* and *L'Autobiographie (fahrasa) du Soufi marocain Aḥmad ibn ʿAǧība (1747–1809).*

KHALIQ AHMAD NIZAMI is an Indian scholar who was formerly professor at Aligarh University and who specializes in Sufism particularly in India. His works, written in both Urdu and English, include *The Life and Times of Shaikh Farīd Ganj-i Shakar* and *Studies in Medieval Indian History.*

JAVAD NURBAKHSH is the present master of the Nimatullahi Order. Of Iranian origin, he was for many years professor of Tehran University but now resides in London. He is the author or editor of some thirty volumes on Sufism in Persian, many of which have been translated into English including *In the Tavern of Ruin, Sufi Symbolism,* and his *dīwān* of poetry.

SAYYID ATHAR ABBAS RIZVI is an Indian historian of Islam and Islamic thought in India. Formerly a professor of Jammu and Kashmir University and Australian National University, he is the author and editor of many works in Urdu and English including *Source Book of Medieval Indian History, Religious and Intellectual History of the Muslims in Akbar's Reign,* and *A History of Sufism in India.*

ANNEMARIE SCHIMMEL is the foremost German scholar of Sufism and Sufi literature of the Indian Subcontinent who has spent much of her life in Turkey and the Indo-Pakistani world. She is professor at Harvard University and the author of many works on Sufism and its literature including *Mystical Dimensions of Islam, As Through a Veil, Pain and Grace,* and *The Triumphal Sun.*

S. ABDULLAH SCHLEIFER is a scholar of American origin who has lived in the Islamic world for over a quarter of a century. He is currently the director of the Adham Center for Television Journalism in the American University of Cairo and author of *The Fall of Jerusalem.*

GÖNÜL A. TEKIN is a Turkish scholar of classical Ottoman and Chaghatay literature who is currently doing research on Ottoman symbolic *mesnevis* (rhyming couplets). She is the co-editor of *The Journal of Turkish Studies* and the series *Sources of Oriental Languages and Literatures.*

MUHAMMAD ISA WALEY is an English scholar of Sufi literature who has traveled extensively in the Eastern lands of the Islamic world and has carried out research on the Sufi orders in that area. He is the keeper of Oriental manuscripts at the British Library in London.

Photographic Credits

The editor and the publisher wish to thank the custodians of the works of art for supplying photographs and granting permission to use them.

1. Ms. Elliott 339, F 95 verso. Courtesy of the Department of Oriental Books, Bodleian Library, Oxford.
2. From the collection of Dr. William Stoddart.
3. Ms. Ouseley Add. 24, F 556. Courtesy of the Department of Oriental Books, Bodleian Library, Oxford.
4. Ms. Ouseley Add. 24, F 78 verso. Courtesy of the Department of Oriental Books, Bodleian Library, Oxford.
5. *Jāmiʿ al-siyar,* volume 2. Courtesy of the Royal Topaki Museum, Istanbul.
6. Photograph by Katherine O'Brien.
7. Photograph by Alexander Upham Pope. Courtesy of the Asian Art Photographic Distribution, Department of Art History, University of Michigan, Ann Arbor.
8. Photograph by Donald Wilber. Courtesy of the Asian Art Photographic Distribution, Department of Art History, University of Michigan, Ann Arbor.
9. Photograph by Eduard Widmer, Zurich.
10. Photograph by Shems Friedlander.
11. Courtesy of the Arthur M. Sackler Gallery, Smithsonian Institution, Washington, D.C. (Vever Collection, Neg. S86.0432 Indian Painting: Mughal ca. 1635. Dara-Shikoh with Mian Mir and Mulla Shah. 17.0 x 10.4 cm.).
12. OR. 2265, F 166. Courtesy of The British Library.
13. Ms. Elliott 287, F 24a. Courtesy of the Department of Oriental Books, Bodleian Library, Oxford.
14. Photograph by Alexander Upham Pope. Courtesy of the Asian Art Photographic Distribution, Department of Art History, University of Michigan, Ann Arbor.
15. Ms. Ouseley Add. 24, F 65 verso. Courtesy of the Department of Oriental Books, Bodleian Library, Oxford.
16. Photograph by Shems Friedlander.
17. Photograph by Shems Friedlander.

Index of Names

Colophon

Islamic Spirituality: Manifestations,
Volume 20 of World Spirituality: An Encyclopedic History of the Religious Quest, was designed by Maurya P. Horgan and Paul J. Kobelski.
The type is 11-point Garamond Antiqua and was set by
The HK Scriptorium, Inc., Denver, Colorado.